AF606960

Earthly Delights

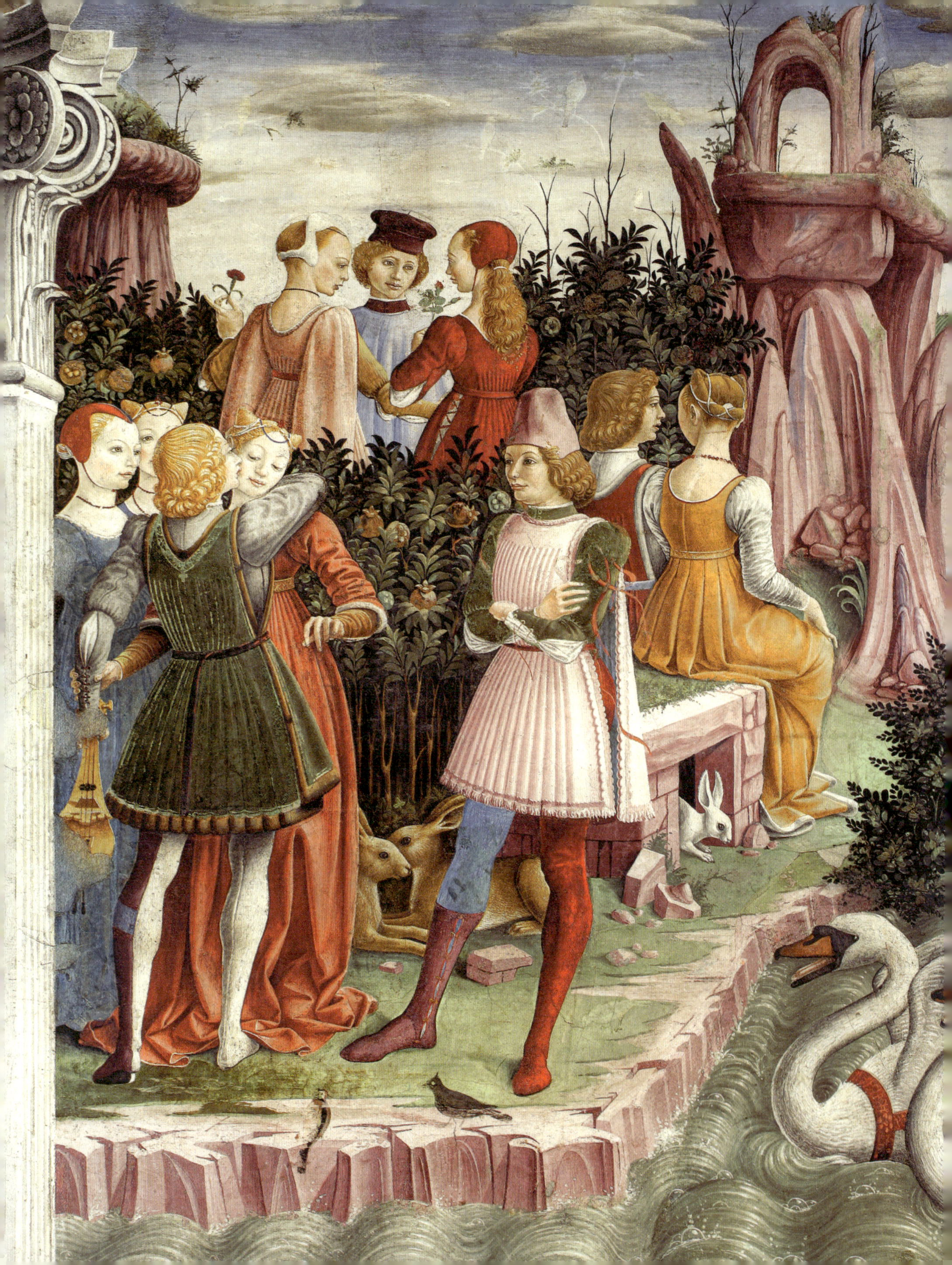

Jonathan Jones

Earthly Delights

A History of the Renaissance

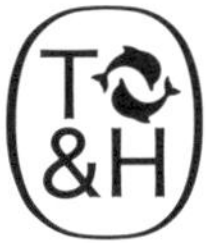

Frontispiece: Francesco del Cossa, *April, Triumph of Venus* (detail), *c.* 1467–70.

First published in the United Kingdom in 2023 by
Thames & Hudson Ltd, 181A High Holborn, London WC1V 7QX

First published in the United States of America in 2023 by
Thames & Hudson Inc., 500 Fifth Avenue, New York, New York 10110

Designed by Adam Brown

British Library Cataloguing-in-Publication Data
A catalogue record for this book is available from the British Library

Library of Congress Control Number 2023934835

ISBN 978-0-500-02313-6

Printed and bound in China by C&C Offset Printing Co. Ltd

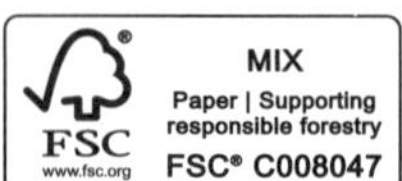

Contents

Introduction: The Birth of Uncertainty 6

1 The Arnolfini Nude 14
2 The Naked Citizen 36
3 The Triumph of Love 60
4 Nature's Child 84
5 Worldly Knowledge 104
6 Haywain to Hell 126
7 The Garden of Earthly Delights 150
8 Render unto Caesar 174
9 Melancholia 200
10 The Pulse of Life 222
11 Judgments 242
12 Carnival and Lent 266
13 Curiosities 292

Notes 318
Further Reading 322
Acknowledgments 324
List of Illustrations 325
Index 331

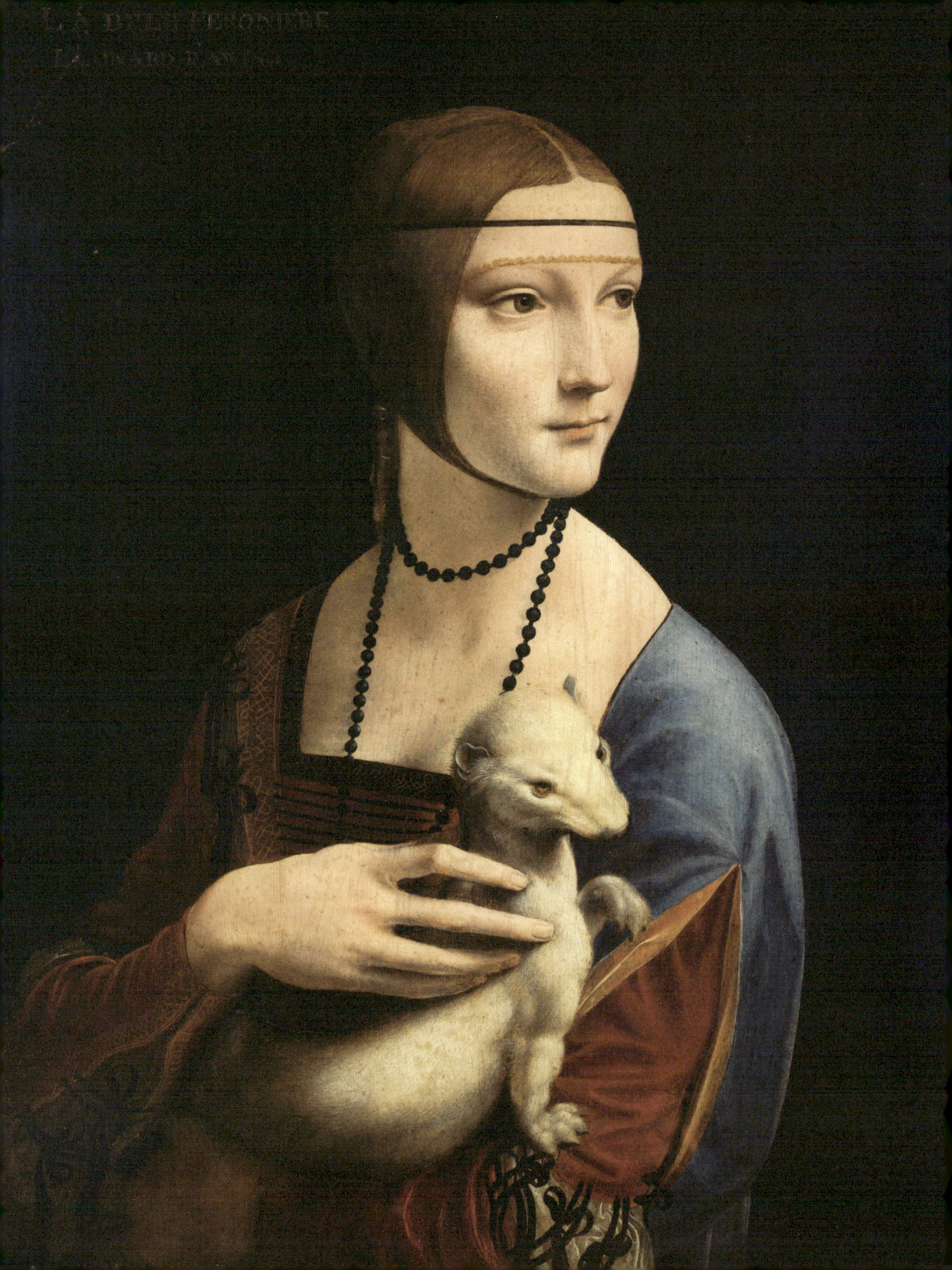

Introduction
The Birth of Uncertainty

She holds the ermine firmly against her chest with long fingers. You can sense its rapid heartbeat and tensile energy at her touch as it digs its claws into the red velvet of her sleeve. Cecilia Gallerani is caught in motion, turning to greet someone while keeping her phallic-snouted pet under control. She beholds this invisible person calmly. Her self-possession is as striking as her gentle mastery of the fierce mammal in her arms.

Leonardo da Vinci's portrait of the mistress of Ludovico Sforza, usurping ruler of Milan, is a secular parody of one of the holiest of Christian artistic themes: the Madonna and Child. In his youth Leonardo made explosively dynamic studies of children holding animals and women playing with children, including designs for a Madonna and Child with a cat. Yet when he first tried to progress from these sketches to painting the Virgin he came, by his standards, unstuck. The *Madonna of the Carnation* and *Madonna Litta* – if the latter is actually by him – are awkward paintings caught between stasis and eccentricity. He could not find in the traditional theme of Virgin and Child what he saw in his brilliant sketches of women, infants and animals on the move. He finds it instead in his portrait of Gallerani, which he painted in Milan *c.* 1489–91. He gives this young woman a squirming animal in her arms instead of a child. Cecilia Gallerani's presence is electric, her nerves, muscles, bones all working

Leonardo da Vinci,
Lady with an Ermine,
c. 1489.

Leonardo da Vinci, *Virgin and Child with a Cat*, c. 1478–81.

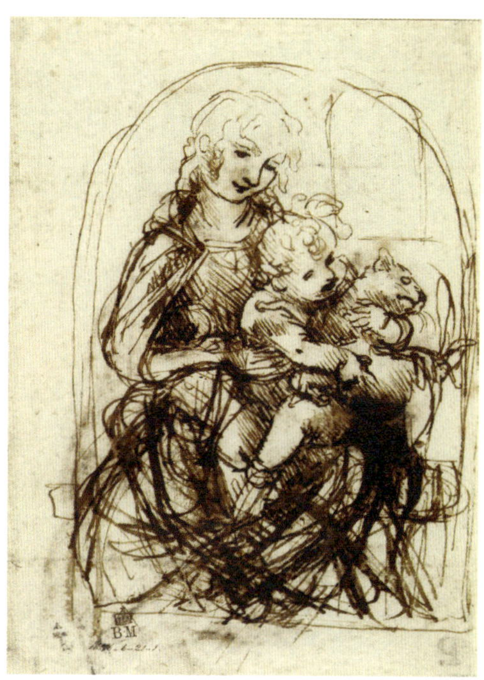

under her skin as she turns her eyes to look at the world. Leonardo frees her from the duty of childcare. Instead, she symbolically exerts erotic power over the beast that embodies Ludovico Sforza.

A decade later, in April 1498, Isabella d'Este, marchioness of Mantua, an avid art enthusiast, wrote to Gallerani asking to borrow the picture. She had just been looking at portraits by the Venetian painter Giovanni Bellini, and

> we began to discuss the works of Leonardo and had a desire to make a comparison between the two; remembering that he painted your likeness, we entreat that, with this rider whom we have sent for this purpose, you kindly send your portrait so we may satisfy our wish to see them compared, and also because I wish to see your face and as soon as we have made our examination we will return it.[1]

Gallerani gladly obliged, although she no longer looked like the same woman – the result of time's changes, she assured Isabella, and not any failing by Leonardo.

She could not even have had such an anxiety a century earlier because in the 1300s there were no convincing portraits to fix a face in time. One of the most instantly popular artistic innovations of the 15th century was the portrayal of people with mirror-like believability. It was not just faces but bodies that became more real; not just bodies but the rooms or piazzas where they posed. Italians called the new method that made all this possible *prospettiva*, 'perspective', an art grounded in the scientific analysis of space that could turn a flat surface into a window on a three-dimensional world. Out of that deep space conjured from flatness real people stared back at you or ignored you as they got on with their business of praying, washing, feeding a baby, holding an ermine.

The new art saw people as unique realities in space – and in time. Gallerani is presented by Leonardo not in some frozen eternity but at a specific moment. Seconds earlier she may have bent down to pick up the ermine. Afterwards the animal may have dug its claws into her arm and broken free. But this is here and now.

This ability to look at the world at a given moment was a distinctive cultural development of Europe in the 15th and 16th centuries. In Italy it was partly achieved by vying with ancient pagan Greek and Roman literature and the ruins of classical civilization. The architect Leon Battista Alberti wrote that Florence in the 1430s was creating wonders like those of ancient times. Botticelli's *Primavera*, one of the best-loved of all Florentine paintings, both celebrates rebirth in nature and 'rebirths' the old pagan gods.

* * *

It was in the 19th century that historians elevated such a 'rebirth' into the historical period they called the 'Renaissance'. The French Romantic writer Jules Michelet celebrated this 'Renaissance' as a secular reaction against the superstition and ignorance of 'le Moyen Âge'. That idea of a glorious escape from the Middle Ages, dancing towards the liberal modern society the Victorian age believed itself to be, is also celebrated in Jacob Burckhardt's 1861 historical classic *The Civilization of the Renaissance in Italy*, which defines the spirit of this age as 'the discovery of the world and of man', and in Walter Pater's sensual 1873 rhapsody on the art of Botticelli and Leonardo, *Studies in the History of the Renaissance*.

Today the very concept of the Renaissance is seen by many historians as a wheezing old steam train, a 19th-century construct that says almost nothing about what university courses define instead as the Early Modern period. If anything, the secular rational 'rebirth' happened in the 18th century – or never did. The Renaissance is still studied, but it is widely seen as a muted, peripheral phenomenon of elite culture rather than an explosive vanguard of modernity. 'To speak of Renaissance may be helpful if we keep in mind the limitations of the context in which we use the word,' J. M. Roberts and Odd Arne Westad warn bleakly in the sixth edition of *The Penguin History of the World*, 'but it falsifies history if we take it to imply a transformation of culture marking a radical break with medieval Christian civilisation.'[2]

As an art critic who has been looking at Renaissance art ever since visiting Florence as a child and falling for Leonardo da Vinci, Michelangelo and Botticelli, I can't share that cynicism. It is impossible to agree with Roberts and Westad when you walk through the chronologically arranged rooms of the Uffizi Gallery in Florence and see how completely the nature of art was revolutionized in the 1400s. In early rooms, the medieval paintings of Giotto, Duccio and Simone Martini have their own power, yet there's a sudden burst into bloom when you see the three-dimensional knights of Uccello's *Battle of San Romano*, the delicate human face of Fra Filippo Lippi's Virgin in front of a window looking out onto a hilly landscape, and soon the early works of Leonardo himself. The change is not a superficial one. Instead, it seems to me, the new eye for nature, reality and individual people reflects, or maybe created, a new way of experiencing the world. Renaissance eyes are fixed on this life, not the next. This is the art of a Europe discovering the world and itself.

That can be seen even more clearly if we step away from the very Italian story the Uffizi tells and head to Northern Europe instead. Perspective, the revolutionary new way of organizing perception, was proudly touted by Florence as a discovery. Yet it was already in use in a more polished form, heightened by the use of glossy oil paints, in early 15th-century Bruges. This is not an attempt to play off Jan van Eyck against his Italian contemporaries. While this

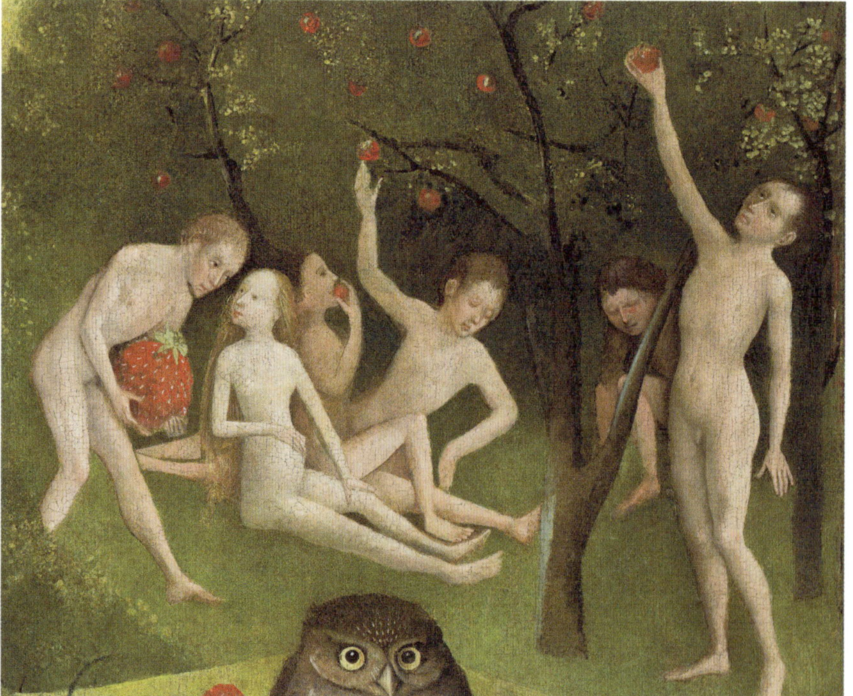

Hieronymus Bosch, *Garden of Earthly Delights* (detail), 1490–1500.

book sets North European art alongside Italian throughout, the point is not to belittle the Italian Renaissance. It is to understand it in Europe's history. For if the same new eye for reality appeared independently at both ends of Europe at the same time in the early 1400s, that suggests the negation of the Renaissance as a historical phenomenon couldn't be more wrong. This obsession with picturing bodies and faces in deep space appears to be nothing less than a transformation in mentalities, of a quite profound kind whose consequences are still reverberating.

* * *

The day I visited Elmina Castle on the Ghana coast, the dark blue Atlantic was driving wild, foaming waves against the rocky shore, and the walls of this 15th-century fortress were turning bronze in the late afternoon sun. It had closed for the day, so I just stood and looked at this West African outpost of Renaissance Europe.

The kingdom of Portugal, which in the 15th century sent its ships ever southwards along Africa's Atlantic seaboard, built the Castelo de São Jorge da Mina in 1482. This was a decade before its Iberian rival, Spain, sent Christopher Columbus in search of a new route to China that instead led him to the New World. El Mina was a permanent base from which to trade in goods, including rapidly increasing numbers of slaves. Before long, slaves purchased in Africa would be taken across the Atlantic to do the work a local population racked by new diseases could not.

The 15th century was when modern history began. Renaissance perspective, with its new clarity about space and objects, played its part in that European 'discovery' of the world. But before you turn away from it on that score, consider that, while some conquistadors undoubtedly cast only dead, gold-addled eyes on new lands, the drive of Renaissance culture, fuelled by news from new worlds, was investigative, curious and attracted to what was different.

* * *

It has been claimed that the perspective picture fixes its ideal viewer as a kind of absolute visual prince, with a uniquely empowered view of events. This is the opposite of what it does. By taking a particular point of view, attempting to show a scene as it would look if you were a spectator in the room, it implicitly acknowledges the existence of other spectators and alternative points of view. In the 1580s the architect Vincenzo Scamozzi created life-sized, eye-fooling perspective scenery for Antonio Palladio's classical Teatro Olimpico in Vicenza; everyone in the audience has a different view of the receding city

Andrea Palladio and Vincenzo Scamozzi, Teatro Olimpico, Vicenza, 1580–85.

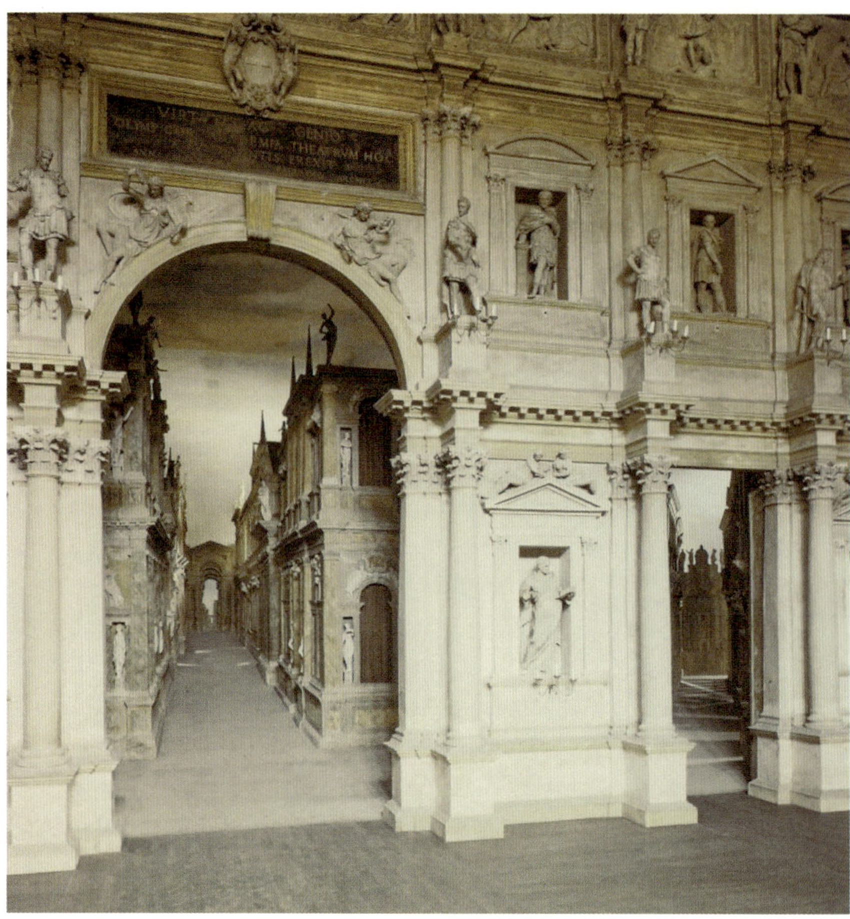

streets it depicts, as they watch a play that itself moves through the spaces the stage creates.

To picture the world in perspective was to abandon a God's-eye, or child's-eye, delusion of omniscience. It was to sense the limits of your knowledge. Leonardo was as aware of this as anyone. When he portrayed Cecilia Gallerani, he was busy pursuing idiosyncratic inquiries, filling notebooks with questions and experiments, dissecting animals, designing clocks and burglar alarms. He never reaches any final conclusions about anything, but rigorously applies an empirical method in which only the evidence of the senses can be trusted.

Leonardo was not the only Renaissance thinker who refused to finish his investigations. None of the great intellectuals of 15th- and 16th-century Europe created a systematic theory to explain everything. That was what medieval theology had excelled at. The *Summa Theologiae* of the 13th-century philosopher Thomas Aquinas synthesizes the doctrines of the church with a finality no Renaissance work achieves, or wants to. Machiavelli, Erasmus, More, Rabelais,

Montaigne and Shakespeare take suggestive, shifting stabs at a reality they know to be many-sided, mysterious and, above all, constantly changing.

* * *

The Renaissance was radical and destabilizing, a liberation of art and thought. It came to an end in the early 17th century, chastened by religious war and crushed by the material misery of a world that, on a technological level, was still medieval, where prayer truly was a needed comfort. Nor was it ever a forerunner of the industrial age. Rather, it was an eruption of curiosity. And that curiosity was relativist, inclined to believe many things at the same time. The great imaginative leap of resurrecting the pagan civilizations of ancient Greece and Rome was not (as we might think now) conservative, let alone self-congratulatory, but the opposite: it meant very consciously recognizing that a remote, distant culture with different religious beliefs might possess a higher wisdom. That was to hold two times, two moral systems, in parallel and move between them. It did not stop at Greek myth. Hermetic writings, talismans and astral spells transmitted from medieval Islam, even Jewish Kabbalah – all were lapped up in a Renaissance Europe where magicians as well as artists were cultural stars. And for the most open minded, it seemed that the customs of 'cannibals' in far-flung American forests might be just as valid as Europe's own equally peculiar ways. It was even reported that they had no property, kindling dreams of a perfect society or – to use the word invented by the Renaissance – a *utopia*.

Leonardo was a rare sceptic where magic was concerned. If necromancy worked, he pointed out, we would see its results everywhere. Who would hold back from using those infinite powers? In the end, the Faustian ambition of the Renaissance was doomed – for Leonardo was right. Necromancy doesn't work. But the appetite for the delights of this world that encouraged people to experiment with the occult or dabble in utopias made the Renaissance a uniquely fertile time. The geniuses in this book boggle our minds. Maybe there will be greater art in the future, but we cannot shake off our justified awe of such prodigious artists. Keeping an open mind is, on their evidence, the best recipe for creative excellence. There are more things in heaven and earth than are dreamt of in your philosophy.

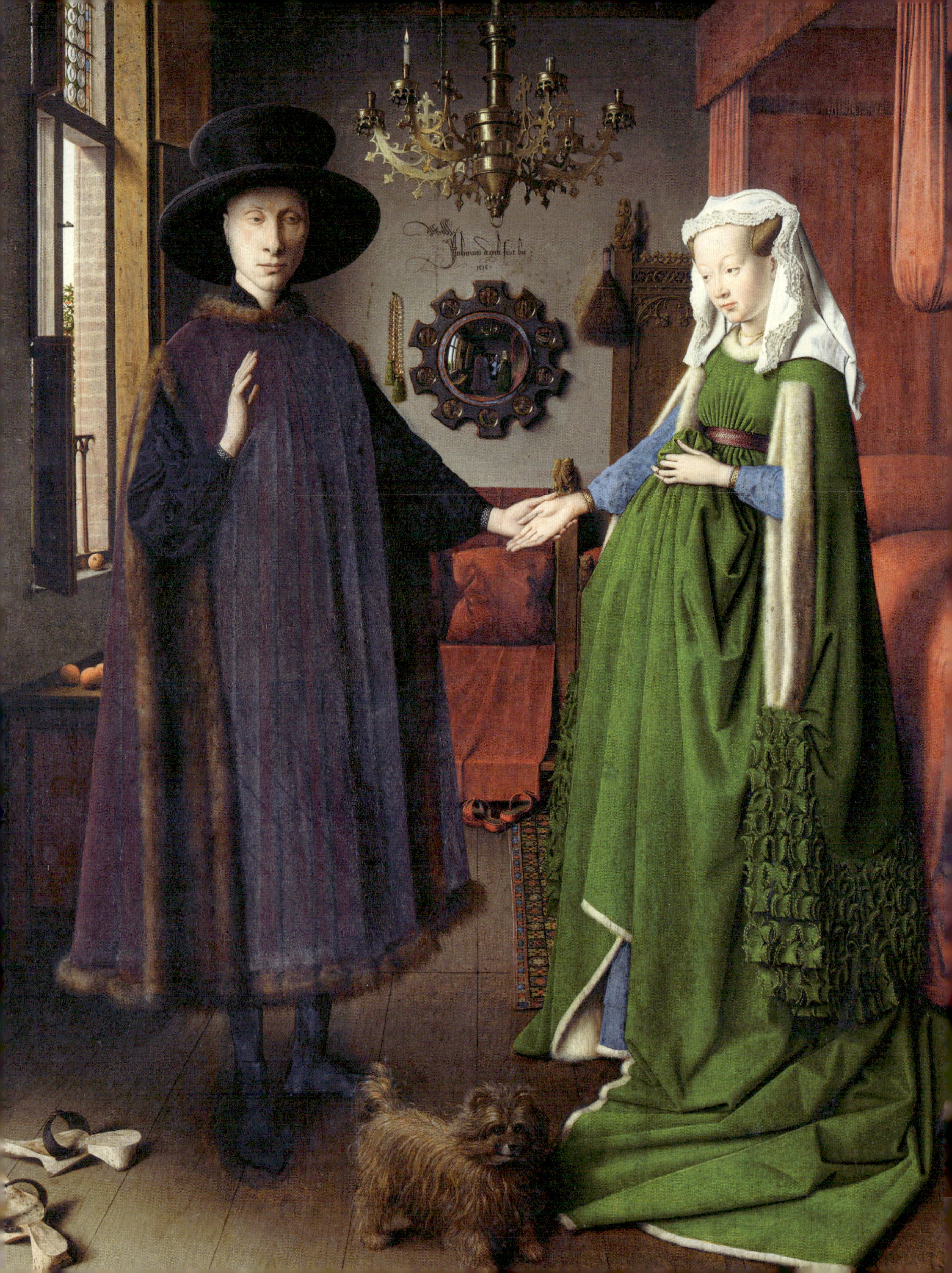
Johannes de eyck fuit hic

1 The Arnolfini Nude

He looks at her sideways with rheumy eyes. They are cold, half-shut, lacklustre. Her face is much brighter and younger, her forehead pale and large – 'almoost a spanne brood', a hand's width, as Chaucer says of the Prioress's brow in *The Canterbury Tales*. Her hair is twisted into two horns that play on the fashionable coned hat called a *hennin*, supporting layers of a neatly arranged white headdress. Her face lowered, she looks at him modestly, deferentially. There's a bed behind her, draped and curtained in red. Yet the couple don't give the impression of being eager to jump into it. Giovanni di Nicolao di Arnolfini – if this is who he is – is so grey and thin it looks like it might kill him. The side of his face closest to his wife, and in shadow, seems palsied.

They stand in their room mantled in thick, warm clothes, his brown, hers green, in both cases well made and expensive. The long fur edging of her sleeve makes a flamboyant ellipse that exhibits the virtuosity of the artist. Jan van Eyck signed this oil painting in large, formal Gothic script right across the back wall of the room, together with the year: 1434. It's a shame he didn't include the precise date, as we could then have identified the very first day of the Renaissance.

No one ever before had portrayed real people in what appears to be their actual house with such a mesmerizingly factual appearance. Nor had any previous painter whose work survives used light and colour to model objects and space

Jan van Eyck,
Arnolfini Portrait, 1434.

so repletely, from glowing spherical oranges to the play of glitter and shadow made by daylight on a chandelier on which a single candle burns redundantly. These are phenomena that would still seem fresh when Johannes Vermeer set his interiors against big daylit windows more than two centuries later. Van Eyck's room is a place mapped like the real world, receding from our eyes in what has been called the first fully realized perspective painting, a consistently eye-fooling illusion of depth on a flat wooden surface.

One thing you wouldn't call the *Arnolfini Portrait*, as it is named today, is sexy. Yet a lost erotic painting with which it had a mysterious relationship changes that impression and bolsters the claim of van Eyck's Bruges to be the true birthplace of the Renaissance in all its earthiness. The 17th-century art collector Cornelis van der Geest, who made his money in the Antwerp spice trade, loved to show off his collection. Luckily there was a genre of painting just for that purpose. To commemorate a visit by the archduke and archduchess of Austria, he commissioned a panoramic *constcamer* (gallery painting) from Willem van Haecht to record the grand room, its contents and its illustrious visitors. Paintings within the painting fill the panelled walls, one above the other, competing for attention. Classical statues are cluttered below them, Renaissance bronzes cover a table, and books and drawings are on every other surface. Among the guests are two men with particularly dapper goatees: Pieter Paul Rubens and Anthony van Dyck, the two most gifted painters in 17th-century Antwerp. The art on show mixes contemporary works by such local stars with paintings from the Renaissance tradition that inspired them. One of the most arresting pictures is comparatively small but glows with vivid colour.

It is a nude by Jan van Eyck.

This depiction of a naked woman hangs, pointedly, above a gathering of nude sculpture, inviting connoisseurs to compare and contrast the ways ancient Greco-Roman artists carved bodies in stone with the way van Eyck enfleshes his model with oil paint. One of the statues directly below van Eyck's picture is a version of the Aphrodite of Knidos, originally created by the Greek sculptor Praxiteles in the 4th century BCE. It depicts the goddess of love – Venus to the Romans – in a very similar pose to van Eyck's bather.

Could this early 15th-century Flemish artist have known of the ancient Greek prototype for his work? Van der Geest's hoard, formed at the end of the Renaissance, expressed what had long become received ideas. The perfection of the nude statues of classical antiquity was, by then, hailed by scholars, hallowed by art. When van Eyck painted his *Woman Bathing* in 1430s Bruges, there was no such common knowledge. It's usually said that Botticelli's *Birth of Venus*, painted as much as half a century later, is the first great female nude

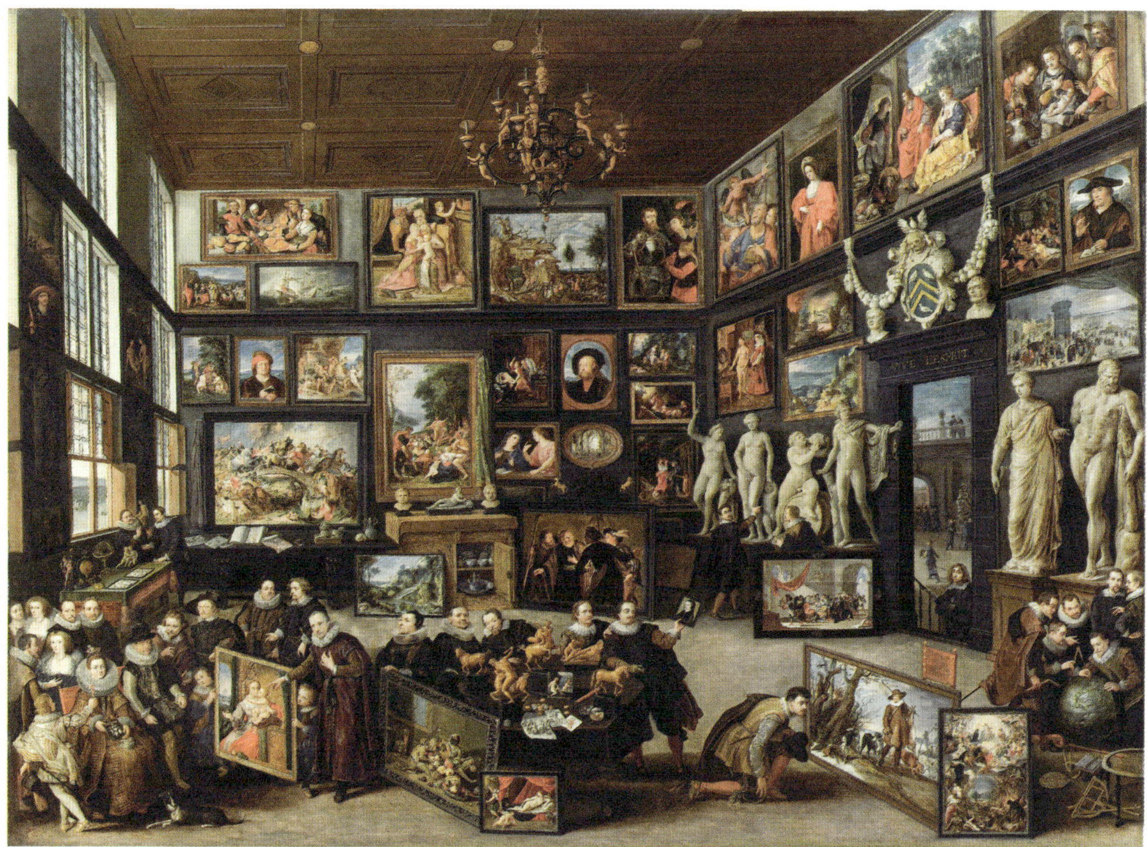

Willem van Haecht, *The Gallery of Cornelis van der Geest*, 1628.

of the Renaissance. Did van Eyck, as the juxtaposition of his painting with a copy of Praxiteles suggests, revive the classical nude as early as the 1430s? Or did he just portray a woman without any clothes on?

* * *

One of the first people to write about van Eyck was an intellectual called Bartolomeo Facio, a secretary at the court of Naples where the art patron Alfonso V of Aragon owned some of the northern master's works. In 1456 he wrote that 'Jan of Gaul' was considered 'the leading painter of our time'.[1] In fact, van Eyck had been dead for fifteen years by then, passing away in Bruges in 1441 at the height of his career. Facio is struck by van Eyck's naturalism: his St Jerome is a 'living being', a portrait subject who 'lacks only a voice'. He goes on to say that Jan was famous for painting 'women of outstanding beauty getting out of the bath. The more secret parts of the body are veiled with fine linen with outstanding decorum.' Of one of them only the face and breast are visible, but 'he shows the behind parts of the body in a mirror painted on the opposite wall. So in this way you may see her back and breast.'

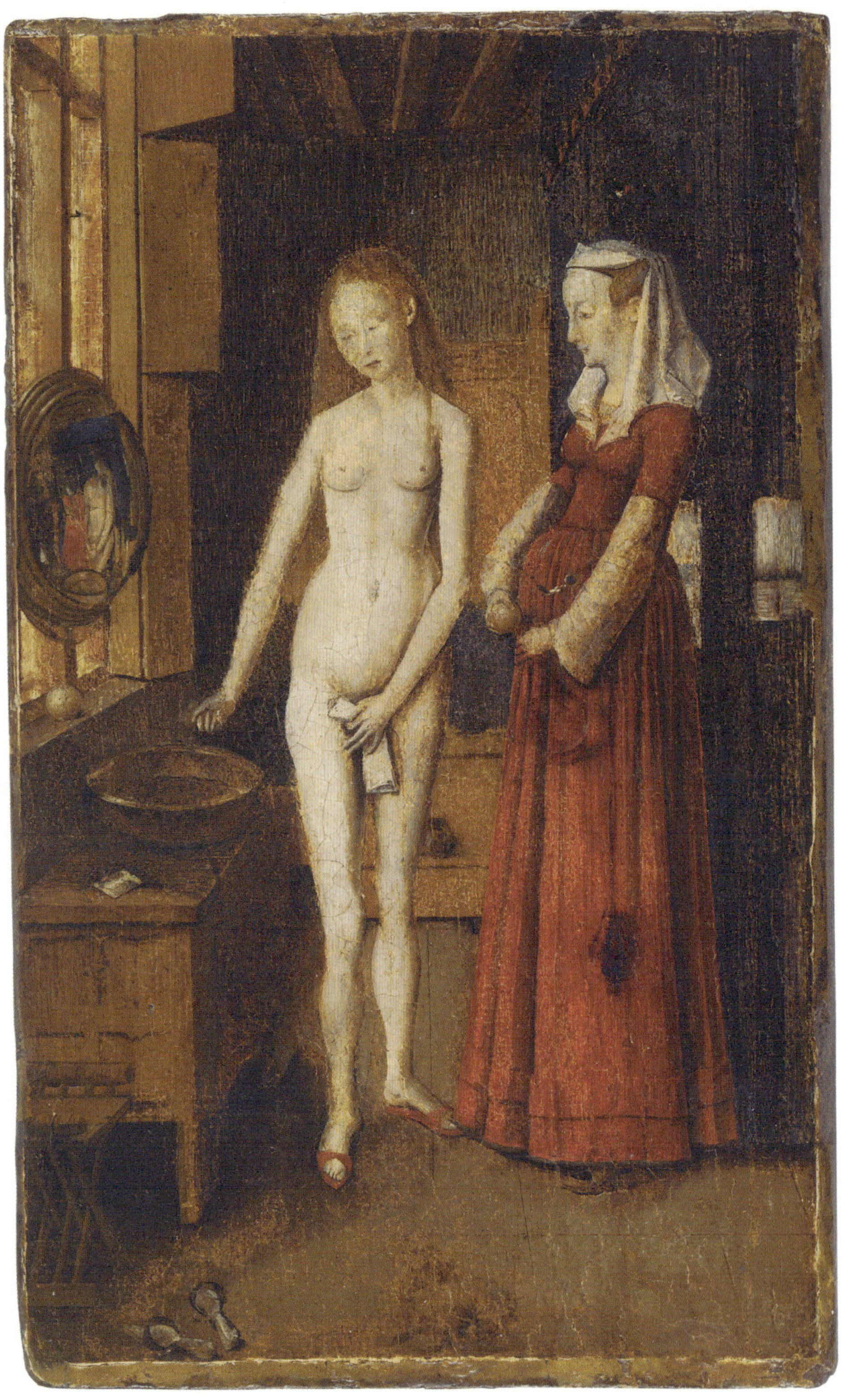

18

That's not all. In the same picture

> there is a lantern in the bathroom that seems to really burn, and an old woman who seems to be sweating. A puppy is licking water. And also horses and men of tiny stature. Mountains. Woods. Villages ... But almost nothing is more marvellous in this work than the mirror in the painting. In it, whatever is depicted you see as if it were a real mirror.[2]

None of van Eyck's bathers survives. The only one of which there is a visual record is the nude with the mirror, preserved in the painting owned by van der Geest and also in a surviving 16th-century copy. Facio implies that the fashion for nudity caught on in Flemish art, describing a picture by 'Rogier of Gaul' – Rogier van der Weyden – in Genoa, 'in which there is a woman sweating in her bath, with a puppy near her and two youths on the other side secretly peering in at her through a chink, remarkable for their grins'.[3] This Italian Renaissance art lover sees nudity as a sensation from the north.

Van Eyck's bather in the two extant versions seems mysteriously connected with the *Arnolfini Portrait* itself, since she poses in what looks disconcertingly like the respectable couple's chamber. The same tall window lets in daylight from our left, as in the *Arnolfini Portrait*. A bed stands at our right. Where fruit is laid on top of a chest in the Arnolfini picture the bather has her washing bowl. A wooden blind next to the window appears in both pictures, flat against the wall in the Arnolfini painting and swinging out in the other. A convex mirror appears in both. In the nude painting it has been brought forward from the rear wall to rest by the washing bowl. As Facio says, it shows the parts our eyes cannot reach. Even the disposition of figures reflects the Arnolfini painting. The bather occupies approximately the same position in the room as Giovanni Arnolfini, while her clothed attendant stands where Arnolfini's wife does, wearing a similar headdress as she casts her gaze towards her.

As she exposes her breasts, the bather holds a comically small cloth that only partly conceals her pubic hair and casts her eyes downwards towards the bowl. She's as reserved as the nameless wife in the *Arnolfini Portrait*. Perhaps the artist wants to emphasize her self-consciousness, to make the moment more real. Not all van Eyck's women look fearful. His wife, Margaret, in a portrait he did of her in 1439, confronts you fearlessly.

Could the resemblance between the naked bather and the Arnolfini bride mean they are the same woman? Van Haecht's painting might suggest this, for it shows the now-lost nude alongside works that survive, enabling us to assess its probable size: it looks to have been close in scale to the *Arnolfini Portrait*, which is 82 cm (32 in.) tall. That adds to the sense that these two paintings

After Jan van Eyck, *Woman at Her Toilet*, early 16th century.

Jan van Eyck, *Portrait of Margaret van Eyck*, 1439.

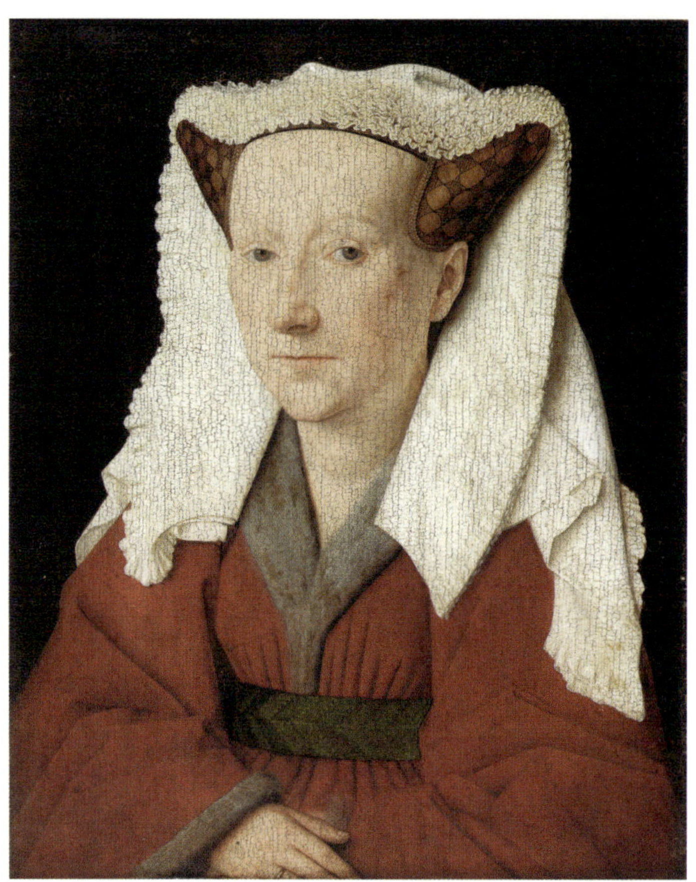

have an intimate relationship with each other. Yet when we compare the bather's convex mirror in the Arnolfini painting with those in van Haecht's painting and in the copy there's a difference. The frame of the Arnolfini mirror contains tiny religious scenes in glass roundels. It's the kind of detail that can make van Eyck seem an intensely religious artist, saturating his scenes with Christian symbols. The nude version of the *Arnolfini Portrait* – if that's what it is – surely subverts that piety. We might even name it the 'Arnolfini Nude'.

The surviving representations of van Eyck's Arnolfini Nude give only an indication of what it looked like: they are just visual notations, with none of his genius. Van Eyck did not invent oil painting, as tradition had it. Instead he took it to new heights, exploring its astonishing power to mimic the living world. Using thin layers of pigment in the translucent medium of oil, he built up staggeringly precise images. What might his bather have looked like in that dazzling style?

We can guess from two great naked figures by van Eyck, male and female, that survive. They are on panels of the complex altarpiece in St Bavo's Cathedral,

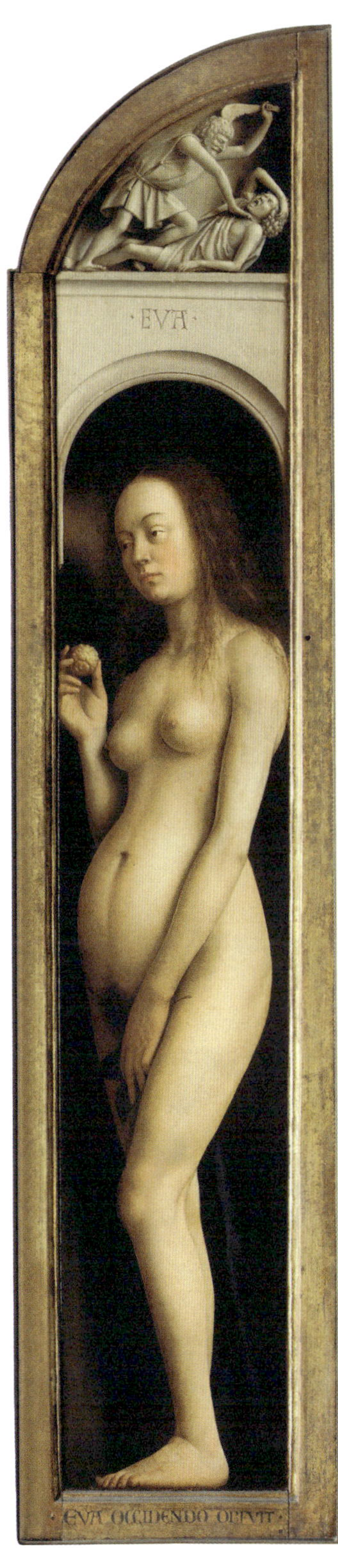

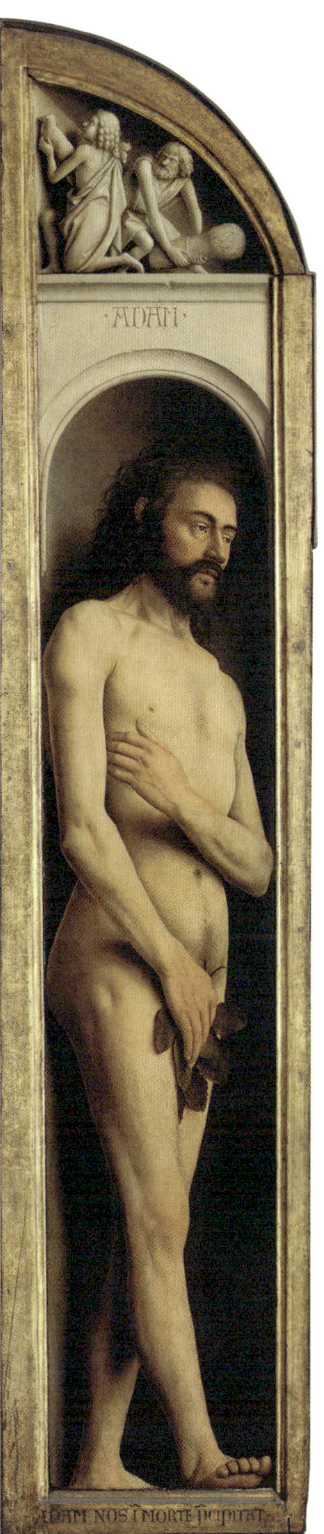

Hubert van Eyck and Jan van Eyck, *Eve* and *Adam*, from the Ghent Altarpiece, 1432.

Ghent, that he began with his brother Hubert and completed alone in 1432 after Hubert's death. Adam and Eve normally stand far from the eye in the upper sections of the Ghent Altarpiece, but when they were displayed up close in an exhibition in early 2020 their sensuality was suddenly exposed to anyone lucky enough to stand in front of their glowing flesh. Van Eyck is one of the very greatest painters of the human body, perhaps the most fanatically exact there has ever been, a master of pores. Every hair on Adam's body stands out in hallucinatory detail (p. 21). Prickly black hairs emerge from pale gold skin, right down his legs. You can even see hair stream over his stomach and under the fig leaf he holds in fallen shame. Eve, holding the apple of temptation, discloses more pubic hair under her sheltering hand. Her belly is prominent, like that of the Arnolfini bride, as she turns towards Adam.

It's a wild thought, but did Arnolfini want his young bride to pose, in the nude pendant to their double portrait, undressed like Eve, in a personal, perhaps heretical interpretation of the meaning of marriage? That can only be speculation. But there is a possible context for such heterodoxy in the world of Arnolfini and van Eyck. Heretics grouped under the label 'the Brethren of the Free Spirit' were punished by the late medieval church, accused of believing that they could not sin and could fornicate without guilt because they were perfectly at one with God. It might explain why in the *Arnolfini Portrait* the merchant raises his hand to bless his wife, like the angel of the Annunciation. Perhaps he believes he is a Free Spirit who can act with divine authority in his own home – and sacralize nudity too.

* * *

The exactitude of van Eyck's brush makes it likely he trained as a manuscript illuminator. This was the most refined form of painting in medieval Europe: it began to flourish before the Vikings and was still coveted in the 1400s, yet its creators got little credit. Van Eyck achieved recognition by leaving illumination behind to become a celebrity in oils. He was employed from 1426 as court painter to Philip the Good, duke of Burgundy, the quasi-monarchical fiefdom that included medieval Flanders and the Bourgogne region in France. At the same time he was working with his brother on the Ghent Altarpiece. The court moved from palace to palace, including those at Brussels and Bruges. It was in the 1420s that van Eyck settled in Bruges.

The landmarks of van Eyck's city are still visible today, all steeped in medieval Christianity: the basilica containing the relic of the Holy Blood of Christ brought back from the Second Crusade in the 12th century; the Beguinage, founded as a refuge for devout secular women in the 13th century; the Jerusalem Chapel, modelled on Jerusalem's Church of the Holy Sepulchre. The chapel was built by members of a branch of the politically powerful Adorno family of Genoa, who would also commission works from van Eyck.

In 1436 a Flemish clergyman who had been a papal scribe in Rome came home to Bruges a rich man. With his wealth he commissioned a portrait from van Eyck, who showed him at prayer in a chapel with a precision that is flabbergasting. Every wrinkle on Joris van der Paele's big, sagging head is mapped, as if van Eyck were scrutinizing him under a microscope. That instrument wouldn't be invented for another two hundred years, but van Eyck refers to lenses in the canon's spectacles and in the swirling discs of glass in the windows beyond, as if to tell us that the rendition of his beefy features is optically momentous.

The place where he kneels may have been a real chapel in St Donatian's Cathedral, which was demolished in 1799 when the impact of the French Revolution reached Belgium. In any case the architecture, in its Gothic complexity, creates a space where heaven and earth meet. In this liminal chamber van der Paele encounters the Virgin Mary with Jesus on her lap, and they both

Jan van Eyck, *Virgin and Child with Canon van der Paele*, 1434.

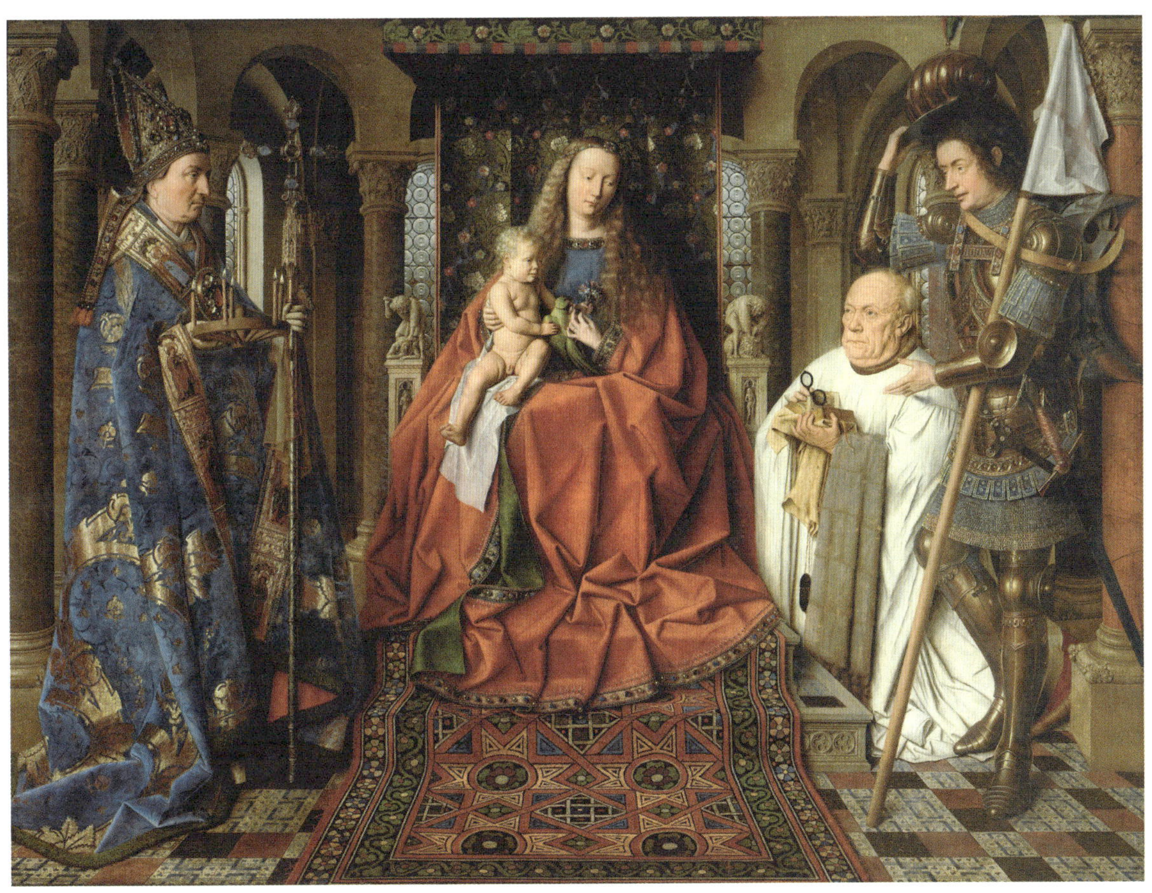

turn their eyes towards him. The sanctuary of the Virgin's throne on its heavenly carpet sets her apart, unlike the two saints who stand in van der Paele's reality and who are depicted with the same material facthood as he is: St Donatian in his golden bishop's regalia, St George in glistening steel armour.

Van Eyck portrays van der Paele with such jowly life that his meaty face imposes itself monstrously on the holy scene. If van Eyck's bathing nudes are lost, here, still, is one of the greatest paintings of flesh of all time – a facial nude. There is nothing transcendent about this masterpiece. Instead we see a man with egotism and worldly experience etched into his stupendous skin, conversing with heavenly visitors who seem as solid as himself. You can't think away the unease of this painting. Van Eyck is so entranced by this world he scarcely attempts to evoke the mystery of the next.

* * *

The Renaissance was a discovery of the physical world and the human body. After a thousand years of obsession with the next life, Europe woke up to this one. This is the story its art tells. Artistic invention was also a driver of the story. The new kind of picture pioneered by van Eyck – spatially deep, optically exact, rich in light, shade and colour – imitated the real world with ravishing immediacy. It could preserve a face in a portrait, fruit that was out of season or a quiet moment when a woman takes a bath.

If the past is another country, medieval Europe is a far-off, semi-legendary land with no decent maps. Medieval geographers put Jerusalem at the centre of the world, knew nothing of any continent to the west of Europe, were barely aware of Africa south of the Sahara. They did know that China and India existed and believed them fabulously rich. To our eyes, the typical medieval map features an undefined blob surrounding the Mediterranean Sea, dotted with turrets to represent famous cities.

Van Eyck knew better, for he was a great traveller. Philip the Good sent him on a series of international trips, most of which were tantalizingly recorded in the Burgundian court records as top secret. He may have got as far as the Middle East. The only journey that was openly recorded took him to Spain and Portugal to portray a new bride for the duke.

While the earth was barely known, the places where medieval souls were destined to spend eternity were mapped in detail. Their greatest explorer was Dante Alighieri, whose *Divine Comedy*, written at the start of the 14th century, recorded a journey through the three otherworldly domains of hell, purgatory and paradise. Dante doesn't just sketch the horrors of hell and the bliss of heaven: he describes them as real, solid places, with lakes, rivers, cities, weather. 'In the middle of the pathway of our life I came to myself in a dark wood,' he began.[4] From there he entered hell and descended through its circular terraces until he reached the frozen lake of Cocytus and the colossal body of Satan. Then everything seemed to invert, as he emerged from the world's lowest point onto an island where the 'Mountain of Purgatory' rose heavenwards.

The concept of purgatory takes us towards the true exoticism of medieval thought. If you sinned 'mortally' and failed to make a deathbed confession, you were sent to hell without any chance of redemption from its torments: 'Abandon all hope you who enter here' are the words Dante sees inscribed above the Gate of Hell.[5] But for the middling sinner there was purgatory, a place where you must suffer for a set term to purge sin before ascending to paradise.

The keys to the next world were held by the church. There was one church, governed from Rome by the pope. Kings ruled in the name of Christ, and their greatest glory, although in practice carried out only between 1096 and the 1200s, was to go on crusade to the Holy Land. Crusading was a military version of the medieval rite of pilgrimage, an act of dedication that wore out your body in this world in order to acquire salvation in the next. 'Purchase' is how later reformers would put it.

Van Eyck didn't satirize or set out to destroy a medieval worldview. Yet he puts to use a technology that was to endanger it. His mastery of methods – and it would take decades, and in some aspects centuries, for other artists to catch up with him – enables van Eyck to picture terrestrial space as a reality, to place bodies within it in ways that imitate life, to reproduce solid objects in an illusion of three dimensions. In the *Arnolfini Portrait* we can see, reflected in the mirror, the door of the chamber. This is where van Eyck stands – apparently one of the two little figures in the doorway whose blurred forms float blue and red in the convex mirror. 'Jan van Eyck was here', declares his inscription on the rear wall. Suddenly the physical world has its day. A room in a merchant's house is made as substantial as Dante made purgatory.

* * *

In a painting that mimics van Eyck, the man at the door at the back of the room is in serious trouble (overleaf). He is spying where he has no business to be and has only himself to blame if he is punished. Meanwhile a naked woman dances alone in a graceful, ecstatic, swaying motion in the middle of her chamber, not washing but enacting a charm, utilizing a heart – can it be human? – in a casket to carry out her forbidden ritual in front of a fire. It is this occult operation that gives the painting, believed to have been done in the Lower Rhineland in about 1470, its modern name: *Love Magic.*

It is clearly an eerie interpretation of van Eyck's Arnolfini Nude. Visual quotations fill this picture showing a narrow room with windows on the right and rear-left wall. Through the windows we see a landscape. Between two windows hangs a small, convex mirror, offering the woman views of herself, and at her feet is a dog, as in the *Arnolfini Portrait*. Roof beams rush away in a slightly clumsy imitation of van Eyck's receding rooms. A cabinet at the back of the room is opened so we can see a luxurious bronze bowl and vessels. They recall a detail of the van Eyck brothers' Ghent Altarpiece: when the wings of that colossal structure are closed, their upper panels display a gripping scene of the

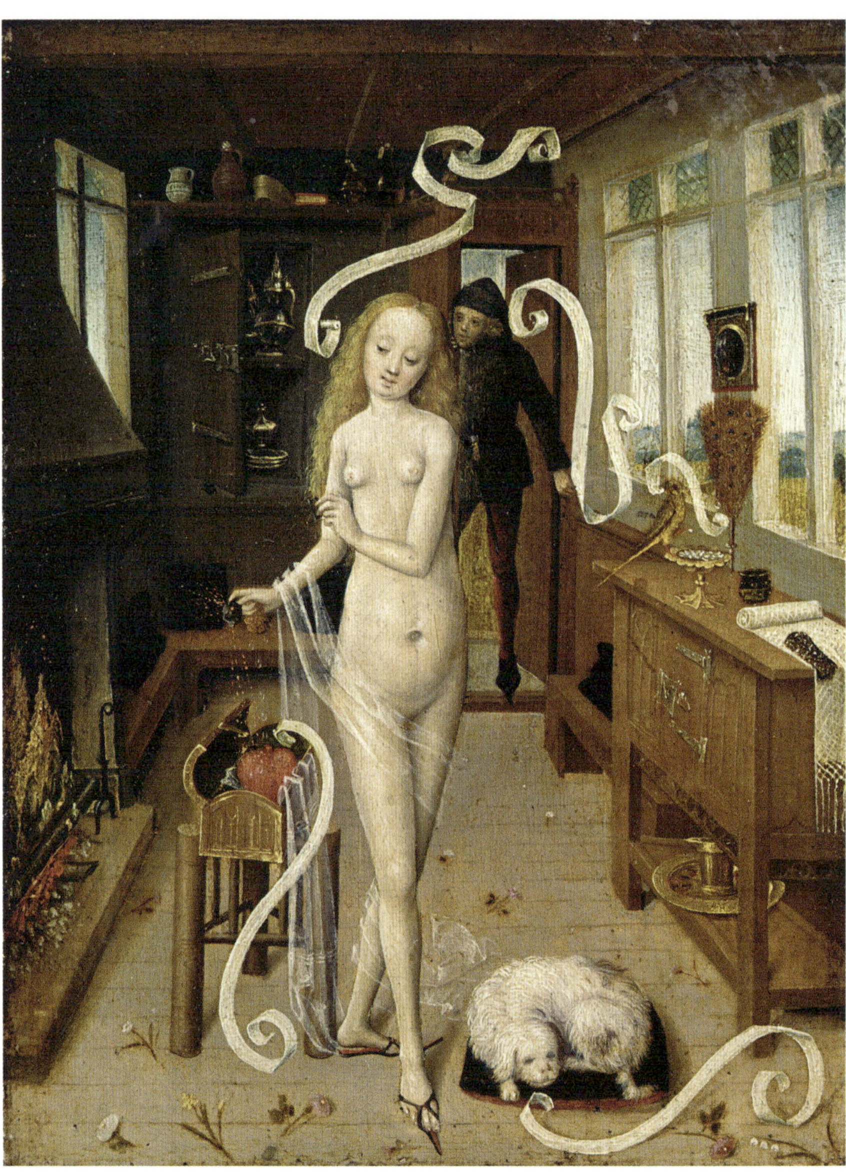

Unknown artist, *Love Magic*, c. 1470–80.

Annunciation set in an high chamber, with windows looking out on the rooftops of Ghent, and, standing in a Gothic niche, a bronze bowl and an ornate ewer. This holy paraphernalia of purification, symbolizing Mary's virginity, resurfaces in the German enchantress's chamber as a corrupt Satanic parody.

The presence of the bowl and ewer draws attention to the way in which van Eyck borrows from his own art. The bronze washing bowl that his Arnolfini Nude uses is also a replica of the one in the *Annunciation*. The Virgin's bowl in the recently restored Ghent scene illuminates the lost beauty this detail would have had in van Eyck's original nude scene. As a shared motif, it invites us to look again at van Eyck's nude. When we do, we see it has a curious formality. We are allowed into the woman's chamber but are not greeted. Her attendant is as grave as she is, and they carry out an ablution more ritualistic than relaxing. This scene hasn't much in common with saucy images of women at their toilette by later artists such as Watteau: if it's erotic, it isn't flippant. The revelation of nakedness is serious. It deserves a baptism of its own. Again, this unfamiliar, far from orthodox mixing of the profane and sacred might hint at a Free Spirit heresy.

* * *

Bartolomeo Facio praised van Eyck's bathers as the essence of his genius. There were examples of them, he says, in the possession of 'that distinguished man, Ottaviano della Carda' – which is how he may have come to see them.[6] Ottaviano assisted his uncle, Duke Federico da Montefeltro, one of the most capable mercenary captains in Italy, in ruling Urbino, his city in the Marche region. That van Eyck's nudes were known at the Urbino court helps us to understand one of the greatest paintings by the most brilliant artist Montelfeltro patronized. It spellbindingly translates the Arnolfini bather from indoors to outdoors, Flanders to Italy, female to male.

In Piero della Francesca's painting the *Baptism of Christ* (overleaf), the Messiah poses semi-nude in a pale, precise, open-air scene. His limbs are almost completely tubular. Such volumetric beauty is typical of this artist and mathematician from the borders of Tuscany and Umbria who wrote books on geometry. Yet the *Baptism* is not an abstract meditation: it is a painting about bodies. It was surely the stilled, sacral quality of van Eyck's bathers that intrigued Piero: the sombreness of the Arnolfini Nude as she washes herself is worthy of the Virgin Mary. In place of the central, upright figure of van Eyck's bather we have a statuesque Christ, praying as he stands, wearing just a loincloth, his pale torso and limbs exposed.

Like van Eyck's bather, Christ stands at the heart of a tall perspective scene, but he is outside, in the country. The landscape of the upper Tiber valley recedes

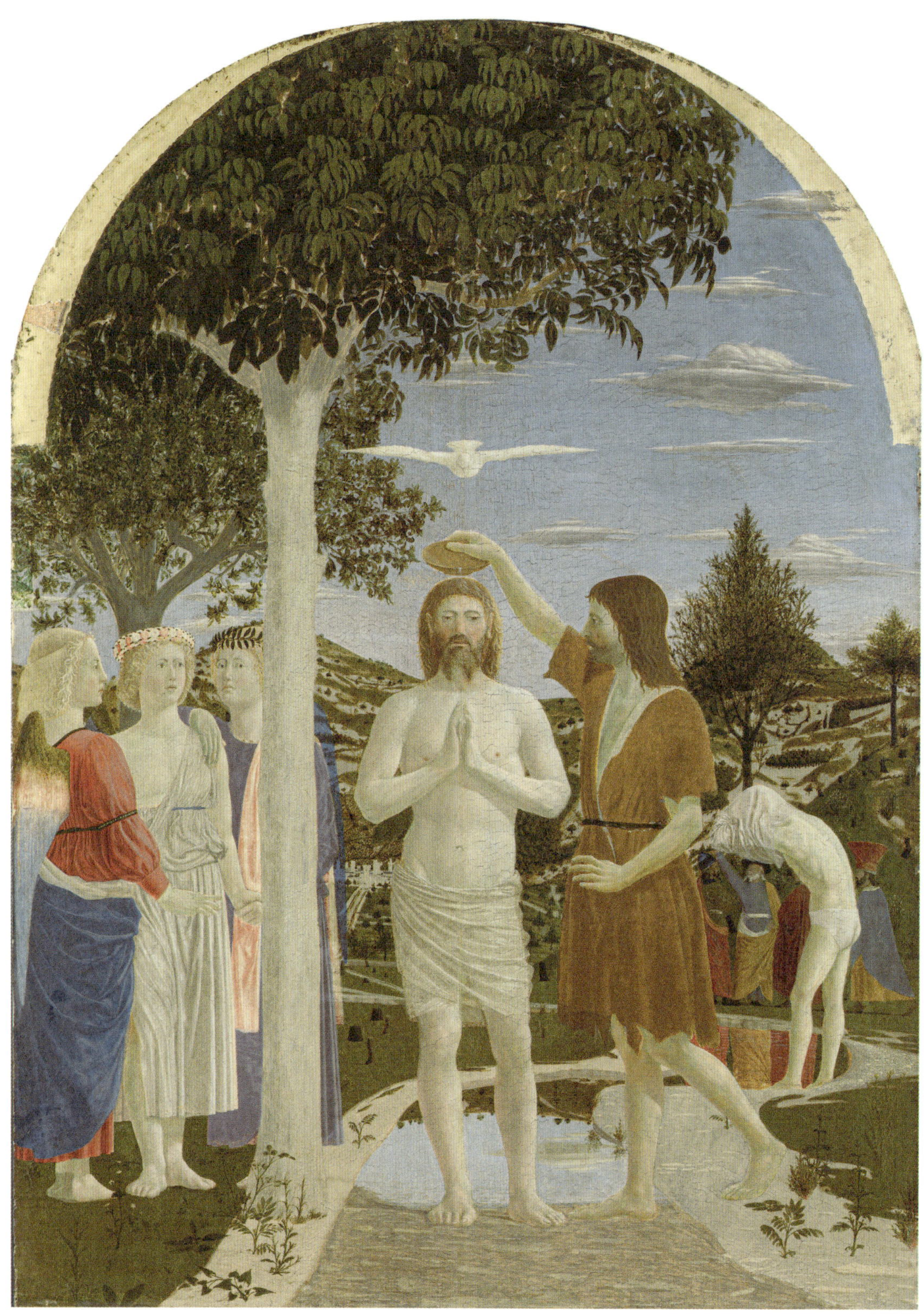

away from us in a deep view of white hills flecked with olive green, towards the tiny-looking walled town of Sansepolcro, the artist's birthplace, on the far side of the valley. This view still exists, and you may well catch it under the same blue sky. Like the Fleming, Piero plays with the optical wonder of reflection. Facio stressed the way van Eyck enhanced his depiction of a nude with the cunning use of a mirror. Piero della Francesca rivals this. Instead of a circular, convex mirror, he doubles the world in the glassy surface of a shrunken summer river. The water is so still that it acts as a perfect reflector. In it, we see upside-down doubles of the sky and hills, and the red and orange robes of the Byzantine philosopher-priests who witness this mystical baptism.

Against their robes and the coloured reflection in the flat water, Piero depicts the chalky skin of another candidate for baptism who leans forward, flexing his knobbly back muscles as he takes off his top. It's a surprisingly corporeal moment in a painting so unearthly – an image that leaps from the past into our own lives. We all put clothes on and take them off. And pulling your top off in the 1400s was, just as it is now, a minor drama of the body. For all the glassy reflective stasis of Piero's scene and the holy rite at its core, he makes us aware of our own bodies, our physical existence, with all its agonies and delights.

* * *

Piero della Francesca trained in the 1430s among the busy, competitive art workshops of Florence, the flourishing centre of international banking, merchant commerce and early industry about 110 kilometres (70 miles) to the west of Sansepolcro. It was a thrilling time for him to be refining his craft under the dizzying red and white dome of the city's cathedral, completed by Filippo Brunelleschi in 1436. This soaring, egg-like cupola paradoxically deployed Gothic building techniques – its arced ribs indebted to the very vaults and buttresses it rendered old-fashioned – to create an image of geometrical harmony and grace, a spectacular symbol of the rebirth of classical antiquity. The theorist and architect Leon Battista Alberti, in a letter dedicating his 1435 book *On Painting* to Brunelleschi, explained that, when he returned home to Florence after his family's exile, he found a city recapturing the glories of ancient Greece and Rome. He recognized in many, but 'first of all in you, Filippo ... there to be a genius for every type of praiseworthy activity not to be regarded as beneath any of the ancients famous for these arts'.[7]

1435, 1436. These dates match van Eyck's exploits in Bruges. The *Arnolfini Portrait* bears the date 1434. Whereas Jan was painting illusions of deep space without any manifestos – indeed, without any written record of his thinking whatsoever – the Florentines were eloquent traders in ideas. We think of Florence

Piero della Francesca, *Baptism of Christ*, after 1437.

as a city of art, but what made its culture so influential was its passion for the spoken and written word. The Florentine writers Dante and Boccaccio and the poet Petrarch from Arezzo made the Tuscan vernacular a trenchant literary language in the 1300s. Florence loved to collect books as well as write them. By the early 1400s its bibliophiles were amassing manuscripts by ancient Latin authors including Cicero, Lucretius and Tacitus, starting to translate the works of Plato from ancient Greek, and attempting to base their civic politics on these lofty models. So it's no surprise that Florentine artists were more verbal, discursive and analytical than any Northern European about the new idea of single-point perspective. As far as we know, van Eyck safeguarded his techniques and, like a magician, kept his powers of mimesis to himself. For the Florentines, keeping knowledge secret would have seemed absurd.

In fact, the reason Brunelleschi is praised in Alberti's book is that in the 1410s he performed a public experiment to demonstrate how a perspective picture could – literally – mirror reality. Brunelleschi drew or painted an image (the work is lost) of the green-and-white octagon-shaped Baptistery of Florence. It was ideal for the purpose: an almost abstract structure, geometric and symmetrical, isolated in the middle of the piazza in front of the cathedral. The picture's viewpoint was the cathedral doorway: this was where you had to stand to look at the little panel, holding it up in one hand. But you didn't look at it directly. There was an aperture in the panel, through which you peered, with the image itself facing away from you – as if you were wearing a mask of the Baptistery. Then, in the other hand, you held a mirror up to the painting. All this so that, by looking from the reflected image to the real Baptistery, you could see how perfectly the perspective method caught the appearances of a three-dimensional world.

At its most basic, a sense of perspective is almost childishly simple, although no child spontaneously makes a picture like this. It means recognizing that objects become smaller to our eyes the greater their distance. The optical science Brunelleschi demonstrated, which had originally been developed by the Arab thinker Ibn al-Haytha (known in Europe as Alhazen), pursued this basic observation to calculate and map the receding shapes of things precisely. Medieval scholars couldn't agree whether optical rays came from objects or from the eye, but this made no difference. The important point to grasp was that these rays travel in straight lines. They fan out in a conical shape, and if a painting reproduces that cone accurately it will resemble the physical world in which we move.

Alberti provides the theory to go with Brunelleschi's practical demonstration. Looking at a perspective painting, he argues, should be like looking through a window onto a receding view beyond. A rigorous insistence on a totally consistent illusion of pictorial depth is what separates Renaissance art from everything that came before. That includes ancient Greece and Rome, where painters created spatial depth yet lightly undermined it by using it as part of decorative fresco designs that spurn systematic unity.

There is undeniably a more considered, mathematical quality to Tuscan perspective than the northern approach pioneered by van Eyck – and no painter shows it more beautifully than Piero della Francesca. You can picture him laying out the landscape of the *Baptism of Christ* on a grid, calculating the scales of near, far and farther objects. It is a systematic approach to space. Despite being hailed by the 20th-century art historian Erwin Panofsky as the first true perspective picture, van Eyck's *Arnolfini Portrait* contains inconsistencies for those who measure it. Where is the chandelier, exactly: above Arnolfini's head or further back? Yet that doesn't matter. What matters is the sense of a chamber, with other places beyond the windows, where we could walk and which we could inhabit – a world held on a panel of wood. If the point of perspective is to fool you into thinking of a flat surface as deep space, no one handles it better than van Eyck. So, for all his grasp of the Florentine science of perspective, Piero seems to reach in the *Baptism of Christ* for something he has seen in van Eyck's nudes.

The way van Eyck makes a world is not by drawing a diagram but by building up colours. The glossy surfaces of his paintings hold light and dark and hard and soft like forms in a mirror that seem substantial but are phantoms. Piero della Francesca explores this idea of painting-as-mirror in the *Baptism*, pondering how red and orange and blue can be held in the reflective water, how these chromatic spectres can imitate nature while having no body. This is a more sensual, immediate way of picturing the world than the calculated scales of Florentine perspective. It's as if northern art captured the true spirit of Brunelleschi's experiment. Brunelleschi used a mirror, with the implication that painting should be one. The allure of van Eyck's nudes for Italians was that he didn't get so distracted by the fussy problems of perspective that he forgot to hold up his glass to beauty.

Van Eyck's impact would be greatest on Venetian painting. Venice and Bruges had a lot in common, and not just their canals. Venetian architecture in the late Middle Ages was all pointed windows and spindly encrustations, a levitating triumph of Gothic: you could almost call it the 'Bruges of the south'. While Bruges connected Atlantic with Mediterranean Europe via its trade network, Venetian ships traded with the Islamic world and established colonies in the Aegean. But, according to the 16th-century author Giorgio Vasari, there was a more specific reason for van Eyck's popularity in Venice.

Vasari's *Lives of the Artists*, published in Florence first in 1550 and then in a much fatter edition in 1568, set out a story of the Renaissance that still endures – and it is an Italian story. He narrates in racy biographies full of adventure and gossip how Italian artists – led by those of his native Tuscany – gradually escaped from crude, lifeless medieval conventions to conquer reality through the discovery of perspective. Northern Europeans barely get a look in. But he pays a backhanded compliment to van Eyck in a fairytale about magic and theft.

* * *

A young painter from southern Italy called Antonello da Messina saw paintings by van Eyck at the Neapolitan court and was dumbstruck. He had to know how these miraculous pictures were done, so he set out on a quest to find Jan and learn his secret. It would seem, after crossing a continent, that he found van Eyck among alembics in a sorcerer's lair of a workshop. The northern artist was a kind of alchemist who discovered oil painting, Vasari says, while boiling up noxious substances. Before him, artists had used egg as the medium for precious pigments but it didn't give anything like the nuance and complexity of thin layers of colour in oil. Antonello charmed the Fleming and got him to divulge his formula. After van Eyck's death, Antonello headed south again, eventually arriving in Venice, where he set up shop, stunning Venetians with his oil paintings – until another artist tricked him and the secret was a secret no more.

It's a fiction. Van Eyck was dead before Antonello reached adulthood. But, like many of Vasari's fables, it has a point. Antonello da Messina was one of the first Italian artists to use oils in the Flemish fashion, and, curiously, the birds that flock in his painting *St Jerome in his Study* are very similar to those that haunt the rooftops of Ghent in van Eyck's *Annunciation*, which he would have had to travel to Flanders to see. What is undeniable is that Antonello looked at van Eyck intensely. His masterpiece, the *Virgin Annunciate*, internalizes the northern eye for solid things, exquisitely imitating a lectern and Mary's smooth skin, and delighting in how definitive oil paints are – while paradoxically suggesting the invisible.

Antonello took his oil paints to Venice and created an altarpiece for the church of San Cassiano, in about 1475–76, of the Virgin and Child enthroned with saints. It was highly influential both in its triangular configuration and in the seductive idea of art as a mirror, holding a sea of colour. In the 1480s, Giovanni Bellini's enormous altarpiece for the church of San Giobbe, in which the Virgin and Child are flanked by St Job and other saints, displayed the potential of oil paint to imitate surfaces (p. 34). Bellini luxuriates in the blue, pink and white robes of the Virgin, angels and saints, and the reflections that shimmer in a golden Byzantine-style mosaic above them. He also proves the

Antonello da Messina, *Virgin Annunciate*, c. 1476.

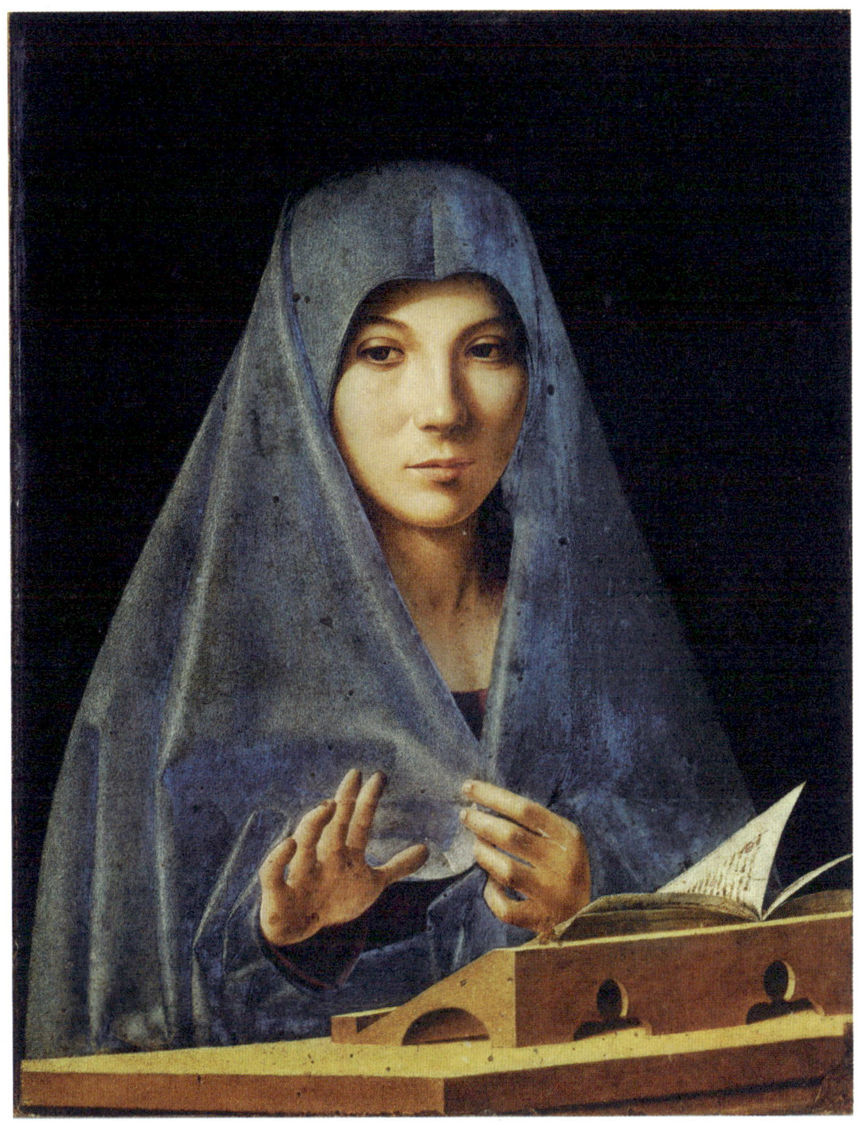

unique power of oil painting to touch on the suppleness and glow of human flesh. On the right, St Sebastian is still standing, despite the arrows shot into him by his fellow Roman soldiers; like Job he is a plague saint, and the altar-piece may have been a response to a recent epidemic in Venice. His skin exudes warmth as it catches the light. Oil paint lets Bellini tint this arrow-pierced male body with eroticism. Compare Bellini's Sebastian with the nudes in Piero della Francesca's *Baptism of Christ*. Piero's male bodies are done in egg tempera, which simply cannot be as sensual as oils. The soft, caressing alchemy of oil colours craves the human body.

* * *

Giovanni Bellini,
Madonna and Child Enthroned, c. 1487.

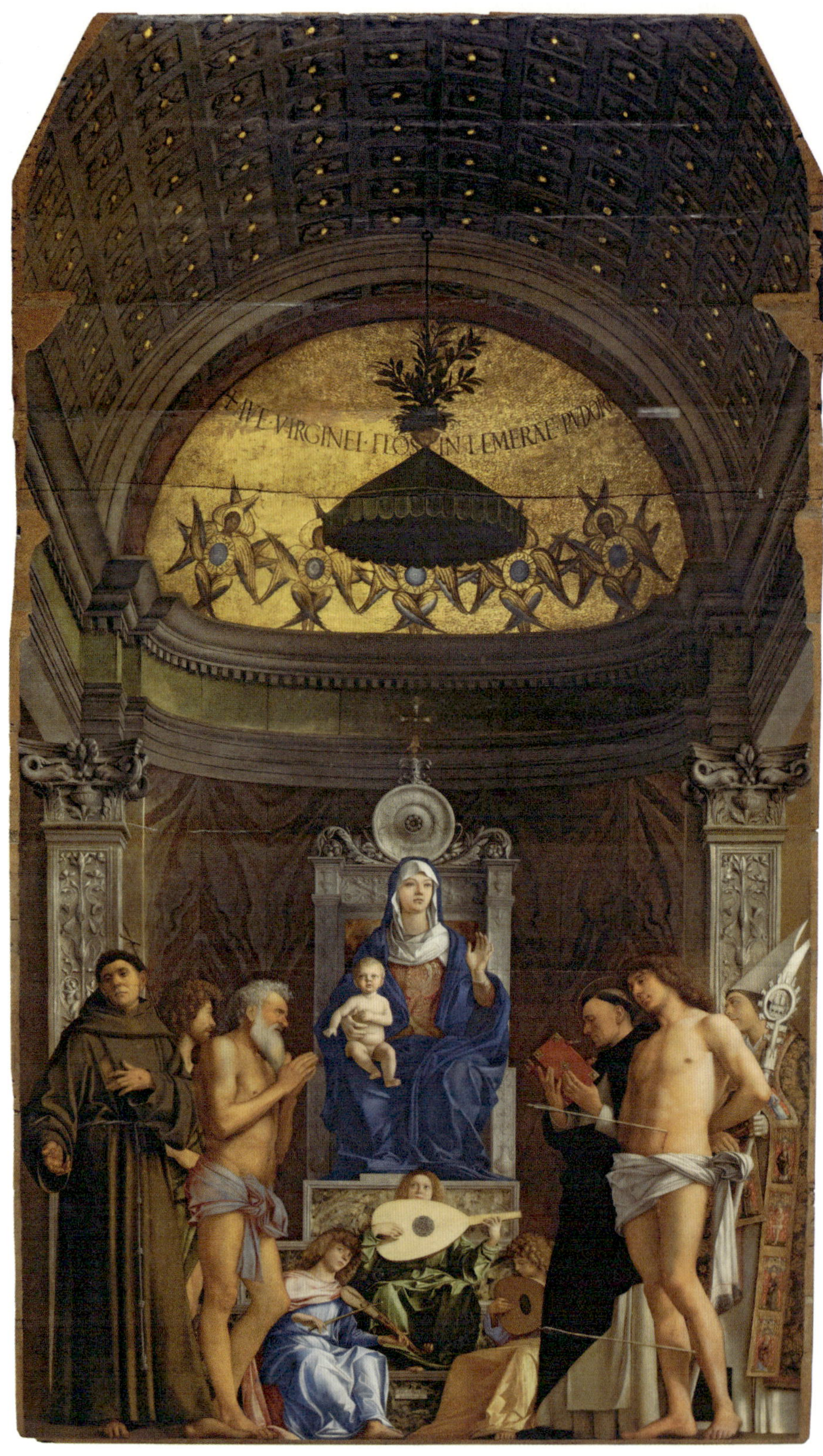

This is why van Eyck's lost Arnolfini Nude is such a seminal painting, even though it's now only a memory of one. Van Eyck died decades before Tiziano Vecellio was born, towards the end of the 1400s. But Titian's lush painting *Woman with a Mirror*, of a full-fleshed beauty and her awestruck lover, is the outcome of an obsession with van Eyck that helped his adopted city, Venice, find its own way to physical beauty.

Titian gives his model two mirrors. The man gazing so devoutly at her holds up a small, flat, rectangular mirror near her face, while at the same time he reaches behind to prop up a round, convex mirror to reflect her hair and bare neck from behind. The two mirrors are arranged so that she can see herself in full. It's different from van Eyck's nude, who lets us inspect her, or the German witch spied on by a male voyeur. She is the looker here. Titian is painting an image of his art: he is the young man with the mirrors, letting this woman see her physical presence.

Yet there's no mistaking the ancestry of that convex mirror. The subtle reflection in its liquid surface reminds you of Facio's praise of van Eyck for using a mirror to provide an additional view of a nude, and his conclusion that 'almost nothing is more marvellous in this work than the mirror in the painting'. Renaissance art from first to last holds a glass to life's beauty.

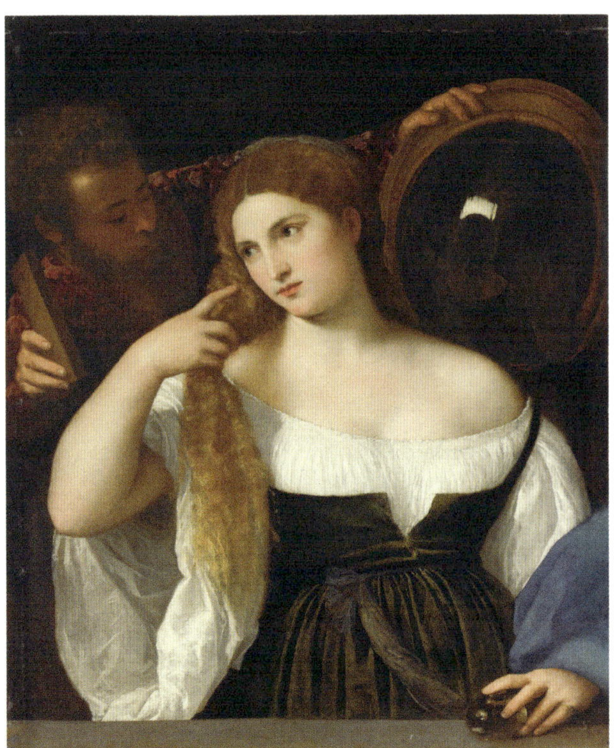

Titian, *Woman with a Mirror*, 1525–50.

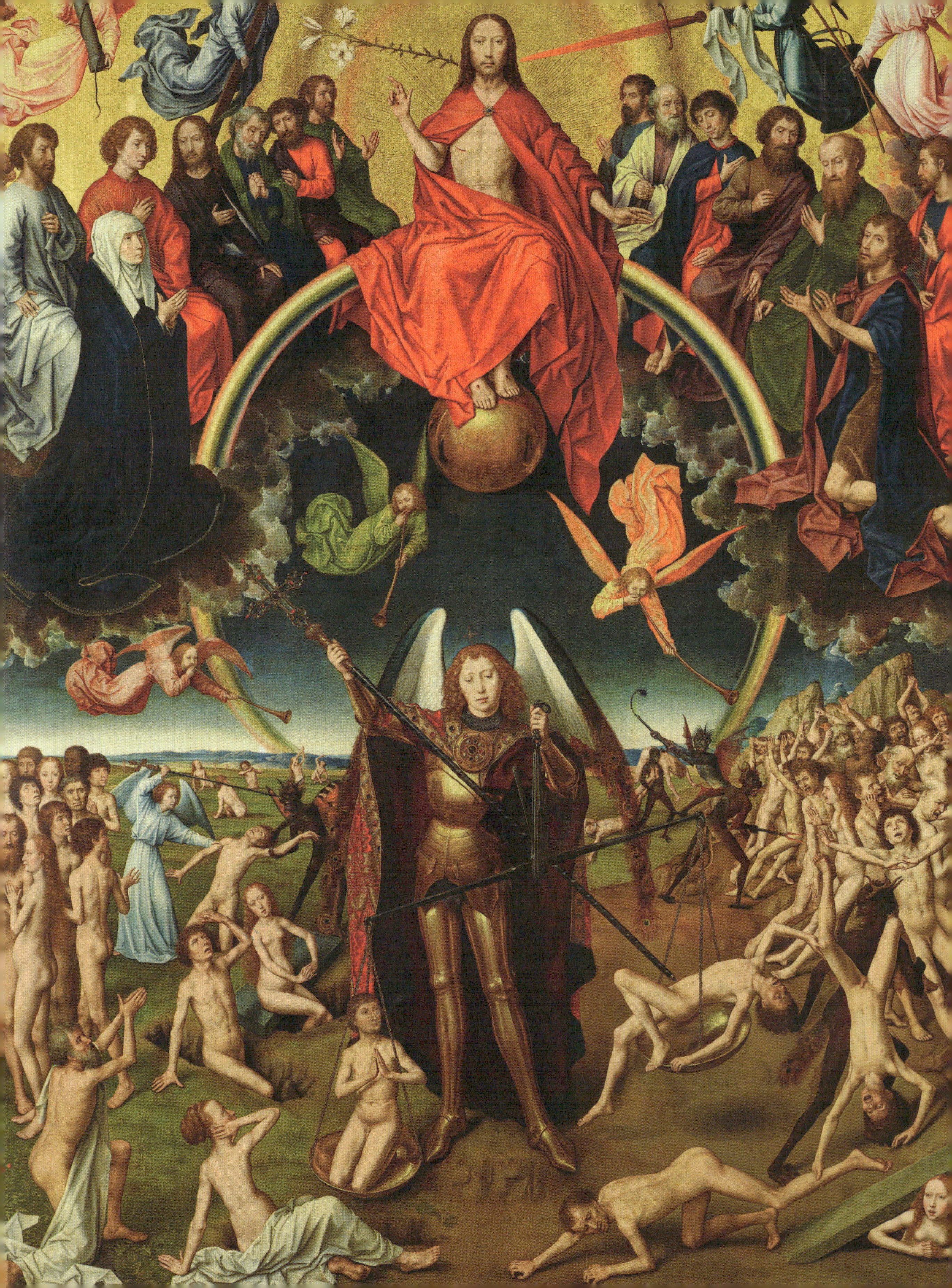

2 The Naked Citizen

Hans Memling, *Last Judgment* (detail), 1467–71.

Angels and devils, the good and the damned pitched and rolled together below decks as the North Sea surged and shrank and vomited itself up. Wrapped in cloth and securely roped in place, the altarpiece was well stowed for its long voyage. But you can't plan for everything. Above the painted bodies, heavy footfalls clumped on the wooden deck. There was a shudder through the timbers.

Pirates were boarding, though they preferred to think of themselves as privateers. In 1473 there was a war on between England and a federation of German trading cities called the Hanseatic League. In their own eyes the raiders, led by Paul Benecke of Danzig (today's Gdańsk), were carrying out a hostile act on behalf of the Hansa. Despite its neutral Burgundian flag, the ship they attacked was bound for the English coast before carrying goods from the Medici bank in Bruges back home to Tuscany.[1] The booty included gold, textiles and the fixative alum, but there was an unexpected bonus: two paintings, one of which was a spectacular three-panelled triptych of the *Last Judgment*. This is how the altarpiece, painted in Bruges by its latest artistic star, Hans Memling, and destined for a chapel in the hills above Florence, ended up in St Mary's Church in Gdańsk. Despite occasional absences (it was looted by Napoleon and the Red Army), Memling's *Last Judgment* has become part of the history

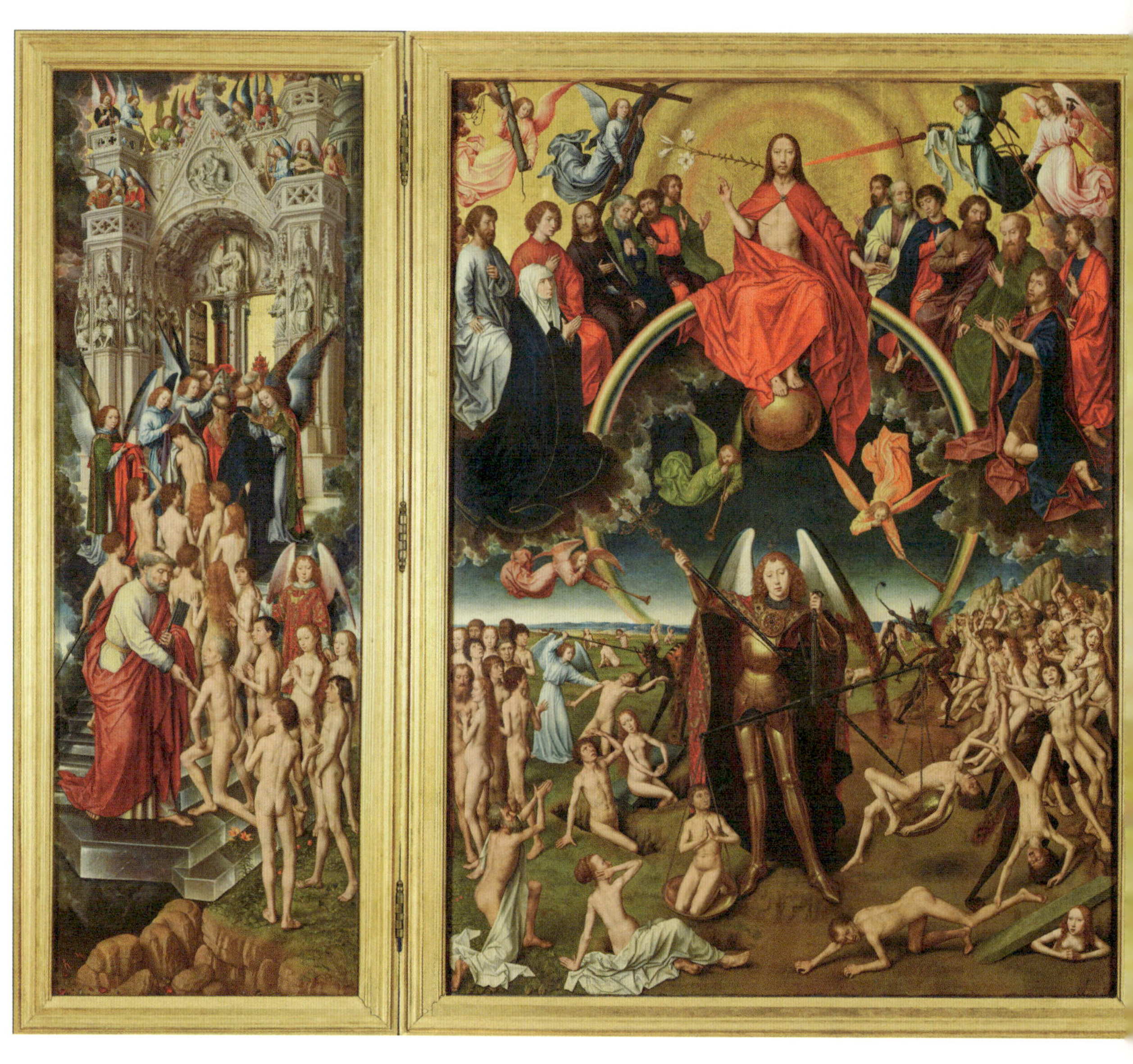

Hans Memling,
Last Judgment, 1467–71.

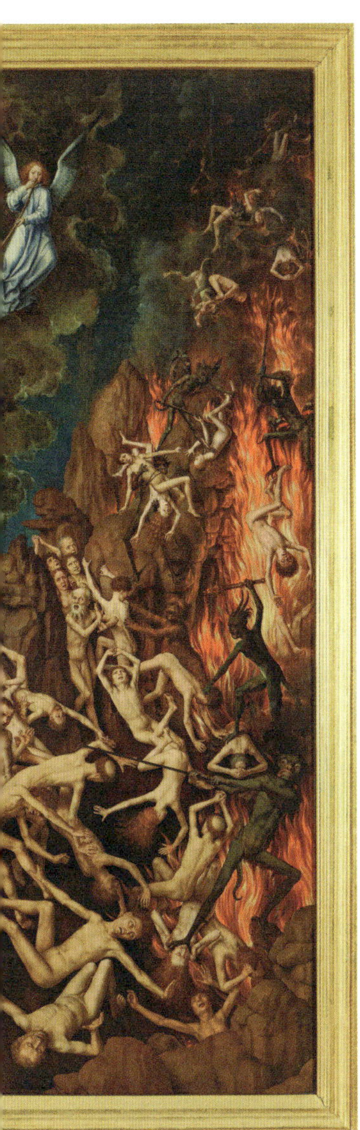

of its adoptive home, its story featuring in Günter Grass's pungent novel of the Baltic port, *The Tin Drum*.

What if the *Last Judgment* had completed its journey to Italy? Today it might be in the Uffizi Gallery in Florence, and the story of the Renaissance that this museum tells so seductively would look very different. Instead of walking through early Renaissance rooms to suddenly turn a corner and see Botticelli's *Birth of Venus*, apparently so unprecedented in its ecstatic hedonism, we would first of all be amazed by this masterpiece done more than a decade earlier: a sensual cascade of bodies whose effervescence comes from the North Sea instead of the Mediterranean and is licensed by Christianity instead of pagan antiquity.

Any excuse to get his clothes off. Tommaso Portinari, assistant manager of the Medici bank in Bruges, would have been easily recognizable to friends and family in Florence, kneeling at the symbolic centre of Memling's triptych in the angel's scales. He is identifiable from another portrait by Memling. In both paintings he prays, hands together, his sharp-nosed face contemplative under his rounded haircut. In the portrait he is soberly clad, as you might expect of a pious bank manager. In the *Last Judgment*, however, he is as naked as the day he was born, his penis recumbent between his legs as he fixes his thoughts on his eternal soul.

Other naked people too appear to be portraits of the Italian mercantile community in Bruges. In front of Portinari a nude sits caressing her head, a sheet over her thighs, as if waking up in a Bruges bedroom instead of rising from her grave. Her complex, tightly wound hairstyle adds to the impression of worldly pleasure rather than holy terror. Yet this is the End of Days, and these souls stand naked before God to face an eternal sorting. Those found to have sinned mortally open their mouths in howls as they are herded by demons with pitchforks. They are carried aloft in hell's bleak sky and plummet into its fires. Two of the most prominent fallen souls have tonsures: they are monks. All the damned are depicted with lavish anatomical accuracy. Memling takes the opportunity to revolve them, showing them from every point of view as they wheel, dive and hang upside down in the netherworld of stone and fire.

The painting in which Tommaso Portinari sent his nude portrait home to Tuscany, only for it to end up in Gdańsk where no one knew him and even Memling's authorship was forgotten for centuries, takes liberties with a sacred theme. It has a sophisticated playfulness, even in its vision of hell. We sense Memling enjoying himself, as well as being happy to oblige clients' egos. What has become of the emotional shock that such a work was supposed to administer?

* * *

It was hard to get bored or doze off in a late medieval church. There was often a ferocious mural of the Last Judgment (called a 'Doom' in England), as well as the rood, a pitiful figure of the crucified Christ suspended from the rafters: a heart-wound of pain and mortality. You were urged to meditate on this body born into agony and death.

Christ's physical being was more enigmatically represented in the Eucharist, the most weighty sacrament of the Western church ever since the Fourth Lateran Council of 1215 had formulated the doctrine of 'transubstantiation' – the miraculous transformation of the bread and wine held up by a priest during Mass into the actual body and blood of Jesus Christ. The body of Christ was also celebrated in its own festival of Corpus Christi.

Artists tried to make the body of Christ so real you shuddered. In Giotto di Bondone's fresco of the *Kiss of Judas*, done at the start of the 1300s in the Scrovegni Chapel in Padua, Christ is about to accept shocking lip contact with a man he knows has betrayed him. As their mouths come close, Christ's stare burns into Judas. Such intimacy electrifies us with Christ's incarnate humanity. His older contemporary Cimabue whips the same fact into us in the *Flagellation*:

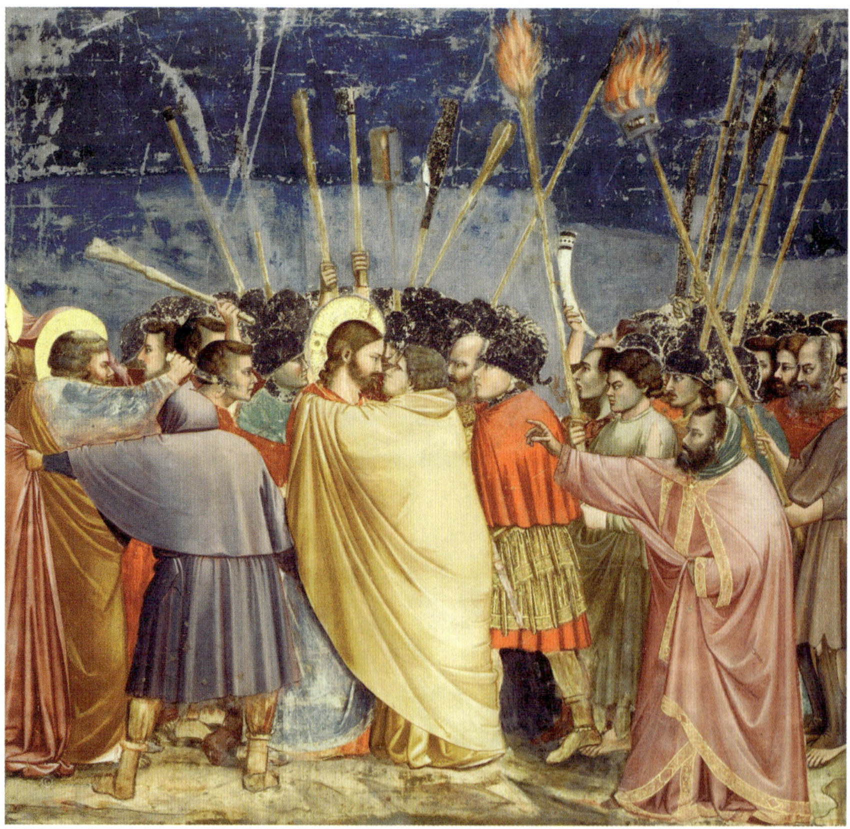

Giotto,
Kiss of Judas, 1304–6.

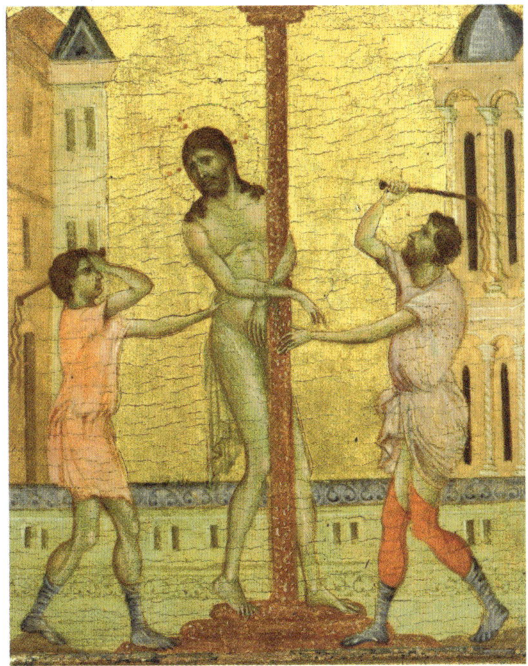

Cimabue, *Flagellation of Christ*, c. 1280.

a slender, anatomically abstract Christ sways at the post to which he is tied as two torturers raise their flails.

'Cimabue thought he was in the lead,' wrote Dante, who lived at the same time as both, 'but now Giotto gets them shouting.'[2] Giotto eclipsed his rival because he made the body of Christ more solid, real and fleshy. Cimabue seems reluctant to show Christ in pain, even as he is whipped: he is loyal to an earlier artistic tradition of Christ in triumph. Giotto, on the other hand, gives Judas's kiss a blunt bodily directness – and a jarring hint of sexuality – that makes Christ's suffering on earth immediate.

That preoccupation with Christ's physical form was given almost grotesque urgency from the 1300s by the North European genre of the *Vesperbild*, named after its association with the 'vespers', or evening prayers, said on Good Friday. The image concentrated not on Christ's suffering but his actual dead body; it was later known in Italy as the *Pietà*. A typical late 14th-century polychrome wood carving from southern Germany depicts Christ as an emaciated corpse with ribs sharply sticking out. Mary cradles this shrunken mummy as if it were her newborn son. It's an astringent attempt to make us see the enormity of death through the eyes of a bereaved mother.

Those who saw this sculpture when it was made around 1375–1400 had grown up in the shadow of the most devastating plague in post-classical European history. In 1347 a Genoese ship brought the Black Death from the Eastern

Mediterranean. It wiped out at least a third, maybe more than half, of Europe's population, scarring the collective imagination with skeletal nightmares. Death grimaces and grins in late medieval art, from cadavers sculpted on tombs to frescoes of death's triumph. It takes on a sublime aspect in the art of Rogier van der Weyden, who was born in Tournai in Flanders and dominated the Brussels art scene from the 1430s until his death in 1464. Van der Weyden took Flemish art in a different direction from van Eyck. He uses oil paints, sometimes with the older tempera colours too, in an art of harrowing expressionism. That 20th-century word – 'expressionism' – does not seem out of place when we look at Rogier's *Pietà*. A red-yellow dawn radiating through blue shadows of night sets this small painting alight. Black, bare branches of winter trees are bitterly defined against the glow; clumps of ragged foliage promise new life, but it's a slender hope. Mary presses her lips to the face of the son she caresses for one last kiss, but he is already gone. Christ's body is discoloured by death, leathery and thin and stiff. Mary cradles his head and stomach while John the Evangelist supports his side, but his body is unnaturally straight and his right arm falls perpendicular to the ground.

Mary Magdalene is the third person to witness this horror. Mentioned in the Gospels as a follower of Christ who was loyal to the end, the first person to see him resurrected, the Magdalene was given a backstory by the church as a reformed prostitute. This profane past haunts her relationship with Christ in art. Here, as in other depictions, her hair is long and sensual, her face young; her grief that of a wife or lover. A pot of perfumed ointment rests on a rock, ready for her to rub into Christ's filthy, bloodied feet.

Rogier brings the same intensity to the *Last Judgment* he painted in Beaune in the 1440s (pp. 44–45). Today Beaune is the capital of the Bourgogne wine region. Six centuries ago this part of France was conjoined with Flanders in the Duchy of Burgundy. Beaune's welfare institution, the Hôtel-Dieu, was built by the duchy's chancellor, Nicolas Rolin. As they endured disease and old age, the poor were encouraged to think of their immortal destiny by the huge altarpiece Rolin commissioned for it. When closed, it shows portraits of Rolin and his wife praying in sparse, contemplative settings. When open, a stupendous nine panels – which put your common-or-garden triptych in the shade – unfurl to announce the End of Days. Under a golden blaze of cloud that mushrooms across all the panels, billowing into heaven and hell, naked women and men stagger in a frieze of hope and terror. Above them towers the Archangel Michael holding scales, which tilt to our right, towards damnation.

Van der Weyden's naked figures carry the weight of this moment in their anguished poses. To stress their emotional isolation and remove any hint of

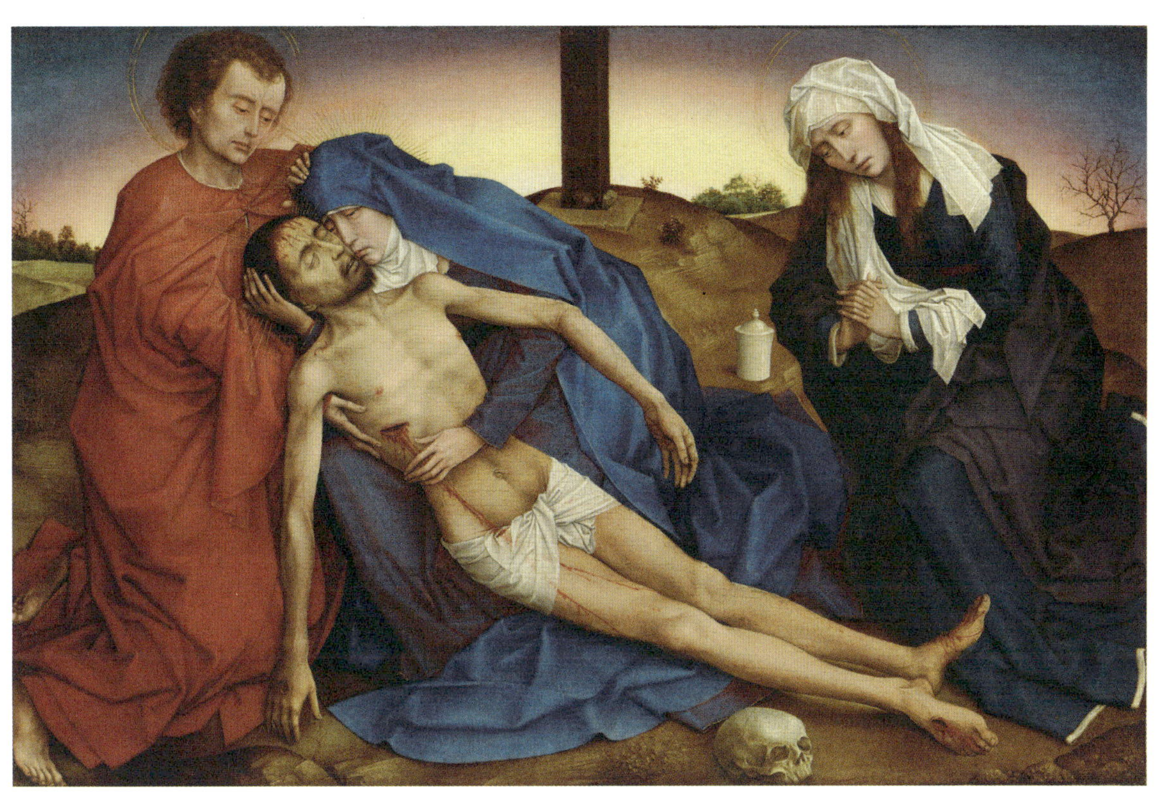

Rogier van der Weyden,
Pietà, c. 1441.

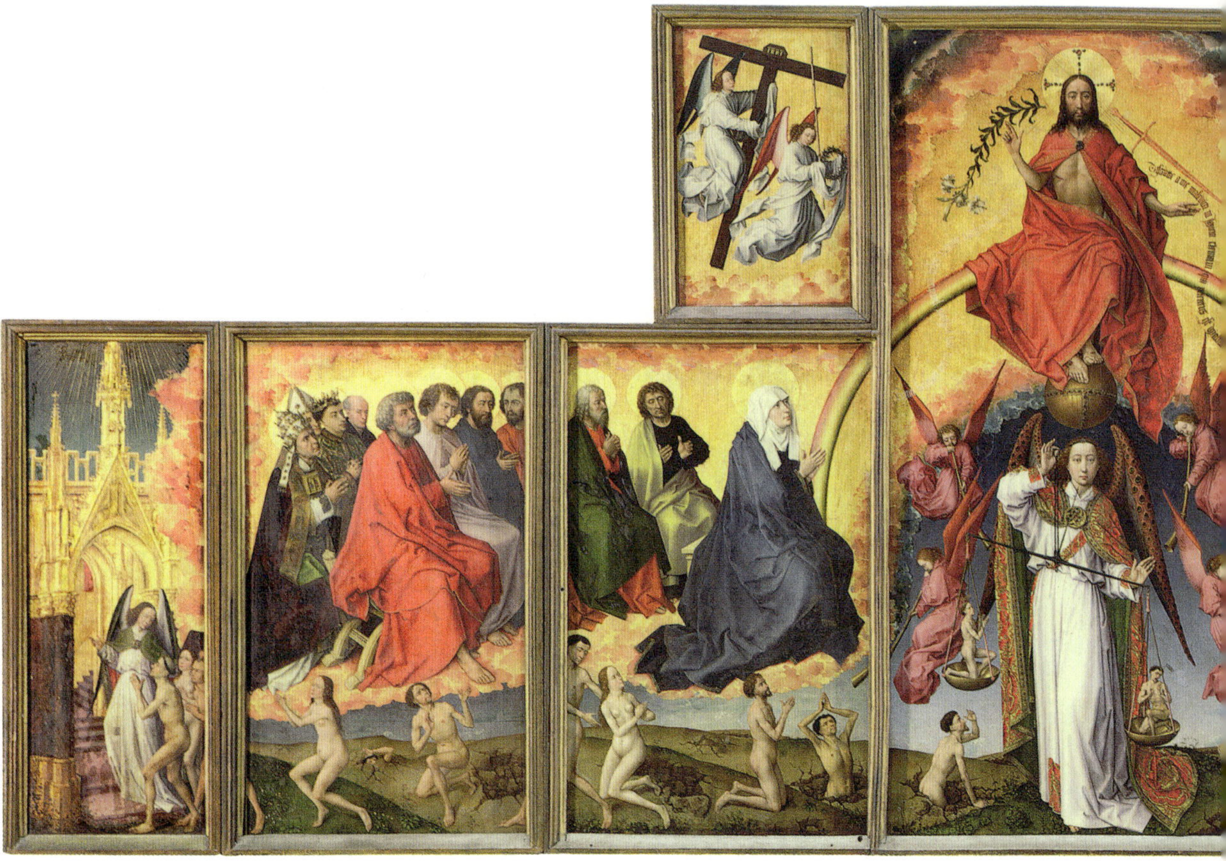

apocalyptic hanky-panky, he separates them in private turmoils across the wide landscape. There's no unseemly crowding, except in the abyss of hell. These nudes are everywoman and everyman, their loneliness urging us to identify with their fate – for it is our own.

* * *

Compared with Rogier van der Weyden's vision, Hans Memling's *Last Judgment* is bustling and lighthearted. We admire the flowing, ingenious arrangement of so many naked bodies, organized in a seamless, graceful river of humanity that starts with the centre panel's landscape of open graves and arcs up heaven's stairs and into hell. Even the damned appear to dance in space, their postures acrobatic. This is an artist enjoying his nudes. Bodies are differentiated, and studied apparently from life. A man stands like a model with his back to us at the foot of heaven's steps, giving Memling plenty of time to analyse his shoulder blades, the canal of his spine and his oblong buttocks. Memling is taking the opportunity to show off his talent as a painter of the nude. You sense the

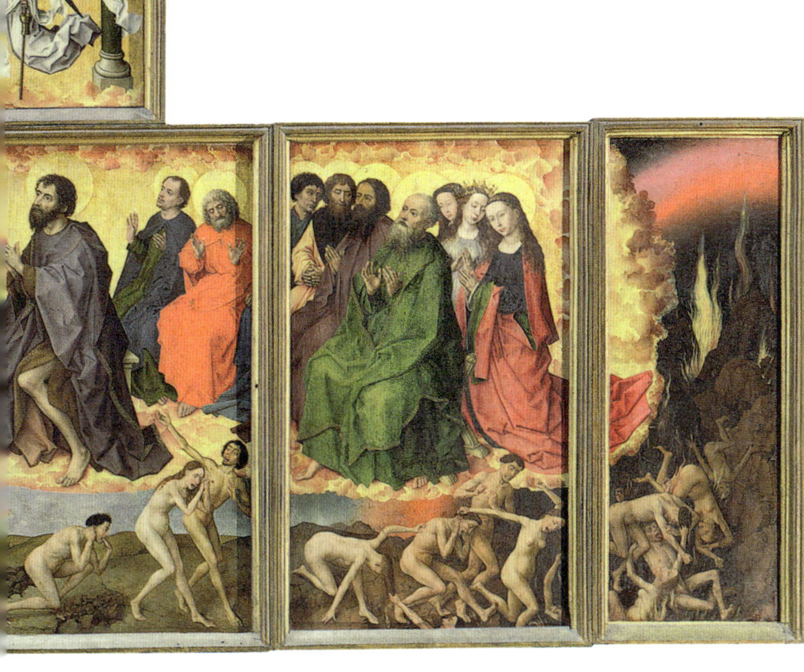

Rogier van der Weyden, *Last Judgment*, 1443–51.

streets of Bruges in this scene's casual crowd, as if this were a market jostling with people all of whom happen to be naked.

The comparison with Rogier van der Weyden is unavoidable, for Memling has obviously adapted his *Last Judgment* from the Beaune polyptych in a dialogue with his late teacher. Born in the 1430s in Selingenstadt near Frankfurt, Memling probably trained in van der Weyden's Brussels workshop before paying to become a citizen of Bruges in 1465, the year after his master's death. He evidently knew Rogier's *Last Judgment*. His own design compresses and crowds it, yet keeps the central figure of a towering angel. The difference is that, instead of having them sinking towards hell, Memling shows the angel's scales tilting to salvation, as the naked man in them is judged to be good. This is Tommaso Portinari, the man from the Medici bank. It's hard to say who had more chutzpah – the painter cramming his religious work with earthly nudes or the Florentine who insisted on being one of them.

* * *

Cosimo de' Medici, the man who put the Medici family at the heart of Florentine life, had never trusted Tommaso. He helped the young Portinari boys after their father died, gave them jobs in the family bank, but he kept Tommaso in a comparatively junior role as assistant manager in Bruges – unlike his older brother Pigello, who had a brilliant career in the Milan branch. Such caution fits the prudent image of a figure who established his family as de facto rulers of supposedly republican Florence: a wise and measured man who thought subtly. In Jacopo Pontormo's portrait, painted long after Cosimo's death, he looks like a philosopher, gaunt and pensive in his wine-red gown. In his own time, the Florentine Republic simply called him, on his tomb, 'PATER PATRIAE': 'Father of the State'.

What was it about Tommaso that Cosimo didn't trust? It can't have been his lineage. The Portinari were a distinguished Florentine family, far older than the upstart Medici. The Portinari bank was flourishing in the 13th century when Dante Alighieri fell in love with Beatrice Portinari. Dante's autobiographical work *The New Life* tells how his ever-deepening love for Beatrice dominated his existence and transformed his soul, turning him into a poet. After her death in 1290, at the age of 25, their unconsummated love became a personal religious cult. Beatrice oversaw his journey through hell and purgatory to paradise in the *Divine Comedy*, ensuring that he had the Roman poet Virgil for a guide and watching sympathetically from heaven as they negotiated hell's surreal terraces.

By Cosimo's time the Portinari bank was long broken. Banking was not a stable business in the Middle Ages. Florentine firms could rise and fall in the space of a generation or two, impaling themselves on the mysteries of credit, not least by lending to Northern European rulers who defaulted on massive sums. Dante's beloved Beatrice, in spite of the poet's adoration, married Simone dei Bardi, creating an alliance between the Portinari and one of the city's grandest banking families. But the Bardi bank was ruined when it lent 900,000 florins to Edward III, king of England, and never got it back.

This was the kind of error Cosimo de' Medici wished to avoid. The Medici bank in Bruges, where Cosimo kept Tommaso on a tight leash, occupied a sprawling Gothic palace with a princely courtyard, gargoyles and sloping tiled roofs. All around it were signs of the city's trading opulence. The busy Kraanplein square took its name from the city's crane that, in Memling's St John Altarpiece, looks like a massive wooden jug with a thick conical spout. Yet for all the prickly Flemish words, grey skies and spiky architecture, Tommaso was not alone in this foreign land. There was a long-established Italian merchant community in Bruges. The Adorno family from Genoa and the Arnolfini from Lucca had been doing business here years before the Medici branch opened in 1439. Bruges was almost the northern twin of Florence, only with crenellations and thin arches instead of the classical columns and pilasters that were all the rage at home.

In other ways the northern city was alien, exotic – and hazardous for a financier. The gold and jewels, carpets and fancy robes we see in van Eyck's paintings are not just evidence of a wealthy mercantile economy but the unvarnished, vulgar display of feudal rule. While Florence governed itself, Bruges owed fealty to the duke of Burgundy, whose court was a fantasy world where birds flew out of pies, funerals were stylized rites of black-shrouded wailing, and dukes started wars as lightly as tournaments. Burgundy was exactly the kind of gold-hungry borrower that had ruined bankers like the Bardi.

In 1464 Cosimo de' Medici died, and his financial acumen was buried with him. Tommaso got promoted and promptly showed why Cosimo's doubts were justified. He ingratiated himself with Charles the Bold, duke of Burgundy, by lending him the bank's money – lots of it. Just like the fallen Florentine bankers of yore, he threw good modern credit into the bottomless pit of medieval chivalry.

Memling's *Last Judgment* actually has conventional donor portraits on the reverse of its two wings, but they do not show Portinari. The people praying here are Tommasso's former boss, Angelo Tani, and Tani's wife, Catarina Tanagli. It was Tani who had commissioned the painting. When Tani was called back to Florence, Portinari made this painting his own by the bold act of having himself painted naked at the heart of it.

* * *

What would Memling's altarpiece have looked like to Florentines if it had evaded the pirates and arrived in the city in 1473 or 1474? Its nudity would have been accepted without much religious scruple, and Portinari's nakedness would have been appreciated by eyes primed to admire the male nude.

This Florentine taste for the male body in art was, at the start, the enfleshing of political ideals. Florence was a republic – a concept of the self-ruling community that went back to Greek and Roman political theory. Just as the Athenians won their freedom from tyrants in the 6th century BCE, so Florence won its freedom in 1343 from the despotic Walter of Brienne, who claimed the title 'Duke of Athens'. To say Florentine politics was a male world is to state the obvious. In modern terminology it seems reasonable to say that the brotherhood of male citizens encouraged a homosocial atmosphere.

The early Renaissance painter who most impressed later Florentine artists was Masaccio – 'Big Tom', as the short-lived Tommaso di Ser Giovanni di Simone was nicknamed. Leonardo da Vinci and Michelangelo worshipped him. When he died in 1428, at the age of only 26, he left behind a handful of severely

Masaccio, *Expulsion from Paradise*, c. 1427.

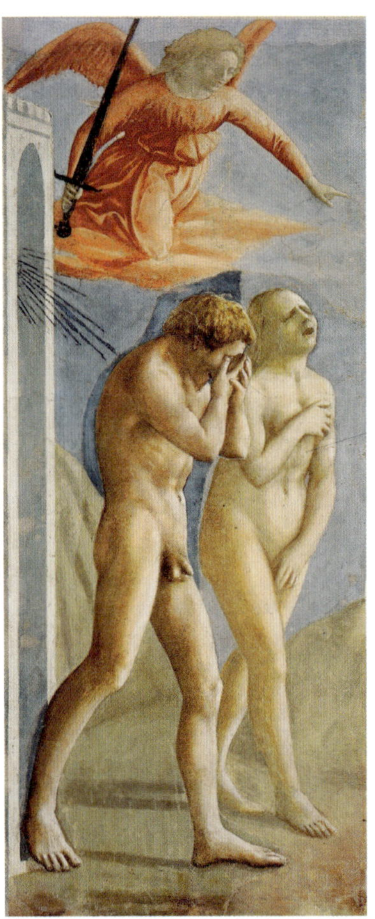

brilliant frescoes, including a naked Adam and Eve in the Brancacci Chapel on the south side of the river Arno. This is a sensuous image – so much so that, in the Baroque age, Adam and Eve would get their private parts painted over, to be finally restored to their full physicality only in the 1980s. While Eve covers herself, howling at the sky as she is overcome by shame, Adam, sobbing into his hands, neglects to hide his penis and globular testicles. Even this early in the century (Masaccio painted the *Expulsion from Paradise* in about 1427), it was the male nude that impressed Florentine artists.

A combination of echoes of ancient republicanism and appeals to male friendship could produce public art with a manly intimacy. Yet just as the Roman Republic in the age of Cicero was under attack from ambitious men including Julius Caesar, so the Florentine Republic had to be on its guard against families and factions that might subvert its freedom.

Some hope. The government was supposedly structured in such a way as to prevent corruption: elections to the executive, called the 'Signoria', and to specialist committees were decided by the frequent, random selection of candidates' names from a bag. The trick was to influence whose names went into the bag. When a faction got into power it tended to exile dangerous rivals. In 1431 the Albizzi dominated the Signoria, and Cosimo de' Medici – after nearly losing his life – was exiled to Venice. By 1434 he had turned the tables, and for the next six decades neighbourhood loyalties, kin connections, business friendships, bribery and occasional bursts of extreme violence kept the Medici in power.

All this was imagined by contemporaries through a lens of Roman history. Leonardo Bruni was the chancellor of Florence, the top civil servant in the Palazzo della Signoria. He wrote a history of the Florentine people in Latin, modelled on the ancient writer Livy's epic history of Rome 'from the founding of the city'. Bruni makes the struggles of rival Tuscan cities seem as weighty as the conquests of the Romans. This emulation of the old Romans can also be seen in portrait sculpture. Florentine artists revived the acutely lifelike style of portrait bust popular in late Republican Rome. Mino da Fiesole's 1464 bust of the anti-Medici politician Dietisalvi Neroni is a warm, intimate portrayal of this 'rebel', with classical-looking short-cropped hair and robe tied at the shoulder.

The Renaissance did not 'rediscover' ancient Rome. The ruins of the ancient empire that rose from a settlement by the river Tiber to rule territories from Britain to Egypt, Judaea and Babylonia were too impressive to ever be quite forgotten. The pagan Saxons in the former Britannia seem to have shunned Roman towns, but by the time of the Frankish ruler Charlemagne the nascent medieval world was already idolizing the Romans. Charlemagne was crowned 'Emperor of the Romans' in 800, marking the start of the Holy Roman Empire – the most ambitious political entity of medieval and Renaissance Europe, which claimed the heritage of the Caesars. The Roman tongue, Latin, was a living language, spoken and read in monasteries and universities, intoned at Mass throughout medieval Christendom. When Cosimo de' Medici and his fellow Florentine bibliophile Niccolò de' Niccoli sought out manuscripts of lost Latin books with the help of the adventurous book hunter Poggio Bracciolini, the reason they could do so was that so many had been preserved throughout the Middle Ages. Vitruvius on architecture, Quintilian on rhetoric, speeches by Cicero and *On the Nature of Things* by Lucretius were among the works these Florentine book lovers found in monastic libraries, neglected but safe. Other texts we think of as archetypally 'Renaissance' had never been lost at all: many a medieval monk was entertained copying out Ovid's the *Art of Love*.

To make such books available, Cosimo created a new public library, designed by his architect Michelozzo, as part of the rebuilding of the monastery of San Marco. This was his most ambitious artistic and architectural commission – and the most profoundly pious. There is no holier artistic destination in Europe than the Dominican convent of San Marco in Florence. The monks' narrow cells were individually decorated between 1439 and 1444 by Fra Angelico, a friar there, and his team. Cell 7 has an eerie fresco of the *Mocking of Christ*: blindfolded like a modern torture victim, he sits impassively while disconnected hands and instruments symbolize his beating and crowning with thorns. A disembodied head spits in his face.

Christ has his entire body hidden under a shroud-like white robe. Several cells are painted with stark scenes of the crucifixion, accompanied by the figures of friars and Dominican saints contemplating the agony of Christ – an aid to prayer for the cells' residents. These pictures too cover Christ's shame with long, white loincloths. His anatomy is formal, almost Byzantine, more reminiscent of Cimabue than of Giotto. Cosimo had his own cell, decorated with a fresco of the *Adoration of the Magi*: the Medici loved to identify with the philosopher-kings who came from the East bearing gifts for the infant Jesus.

Maybe the spiritual visions at San Marco protest too much, going out of their way to avoid stimulating the eyes of the Dominicans. Fra Angelico seems to be imposing a discipline on the bodies of his fellow friars: they had best keep their hands for praying. The presence of licentious pagan books (Lucretius's *On the Nature of Things* begins with a prayer to Venus) so near to the monks' cells only made this purifying art more urgent.

As the wealthy Classics fans of 15th-century Florence pored over Latin texts, they wondered about the older civilization of the Greeks that lay behind them. In this they were following the Romans themselves: even as they annexed Greece, the Romans honoured Greek literature, architecture and art. They turned them into the style we call 'classical', which they reproduced wherever they conquered. Romanized Greek gods are still being excavated in British fields and North African deserts.

In 1400 the language of the Greeks was barely known in Western Europe. Where the Roman church and Carolingian court had preserved Latin texts, the manuscripts and language of ancient Greece were safeguarded by the Byzantine Empire, which had its capital at Constantinople. There wasn't much love lost between Eastern and Western Christians. But as the Byzantines faced being overwhelmed by the Ottoman Turks an attempt was made to reconcile the two churches. It brought some of the greatest Greek scholars to Florence and, with them, ideas that were both enthralling and disturbing.

* * *

Fra Angelico,
Mocking of Christ,
1440–42.

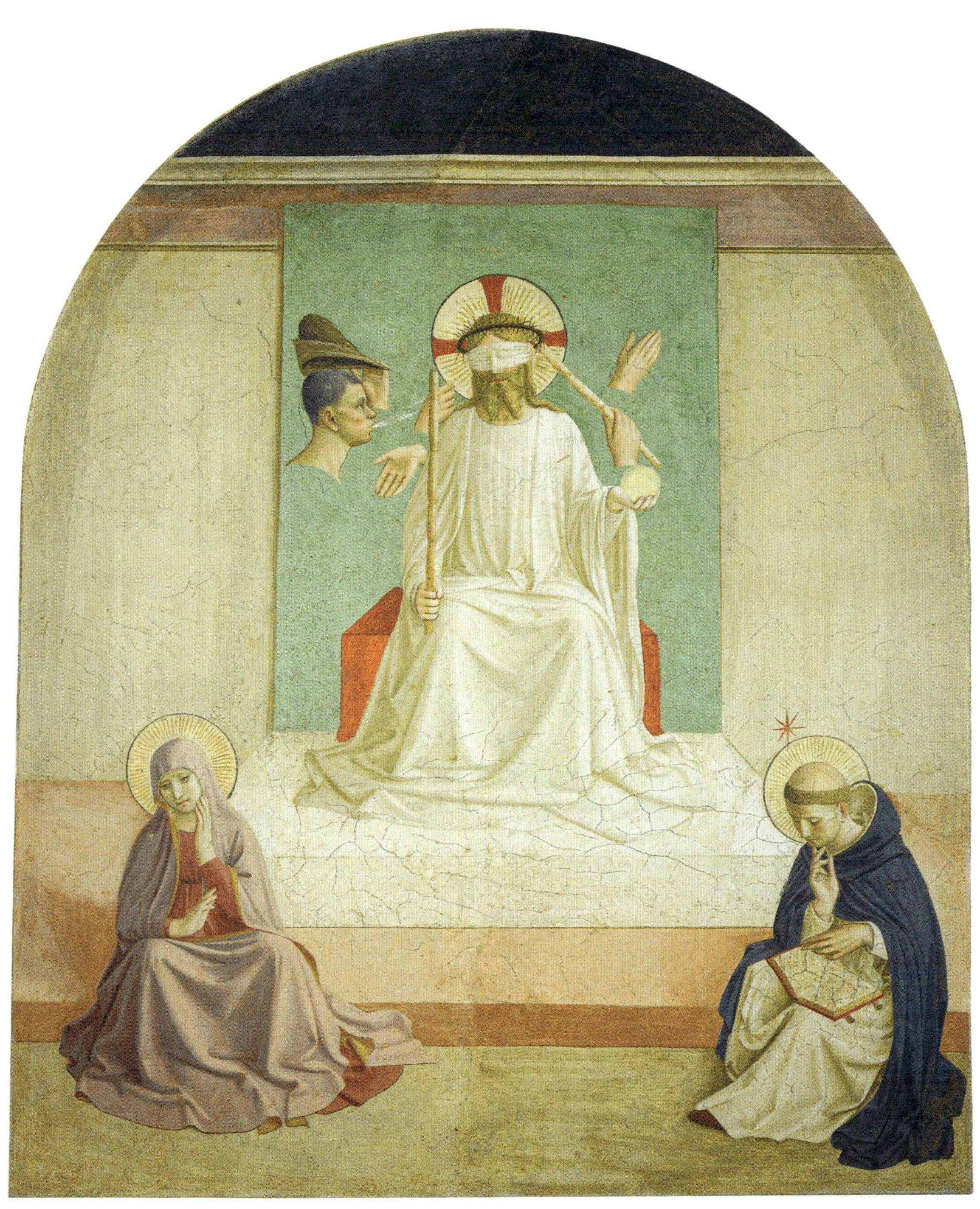

The wise men in Piero della Francesca's *Baptism*, with their Byzantine-style hats that are fatter at the top than bottom, appear to commemorate this meeting. Piero was probably in Florence in 1438, where a tense conference between the Roman and Byzantine churches had been relocated from plague-stricken Ferrara. The Byzantines spoke Greek as their living language. Their delegation included George Gemistus Plethon, a daring philosopher who electrified Florentines with his radical understanding of ancient Greek thought. For a start, he explained the difference between Aristotle, the one Greek philosopher who was not just known but exalted in the West, and his elder Plato. Even from a slight acquaintance, the Florentines could see that Plato was a more poetic, suggestive, unpredictable thinker. Plethon was also a devotee of the Persian prophet Zoroaster and aspects of Islam, and may have put the idea into Cosimo de' Medici's head that Platonism could be combined with magic and occult lore from Egypt and Babylon. In an unpublished work that was largely destroyed after his death, surviving only in provocative fragments, he went much further, proposing a return to paganism that would be the salvation of decadent Byzantium.

The agreement reached at the Council of Florence on 6 July 1439 is remembered in Filippo Brunelleschi's Old Sacristy (a chamber where priests donned their vestments), commissioned by the Medici for their parish church of San Lorenzo, around the corner from their old family home and the new palace Cosimo built in the 1440s. A painted dome over the altar shows constellations, gold on blue, as they appeared on the date the concord was made. It is both an acute manifestation of astronomy and a mystical vision. This meeting of East and West is memorialized as a world historical event like the birth of Christ, witnessed by modern magi who have tracked and recorded the prodigious moment in the heavens.

The fresco suggests a realm beyond clerical politics, for on a practical level the agreement turned out to be worthless. It suggests the thrill of philosophical discovery as ancient Greek learning came closer. Cosimo, the story goes, couldn't stop there. Plethon inspired him to refound the Academy – Plato's school in Athens – and to commission a brilliant young Tuscan scholar called Marsilio Ficino to translate Plato into Latin, and, while he was about it, a late antique body of magical writings attributed to a Greco-Egyptian semi-divine figure named Hermes Trismegistus.

* * *

Ficino is the quintessential 'humanist', a term coined in the 19th century for the new breed of classical scholar seen as the intellectual vanguard of the Renaissance. It comes laden with assumptions, suggesting a new belief in 'humanity' and our capacity to reason. As the case of Ficino shows, the reality was more complicated: he revived the practice of Hermetic magic and demonstrated how to make talismans that draw down astral powers. He also fervently sought to reconcile Plato with Christianity.

It's hotly debated whether Cosimo truly recreated the Platonic Academy or just invited friends around to chat about Plato over a glass of wine. But he did set Ficino to his great labour. By the time of his death in 1499, Ficino had translated Plato's works and written influential commentaries on them in a project that transformed European high thought. The appeal of Plato for the Renaissance was precisely that he is less systematic than Aristotle: where medieval universities enshrined Aristotelianism as a dogmatic theory of everything, Plato, with his enigmatic images, dramatic dialogues and assertions that ecstatic fury and love can lead to truth, opened up new freedoms.

Ficino would merge Christianity and Platonism, to his own satisfaction at least. But the impact of Plato could be dangerous. One early Italian fan was Sigismondo Malatesta, the lord of Rimini. Malatesta so admired Plethon, who by the end of his life wanted to roll back Christianity, that he recovered his body from the East and constructed a tomb for him in the Tempio Malatestiano, a church in Rimini designed by Alberti with a façade modelled on the triumphal arches of pagan Rome. It is fairly pagan inside as well, decorated with zodiacal reliefs that include a crab crawling up the wall – hardly traditional for a church.

As far as the pope was concerned, excommunication wasn't bad enough for Malatesta. He is the only person in history who has ever been 'infernally canonized' – that is, condemned to hell while still alive.

* * *

The first Greek manuscript of Plato's complete works had reached Florence in 1423. A year later Leonardo Bruni issued a quick, partial translation of what people were presumably most eager to read, the *Phaedrus*. Plato's dialogues are intellectual dramas, realistically set in classical Athens, and star the sage Socrates, who expounds his ideas by subjecting people to playful interrogations. *Phaedrus* is a rich, complex, paradoxical dialogue that deals with love, rhetoric and different types of divine madness, or *mania* (*furor*, as it was translated into Latin), including poetic 'fury'. The dialogue includes the evocative image of the winged soul. Bruni later sent Cosimo his translation of the concluding speech of the *Symposium*, in which the general and politician Alcibiades describes his erotic pursuit of Socrates. In both cases Bruni had tried to expunge the dialogues' homosexual content. Despite his efforts, however, there was no getting away from the fact that, in exploring Plato, the humanists were encountering the ancient Greek openness to what the church considered the mortal sin of 'sodomy', a crime punishable by death.

That the threat from Plato was erotic as well as theological may have had an emotional urgency for Marsilio Ficino, who desired men. The model of love presented in the *Phaedrus* is that between an older man and a younger man of the same class. Such love can lead the soul upwards, to a higher truth.

The firebrand 15th-century preacher Bernardino of Siena had a gripe with Florence: why did it countenance sodomites? This tolerance went at least as far back as Dante, who shows compassion for homosexuals in hell, especially his mentor, the scholar and writer Brunetto Latini. All those being punished by fire alongside him, says Latini in the *Inferno*, are cultured men like him:

> 'In sum, know that all were clerks
> and great literary men, of great fame,
> Yet by the same sin were filthy to the world.'[3]

It seems that Dante's trust in divine justice is being tested, for it was Latini who taught him the nature of morality and goodness.

By the 1400s the republic's tolerance of homosexuality was so notorious that it was being condemned from Bernardino's pulpit. It was in this charged moment, when Florence was first encountering Plato, that Cosimo de' Medici appears to have commissioned a statue that frankly explores not only Greek art but Greek love. Donatello's *David* stood on a column in the new Medici palace. Its sensational departure from a thousand years of Christian artistic tradition was an assertion of the new learning that the Medici sponsored. It depicts the moment when the biblical David, having killed Goliath with a stone, slices off his head with the giant's own sword and rests his foot on it in triumph. What we see, though, is a cocky boy, hand on hip, without clothes. This is how the ancient Greeks liked their statues: nude. And this polished figure of a beautiful youth left no doubt that classical nudity was perilous.

Donatello is the greatest artist of the early Florentine Renaissance because his use of classical harmony is always in creative tension with a Gothic energy. His marble statue of a defiant *St George*, for instance, has the poise of ancient sculpture yet wears armour and carries a shield. Donatello's bronze *Judith and Holofernes* (p. 56) was commissioned, like the *David*, by Cosimo de' Medici for his palace. It too is positively alarming in its collision of flesh and justice: the muscular, hulking mass of Holofernes is gripped and held up by his matted hair, as the avenger Judith raises her sword to chop his head off. Judith is completely covered up; Holofernes is naked. In the Apocryphal Old Testament story, the heroic young widow tricks this oppressor of the Israelites, gets him drunk then kills him. Does Donatello have more sympathy for the drunkard than the killer? That possibility was not conceived of by those who placed inscriptions beneath the statue. One celebrated the defeat of pride by humility; another praised Judith as a model of republican virtue. Manuscript evidence has shown that *David*, too, had a similarly stirring inscription, praising the boy who overcame a tyrant and urging citizens on to conquest.

* * *

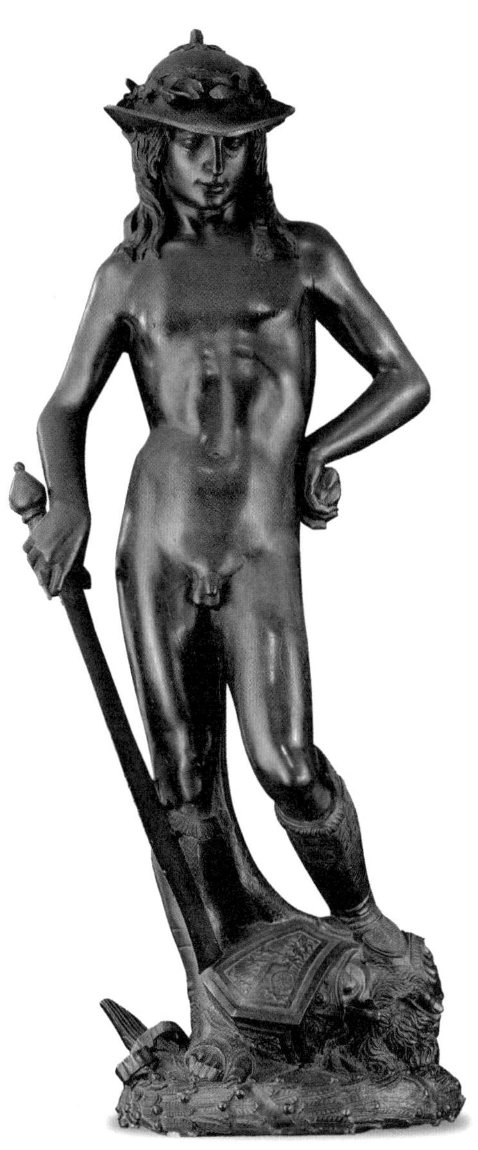

Donatello,
David, c. 1440.

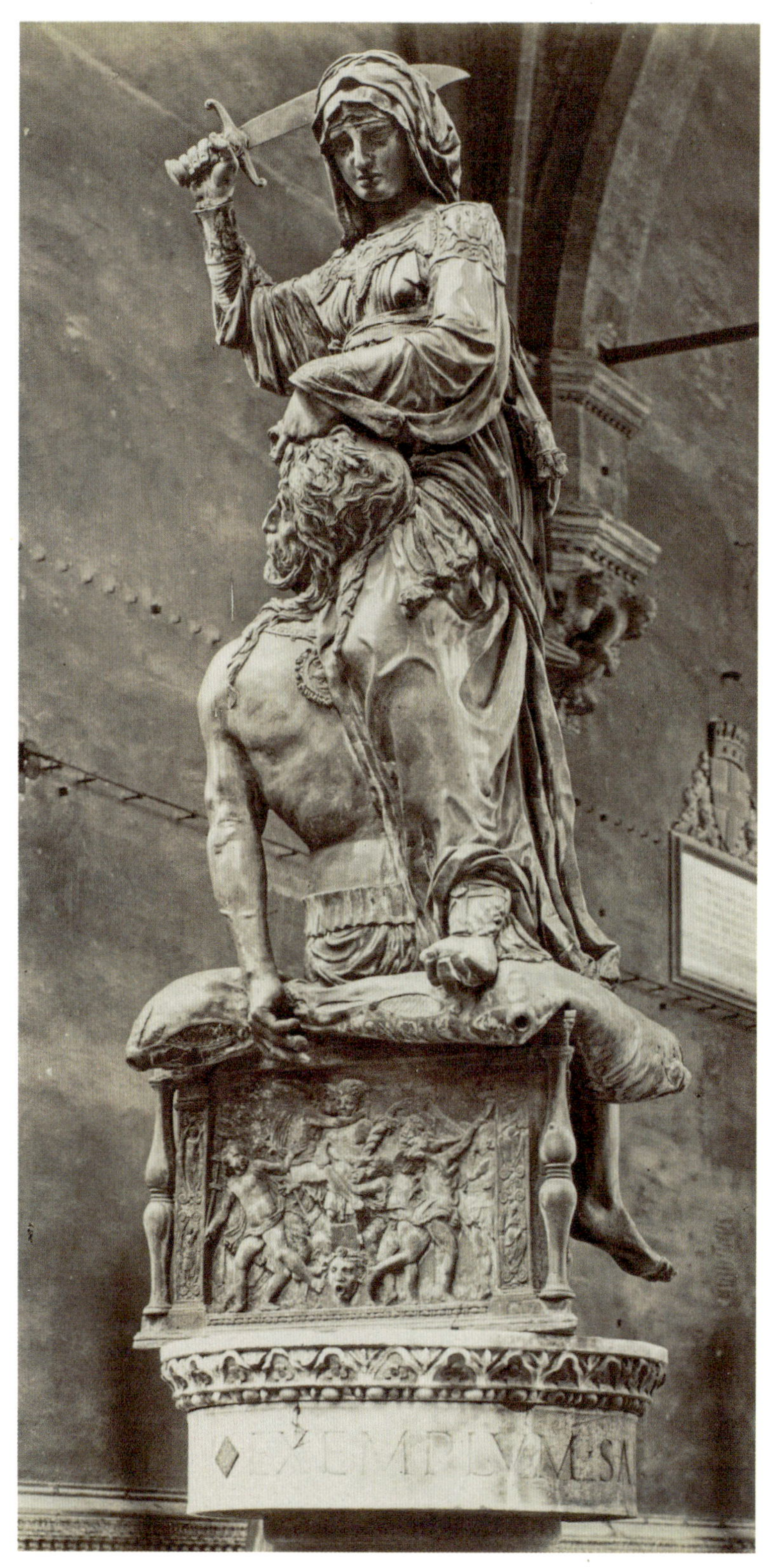

Donatello,
Judith and Holofernes,
1455–60.

Judith and David were obvious heroes for Florence, a city republic facing mighty enemies including Milan and the church. The two statues were surely intended by Cosimo to reassure citizens that the Medici backed the republic. Their inscriptions made the politics explicit, but the symbolism was clear to everyone. These commissions were exercises in political hypocrisy, the subtle tyrant proclaiming a hatred of tyranny. Yet they exceed such simple rhetoric and are full of aesthetic ambiguity.

It's not that *Judith* or *David* are perverse celebrations of sensuality. To claim this simplifies the contradictions that make these masterpieces from six centuries ago still throb with artistic life. *Judith* juxtaposes pleasure and punishment. This dissolute Holofernes is a long-haired, fleshy sinner, a cushioned sensualist, about to be beheaded by a nun-like spectre. Far from denying the doctrine of sin, Donatello stresses the conflict between the classical nudity of Holofernes and the rigour of Christian morality. He does this more candidly, even embarrassingly, with the *David*. This is the first free-standing nude in European art since the fall of Rome. It emulates classical statues, yet does not ask you to forget why they had been considered shameful for the past millennium. In Plato's Athens, a world being explored under the leadership of Donatello's patron, Cosimo, male nude statues went hand-in-hand with homosexual relationships. Can beauty provoke sodomy?

Donatello outrageously suggests it can. He communicates the sinfulness of the male nude by dressing it up in skimpy attire. David sports a stylish, garlanded hat and luxurious sandal-boots that encase his calves but allow his toes to steep themselves in the flowing beard of his enemy's severed head. The leather and metal accessories all heighten the impact of his flesh. David's superbly modelled torso and relaxed pose pay homage to classical sculptures the artist can have known only slightly. Most of the classical statues that later became famous had not yet been excavated, and the artist's best sources were probably marble reliefs on sarcophagi from the Roman Empire that were reused by wealthy families in Pisa's monumental cemetery,[+] maybe the *Spinario* in Rome (a bronze figure of a boy removing a thorn from his foot), and a few figurines and vases. Donatello, from such scant evidence, intuits the formal grace of the classical nude and amplifies it. *David* possesses the mathematical harmony of classical nudes, which were balanced to create perfect proportions. The Roman architect Vitruvius described the Canon of the ancient Greek sculptor Polykleitos, a mathematical analysis of ideal human proportions. Donatello's youth looks canonical, his ribcage symmetrical, his nipples as regularly spaced as temple columns. His left leg is casually raised in a contrapposto pose, with weight more on one foot than another, that shows off his easy balance.

Yet this is art that wants to unnerve. As you walk around the statue – for it is indeed free-standing, fully portrayed in the round as an autonomous entity – your eyes move over smooth buttocks, an unveiled penis. This is a rebirth of the sensual art of pagan antiquity, and Donatello insists that you should be a little uncomfortable. The sandalled foot that David rests in the soft beard hair of Goliath suggests not enmity but another kind of triumph.

David is an interpretation of classical culture. Behind the gravitas of the Romans lies the true genius of the Greeks, and it is mercurial, poetic, erotic. The meaning of nakedness can't be controlled, whispers Donatello; your moral hero may be someone else's sexual ideal. In the depiction of a youth's destruction of an older man there could be a hint of Donatello's relationships with his apprentices. Anecdotes from a source close to the Medici in the late 1400s tell of his turbulent love affairs with male pupils.

So why did Cosimo, the canny merchant prince, risk associating himself with such an image? Because *David* is nothing to do with 'real life' at all. Because it is art. The biggest gulf between Florence and Bruges was that classical culture gave the Tuscan republic a distinctive understanding of 'art' as existing in its own right, for its own sake. It didn't need to serve religion or politics. It was not functional. It existed for contemplation and pleasure.

That elegant otherworld was what artists and humanists perceived in the classical past. Donatello was himself a kind of humanist who studied the ruins of antiquity. He and Brunelleschi went to Rome to draw and measure its majestic remains. To their Renaissance eyes, the old Gothic churches of the recent past did not seem to be architecture at all, just chaotic masses of stone. But classical buildings, even in ruins, *were* architecture: they were designed, they represented the human mind, rather than existing as an agglomeration. Brunelleschi, Michelozzo and Alberti were reshaping Florence with interpretations of the classical orders not as builders but as architects. The most avant-garde example is Alberti's façade for the medieval church of Santa Maria Novella, which imposes classical flourishes on a Gothic hulk in a gratuitous way. This is how classical antiquity gave the Florentine Renaissance a sense of art as an autonomous creative reality. Like the massive flowing volutes of Alberti's design, a classical nude was a human creation, a willed form.

* * *

By the time Portinari sent the *Last Judgment* on its doomed voyage, the fusion of classical and Christian responses to the body begun by Masaccio and Donatello was becoming almost casual. In a 1475 painting of the *Martyrdom of St Sebastian* by the brothers Antonio and Piero Pollaiuolo, the saint is not

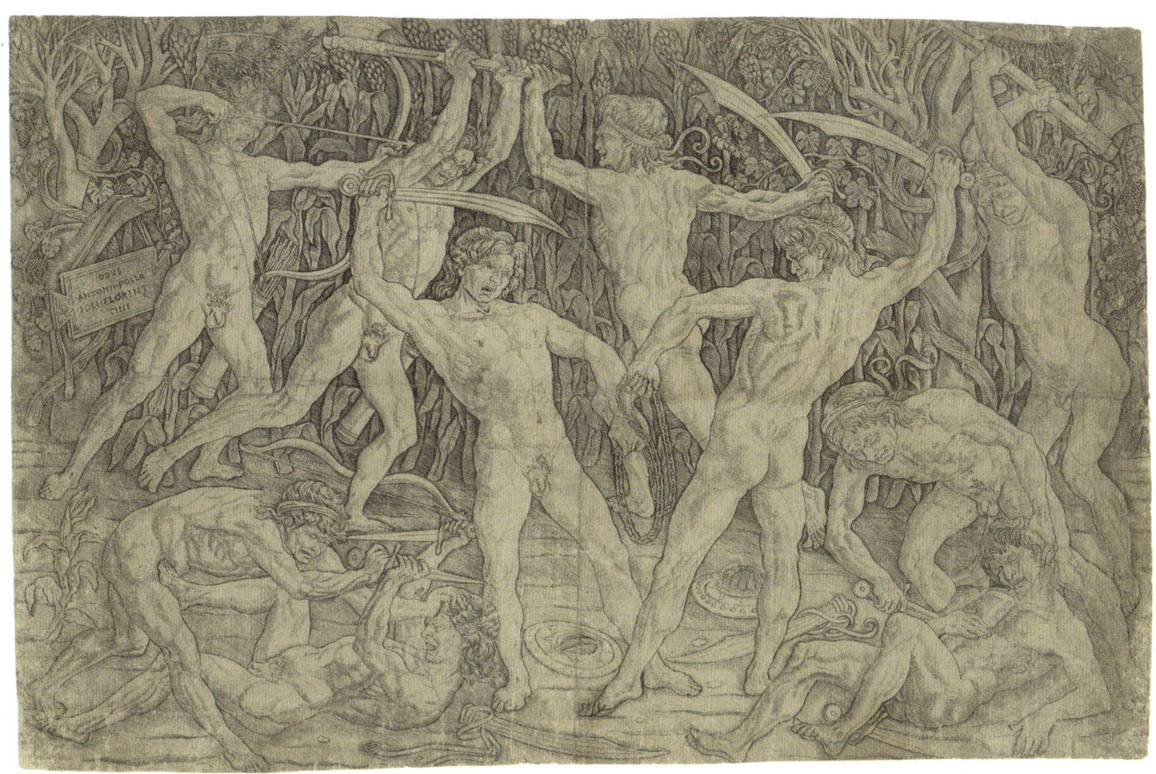

Antonio Pollaiuolo, *Battle of the Nudes*, c. 1470–90.

just a classical nude but an oddly placid one, as if beauty had immunized him against the arrows that crossbowmen are firing at short range. Their weapons are shiny, fetishized, their bodies ripe as they load their bolts. This altarpiece was commissioned by the Pucci family, allies turned rivals of the Medici, for an oratory – a private chapel for prayer – that held a relic of Sebastian's arm bone. Yet piety is dissolved by an almost jokey sensuality. A print by Antonio Pollaiuolo, the *Battle of the Nudes*, takes the male nude out of any context whatsoever into a realm of unmoored art: warfare is just an excuse to explore muscled bodies in various poses. This liberation of male nudity goes where Donatello's *David* led the way.

Looking at the early Florentine tradition of male nudes, it makes sense that Tommaso Portinari wanted to send his naked portrait home. Nudity spoke the artistic language of citizenship. Portinari was offering Florence a testimony to his upright character and open hand. He conceals nothing, Memling's nude portrait tells the Florentines, because he has nothing to hide. But since the arrival of Plato and of Donatello's *David*, the male nude in Florence was no longer so simple. If his naked image had ever got there, it might have been not so much morally admired as enjoyed.

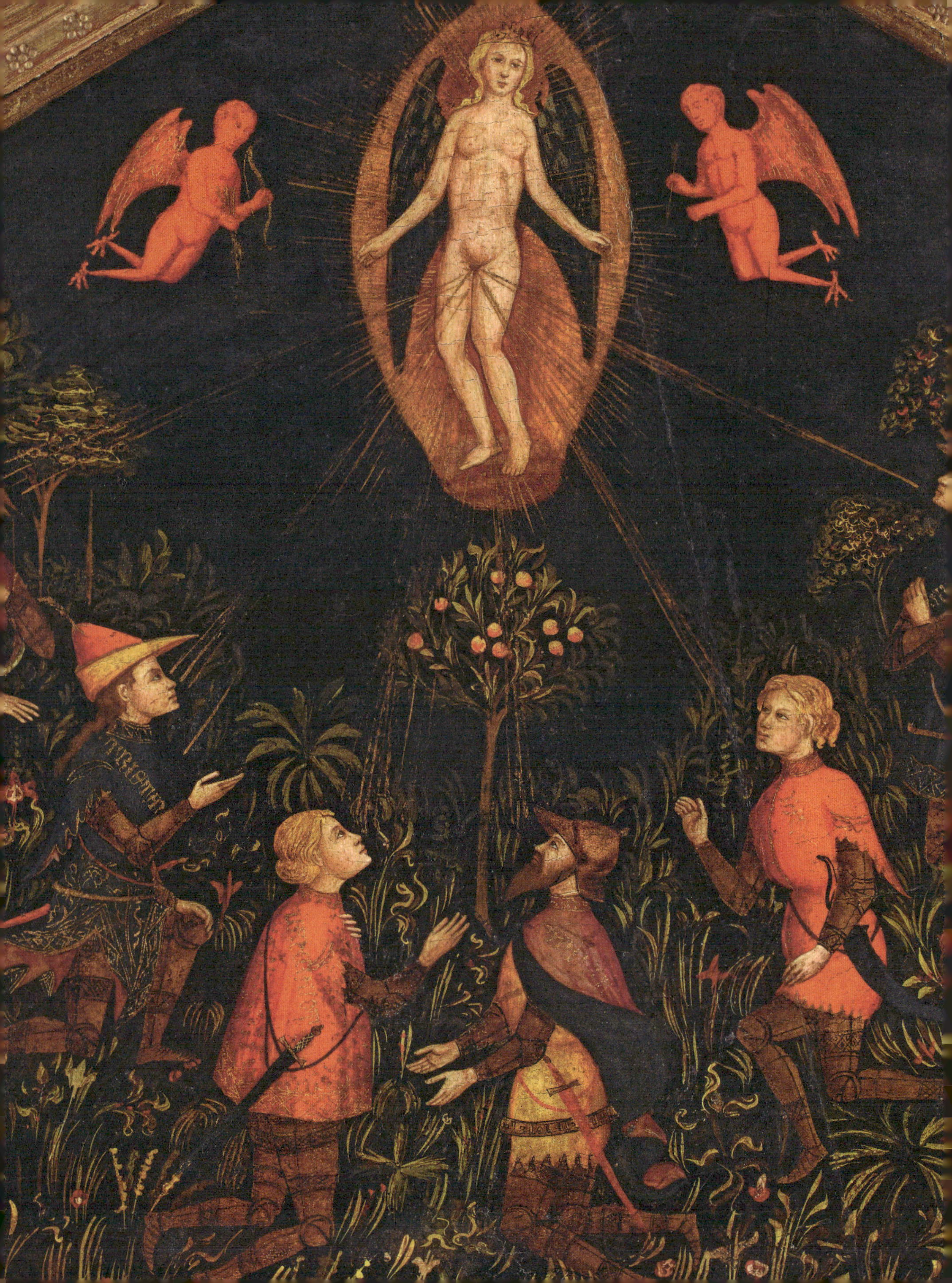

3 The Triumph of Love

Florence did not let go of Memling's pirated masterpiece easily. It negotiated with the Hanseatic League for its release. When talks failed, Tommaso Portinari commissioned a new altarpiece from the latest Flemish art star, Hugo van der Goes. A decade after the abortive first voyage, a massive triptych was again loaded onto a ship in Bruges. It was carried across the Bay of Biscay, round the coasts of Spain and Portugal, through the Straits of Gibraltar, and all the way to Sicily. Then it sailed to Pisa, and was put on a barge up the river Arno. It arrived in Florence on 28 May 1483.

What a difference a decade makes. The Portinari Altarpiece, as it is known in memory of its dodgy patron, was carried in state to the church of the Santa Maria Nuova hospital and has been the most famous example of Flemish art in Florence ever since. It came too late, however, to have much impact on the city's art scene. In the early 1470s Memling's *Last Judgment* was advanced stuff that might have caused Florence to defer to the Flemings. A decade later, the art of the north looked suddenly out of date. The Portinari Altarpiece – van der Goes's sweet, rich, humble painting – was magnificent yet archaic.

Master of Charles of Durazzo, *Triumph of Venus* (detail), c. 1400.

By the end of the 1470s, while the painters of Bruges were stuck in a Gothic mental world, Florence was the centre of an artistic revolution. The Renaissance we think we know – Italian, above all Tuscan, enthralled by pagan antiquity – was in full bloom. It was not, however, the product of a select coterie of patrician men and their erudite advisers. Some of its first patrons and enthusiasts were women. The art of myth born in Lorenzo de' Medici's Florence was a bright new decoration for the rites of courtly love, a chivalric stylization of sexuality that was already several centuries old. Courtly love not only shaped how Greco-Roman mythology entered Italian art, but ensured it would centre on images of female power.

* * *

When Francesca Pitti, the wife of the eminent Florentine citizen Giovanni Tornabuoni, died in childbirth in 1477, he honoured her as a hero. Tornabuoni commissioned a marble relief for her tomb from the sought-after artist Andrea del Verrocchio. It depicts the moment of her death with startling intimacy. She sits up one last time, supported by a sobbing friend – but she's already gone. Her eyes are closed, her face expressionless. We are witnessing the end of a tragic struggle. The weeping figures around her are fit for a Lamentation of Christ. One mourner claws at herself, opening her mouth in a howl; another tries to pull her hair out by the roots. A fellow griever sits on the floor, head in hands, crushed by despair. An older woman, apparently the midwife, cradles the outstretched arm of the corpse.

A second scene shows the midwife presenting to Giovanni Tornabuoni the new life for which his wife gave hers. Francesca's tiny baby has survived. It is held out in the old woman's arms, but this is no moment of joy. Tornabuoni is grave, trying to balance his monumental loss with a welcome to the newborn. The man behind him is less dignified, his body quaking.

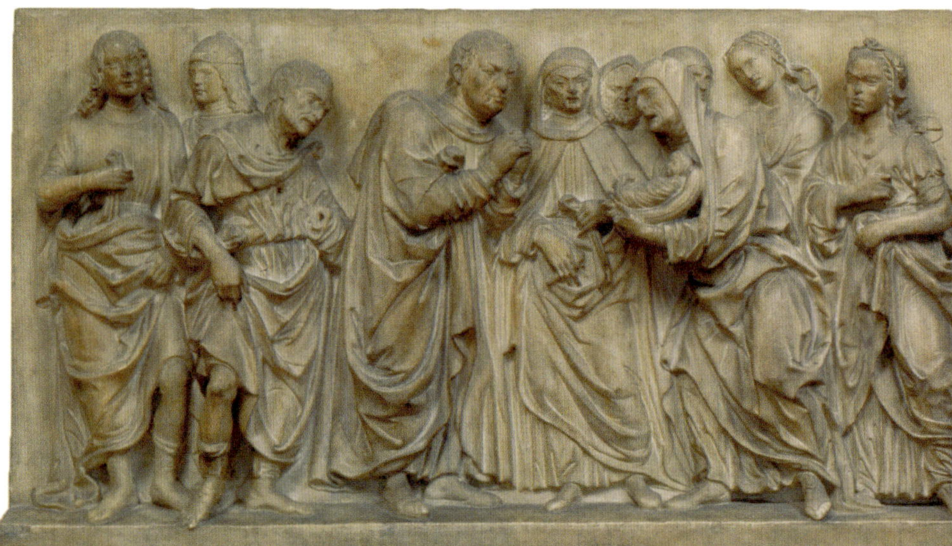

Andrea del Verrocchio, *Death of Francesca Pitti Tornabuoni*, c. 1477–80.

It is all highly classical. Tornabuoni and his male company wear togas like old Romans. Verrocchio's marble relief is modelled on ancient carved sarcophagi, which were among the most visible classical remains in 15th-century Italy. This is a classicism under the fierce influence of Donatello, who had imitated them in the 1430s in his explosively powerful *Cantoria*, a singing gallery for Florence Cathedral, across whose parapet stone boys run and leap with infectious energy.

That same salty stew of classicism, Christianity and brute reality is what makes Verrocchio's relief of Francesca Pitti-Tornabuoni's death such a harrowing glimpse of the lives of Renaissance women. It was all very well for Florentine men to clad themselves mentally as ancient Roman senators and Republican heroes, it seems to acknowledge. Their wives were the true heroes, enduring the risks of childbirth to perpetuate such families as the Tornabuoni, Pitti and Medici.

Tornabuoni's grief shows that, for all the inequality of Renaissance marriage, shared emotions connected men and women. Nor did this tomb exhaust his grief. A few years later he brought Francesca back to life in paint in a donor portrait in the family chapel at the church of Santa Maria Novella in Florence, frescoed by Domenico Ghirlandaio and his team in the later 1480s. She kneels in prayer with head covered and her body robed in cloth of doleful hue. Older now. And a ghost.

As if to put right what had happened, there are two depictions of births in the Tornabuoni Chapel. Both are happy events in which mother and child survive: the *Birth of the Virgin* and *Birth of John the Baptist*. Ghirlandaio sets the *Birth of the Virgin* (overleaf) in a palatial chamber decorated with a relief of playing infants reminiscent of Donatello's *Cantoria*: a benevolent augury for a

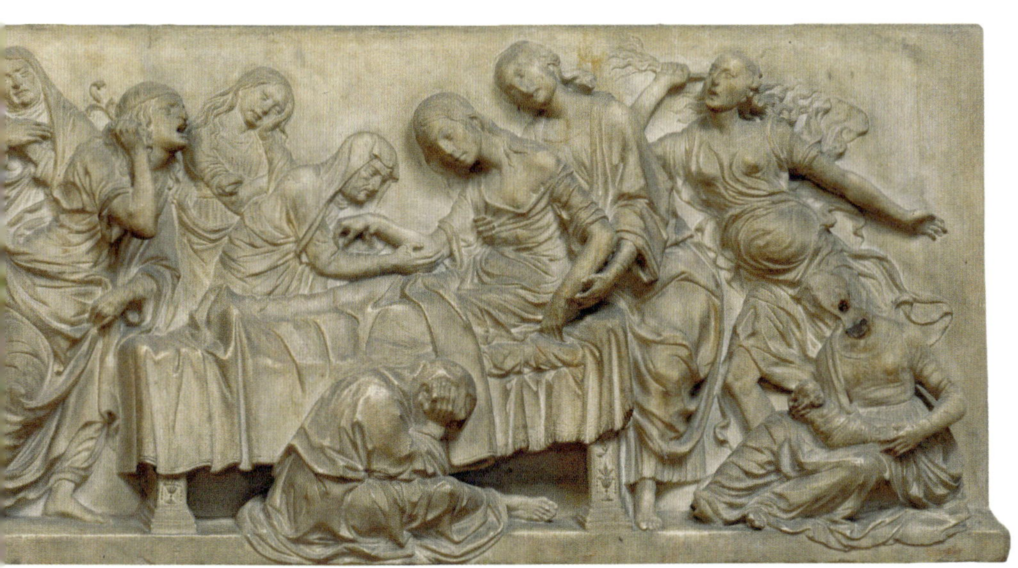

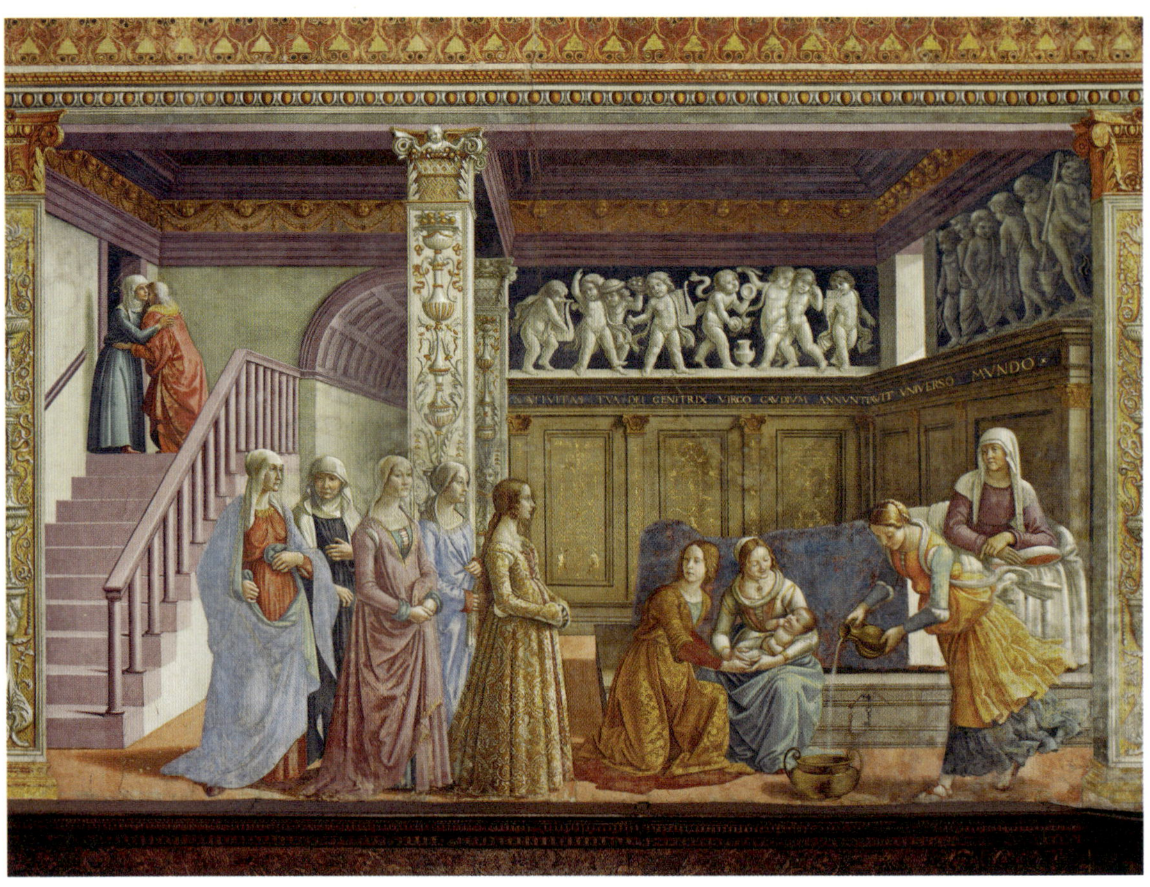

Domenico Ghirlandaio, *Birth of the Virgin*, 1486–90.

healthy birth and happy childhood. He lovingly pictures the rituals surrounding birth in a well-off Renaissance home. A servant pours water into a bowl while two friends look after the newborn child. The mother watches while she rests. More women are on hand, in an all-female company. The second birth – that of John the Baptist – adds details of real life to formal splendour. On the far side of the bed, a servant fetches wine. A young woman dressed in blue enters with a tray of fruit balanced on her head: succulent foods to revivify the mother.

We can see the golden edge of the tray. This is not any old utensil, but a specially made, finely painted *desco da parto*, or birth tray. In a world without real medicine, the best remedy for an exhausted new mother was thought to be sweet food and drink. In Florence, they were presented on such a tray, which would be kept as a family treasure. Examples survive in museums – often hanging on the wall, as if they were conventional paintings that just happen to be circular or hexagonal or even dodecagonal. They tend to be painted with amorous themes taken from poetry and myth, such as the abduction of Helen of Troy or the Triumph of Love. On a birth tray from the 1450s Helen, who has

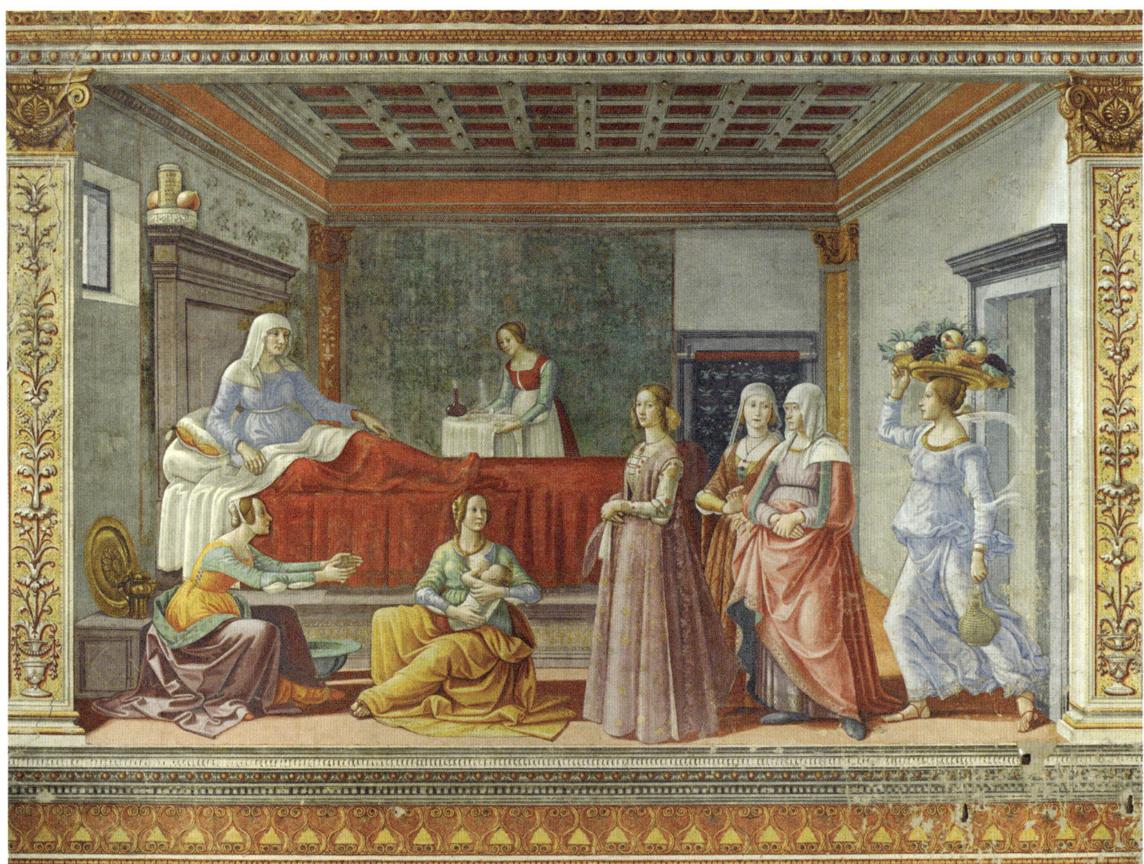

Domenico Ghirlandaio, *Birth of John the Baptist*, 1486–90.

deserted her husband, Menelaus, rides piggyback on her lover Paris as he runs for his ship. He shows a bit of red-hosed leg.

* * *

A *Triumph of Love* of a similar date, painted on a birth tray in Florence (overleaf), mixes eroticism and subversive humour. Cupid, a naked youth, fires his bow at a crowd of courtly sophisticates. In the foreground we see how those arrows can disempower men. A woman sits on a man's back, riding him like a horse as he crawls on hands and knees: she is Phyllis, and he is the Greek philosopher Aristotle. According to a medieval fable, Aristotle warned his pupil Alexander against this temptress, but then fell for her himself and submitted to being ridden. Another woman on top on the tray is Delilah, cutting the sleeping Samson's hair after lulling him with love. The Triumph of Love was obviously a popular subject: another birth tray by the same workshop also focuses on Phyllis riding Aristotle and Delilah unmanning Samson, who is shown as a good-looking male nude. It's hard to avoid the conclusion that these images were created

Apollonio di Giovanni,
Triumph of Love,
c. 1460–70.

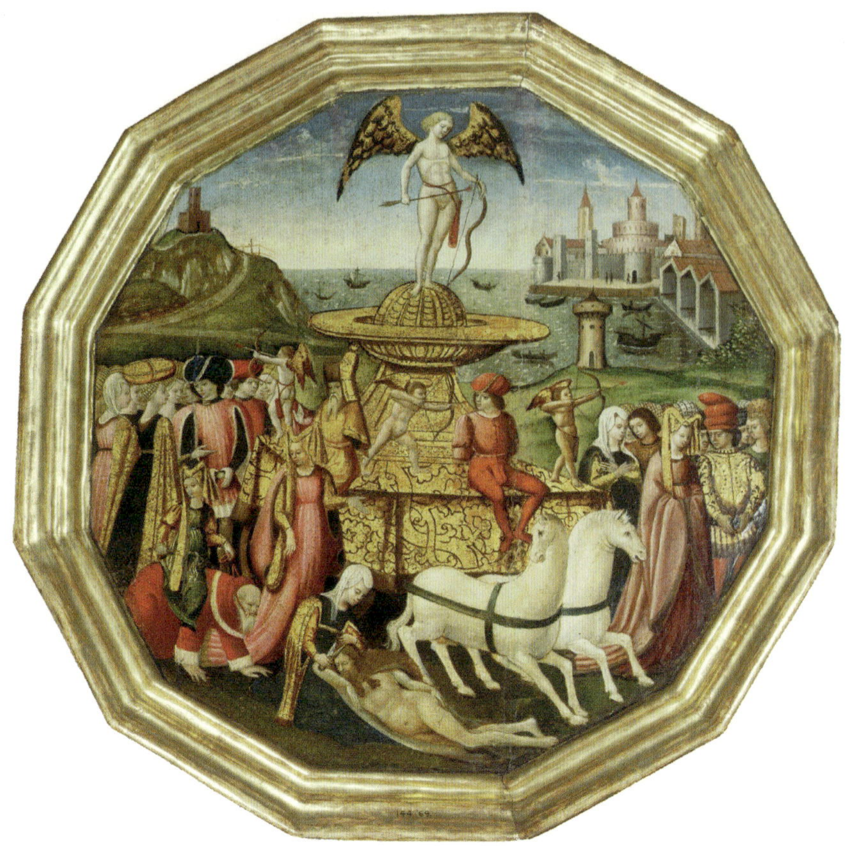

for the enjoyment of female eyes. It's tempting to picture the companions at the birth joking about these pictures of women escaping their husbands or humiliating a lover. As the sweetmeats were eaten, the playful, even ribald images would emerge.

The art of the birth tray is aimed at a literate female audience who read poetry in the Tuscan vernacular. That doesn't mean that there were no female students of Latin in 15th-century Italy: one such was the humanist Laura Cereta from Brescia. But ever since the time of Boccaccio, who addresses his female readers directly in the *Decameron*, writings in the Tuscan vernacular had been imagined as a literature for women as well as men. The popular birth-tray subject of the Triumph of Love illustrates one of the *Triumphs* described in a 14th-century vernacular poem by Boccaccio's contemporary Francesco Petrarca, known in English as Petrarch. The poems of Petrarch are lyrics of obsessive love. Just as Dante worshipped Beatrice, Petrarch adored a woman he called Laura, whom he first met at the pope's court in Avignon during the period of the papacy's relocation to France. Petrarch spent a lifetime writing poems about her, establishing the love sonnet at the forefront of European literature. Emulated by poets from

Michelangelo and Vittoria Colonna to Shakespeare, Petrarch attained a cult status that went beyond his literary significance. He provided a template for passion, the pattern for every lutenist under a midnight balcony. As the popularity of his *Triumphs* on birth trays proves, women were among his most avid readers. A 16th-century portrait by Andrea del Sarto shows a young woman pointing to lines in a book of Petrarch's sonnets as she looks sensitively at us. Petrarch by this time was synonymous with the language of love, the heartbeat of the soul.

For some births, however, the language of love was not quite lofty enough. When Giovanni Tornabuoni's sister Lucrezia gave birth to a son on 1 January 1449, the scene shown on the birth tray was based instead on another of Petrarch's *Triumphs*: that of Fame. A gathering of armoured knights on horseback pays homage to an allegorical statue of Fame in a perspective landscape. It's a very fine example of birth-tray art. Lucrezia's husband, Piero, was the son and heir of Cosimo de' Medici, and the little boy to whom she gave birth that day would indeed win fame, as Lorenzo the Magnificent.

* * *

Petrarch's poetry of desire was an elegant refinement of the medieval chivalric game of courtly love. In this ritualized upper-class culture, the primitive warrior roots of the knights and lords who dominated feudal society were civilized through poetry, play and eroticism. In an era when so much art and architecture was controlled by the church, the chivalric arts of love and war provided an earthly antidote. Castles were not just functional defences but full of romance and symbolism, as their turrets and dreamy moats mirrored the popular romances of King Arthur and his knights. The figure of Arthur, possibly a distant memory of an ancient British warlord, was dredged out of the bogs of time by the Welsh chronicler Geoffrey of Monmouth. Yet it was in French romance literature from the late 12th century onwards that he became the perfect king, served by knights who fought brave jousts and went on perilous quests. Camelot had it all, including sex. Arthur's queen, Guinevere, has a fatal affair with his best knight, Lancelot. To Dante it was dangerous even to read the sensual story of Guinevere's adultery. In the *Inferno* Dante meets Francesca da Rimini, doomed to spend eternity in a swirling dust cloud in the circle of the lustful. She was married to Giovanni Malatesta, the son of the lord of Rimini, but fell in love with his brother, Paolo. Their adultery began with a manuscript. The shade of Francesca explains to Dante that

> 'We were reading one day for our delight
> Of Lancelot how love seized him;
> We were by ourselves and without a shred of suspicion.

Enamelled casket, Limoges, c. 1180.

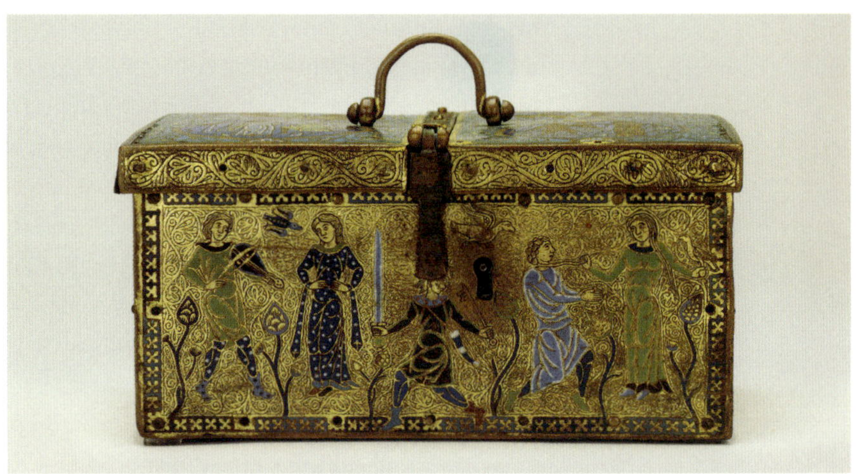

> Again and again that reading made our
> Eyes meet, and paled our faces ...
> We read no more that day.'[1]

Dante pities Francesca, for he too had a heart. His autobiographical work *The New Life* is about his self-discovery through the blazing rapture of being in love with Beatrice. The younger Petrarch modelled his whole life of overpowering love on this text.

In chivalric images, women rule their devoted knights and adoring troubadours. An enamelled metal casket made in 12th-century Limoges depicts a woman holding her lover by a leather leash about his neck. A 14th-century ivory casket is covered with love scenes, including Phyllis riding on Aristotle's back. It also depicts knights fighting with long lances at a tournament while a group of ladies look on. The stylized – but dangerous – mock warfare of the lists may have started as training for knights, but by the later Middle Ages the tournament was like a mating ritual performed by brightly feathered hummingbirds. Knights wore heavier, more ornate armour than they did in battle. Their helmets had extravagant plumes. They were watched by women, including their chosen mistresses, who were often married to someone else. Everyone present was acting out romance literature, from the knights jousting like Lancelot to the Guineveres in the gallery. One 15th-century knight commissioned a Flemish artist to paint his shield with a febrile confession: 'Vous ou la mort': you or death. He kneels at his lady's feet in shining armour while she towers above him with a tall, conical hennin on her head, toying with the golden rope that hangs from her waist as if she means to tie him up. Death as a skeleton stalks the knight to redeem his rash vow.

Such images of abasement and dedication might not mean much. Then again they might. A knight's devotion to an unavailable woman could be abstract. Or, like the passion of Paolo and Francesca, it could become dangerously real: 'We read no more that day.'

* * *

The painted trays on which post-partum snacks were brought to Florentine women are playful artefacts of courtly love that include some of the first Renaissance images of classical mythology. On a twelve-sided birth tray made in about 1400, six men adore the goddess Venus. They are Achilles, condemned by Dante to the second circle of hell for lechery; Tristan, the doomed lover of Iseult; Lancelot; Samson, betrayed by Delilah; Paris, the abductor of Helen, who died at Troy; and the Trojan Troilus, the lover of faithless Cressida. All were men brought low by love. Floating above them in the night sky over an orchard is the divinity responsible for their destruction. Venus, the ancient goddess of love and desire, shines naked, her body golden inside a flaming nimbus resembling a seed pod. Devilish red cupids fly around her. Lines of

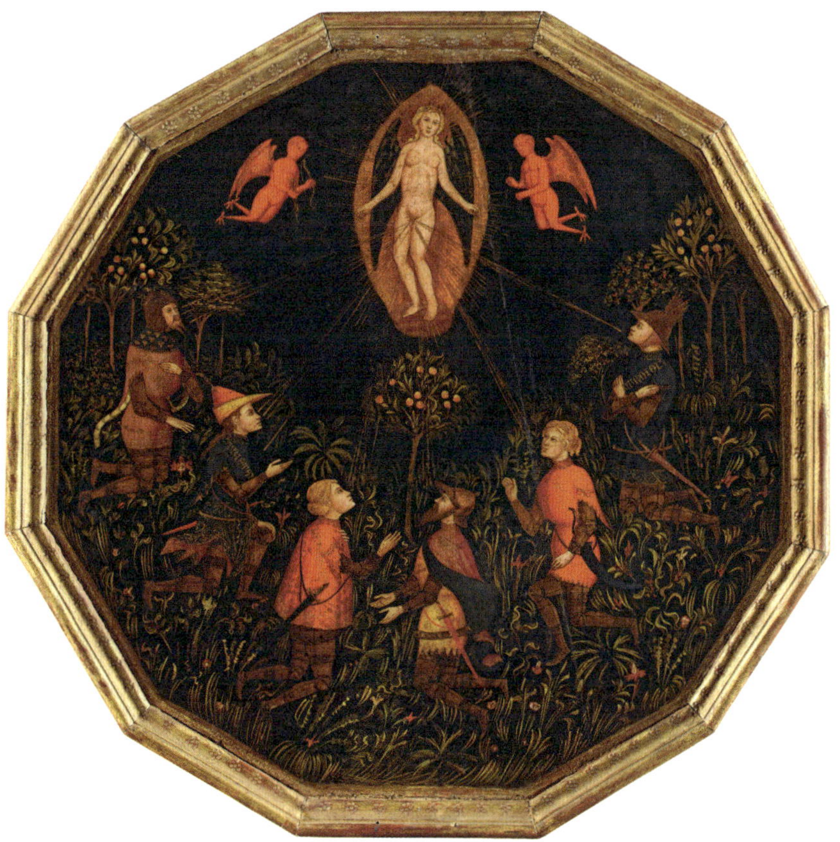

Master of Charles of Durazzo, *Triumph of Venus*, c. 1400.

gold light, the laser beams of love, connect the eyes of her admirers with her vagina, from which these shafts radiate. This Venus is a cruel mistress. Her nudity gives her hypnotic power over the eyes of men and total dominion over their fate. That is how Venus looked to an audience of Florentine women at the start of the 15th century: a symbol of sexual power who turns the world upside down. Men, watch out.

The Venus on this birth tray was inspired not by the Greek and Latin texts that were the intellectual property of university-educated male humanists, but by love poetry in the vernacular, whose readers included women. The rebirth of myth in Italian art occurred organically, emerging from a stylized culture of chivalry that licensed unpredictable, playful relationships between men and women.

* * *

Courtly love is in full bloom in all its civilized sado-masochism at the Palazzo Schifanoia in the city of Ferrara. On a wall of the Hall of the Months, the war god Mars has been subdued by Venus. She sits on a throne, and he kneels before

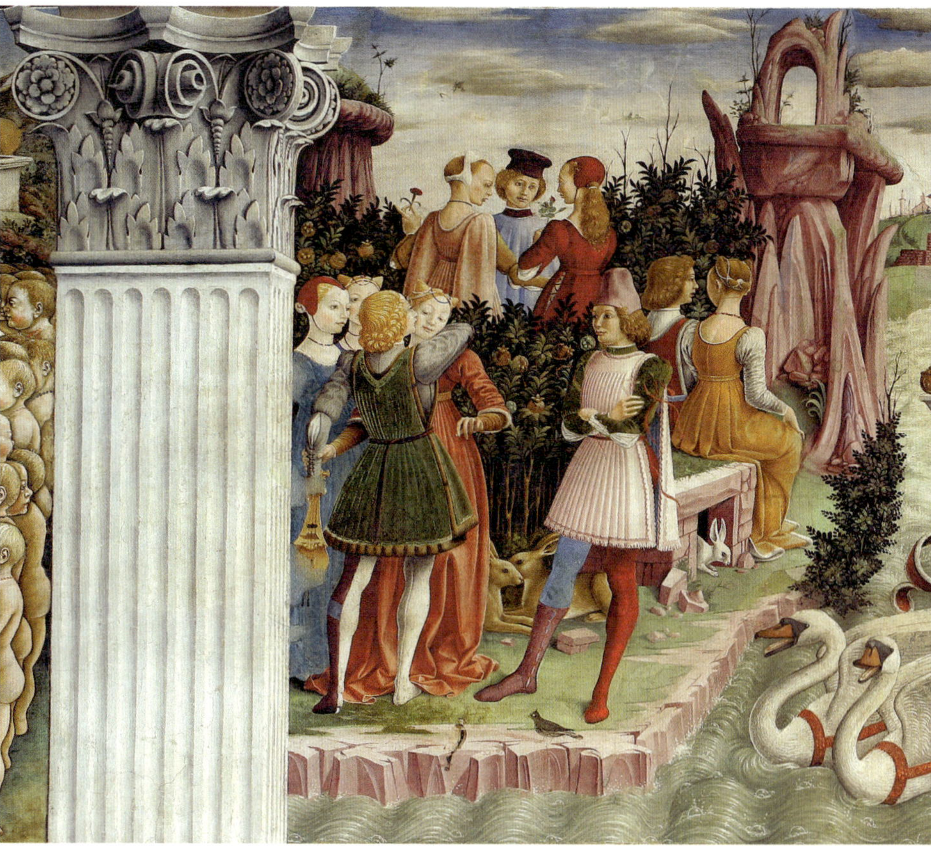

Francesco del Cossa, *April, Triumph of Venus*, c. 1467–70.

her, a prisoner of love. He is held securely by a chain that binds his arms to his sides and is attached to her car. The war god's submission takes place on a triumphal chariot or raft, pulled by swans between two shores where young men and women talk intimately on a bench, or cuddle and kiss. Some of the women play lutes. It is a court under the rule of Venus, and every figure looks like a portrait from life.

The *Triumph of Venus* fresco is visibly in the tradition of courtly love images but is executed with a new painterly confidence. The artist, Francesco del Cossa, creates an atmospheric perspective landscape full of lifelike people and details such as the flapping draperies on the triumphal barge. Mars may be god of war, but he is also a man felled by love, like Aristotle with Phyllis on his back.

And this is spring, the season when nature itself tells its creatures to make love. The *Triumph of Venus* represents April. Its meaning was easy for anyone to read: the courtiers who danced and banqueted here did not need Petrarch to associate April with sexuality. It was a ritual awareness that everyone shared in a world closer to nature than ours, where the fields and meadows were never

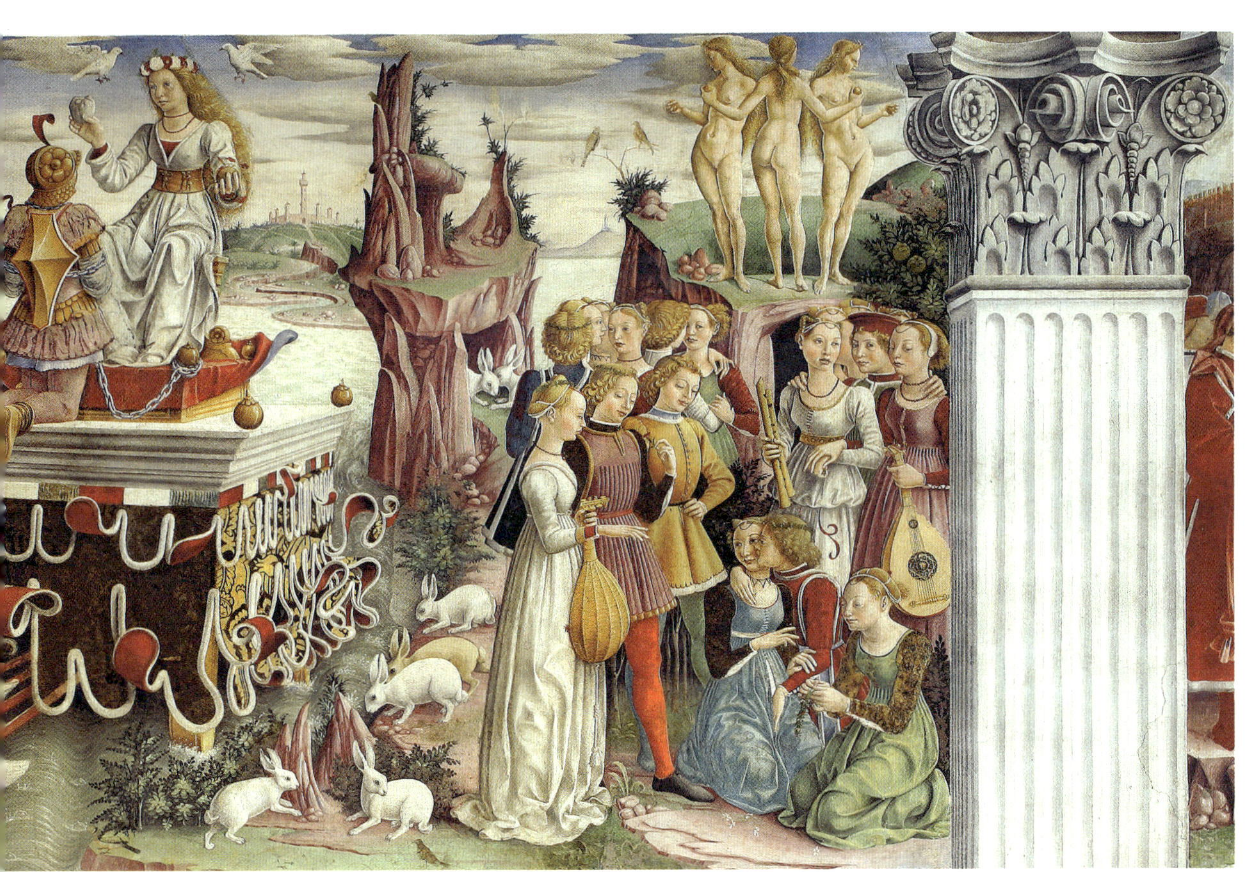

far away. In the 14th century Chaucer wrote of April, when sweet showers bathe the veins of plants in the liquid by which 'engendred is the flour'.[2] The young men at Venus's court are keen to 'engendre' the women. Yet they are ruled by Venus, who offers her delights only in return for total submission.

* * *

Andrea Mantegna's Chamber of the Newlyweds, completed in 1474 in the palace of the Gonzaga, rulers of Mantua, does something that the Ferrarese court artists could not match. While the paintings in the Palazzo Schifanoia are bursting with detail, they don't do anything to the space of the room: they just cover its walls as if they were tapestries. By contrast, Mantegna sets the Gonzaga family, their dogs and court entertainers inside an eye-fooling carnival of architectural fantasy, with the real Gothic vaulting of the ceiling transformed into a gallery of *trompe-l'oeil* statues. At the summit is Mantegna's showstopper: a circular 'hole' in the ceiling from which women of the court look down laughing among cupids and clouds and a precariously balanced potted plant.

The oculus, to use its Latin name, is a miracle of perspective. Mantegna lets us look up through a fat, circular parapet that recedes from the painted vault and see foreshortened faces and bodies, as if we were viewing living figures from below. The women seem to share the joke with us. They look like portraits of real ladies-in-waiting. An African man gazes at his female companion with unconcealed desire while another man accompanies two women. It looks like there may be some courtly love going on up there.

Mantegna touches on mythology so lightly that you barely notice it. The *putti* – little boys, usually winged – who defy gravity to balance on the inside ledge of the parapet express the spirit of classicism rather than the letter: a feeling of freedom and joy, as if it's spring all the time. The model for the painter's fantasy is surely the real oculus of the ancient Pantheon in Rome. That vast hole in a shadowed vault is an uneasy circle of constantly changing sky, and when it rains it pours inside the building. By contrast Mantegna's sky is fixed for ever in the same perfect moment, a circle of blue brought to life by gentle puffs of cloud, on a fine day, when the gods are smiling.

* * *

Andrea Mantegna, ceiling fresco, Camera degli Sposi (Chamber of the Newlyweds), c. 1474.

Mars is in a stupor. He lies there naked and dissipated. His lance is abandoned, his helmet a plaything for little goat-legged fauns who mock the sleeping war god. Venus is too dignified to laugh at him. She lies opposite her spent lover, her white dress unruffled, her face impeccable.

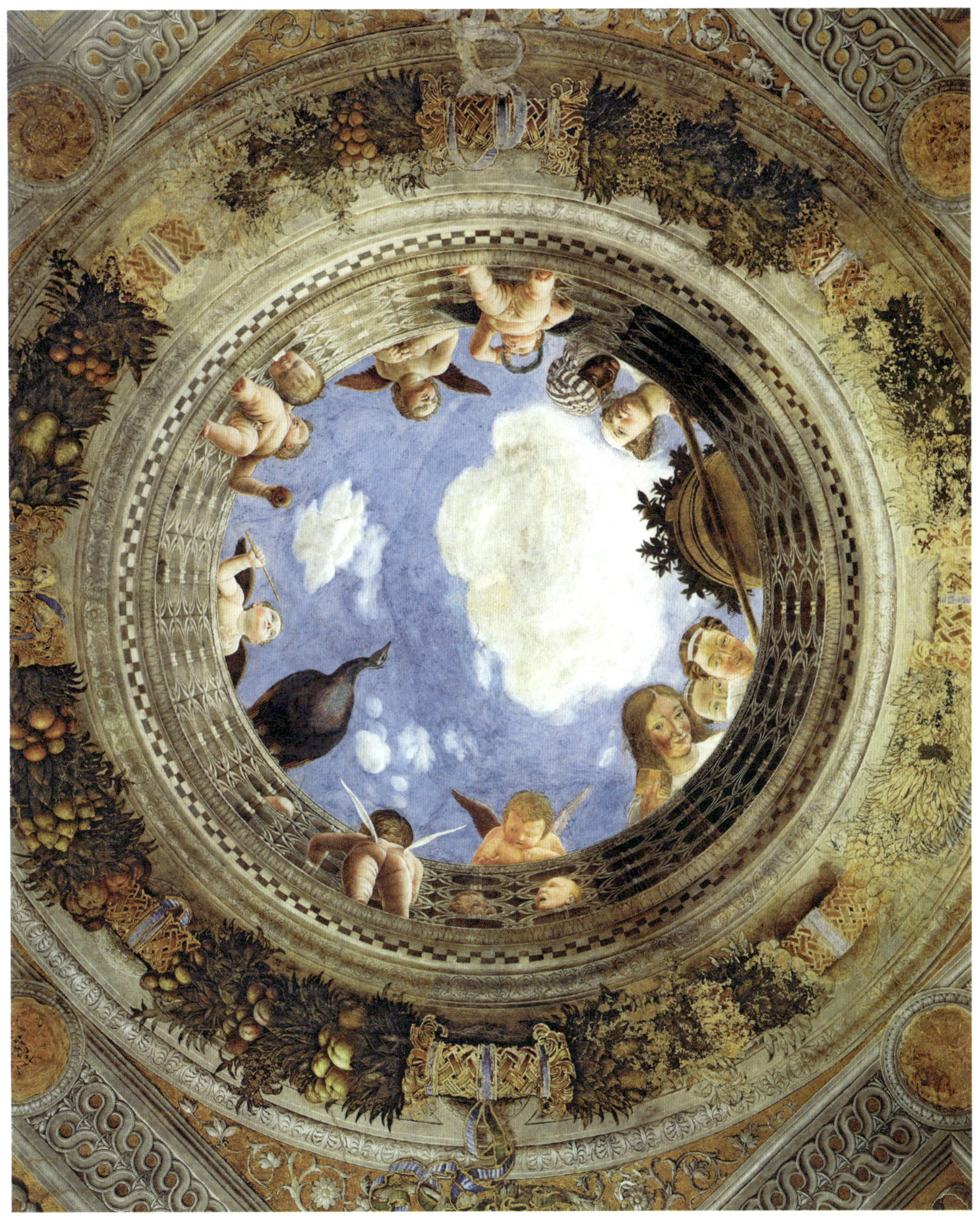

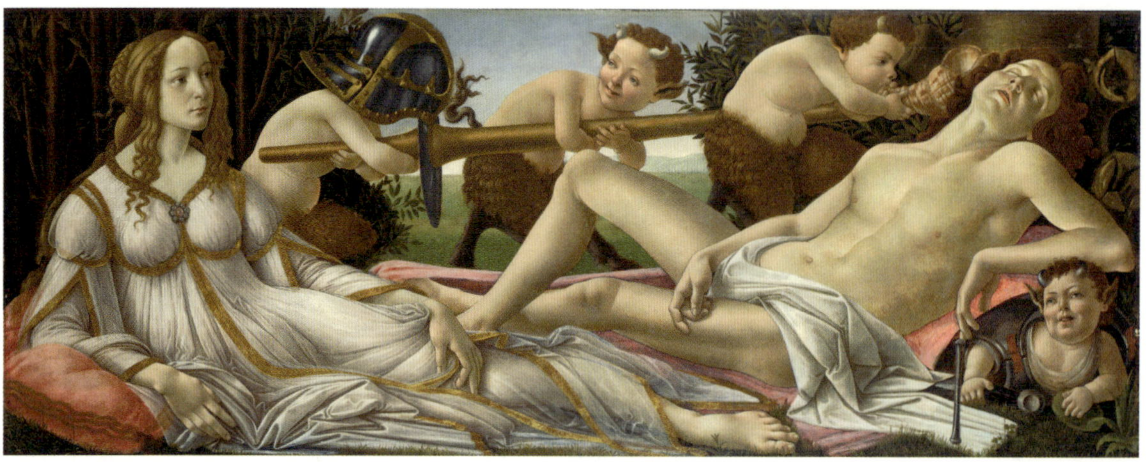

Sandro Botticelli, *Venus and Mars*, c. 1485.

Sandro Botticelli's *Venus and Mars*, painted in about 1485, is both a consummate re-creation of classical myth and a triumph of courtly love. She may not have Mars on a chain or shoot bolts of light from her vagina, but this Venus is recognizable as the goddess of courtly love, effortlessly dominating the man she has unmanned. It is Mars who is nude and vulnerable, Venus who is self-possessed. She is a variation on Phyllis riding Aristotle, but where that was a bit of medieval folklore, this is an interpretation of a Latin text of the 1st century BCE. Lulling Mars is one of the powers for which Lucretius praises Venus in his poem *On the Nature of Things*. Addressing her, Lucretius describes how weapon-wielding Mars, chief of all military affairs, 'often throws himself into your lap, conquered by the eternal wound of love'.[3]

The imagery in the Hall of the Months (pp. 70–71) had awkwardly yoked the gods' passion to a traditional chivalric image of a man held on a chain. Botticelli is more explicit about the nature of Venus's victory. Mars is shattered by sex with a goddess, just as Lucretius says. The style too is more classicizing. The lovers are elegantly disported across the panel like entwined figures on an ancient sarcophagus, cameo or vase. The balanced composition, brought to life by the comical fauns, has the symmetry of a classical temple. Yet this does not mean that Venus and Mars was painted for male scholars.

Botticelli's *Venus and Mars* was part of the furniture. It was made as a decorative backboard for a chest, day bed or settle, meaning it was there to be seen and chatted about by everyone in the family, not hidden away in a patriarch's *studiolo* to be pompously decoded or slavered over. In any case, by dressing his Venus and leaving his Mars nude, as with the naked Samson on birth trays, Botticelli's work is surely aimed at the eyes of women, or men who liked men. A mirror frame made in Florence a few years earlier, surely intended for a woman, has a similar depiction of Venus and Mars – except that the artist, thought to be Antonio Pollaiuolo, has made the goddess as naked as her slumbering post-coital partner. The connection with light-hearted, courtly love images is even clearer, and so is the everyday domestic context.

One intriguing fact about Pollaiuolo's frame is that it is in the shape of a diamond ring, one of the heraldic emblems of the Medici. Botticelli's painting may also have symbols of a famous family buzzing through it. The wasps (*vespe*) that circle a nest behind Mars's unconscious head seem to allude to the Vespucci family and their house, their 'nest'. These two houses, Medici and Vespucci, are linked by one of the most mythologized courtly love stories of all time.

* * *

In February 1469 the Middle Ages made a comeback in Florence. Gone were the short haircuts and grave demeanours with which patricians in the age of Cosimo the Elder had aped the senators of Republican Rome. Long-haired youths gathered in the Piazza Santa Croce, a long, open space with windows overlooking it from which the women of wealthy families watched. Wooden barriers were placed along the makeshift arena in front of the black-and-white façade of the church. Young men from some of the finest families in Italy, strapped into armour, mounted their horses and took up their lances to joust in the names of their chosen mistresses.

Lorenzo de' Medici, just turned 20, was the star of the tournament, which had been paid for by his family. His father, Piero, current head of the family business and political system, was ill with the family affliction – a form of gout – and would not outlive the year, so it was a good time for young Lorenzo to be promoted as the Medici golden boy. He won the day: as victor of all the jousts, he received a golden helmet with a crest representing Mars.

Lorenzo dedicated his arms to the lady of his heart, Lucrezia Donati, a married woman he showered with sonnets. He was scribbling the same literary version of courtly love pioneered by Dante and Petrarch, and was talented enough to get away with his versifying. Whether his love was chaste or not is another question. Lucrezia was married to the rich merchant Niccolò Ardinghelli, and there's no record of Lorenzo – who married Clarice Orsini in June 1469, just a few months after his joust – siring any illegitimate children. So perhaps their courtly love remained a game. However, Alessandra Strozzi, the matriarch of one of the wealthiest families in Florence, whose letters afford gossipy insights into top-drawer life, had remarked teasingly in 1465 that Ardinghelli was spending far too much time away from his fiancée on business, and if he didn't watch out young Lorenzo would find a way to please Lucrezia.

This was the delicious ambiguity of courtly love: it might be all fine words and gifts and dancing, or it might veil a steamy sexual relationship. The licence of supposed chastity, on her part rather than his, let Lorenzo carry on his sophisticated flirtation with Lucrezia Donati long after he married Clarice. In the later 1470s, according to his long-term houseguest the poet Angelo Poliziano, 'Lauro' ('Laurel', a suitably Petrarchan nickname for Lorenzo) 'still for the beautiful Lucrezia burns', but Lucrezia 'still shows herself hard to Lauro'.[4]

* * *

In the 1520s Niccolò Machiavelli, notorious author of the handbook for tyrants, *The Prince*, remarks with characteristic cynicism in his *Florentine Histories* that Piero the Gouty staged the 1469 joust to distract the people from a political crisis. It's a razor-sharp insight into a transformation of Florentine culture. Where once this city compared itself with ancient Athens or Republican Rome, now the dominant family was coming on like a feudal dynasty, celebrating its young heir with a full-on chivalric tournament in a new dramatization of the personal nature of Medici rule. Even Lorenzo's sex life was entwined in this public ritual. The rational, money-based influence of Cosimo the Elder was giving way to Lorenzo's charismatic authority.

That authority was fully established by the time the Medici staged a second joust, in 1475. Lorenzo had taken power decisively following his father's death nearly six years earlier. Now he put on an extravagant tournament in honour of his brother, Giuliano, a rite that gaudily proclaimed the rule of the Medici. A city that was still supposed to be a republic was being asked to kneel not just to Lorenzo but to his proud, athletic brother too.

This was where Sandro Botticelli came in. Quite how a tanner's son, born in 1445 to the stink of urine, eased his way into the city's gilded elite is a mystery. But there he is, in his painting of the *Adoration of the Magi*, done around the time of Giuliano's tournament. He preferred to be addressed by his full first name, Alessandro – and in the self-portrait he included in the work he looks every bit an Alessandro, lofty and classical, regarding us proudly as he stands nobly robed at the right of the Magi and their retinue. The purportedly devotional scene is packed with portraits, and they emphasize the painter's ascent. Lorenzo de' Medici, with his sallow looks and mane of dark hair, stands introspectively to the left of Botticelli. Near him, in a red cloak at the centre of the scene, kneels his father, Piero the Gouty, in a posthumous performance as one of the Magi, while the even longer-deceased Cosimo the Elder kneels directly before Christ. At the other side of the group stands Giuliano de' Medici, his expression almost sneering so proud is his bearing; he wears the short tunic and elegant hose of a knightly youth, with a white horse at his right shoulder ready for hunting or jousting. Between his legs he holds a long sword. He is portrayed as the muscle of the Magi and of the Medici: the riding and fighting man to complement his elder brother, the thoughtful poet-prince.

Yet Giuliano lets Angelo Poliziano rest his head on his shoulder and put an arm round his back in a very familiar way. It is the intimacy between a poet and his epic hero. If Botticelli's rise was impressive, so was Poliziano's. Born in Montepulciano in the Tuscan countryside in 1454, he came to Florence as a penniless child after his father was murdered. Poliziano had a gift for languages and as a teenager started translating Homer's *Iliad* from ancient Greek into Latin, which many more people could read. He also wrote in the Tuscan vernacular and had a talent for popularizing the classics, mixing them with folk culture, as in his song 'Welcome May' ('Ben venga maggio'), which gives a mythic grace to what's essentially a raucous celebration of springtime courting. This accessibility eased his dialogues with artists. In 1475 Poliziano started a poem in Tuscan telling of Giuliano's joust and the love that inspired him. This is the bond between Angelo and Giuliano that Botticelli depicts – and it was a collaboration that involved Botticelli.

When Giuliano de' Medici rode into the tournament in 1475 he carried a banner painted by Botticelli depicting the goddess Minerva – the Roman counterpart to Athena – who plays a commanding role in Poliziano's poem. The banner does not survive, although there may be an echo of it in his later painting *Pallas and the Centaur*, which shows Pallas Athena, goddess of wisdom, reason and virtue, holding a male centaur – image of all that is antagonistic to those qualities – by his shaggy hair (overleaf). As she effortlessly controls this violent, impulsive beast, whose human top half is sutured at the groin, her face is calm and impassive, its beauty severe. Her dress is covered in Medici diamond rings.

In Poliziano's unfinished *Verses for the Joust of Giuliano de' Medici*, Julio (as the poem calls Giuliano) dreams that he sees his beloved in the persona of Minerva punishing the love god Cupid in just such a crushing way. She was Simonetta Cattaneo, the wife of the Florentine citizen Marco Vespucci, whose family seems to be symbolized by the wasps in Botticelli's *Venus and Mars*. Born in Genoa in 1453, Simonetta was the same age as her courtly lover Giuliano. As Poliziano tells it, he was a harsh misogynist before he saw her, despising men who fall in love and go mushy. He preferred to hunt in the woods. But Cupid struck him down, and he was instantly dazzled by a young woman he saw wandering in the greenwood outside Florence:

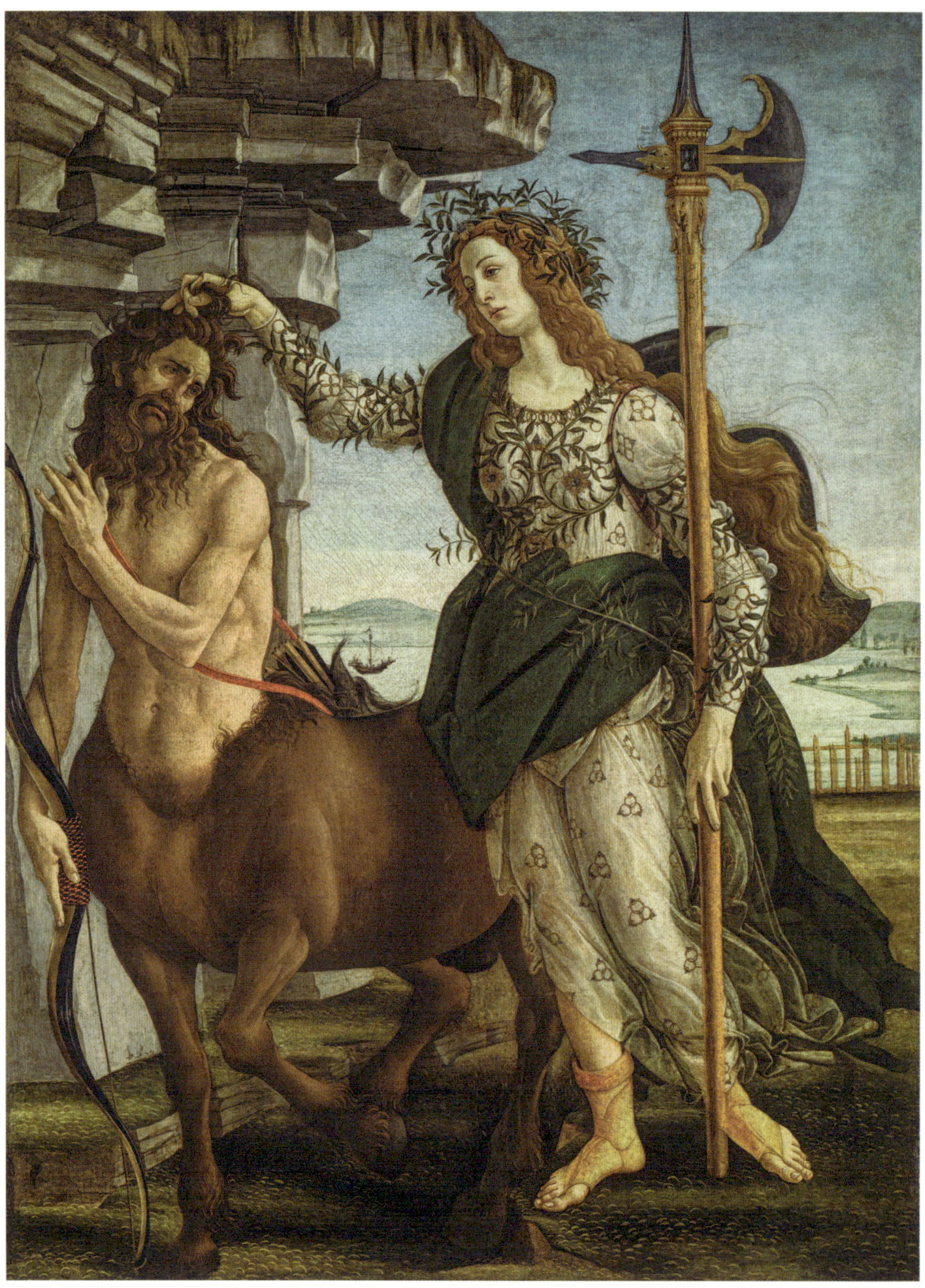

Pure white is she, and pure white her dress,
but painted with roses, flowers and grass;
the ringlets of her golden hair
fall on her brow with humble pride.[5]

He thinks she is a nymph or goddess, but she explains that she is a real woman who lives in Florence by the river Arno, under the 'bond' of marriage, though born by the sea in Liguria. She loves the woods, for

'Here the grass and flowers and fresh air please me;
the way to my home is quick,
here I rest easy: I, Simonetta,
in the shade by some cool fresh stream.'[6]

Poliziano weaves a garland of pastoral reverie. Simonetta spends much of her time in the green of nature and even wears a gown 'painted [*dipinta*] with roses, flowers and grass'. As the painter of decorations and heraldry for the joust commemorated by these verses, Botticelli helped to fashion this image. He recreates it in his most ambitious painting. A flowery dress, like the one Simonetta wears in Poliziano's poem, is worn by Flora, the Roman deity of spring and flowers, in Botticelli's *Primavera* (overleaf).

This work has been known as a celebration of *la primavera* – spring – ever since the Renaissance. Giorgio Vasari saw it, along with Botticelli's *Birth of Venus*, in a Medici country villa at Castello outside Florence, describing the scene as 'Venus, whom the Graces are covering with flowers, as a symbol of spring'.[7]

Vasari may be giving us the original name of the painting, accurately handed down. Botticelli's shady grove is certainly like one Poliziano describes on Cyprus, the isle of Venus, from which

happy Primavera never departs,
She releases her blond curls in the fresh breeze
And a thousand flowers in a garland gathers.[8]

Botticelli's 'symbol of spring' is so much more convincing than previous 15th-century paintings of the pagan gods. Venus stands at the centre of the scene, with Cupid flying above her head. The Three Graces dance on one side of her, with Mercury at the far left. On the other side of the big wooden panel a blue, male figure – the wind god Zephyr – chases the nymph Chloris while Flora in her painted dress, a garland in her blonde hair, smiles inscrutably. Botticelli views his classical sources through the enchanted glass of courtly love. Like Poliziano, he weaves ancient mythology into a sweet, sad, romantic vision. This can be seen in his portrayal of Flora. There is a floral tendril

Sandro Botticelli,
Pallas and the Centaur,
c. 1480–85.

Sandro Botticelli,
Primavera, c. 1480.

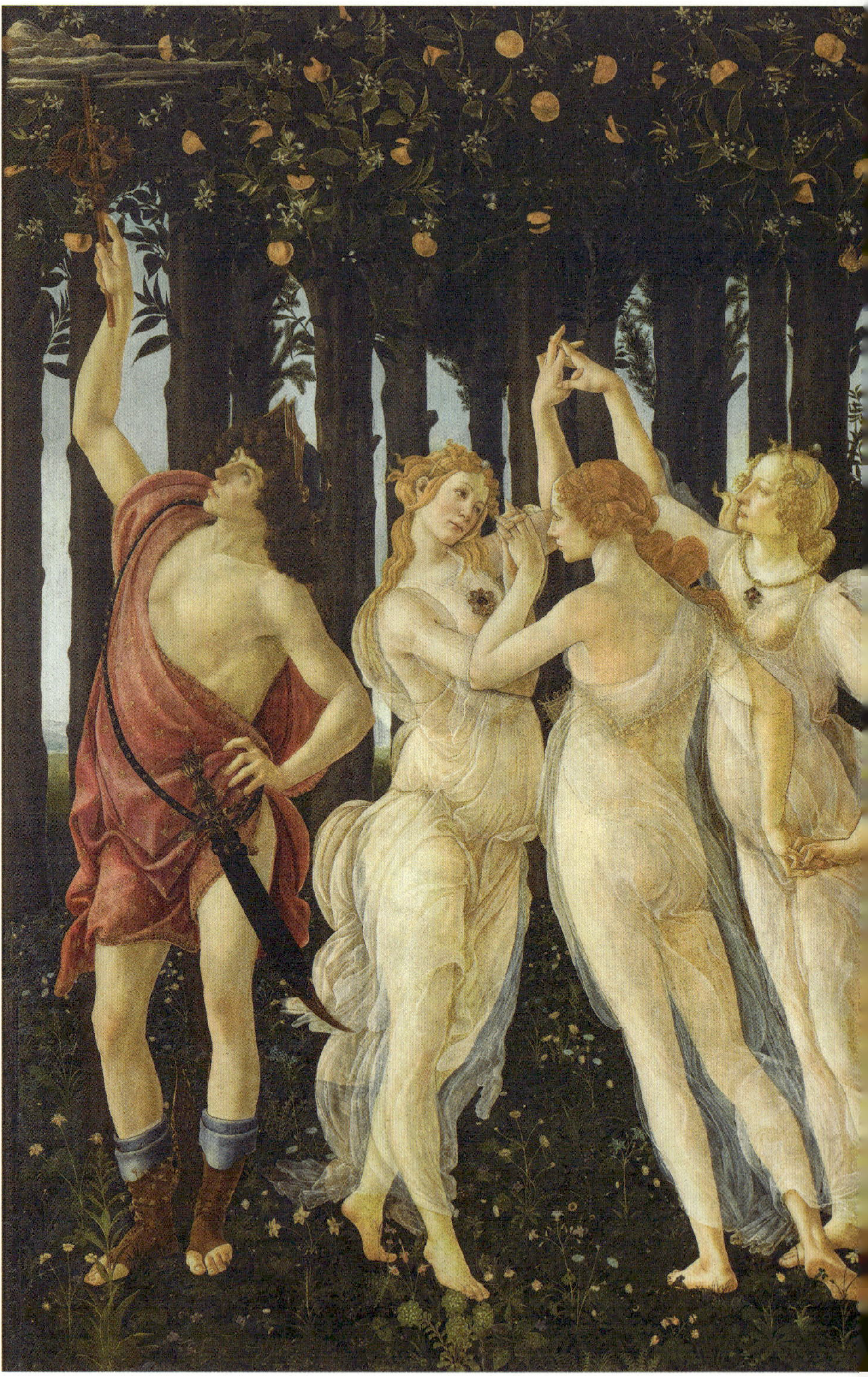

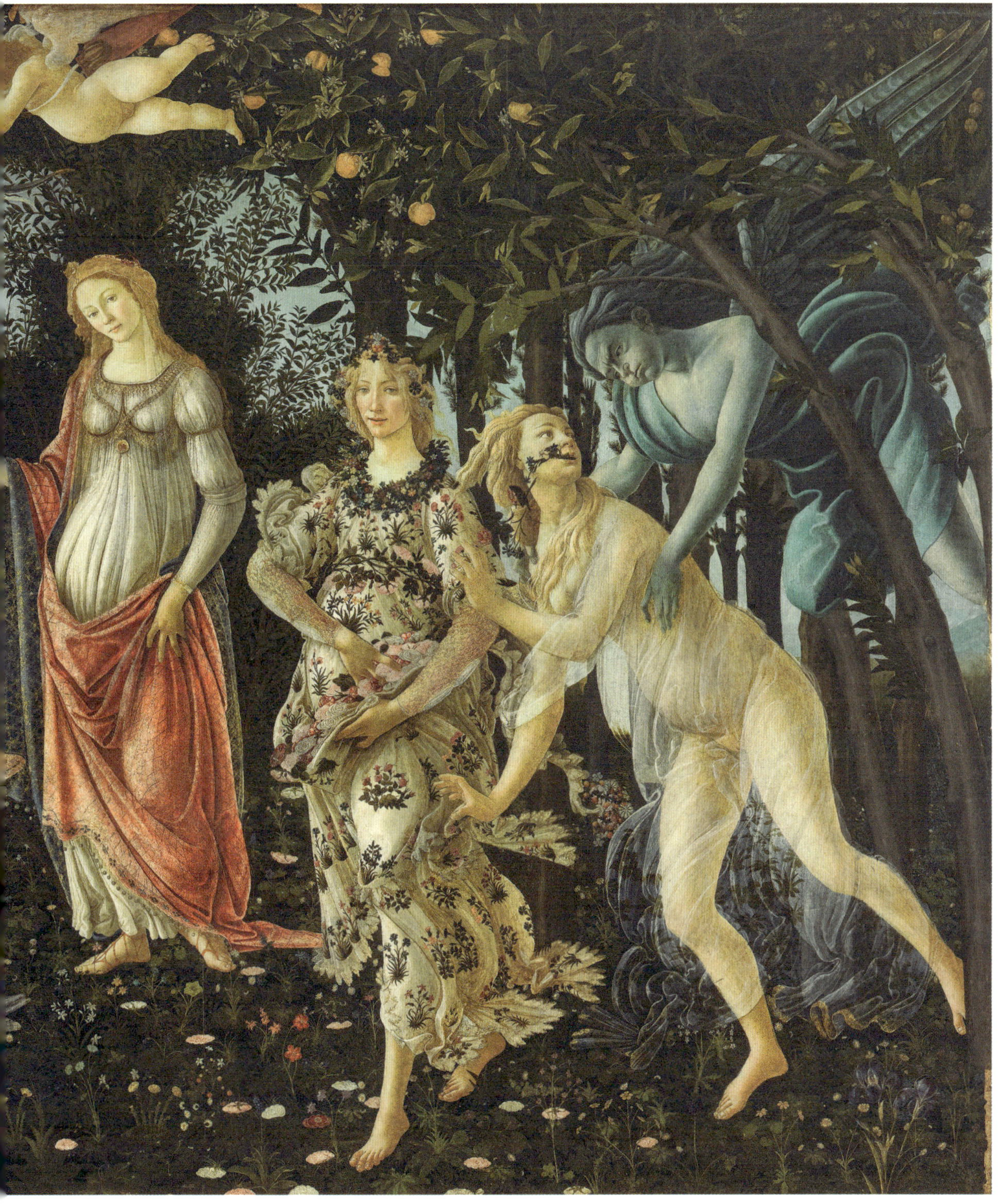

flowing from the mouth of the fleeing nymph and becoming the pattern on Flora's dress. They are in fact the same person. We are seeing a *metamorphosis*, one of the first Renaissance pictures of a phenomenon in classical myth that was to spellbind artists. According to Ovid's calendrical poem the *Fasti*, after the wind god Zephyrus chased and caught the nymph Chloris he made her a goddess and charged her with tending his garden.

The account in Book 5 of the *Fasti* is brutal. Ovid, writing in the age of the Emperor Augustus to explain Rome's old festivals, tells how the Floralia, in which prostitutes took a leading part, commemorated the rape of Chloris by Zephyrus and her blossoming as Flora. Botticelli does not show it like that. His flying Zephyr grabs the running Chloris, yet he is a spirit, a ghost, more air than flesh. He becomes incorporeal so that we concentrate on the triumph of Flora who is also Spring, 'La Primavera', herself. The emphasis is on her radiance and tranquillity. She is a supernatural being, a lady worshipped by a poet, a knight's enchanting mistress. In depicting classical myth, Botticelli is serving the game of courtly love.

Lucretius began his poem with a prayer to Venus. She is more than just a love goddess for him: she is the spirit of creativity, identified with nature itself. But Lucretius does not believe in her or any other god in a literal sense: everything is made of atoms, according to his ancient Greek philosophical heroes Democritus and Epicurus; matter forms itself without divine aid. The gods get more respect in Poliziano's *Joust*. Poliziano makes no effort to Christianize them. Unlike his contemporary Marsilio Ficino, who worked to find Christ in Plato, he puts all his effort into creating a classical dreamworld of the senses, ruled by ancient deities whose beauty is the embodiment of nature's fertility. This non-Christian Arcadia is the place Botticelli paints.

This approach is even clearer in the *Birth of Venus*. Botticelli's love goddess may not be the first 15th-century painting of a bare body, yet for the first time in the Renaissance an artist convincingly creates a female nude with the balanced musicality of classical sculpture.

In Poliziano's *Joust* we enter the palace of Venus, created by her husband, the divine artisan Vulcan, where wondrous reliefs of the gods include the birth of the love goddess herself. First we see how the penis and testicles of the sky god Uranus, severed by his son Cronus, create a 'foam' in the Aegean sea, from which Venus is born. Then Vulcan portrays the newborn yet adult love goddess gliding to her home, Cyprus, on a conch: 'a young woman not with a human face, / by lusty zephyrs pushed to shore'.[9]

It could be a description of Botticelli's *Birth of Venus*, in which the zephyrs blow to speed Venus on her way. Botticelli is directly rising to the challenge

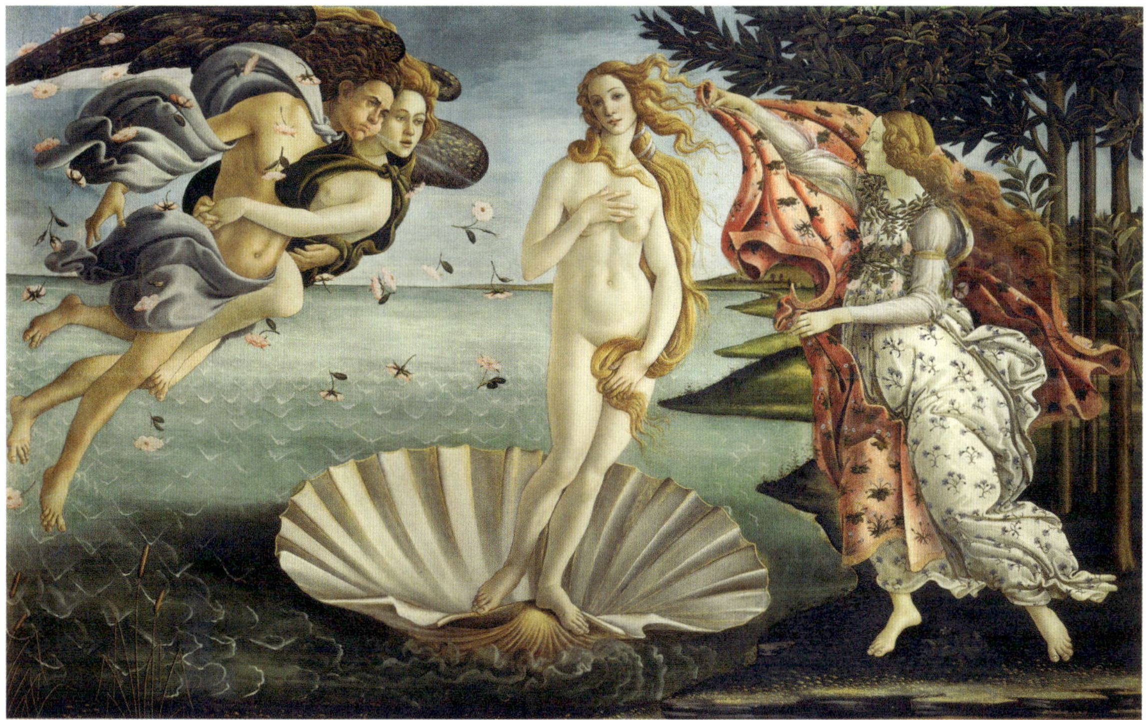

Sandro Botticelli,
Birth of Venus, c. 1485.

Poliziano poses in his poem. The image of Venus on her shell created by Vulcan is miraculously real, or *vero*:

> Real the foam and real the sea you'd say,
> And real the shell and real the breaths of the winds.[10]

and this is the precise quality that makes Botticelli's Venus so alive and so unforgettable, even after more than five centuries. Consciously competing with Poliziano's description of a divine pagan masterpiece, he makes everything in the *Birth of Venus* real. She floats towards us, a pre-Christian, natural deity of love and desire. Behind her, flecking the green sea in little fast splashes of white paint, we see the sperm from which she arose – the physical reality of her genesis. For the paganism that Poliziano showed to Botticelli was not a spiritual religion like Christianity: it was a cult of the natural world.

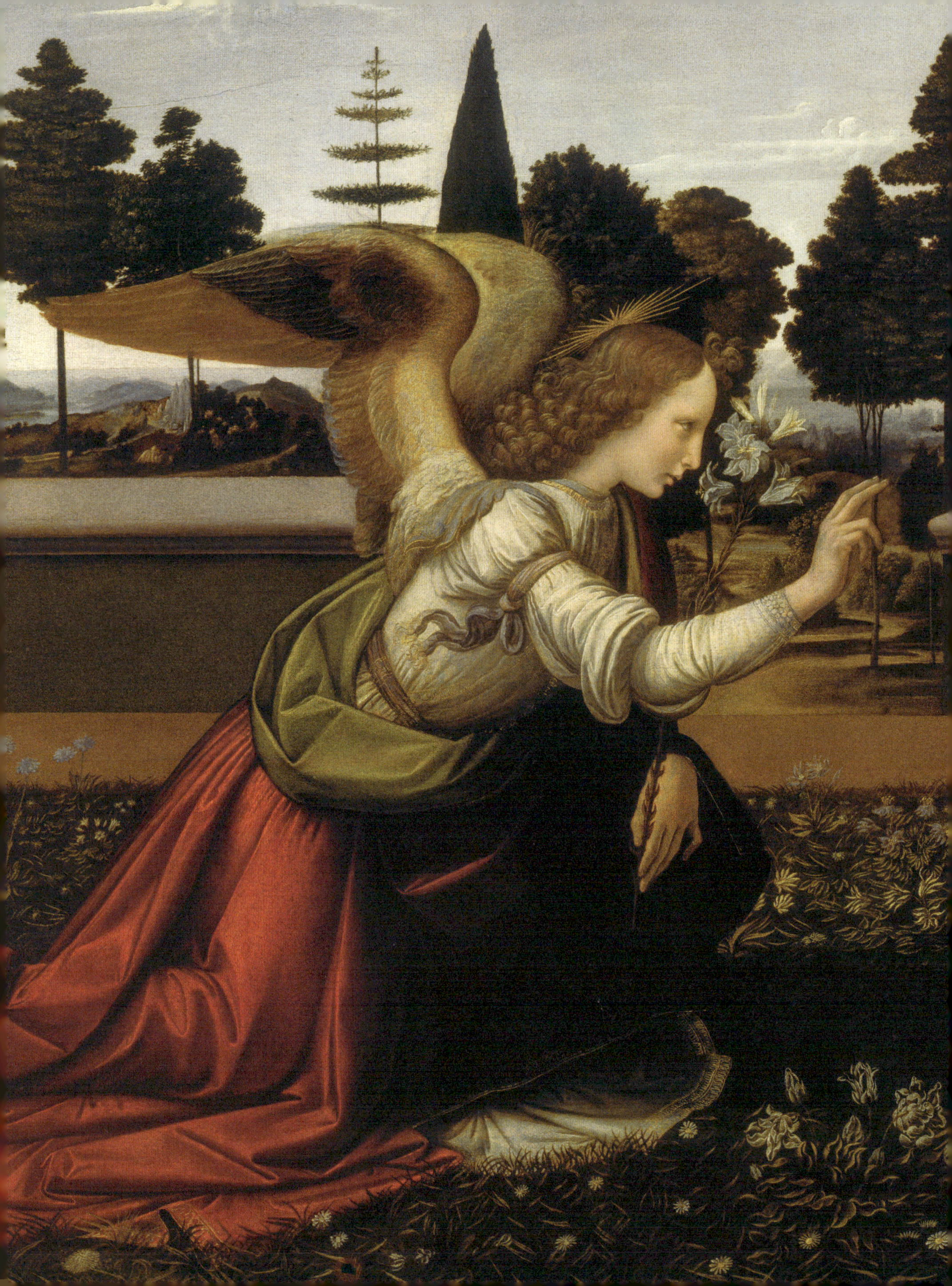

4 Nature's Child

Leonardo da Vinci often spoke to Botticelli in his head. Long after the days when they were up-and-coming painters in 1470s Florence, he would pen acerbic notes addressed to 'Sandro', as if repeating or inventing a debate between them. He appeared locked in an argument he could not end. In the most extended note, he rails at Botticelli's casual approach to landscape painting. You cannot be a true artist if you trivialize landscape, Leonardo insists, complaining about Botticelli's view that such study was futile

> because just by throwing a sponge full of diverse colours at a wall it left a stain on that wall where a beautiful landscape could be seen.[1]

Botticelli must have once sneered that it was as easy as throwing a paint-soaked sponge to daub a few trees and mountains in a picture's background. You can get ideas by looking at marks on a wall, Leonardo adds, but as a stimulus to the imagination, not the quick cheat Botticelli joked about. In the privacy of his notebook, Leonardo gives himself the last laugh: 'And such a painter makes very poor landscapes.'[2] We are left with the impression of Botticelli, the darling of the Medici, holding forth to Leonardo, his junior by seven years, on a subject sure to provoke the younger man. For in Leonardo's mind the landscape was much more than a background.

Leonardo da Vinci, *Annunciation* (detail), c. 1472.

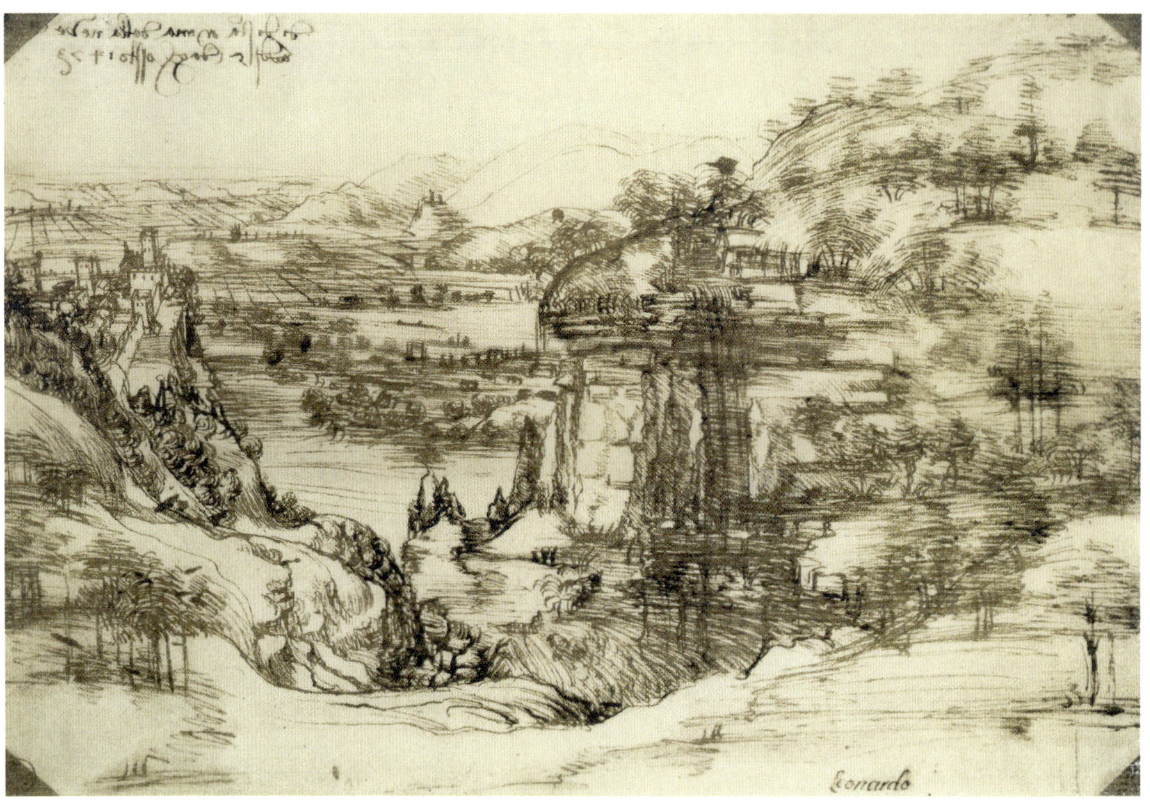

Leonardo da Vinci, *Drawing of an Arno Valley Landscape*, 1473.

* * *

Born in the Tuscan hills in 1452, the illegitimate son of a notary called Piero da Vinci and a peasant named Caterina, Leonardo seems to have spent much of his childhood at the family's country house in Vinci, a little town perched above rugged slopes. The earliest dated drawing by him that survives, done on 5 August 1473 soon after he started his career as a painter, seems to depict his childhood world of hilltop towns, lofty rocks, lush foliage, a river at the foot of the steep terrain and, beyond it, cultivated fields and the distant sea. That doesn't mean it is an exact picture of Vinci or any specific place; but it is a detailed, utterly absorbed attempt to see scenery in its own right, not just as a setting for a story. To Botticelli's eyes, such an appetite for topographical detail was pedantic, even pointless.

Leonardo had been enrolled in Florence's Guild of St Luke as a professional painter the year before drawing this quietly revolutionary landscape. He was probably living with his master, Verrocchio, whose workshop he joined at the age of 17. How he was educated before that is unknown. Presumably he was taught basic literacy, and numeracy (valued in commercially minded Tuscany). All his life Leonardo's lack of an academic education would both impede and

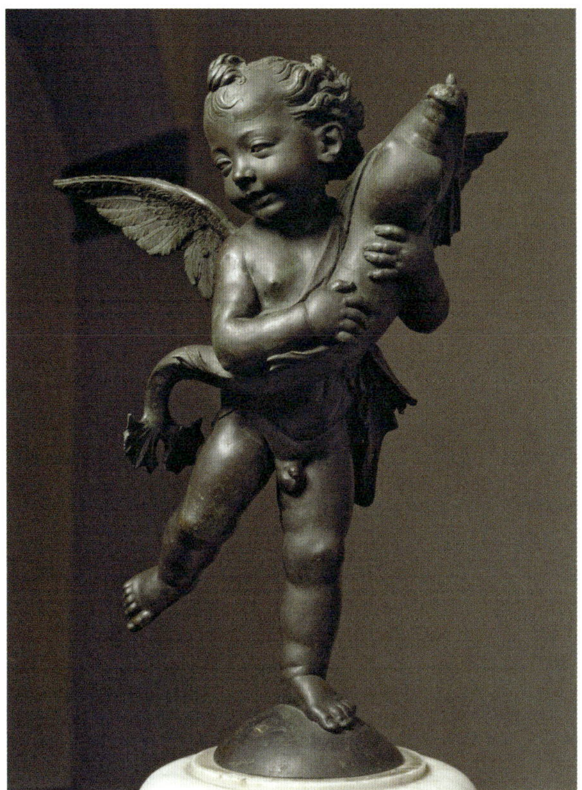

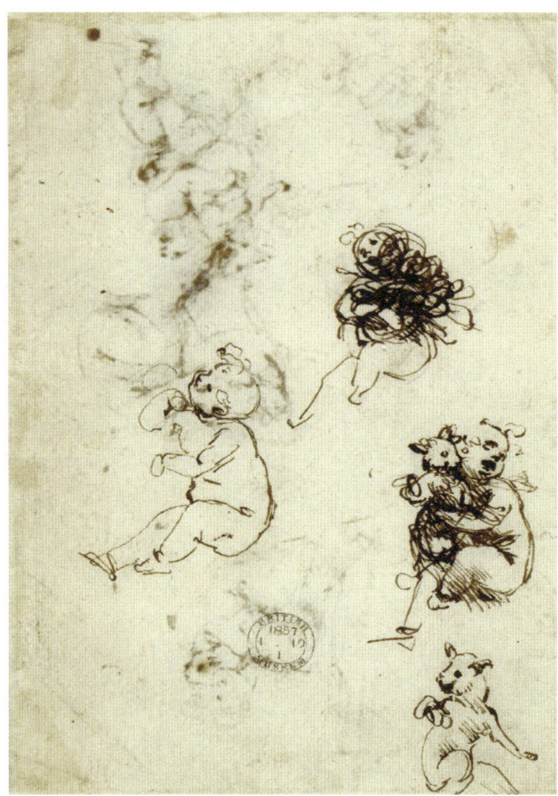

Andrea del Verrocchio, *Putto with a Dolphin*, c. 1470.

Leonardo da Vinci, *Study of the Christ Child with a Cat*, c. 1478–81.

impel his inexhaustible studies. It was during his childhood that he must have started the habits of independent research that he never lost: wading in streams, collecting frogspawn, drawing flowers and trees.

Verrocchio's workshop rolled out graceful neo-pagan artworks alongside a production line of sweet Madonnas. Verrocchio made a bronze David that is decorous and tame compared with Donatello's. His bronze putto holding a dolphin is more fun, an energetic, bubbling homage to childhood play. It was made for a fountain at a Medici villa in Careggi, in the hills outside Florence. Its effervescence would echo in Renaissance fountains and gardens for a long time. Leonardo, however, always looked for something more real, the pulse of life itself. You can see how he took Verrocchio's *Putto with a Dolphin* as a prototype for a sheet of rapid sketches of a child playing with a cat. Yet he adds new dimensions, new universes of possibility to his teacher's slick sculpture. Instead of recording a single pose, the most spectacular drawing on the page tries to capture the cat struggling in a flurry of superimposed limbs. He sees both cat and baby as beings full of their own purpose: you can sense the tension and vitality as both try to get their way. Verrocchio's sculpture seems limited by comparison. So do most works of art that have ever been created.

* * *

In Lorenzo de' Medici's Florence, where Leonardo was trying to establish himself, you were nobody if you could not name your courtly lover. The new Venetian ambassador to the Florentine Republic, who took up his post in time for Giuliano de' Medici's joust, played the game well. Bernardo Bembo let it be known that he loved a young Florentine woman called Ginevra de' Benci. His passion so impressed the Florentine poet and scholar Cristoforo Landino that he addressed poems in Latin to the diplomat celebrating his great love. Ginevra de' Benci was married, but no need to fret, explains Landino, who stresses the chastity of Bembo's adoration: it was 'such as the divine page of Plato expresses with the eloquence of Socrates'.[3]

Landino uses what he has learnt from Marsilio Ficino, translator and interpreter of Plato, to justify Bembo's obsession with a married woman. Bembo does love Ginevra's physical beauty, but such love, as discussed in the *Symposium*, leads him upwards, towards a love for her soul and towards what is virtuous, away from anything morally wrong.

It was not the only type of otherwise illicit relationship to be justified by love as it appears in the Platonic dialogues. Some of the pioneers of Neo-Platonism in 15th-century Florence were men who desired men, including Ficino. It was he who invented the term 'Platonic love' – or, more precisely. 'Platonic and Socratic love'– in his commentary on the *Phaedrus*. There he asserted that a chaste love of physical – specifically male – beauty can lead upwards to the love of the soul, and ultimately to the love of God.[4]

Landino here gives courtly passion the philosophical justification that was to legitimize many otherwise unlawful Renaissance loves. It was a lot to load onto a love affair, chaste or not. It is uncertain whether Leonardo's portrait of Ginevra from the mid-1470s was commissioned by Bembo, although on the back of it her namesake juniper – *ginevra* – appears between the laurel and palm branches of his coat of arms. Leonardo certainly makes her look like a woman with the character to inspire homage. Her eyelids have the heaviness of thought. Her eyes, meanwhile, are depicted with scientific accuracy as shimmering, translucent and reflective lenses. Ginevra looks out of the painting critically from her natural seeing-machines of soft jelly. No artist had ever before painted the human eye like this. Had the young Leonardo already dissected one?

Ginevra de' Benci's solemn regard is amplified by her tall brow and long nose. Her beauty is a complex phenomenon, her lips a pink study in themselves. Her hair, bound tightly on her head, bursts at the fringes into curls that resemble the whirlpools and rapids of a raging river. Behind her rises the spiky juniper

Leonardo da Vinci,
Ginevra de' Benci,
c. 1474–78.

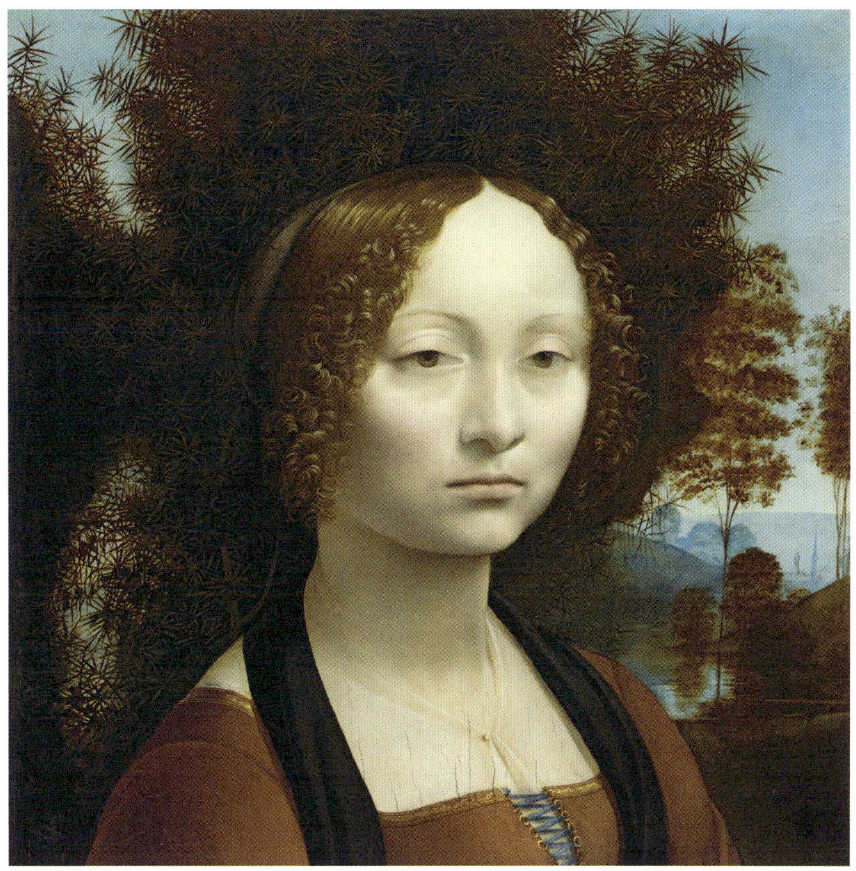

bush, her symbol. It merges her with the reflective water beyond, in which we see an upside-down tree. The landscape melts to blue. A town lingers in its mist like an evening shadow.

To a contemporary, Leonardo's method must have seemed as novel as his subject is dramatic. It was certainly new in Florence. *Ginevra de' Benci* is an oil painting built up in layers of glaze on a panel of wood. The new medium is more than a technique. It lets Leonardo see what he otherwise might not: reflections, shadows, a flash of light in a filament of hair. At last, in this work, the discoveries of Jan van Eyck are rivalled in Florence. Leonardo has looked hard at Flemish paintings. He experiments with the medium they used to mirror reality – and goes further. His restless mind sees more enigma and paradox in the art of oil painting than anyone had previously conceived.

Portraiture was one of the most magical tricks at the disposal of Flemish painters. In a world without cameras or screens, the memory of faces could easily fade. 'Léal Souvenir' – 'loyal memory' – says the inscription on a portrait of a man by van Eyck from 1432. If this portrait is posthumous, the motto is not only a declaration by the person who commissioned it, but a professional promise by van Eyck. The oil painter could reproduce every hair and blemish, make memory permanent.

Simple portraits whose sole purpose is to record someone's appearance are among the earliest northern oil paintings. In about 1435 Robert Campin portrays a married couple facing each other in two matching panels, their plain, arresting faces within red and white swathings of drapery. Around the same year Rogier van der Weyden paints a woman looking straight at us from under her elaborately pinned headgear. She looks jovial, smiling inwardly at a private joke. Her glossy lips and fine nose have some of the hypnotic beauty Leonardo would make his own.

Portraiture was a precious mirror of fleeting life. The English diplomat Edward Grimston, a Lancastrian supporter of Henry VI, went to Bruges to be portrayed by the painter Petrus Christus. It's possible the unknown young woman who posed for this artist in about 1470 was also English. The result is the most Leonardesque portrait that survives by a 15th-century artist who was not Leonardo. The young woman is almost comically characterized – a teenager, maybe, looking off to one side. She's hypnotically real. Petrus Christus peers into an ear with the microscopic detail of a Leonardo drawing, and sculpts her nose and lips with the opulent precision only oil paint can give.

* * *

Leonardo may have been shown Flemish portraits of this quality, or told about them, by Bernardo Bembo, whose diplomatic posting before Florence was to Bruges. Even without Bembo as middleman, or Portinari sending triptychs, there was Flemish art to study in Florence. The Medici owned an altarpiece that Rogier van der Weyden had painted, possibly while stopping at Florence on pilgrimage to Rome in 1450. It is another of his devastating images of the near-naked, dead Christ. This treasure was done in oils. The first family of Florence also owned a painting of *St Jerome in his Study* by van Eyck, listed in an inventory of Lorenzo de' Medici's possessions.

The puzzle is why it took a Leonardo to fully embrace the oil technique. Even after he had painted Ginevra de' Benci it did not instantly catch on in Florence. Botticelli mostly stuck with tempera. Partly this was down to local pride. Florence saw itself as the place where ancient beauty was being revived, and copying ideas from Bruges and Brussels was a betrayal of the lineage of Giotto and Masaccio. And Leonardo didn't exactly help make oil painting respectable, for what he did with it was unsettling.

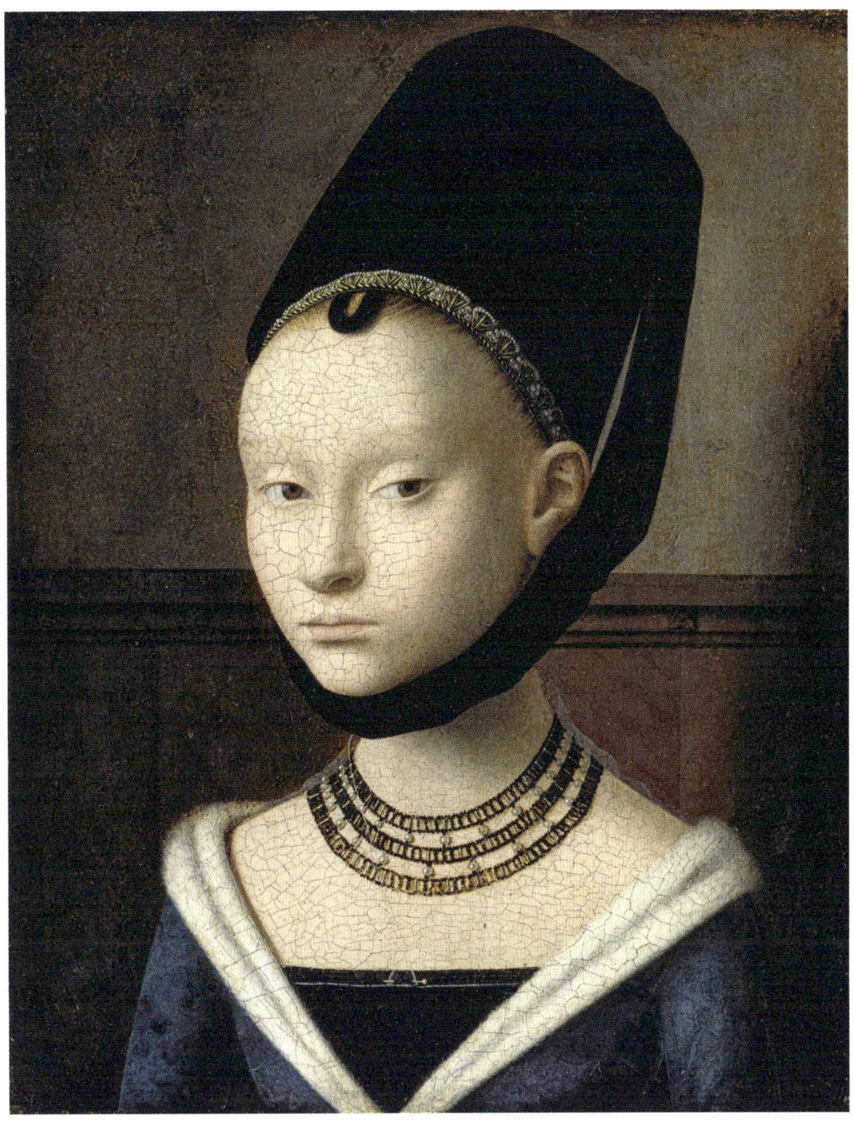

Petrus Christus, *Portrait of a Young Woman*, c. 1470.

One person thrown into confusion by the young Leonardo's brush was his teacher, Verrocchio. As Vasari tells the story, the successful older artist took on a commission in about 1472 to paint the Baptism of Christ and 'was assisted by Leonardo da Vinci, his disciple, then quite young, who painted therein an angel with his own hand, which was much better than the other parts of the work'. In response Andrea 'resolved never again to touch a brush, since Leonardo, young as he was, had acquitted himself in that art much better than he had done'.[5]

It was the greatest upstaging in art history. Verrocchio's humiliation is preserved in painful perfection in the *Baptism of Christ* (overleaf). The angel in profile on the far left is unambiguously by Leonardo and makes other parts

Andrea del Verrocchio and Leonardo da Vinci, *Baptism of Christ*, 1470–75.

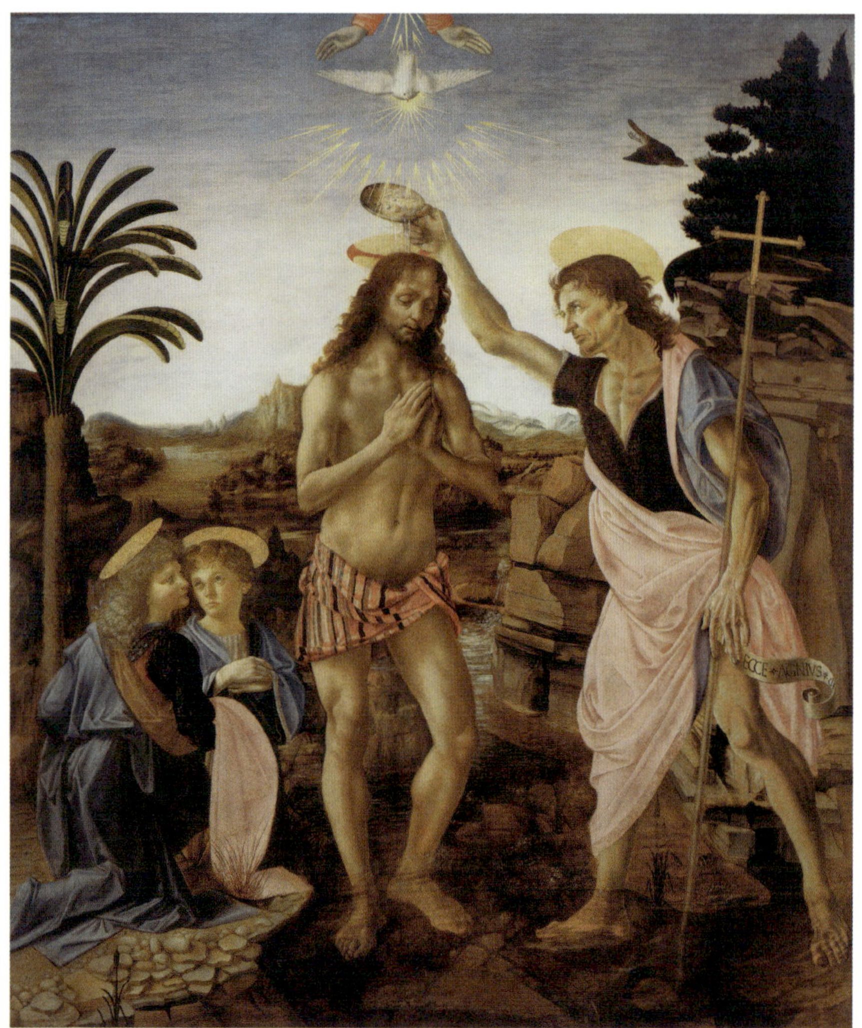

of the picture seem dead. Yet it is not just the quality that startles. Verrocchio's stern, muscular John the Baptist is a figure of sombre asceticism, piously holding a tall cross. Leonardo's angel, by contrast, seems decadent and corrupt.

Flemish oil painting is realist. Leonardo, however, uses oils in a different way, to create trembling images of infinite ambiguity. His angel is painted with a heady, sensual sense of play. An angel in a religious scene really doesn't need to be so softly androgynous. This flight of painterly freedom is a manifesto of art for art's sake. The angel is not only Leonardo's triumph over his master, but the emergence of the artist from behind the work of art. Up to now every painter and sculptor, even the most famous, remained faithful to an impersonal sense of craft. A painting should be consistent across its surface, a well-made artefact for a church or a palazzo. The maker might be renowned for a style, but this style could be reproduced by assistants and disciples. Leonardo's angel explodes this convention. All of a sudden the artist is an astonishing individual painting a performance that needs no justification but its own beauty.

Verrocchio might reasonably have expected Leonardo to paint the angel in his master's style. A glance through the young artist's drawings would have shown him that Leonardo couldn't be trusted. The budding genius was constantly taking Verrocchio's elegant ideas and improvising on them.

Verrocchio was commissioned by Lorenzo de' Medici to make bronze heads of the ancient rulers Alexander the Great and Darius to send to the cultured king of Hungary, Matthias Corvinus. They do not survive, but copies, probably from Verrocchio's workshop, do. The finest has a youthful warrior in profile in an ornate helmet and cuirass. It is obviously connected to an early drawing by Leonardo of a man in florid classical armour. Leonardo's old and battleworn warrior, his skin like leather, his helmet squirming with scales and wings, is a hyperreal fantasy that trumps Verrocchio's neoclassical grace. Or, as Leonardo puts it succinctly, 'He is a poor disciple who does not excel his master.'[6]

It was an insight learned in Verrocchio's workshop, where Leonardo could see the difference between apprentices who just followed instructions and those who challenged themselves to innovate. His angel in Verrocchio's *Baptism* insists with every golden hair that artistic personality is unique and unconventional.

The angel's light-catching locks, like the flaming fringes of Ginevra de' Benci's hair, don't conform to any customary way of showing angel hair. Curls are already an obsession with Leonardo, a phenomenon he grafts onto any head he pleases because it embodies his train of thought. Vasari saw it as a sexual fetish: Leonardo delighted in fine tresses, flowing in ringlets, on young men. But there was more to it than sex. The spiralling of hair reminded Leonardo of other rotating, wavy phenomena he observed in nature, from the flight of birds to the movement of water. One of the reasons his angel has more life than anything else in the *Baptism of Christ* is that every detail, from those bright eyes to the legs kneeling under silken drapery, reflects Leonardo's intellectual and artistic character.

Numerous drawings of drapery from this period attributed to Leonardo match the angel's skirts. They are acute analyses of light and shadow and the way the folds and recesses of hanging cloth can at once hide and reveal the body underneath. This theme haunts Leonardo's *Annunciation*, painted in around 1472 (overleaf). Mary's lap is covered with a skirt that is not a skirt but a massy, blue-grey silken hanging that drapes over the furniture beside her (or is it suspended by something ghostly?) and is slung over her right arm. Between her

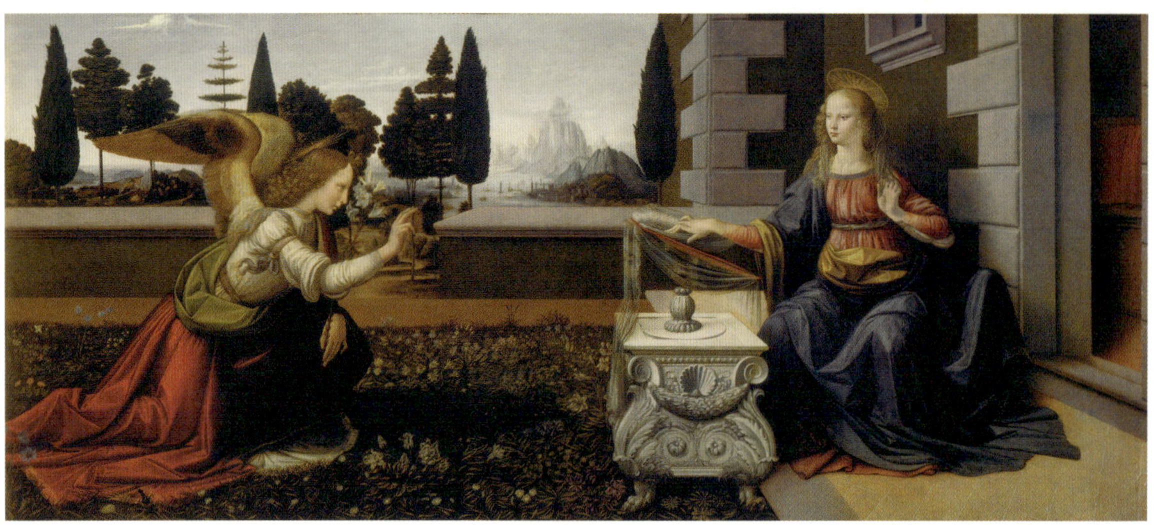

Leonardo da Vinci, *Annunciation*, c. 1472.

legs it falls in a deep, dark valley. Above, the crimped silk of her dress bursts out from a belt to form two lip-like rednesses. Mary isn't so much wearing clothes as defined by an arrangement of fabric foldings.

The angel too is swathed in linen, red set off by green, and has the requisite curly hair. Its face in profile possesses both male and female qualities, yet there's a more extreme example of hybridization. What grips Leonardo is the nature of the angel's wings. Botticelli could paint a centaur and make the splicing of horse and man look absolutely real. Here Leonardo does the same with human and bird, but with greater anatomical detail, crueller precision. We can see the roots of the wings where they burst from the angel's back: it's easy to believe that the young artist looked at the severed wings of real birds before he painted them. The solid, skeletal structure under the feathers, the almost painful way they join the angel's body as if stitched on, clashes with the idea of an angel as a supernatural being. This messenger is more Frankensteinian experiment.

Vasari describes the teenaged Leonardo carrying out such researches in preparation for decorating a shield, relating how

> he began to think what he could paint on it, that he might be able to terrify all who should come upon it, producing the same effect as once did the head of Medusa. For this purpose, he carried to a room of his own into which no one entered except himself, lizards great and small, crickets, serpents, butterflies, grasshoppers, bats, and other strange kinds of suchlike animals, out of the number of which, variously put together, he formed a great ugly creature, most horrible and terrifying, which emitted a poisonous breath and turned the air to flame.[7]

Leonardo darkened the room before inviting his father to enter and look upon the creature he had made. His father was terrified. Was it is living or dead, a reanimated beast or the painted image of one? Vasari seems unsure.

Leonardo traced his particular lifelong fascination with birds and flight, specifically the kite, to an early memory. He wrote that: 'Among the first recollections of my infancy it seemed to me that as I was in my cradle a kite came to me and opened my mouth with its tail and struck me several times with its tail inside my lips.'[8] Whatever the meaning or origin of this reminiscence, it confesses the intense psychological drive behind Leonardo's interest in birds. We see that infatuation in this very early work, painted when he was only about 20 years old. It makes no sense to explain the angel's wings in terms of theological or classical iconography. Their source is Leonardo's study of nature. The angel is his first flying machine.

The *Annunciation* has elements that will recur in Leonardo's other religious scenes: the dreamy blue landscape, the sculpted draperies. It is the angels in this painting and in Verrocchio's *Baptism* that are a breakthrough. They are messengers of desire, embodying a new kind of being, androgynous and gifted, with the ability to fly. To become such an entity is a manifestation of the artist's dreams of flight that began when a kite visited him in his cradle.

* * *

On 9 April 1476 those dreams nearly came crashing to earth. Leonardo was accused of sodomizing a male prostitute called Jacopo d'Andrea Saltarelli. Three other men were accused with him: a goldsmith, Bartholomeo di Pasquino; a tailor named only as Baccino; and Leonardo Tornabuoni, one of the wealthy Tornabuoni family who were related by marriage to the Medici. The anonymous nature of the evidence weakened any case, and the power of the Tornabuoni may also have helped. All four were warned not to come before the city's Office of the Night again. This piquantly named magistracy was specifically created to control what was feared to be an epidemic of male homosexuality in Florence. The social mixture of the four men arrested – two artisans, an artist and a patrician – suggests a nocturnal subculture that crossed class lines, bringing different men from varying milieux together to pursue illegal pleasures. There's evidence that Saltarelli served such needs for cash. On the back of a draft letter asking for support against the sodomy accusation, Leonardo meditates: 'If there is no love, what then?'[9]

Another fact recorded in his sex crime accusation is that Leonardo, at nearly 24, was still living with Verrocchio. His vision had not captivated Lorenzo de' Medici's Florence. He was not cosy with the elite like Botticelli; there were no

Medici commissions. And he was slow. His early paintings amount to just a handful of works, each one wrought with idiosyncratic intensity. Other artists, meanwhile, were producing Madonna after Madonna.

Leonardo was still studying, still learning. He didn't aspire to become a busy craftsman running a workshop to supply wealthy Florentines with painted chests and backboards, mirror frames and other household wares. His relationship with the classical revival to which Botticelli gave such ravishing form was also knotty. The most ambitious image of the antique in his early art is the fantastical marble lectern in the *Annunciation*. Yet this embellishment of ancient sculpture tumbles into his own scientific obsessions with its scallop shell, foliage and animal feet.

Those animal feet on which the structure rests are carved with such realism you could believe them to be real paws. They resemble Leonardo's earliest surviving anatomical drawings, in which he studies the feet of bears and wolves or dogs. These sketches are usually dated to about 1480, but the clawed lectern suggests that he may have been studying animal feet eight years earlier. Again we glimpse the young polymath creating incongruous, hybrid beauty from his passion for nature.

* * *

In the second half of the 1470s Leonardo spent time working at Lorenzo de' Medici's sculpture academy. Lorenzo didn't just write poetry and sponsor philosophy in his quest to revive the mythology and ideology of the Greeks and Romans. He also created this art school close to the convent of San Marco, a short walk from his home, specifically to educate young artists in the classical tradition. It was full of ancient statuary and decoration for them to copy. It didn't make Leonardo a painter of gods like Botticelli. His brashest attempt to get Lorenzo de' Medici's attention was instead a depiction of brutal fact.

All the jousts and classicized chivalry in the world couldn't stop rivals from plotting. On 26 April 1478 they struck. The Pazzi family, who had recently usurped the Medici as bankers to the pope, led an ambush on Lorenzo and Giuliano de' Medici in Florence Cathedral. Giuliano was stabbed to death. Lorenzo got away, re-established his control of the Signoria and plotted his violent revenge.

It wasn't enough just to hang the conspirators from windows close to the Palazzo della Signoria. Their dangling corpses were also painted on public walls in a macabre Florentine tradition that functioned as a curse through portraiture. Their shame was immortalized through this second 'execution' – at least symbolically, for the open air frescoes wouldn't last. The drawing Leonardo did in the courtyard of the Bargello, the palace of justice, in December 1479 is a portrait of Bernardo Baroncelli, the last

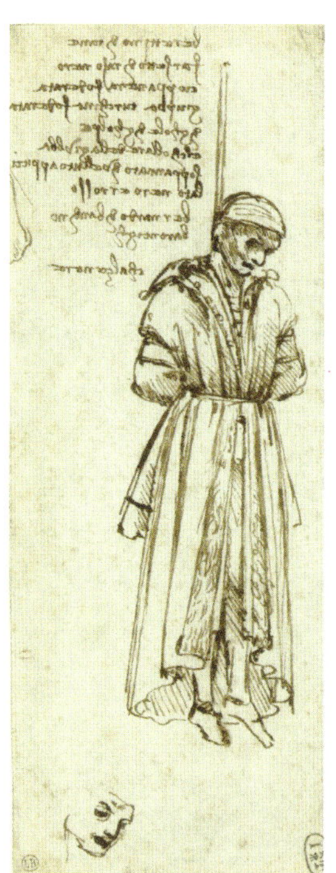

Leonardo da Vinci, *Study of the Hanged Bernardo Baroncelli*, 1479.

of the Pazzi conspirators to be caught, swinging by the neck. His face is hollowed, the dead skin shrinking back onto the bone below, his eyes inky voids.

Painting the hanged was dirty work. An earlier artist charged with such frescoes was known ever after as 'Andrea of the Hanged Men'. Lorenzo had hired his family artist to portray other conspirators: Botticelli, the magician of beauty, who painted visions of enchanted femininity and courtly love. Pictures of the executed were surely an awkward job for him, and it's perfectly possible that Botticelli hated it. Leonardo was apparently pitching for this work, and it suits him perfectly. His clinical eye, which would later enable him to dissect and draw corpses in hospitals, responds to the visible decay in this dangling body. Death is a part of nature, whose secrets he longs to understand. You can almost imagine him reminding himself to 'study the way nature ruins a dead body'. In the note he actually made, he lists the clothes the dead man was wearing, and their colours. Baroncelli had been dragged back to Florence from distant Constantinople and was hanged in his Turkish clothes just to emphasize how far Lorenzo's revenge reached. Leonardo lovingly notes his black serge doublet, jerkin with black and red velvet collar, blue coat with fox-fur lining and black hose.

He didn't get the commission. Perhaps his entrancement with the exotic clothes was too sensual, even odd, when he was supposed to be demonizing the dead man.

* * *

Can we really know anything about the sex life of Leonardo da Vinci? Do we need to? Sigmund Freud was the first writer on Leonardo to see his homosexuality as crucial to understanding his art – or at least the earliest explicitly to say so. Before him, the Victorian critic Walter Pater implied plenty in a sensual essay on Leonardo published in 1873. In fact, the gossip goes back to the Renaissance. Vasari and another 16th-century writer, Giovanni Paolo Lomazzo, both suggest that Leonardo's assistant Salaì, noted for his curly ringlets, was a boyfriend. Vasari also stresses the beauty of his pupil Francesco Melzi.

Perhaps Leonardo's private life should be left in twilight. He liked painting androgynous figures with long, soft hair and smooth faces. He was accused of sodomy but never convicted. There was some talk. If that were all, you could call it prurient to dwell on the elusive sexuality of a genius. However, that is not all. The ambiguous angelic faces in Leonardo's early art continued to hold him spellbound. As he became more artistically confident, he started to refine these personae in fearless and even heretical visual arguments that would culminate in a direct, if widely misunderstood, theological justification of homosexual love in one of the world's most treasured masterpieces.

* * *

By the beginning of 1483 Leonardo was settled in a new city where he didn't have to compete with Botticelli. Milan was bigger than Florence but had fewer good artists. According to Vasari, Leonardo was sent there by Lorenzo to play upon a lyre of his own invention for Ludovico Sforza, Milan's de facto ruler. If so, the duke must have been charmed, because Leonardo was able to ensconce himself as a court artist in the chunky-towered, Gothic Sforza castle that dominated the city.

Being a court artist was much more suited to Leonardo's polymathic interests than trying to fulfil one painting commission after another: he left an

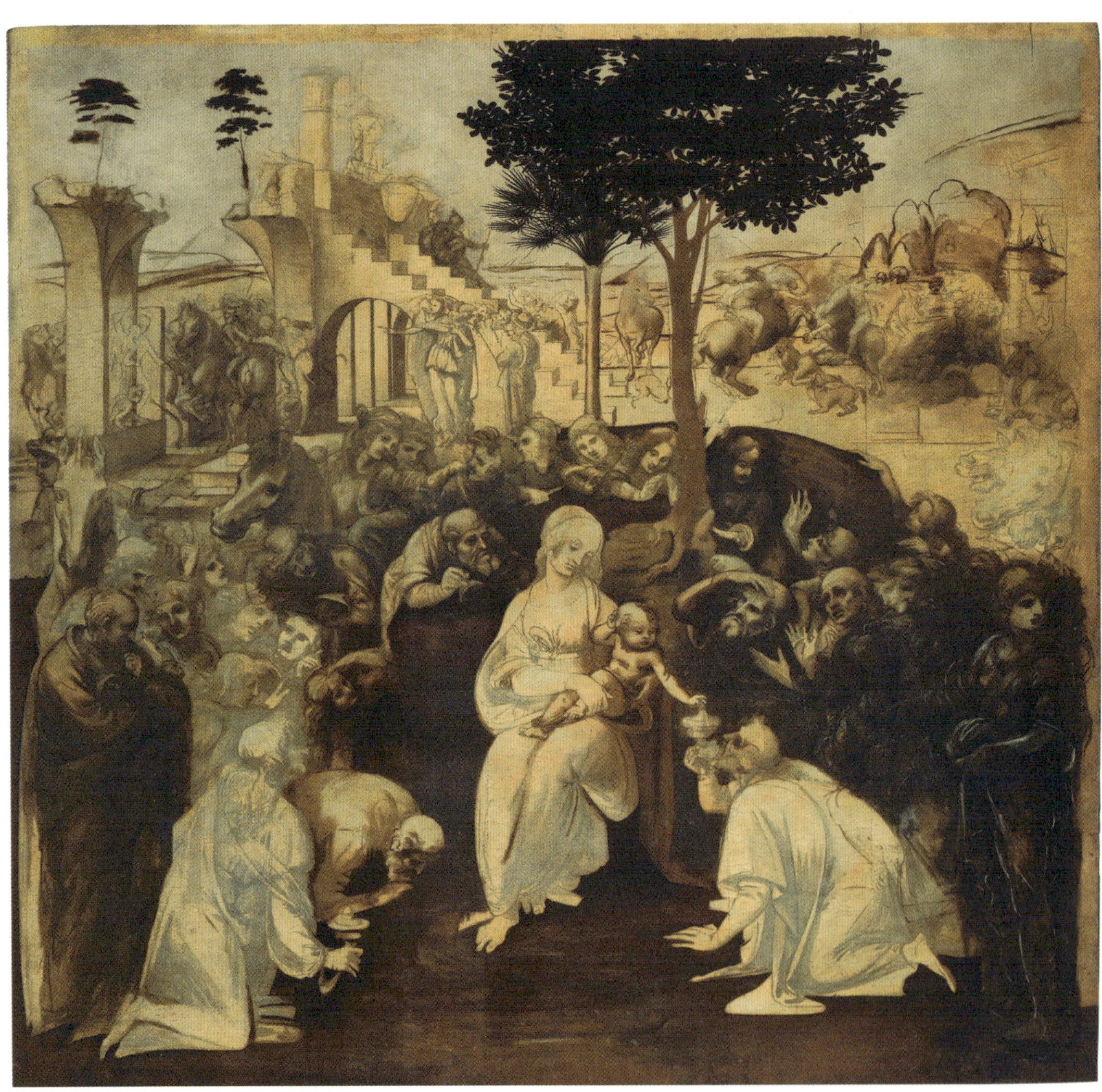

Leonardo da Vinci, *Adoration of the Magi*, c. 1482.

Adoration of the Magi unfinished in Florence, its surface pulsating with figures in a state of quantum uncertainty. In Milan he might be designing tournament costumes or theatre sets one day, and left to his own devices to work on flying machines the next.

In April 1483 he teamed up with two local artists to make an altarpiece for a chapel in the church of San Francesco Grande in Milan. It was commissioned by a confraternity, a lay brotherhood, dedicated to the doctrine of the Immaculate Conception – the belief that the Virgin Mary was conceived without original sin. Leonardo was to paint the central panel. Unusually for him, he actually completed it over the next few years. Yet the choices he made were eccentric, and he and his assistants would eventually have to paint the whole work again, producing a second version with highly significant changes.

The brothers were specific about what they wanted. For one thing it had to be painted in oils, they stressed in the original commission.[10] While Florence was still unsure about adopting the innovation of oil painting, the Milanese were all for it – perhaps because this powerful city was close to the Alps and thus open to the influence of Northern Europe. Milan itself had a Germanic flavour, its cathedral a thorny nest of spires and pinnacles. The most classical building in the city when Leonardo arrived was probably the local branch of the Medici bank, with its door based on a Roman triumphal arch.

The contract with the confraternity also specified what Leonardo should put on his central panel: Our Lady with her son and angels. Leonardo provided an oil painting as asked, but he also took the innovations of Jan van Eyck into the realm of subversion. The ability of oils to suggest sensuality in unlikely contexts and probe the mysteries of nature was apparent in Leonardo's first paintings. In the *Virgin of the Rocks* he explores further.

Ignoring the brief, Leonardo painted Mary cuddling a child while an angel shelters a second child and points towards the first (overleaf). To judge from the clarification of their identities in the second version of the picture (p. 106), the child under Mary's arm is John the Baptist, while the boy beside the angel is Jesus. The setting is a post-apocalyptic hideout, a grotto in a rocky wasteland with views of distant mountains rising from an amniotic sea; these might be the last survivors of a nuclear war. In this refuge, plants and flowers sprout, signs of life bursting from the rocks. The angel is descended from those he had painted a few years earlier, yet the androgynous face is more real. Whoever posed as this calmly pointing messenger would have had to look both male and female, yet the chances are there was no single model. The greater precision of this supernatural visage emerges from Leonardo working to crystallize his fantasy.

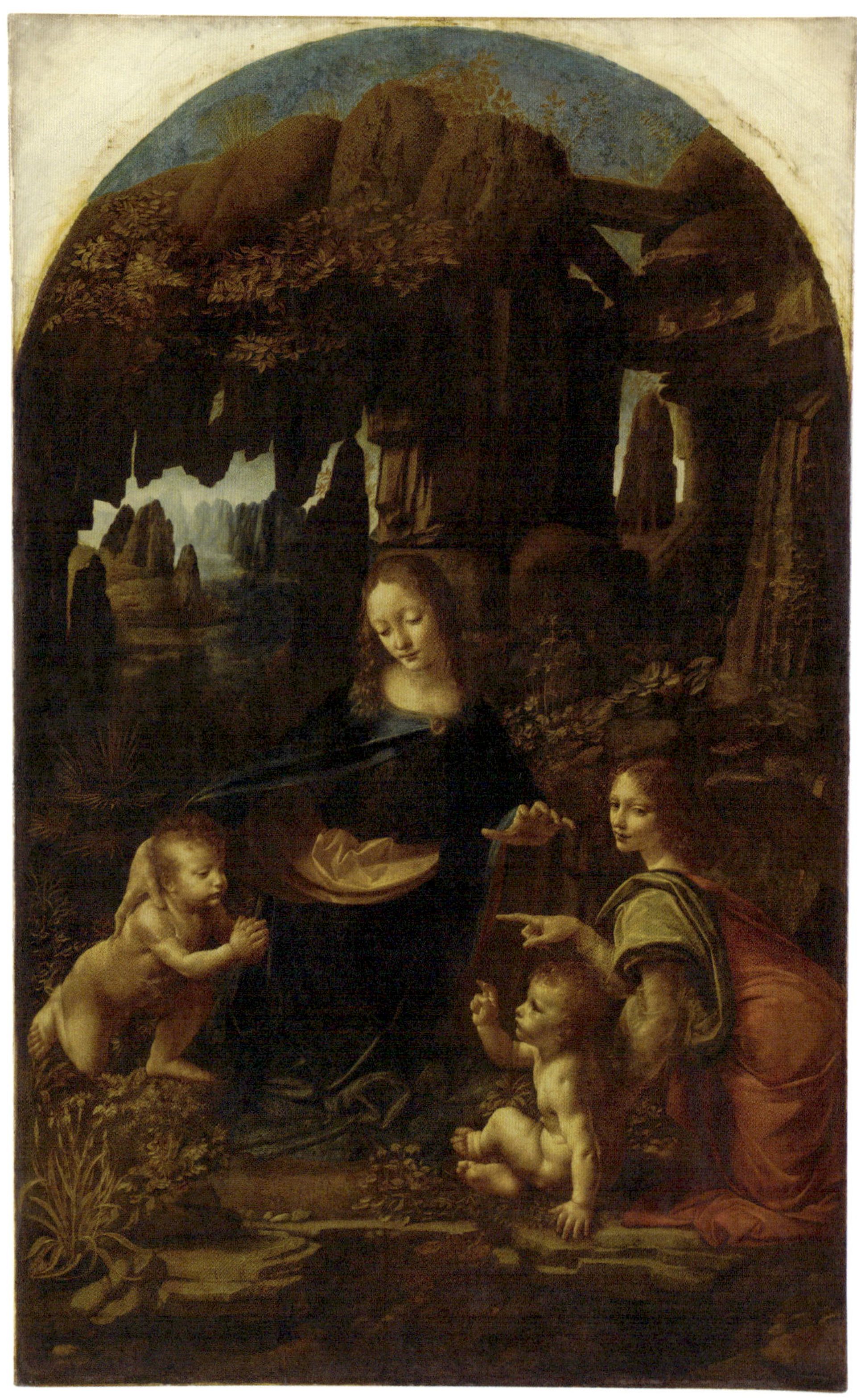

The angel is Uriel. According to the Apocrypha, it was Uriel who rescued the infant John the Baptist, the cousin of Jesus, from the Massacre of the Innocents. Uriel brought the child to Mary and Joseph on their flight into Egypt. So this is an Egyptian refuge, and it is not war but Herod's mass infanticide they are hiding from. What is perplexing is that it could look as if Jesus, under Mary's arm, were clasping his hands in prayer to John.

This difficulty is avoided in the second version of the painting by giving the child on the left a cross, the attribute of the Baptist. But if this child is John, why does the angel point towards him and not Jesus? The angel's pointing finger was removed in the second version, presumably to eliminate doubt as to who is who and who is the more holy.

There is an ancient offshoot of Christianity that survives in Iran and southern Iraq called Mandaeanism, which holds Christ to be a false prophet and instead worships John the Baptist. The Mandaeans have their own holy books that celebrate the superiority of John. This is a Gnostic belief system – one that favours personal knowledge (*gnosis* in Greek) of the divine over traditional teachings and rejects the material world. Any such ideas that reached Western medieval Europe were reviled as heresy. The confraternity surely cannot have thought Leonardo was propagating a heretical conception of the divinity of John the Baptist, yet the first finished version of the *Virgin of the Rocks* was not installed in San Francesco Grande, and a second version commissioned instead. Why precisely remains obscure.[11]

Even if Leonardo did remove troubling, even potentially heretical details in the new painting, his treatment of Uriel remained challenging. This supernatural being is John the Baptist's saviour from Herod's vicious mayhem. We should see such an archangel as purely, wholly good. Yet this supernatural being has the hairstyle and complexion of a sensationally non-binary Renaissance courtier.

It was assumed that most of Leonardo's second version of the *Virgin of the Rocks* was painted by his assistants. Restoration and scientific analysis have been used to try to show that his hand is present throughout the painting. Yet there's a huge difference between most of the work and the one part that has always been recognized as pure Leonardo: the angel's face. In painting Uriel again, he used even more subtlety to create a face of transcendental beauty that isn't male or female but something new.

* * *

Leonardo da Vinci, *Virgin of the Rocks*, 1483–94.

Leonardo is not questioning gender in some precociously 21st-century way. He is looking for a way to depict, and vindicate, men who were called 'sodomites'. Portraying such men as 'feminized' was one way to do so. In his most ambitious religious painting of all, he finds a clear theological justification for his choice. The *Last Supper* consummates Leonardo's persistent attempts to gender-bend Christianity. Its representation of sexual ambiguity is so conspicuous that it must have been intended as a talking point.

Leonardo painted the *Last Supper* on the refectory wall of the Dominican friary of Santa Maria delle Grazie, Milan, achingly slowly, said an eyewitness. He worked like a philosopher, sometimes staring at his mural for hours before even touching it with his brush. That contemplative mood survives in the painting. Even in its fragile, damaged condition, it soothes you into meditation. Might prelates and dukes be able, in this rarefied atmosphere, to consider a truly radical idea?

Next to Jesus, on his right, sits St John the Evangelist, with a pink robe over his shoulder and long flowing locks that were surely full of curls when the painting was in pristine condition. John is so feminized he has even been seen as a woman (in Dan Brown's *The Da Vinci Code*, s/he is really Mary Magdalene). That misses the point. He is portrayed by Leonardo as nothing less than Christ's same-sex lover.

At the Last Supper as related in John 13, Jesus says that one of the gathered disciples will betray him. They are described as lying on couches, dining in the style of the ancient Romans: 'Now there was leaning on Jesus' bosom one of his disciples, whom Jesus loved.' This has traditionally been identified as John himself, the purported author of this account. Peter asked the beloved John to ask Jesus who the traitor was: 'He then lying on Jesus' breast said unto him, Lord, who is it?' This intimacy between Christ and John was no heretical secret: it is recounted in the Gospels themselves.

The medieval compendium of saints' lives and folkloric religious tales in Latin known as the *Golden Legend*, by the Genoese bishop Jacobus de Voragine, stresses this closeness as the first of John's qualities. This was a mainstream Christian source designed to provide readings from the pulpit. In William Caxton's translation of 1483, we learn that John had 'four privileges', of which the first was 'the noble love of Jesu Christ, for he loved him more than the other and showed to him of greater love ... And to him he was more gracious than to Peter, for he loved him much.'[12]

Leonardo illustrates this moment when Peter asks John to help find the traitor's name, except that they are seated at a table, not lying on couches. Peter, angry and armed, speaks close to the soft and delicate John, while Judas, right by them, is alarmed at his potential exposure. Leonardo is at once highly orthodox here and completely subversive. He directly refers to the account in the Gospel – John sits at Christ's right hand because he is the disciple 'whom

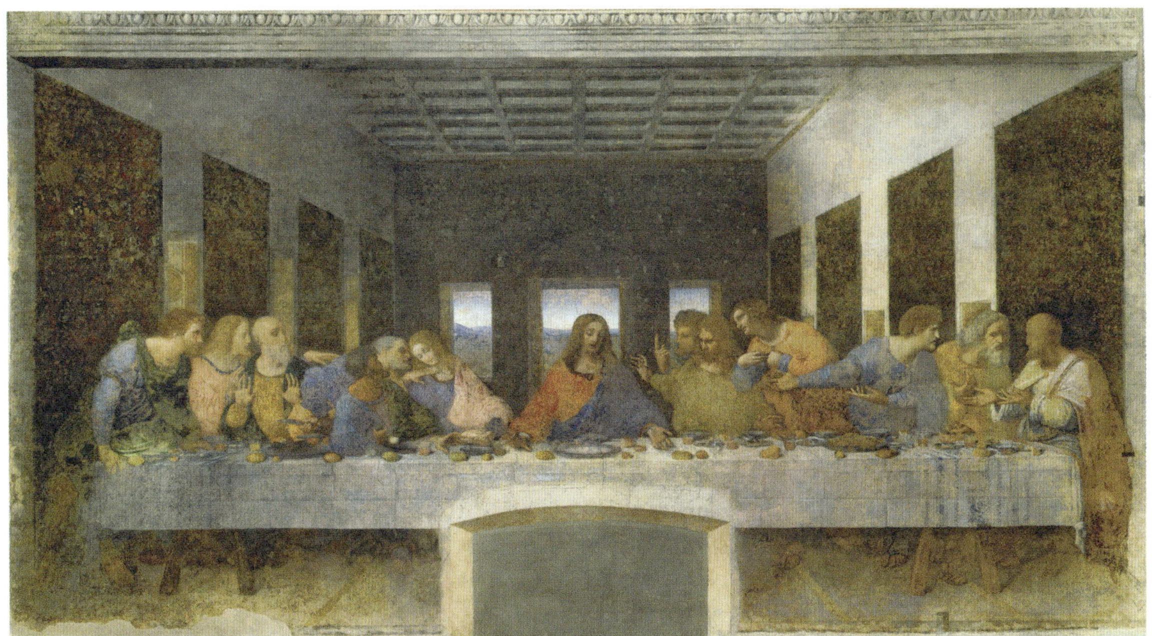

Leonardo da Vinci, *Last Supper*, 1495–98.

Jesus loved' – yet the way in which John is depicted rejects any pusillanimously 'spiritual' interpretation of the nature of that love. John is an androgynous, beautiful youth. He conforms to Leonardo's personal homoerotic iconography. He is the lover of Jesus.

Leonardo was not the only Renaissance man to see this possibility. In 1593 an informer called Richard Baines claimed that the spy and playwright Christopher Marlowe had told him John 'was bedfellow to Christ'. The dramatist Thomas Kyd also said that Marlowe spoke of Christ's 'extraordinary love' for John, meaning carnal lust.[13]

Marlowe, who was also accused of giving 'reasons for Atheisme', was murdered soon after these allegations; his complex life on the edge caught up with him. Leonardo got away with his casual image of homosexuality in one of the world's most celebrated religious paintings, yet his intent is lucid and unconcealed. There it is: a hymn to the holiness of love as he knew it.

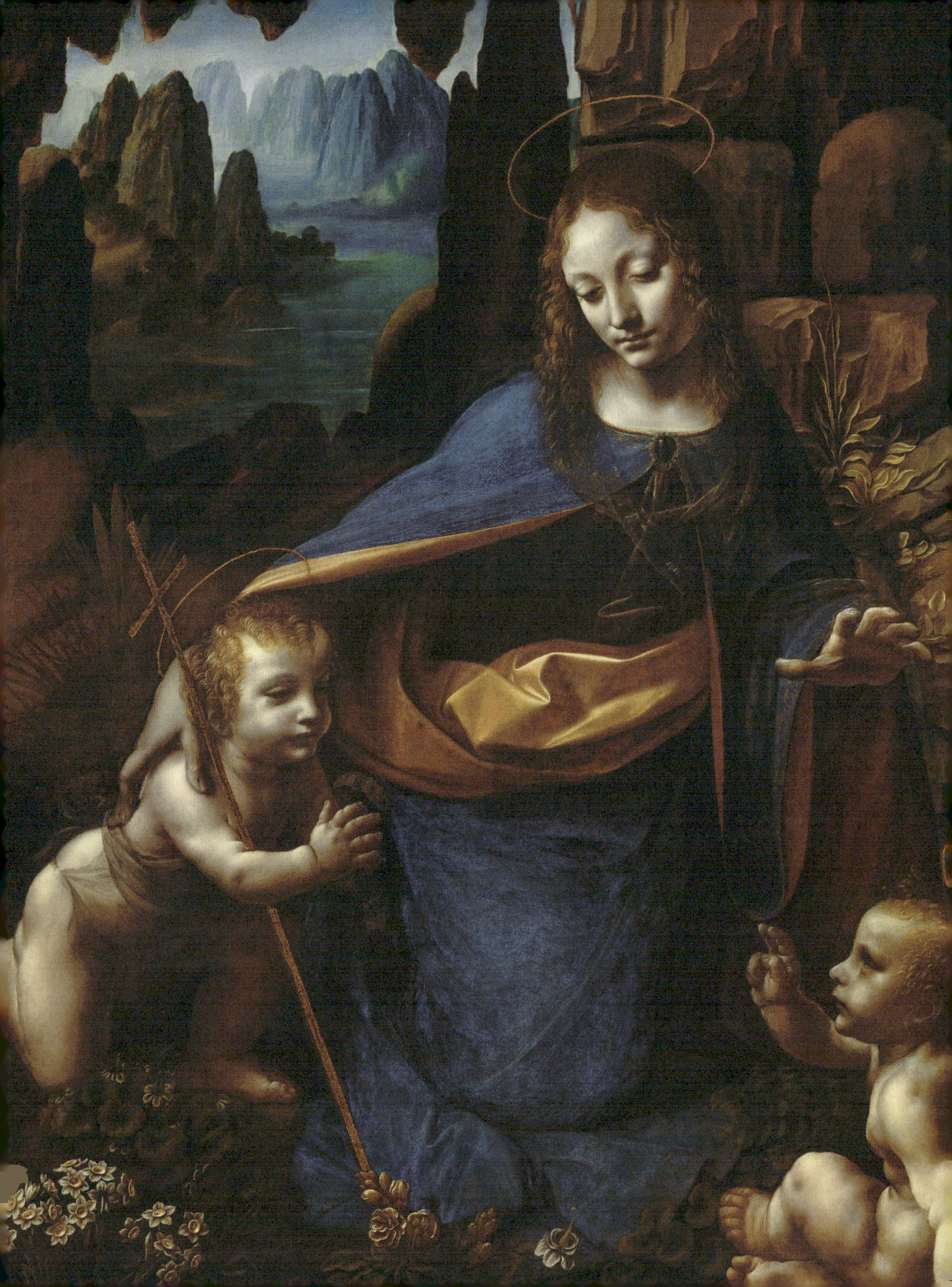

5 Worldly Knowledge

The rocks are like fingers, or even penises, sticking up out of the earth and hanging down to form a toothy mouth looking over a still, green sea and blue peaks beyond. It's debatable how much of Leonardo's second version of the *Virgin of the Rocks* was painted by him, but it is saturated with his thinking. He sharpened and emphasized the strange mountain world where he placed the holy group, casting the rocks a deeper brown, the distance a purer blue. Perhaps it is an ecstatic vision, a hallucination. The reason Leonardo was so annoyed by Botticelli's sneer that you can create a landscape by chucking a paint-soaked sponge at a wall was that it parodied his own method. If you stare long enough at cracks and stains, he wrote, you might see faces, landscapes, battles. If you draw these shapes you can organize them into compositions. Try squinting at the *Virgin of the Rocks*, or looking at it in low light. The landscape is almost a blot of ink, a murky stain disinterred from primeval swamps.

If Leonardo saw a trancelike vision of a cave above the sea when he gazed at a dirty wall, that may have been because he spent so much time walking in the mountains and contemplating his collection of fossils. He explored the Alps as well the hills of Tuscany in a lifelong attempt to understand the forces that raise mountains from the sea and erode them to rubble. He could see for himself

Leonardo da Vinci, *Virgin of the Rocks* (detail), c. 1491–1508.

that the earth was constantly mutating, seas and rocks changing. How else, he asked, can fossil sea creatures be found on top of a mountain?

Leonardo was not the first person to notice fossils, rather the first to start to understand them. In medieval England it was said that St Hilda had turned snakes to stone, creating the coiled ammonites that were common around Whitby. Leonardo in his notebooks gives superstitions like these very short shrift. He's interested only in a material explanation for why he sees seashells preserved

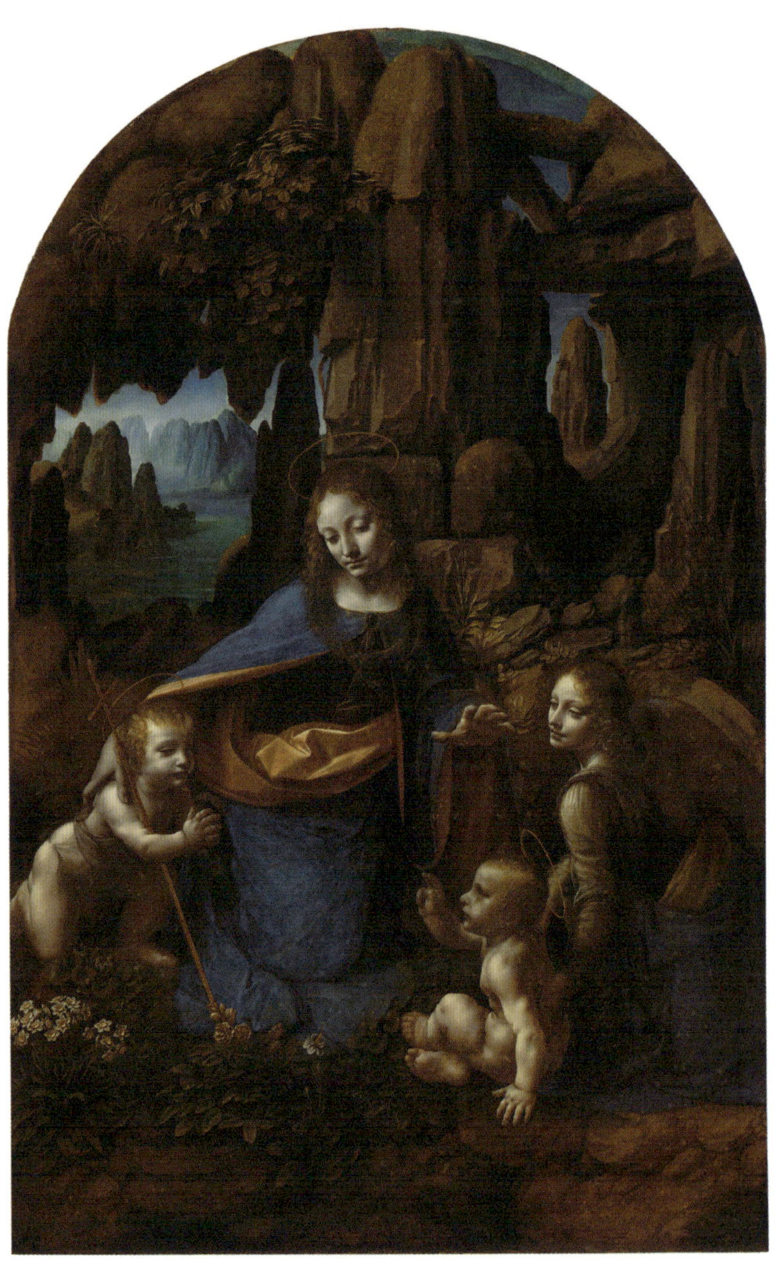

Leonardo da Vinci, *Virgin of the Rocks*, c. 1491–1508.

in sedimentary rocks up in the hills. He dismisses the 'ignorant people' who think they might have been put there 'through the influence of the stars, as if we didn't find in those places how the bones of fishes have grown with the length of time, and as if you couldn't enumerate the years of the lives of the shellfish and molluscs from their outer crusts.'[1]

In other words, Leonardo has seen clear evidence that sea creatures found in the mountains passed their entire natural lives there, when those places were underwater long ago. He has looked carefully, and what he observes appear to be the hard remains of creatures that were once alive – not symbolic objects put there by heaven. Close scrutiny of the shells preserved in rocks makes it plain that they were deposited over a long time, layer upon layer, and not in a miraculous instant, for

> How would you find so many pieces and whole shells amid stratum [*falda*] upon stratum of stone, if they were not covered on the shore by new earth thrown by the sea, which then came to be petrified?[2]

These observations prove they were living creatures that existed in the sea before they died. Thus Leonardo dismisses the 'celestial' explanation in his notebook known as the Codex Leicester, written towards the end of the first decade of the 1500s. Yet his real target is much more dangerous: the biblical Flood. Centuries later, when mainstream science finally caught up with Leonardo's astonishingly advanced understanding of fossils and rock strata, geologists and theologians would argue about the Flood, as religious conservatives tried to reconcile Genesis with mounting contradictory evidence. Yet it is obvious to Leonardo that such an event cannot account for what he has seen. The shells are found in multiple strata:

> And if the Flood already mentioned had carried them from the sea to such sites, you would find these shells at the limit of one stratum alone, and not the limits of many, where it is possible to enumerate the winters of the years that the sea has multiplied the strata of sand and mud ... And if you wished to say that numerous Floods took place to produce such strata and the shells in them, you'd have to also say there was a deluge a year.[3]

Once you get over the shock of a Renaissance mind pouring scorn on the Flood – the central event in the history of earth according to the Bible – the sophistication of this passage begins to sink in. Leonardo not only perceives the strata of the earth exposed by cliffs and gullies but understands that they were laid down in different temporal phases: layers of time. He guesses that this time was vast. Fossils are evidence of impossibly ancient events that stretch back before written records: 'Since things are much older than letters, it is no marvel if in our days no writings record how in former days the seas filled so many countries.' Instead we must look at the physical evidence, because 'for us the testimony is enough of things born in the salt waters, rediscovered in the high mountains, sometimes far from the seas'.[4]

Everything about these writings on why seashells are found in the mountains is startling. Leonardo applies a rigorous scientific method, insisting on a natural rather than a supernatural explanation, refusing to accept any theory unless it fits the evidence to which he has applied his acute observational skills.

He depicts the strata of an exposed hillside in a drawing from about 1510–13, soon after making these notes, that shows shale-like flakes layered over each other where the grass and soil have been swept away. It is a scientific drawing, not a preparation for a painting: no painting required this knowledge. He put it in one anyway. The *Virgin and Child with St Anne* is more geologically precise than the *Virgin of the Rocks*. Created in his last two decades and informed by his research into rock stratification, this is a document of everything he had discovered about the inner life of the earth. Specifically, it is an epic vision of geological time.

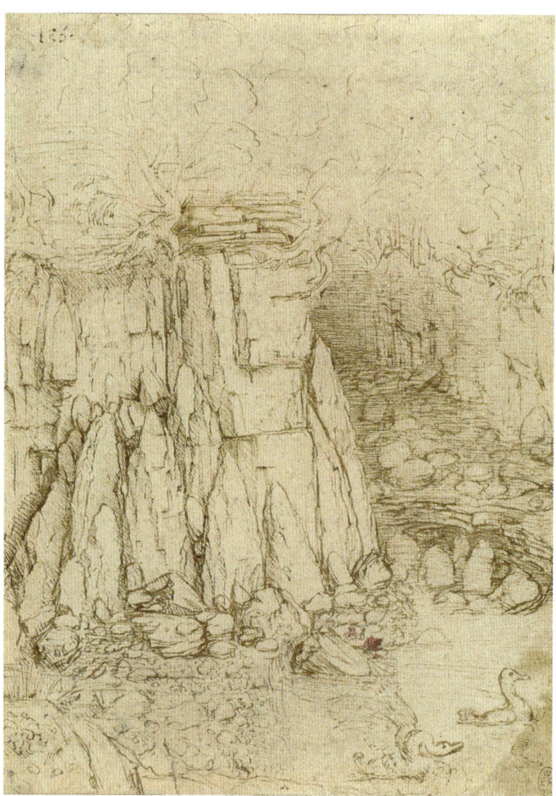

Leonardo da Vinci,
A Ravine, c. 1482–85.

Leonardo da Vinci, *Virgin and Child with St Anne*, 1503–19.

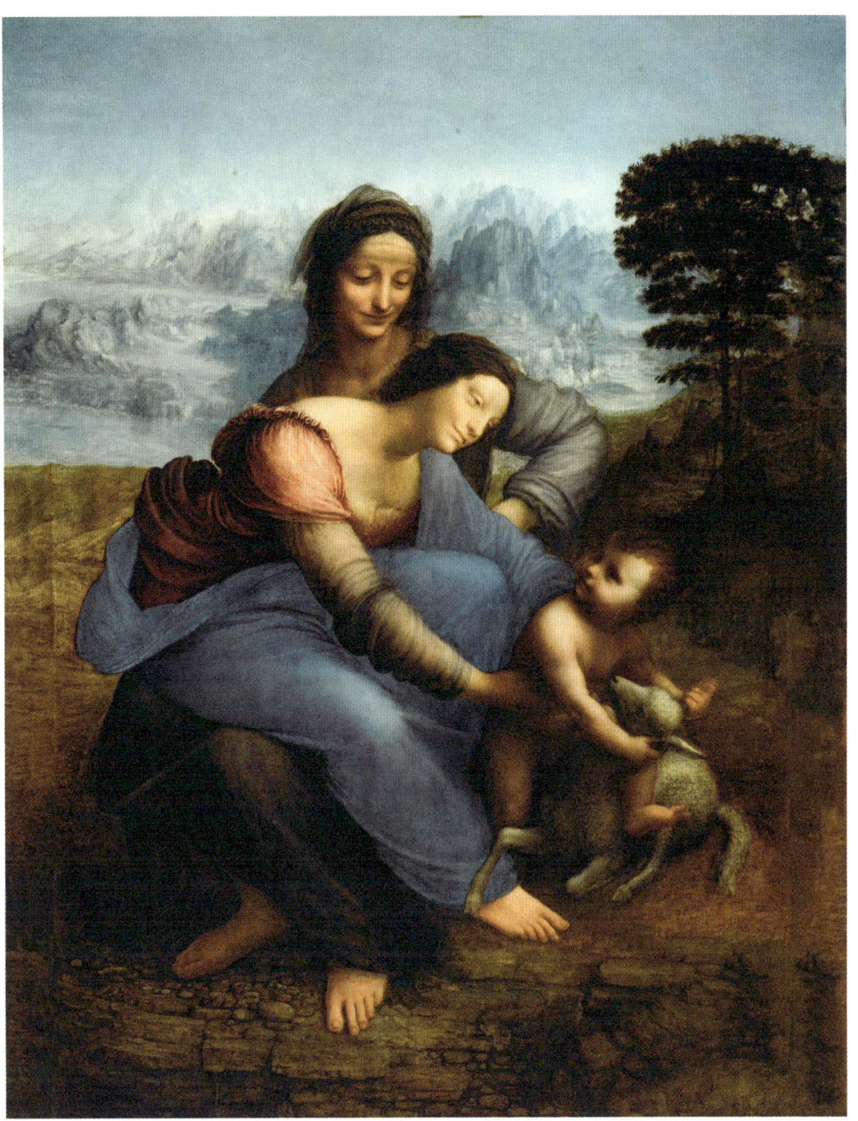

Mary, her mother Anne, Jesus and a lamb have climbed high into the Alps. They rest and play on a mountain ridge whose innards are exposed in the vertical drop of the foreground. We see strata laid on top of each other over aeons of time, the compressed layers falling away into darkness. At Mary's feet are myriad pebbles, worn smooth by an ancient river bed and deposited on what is now a lofty crag. Leonardo had shown a river smoothing pebbles in a drawing from the 1480s; here he celebrates the exquisite results of erosion in glistening minerals polished by nature – a treasure for the Virgin. It is also evidence of geological processes that leave theology far behind. Those processes sculpt the earth on the grandest scale, we see, when we look further into the painting. In the blue distance is an expanse of mountains under the azure sky. They too are stratified, folded, pushed from the earth in layers that expose their antiquity. Their blueness makes them seem an almost submarine mountain range, perhaps reflecting Leonardo's argument that mountains can bear shells only if they were once underwater.

* * *

The *Virgin and Child with St Anne* almost seems an attempt by Leonardo to preserve his geological and paleontological discoveries visually in case his manuscripts were lost. Luckily many of his manuscript notes have survived wars, disasters and censors, pulsing with curiosity, a boundless delight to explore. The notebooks were rebound and sold after his death, many ending up in two great albums: one in the Ambrosian Library, Milan (known as the Codex Atlanticus), and the other in the Royal Library, Windsor. There are more in Paris, Madrid and Turin. The Codex Leicester was bought by Bill Gates, and separate sheets can be found in other collections. To judge from this body of work, Leonardo started creating his illustrated manuscripts when he settled in Milan. Before that, his final project in Florence, to paint an *Adoration of the Magi*, generated a feast of drawings that suggest he was increasingly preoccupied with putting his unfettered thoughts on paper. One study in particular lets us witness the birth of a scientist.

Riders flash into existence from another universe. They float in the ether, both real and not; a camel has seen them, just as dogs are said to see ghosts.

Leonardo da Vinci, *Perspectival Study for the 'Adoration of the Magi'*, c. 1481.

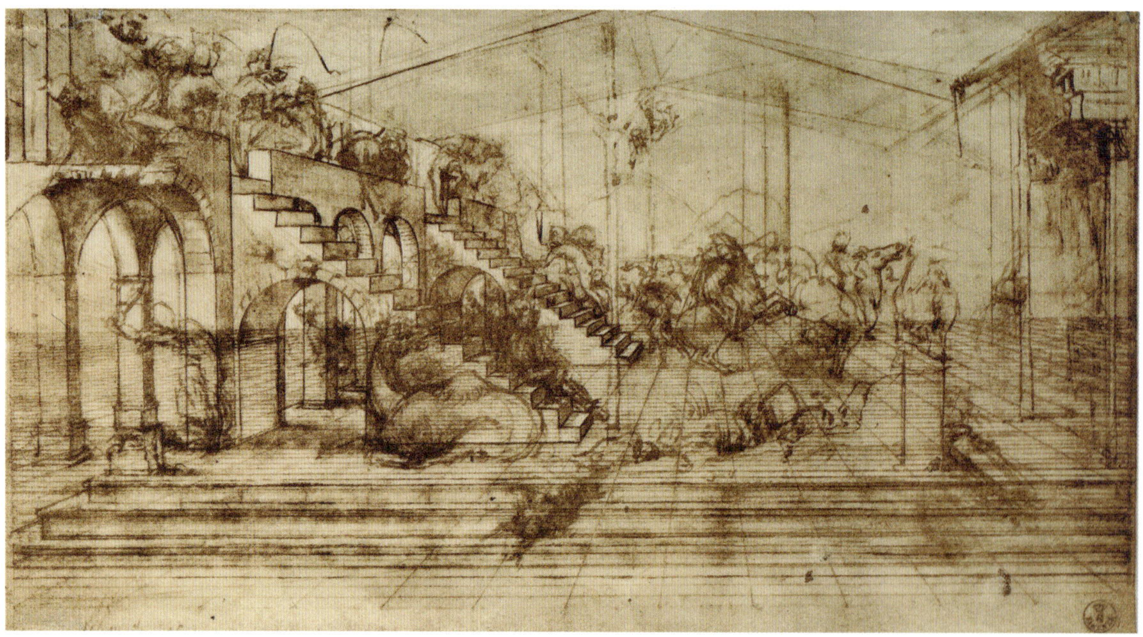

Then you notice that, for all their ambiguity, the hooves of the rearing horses are planted firmly on the ground – except that the ground is an abstract grid of intercrossed lines rushing away from the eye, a mathematical figment. For across the bottom half of this wide sheet of paper Leonardo has plotted radiating straight lines that all begin – or end – at a single point behind the mouth of a rearing horse. Sketched mountains rise in the distance. Horizontal lines crisscross the receding verticals. And on the vanishing grid, or under it, are staircases to nowhere, crumbling arches, blotches of people.

This is a diagram of a world in perspective. Leonardo started by sketching a roof over it all, planning a conventional scene in a ruinous stable. But this design has escaped that box. Instead, it opens out onto a vista of battling horsemen, philosophical witnesses, paradoxical architecture; its potential chaos is held together only by the rational space he plots out.

The Florentine theory of perspective always had aspirations to be scientific. Brunelleschi's demonstration and Alberti's book emphasized that it required mathematical precision to mimic the world in depth. Perspective was rooted in the science of optics. Most of all it was a cognitive leap: in one telling passage Alberti explains that, in a perspective painting, you must not see around corners or through solid buildings. This is a new way of thinking about reality: perspective depends on the acceptance that we cannot see everything, only what the 'rays' of vision permit us.

For Leonardo there is no end to the new discoveries perspective makes possible. His unfinished, 'final' version of the *Adoration of the Magi* (p. 98) is just as swarming with life as the preparatory sketch. It is a conscious demonstration that perspective lets you see new worlds. For perspective, he writes, models the way the eye sees. Painting is 'based primarily upon perspective which is nothing else than a thorough knowledge of the function of the eye'. This function 'simply consists in receiving in a pyramid the forms and colours of all objects placed before it'.[5]

Leonardo never lost his wonder at how perspective can imitate the way we see. He returns to it time and again in his notebooks. His experiments widened the possibilities for what had started as a simple recognition that objects look smaller the further away they are. As an oil painter he explored how colours change and the contours of objects get softer as they recede from the eye: the blue mountains and fuzzy hills in his landscapes are not random effects but demonstrations of these subtle aspects of vision. He says there are actually three kinds of perspective: 'Linear perspective. The perspective of colour. The perspective of disappearance.'[6] All are developed superlatively in his art.

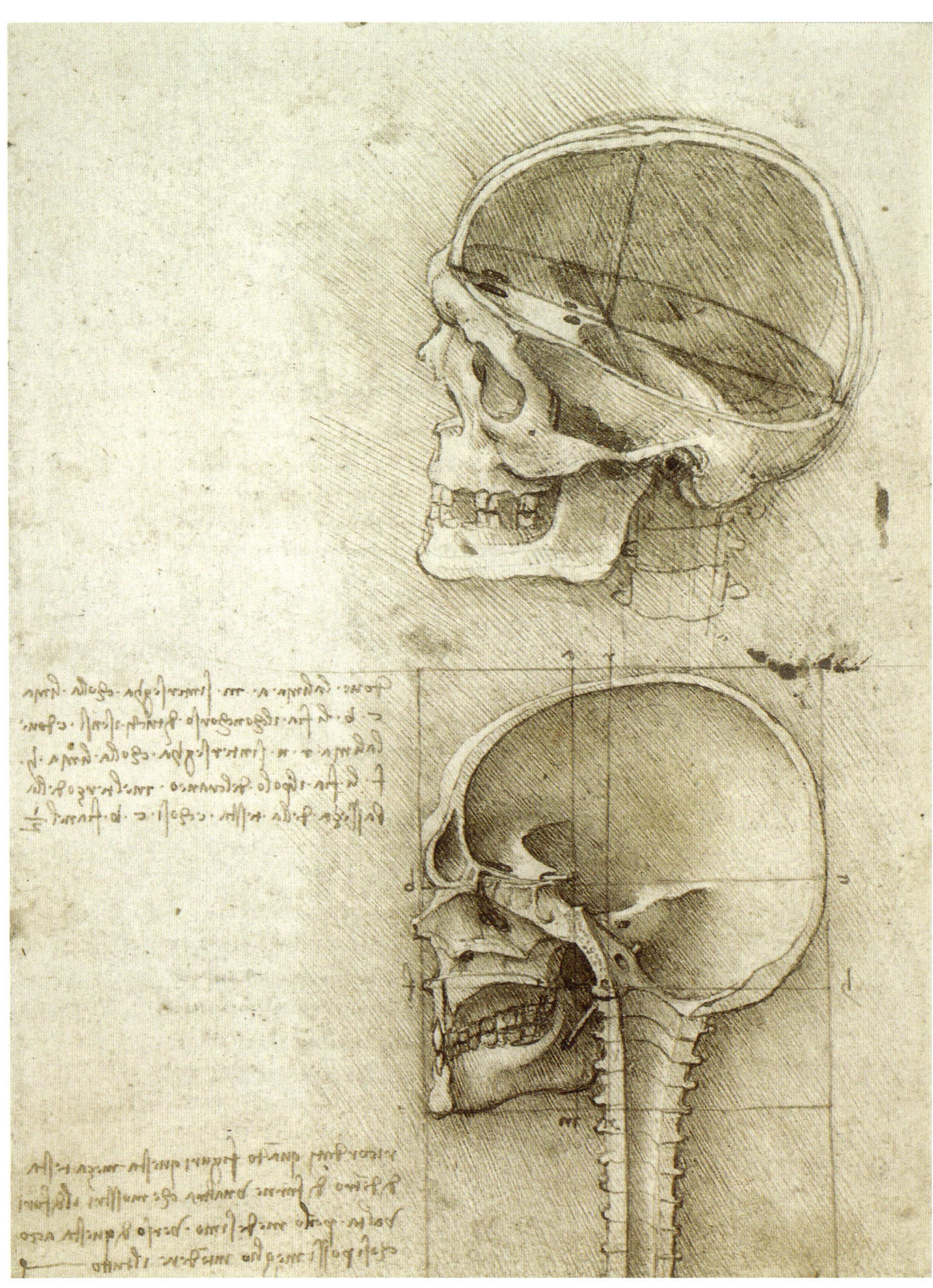

Leonardo da Vinci, *The skull sectioned*, 1489.

Leonardo da Vinci, *The layers of the scalp and the cerebral ventricles*, c. 1490–92.

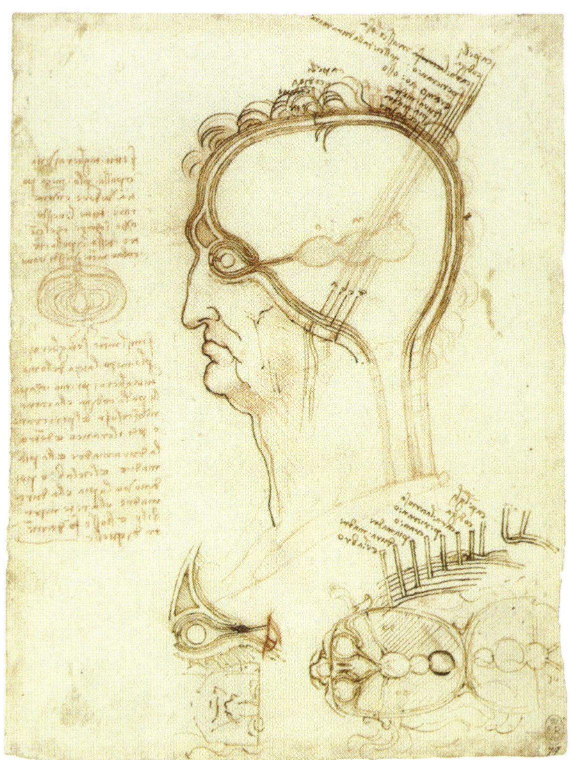

Leonardo keeps widening the topic. Perspective is based on the human eye. So how does the eye work, and how does it send information to our brain? One of his first anatomical drawings, done in the early 1490s, is a side view of a human head showing a thick optic nerve leading to three connected chambers in the brain. Already, in the late 1480s, he had cut apart a human skull to see what he could learn. His drawings of the exposed inner dome of the cranium (sensitively shaded to show how it curves), the recessive eye sockets and a section cut into the jaw display the stunning power of perspective to analyse nature: this is a new kind of scientific drawing, a foreshortened, spatially real simulacrum of the skull.

That was just the start. Later Leonardo thoroughly dissected human bodies. His drawing from around 1506 of a head sawn in two horizontally (overleaf) shows what looks at first like an alien architecture. Two glistening spheres are eyeballs, exposed from below by his cutting but still fitted snugly into the bone. Nerves like tree branches emerge, intercross and lead from the eyes into the brain. An art that models itself on the eye reveals the mechanics of eyes.

* * *

Another way to understand the eye was through an experiment Leonardo describes. Make a small hole that lets light into 'a very dark chamber'. You can

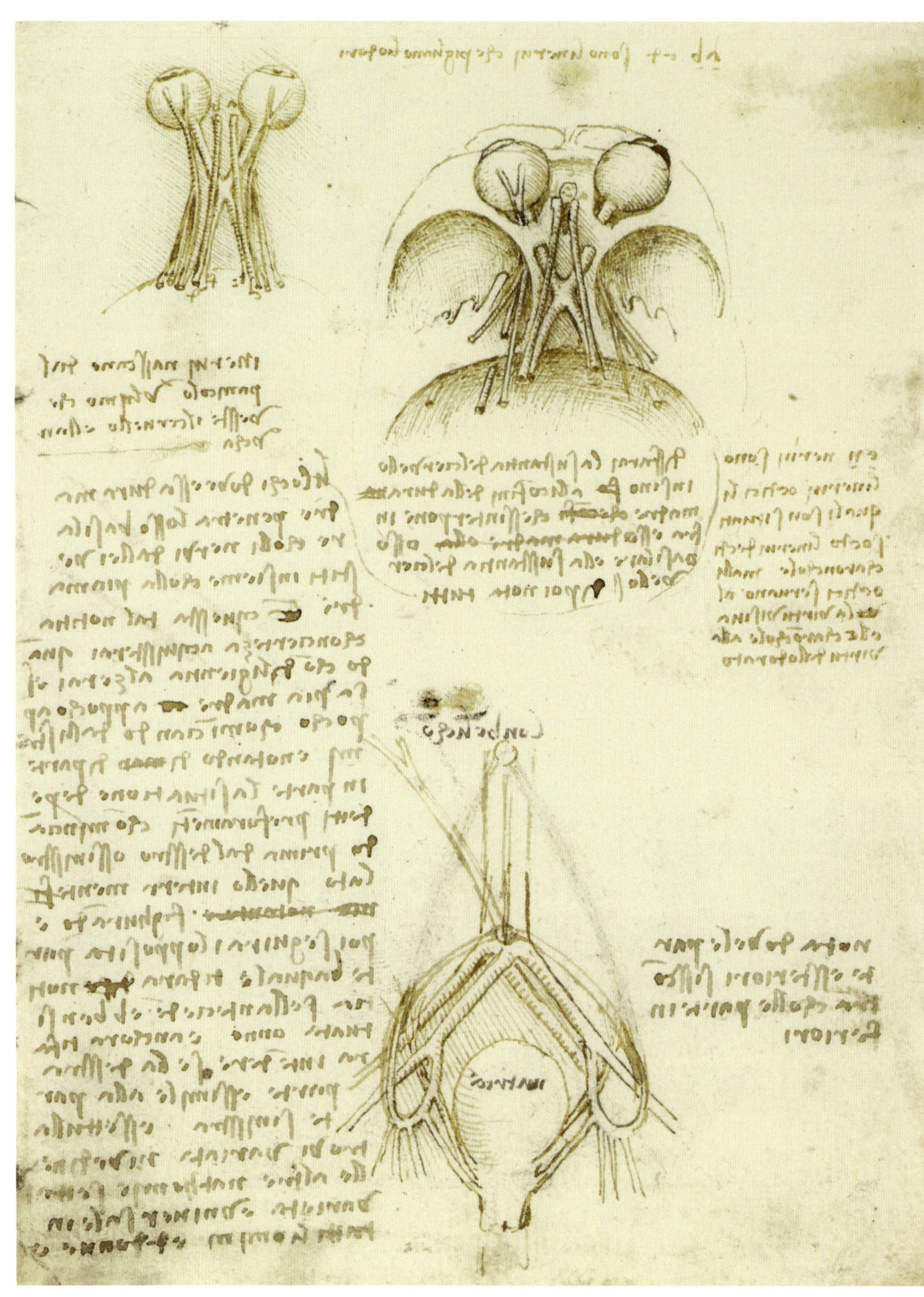

Leonardo da Vinci, *The cranial nerves*, c. 1506.

then capture the bright images it lets in with a sheet of paper, and 'you will see all the objects on the paper in their proper forms and colours, but much smaller; and they will be upside down.'[7]

This idea of the eye as a camera obscura, letting images into the dimness of the skull, is reminiscent of the *Virgin of the Rocks*, with its bright landscape visible though an opening in the shadowy grotto. That is not because Leonardo used a camera obscura. If he did, he would have said so in his notes. (He had no need to hide anything in writings done in reverse, so that you needed a mirror to decipher them.) He is frank about artistic techniques, including how to measure perspective using a gridded screen placed between you and the model. He is not advocating the artistic use of a camera but using the analogy to explore the riddle of visual perception itself.

* * *

The science of perspective gave Leonardo a mind-boggling ability to design machines that look as real as his angels. Just as he can draw skulls and dissected body parts, so he can draw masterpieces of engineering studies. In the Codex Atlanticus there are designs for a goods lift, a rope-making machine, a cloth-cutting machine, a spinning machine, a canal-digging machine, clock mechanisms. Leonardo was not just a scientific speculator pondering his fossils: he believed in using science to make a new world where technology would transform human existence.

The world he lived in had next to no machines. The fastest transport on land was the horse. On the Mediterranean, large ships relied on galley slaves as much as sails. Windmills, waterwheels, iron clocks and the occasional fountain were the only instances of technological know-how in the daily grind of back-breaking labour and repetitive routine. Leonardo cast his eyes on the arduous lives of manual workers and drew physical tasks such as hoeing, cutting down trees, pulling loads – the everyday toil of peasants throughout pre-industrial Europe. Another sheet of studies concentrates on a woman cleaning a step. One day, his inventions dream, such dreary tasks will be done by machines.

The despotic princely rulers of Italian Renaissance micro-states were unlikely, however, to sponsor an industrial revolution to liberate their peasants from toil. The machinery they wanted was anything that might give them an edge in warfare. Here technology really was changing the world. Improved designs for bows had been destroying the era of knighthood since around 1300, but there was a still more devastating military revolution afoot. Gunpowder reached Europe from China in the 14th century. By the mid-1400s European guns were

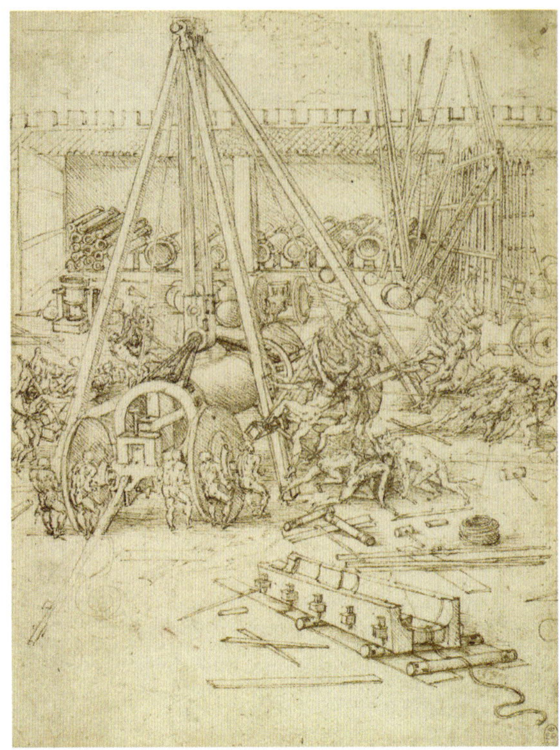

Leonardo da Vinci, *A scene in an arsenal*, c. 1485–90.

becoming formidable, if cumbersome. They could reach immense sizes, as they were made to be stationed in one place, to terrorize besieged castles. In 1449 Philip the Good of Burgundy had a huge bronze gun cast with a barrel 48 centimetres (19 inches.) in diameter as a gift for the king of Scotland: Mons Meg, as it is known, survives in Edinburgh Castle. This 15th-century superweapon is reminiscent of a drawing by Leonardo that takes the late medieval arms race to science-fiction extremes. It portrays a crew of tiny workers dwarfed by the colossal tubular bombard they are trying to move.

It is another example of how Leonardo can use his grasp of technical drawing to make his inventions look as if they were already built. Milan was a strong military power, with many armourers' workshops. Ludovico Sforza stockpiled armaments and nursed audacious schemes in an age when Lorenzo de' Medici was credited with keeping Italy peaceful through a balance of power. So the best way of obtaining employment from Milan's despot, it must have seemed to Leonardo, was to stress his expertise in warfare. In about 1482 Leonardo wrote to Ludovico offering to share his 'secrets' as a military engineer. He claims to have invented new kinds of portable bridges, siege machines, mortars, cannon, fireproof warships, armoured cars, catapults and trebuchets. He knows how to undermine fortresses and get to places by subterranean ways.

Architecture, sculpture and painting, in that order, come afterwards in his offer of skills.

By far the most original of the military inventions Leonardo describes in his letter is the armoured car or tank. In his mind's eye he paints a picture of these machines leading an attack, 'which, entering among the enemy with their artillery, there is no company of men at arms so great but that they would break them. And behind these, infantry could follow quite unhurt and without any hindrance.'[8]

Leonardo did superb drawings of this new secret weapon and, in the most detailed, of the mechanism inside. Soldiers have to power the machine manually by turning crank handles. A sturdy wooden roof is placed over them, with small guns arranged under the canopy to fire in all directions. He notes that eight men will go inside – maybe half of them to move it, the others to fire the guns. Infantry need to follow it up. It's a shock weapon, a sinister novelty to confuse an enemy.

It may seem disturbing that Leonardo lent his unique talents to devising new ways of killing, but the coming of artillery posed serious mathematical problems that stimulated early science. Ballistics – the science of trajectories from an angled gun – was not just essential for gunners, wrote Galileo in the

Leonardo da Vinci, *Mortars firing into a fortress*, c. 1503–4.

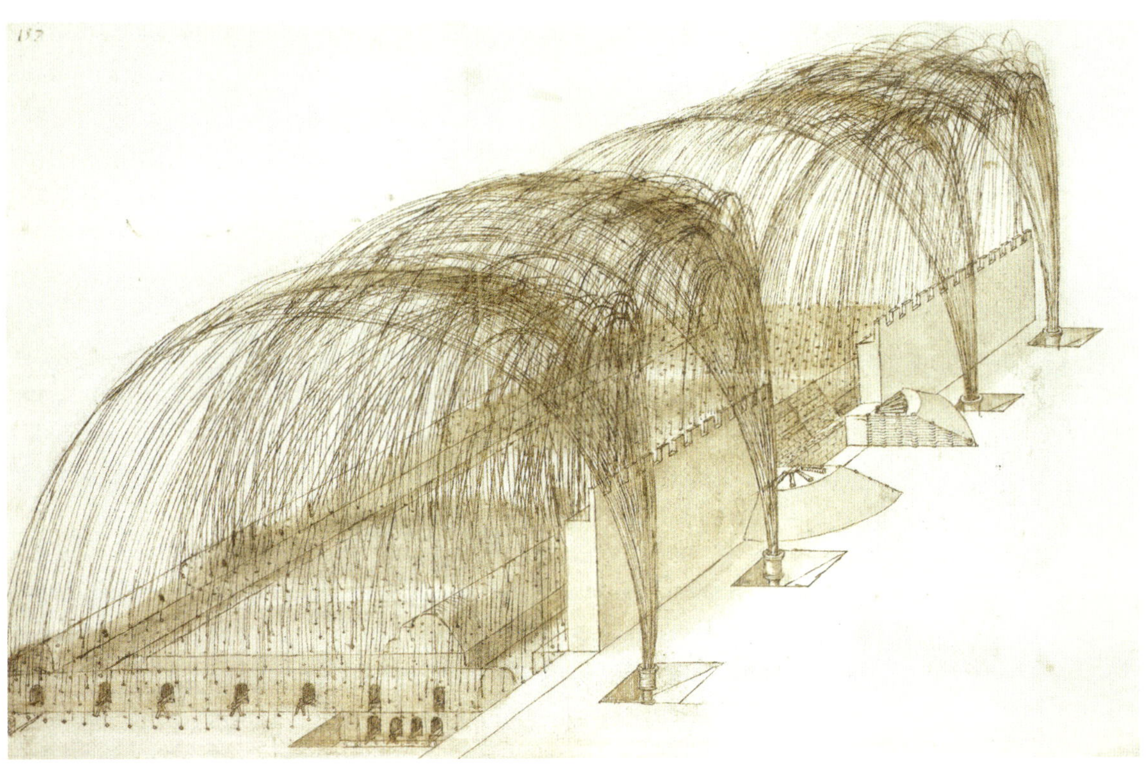

17th century, but of interest to 'philosophers'. It stimulated the founders of modern physics to think about the nature of motion and reject what had been said about it by the ancient authority Aristotle.

Leonardo had quizzed himself on ballistics more than a century earlier than Galileo, pondering: 'If a bombard fires at different distances with different curves of movement, I ask in what section of its course will the curve attain its greatest height.'[9] Yet he thought in a different way from a university graduate. His was the training of a skilled artisan, not a scholar. The specialist knowledge he possessed was how to draw in perspective, and this was the tool he used. His questions about ballistics are beautifully expressed in drawings of mortars firing projectiles high in the air (previous page).

Leonardo is a *visual* thinker, his notebooks a miracle of the mind's eye. For the eye, he argued, is the true window of the intellect and 'the prince of mathematics, and its sciences most certain. It has measured the heights and sizes of stars.'[10] That was no idle example. In 1471 the astronomer Johannes Müller von Königsberg, later known as Regiomontanus, used parallax – measuring the angle between two sightings of an object from different positions – to calculate the distance of a comet from earth. It was the first demonstration of a method that is still used in astronomy. Looking really was central to the birth of modern science, a discipline that was just getting started as Leonardo opened the sacks of fossils that Lombard peasants brought him. Observing the sky, studying fossils, dissecting the body were visual endeavours. As a supreme looker, Leonardo could see things that escaped others.

Leonardo's clearest scientific insight is his declaration of the scientific method itself: all knowledge comes from experience, and every idea must be tested against evidence. He concludes that 'Experience never errs: it is only your own judgments that err by promising themselves effects such as are not caused by your experiments.'[11]

Today this is the accepted basis of all science. Yet its early pioneers were rarely as consistent as Leonardo: Regiomontanus was a noted astrologer; the great Renaissance medical pioneer Paracelsus practised alchemy; and in a work called *Natural Magic*, published in 1558, Giambattista della Porta mingled genuine scientific findings with the occult.

Leonardo owned a book on chiromancy, or palm-reading, and maybe had fun impressing the court with this trick. He conceded that alchemy produced useful things, although there's no sign of him practising it. Yet his notebooks are amazingly free from supernatural speculation. In a radically materialist argument, he scorns necromancers for claiming that spirits can speak without tongues or any physical organ when it is impossible. In fact, his most ruthless writings on the impossibility of 'spirits' intervening in the material world appear among his drawings of anatomical dissections, which explore the physical body in minute detail, from bones to blood, lungs to womb. The idea of a spirit moving without a body is nonsense, Leonardo argues as he works late at night among bloody corpses. For one thing it would just be 'vacuum'; it would be torn to pieces by the winds. And how could it speak without a tongue, like the one he has cut out at its root to study? It takes friction to make sound. Air must be expelled from the lungs: 'We may say therefore, that the spirit cannot produce a voice without movement of air, and there is no air within it, and it cannot expel air from within it if it has it not.'[12] You can almost sense him banging his head in frustration as he tries to refute a non-scientific belief scientifically.

The most radical implications of such passages in Leonardo's notebooks reached Vasari, who, in the first edition of his *Lives* of 1550, makes a dramatic assertion that

> in his mind he had such heretical thinking he did not approach any religion whatsoever, reckoning it much better to be a philosopher than a Christian.[13]

Vasari excised this statement from his second edition in an age of increased religious scrutiny, perhaps urged by Leonardo's heir, Melzi, who wanted to protect his reputation. Although there are deistic references to a prime mover in Leonardo's notebooks, the absence of theological interest is extraordinary by the standards of the time. Worship was not passive: people worried about life after death, wrote down prayers, analysed their immortal souls. Leonardo prefers to be a philosopher.

* * *

That might make him seem a marginal figure, outside the culture of his time, but no one embodies the Renaissance like Leonardo da Vinci. He befriended soldiers and mathematicians, took part in court entertainments and canal-digging schemes, designed domes and stables. Through his eyes we start to get the full measure of what the Renaissance was by the 1480s. It was much more than a change in artistic style or a revival of learning. The range of Leonardo's interests, activities and networks give a picture of new energy and ideas across many practical fields. What it comes down to is optimism. The inventions of Leonardo assume a belief that unheard-of achievements are just around the corner. Renaissance minds like Leonardo's were able to believe in progress without much evidence of it happening.

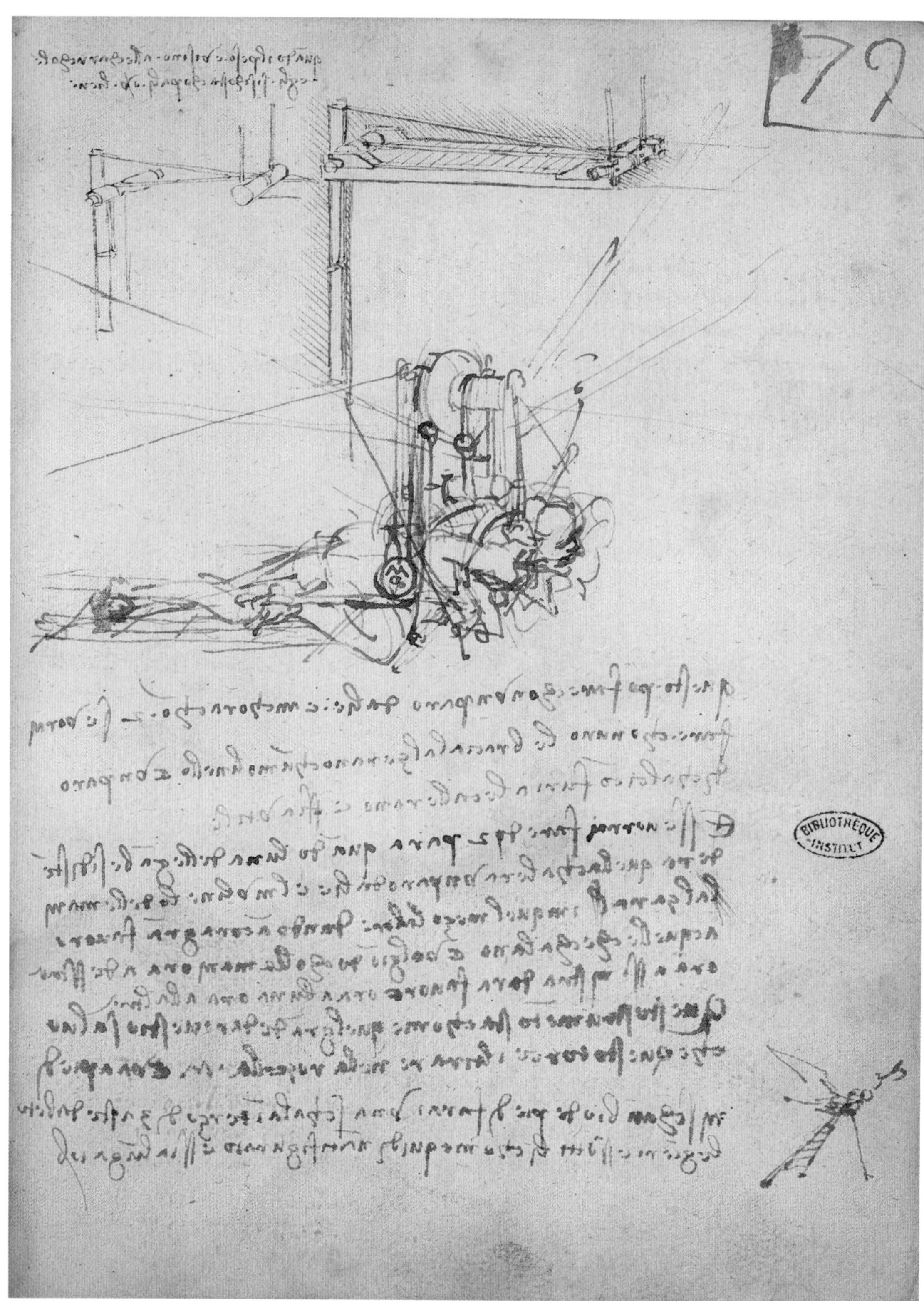

Leonardo da Vinci, *Study for a flying machine with a hand- and foot-driven mechanism*, c. 1487–90.

Nothing captured this sense of escape from tradition, this almost insane self-confidence, like Leonardo's attempts to build a flying machine. The fantasy that possessed him from childhood – even from the cradle, where he remembered being visited by a bird of prey – turned into a real project at or, rather, beyond the limits of medieval engineering. Under a sketch of an armoured vehicle is a wide screw-like mechanism with a wooden capsule suspended underneath: it resembles a helicopter. In fact, it impossibly attempts to use Archimedes' screw to pull itself upwards.

It doesn't look impossible. The sharp pen and ink study, with its bold shading and solid foreshortened details, seems so practical. However, Leonardo quickly abandoned this dream machine and started designing winged craft. A wooden frame big enough for a pilot to lie flat supports hinged wings designed to flap up and down; another design from the same years, made at the end of the 1480s, shows how the wings would be covered in leather like those of a bat. The problem was that these wings had to be moved up and down by human power. Another sketch shows him working out an elaborate gear mechanism to make that possible. Every bit of machinery meant more weight to get off the ground.

The pilot lies under all this gear, suspended in the air, his eyes pools of brown ink: a new human entering a new element. Leonardo is not just playing. He intended to build and use his machine. He was planning an unprecedented adventure, a journey into the element of air, at huge risk. He was, claims Vasari, a great talker. He could describe the most unlikely schemes, and when they were listening to him people believed the impossible.

Leonardo might have got on with another persuasive Italian talker who was shortly to sell an equally impossible-sounding voyage.

* * *

On 2 January 1492 the Emirate of Granada, the last outpost of Islam on the Iberian peninsula, surrendered to Queen Isabella and King Ferdinand of Spain. The 'Catholic Kings', as they were officially titled by the pope two years later, had sworn a crusade against this remnant of al-Andalus after uniting Castile and Aragon in their married persons. Granada was dominated by the ravishing Alhambra, a clifftop palace with interiors decorated in a celestial geometry of tessellated tiles and crystalline stuccoes. Now the last Muslim ruler gave the keys to Ferdinand.

The Reconquista of Spain for Christianity had taken centuries. Now it was over, the monarchs were ready to give serious consideration to the man from Genoa who had been pestering them with his audacious plan. Christopher

Columbus claimed that he could sail westwards to China: set out on the Atlantic, keep a course west, and you were bound to reach the Spice Isles and the fabled wealth of Asia.

There was growing evidence that sea voyages could find new realms and opportunities beyond the Mediterranean world and its centuries-old struggle between Christianity and Islam. Since 1418 Spain's rivalrous neighbour Portugal had been sending caravels around the west coast of Africa, gradually pushing further south and creating a permanent coastal base, Elmina Castle, in modern Ghana in the 1480s. They kept on going further: in 1488, while Leonardo was designing his ornithopter, Bartolomeu Dias rounded the Cape and reached the Indian Ocean.

Columbus's proposal was stranger. Instead of hugging the African coast, he planned a voyage into the unknown. For all his fanatical claims that it would lead him to China, no one knew what lay beyond the Canary Islands and the Azores. He was driven by a quirky cocktail of beliefs and thought that his new route could bring about the End of Days. Yet Columbus was also a skilled navigator, a citizen of the republic of Genoa that had fought for control of the Mediterranean for centuries.

Ferdinand and Isabella, fuelled by confidence in the new martial Spain forged by the Reconquest and eager to challenge the maritime successes of Portugal, agreed to pay for Columbus's voyage. His three small ships set sail from Palos de la Frontera, in the kingdom's south-west, on 3 August 1492.

It was like flying into the blue.

* * *

'My map of the world which Giovanni Benci has', wrote Leonardo in a to-do list in about 1505.[14] Benci was the brother of Leonardo's early portrait subject Ginevra de' Benci, and at this point Leonardo was back in Florence. But what was the world map? A couple of years later, in 1507, the most important map of the Renaissance world was published by the German cartographer Martin Waldseemüller. For the first time a map names the new continent of America, even if it depicts it as just a sliver of landmass stretching from north to south; Europeans had still not seen much beyond the eastern coast. Columbus never accepted that he had found a new continent. He insisted the islands and mainland he eventually set foot on were a way to Asia, or maybe the Four Rivers of Paradise mentioned in the Book of Genesis. It was a Florentine explorer following rapidly in his footsteps, Amerigo Vespucci, who wrote letters home declaring the western discoveries a 'New World' and after whom the continent was named.

Vespucci, from the family of Simonetta Vespucci, had a cousin who worked in the Signoria, Agostino, who wrote in a friendly and complimentary way about Leonardo. The artist's curiosity about maps is likely to have been stimulated by stories from the New World, for which Agostino may have been one source, even before Amerigo's works were published. Leonardo's surviving designs for maps all date from after 1500. Suddenly, as news from America spread, revealing that the very shape and extent of the earth's land masses was totally different from all medieval conceptions, he started a flurry of cartographic research.

Leonardo's investigations fed his obsession with flight. His maps imagine a flying machine's view of landscapes and cities and can persuade you that he has actually seen the earth from above. He does not design maps of the world but, perhaps goaded by them and descriptions of the New World, he focuses in empirical detail on Italy itself. Leonardo experiments with how much knowledge a map can give, how it enhances our picture of where we are.

* * *

Such knowledge can be power. So says Niccolò Machiavelli in *The Prince*. Study the landscape well, he urges the despot, for the lie of the land is critical in warfare. Ride to hunt to find out 'how the mountains rise, how the valleys open out, how the plains lie, and to understand the nature of rivers and marshes'[15].This is not the only landscape image in *The Prince*. In his dedication, Machiavelli makes a specific allusion to map-making. He asks forgiveness for his audacity in telling rulers how to act even though he is a former civil servant forced into retirement, explaining that

> Just as those who draw landscapes place themselves below in the plain to contemplate the nature of the mountains and of lofty places, and in order to contemplate the plains place themselves upon high mountains, even so to understand the nature of the people it needs to be a prince, and to understand that of princes it needs to be of the people.[16]

Looking at a map of the hills around Arezzo that Leonardo drew in about 1502, you get just such a picture of a world arranged into lowland valleys and rugged peaks. This is surely no coincidence. For Machiavelli and Leonardo met that year in the camp of Cesare Borgia, the son of a pope and a ruthless empire-builder who had plenty of use for a good map.

Cesare's father, Rodrigo de Borja, was elected pope in 1492 – the year Columbus made landfall in the Caribbean – and took the official name Alexander VI. He already had adult children, born to his mistress when he was rising in the church hierarchy. This wasn't so unusual. What made the Borgias (as

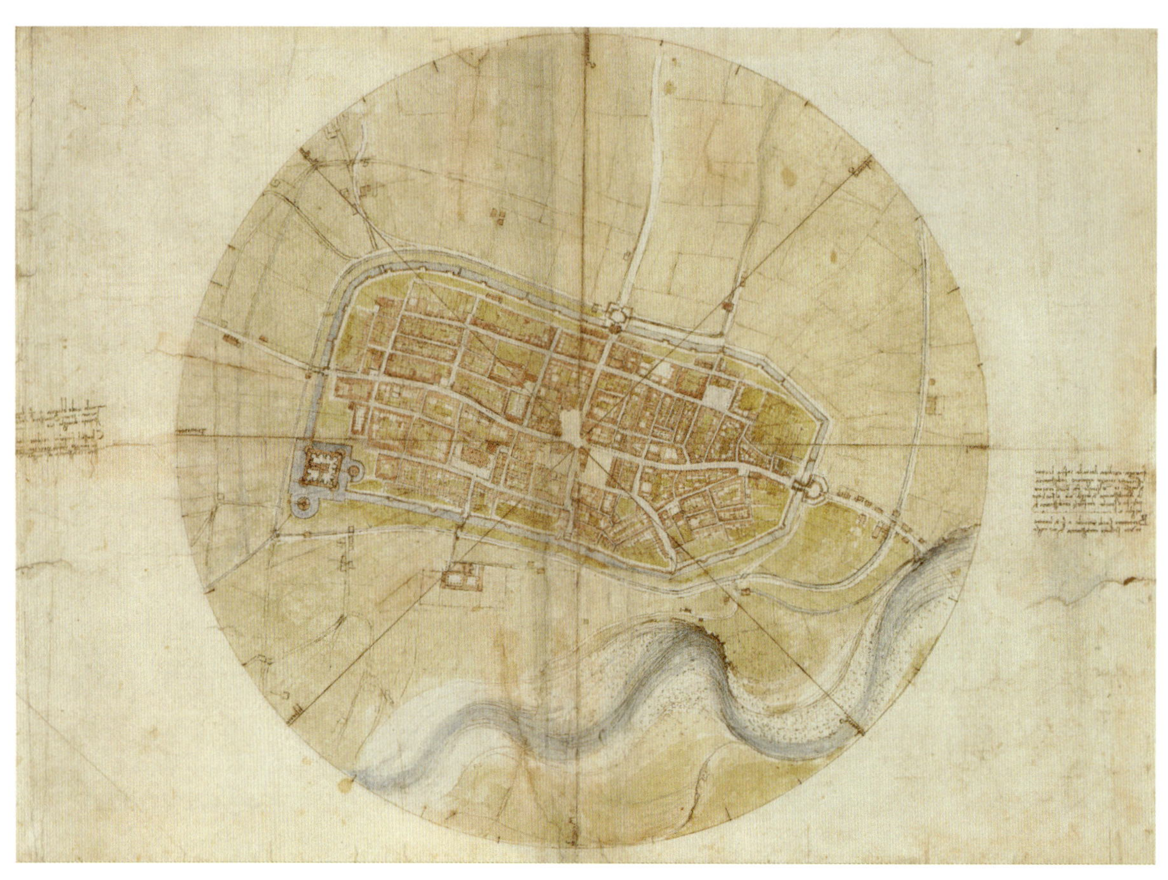

Leonardo da Vinci,
A map of Imola, 1502.

their name was Italianized) so notorious was that Alexander not only openly acknowledged his offspring, but sought to advance them using the wealth and power of the papacy. The church became, briefly, a Borgia empire. Cesare was a cardinal, destined to follow his father's path, but he had other plans. After his brother Giovanni, the duke of Gandía, was murdered – some said by him – he asked to exchange his cardinal's hat for a sword. Alexander VI put him in charge of the papal armies, and he set out to conquer a string of cities in central Italy. Leonardo joined him as a military engineer.

It can't have been relaxing. A drawing by Leonardo shows 'Valentino', as Cesare was known, as a forbidding, bearded, rapacious tough. Machiavelli saw his good qualities. He found Valentino to be daring, intelligent and effective, an excellent example of a prince, he insists, in all his actions. One example is when Cesare got rid of an underling who had terrorized the local population a little too much. He arranged for the unpopular officer to be found one morning in a piazza, cut in two. The people were 'both satisfied and stupefied'.[17]

Leonardo needed to deliver if he wasn't to meet some bloody fate in a small town in the Romagna. Cesare was too impatient to wait for wooden tanks and flying machines: instead he got maps. Leonardo's plan of the small city of Imola is the most remarkable. As if he were viewing it from above, he plots every street and building in a perfect circle, providing instant information for the eyes of the prince.

Leonardo also shared his maps with Machiavelli and discussed this exciting new science of cartography. They had a lot in common. The reason Machiavelli upset so many readers is that he analysed politics scientifically, not morally. As with Leonardo, it is hard to categorize Machiavelli as a Christian thinker. He comments on spiritual matters with heavy irony and discusses the church as a pure system of power. Before 1492 power in Italy was balanced between several states, he says, but 'Alexander VI arose afterwards, who of all the pontiffs that have ever been showed how a pope with both money and arms was able to prevail.'[18] Since then, the church has been a massive secular force.

That dominion is made visible in the Vatican, to this day, by its seemingly endless Gallery of Geographic Maps, created in the late 16th century. Frescoed charts of Italian regions define the peninsula while also creating the illusion that it can be controlled. Philip II of Spain also sponsored a complete mapping of his domains. Leonardo was a pioneer of this new science of political geography and apparently discussed it with Machiavelli while they watched Cesare Borgia plan to strangle his disloyal captains.

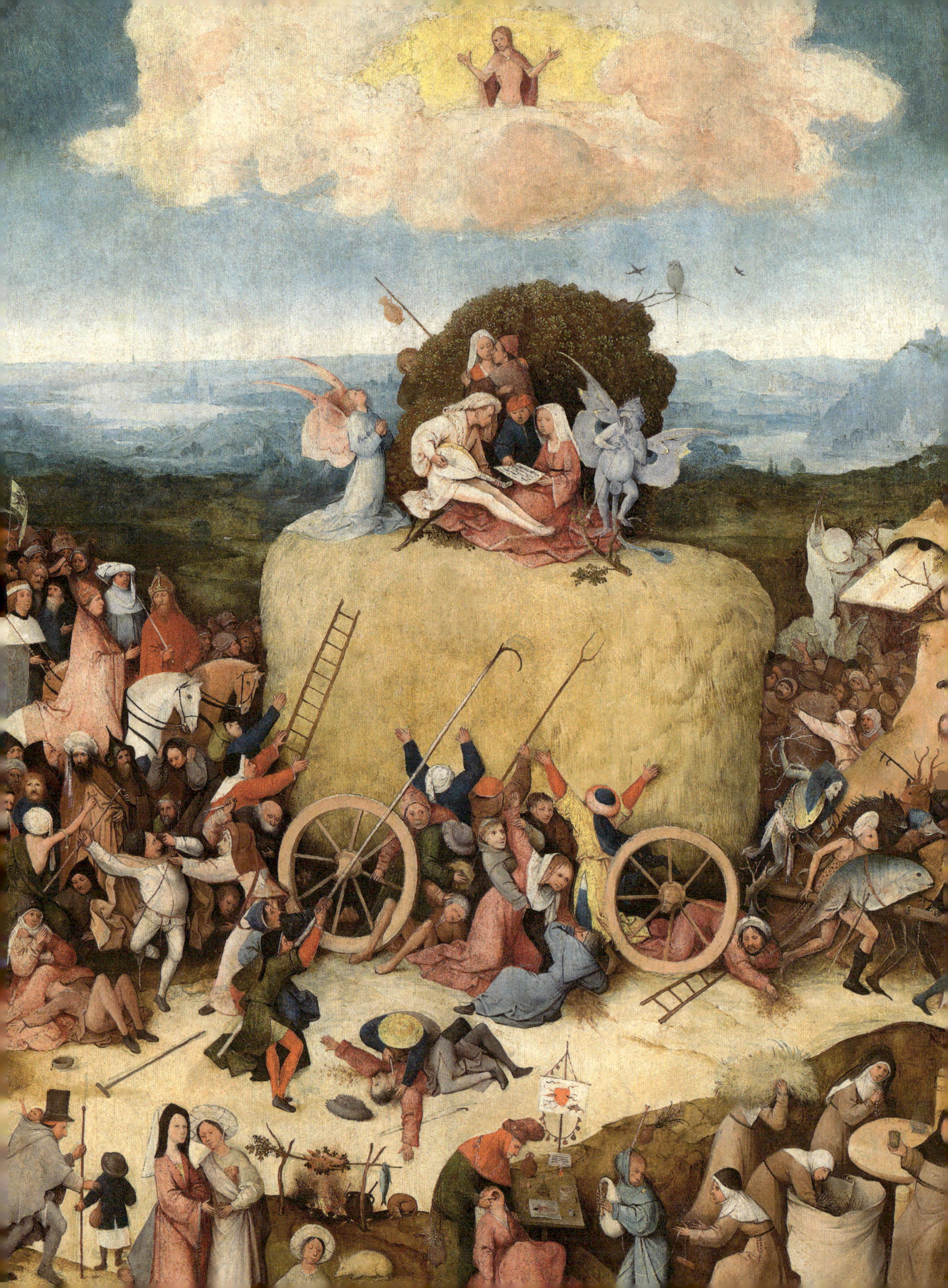

6 Haywain to Hell

In Antwerp in the early 16th century, three men sat and talked in a garden. Thomas, who was on a visit from England, had just been to Mass at the city's biggest church when he spotted his friend Peter Giles chatting to a sunburnt, unshaven, dishevelled old man. The mysterious stranger looked to Thomas like a sailor. Giles spied his English friend and said he must meet this character, 'for there is no man thys day livying that can tell you of so many straunge and unknown peoples, and Countreyes, as this man can. And I know wel that ye be very desirous to heare of such newes.'[1]

It turned out that the shabby 'blacke' man, whose name was Raphael Hythloday, had travelled to the New World with Amerigo Vespucci. Left behind as part of a garrison on Vespucci's fourth voyage, he had a chance to explore new lands for himself before making his arduous way home via Ceylon and India.

Intrigued, the Englishman invited them to his lodgings where, as it was summer, they sat outside on a turf-covered bench. Hythloday talked of the island of Utopia, whose people lived like true Christians despite knowing nothing of Christ. Free from the brutality and corruption of contemporary Europe, they arranged their society along philosophical lines, reminiscent of those in Plato's *Republic*: they shunned private property, lived communally, dined together in

Hieronymus Bosch, *The Haywain* (detail), 1512–15.

big refectories and worked happily for the common good. Children were taught that jewels and gold are worth precisely as much as excrement.

* * *

Peter Giles (or Pieter Gillis) was real enough: he was the clerk to the city of Antwerp and a good friend of Thomas More, who tells this story as the framing device of his masterpiece of political thought, *Utopia*. More, a rising public servant and humanist author from London, visited him in Antwerp in 1515. But there was no Raphael Hythloday. As for Utopia, its name, invented by More, is a joke in ancient Greek that combines the words *ou*, 'not', with *topos*, 'place': it is not a place.

Yet More sets up his fiction with careful attention to detail. If you wanted to hear a wild story of distant realms in the early 1500s, Antwerp was as likely as anywhere to be the place you would meet a weatherbeaten global traveller. This bustling North Sea port was full of Portuguese merchants importing goods from Africa and Asia. There were Africans too, who might be slaves or servants or free. Germans got here by sailing up the Rhine, and the English, like More, crossed the narrow, rough sea. You could get exotic fruits and spices and curios. Antwerp had taken over from Bruges by the late 15th century as the commercial conduit between Northern and Southern Europe. It was a humming cosmopolis in an age when the Mediterranean was becoming a lot less dynamic than the Atlantic.

The small city of 's-Hertogenbosch was 80 kilometres (50 miles) north-east of Antwerp, close enough to pick up some of its news, wealth and trade. It was a busy community, centred on a market square packed with cloth stalls. The two places were well enough connected for wealthy Antwerp burghers to commission paintings by 's-Hertogenbosch's most famous artist, a man so rooted in his little community he took the last part of its name as his own. We know him as Hieronymus Bosch.

Among the Antwerp citizens who hired Bosch were Peeter Scheyfve and his wife, Agneese de Gramme. Scheyfve was a great success in the cloth industry, becoming an official of the Antwerp weavers' corporation, rich enough to buy a manor outside the city. The painting he commissioned, in which he and Agneese are portrayed praying on their knees, he in a fur-collared robe, she in black and significantly younger than him, is an *Adoration of the Magi*. It's also an outpouring of the artist's hallucinatory imagination, which seems stimulated by exactly the kind of global comings and goings that inspired More to have the tale of Utopia narrated in Antwerp. It is a big, ambitious triptych. Perhaps the couple brought Bosch to Antwerp to paint it: you can almost sense a harbourside bustle.

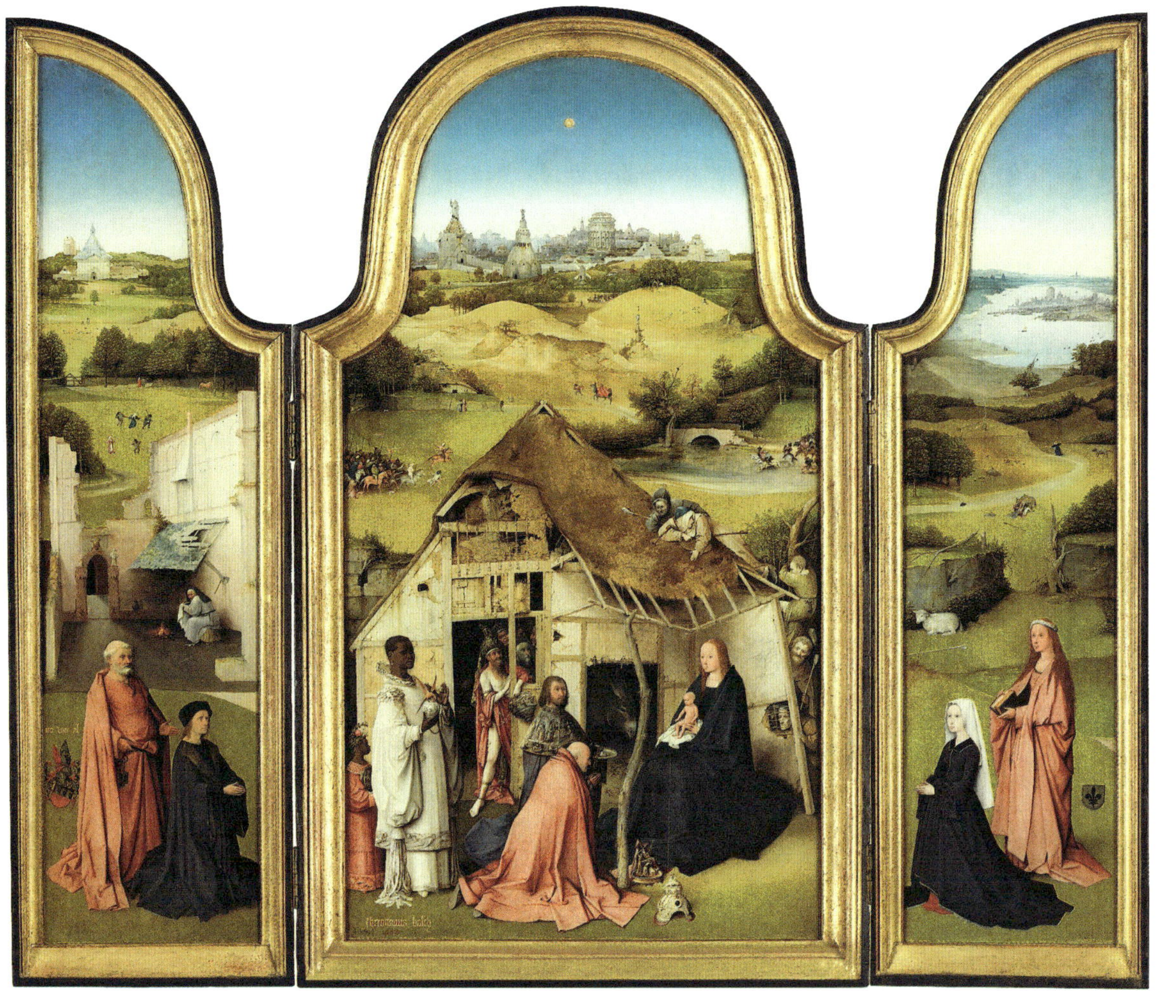

Hieronymus Bosch, *Adoration of the Magi*, c. 1494.

Balthazar, the black Magus (as he was said to be in medieval lore), looks like a portrait of an African whom Bosch may have encountered in Antwerp. His features are surely depicted from life. Yet if Balthazar looks like a plausible portrait, his ornately cut white garment, with its motionless folds, stiff collar and pauldron of thistly leaves, is chimerical. It doesn't seem like cloth at all. It appears carved rather than cut, as if it were made of ivory.

The trade in ivory was already ancient when Portuguese ships started navigating Africa. In Roman times it mostly came from North African elephants – which is why there are no more North African elephants. In the early Middle Ages Arab caravans brought ivory across the Sahara. Medieval elephant-ivory objects abounded, including drinking horns called 'oliphants' that were made from whole tusks. Portugal's navigators in the 1400s gained direct access to ivory from sub-Saharan Africa, cutting out the Islamic middlemen. They now traded face to face with rulers who understood how much the newcomers coveted this material.

Some of the first African works of art to reach Europe were spectacular ivory objects carved in West Africa for the European market. Some depict Portuguese soldiers and ships; others are fanciful flights of form. Many were made as salt cellars for the banqueting table. One such 'salt' from Sierra Leone is a phantasmagoric fusion of African and European images. Snakes, which symbolized wealth for the Sapi peoples who made it, face down dogs that could be Portuguese hunting hounds, except that they have dragon spines on their backs. A Sapi man and woman pose formally for their portraits, the warrior in armour leggings, the woman bare-breasted. Could her skirt be Portuguese? Yet these figurative details are just part of an extravagant, abstract invention. Rope-like tubes extend from the dogs' haunches. Four snakes are coiled around a bulging, bearded doughnut that hangs over the heads of the human figures, from which a collar rises to support a hollow sphere. The top half of this object is a removable lid to cover the salt inside. It is carved with beads and flowers and topped by a spindly spire.

Unknown Sapi-Portuguese artist, lidded salt cellar, 5th–16th century.

It's not only the creamy, immovable sculpture of Balthazar's robe that intimates ivory. The pale hue of the gift he presents to the infant Christ, though it is made of silver and gold, could also suggest the West African carvings that were being imported by the Portuguese to Antwerp and other cities. Balthazar's gift is also shaped like a coconut shell. These were precious rarities in themselves. Some ivory salts from Sierra Leone had coconut-shaped containers; one that survives has crocodiles crawling around the vessel and is topped with a magisterial figure of a nude African woman.

When the German artist Albrecht Dürer was staying in Antwerp in 1520, the gifts he received included an 'Indian nut' – that is, a coconut. It was Portuguese ships that introduced the coconut to Western Africa from their trading bases in Asia: *coco* comes from the Portuguese for 'head' or 'skull'. One of the Portuguese merchants Dürer befriended in Antwerp also gave his wife, Agnes, a green parakeet.

* * *

The theme of the Adoration of the Magi was a medieval opportunity to depict the 'exotic', from the black king Balthazar to the Babylonian traditions of astronomy that guided the Eastern philosopher-rulers. For Bosch, however, these images of elsewhere are symptoms of a rapidly changing world. Antwerp is full of news from far-flung places. In his turbulent imagination that can only mean one thing: the end of the world.

The universe Bosch depicts is on the edge of a revelation. Christ's birth is not a simple, happy event but a rupture in history that will, soon enough, lead to the final cataclysmic events of human time. Mary sits in front of the stable with her baby, as the grave figures of the Magi pay court. Jesus is bolt upright on her lap, aware of everything. From inside the stable a motley gathering of seedy characters watch – at least most of them do: one face is turned away, refusing to be interested in this epochal moment. The leader of the crew is a half-naked man wearing a bulbous, thorn-covered crown and a peculiar smile, sticking his bare leg into the gathering of Magi. He is the Antichrist. In the Last Days, according to the biblical Book of Revelation, this diabolical character will rule briefly before the final triumph of heaven, the rise of the New Jerusalem and the Last Judgment.

Beyond the peasants on the roof, Joseph washing a nappy in a ruinous courtyard, a group of people dancing ecstatically and squadrons of soldiers, a city rises like a glittering mirage under a winter sun burning in a gelid sky. Its weird domes, towers and spires don't look like any style from the Europe of Bosch's time. They are neither Gothic nor classical. If anything, a building that tapers in a pear shape resembles the mud mosques of Timbuktu, which reached their distinctive form in the 15th and 16th centuries. Yet there's a European windmill nearby. Technically, this miraculous city is Bethlehem, where Mary and Joseph, summoned for the census, had to shelter in a stable. But its marvellous appearance is a premonition of the New Jerusalem. According to the Book of Revelation, this will be a city of gold and jasper, with a wall and gates and the river of life: a utopia at the end of time.

* * *

The artist who became known as Hieronymus Bosch was born Jheronimus Anthoniusz van Aken sometime in the mid-1400s. His grandfather had moved to 's-Hertogenbosch in the 1420s and created a family business providing solid works of art for the town: all Hieronymus's male relatives were painters. It was also a family tradition to belong to the Brotherhood of Our Lady, a religious and social fraternity that seems to have had the town sewn up, staging annual swan banquets as well as religious processions. 's-Hertogenbosch's fine Gothic chapel, built in Bosch's time adjacent to the cathedral, still survives. Belonging to the brotherhood helped the van Akens get regular commissions. Bosch joined it too in the mid-1480s, then soon afterwards rose to join the inner elite of sworn members whose duties included providing a swan every year for the banquet.

Bosch could afford the swans. He married Aleid van der Meervenne, whose family were well-to-do merchants. She inherited an impressive house on the market square that had room for workshops and cellars for storage, and this was where Bosch lived and painted. The couple also had an income from other property inherited by Aleid. They had no children. And there you have it: a middle class, respectable man who lived in a tight-knit Christian community in which he played a leading role. Yet the restless imagination of Hieronymus Bosch wandered far from his small city, through landscapes of war and madness, across seas filled with peculiar fishes, riding on the backs of flying monsters.

* * *

In one of Bosch's most famous inventions, a hunchbacked creature with a bird's face and red robe skates on a frozen river to deliver a letter it holds in its beak. This post-bird is bringing news from a world full of prodigies and signs. New media were speeding up the transmission of information but also disseminating fantasy. The first movable-type printing press in Europe was set up by Johannes Gutenberg in Mainz in the late 1440s. Gutenberg brought out his epoch-making printed Bible in 1455, proving the power of this new technology and defining a new age: the Gutenberg Age.

Printing multiplied the image as well as the word. The first European woodcuts, made by inking incised blocks of wood and stamping them on paper, predated Gutenberg. They illustrated books and tracts but also circulated as standalone works of art, popular icons, instant news images. Printing from engraved metal plates achieved more refined results, with sharper lines and greater nuance. The German artist Martin Schongauer showed how the black-and-white intensity of the new medium could give images firmness and imaginative force when in the 1470s he engraved the hermit St Anthony patiently bearing his torment by a gang of flying demons who carry him aloft in the empty white sky. Their forms are delineated in spine-tingling detail: foul mixtures of hedgehog spines, ram's horns, bat wings, reptilian claws, fish eyes, skeletal arms, chicken legs. One demon has a second face that sprouts from its anus. The creatures revolve round the flying saint in an elegant circle, beating him with clubs and pulling at his robes and beard while he endures it all, refusing to look at them.

The information that printing spread in words and pictures was eschatological. Such new and strange things were happening that it was reasonable to expect the Last Trump at any moment. Schongauer's devils announce a flood of fiendish images. The Devil appears, claw-footed and tentacle-faced, speaking with

Martin Schongauer, *Temptation of St Anthony*, 1470–75.

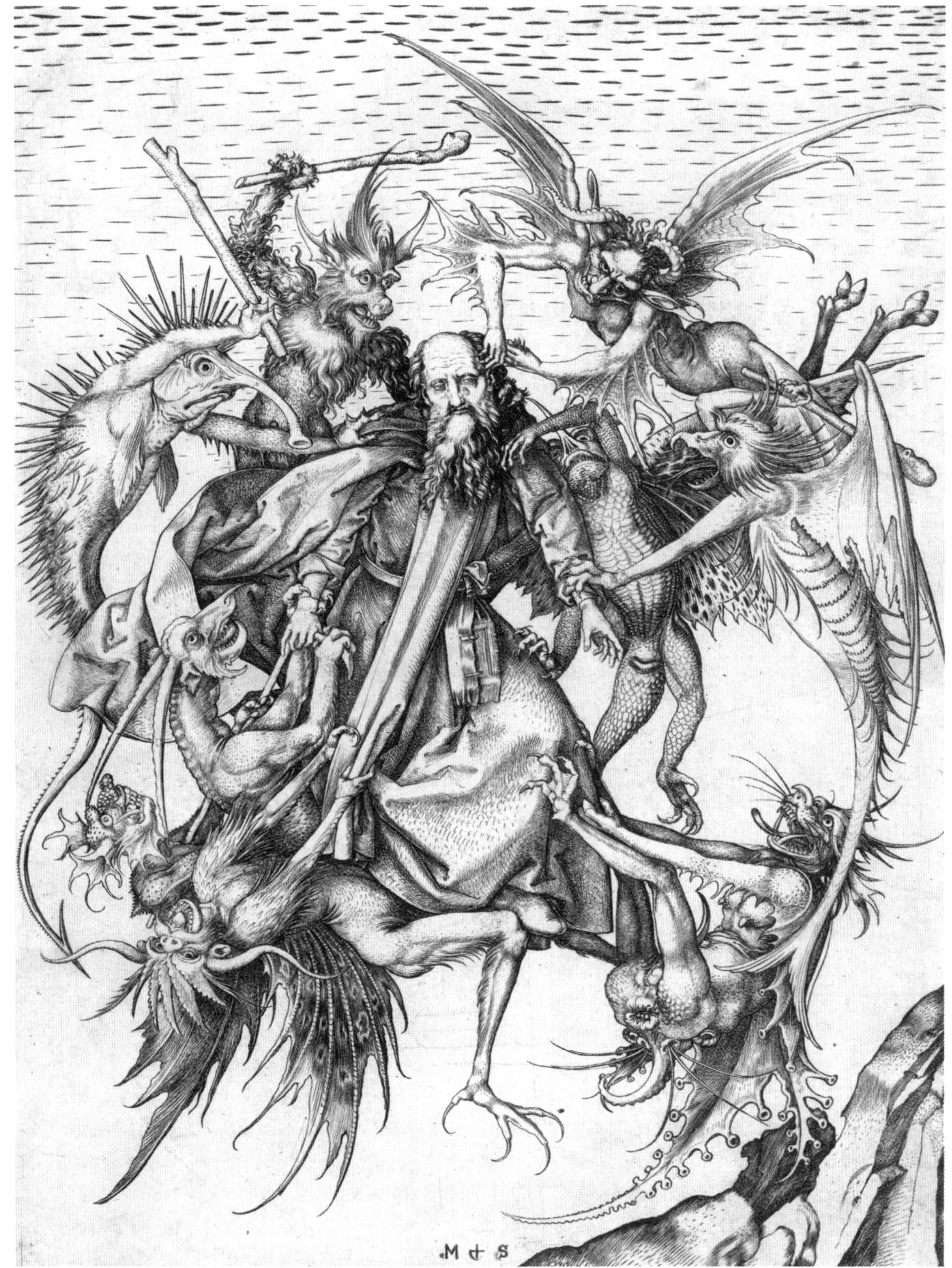

Christ in broad daylight in a print by the anonymous German engraver known only as 'Master LCz'. Spookily real, it seems more news story than Bible illustration. One of the many woodcuts in Hartmann Schedel's *Nuremberg Chronicle*, printed in 1493, depicts Jewish men sacrificing a Christian child. This blood libel supposedly reports an atrocity that took place in Trento in the 1470s. It is an item of Apocalypse news, for the *Nuremberg Chronicle* tells the story of the world from Genesis to the Last Judgment: past, present and prophetic future.

The woodcuts in a book published in Basel in 1494 were equally indicative of history hotting up, hurtling towards the Last Days. This was a Latin version of a letter from Christopher Columbus telling of his voyage to previously unknown islands on the far side of the Atlantic. Its illustrations include Columbus's ship, the *Santa Maria*, with a square cross on its sail. The great navigator corrects its course towards islands between which the sea flows like a narrow river. Another woodcut of Columbus, published in Florence in 1493, shows King Ferdinand on his throne ordering the Genoese admiral's voyage. The three ships in his fleet instantaneously arrive at a tropical island, where a host of naked people flee.

* * *

In a *Last Judgment* by Hieronymus Bosch, painted around 1495–1505, a vessel like a pink marquee ferrying the blessed to paradise has a small wooden sailing ship balanced on top as a crow's nest, with a flag suspended from its stern. The flag shows the same red crusader cross that emblazoned Columbus's vessels. If it is an allusion to the discovery of new lands across the ocean, it's appropriate, because Columbus himself was a millenarian thinker attracted to the ideas of the medieval prophet Joachim of Fiore. Joachim argued that the events foretold in the Book of Revelation were imminent. Columbus claimed that, by opening a new route to Asia, Christendom could go behind Islam's back and take Jerusalem by surprise, triggering the End of Days, the creation of a New Heaven and a New Earth, and the Last Judgment.

Columbus was not alone or culturally backward in his thinking. Florence was increasingly in thrall to the apocalyptic preacher Girolamo Savonarola. Despite being denounced by this formidable Dominican friar, Lorenzo de' Medici supported his appointment as prior of San Marco, his tolerance perhaps influenced by a remarkable humanist thinker named Giovanni Pico della Mirandola. This intellectual nobleman had a very open mind. Educated at Padua University and partly influenced by the Jewish philosopher Elia del Medigo, Pico was fascinated by Judaism and Kabbalah, the mystical interpretation of Hebrew scripture. He was also interested in Islam, and recognized the interconnectedness of medieval thought in which Aristotle had been rediscovered by Muslim and Jewish scholars before being lionized by Christian Europe. It goes without saying that, as a humanist, he hallowed pagan antiquity. Innocently thinking the church was ready to hear all this, in 1486 Pico published a book in Rome presenting *900 Theses* taken from classical pagan, Christian, Muslim and Jewish beliefs, all of which he claimed were reconcilable. He emphasized Kabbalah, which had never before been disseminated in Christian Europe, where antisemitism was religious doctrine. Pico wanted to pay for a conference in Rome to debate these plural, rangy views. Instead, he was condemned by the pope and hounded out of the city, fleeing to Florence, where he was protected by his friend Lorenzo the Magnificent.

Pico della Mirandola's inquisitiveness made him interested in Savonarola's prophecies. Might this harsh critic of Medici rule truly be able to speak to God, as he claimed? During Lorenzo's lifetime it was an intriguing question for dinner-table debate. It was different when the Magnifico succumbed to the family gout in 1492, for then all hell broke loose. Lorenzo's son Piero had none of his political insight or diplomatic finesse. In 1494 Charles VIII of France invaded Italy to lay claim to the Kingdom of Naples. As Charles marched south, his army spearheaded by a new kind of portable artillery called cannons, he approached Florence. Piero de' Medici, trying to be clever, rode out to negotiate – but the Florentine people feared treachery. There was an uprising that ended Medici rule and established a radical holy republic. Pico didn't live to see it, as he died that autumn – poisoned by arsenic, according to a 21st-century examination of his remains.

Savonarola dominated the new regime and effectively controlled the city from his base at the monastery of San Marco. His authority stemmed from the fact that he had predicted the invasion of Italy by France. Now his prophecies of disaster for corrupt Florence, which included an angel descending with a fiery sword, consumed his followers, who were nicknamed 'weepers' by more cynical souls. One of the 'weepers' was Sandro Botticelli, no longer an artist of classical myth but an introspective Christian mystic. His paganistic poet friend Poliziano died, like Pico, in 1494: he too may have been poisoned. Botticelli himself had become obsessed with Dante. He spent much of the 1480s drawing illustrations for the *Divine Comedy* that are second only to the studies of Leonardo as miracles of draughtsmanship, as well as being subtle interpretations of Dante's theology.

After the 1494 revolution, Botticelli made woodcuts for Savonarola's pamphlets and simplified his painting style, as if turning the clock back to a pristine world before perspective was invented. His painting of the *Mystic Nativity* mixes figures on different scales, reflecting their holiness rather than distance from

Sandro Botticelli,
Mystic Nativity, 1500.

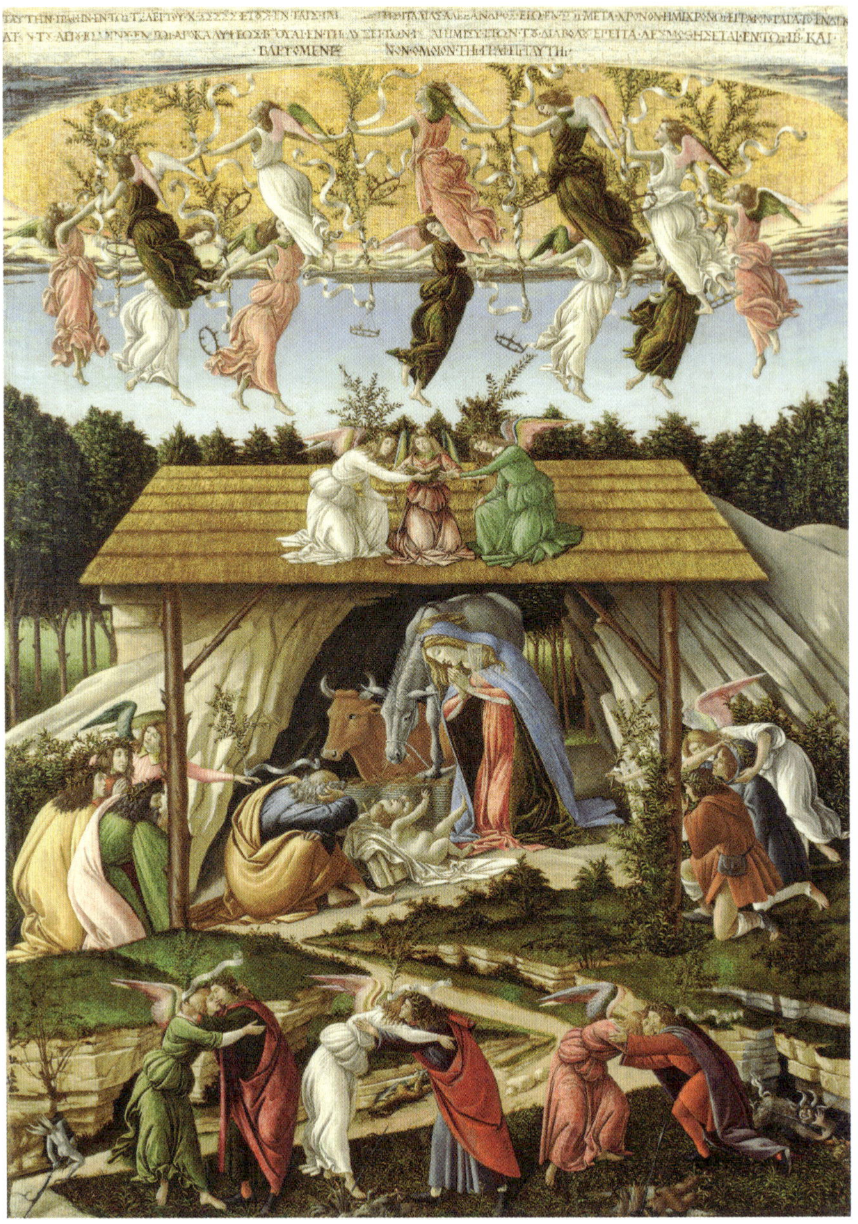

the eye. Like Bosch in his *Adoration*, he sees the birth of Christ as the start of the countdown to the Last Days. He wrote an explanation at the top, in Greek, that proclaims his own prophecy:

> I, Alessandro, painted this picture at the end of the year 1500, in the troubles of Italy, in the half-time after the time, according to the eleventh of St John, in the second woe of the Apocalypse, during the release of the Devil for three and a half years.

The 'troubles of Italy' he is talking about were indeed perturbing. Savonarola became increasingly controversial, commanding trinkets and treasures to be burned in 'Bonfires of the Vanities', attacking the pope and spreading scandal about the Borgia family. In 1498 a faction in the Signoria seized him from San Marco and burnt him alongside two supporters in the middle of the city's main square: mercifully they were hanged first. Botticelli read the Revelation of St John for himself. The 'half-time after the time' is the year 1500: a millennium and a half has transpired since the death of Christ. The Apocalypse has started: we are in the times of the Antichrist, by which Botticelli means Pope Alexander and his demonic son, Cesare Borgia.

* * *

The Apocalypse also caused Nuremberg to tremble. This southern German city was at the forefront of the printing revolution. The *Nuremberg Chronicle* not only illustrated biblical stories and antisemitic myths, but also presented woodcuts of great cities including Constantinople, Kraków, Paris and Nuremberg itself, a crowded constellation of towers and spires and steep-roofed houses inside its high walls. The city was part of the Holy Roman Empire, the elective Germanic super-monarchy established in the early Middle Ages, but like other imperial cities it was highly autonomous. The *Nuremberg Chronicle* encapsulates the dizzying mix of fact and fantasy that drove the feverish mood of the years approaching 1500. One enterprising young Nuremberger cashed in on the anxious atmosphere by offering an illustration of exactly what the Book of Revelation predicts.

Albrecht Dürer's family were, as far back as he knew, cattle and horse breeders in Hungary. His grandfather had left their village to become a goldsmith, and his father, following the same profession, migrated to Nuremberg. Dürer wrote in an open, tender way about his relationship with his father, who was also called Albrecht. The artisan had hoped that his son, Albrecht junior, born in 1471, would succeed him in his business, but the boy said he wanted to be a painter, so he arranged an apprenticeship for him with a local artist, Michael Wolgemut. When the young Albrecht was 13, both he and his father drew self-portraits in silverpoint: the father's is impressive, but the 13-year-old's is prodigious.

For all his desire to paint, Albrecht could not avoid printing, which offered a halfway house between hardheaded, practical work and his aesthetic ambitions. His teacher Wolgemut did the woodcuts for the *Nuremberg Chronicle*; his godfather, Anton Koberger, was its publisher.

Dürer maintained a businesslike attitude to printmaking all his life. Long after he had become wealthy and famous, when he and his wife sailed up the

Albrecht Dürer, *St Michael Fighting the Dragon*, from the *Apocalypse* series, 1498.

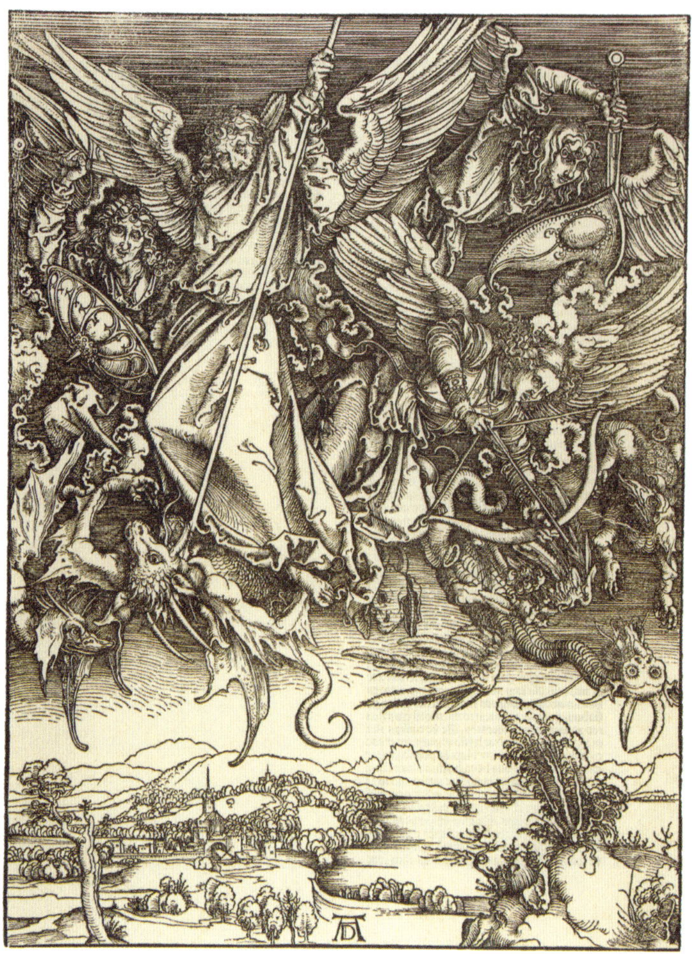

Rhine to the Low Countries, he took a hoard of his prints to sell and give as gifts to useful friends. He co-opted his mother, Barbara, to sell his prints at market and employed a brother as a travelling salesman. So it's fair to see his *Apocalypse*, first published in 1498, as a well-timed economic move as well as an exceptional essay in the power of images. Alongside the text of the Book of Revelation, Dürer recreates its prophecies in sixteen full-page woodcuts.

It is astonishing how much information Dürer can distil into each black-and-white image. He has learned this partly from Martin Schongauer's formidable instinct for selection and emphasis: when he went travelling after his apprenticeship, it's said that he headed for Colmar to find Schongauer, but the creator of the *St Anthony* had recently died. Yet Dürer adds more layers and shifts, using the techniques of perspective to create huge spaces on a sheet of paper. His woodcut of *St Michael Fighting the Dragon* shows the angels and their demonic foes battling in the sky and simultaneously maps the earth below them, from foreground trees to a little town to ships on the sea. This serene landscape contrasts starkly with the war in heaven, as if the struggle could be going on now, above our heads, and we don't know it. You can actually feel a sense of vertigo if you look from the fields below to the lofty angels – yet this is just an inked sheet, not a vast fresco.

Down at ground level run-of-the-mill, plump people witness and suffer. A crowd, who might easily be well-off Nurembergers, hear the oratory of the Antichrist, while the Whore of Babylon appears next to the Seven-Headed Beast as an army descends through the clouds and a distant city bursts into flames as if struck by the latest artillery. In the most brutal clash of prophecy and day-to-day life, common folk, as well as a prelate of the church, are crushed under the hooves of the Four Horsemen: Death, War, Famine and Pestilence.

Dürer makes sense of the complex imagery of Revelation and relates it to the quotidian. This is what the Apocalypse will mean to you and yours, this tabloid from the future tells its audience with an unerring instinct for journalism.

* * *

No one ever accused Bosch of excessive clarity. Where Dürer's woodcuts help a confused reader (or someone unable to read) to comprehend the prognostications vouchsafed to St John on the island of Patmos, Bosch's paintings sow endless mystery, create entangling chaos. His landscapes are rooted in the ponds and rivers, woods and timber buildings of his Netherlandish world, but are filled with freakish prodigies to confound even the most jaded connoisseur of the impossible. His triptych of the *Temptation of St Anthony* (overleaf) is not immediately identifiable as the same story Schongauer depicted; there are so many distractions. In the central panel a town is in flames against a sky that is turned brown by its smoke. What catastrophe is this? You then notice, as the smoke clears, that a deep-blue sky melting to a pale horizon is dotted with flying creatures and machines. A man and woman ride a giant fish in the sky; high above passes a form, part sailing ship, part swan; a flying tub is borne aloft on the back of a monster carrying a naked man who bends over, his head between his legs, showing his buttocks.

Below, a fish lies helplessly on the ground, plate armour and a red cloak strapped to its back. Unlike the ice-skating bird-postman in the left-hand panel, this dying creature at the centre of the triptych looks at you with a cold, empty eye, a fish out of water. Just above it is a ray, its white belly turned towards us and guts exposed: a horror not so different from the daily North Sea catch. As your eyes take in one unlikely sight after another, you start to see a method in

Hieronymus Bosch, *Temptation of St Anthony*, 1505–6.

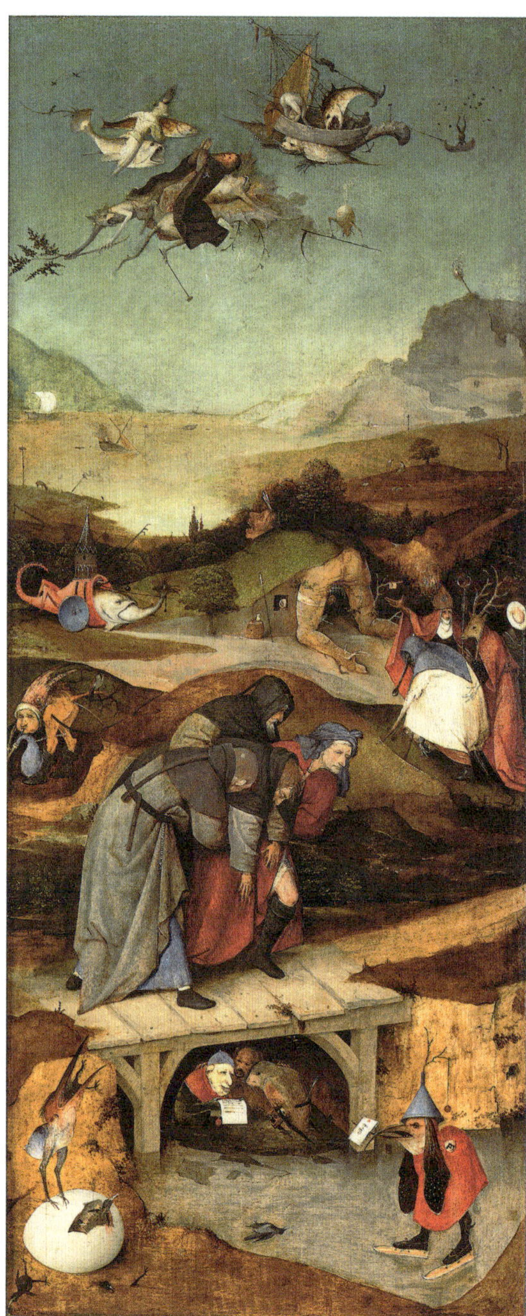

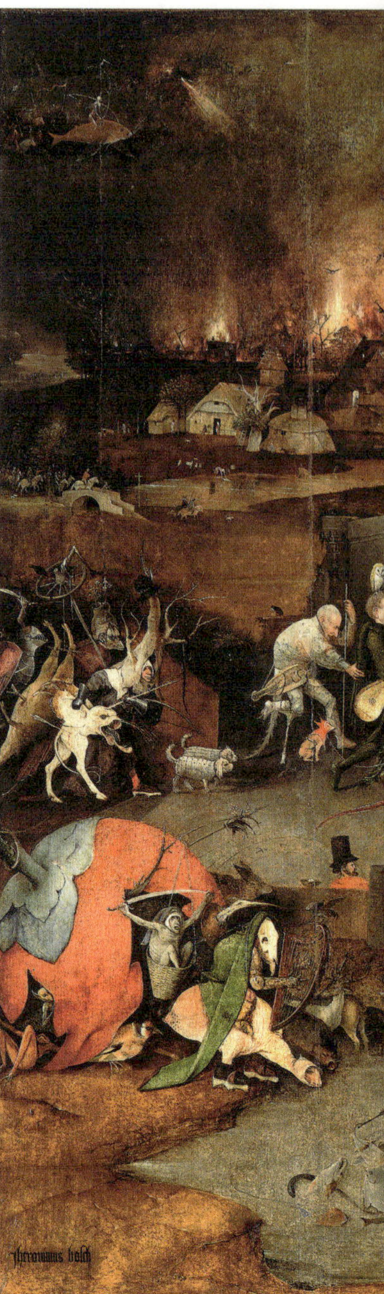

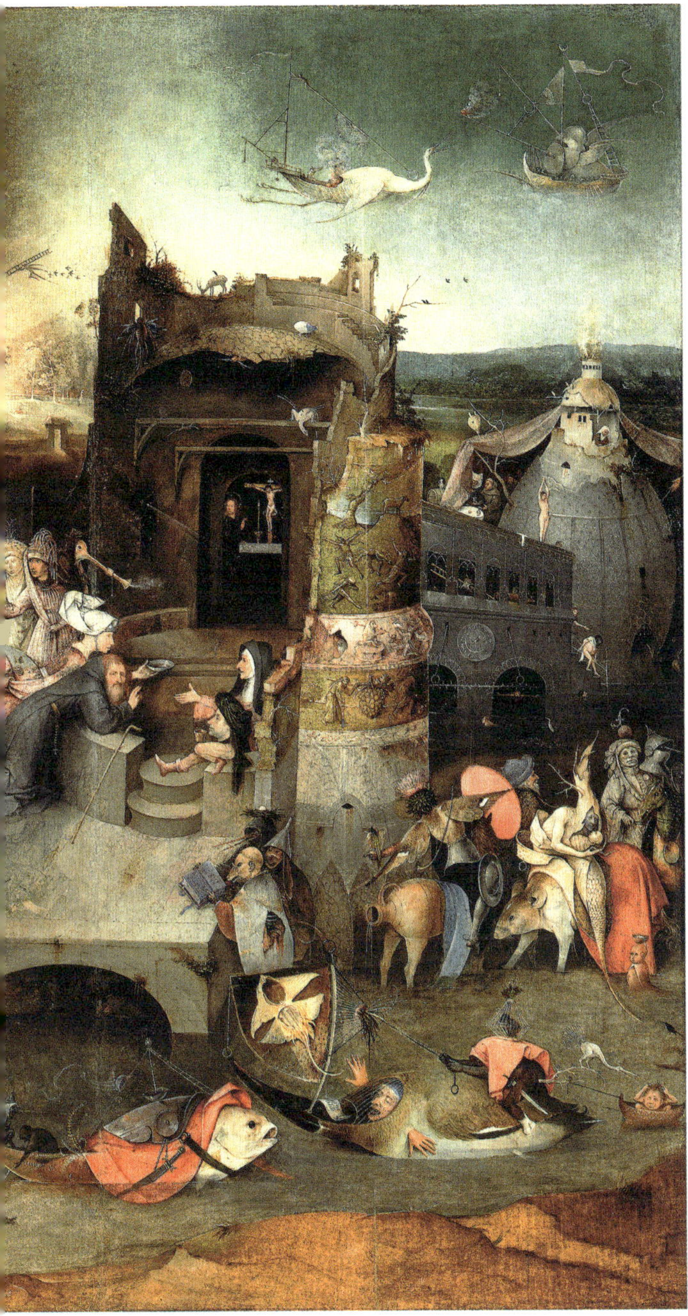

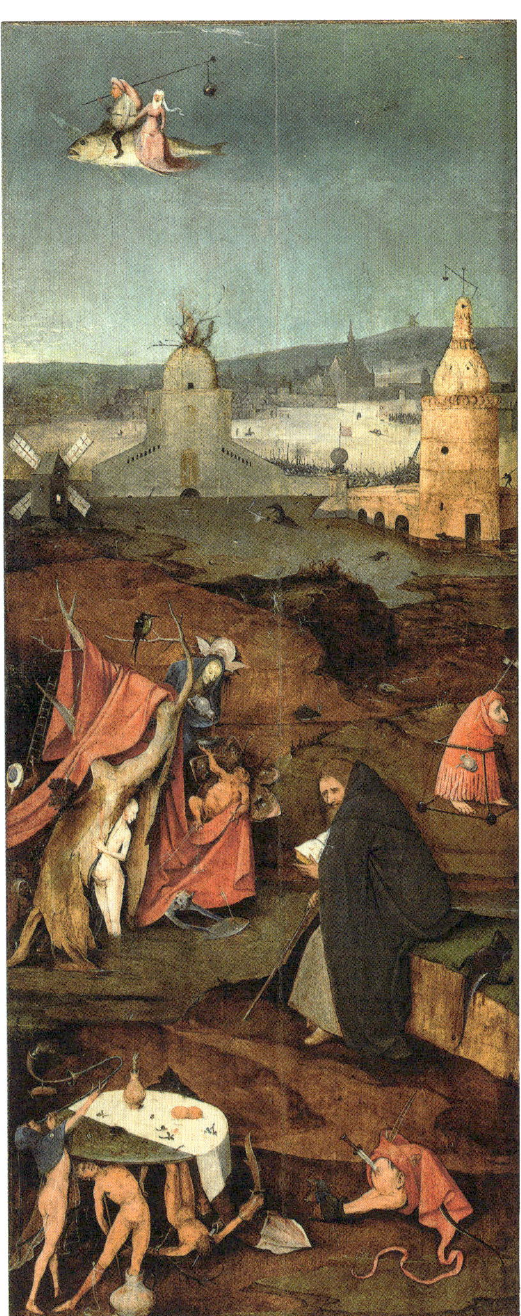

Hieronymus Bosch, *The Wood has Ears, the Field has Eyes*, c. 1500.

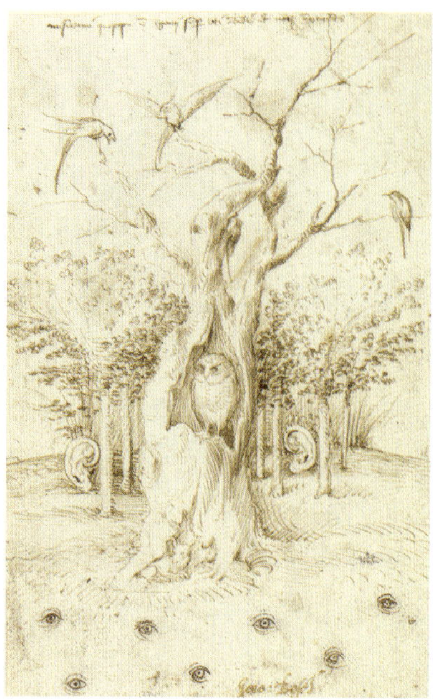

the madness – not a key to Bosch's meaning, rather the means by which he creates the unexpected.

Bosch is not a random fantasist but a patient realist. His hilarious, frightening images are born from close studies of the humdrum material around him. A funnel worn by a bird as a hat; a tree with a face in its trunk; a head with no body, just a pair of legs – all conjoin perfectly common things to create the marvellous.

An extraordinary drawing by Bosch takes us closer to his distinctive experience of reality. It illustrates a proverb: 'The Wood has Ears, the Field has Eyes'. An owl perches inside a hollow tree, staring at us. Beyond is a woodland where two giant ears grow from tree trunks. Most unpleasantly of all, human eyes float unattached in the foreground. The way Bosch transforms a homely warning about eavesdroppers into a paranoid, nightmarish vision might suggest a heightened sensitivity to, or a distaste for, the folk culture that surrounded him. It might even imply a capacity to go into a dream state as he walked through the woods and the fields, like Leonardo staring at a wall. Like Leonardo, Bosch has covered the other side of the sheet with drawings as though he has more ideas than he knows what to do with.

* * *

Bosch is a subtle colourist who paints landscapes that have what Leonardo defined as 'atmospheric perspective' as well as the 'perspective of distance': look past the tragicomic grotesqueries and you see lovely horizons, shimmering blue distant waters, smoky far-off trees. This quiet undercurrent of pastoral beauty served to stage the chaos with all the more hypnotic factuality. In the central panel of Bosch's *Last Judgment*, the common or garden is as out of place as ears in the wood, eyes in the field. A giant clog, comprising a pink cloth upper nailed onto a wooden sole, crushes naked bodies. A rat with floppy rabbit ears and a hollow stomach carries a cauldron, inside which a monk and a nun canoodle. In the distance a naked man is laid over an anvil to have his bottom beaten with a hammer by a monastic figure cowled in white. Another naked man is crucified across the strings of a giant harp. Beside him nude figures dance hand in hand around blue bagpipes on top of a tent on top of a cabinet in which we see more cavorting clerics. This is daily life on earth, according to Bosch: an insane world of violence and cruelty, religious hypocrisy and crazed lust.

Bosch himself must have felt like a lonely pilgrim negotiating a deranged country. His painting *The Wayfarer* portrays a thin, white-haired man with a heavy pack on his back, walking bent and saddened along a country road past an

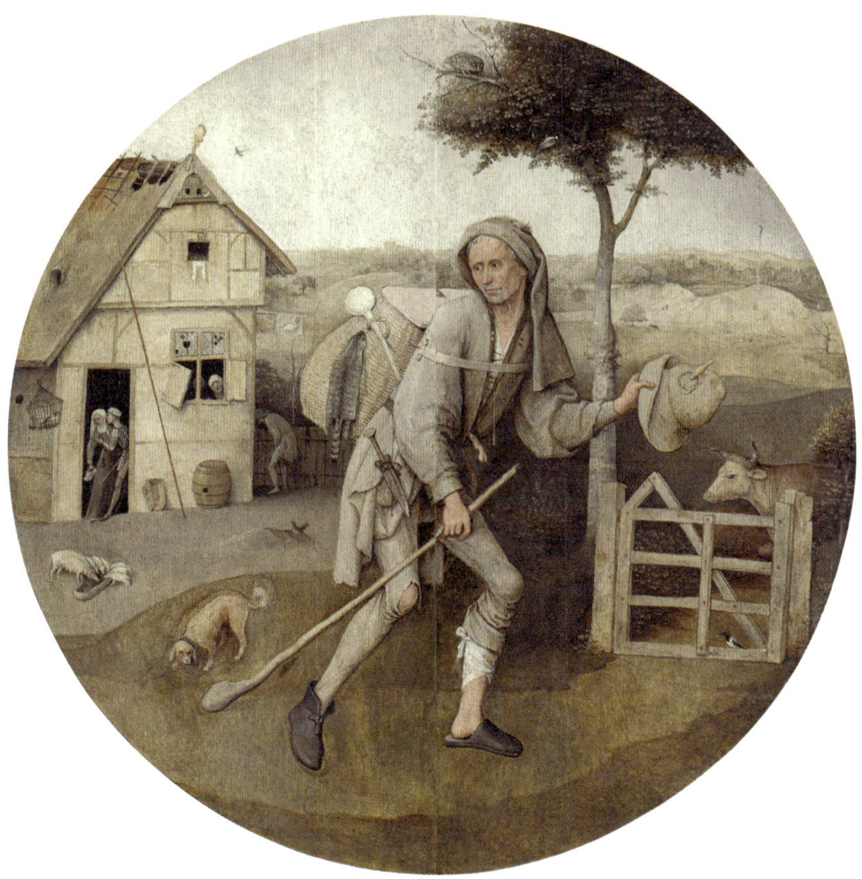

Hieronymus Bosch, *The Wayfarer*, c. 1500.

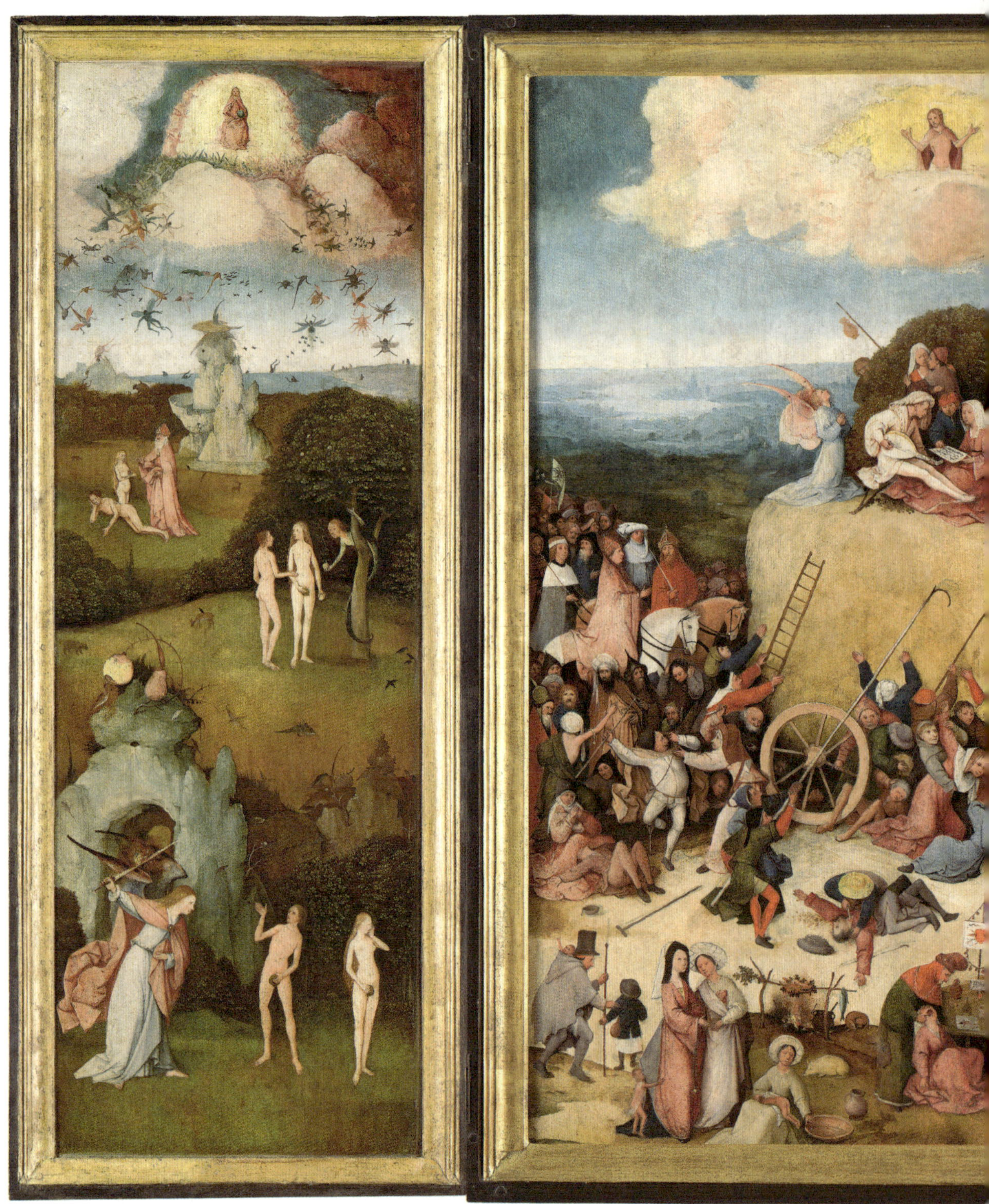

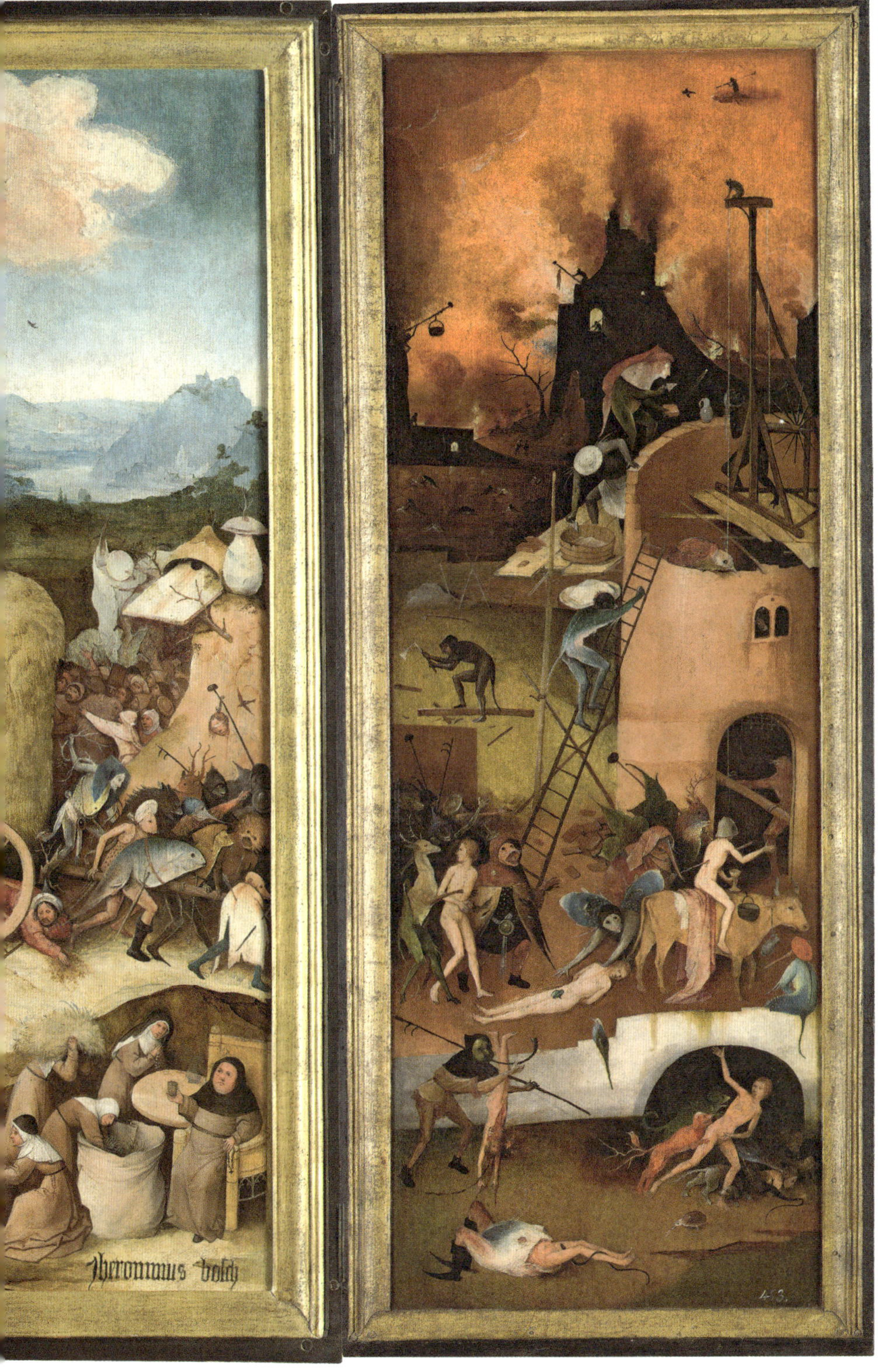

Hieronymus Bosch, *The Haywain*, 1512–15.

inn where lovers cuddle in the doorway. A woman looks at him from a window, and a man urinates against the side of the dilapidated structure. The traveller turns his back on them, searching for something else.

This figure also appears on the closed doors of Bosch's triptych *The Haywain*, making his way past outlaws who have tied up a man to rob him, and a man and woman dancing to bagpipe music. Open, the triptych shows human life as a frenetic hayride, with crowds of rich and poor gathered round a swaying wagon full of hay, on top of which courtly lovers are accompanied by a music-making devil and an angel with eyes on heaven (pp. 144–45). In the procession that follows the tottering wagon, the pope and the Holy Roman Emperor ride along complacently, without any awareness of where they are headed: hell.

Like so many of Bosch's triptychs, *The Haywain* depicts the Garden of Eden on its left wing, with hell on the right. The central panel is not, however, evenly poised between the two. Everyone is headed for hell in a riotous cavalcade. The haywain is pulled by demons – a mouse-headed figure who carries a giant fish; a tree-man whipping the creatures on; another figure carrying a blindfolded, severed head on a pole. So determined is the crowd to reach hell that no one cares about the people crushed under the haywain's wheels.

The purpose of paintings showing the Last Judgment was to remind Christians of choice and consequence. Pray, attend Mass, do good works, pay for a chantry chapel so your soul can be remembered in prayers after death, and paradise awaits, even if you have to spend centuries in purgatory first. Dirk Bouts's painting the *Fall of the Damned*, a spectacular vision of naked souls tormented by multiform devils in a scintillating infernal landscape, done around 1468, seems to anticipate Bosch in its preoccupation with the outlandish and macabre. Yet this is an optical illusion: it has been separated from a conventional *Last Judgment* in which it was balanced by a scene of paradise into which the blessed parade in their solemn nudity.

Bosch's triptychs destabilize this divine order. Even his Last Judgments are odd, with their manic carnivals of human life spilling over into hell's chaos. *The Haywain* makes his disagreement explicit. It imitates – it's tempting to say, parodies – the structure of a Last Judgment, yet instead of presenting a choice between heaven and hell it narrates a bleak history of the world from creation to universal destruction. Even the 'paradise' panel depicts the origin of sin. In the distance, land and sea are separated from primal chaos. Then, in the quiet of Eden, woman is created out of the body of sleeping Adam. The serpent offers her the apple, and innocence ends. In the foreground the angel drives Adam and Eve out of paradise. It's all downhill from there, as the unthinking, greedy, lustful human multitude follow the haywain to hell.

Dirk Bouts,
Fall of the Damned,
c. 1468.

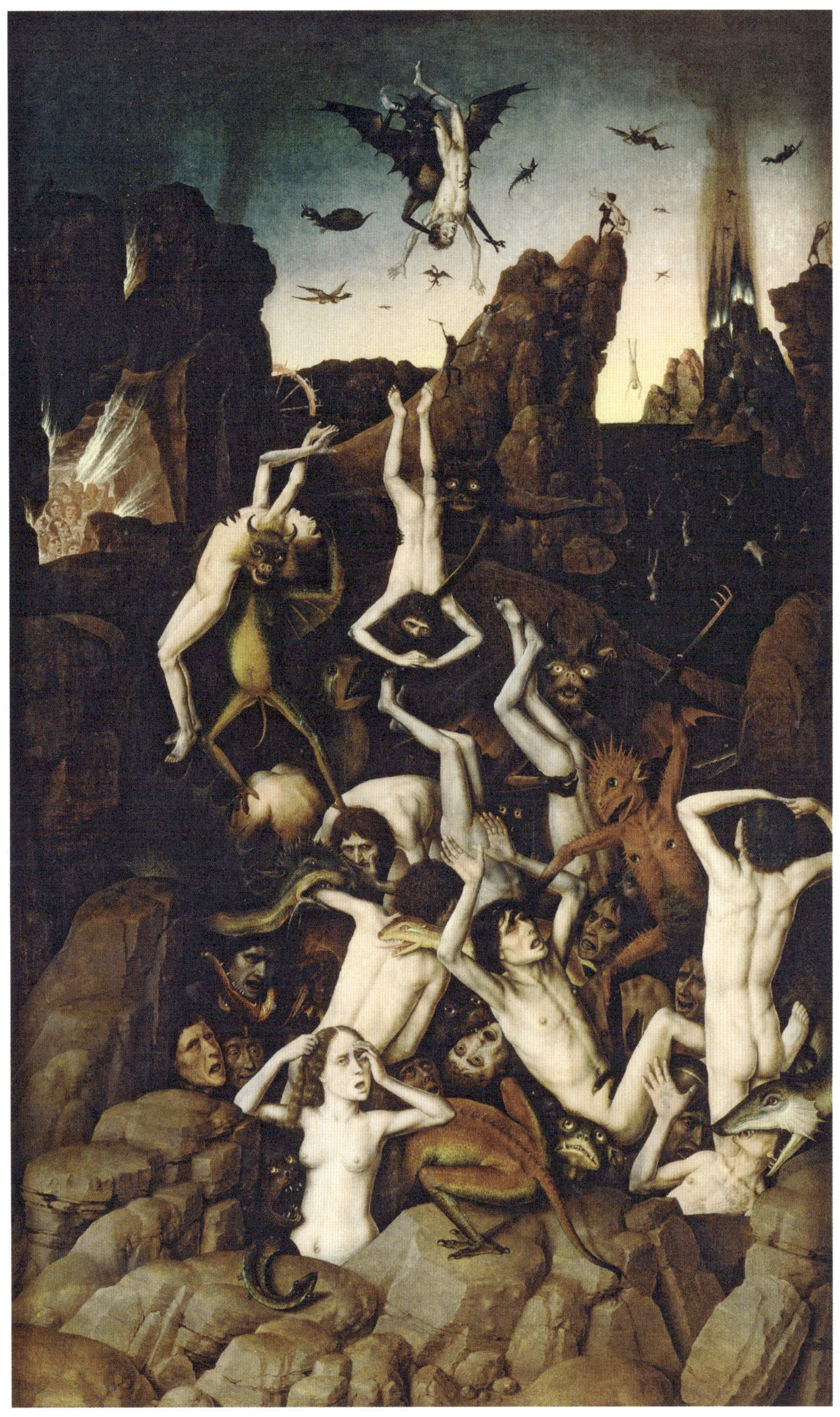

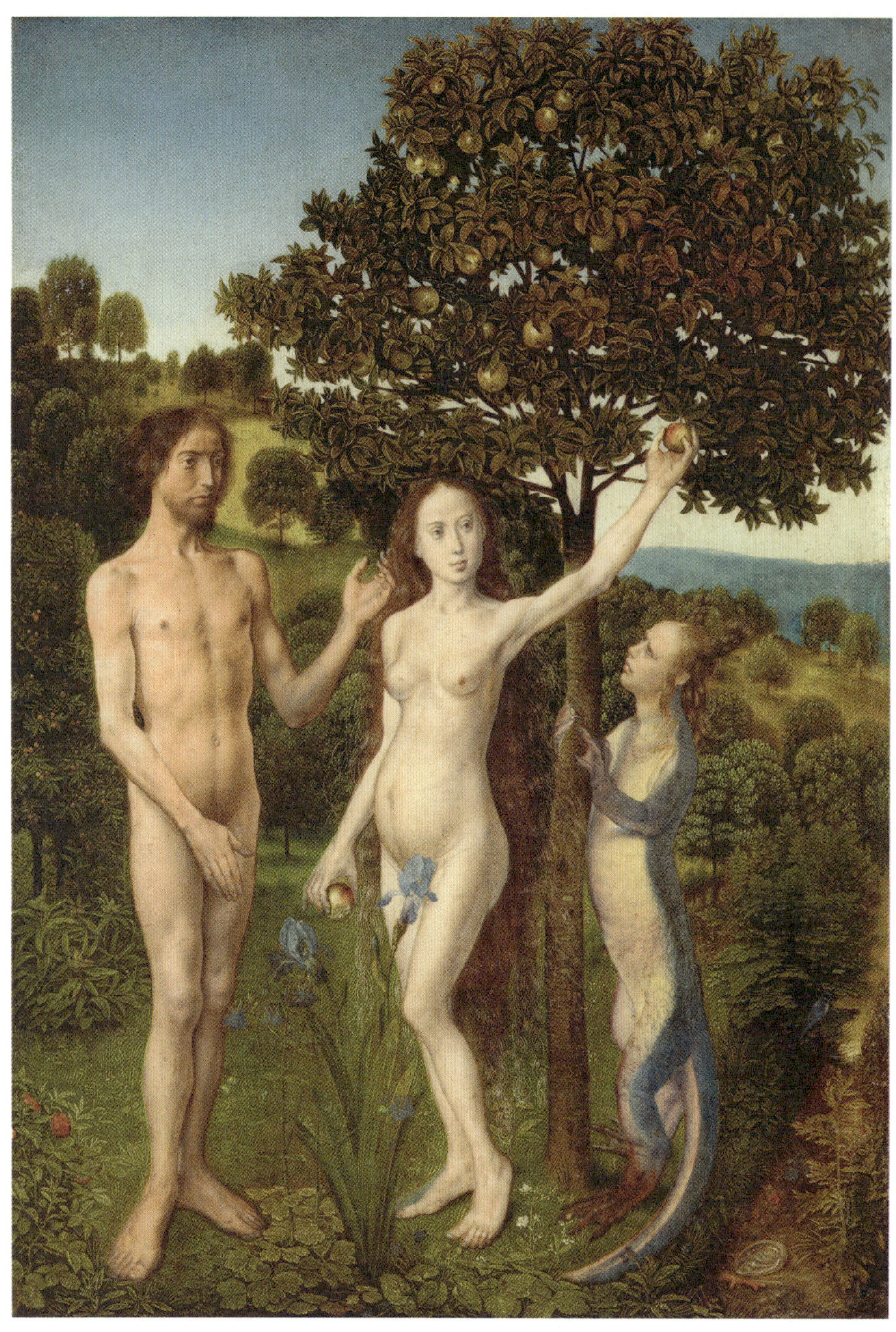

Hugo van der Goes,
Fall of Man, c. 1470–75.

* * *

The serpent that slithers round the apple tree in Eden has a woman's upper half emerging from a reptilian tail. This is a rare example of Bosch borrowing from an earlier artist. Hugo van der Goes, the painter whose *Adoration of the Shepherds* was shipped to Florence by Tommaso Portinari in the 1480s, had painted a precise vision of the tempting serpent. In his *Fall of Man*, the Devil is a hybrid of human and reptile, more salamander or monitor lizard than snake, out of which a woman's head emerges. Van der Goes follows a medieval tradition, but his verisimilitude in oils gives it disturbing intensity.

It is not completely surprising to learn that Hugo van der Goes had mental health problems. At the peak of his highly successful career he experienced a spiritual crisis and entered the Rood Klooster (the 'Red Cloister'), a monastery near Brussels. He still painted, and entertained high-ranking visitors from as far afield as Scotland, whose king commissioned an altarpiece from him. But on his way back from a trip outside the Cloister, recorded the medic of the monastery, Gaspar Ofhuys, poor Hugo was 'seized by a strange illness of his mind'. It took the form of a conviction that he was damned, and he had to be restrained from killing himself. The prior tried to heal, or at least soothe, him by breaking the monastery's ascetic rules and getting musicians to play and sing sweet harmonies. But it didn't work. According to Ofhuys, Hugo 'uttered unceasing laments about being doomed and sentenced to damnation ... he continued to rave and pronounce himself a child of perdition.'[2]

Hugo's certainty that his sins lay so heavy on him that he would spend eternity in hell is not so different from the pessimism that unbalances Bosch's art. There's no record that Bosch ever experienced a collapse. On the contrary, all the documentary evidence paints a picture of an affluent burgher who married well and was the life and soul of the swan banquets. Instead, it is Bosch's art that is 'mad'. His creativity is a crazed fugue in which the wood has ears, the fields have eyes, and an ice-skating bird delivers the post. The same fear that paralyses Hugo consumes Bosch. As he makes explicit in *The Haywain*, he is not persuaded by the remedies of the church. Just as the abbot's musicians could not calm Hugo, the late medieval religious institutions that offer salvation in return for chastity, charity, communal kindness, and even the purchase of pardons and relics don't reassure Bosch that anyone is going to heaven. The world looks to him utterly hellish, and hellbound.

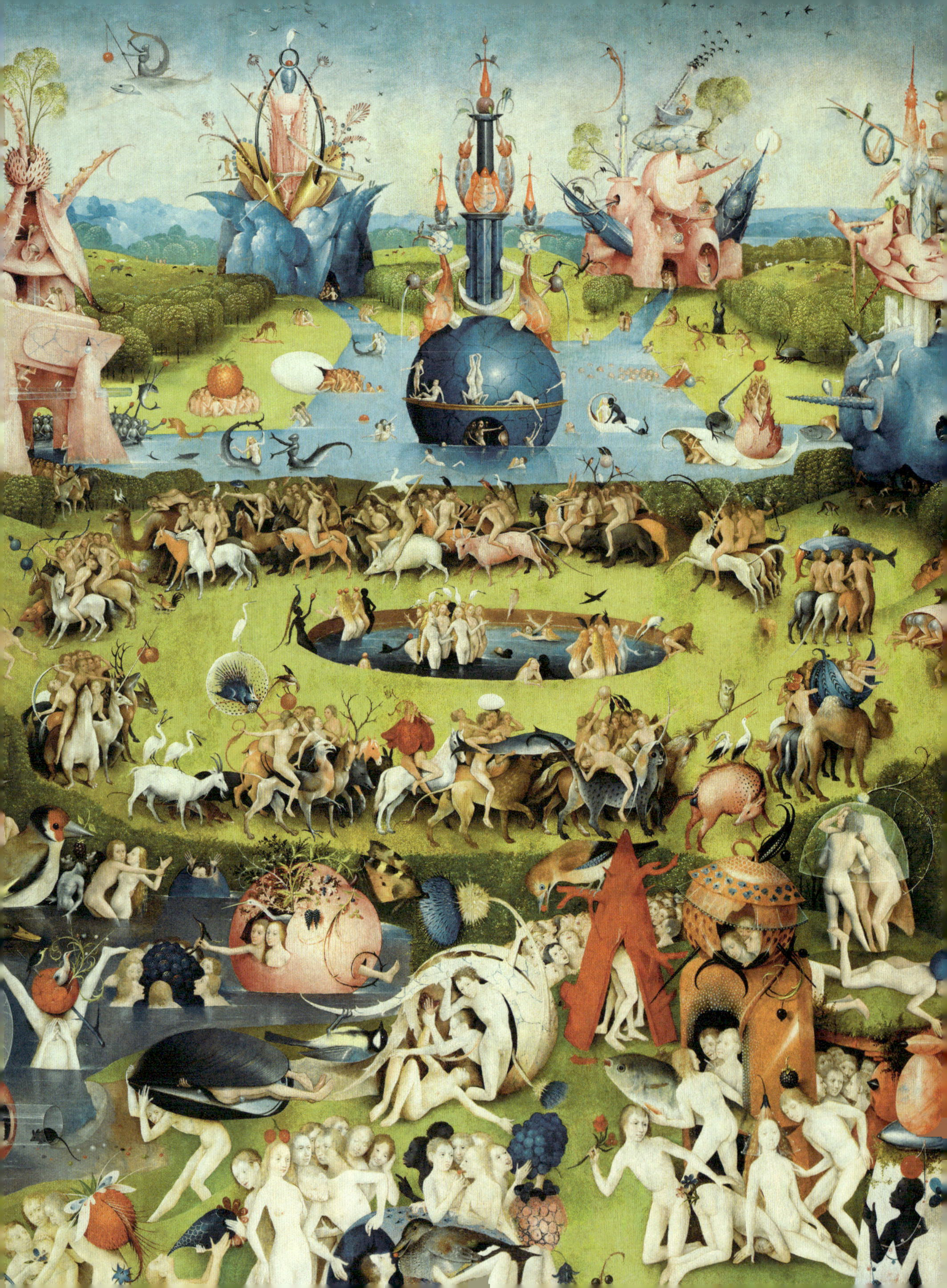

7

The Garden of Earthly Delights

The church gets a rough ride from Bosch. In the foreground of *The Haywain*, a monk sits in a comfy chair savouring his drink, attended by a doting nun; they couldn't care less about the doom of humanity. In the *Ship of Fools*, a nun playing the lute and a tonsured monk sing lustily together (p. 152). Monks and nuns also kiss and play together in the *Last Judgment*. And in the most awe-inspiring of all his visions, a naked man tries to escape the attentions of a pig in a nun's habit.

When the *Garden of Earthly Delights* – the great triptych that contains that last phantasm – is closed, you see the earth floating like a bubble in space (p. 153). God the Creator looks down from his spherical spaceship on the reverse of the wings, shaping a world out of nothingness: 'For he spoke and it was done,' says the Latin inscription.[1] Broiling black and grey clouds flow above a monochrome, circular island surrounded by water that fills the bottom part of the earthly sphere. The land is hilly and healthy, with clumps of trees dividing tranquil meadows. Sensual structures sprout near the water's edge.

Hieronymus Bosch, *Garden of Earthly Delights* (detail), 1490–1500.

On the right-hand wing we read: 'He commanded and it stood fast.' Yet the *Garden of Earthly Delights* stuns eye and brain with worlds that seem anything but stable. Open, this physically imposing triptych (pp. 154–55) depicts Christ

Hieronymus Bosch,
Ship of Fools,
c. 1475–1500.

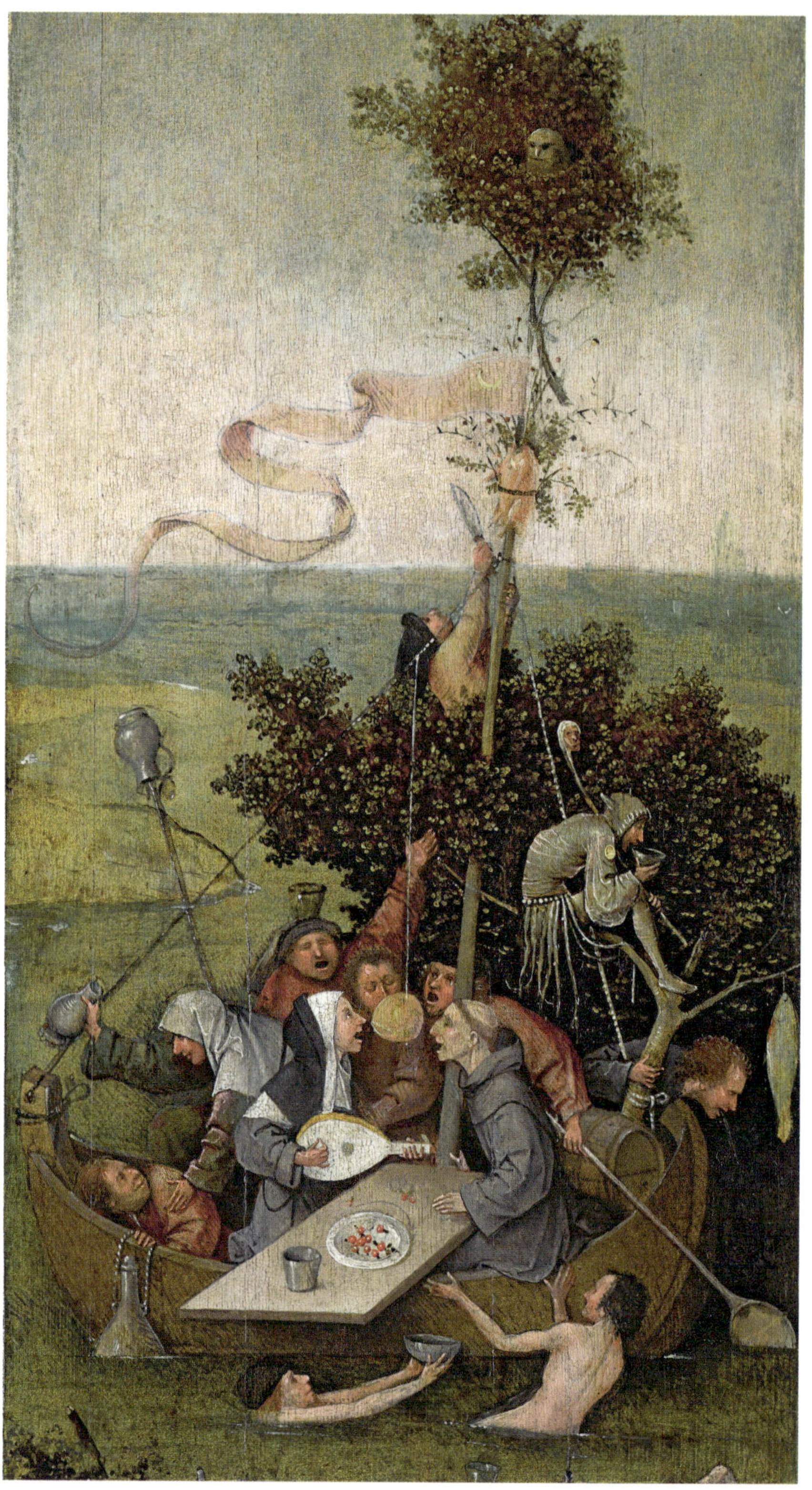

with Adam and Eve in the left panel and hell on the right, while in the centre is a staggering realm of carnality and bliss. There, more naked people than it's possible to count engage in a communal frolic among gargantuan fruit and outlandish architecture, without any apparent awareness that sin or damnation even exist.

The earliest description of the painting was written in 1517 by a cleric called Antonio de Beatis, who was engaged as part of a cardinal's entourage specifically to produce an account of the long, leisurely journey they were taking north of the Alps. His employer, Cardinal Luigi d'Aragona, may not have been the best of Christians: according to the *Novellas* of the gossipy storyteller Matteo Bandello, he ordered the murders of his sister and her children. The case was immortalized in John Webster's bloody late Renaissance tragedy *The Duchess of Malfi*.

In Brussels the party visited the palace of the powerful aristocratic dynasty the counts of Nassau, where Antonio was left stupefied by an outlandish painting, with its

> various bizarre images, with pictures of seas, skies, forests, fields and many other things; some [people] come out of a mussel shell; others shit cranes;

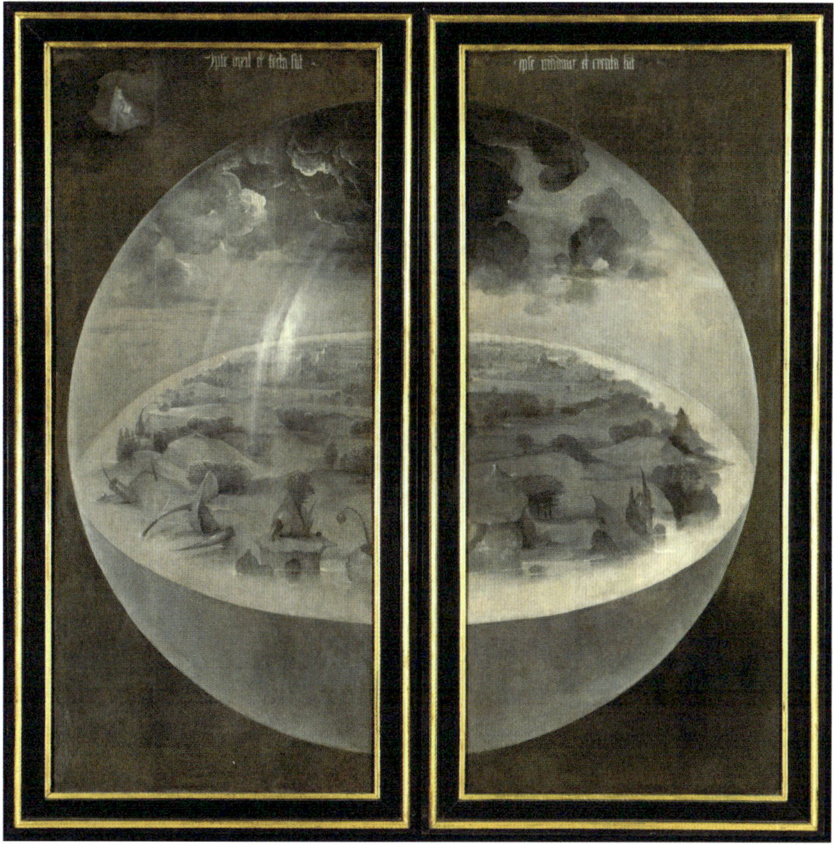

Hieronymus Bosch, *Garden of Earthly Delights* (with panels closed), 1490–1500.

Hieronymus Bosch, *Garden of Earthly Delights*, 1490–1500.

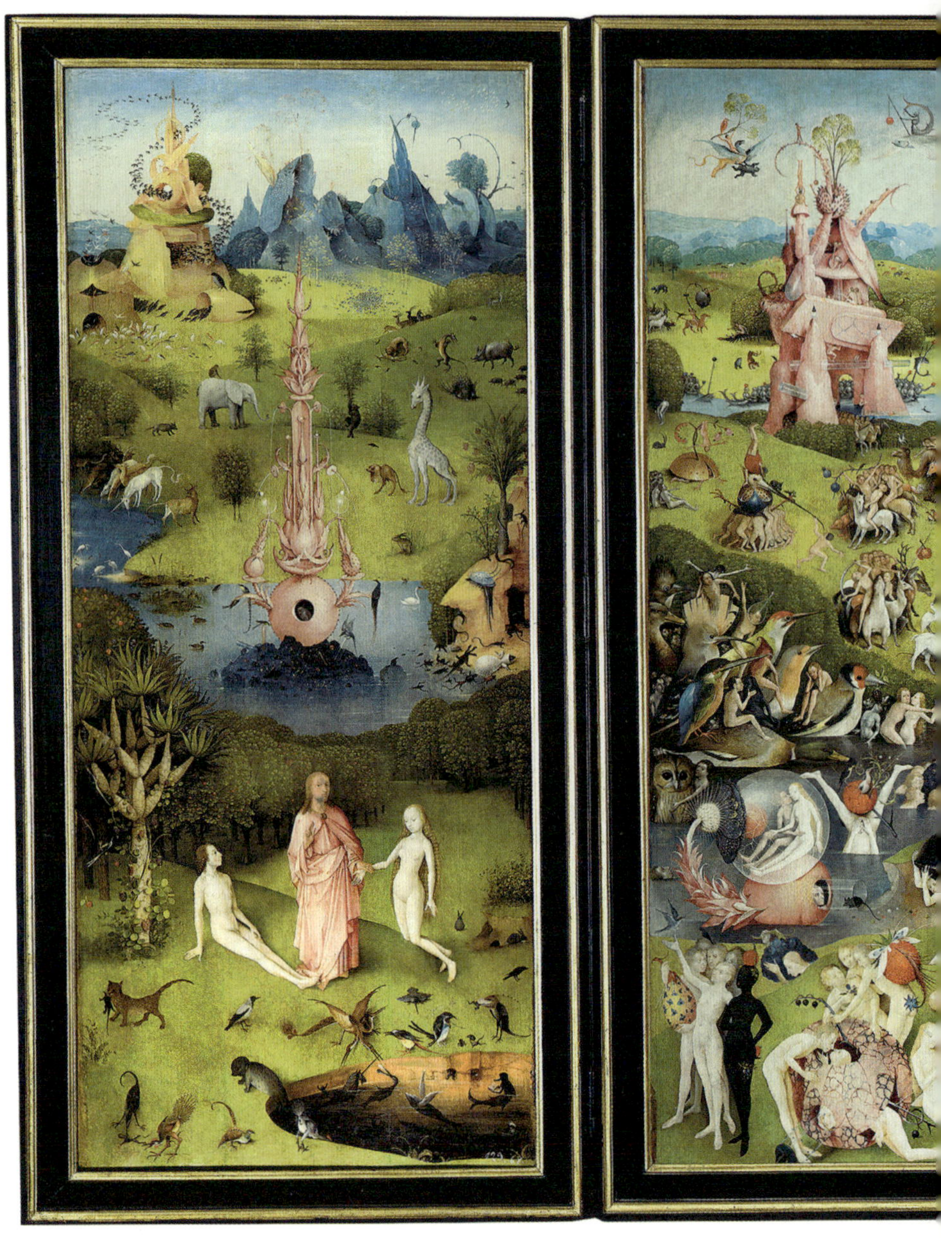

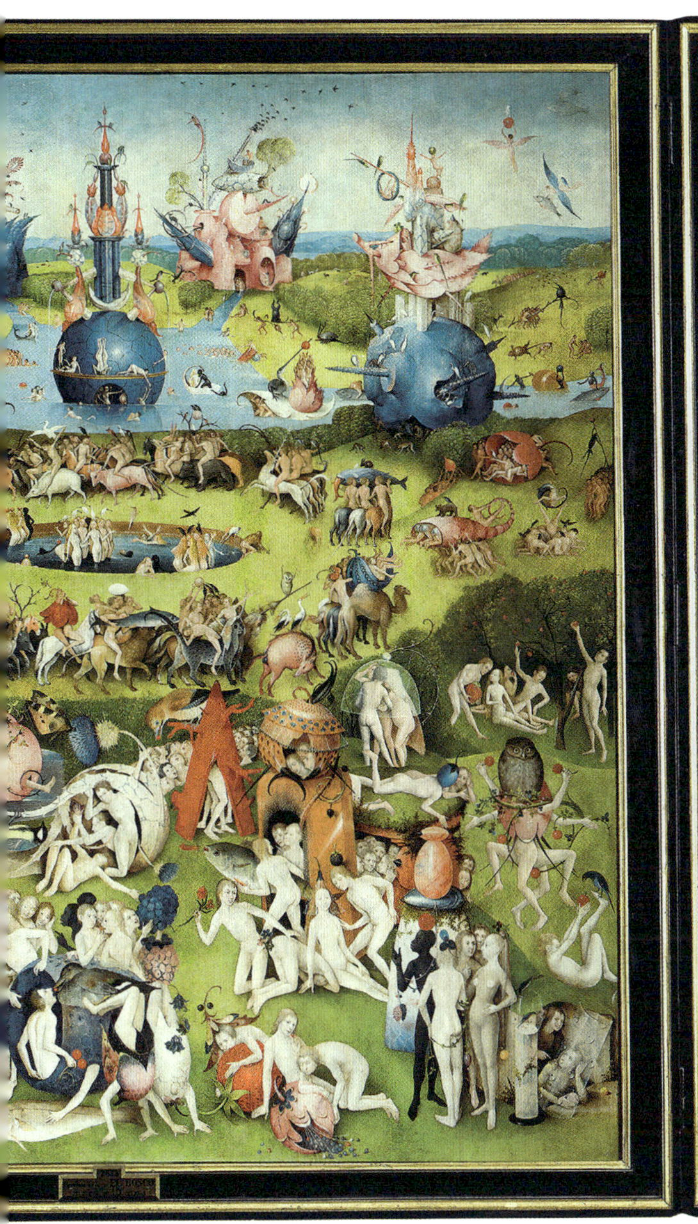

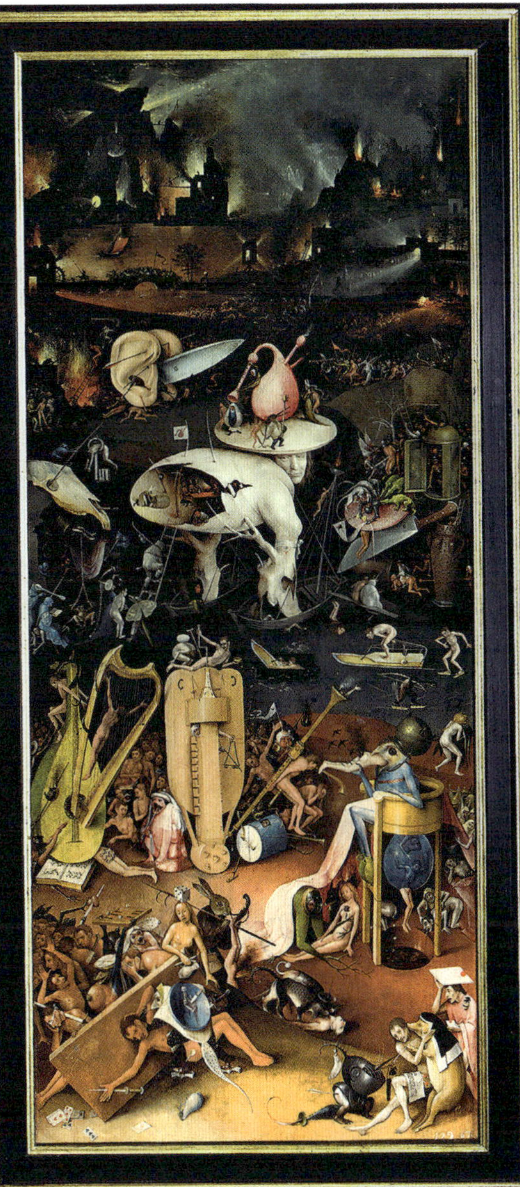

men and women and whites and blacks in various actions and poses; birds and beasts of every kind and with much naturalism; things so charming and fantastic that they could not be properly described in any way to those who do not know them.[2]

The image of a nude emerging from a giant mussel shell is easy to recognize, even if the people who excrete birds are harder to find (on the contrary, a bird excretes a man). De Beatis does not know it as the *Garden of Earthly Delights*, a title it acquired later, nor does he seem to know who painted it; he was writing just a year after Bosch had died in 1516. Yet he sees this delirious masterpiece with great clarity. The first details he singles out are likely to be taken for granted by us today: the 'seas, skies, forests, fields' are for us a mere background for all the action – nude animal-riding, giant strawberry-guzzling, a man being fondled by a pig-nun.

Yet as Antonio saw through Renaissance eyes, Bosch maps out his creation in convincing landscapes. Bodies of water, woodlands, greenery and mountains recede to a distant horizon. As de Beatis observes, Bosch depicts everything with great *naturalità*: robin redbreasts, owls, semi-tropical trees, ears, cooking pots, pigs, glass tubes and bagpipes are meticulously observed in three-dimensional solidity even as they are absurdly enlarged or combined (the giant severed ear has a blade through it; the brass pot is worn as a hat by a bird-monster). In a way, the *Garden of Earthly Delights* is an unholy marriage of a landscape and still life, their different scales colliding to breed monsters.

Yet it is also a vision of all human life: 'men and women and whites and blacks', as Antonio puts it, cavort together on the orgiastic central panel. As they bathe in a central sea and climb on towers that look as if they have grown from bodily organs, these revellers look rapturously ignorant of sin, gorged on prodigiously scaled fruits and intoxicated by unabashed desire. This early tourist appears to have been as excited and nonplussed as we are by it all.

* * *

One stable fact about this enigmatic marvel is that it must have been painted after Christopher Columbus sailed to unheard-of realms. A tree in Bosch's Eden with spiky leaves and bulbous branches is a dragon tree from the Canary Islands off the north-west coast of Africa, conquered by Spain in the 15th century with catastrophic results for the indigenous Guanches people. Bosch's depiction has an unmistakable visual source: the same tree with weird tubes and hard leaves is depicted in the *Nuremberg Chronicle*, published in December 1493. He must, therefore, have painted his delirious masterpiece in 1494 at the earliest, two years after Columbus made landfall in the New World, when stories were circulating of naked people who lived in vulnerable innocence in far-off lands.

Is it fanciful to see the central panel of the *Garden of Earthly Delights* as a dream of that New World, an apparition of a terrestrial paradise? There are still many art historians who uphold the moralizing view of the 17th-century Spanish friar José de Sigüenza. He saw this treasure of the Spanish royal collection at the Escorial – Philip II's palace and monastery complex – as a stern satire on those who dedicate themselves to ephemeral joys and forget 'that brief, insignificant pleasure will be transformed into eternal, incurable and implacable wrath'.[3] So the naked feast at the heart of the *Garden of Earthly Delights* is just another of Bosch's epic tragicomedies of fallen humanity, another haywain to hell.

Yet if you compare crucial details of this painting with *The Haywain* and other depictions of human sin by Bosch, it's abundantly clear that he is doing something different this time. This is a vision of another country, where the customs are different, the fruit bigger, where there is no madness or sin because the concepts do not exist. The pig-nun, the most outrageous of Bosch's anti-clerical satires, appears in *Hell*. But why isn't she in the central panel if it shows the vanity of our human carnival? For the middle, 'earthly' panels of other Bosch triptychs are crammed with such grotesques. The *Last Judgment*, *The Haywain* and the *Ship of Fools* all associate monks, nuns, bishops, and even the pope with earthly corruption in their centre panels.

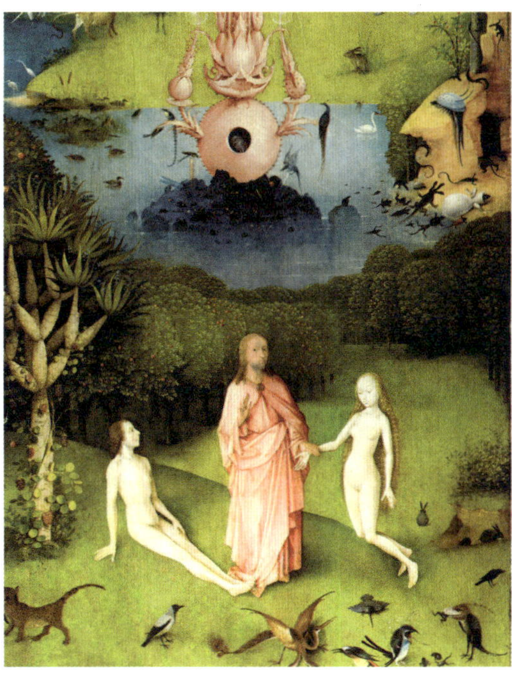

Hieronymus Bosch, *Garden of Earthly Delights* (detail), 1490–1500.

Hieronymus Bosch, *Garden of Earthly Delights* (detail), 1490–1500.

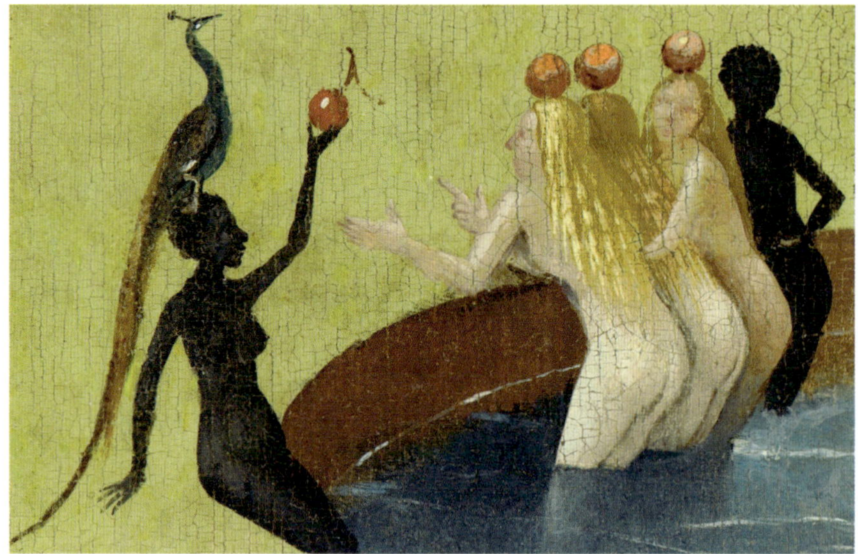

There isn't one tonsured monastic head or nun's habit in the frantic party at the middle of the *Garden of Earthly Delights*. There are mermaids and mermen, black and white people, bird-headed humans, bareback riders – but no clergy. Clerical misdemeanours are so much a part of Bosch's landscapes of sin that their absence has to be significant.

And there are other differences from Bosch's typical painted worlds. Where are the objects that usually fill his earthly landscapes – the ice skates, clogs, steel helmets, iron cauldrons, wheels and knives he lifts out of daily life and puts to strange new uses? The people here simply do not have – or need – these things. Instead they live off the stupendous bounty of nature, which supplies apples to pluck from trees and grapes to take from the beak of a giant bird.

They don't have windmills either. These familiar sights of north-western Europe often appear in Bosch's landscapes; so do inns, cottages, stables. But no such familiar structures appear in the green, generous natural world where these nudes live without shame, hunger or toil. The explanation is unavoidable. We are not in Europe anymore.

* * *

Enlarged and transformed pieces of everyday technology do appear in the *Garden of Earthly Delights*, but they constitute hell. *The Haywain* shows how close Bosch felt to hell, and it is there that we see the familiar apparatus of Bosch's universe. One poor soul is crucified on a giant harp – a motif borrowed from the *Last Judgment*. Another man is tied to a colossal lute. A bird creature with a cauldron for a helmet sits on a raised wooden chair through which it excretes a man from a bubble. Ice skates, boats, a giant knife, an overturned table, playing cards, a drum, bagpipes – all the paraphernalia of sinful workaday life that he usually puts in his terrestrial landscapes appears here. The landscape too is familiar. There are bridges and buildings, as you would see in the Netherlands, lit up by the fires of a dreadful war as armies are silhouetted against the night.

The *Hell* panel is Bosch's own world. It is full of material possessions that turn on their owners. Bosch is not just here in spirit. In the centre of the panel is a hollow, bony, arboreal structure into which denizens of hell climb via a ladder to indulge in ghastly, futile pursuits. A wry face peers round from it with the ironic intimacy of a self-portrait.

* * *

If hell looks like home and the land of the naked fruit-eaters a distant earthly paradise, the key to this phantasmagoria may lie in Eden. The pristine landscape of the left-hand panel, taking shape from blue and gold mountains in the distance, resolving itself into a pastoral realm full of newborn beasts, is the source of all earthly life. And not just the kind you would meet in 's-Hertogenbosch, or even in Antwerp. An elephant and a giraffe are prominent among the novel creatures, not to mention a unicorn and beasts crawling out of the water like evolving forms. A leopard carries its prey in its mouth near Adam, who sits under the dragon tree. So this is not just a random borrowing from the *Nuremberg Chronicle*: Bosch has copied it because he wants to incorporate the variety of plants and animals that now fill different parts of the world. In the same vein he peoples the central panel with black as well as white nudes. Black and white women bathe together in a pool, and a white woman is embraced by a black man on a boat.

The 'nakedness' of New World peoples was one of the first pieces of news about them to reach Europeans. In 1493 Columbus sent a letter to Ferdinand and Isabella concerning the Caribbean islands he had claimed for them, describing how

> the inhabitants of both sexes of this and of all the other islands I have seen, or of which I have any knowledge, always go as naked as they came into the world, except that some of the women cover their private parts with leaves or branches, or a veil of cotton.[4]

It was an observation given greater prominence at the start of the 1500s by the Florentine New World explorer Amerigo Vespucci, whose account was a widely pirated European-wide bestseller.

Columbus in his letter grows lyrical about the island of Juana – Cuba – with its 'health-giving rivers' and 'lofty mountains'. In fact,

> All these islands are very beautiful, and of quite different shapes; easy to be traversed, and full of the greatest variety of trees reaching to the stars ... looking as green and lovely as they are wont to be in the month of May in Spain. Some of them were in leaf, and some in fruit; each flourishing in the condition its nature required. The nightingale was singing and various other little birds, when I was rambling among them in the month of November. There are also ... seven or eight kinds of palms, which as readily surpass ours in height and beauty as do all the other trees, herbs, and fruits. There are also wonderful pinewoods, fields, and extensive meadows.[5]

A garden of earthly delights, no less.

A woodcut, also from 1493, has King Ferdinand pointing to Columbus, who is about to make landfall on a coast where Caribbean islanders – a naked, close-packed, longhaired crowd – are either gathering or fleeing. It looks like a kind of Fall: Europeans are transgressing on an unspoiled Eden, and Columbus is the serpent. In Bosch's earthly paradise there is no Columbus. These naked people have no visitors, no conquistadors. Except perhaps us, as we look at them without their knowing.

Columbus saw the New Worlders as benighted, in need of conversion and easy to conquer. The more intellectual Vespucci saw a potential superiority in their physical grace. Both men and women were fleet of foot and superlative swimmers: 'and herein they have a very great advantage over us Christians'.[6] They also have no interest in riches – an obvious source for More's *Utopia*. Vespucci deems their ethos to be 'Epicurean', and that pleasure-centred philosophy gets a wild spin in Bosch's primitive playground.[7]

Bosch's new-found land is a parade of ingenious ways to enjoy yourself. Lovers float in a translucent bubble, disappear into a coral teepee, consume immense shellfish. They swim, ride and climb in childlike fun. If there are no European-style houses, the horizon is dominated by pink and blue towers with spindling, tentacular protrusions and moist, shiny surfaces. These are not man-made structures. In this warm and sunny paradise, fed by pure blue water, the earth itself grows living buildings to shelter and amuse the lucky inhabitants.

What does Bosch think of all this? The same face that peers at us from the empty tree-man in hell looks out of a grotto at the bottom right of the orgy, pointing at a woman who toys with fruit. He may be reminding us of Eve and the apple. That doesn't mean this paradise of uninhibited innocents is a fraud; it's just that Bosch himself doesn't belong there. Innocence exists only for the innocent.

There is no Fall in Bosch's painting. Eve is not being tempted, nor do we see her and Adam driven out of paradise. Instead, a God with the merciful face of

Christ introduces the first woman to Adam. The naked man looks at her with bland, happy interest.

* * *

There is no hint of classical learning in any of Bosch's works. His naked people owe nothing to the classical nude. And yet his depiction of a prelapsarian paradise of free fruit and free love has a lot in common with the dream of Arcadian bliss that was taking shape in Italy's classicist art. In fact, Bosch had a soul brother in Florence, an artist for whom the ancient world was an escape from the wretchedness of contemporary life.

Anyway, this is how Vasari portrays the painter Piero di Cosimo. Born in 1462, Piero seems to have had characteristics in common with Leonardo da Vinci. Vasari even attributes to him Leonardo's method of staring at walls until he hallucinated. Except it's much more disgusting: Piero studied globs of phlegm. He

> would sometimes stop to gaze at a wall against which sick people had been for a long time discharging their spittle, and from this he would picture to himself battles of horsemen, and the most fantastic cities and widest landscapes that were ever seen, and he did the same with the clouds in the sky.[8]

Piero's apparitions – armed horsemen, unreal cities, vast landscapes – are distinctly Boschian. Such eccentricity was typical of this oddball. He was nervous and anti-social, locking himself in his house and letting the garden go to seed. People thought him 'a madman'. He was so lost in his work that he lived on boiled eggs, cooking them in a big pot in batches of fifty. Noises offended him: he couldn't stand to hear children laugh, men cough, bells ring, monks chant.

These last two suggest that Piero was uncomfortable with the Christian world itself. As the great cultural historian Johan Huizinga observed, the omnipresence of church bells and their domination of a soundscape that lacked competing noises is one of the differences we need to remember as we try to imagine life in medieval Europe: 'Everyone knew their individual tones and instantly recognized their meaning. People never became indifferent to these sounds.'[9]

Vasari claims in his life of Piero di Cosimo that he has spoken to 'certain old men' in Florence who remember this eccentric figure. The impression of an artist retreating from society, even from Christendom itself, may reflect reputation rather than reality, but it's how his contemporaries perceived him.

Piero di Cosimo's favourite subject matter is classical mythology. In it, he finds haunting images of grief and loss: a female centaur cradling her dying love; a goat-legged satyr kneeling sorrowfully over a dead nymph; animals fleeing a forest fire. He inhabits this other world in his mind, setting the loves and

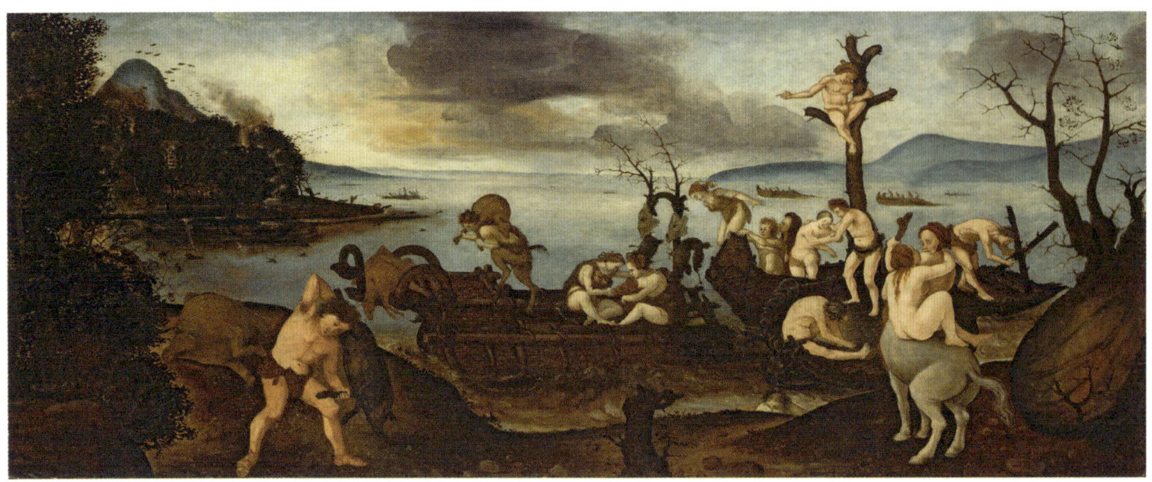

Piero di Cosimo, *Return from the Hunt*, c. 1494–1500.

battles of half-human, half-animal beings in palpably real pastoral landscapes. Its dreamlike conviction may owe something to the method Vasari says Piero used, discerning forms through half-closed eyes in a pool of spittle. A dense fighting mass of figures in his painting the *Battle of the Centaurs* congeals like a stain in the centre of a landscape.

Like Bosch in the central panel of the *Garden of Earthly Delights*, Piero pictures a simpler, less 'civilized' world. This, too, is a fantasy, animated by the discovery of the Americas. Piero explores the idea that ancient peoples had once lived in a purer, healthier way, close to nature, free from civilization's sophistication and decadence. The idea of a prehistorical Golden Age recurred and developed in classical literature, beginning with the early Greek poet Hesiod's *Works and Days*; the earth was then so fertile that it produced crops without labour, and the people of the Golden Age spent their time feasting and were never tired. The Golden Age gave way to a series of other Ages, of Silver, Bronze and Iron, and to different peoples who were now tainted by violence and corruption. Worst of all is the current Iron Age, where people live in misery and toil, tell lies and violate every social convention. This model was refashioned by the Roman poet Ovid in his *Metamorphoses*. He adds a detail that would be fitting for the late 15th century: navigation was an invention of the Iron Age.

Such classical texts now seemed substantiated by encounters with the peoples of the New World; both Columbus and Vespucci comment on the absence of iron. Bosch takes care to show iron and metal technology – even something as basic as a kitchen knife – only in the *Hell* panel of the *Garden of Earthly Delights*. Hell belongs in the modern Iron Age; the naked paradise is a Golden Age.

In the *Return from the Hunt*, painted in about 1494–1500, Piero shows early people, nude or clad in furs, gathered on a shore. It's not so far from how a 21st-century archaeologist might picture a community of hunter-gatherers – except that some are satyrs and centaurs. A fully human woman has jumped on her centaur lover's back to embrace him, her fleshy hips straddling him as her bare breasts press against his muscular torso. Meanwhile a satyr carries a dead deer for the communal supper, two women in furs converse, and another group disembarks from one of two boats. Lashed together with vines, their hulls made of wicker, and one of them decorated with animal skulls, these inventions are ingenious attempts to visualize 'primitive' craft. More boats, resembling canoes, can be seen in the distance. The sea-going vessels encountered by the first Europeans since the Vikings to arrive in the Americas were pictured in one early woodcut as if they had been Italian galleys. Much later, the English traveller John White would more faithfully depict Americans fishing from a bark canoe. Piero does a plausible job here of picturing New World watercraft.

This is a romance of the New World seen through the myths of the ancient one. Yet Piero is not naive. The pendant to this painting, a *Hunting Scene*, shows primal people and their half-bestial friends doing dreadful violence to nature. A man holds a wounded lion by its tail so that his satyr associate can beat it to death; another man tries to strangle a bear. The satyrs are more accomplished in tool use than the men: while humans grab animals with their bare hands or leap on their backs, two bearded, goat-legged characters enter the scene in more meditative poses, armed with the latest in wooden clubs. The beasts have been driven out of their forest by a fire.

Fifteen centuries earlier, Lucretius in his philosophical poem *On the Nature of Things* suggested it was by seeing such natural catastrophes that humans learned about fire. This was the start of a more complex society: 'As time went on, they sought to change their former way of life by new methods including fire.'[10] Spurning superstition and following Democritus's theory of atoms, Lucretius offers a rational, materialist account of human development, reasoning that early

Piero di Cosimo, *Forest Fire*, c. 1505.

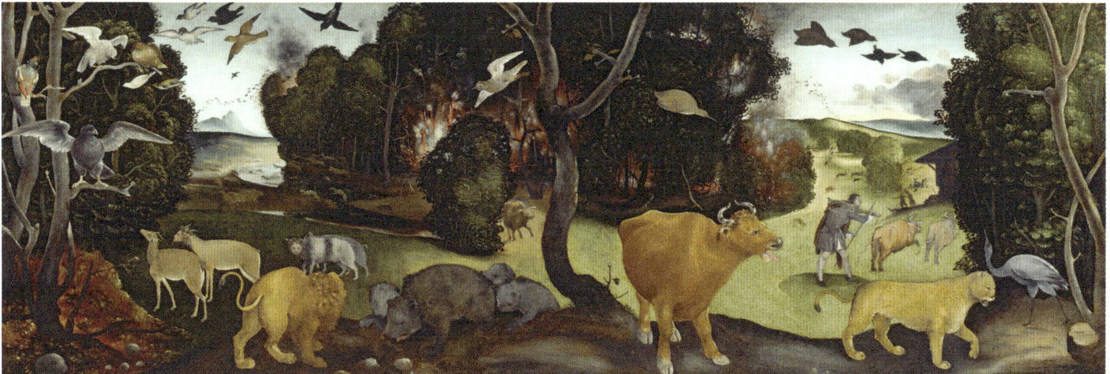

society gradually became more organized and technological. Piero appears to have read enough Lucretius to know about forest fires in his account of human evolution. It's the central theme of his painting the *Forest Fire* (previous page), in which a glowing red and yellow blaze in a smear of woodland sends a variety of beautifully observed species fleeing in dumb panic.

Yet it is never a good idea to be pedantic in identifying the 'sources' of Renaissance art. Piero di Cosimo is not an illustrator of texts but an expressive artist. His paintings do have strong echoes of Lucretius, but whereas the Roman writer says there never were such half-human monsters as centaurs or chimeras, Piero can't get enough of these mythical beings. In the *Battle of Lapiths and Centaurs* he depicts the moment early people fell out with their semi-equine allies. The Lapiths, a human tribe, invited the centaurs to a wedding, but the wine was a toxic goad to lust and violence for creatures so close to the irrationality of beasts. In Piero's painting they go wild and the Lapiths answer in kind. People have weapons now. They not only batter the centaurs with clubs, but smash them with heavy picnic-ware and cooking gear. It is all desperately sad. You sense Piero's melancholy at this fall from grace. He feels it as a tragic loss of innocence.

* * *

The classically informed pastorals of Piero di Cosimo may seem remote from the apocalyptic havoc of Bosch, even if they were both inspired by the 'naked peoples' of the New World. Yet a lost ephemeral creation by the Florentine artist has a suggestive affinity for the *Garden of Earthly Delights*.

Vasari's elderly informants told him another Piero anecdote: that at carnival time he shut himself away, not at home but in a government-run workspace, the 'Room of the Pope', next to the church of Santa Maria Novella. There he secretly sawed, hammered and painted away to create a ceremonial float for the carnival parade. Finally he unleashed

> an enormous car drawn by buffaloes, black all over and painted with skeletons and white crosses; and upon the highest point of the car stood a colossal figure of Death, scythe in hand, and right round the car were a number of covered tombs; and in all the places where the procession halted for the chanting of dirges, these tombs opened, and from them issued figures draped in black cloth, upon which were painted all the bones of a skeleton.[11]

Piero's float may have been a satirical vision of doom at a moment in the early 1510s when the Medici were threatening to overwhelm the Florentine Republic. It was also a macabre joke that went down well at the festival of carnival, when the social and moral order was turned upside down and pent-up tensions were transformed into deranged comedy. The Florentine Renaissance may seem like an elite culture of great refinement, but Piero di Cosimo was not too civilized to provide a preposterous entertainment in the spirit of Bosch. Their worlds were connected by carnival, a regionally varying yet pan-European ritual.

The ultimate artist of carnival would be Pieter Bruegel the Elder. This glorious 16th-century painter provides the most comprehensive visual document of Europe's festive customs in the *Battle between Carnival and Lent*, with all its masks, pancakes, beggars, plays, drink and mock war. Bruegel was a brilliant interpreter of his northern predecessor. His art is full of structural echoes and reworkings of Bosch's madcap triptychs. In fact, his painting of a Flemish carnival can be seen as a more homely version of the *Garden of Earthly Delights*. Through this Bruegelian lens, Bosch's upside-down vision, in which Christian scenes of Eden and hell are confronted by a vast tableau of riotous sensuality, is itself a battle between carnival and Lent. Bruegel helps us decode the carnivalesque in Bosch.

In life Bosch was an ultra-respectable figure, his piety on record. In art he mocks with abandon monks, nuns, and higher clergy all the way to the Vatican. He unleashes perplexing, outrageous inversions and distortions of the 'real' world: the kinds of jokes people acted out at carnival time. An old woman looks out of the window of her house in the *Temptation of St Anthony*: its door lintel is the naked bottom of a giant man. Such absurdities appear everywhere in his works. Even *The Haywain*, his grimmest religious statement, can be seen as a huge jest, its depiction of a manic crowd obsessed with a wagon of hay just as laughable as Piero di Cosimo's Car of Death.

Bosch may have been a pillar of the community in 's-Hertogenbosh, but his scabrous, eye-popping humour is nothing if not carnivalesque. The *Garden of Earthly Delights* is the most spectacular depiction of carnival pleasures in Renaissance art, a collective dive into food, drink and copulation. It is also a representation of the longings to which this rollicking festival gave expression.

The clue to its roots in popular culture is offered by the food fantasy it taps into. A group of naked people gather round a giant strawberry as if worshipping it; there are colossal oysters, an infinity of apples. Such delicious gratification is the stuff of folk tales manifested in the 'Land of Cockaigne', a dreamworld of plenty without the need for labour. Such seventh heavens could be found throughout Europe and often adopted a flavour of the region. In a poem from medieval Ireland, 'Aisling Meic Conglinne' (The Vision of MacConglinne), the hero is granted an apparition of a country made entirely out of food, including bacon, butter and cheese. That such mirages could be framed as a condemnation of gluttony makes no difference: these are yearnings from the bellies of peasants who knew what it was like when food was scarce.

At real northern carnivals, people guzzled pancakes and roast meat and quaffed beer. They also made obscene jokes. Bosch simply takes it one step further. Everyone is naked, and everyone is making love, resting from it or will soon be at it. His world-turned-upside-down is a distant place, free of European tools, weapons and rules. From what Bosch hears, in the New World it's carnival all the time. Who knows? Perhaps there is wisdom in such folly.

* * *

Albrecht Dürer was less convinced that primitive characters deserve respect. In his engraving *Hercules at the Crossroad*, published in about 1498, a satyr and his lover have been surprised in their rustic retreat by the musclebound hero and a female companion. These moral vigilantes are about to beat the lustful goatish creature and the woman he has tempted with heavy wooden clubs. The satyr has his hand on his own weapon, an animal jawbone, but doesn't seem to be making a move: he simply sits there, waiting to be battered to death. It is a confrontation of virtue and vice, between the higher faculties of civilization and the sexual abandon of savages – but it does not take place in far-off America or a mythic Arcadia. This is the Europe of Dürer's own day. The punishment is happening in a mountainous German landscape. Beyond the clump of trees where the satyr and nymph skulk, a road leads to a hilltop castle. Cupid the love god runs away towards a river flowing from the distant hills. We might be in the foothills of the Alps.

This scene is Dürer's invention, not a specific classical myth. It expresses feelings that are very much his own. And the longer you look, the more ambivalent Dürer seems. The artist's advocacy of slaying satyrs, subduing the lower urges that their stinking hairy legs and horns embody and making of yourself a fortress of chastity like the city on the hill, is undercut by the way his picture entertains the eye with a male and female nude. Hercules is naked, his buttocks on view, the rich musculature of his back and legs eagerly explored in supple ink. The satyr's bride too is a sumptuous nude, her breasts exposed, her curvaceous form framed by foliage. There are emotional as well as erotic ambiguities. The satyr and nymph don't seem to be doing any harm. He may be part beast, his huge hoofed leg full of animal power, but his face is passive and fatalist. Does lust in the bushes really deserve such violent retribution?

When Dürer created this image he was wrestling with his own tortured infatuation with pagan myth, classical nudes and the sensuality of the south. In the mid-1490s – probably between summer 1494 and the summer of the following year – the young Nuremberg craftsman made the tough mountain journey across the Alps to Venice. He had just married Agnes Frey, daughter

Albrecht Dürer, *Hercules at the Crossroad*, c. 1498.

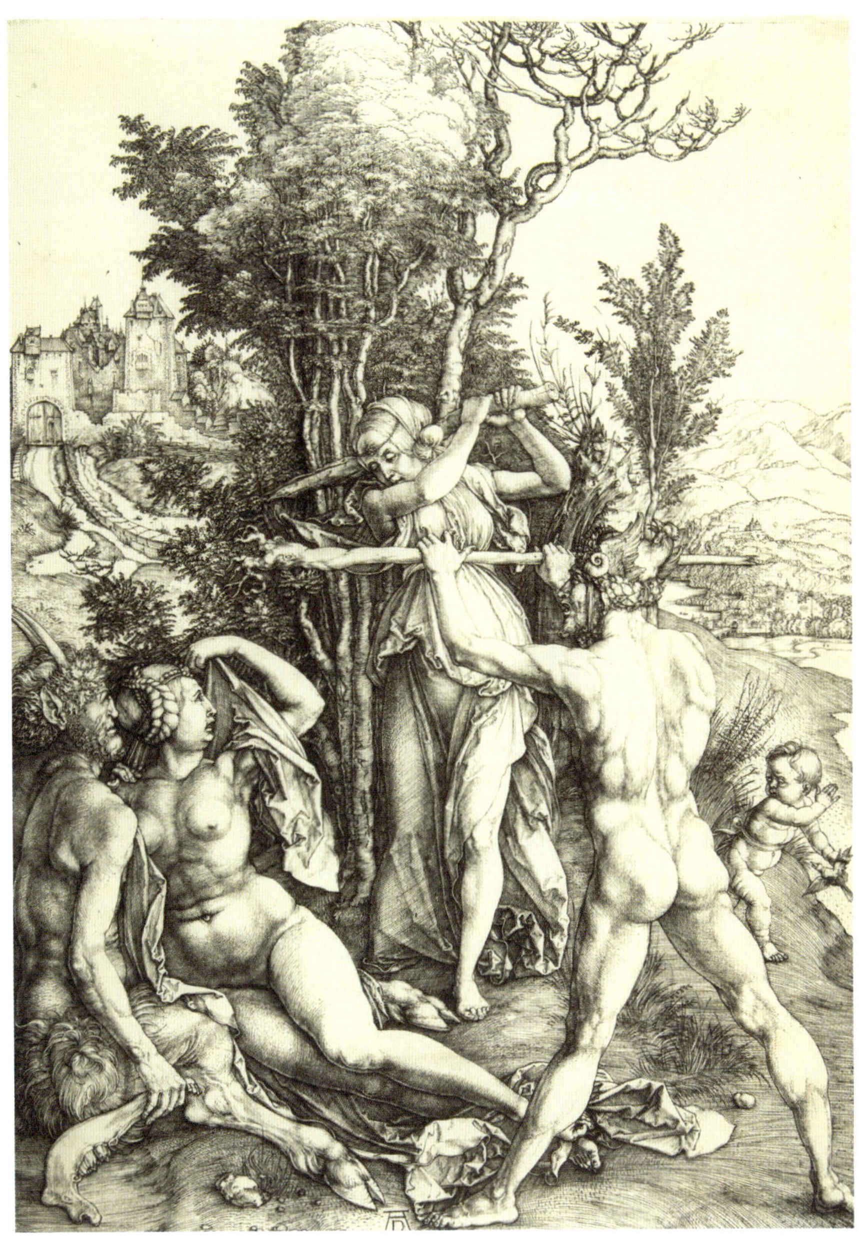

of a wealthy Nuremberg artisan and town dignitary – a socially useful alliance, like the marriage Bosch made – but he couldn't resist this adventure. He would never forget it.

Watercolours of Innsbruck, with the snowy Alps twinkling beyond its towers and, in northern Italy, of Trent and the Cembra valley record his route. There are no written records of his experiences in Venice on this trip, although he recalls it fondly in a letter from his second visit eleven years later. His prints

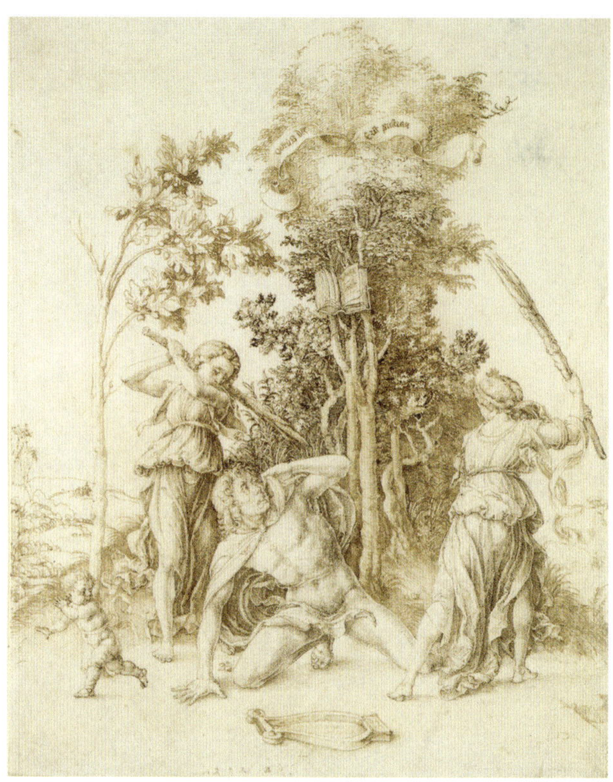

Albrecht Dürer,
Death of Orpheus, 1494.

and drawings glow with delights he found there – and shudder with moral unease. A drawing he probably did in Venice shows a fashionable Italian woman with her dress low on her shoulders, a huge necklace, and her hair hanging down in ringlets. He gives the Whore of Babylon just such a Venetian hairstyle in his woodcut *Apocalypse*, as if he were haunted by this city renowned for its courtesans.

Venice was also a city of artist's models, who may have been the same women. Depicting nudes from life was by now a recognized practice in Italy. A drawing by Dürer from 1495 shows a model with her back to us, resting one arm on a pole in the kind of pose life classes would repeat for centuries to come. He has heavily reworked her back, bottom and legs. In the process she has become almost masculine.

Dürer made a copy of a lost engraving of the *Death of Orpheus* by Andrea Mantegna, one of the few great Italian artists who embraced print, producing sharply incised, rugged images of Greek myth. Albrecht's Orpheus has been surprised by two Maenads – frenzied followers of the wine god Bacchus – who are about to club him to death. He kneels helplessly before their wrath, his lyre no defence against their weapons. What has Orpheus done to deserve this fate?

Dürer has written the reason on a banner in the trees: 'Orpheus, der Erst puseran' ('Orpheus, the first pederast', or 'Orpheus the first sodomite').

The version of Orpheus's death Dürer so graphically illustrates was told in Ovid's *Metamorphoses*: the poet was killed by Maenads because he had rejected women in favour of the love of boys. Drawing the poet's punishment so soon after his marriage to Agnes Frey, which was negotiated between her father and his while he was out of town, Dürer seems to be exploring some fraught personal issues, finding a landscape for his complex nature in the mythological art pioneered by Italians such as Mantegna. The rediscovery of classical art and myth that had been happening for decades south of the Alps filled him with excitement and dread. It was nakedly sensual and explored all human beauty, male and female.

Back in Nuremberg in about 1496–97 Dürer depicted male and female public baths, exploiting a real-life, northern opportunity to see groups of nudes relaxing together. The women bathe indoors in a heated room, unselfconsciously

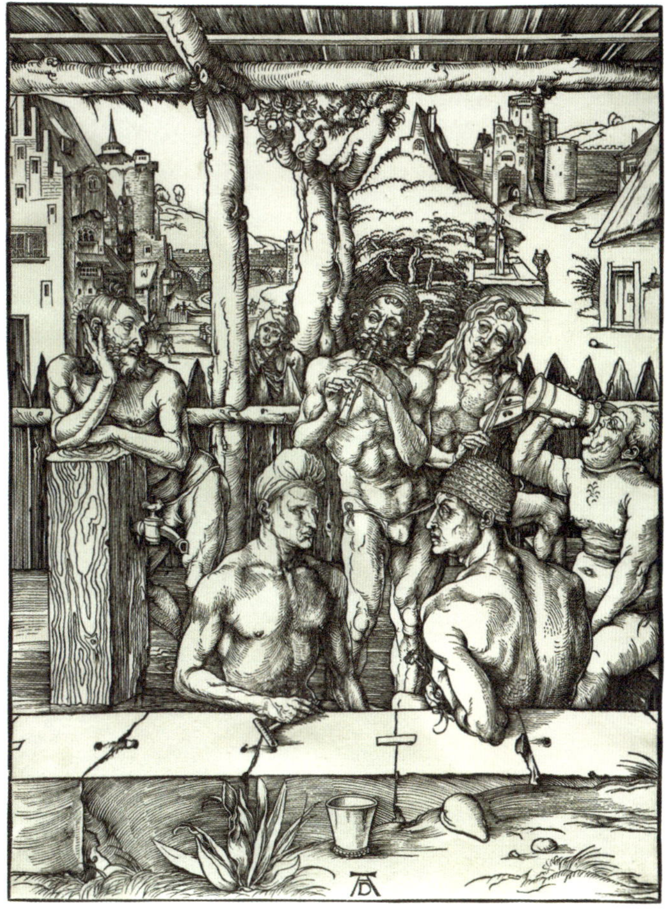

Albrecht Dürer, *Men's Bath*, c. 1496–97.

showing different parts of their bodies, one woman looking directly at us as she confidently displays her breasts. Yet this drawing is less charged than Dürer's woodcut of the *Men's Bath* (p. 169). The men are audacious enough to strip off under an open wooden roof with a water tap. They pose and preen and pretend it's Italy: one plays the flute, and another long-haired figure beside him draws a bow across a stringed instrument. The symbolism is clear enough: this is Orpheus, right here in Nuremberg. Another man, who looks like Dürer, leans languidly against the tap post, engaging the flautist in an intimate mutual gaze. The tap is aligned to his genitals and has a sculpted cock on it to emphasize the phallic joke. The baths at Nuremberg were closed in 1496 to stop the spread of syphilis, which suggests that they were suspected of being a sexual hangout. A pear in the foreground resembles testicles and a penis. A cup beside it could be an anus.

If that sounds overly ripe, consider Dürer's note in Greek on a 1503 portrait drawing of his close friend the high-ranking Nuremberg humanist Willibald Pirckheimer: 'With erect penis into the man's anus'. It's a fleshy, close study of Pirckheimer's face. The two joked together about sex, their comments displaying overtones of a shared misogynistic resentment of Dürer's wife and an interest in men. Writing from Venice in 1506, Dürer tells Pirckheimer not to give Agnes a 'washing' – that is, not to copulate with her – unless it's to the death.[12] He also teases the scholar about the good-looking soldiers in Venice. Flirting with men was a style copied from Italy, like the classical nude. So too was long curly hair and a dashing beard, which Dürer sports in a self-portrait from 1498.

The artist was depicting plenty of female nudes, but in ways that dramatize the tension between Christian Nuremberg and classicist Italy. The *Dream of the Doctor*, created in around 1498, depicts a scholar asleep. After all the Ovid and Lucretius he has read, he dreams into existence a long-haired, naked woman who beckons to him graciously while Cupid uses his arrows as stilts. But this mythological apparition is not innocent. A demon, who could have come straight out of Martin Schongauer, blows a bellows in the sleeper's ear. The Devil makes an even more hair-raising appearance in Dürer's engraving of four women dancing in a circle in a room, all nude like the classical Graces. Yet beautiful as they are, there is something amiss. A human skull and thighbone lie at their feet. A globe hangs above them. They are witches, weaving a spell. Their master, Satan, watches from a cellar that is a portal to hell.

* * *

Bosch had no interest in classical nudes. The people in the *Garden of Earthly Delights* are painted in a direct way that goes back to van Eyck. To Dürer, however, the nude is a classical ideal that comes from Italy. He has learned that ancient

Greek artists tried to give their nude statues the proportions of the perfect human body as mathematically analysed in the Canon of the sculptor Polykleitos, which reached the Renaissance via the Roman architectural writer Vitruvius. Leonardo's drawing known as 'Vitruvian Man' was a star-shaped attempt to make visual sense of the ideal proportions of a man. Dürer was just as keen as Leonardo to get the maths right when he designed his nudes. He wrote on human proportions and did some ugly, awkward drawings to analyse them.

What makes Dürer's art so absorbing is the combination of this geometry of the body and the religious and folkloric traditions of Nuremberg. He brings nude statues to life like a sorcerer and sets them in a lush Germanic world of castles and forests. One folk legend that fascinates him is that of the Wild Man, a hairy, primal variant of humanity that lives in the woods. Dürer's portrait of the merchant Oswolt Krel, dated to 1499, seems respectable enough, except that it is flanked by side panels of fearsome wild men bearing clubs. When you look again at Krel's intense, sideways stare, you sense there may also be a hairy savage inside him.

Dürer also invents, or excavates from popular culture, still weirder hybrids of classical myth and gothic fantasy. In his engraving *The Sea Monster*, a poised, curvy and ample nude – for once a woman he seems to crave – rests on the back of a creature who's carrying her away to sea. He is a primeval synthesis

Albrecht Dürer, *Portrait of Oswolt Krel*, 1499.

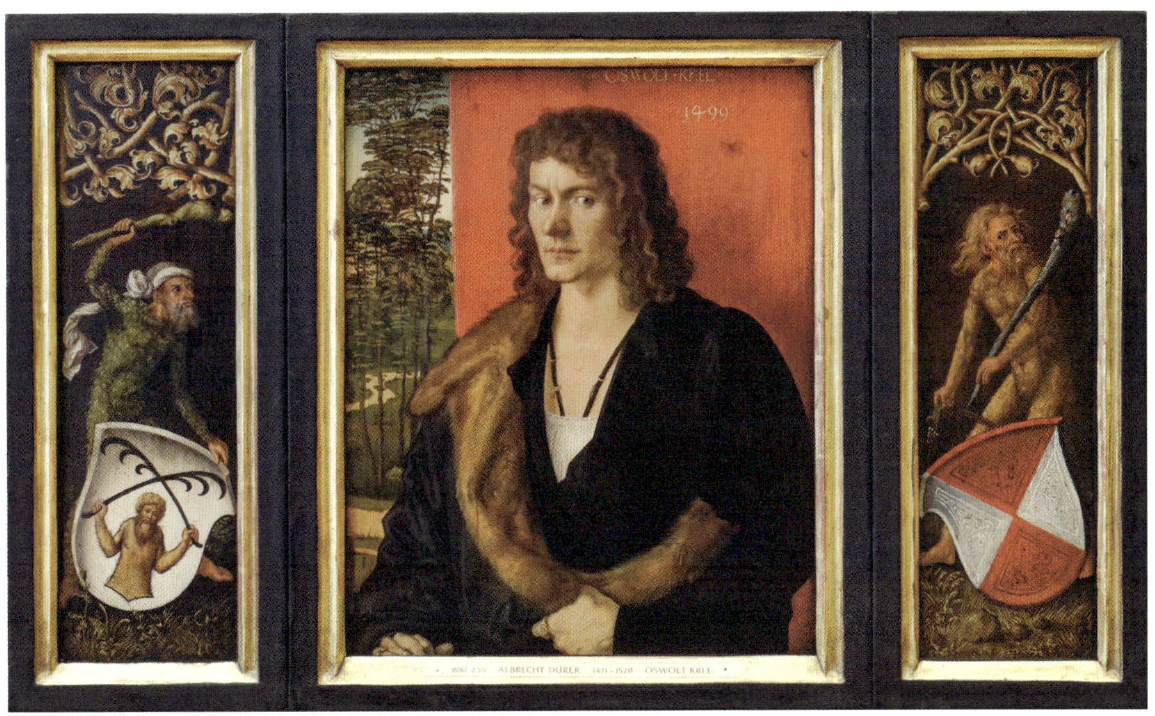

Albrecht Dürer,
The Sea Monster,
c. 1498.

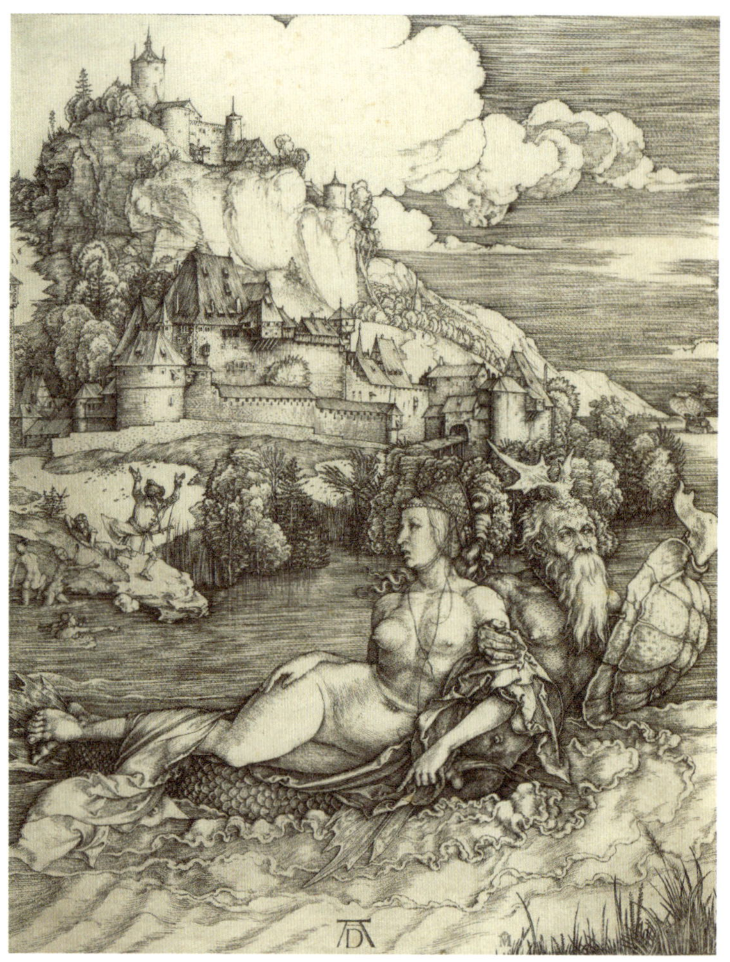

of animal and human, with an antler-like growth sprouting from his head, a scaly tail and a long, white beard. The animal in us, it implies, takes as many forms as there are desires.

* * *

Hieronymus Bosch, Piero di Cosimo and Albrecht Dürer all explored uncharted realms and participated in exotic carnivals – in their heads. Bosch painted travesties of traditional religious triptychs and not only got away with it but was in demand. Those who paid for his paintings were buying his creative extravagance, his artistry. Piero di Cosimo too travels into worlds that have little to do with tradition or patronage, absorbing classical myths into his own vision. In their discoveries of a new world of the mind, these artists probe dreams, terrors and desires. They cannot be classed as artisans carrying out work for hire, like Bosch's family of jobbing painters. They are seers, visionaries.

It was the intensely self-conscious Dürer who asserted this new identity. In the half-millennium year of 1500, about to turn 28, he portrayed himself with daunting intensity. He stares at you from brown, translucent eyes, under his shamanic mane of artfully curled locks. He looks, as everyone thinks the first time they see it, like Jesus Christ. And who knows, perhaps he is bigger than Jesus. Albrecht himself is awed by his face in the mirror, painting this. He feels an almost messianic power, an ability to conjure worlds in and out of being, to shapeshift and see the invisible. He is an artist.

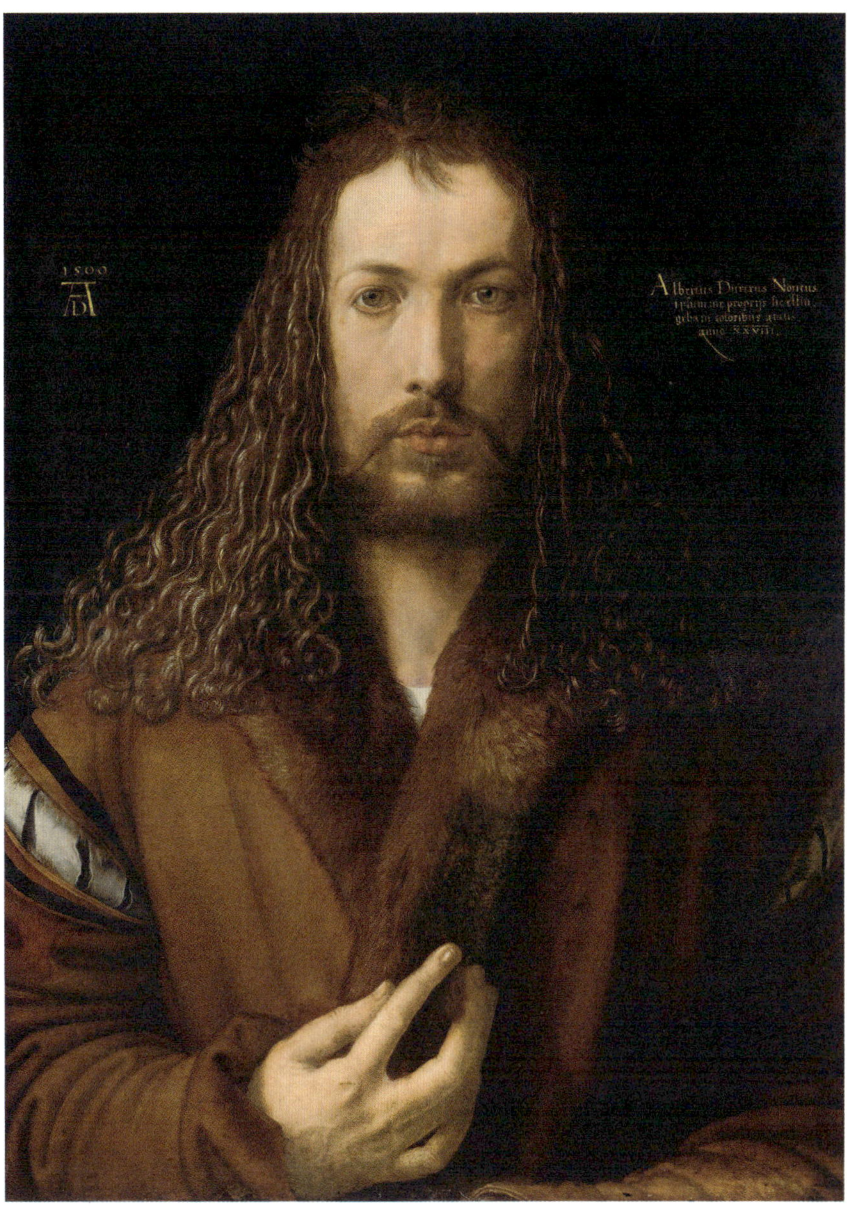

Albrecht Dürer,
Self-Portrait, 1500.

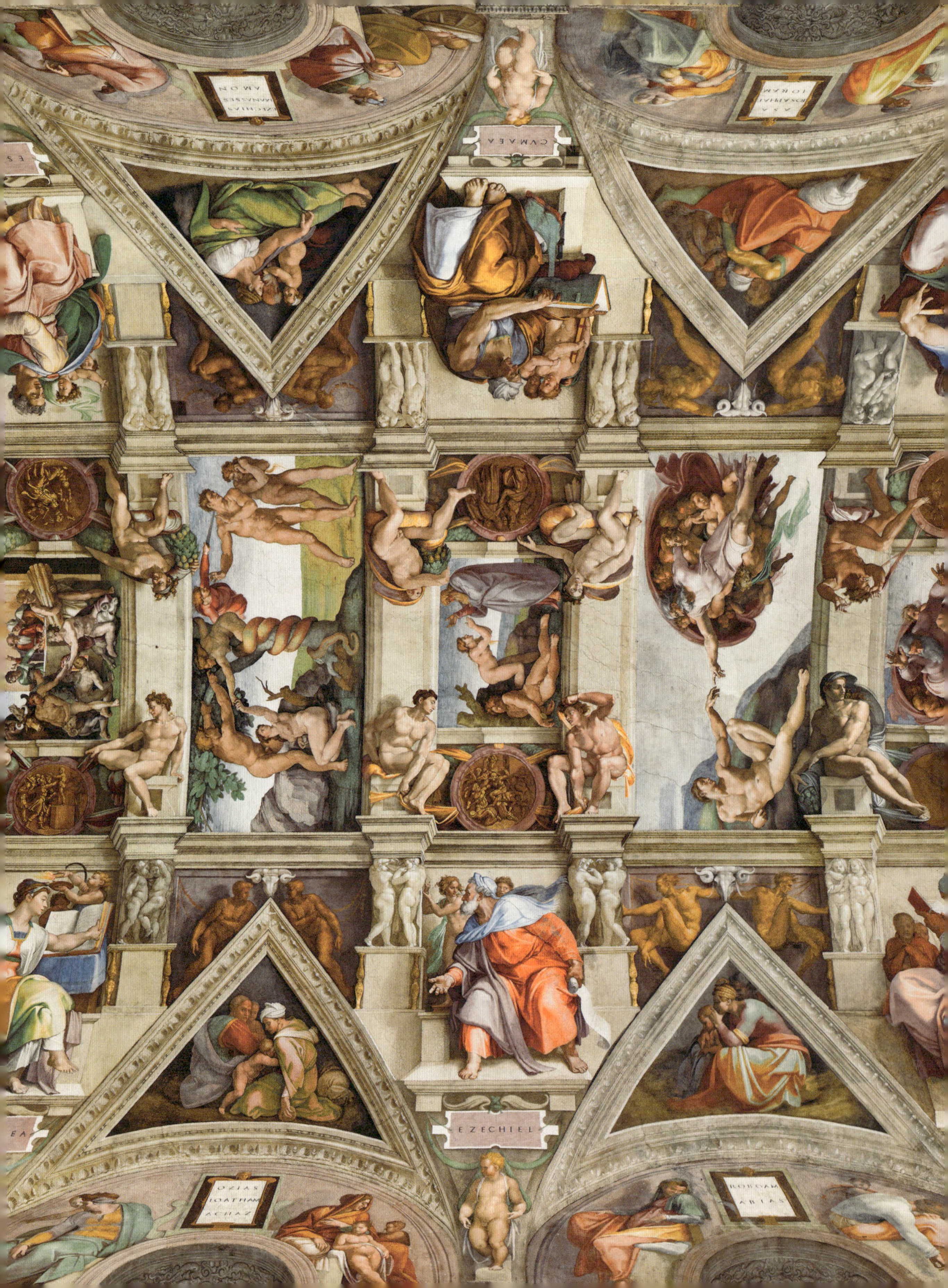

EZECHIEL
OZIAS
IOATHAM
ACHAZ
ROBOAM
ABIAS

8 Render unto Caesar

Michelangelo Buonarroti hated his teacher. He refused even to acknowledge that he, a poet, architect, sculptor and painter, friend of nobles and pontiffs, had once been the humble apprentice of the Florentine craftsman Domenico Ghirlandaio. It was one reason that, on reading Vasari's *Lives* in 1550, in which this detail was included, he encouraged his pupil Ascanio Condivi to write an alternative account; it didn't matter that Vasari celebrated Michelangelo as the greatest artist of all time, 'who takes the palm from both living and dead'.[1] With the septuagenarian Michelangelo's voice echoing in his ears, Condivi explains in his 1553 *Life of Michelangelo* how the spiteful Ghirlandaio and his family made false claims about teaching the young genius. Instead, Michelangelo's first inspiration was an artist he never met, whose nationality or even his real name he didn't know. It took the form of a print.

* * *

Printed images could cross mountains and language barriers, sending visual ideas to different ends of the continent. One centre of printmaking in Italy was Mantua. When Vasari visited the city before publishing his second, expanded version of his *Lives*, he met the sculptor and engraver Giovanni Battista Mantovano – and, 'what is even more astonishing', his daughter Diana, 'who also engraved so well

Michelangelo, *Ceiling of the Sistine Chapel* (detail), 1508–12.

it is a thing to marvel at'.[2] Diana Mantovana, or Mantuana, would go on to have a highly successful career in Rome, producing forceful engravings on religious and mythological themes, some based on works by her teacher Giulio Romano. Print was accessible, but images were often bootlegged, frustrating their creators who were left out of pocket even as it enhanced the flow of ideas. The pioneer of printmaking in Mantua was Andrea Mantegna, and he had tried to enforce control. He was a powerful man in the little lakeside city, as is attested by his house, a fanciful reconstruction of a Roman villa. When he discovered that the printmaker he employed was working for a rival, he hired a gang to attack the hapless engraver then accused him of sodomy. It was one way to regulate the print business.

It's impossible to know if the version of the *Temptation of St Anthony* by Martin Schongauer that came into Michelangelo's hands in the 1480s when he was just a boy was authentic or plagiarized, but it engrossed him. Condivi, relaying Michelangelo's memory, calls the artist 'Martin of Holland', on the principle that any good art from beyond the Alps must be Netherlandish rather than from somewhere as specific as Alsace, where Schongauer actually worked. Michelangelo found this remote, uncanny image more absorbing than anything his Florentine elders were doing. Its image of an old man suspended in the air, molested by demonic beings, kindled his imagination. He challenged himself to make a full-colour painting based on the black-and-white design, and to help recreate the persecuting fiends he headed to the fish market, 'to examine the form and colour of the fins of fishes, what colour their eyes were and every other part'.[3]

Michelangelo's panel has gleeful, radiant colours that do justice to those glistening market fish. Yet there is another reason to see this as the seed of his most ambitious paintings. Schongauer's little print is a vision of bodies floating free in empty space. This depiction of flight, a magical suspension in the void, is a prototype from which Michelangelo would go on to create art that can give you vertigo just to look at it.

Two decades later, in 1509, Michelangelo is balancing on a wooden platform under the vaulted ceiling of the Sistine Chapel in Rome, suffering from a crick in his neck from constantly looking up to concentrate on the immense images he is painting above his head. He has to keep in mind how they will look from the ground – from up here, the robes of God are a swirling purple cloud, and Adam a naked giant close to his face – not to mention measuring out the intricate design of animal skulls, gold medallions, *trompe-l'oeil* capitals, and illusory niches flanked by painted sculptures of putti that he's set himself to create in an impossible act of solo physical and mental daring. His beard is covered in paint, he writes in a rueful poem that he probably composed in his head while

Michelangelo, *Torment of St Anthony*, 1487.

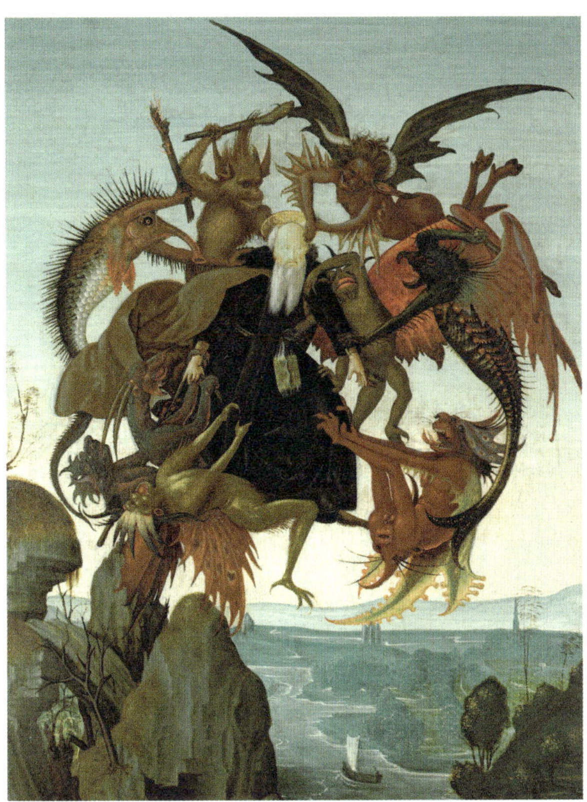

he worked and wrote right here in the chapel during a break. He's so tired he doesn't see where he's going as he walks along the precarious platform.

* * *

Pope Alexander VI tried to create an empire for his family but ended up carving out power for the church. The ambitions of the Borgia family came to a crashing halt in August 1503 when the pope and his son fell gravely ill. Fevers were not uncommon in Rome, a city where tourists could succumb to malaria into modern times, but that didn't stop rumours that they had accidentally poisoned themselves. The pope died, and Cesare Borgia lay stricken as rival factions moved in to select a successor. In the event, the new pope, Pius III, would reign only twenty-six days before himself expiring. When a new conclave met in October, Cesare was fit enough to manipulate the outcome, but he made a big mistake in the candidate he supported. As Machiavelli saw it,

> He ought never to have consented to the election of any cardinal whom he had injured or who had cause to fear him if they became pontiffs. For men injure either from fear or hatred. Those whom he had injured, amongst others, were San Pietro ad Vincula, Colonna, San Giorgio, and Ascanio.[4]

'San Pietro ad Vincula' was a reference to Cardinal Giuliano della Rovere, whose uncle, Pope Sixtus IV, had built the Sistine Chapel and the Sixtus Bridge – both hinting at a future resurgence of Rome. Sixtus had given della Rovere the cardinalship (named after the church on Rome's Esquiline Hill) when he was not yet 30 years old. That was typical of the way leading Italian families played politics with sacred offices. It was also typical that della Rovere had fathered at least one illegitimate child while a cardinal. Yet there were some unusual qualities to the new pope. Giuliano supposedly chose to rename himself after Julius Caesar, the greatest of all Roman generals, whose account of his victories in Gaul and Britain paints a picture of unrelenting imperial aggression. Once enthroned, Pope Julius II did indeed ensure that Cesare Borgia never got to exert his power or influence again, and Machiavelli's dark prince died in an ambush in Spain in 1507.

The new pontiff also learnt from the distinctly temporal achievements of the Borgia papacy. Alexander VI had licensed his son to conquer central Italian territories, which had a history of direct rule by the church. Julius liked the Borgia plan to reimpose papal control – not for his family, but for the church. Here was a dramatic way to resurrect the authority of Christ on earth.

Christendom had been in retreat for decades. In 1453 the Byzantine Empire, which had preserved its versions of Hellenism and Christianity for a millennium, came to an end when its capital was conquered for Islam. The Ottoman Turks made Constantinople their capital and designated its 6th-century domed cathedral, Haghia Sophia, a mosque. In 1480 an Ottoman fleet set out to conquer Rome, taking the city of Otranto on Italy's heel and killing more than half the population. Only then did the pope get a crusade together to drive them out.

Yet this was no war of civilizations. As Turkish rule absorbed much of Balkan Eastern Europe, realpolitik ruled the Italian response. In the early 15th century attempts were made to reconcile the Western and Eastern churches, but the fact was that Byzantium and Rome had never got on. And to Venetian and Genoese merchants, control of trade routes mattered more than theological niceties. When war broke out between the Republic of Venice and the Ottomans in 1499 it was over control of islands and trade, not articles of faith. Leonardo offered to assist Venice with a submarine attack on the Turkish navy.

Leonardo was looking for work because that year France, under its new king Louis XII, invaded Italy again and took Milan, toppling his employer, Ludovico Sforza. For target practice French archers used the clay model of a colossal equestrian statue Leonardo had been working on for years. Italy was turning into a laboratory of modern warfare. It was a playground for great powers where the machinations of France, Spain and Venice dwarfed the freedom of smaller city-states that didn't have Venice's shipbuilding *arsenale* or its colonies.

Another mighty power was rising in the north. The Holy Roman Empire was not exactly an upstart, having been founded by Charlemagne at the start of the 9th century, but the Emperor Maximilian I was giving it new life as the dynastic vehicle of his house of Habsburg. He married Mary of Burgundy and arranged for his son Philip to marry Joanna, heir to Castile, thus mapping a future in which the Habsburg crown would include not only the Central European lands of the Holy Roman Empire, but also Flanders, Spain and Spain's global possessions.

Maximilian saw the power of print. He commissioned Dürer to create for him an imposing work made of thirty-six separate sheets of woodcuts that fitted together to create a representation of a triumphal arch, emblazoned with images of his world empire, including New World peoples. As a multiple image it could be displayed in castles and council chambers throughout his dominions.

In this age of bully states, Julius II saw the Borgia conquests in the Romagna as a model for turning the church into a true military power capable of fighting off Italy's invaders. He also enjoyed war. He led his own armies into battle, despite turning 60 the year he became pope, in campaigns to subjugate Bologna and Ferrara. If the church was to become an imperial power, then Rome must regain the splendour it had enjoyed under the Caesars. Julius took up his papacy in a city that was still a chaotic medieval community among the mouldering yet awe-inspiring ruins of antiquity. Even after it had been used as a stone quarry for centuries, the Colosseum eclipsed everything around it. The Roman Forum might have been used for grazing cattle, but its triumphal arches made more recent constructions look feeble. The Pantheon and Mausoleum of Hadrian were better preserved, their engineering genius an accusation of decline and impoverishment since the fall of ancient Rome. Julius II had the ambition and ruthlessness to transform this degraded Rome and make it a new kind of Renaissance city, taking the aspirations of his uncle Sixtus to new heights. All he needed was an artist of genius.

* * *

Michelangelo got his foothold in Rome with an art forgery. In 1496 Cardinal Raffaele Riario paid 200 ducats for a marble sculpture of a Sleeping Cupid that he thought was a classical antiquity. In reality it had been made in Florence just a few months earlier by Michelangelo. Riario found out and invited Michelangelo to come and see him in Rome.

Was the young artist in on the joke, or was he innocent in the whole affair, as Condivi implies? Forger or not, Michelangelo at the age of 21 was creating imitations of classical sculpture that could pass as the real thing. His mentor was Lorenzo the Magnificent. The highbrow ruler's sculpture garden near San Marco in Florence was a conscious attempt to encourage students to study Greek and Roman art with the rigour classical scholars brought to texts. It was the most successful art school in history because this was where Michelangelo learnt to sculpt. Of course he was lying when he denied being taught by Ghirlandaio – in the second edition of his *Lives*, Vasari reproduced the bond of apprenticeship – but in the Medici garden Michelangelo discovered a new skill when he took up a chisel and started hammering.

Lorenzo even invited Michelangelo into the intellectual atmosphere of the Medici palace itself. Michelangelo remembered how much he learned from the talk at the Magnifico's dinner table, where democratic seating arrangements meant that he was sometimes placed above Lorenzo's sons, two future popes among them. The voice he remembered most fondly was that of Angelo Poliziano. The poet who had inspired Botticelli now encouraged Michelangelo. Poliziano took the teenager under his wing,

> always explaining things to him and giving him things to do. Among these one day was his proposal of the Rape of Deianira and the Battle of the Centaurs, and he explained the whole story to him stage by stage.[5]

Poliziano perhaps related to him two tales of thuggery by centaurs, including their battle with the Lapiths. Or perhaps this is a reference to a less familiar myth concerning Hercules' rescue of Deianira from the centaur Eurytion and a subsequent punch-up. It hardly matters, because in the marble relief Michelangelo sculpted when he was 17 at the oldest there is no obviously discernible narrative. The struggling bodies are overwhelmingly male, overwhelmingly human and overwhelmingly naked. Only if you look for a while do you notice the equine rump of a centaur.

Yet there is one detail that surely came from Poliziano: a bald, bearded man at the left, heaving a rock. This must be a reference to a self-portrait by the Greek sculptor Pheidias, which he was said to have included on the Shield of Athena inside the Parthenon, the temple to the goddess on the Acropolis in Athens. According to the ancient historian Plutarch in his *Life of Pericles*, when Pheidias 'wrought the battle of the Amazons on the shield of the goddess he carved out a figure of himself suggesting a bald old man lifting a stone on high with both hands'.[6] Michelangelo's visual quotation is exact. Did Poliziano tell him about this image of the artist as fighter because he recognized a fiery and combative spirit in the teenaged sculptor? It suggests genuine understanding and sympathy.

There's no doubting the energy and vehemence that pounds in the marble. The *Battle of the Centaurs* rejects the very idea of a picture – as the early Renaissance

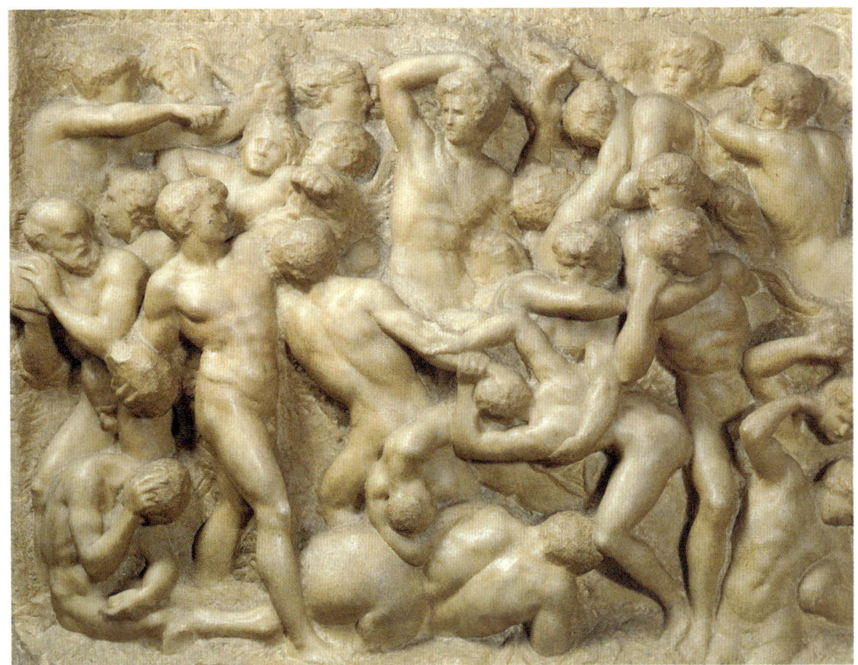

Michelangelo,
Battle of the Centaurs,
1490–92.

had created it – by refusing to neatly order its figures in a deep space. This was as true of reliefs as paintings: the textbook example of perspective art was a set of bronze reliefs by Lorenzo Ghiberti for the doors of the Florentine Baptistery that Michelangelo nicknamed the *Gates of Paradise*. Michelangelo does not create a perspective scene, or a landscape, or a room. He lets a struggling mass of human flesh emerge, as if in a chemical reaction, from the block. Figures seem to have been discovered instead of carved, except that you can see his chisel marks on the sides of the shallow void.

Here, in this heaving mass of limbs and backs, are Michelangelo's nudes in their primordial form, without much in the way of symbolic justification. A youth raising a rock has a rippling torso and his genitals poking out from between his legs, while the figure by him shows us a surging, heaving back, its muscles divided by the spine's deep valley, as he pulls another male nude by the hair. On the ground is a centaur's massive human back. All these are aspects of male anatomy to which Michelangelo would keep returning. As he confesses here in stone, the bodies of men arrest him. Michelangelo has 'loved the beauty of the body', writes Condivi,

> and has loved it in such a manner, that among certain gross men, who do not know how to comprehend the love of beauty unless it is lustful and corrupt, there has been occasion to think and speak evil of him,

> as if Alcibiades, a most comely young man, had not been loved most chastely by Socrates, from whose side, when he rested with him, it was accustomed to be said that he did not rise other than he would from the side of his father.[7]

* * *

Here is another way the humanists put their mark on Michelangelo. The story of Socrates sleeping with Alcibiades comes from Plato's *Symposium*, one of the works Marsilio Ficino translated for the Medici. At a drinking party where the snub-nosed philosopher and his friends have been giving speeches in praise of love (*erōs*), Alcibiades shows up late, and the two of them tease each other about their relationship. Alcibiades drops the joshing and makes a heartfelt speech in praise of Socrates, contrasting his outer appearance and demeanour with his inner self. Socrates likes the company of good-looking young men: 'See you how fond he is of the fair? He is always with them and is always being smitten by them.'[8] Yet this masks Socrates' real passion: truth. The handsome Alcibiades found out the hard way by pursuing him, taking him to the gymnasium and manipulating him into sharing a bed. Socrates refused to be seduced, rejecting Alcibiades' spurious bargain of physical for spiritual beauty. Alcibiades confesses that 'in the morning when I awoke (let all the gods and goddesses be my witnesses) I arose as from the couch of a father or an elder brother'.[9]

So Condivi, under Michelangelo's influence, is playing with the idea that Michelangelo loves male beauty but also doesn't care about it all. He adores the body but looks past it to make art about the soul. That was what Michelangelo said of his sexuality when, in his seventies, he spoke to his biographer. In old age he even looked like Socrates, with his wrinkled nut of a face and broken nose, as a cast of his features by one of his pupils proves. When he was 17 he probably felt less like Socrates in every way.

Michelangelo was a teenager when he got his nose broken. A fellow student from the Medici garden called Pietro Torrigiani punched him in the face for getting too big for his boots. Worse was to come. Lorenzo the Magnificent's death left the young artist suddenly without his greatest supporter, back in his father's house and too proud to rejoin the Florentine workshop system. Piero de' Medici showed his shallowness by asking him to make a snow sculpture in the Medici palace courtyard. A snowman! By him, Michelangelo! When Piero's idiocy got the Medici chucked out of Florence, their greatest artistic protégé set his sights on a career elsewhere. The affair of the Sleeping Cupid got him a stylish debut in Rome as an instant celebrity. This was more like it.

* * *

The duped cardinal was big about the affair. Riario purchased 'a block of marble suitable for a life-sized figure', wrote Michelangelo from Rome in July 1496, and challenged him to make 'some beautiful work' from it. Even at this early stage he was not being given orders but asked to follow his genius. There was no tedious contract specifying a subject. He was free to create anything – as long as it matched the ancient statues in the cardinal's collection. In the event the work he produced assimilated the perfections of classical art almost to the point of parody.

Bacchus totters in space, his balance unreliable, connected by a hanging drapery to a young satyr who acts as a brace for the heavy statue. This is a sculptor's joke. Michelangelo could make a statue stand strong without any external support, but he's imitating Roman statues, mostly copies of lost Greek originals, that lazily use trees or wooden clubs as buttresses. The prop becomes a virtue, as the bunch of grapes being munched by the satyr with his wicked little horned face add to the work's insouciant vitality. Its comedy contrasts with the otherworldly features of the drunken god.

The face of Bacchus is cocked awkwardly on his neck, disturbing the smooth stone's promise of harmony. His eyes, with drilled holes for pupils, are drifting off

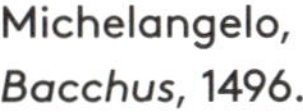

Michelangelo, *Bacchus*, 1496.

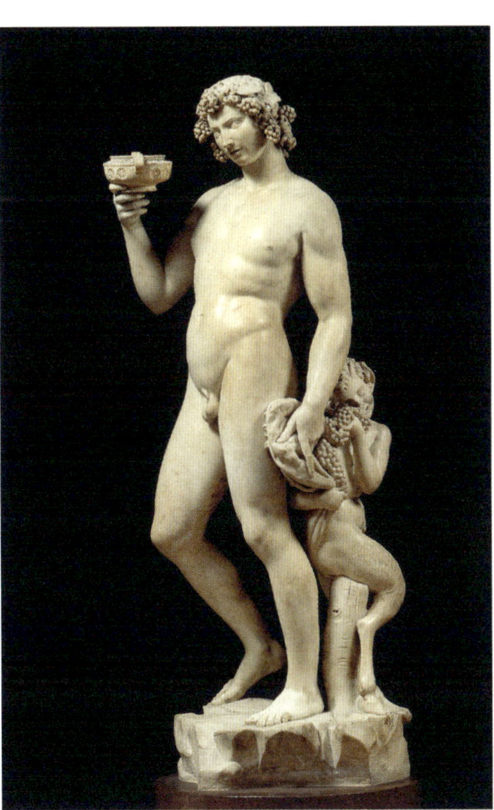

into a psychotic dream. He appears lost in perilous ecstasy, the cheery bunches of grapes in his hair failing to reassure us that it's all in good fun. The depiction of classical gods has entered perturbing new territory. Like Botticelli's *Venus*, Michelangelo's *Bacchus* confronts us as a pagan deity reborn, large as life (p. 183). Yet instead of creative love, he personifies intoxication, abandonment, the triumph of irrationality. It is a statue of insanity as much as drunkenness.

Michelangelo is again applying humanist ideas he picked up at Lorenzo the Magnificent's palace. Plato in the *Phaedrus* has Socrates discuss types of divine fury, or *mania*. These include a mania that comes from Bacchus of cultic initiation, and a mania that comes from the Muses that is poetic. *Bacchus* insinuates the mania of the initiate, but perhaps it was also created through poetic mania. And Michelangelo is its furious creator, who plunges into madness, oblivion, the abyss. Perhaps Cardinal Riario saw that abyss in this uneasy masterpiece; he was certainly troubled or confused enough to reject the *Bacchus* in what seems to have been a moment of papal suspicion of pagan art, and almost immediately sold it to the banker Jacopo Galli. Not every Italian Renaissance work of art can be explained in relation to Plato. But Michelangelo really did encounter humanist thought as a teenager. *Bacchus* is a deep draft of wine-dark intellect, as he depicts the risk and estrangement of creative frenzy.

It was not such a huge step from a drunken god to a dead one. Yet the sculpture of the dead Christ in Mary's lap that Michelangelo carved in 1498–99 represents a leap in how he conceives the nude. *Bacchus* is the climax of pure classicism for Michelangelo: he has perfectly recreated, yet also improved on, a classical statue. Why do it again? The *Pietà* approaches nakedness from a completely different, medieval starting point. Michelangelo heads north.

The *Vesperbild* or *Pietà*, that old German and Flemish favourite, was an attempt to harrow the soul into seeing death. A successful work on this theme should leave you shaken by the recognition of mortality. Michelangelo's awareness of such northern art was more precise than you might think. Lorenzo de' Medici owned Rogier van der Weyden's *Deposition*, showing Christ being taken down from the cross. It was a much more expressive response to a painting of the Deposition by Fra Angelico, in which the dead Christ is held up vertically, stiff as a board. Rogier tried the same idea of Christ's body suspended upright but succeeds in making it moving and desolate. Christ's lightly bearded face flops to the side in Rogier's *Deposition*, while his arms, held up by his mourners, have a distressing looseness.

Michelangelo was clearly struck by van der Weyden's painting because he imitates it in an unfinished, sketchy early painting known as the *Entombment*. He also remembered those lifeless arms when he created his *Pietà*. The right

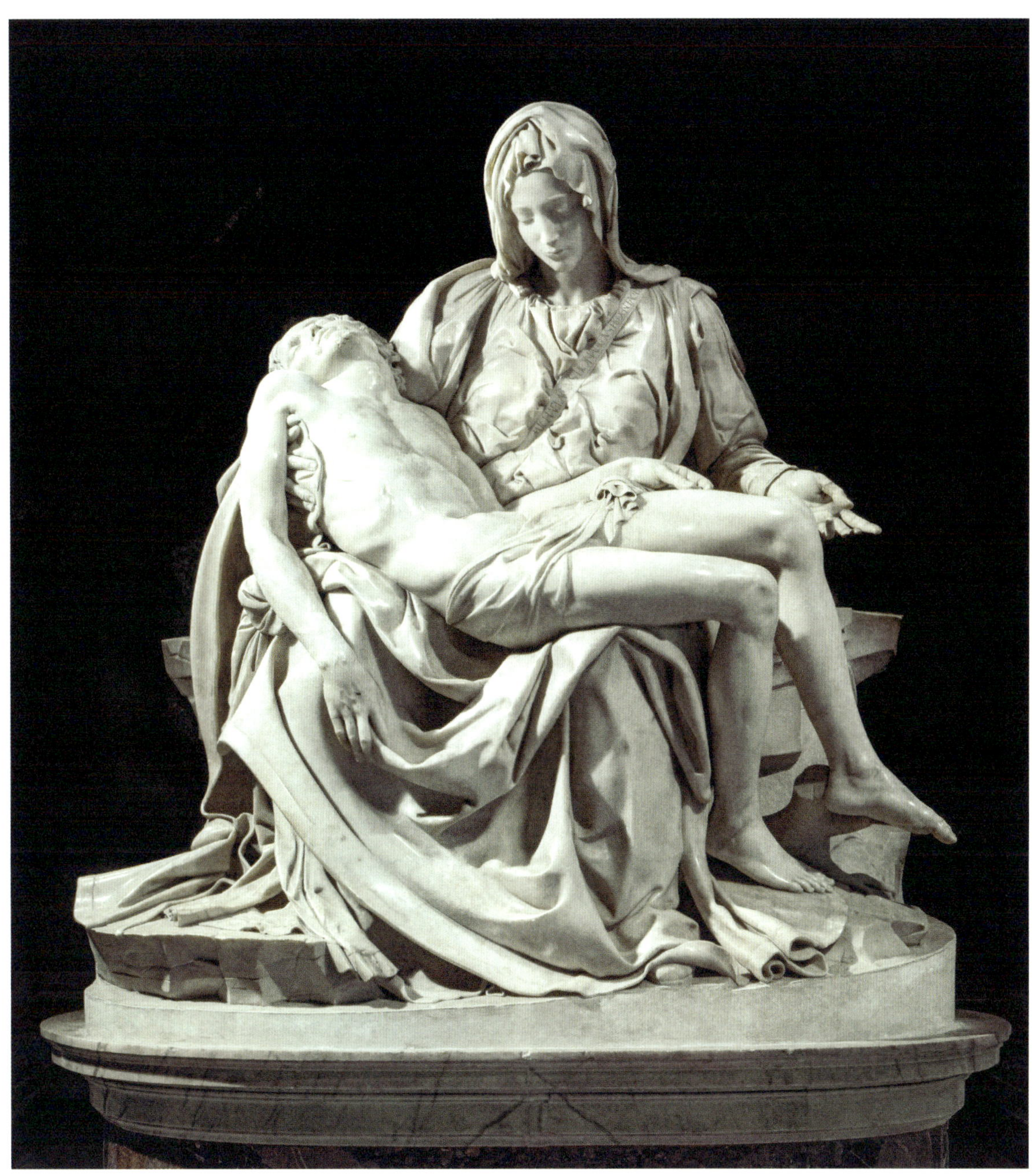

Michelangelo,
Pietà, 1498–99.

arm of his Christ hangs down alarmingly, falling over Mary's hand as it clasps his ribcage. The flesh under his shoulder bulges over her finger, a detail that clutches at your heart because it is so lifelike. Yet the instant you think that, you realize this is not life – it is after life. Like Rogier, he forces that realization on us with a natural yet unnatural fall of the limbs: the left arm lying against Christ's lap, the legs dangling over Mary's lap. Christ's head falls right back, a posture only someone profoundly unconscious could assume.

One response to Michelangelo's *Pietà* is to say that he takes a coarse northern genre and gives it classical grace. In reality Flemish painting had already made the death of Christ hypnotically beautiful. And far from being a Greek nude, Michelangelo's Christ is a real corpse, observed with unflinching anatomical clarity, not idealized but seen through eyes of love. Mary has a superhuman strength in her grief: she takes away the supporting hand from his legs as if they can float for themselves and gestures to us to behold her boy.

* * *

For all the greatness of the *Bacchus* and the *Pièta*, they are experiments. Part of the allure of sculpture for the young Michelangelo was its unpredictability. He would start with a block of stone and see what he could find. He was drawn back to Florence at the start of the 16th century by a block of marble in the cathedral workshops that another artist had made a bad start at sculpting. The damage enhanced the challenge. When leading Florentine artists were consulted in January 1504 on where the 'giant' that Michelangelo had created should stand, there was an aura of dread about what he had released, as if it were a living creature with a basilisk stare.

David is eyeing up the enemy, fixing his attention on the oppressor Goliath as he calculates the trajectory for his slingshot. His weapon is draped over his left shoulder, while in his right hand he hides a stone. Apart from that he is naked, a quivering, taut colossus of closely observed flesh. His chest is so lifelike it's hard not to imagine a heartbeat. The prodigious veins in his hand, the wild curls on his head, the flame of his pubic hair might seem excessive if they were not so acutely observed, but everything that is exaggerated in this nude serves only to make him seem full and alive. That's why a statue 3.4 metres (17 feet) tall never strikes anyone as gargantuan or monstrous. He is big enough to stride out of the world of art and meet us as an equal. He's no bigger than that.

David has the poise of an ideal Greek nude, his physical proportions graceful and confident, an athlete at ease with his body that could have graced the gymnasium where Alcibiades took Socrates. Yet a panoply of quirks, from the slight inclination of his shoulders and his out-of-proportion right hand to his

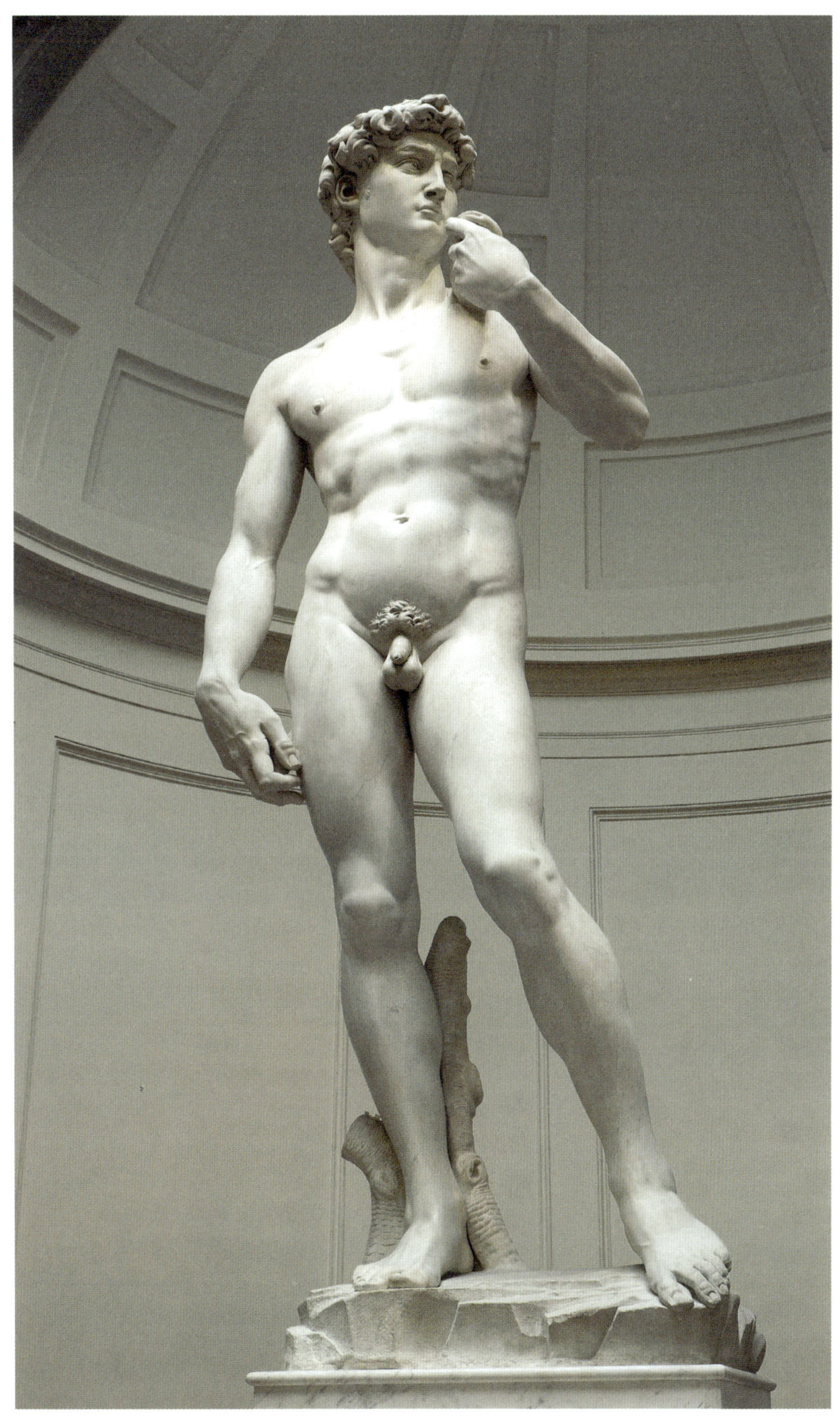

Michelangelo,
David, 1501–4.

knobbly knees and the barely suppressed anger of his face, take him out of the calm perfection of classical nudity into a more earthly, flawed realm. This hero is a frail mortal, his strength and self-control hard-won in a world of tough moral choices.

* * *

The 'naked peoples' of the New World helped inspire this new image of humanity. Florence's son Amerigo Vespucci wrote to his home city about the voyages he claimed to have undertaken between 1497 and 1504. (He seems to have reached the American mainland, but possibly not as early as he boasted.) Vespucci's *Letter to Piero Soderini*, published in 1504, was addressed to the head of the Florentine Republic, who was Michelangelo's friend and supporter. Vespucci's first sight of the 'natives' was of

> many men walking along the beach, at which we were much pleased; and we found that they were naked, and they showed fear of us, I believe because we were dressed and of a different stature.

This first impression was reinforced, for

> they all go naked, as well the men as the women, without covering anything, no otherwise than as they come out of their mothers' wombs. They are of medium stature, and very well proportioned. The colour of their skins inclines to red, like the skin of a lion, and I believe that, if they were properly clothed, they would be white like ourselves.[10]

David was created in the context of this expanding world, but he is not exotic or other. The hint of wildness in his defiant nudity suggests that true humanity is raw and natural, shorn of fine clothes, naked like Adam or the New Worlders.

Anyone who looks at *David* knows, however, that he is not just a body: he is a consciousness. The great art historian Jacob Burckhardt quoted Pico della Mirandola, whom Michelangelo probably met at Lorenzo the Magnificent's palace together with their mutual friend Poliziano, to sum up the discovery of human potential that Burckhardt believed occurred in the Renaissance. 'The brutes bring from their mother's body what they will carry with them as long as they live,' said Pico. But humanity is defined by choice: 'The higher spirits are from the beginning, or soon after, what they will be for ever. To thee alone is given a growth and a development depending on thine own free will.'[11] We can sink to the beasts or rise to the angels, depending on our actions. *David* can make you believe that.

That was all very well for Florentine intellectuals, but for Julius II it was probably the sheer heft of *David* that clinched his interest. The sensational statue in Florence was generally called 'the Giant'. To the embattled Florentine Republic, still liberated from Medici rule a decade on from its revolution, *David* symbolized a free city seeing off powerful enemies. This was confirmed in a backhanded way when Medici supporters stoned the statue as it was moved on rollers to the Piazza della Signoria. Soderini commissioned Michelangelo to cast a second *David* in bronze, rivalling Donatello's, just to underline the republic's identification with the plucky biblical hero. Machiavelli, one of Soderini's chief public servants, offers a highly political interpretation of the shepherd boy's victory over the Philistine. David's rejection of Saul's offer of armour is an example of why a state should take care of its own defences and never rely on mercenaries or bigger friends:

> David offered himself to Saul to fight with Goliath, the Philistine champion, and, to give him courage, Saul armed him with his own weapons; which David rejected as soon as he had them on his back, saying he could make no use of them, and that he wished to meet the enemy with his sling and his knife. In conclusion, the arms of others either fall from your back, or they weigh you down, or they bind.[12]

Such nuances of republican ideology were lost on Julius. Hearing about *David*, the ambitious pontiff may have asked himself: if this guy could make the shepherd boy 17 feet tall, what might he do for Goliath?

* * *

In 1505 the Warrior Pope ordered Michelangelo to work on a massive project that would return Rome to its days of imperial splendour and leave no doubt as to who had restored the city of the Caesars: a tomb for himself. The mausoleum of Julius II was to stand in the crumbling Basilica of St Peter's, founded by the Emperor Constantine over the tomb of the disciple Peter – and totally dominate it. The plans were startling. A huge, free-standing structure, like a giant coffer, would be surrounded by slightly larger-than-life statues of bound prisoners, with a higher tier of biblical prophets, angels and a colossal figure of the pope himself at the top. There would be forty statues in all.

Michelangelo was uneasy in Rome, as he negotiated the paranoid atmosphere of the papal court. It was probably a relief to escape to the quarries at Carrara, Italy's best source of marble since ancient times, to supervise the cutting of blocks of stone for the tomb. Spending days on end in this hollowed rocky wonderland near the sea between Genoa and Pisa, he daydreamed of making a truly titanic figure like the ancient Colossus of Rhodes. The spectre of gigantism seemed to haunt him as a possibility he had at his disposal: how big was too big? If *David* was large enough to seem alive, an even bigger statue might resemble a god – or a monster.

* * *

When all the marble was ferried down the Mediterranean coast, up the river Tiber and laid out in front of St Peter's, the pope was overjoyed. The 'impetuous' Julius now took a warm interest in the 30-year-old artist's work and visited his workshop frequently.

That was when the envy started, believed Michelangelo. He blamed the architect Donato Bramante, who had put forward his own artistic manifesto for a new Rome in 1502 with the comely little tomb he built over the site of the crucifixion of St Peter on the Janiculum Hill. Bramante's Tempietto – 'Little Temple' – is a miniature demonstration of geometrical sublimity, a perfectly circular gallery standing on regular columns enclosing a circular building capped by a dome. It took Renaissance architecture to a new level of geometrical grace. Picture this on a colossal scale, Bramante seems to be saying to Pope Julius.

Michelangelo later claimed that Bramante schemed against him and dripped poison in the pope's ear. By spring 1506 his anxiety and sense of alienation had got so bad that he made a secret dash on horseback to the safety of the Florentine Republic. Here he received the protection of Soderini. From Florence on 2 May 1506 he wrote to the architect Giuliano da Sangallo in Rome to explain his flight. He writes how, to his astonishment, he had overheard the pope saying to a 'jeweler' and his master of ceremonies that he didn't want to spend another penny on stone for the tomb, neither small nor big pieces. Cash for materials suddenly seemed unforthcoming, and the artist found himself denied access to the pope, like a nobody.

This humiliation left Michelangelo in 'great despair'. There was another reason for his fleeing Rome, he tells Sangallo, but he doesn't wish to write it down. It was enough to say that 'I thought that if I stayed in Rome that my tomb would be made before the pope's.'[13] He proposes to work on the tomb from Florence, pay for the marble to be shipped there, and then send each statue to Julius as he does them. Instead, an uneasy standoff developed in which the safety and happiness of one sculptor became a diplomatic issue between Rome and Florence.

Whether or not Michelangelo genuinely feared he would be murdered, this marked a turning point for the Renaissance cult of the artist. Dürer had depicted himself as a Christlike visionary; now Michelangelo proved in the most dramatic way that a great artist was not someone to be turned away by a flunkey but had to be handled with respect and sensitivity. His inner turmoil was not a shameful weakness but the soul of an artist and poet, inspired by fury – a fact that his patron simply had to accept. When Soderini brokered a meeting between Michelangelo and Julius in Bologna, the pope welcomed and forgave his rebellious artist.

Julius was in a good mood because he had just overthrown the ruler of Bologna and taken the city for the church. He wanted Michelangelo to make an outsized bronze statue of him in Bologna to remind the city who ruled it. The artist agreed, and Julius headed back for Rome. Michelangelo stayed eighteen months in Bologna to finish the hot, intricate work of casting a bronze figure over three times life size. It was placed above the door of the cathedral for all to admire and fear. When Bologna overthrew papal rule soon afterwards, its citizens pulled the statue down, broke it up and sold it to Alfonso d'Este of Ferrara, who used the bronze to make a gun mockingly named 'the Giulia'.

* * *

Michelangelo might be a less attractive artist if his statue of Julius had survived. It sounds like it was a bombastic image of a tyrant, the opposite of *David*. The planned mausoleum sounds like that, too. It is tempting to wonder if, behind his quickness to take offence, he was troubled by the commission itself. The works Michelangelo made for it are doubting, melancholy, unfinished. It is as if he were melting the image of power, recasting it in glimpses of suffering and desire.

The tomb was now on hold. One problem was that there was no longer a basilica for it to stand in. Julius had commissioned Bramante to begin completely rebuilding St Peter's. The same architect was working on a splendid classically inspired papal palace, the Belvedere; the new Rome was taking shape. Julius now wanted Michelangelo to fresco the ceiling of the Sistine Chapel while a rising star from central Italy called Raphael painted rooms in the Apostolic Palace nearby. The pope gave Michelangelo a freedom no artist had been allowed before. A fairly dry plan for decorating the Sistine ceiling with portraits of the twelve Apostles had been drawn up. Michelangelo told the pope it wouldn't work; Julius told him to paint what he liked.

You can tell the Sistine ceiling is Michelangelo's design simply by looking at it (overleaf). The complex, many-layered richness of this immense fresco flowing in one organic whole is a perfect synthesis of content and form, with an inseparability of narratives and personae from the logic of paint and architecture that only the artist can have conceived, as opposed to some putative clerical advisers telling him what to depict. There are startling elements of spontaneity. When modern restorers examined the painting, they found that the brushstrokes, especially in the *Creation* sections that Michelangelo painted last, are energized by improvisation. The plurality of narratives and times he created might even

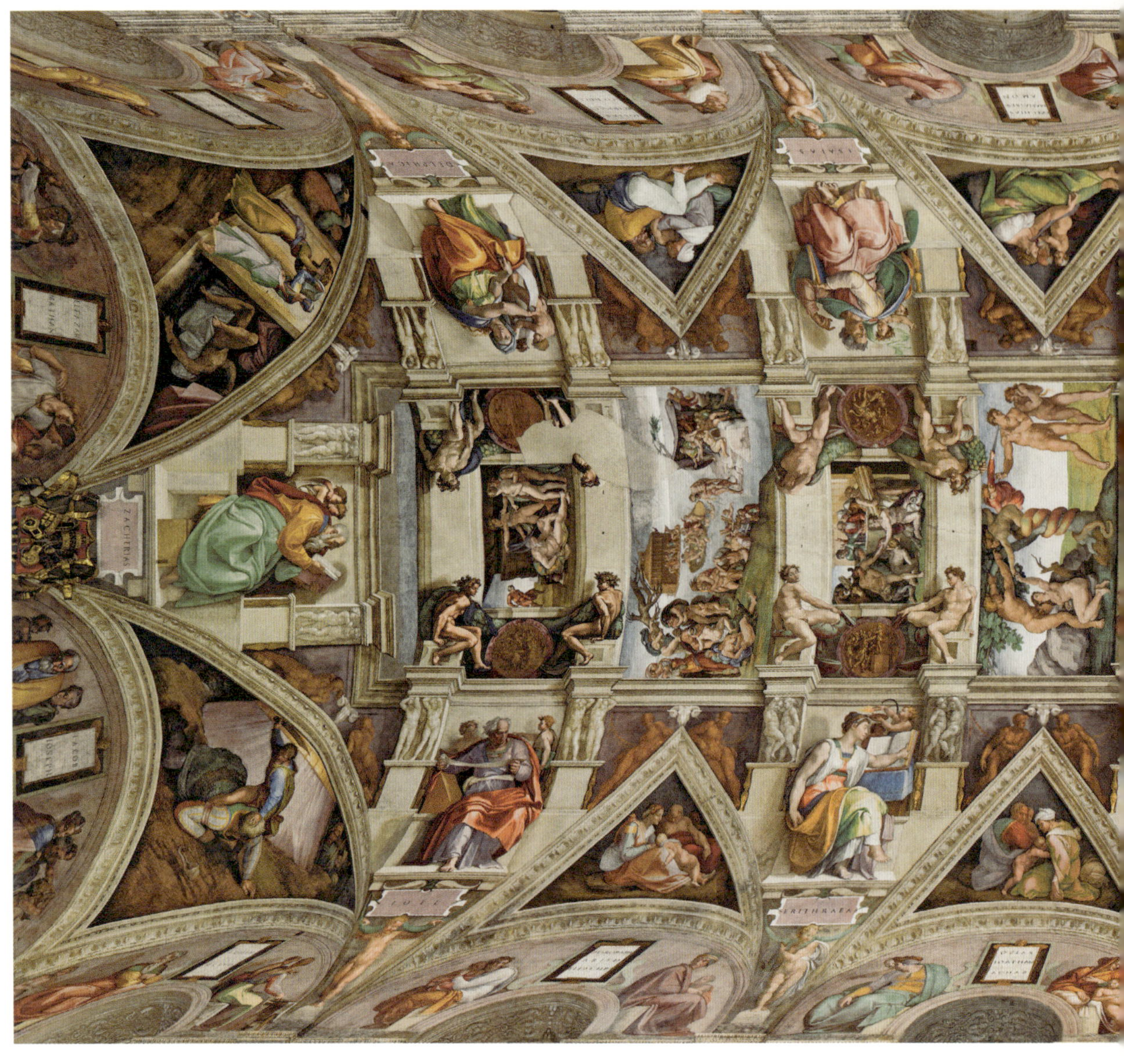

Michelangelo,
Ceiling of the Sistine Chapel, 1508–12.

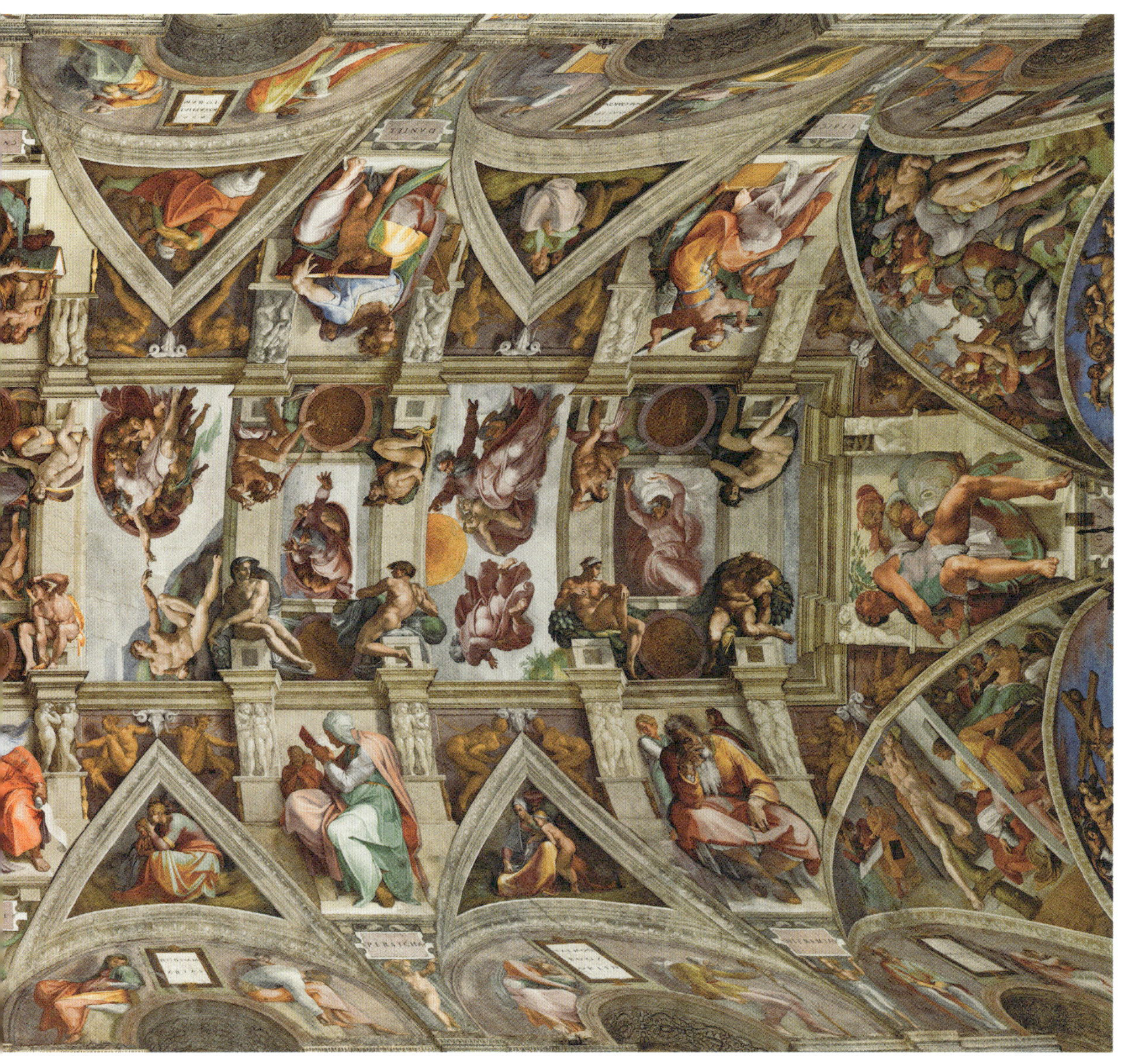

echo the ideas of Pico della Mirandola, who in the early 1490s was very close to Michelangelo's mentor Poliziano and so could have been known to the young artist. Below the main thrust of scenes from Genesis are depictions of prophets, including pagan Sibyls and Old Testament seers, implying a multitude of oracles. Most personal of all are the male nudes, whose holy innocence he proclaims from on high even as he delights in their bodies.

Raphael watched this audacious feat as he worked on his own gracious, calmly classical fresco of ancient Greek philosophers under a light-filled vault, the *School of Athens*, in the pope's palace. He included an awestruck if satirical portrait of Michelangelo as Heraclitus, sitting by himself on the steps, writing a poem, as he might have done in a break from his heroism in the heights: the artist as a baffling, creative 'maniac'.

In 1513, the year after Michelangelo completed the ceiling, Pope Julius II died. Michelangelo carried on working sporadically on the tomb, including its most sensational and perplexing figures: the naked *Prisoners* tightly tied up. In the first edition of the *Lives*, Vasari claims that these captives symbolized the provinces conquered by Julius for the church. Three years later Condivi offered an alternative interpretation: that they were personifications of the 'liberal arts' of the education system, supplemented by painting, sculpture and architecture, signifying that the arts too were subject to death and would never again find a patron like Julius to sustain them. Was Condivi thinking of Antonio del Pollaiuolo's tomb for Sixtus IV? This bronze monument was the only papal sepulchre preserved when Old St Peter's was demolished and has the liberal arts, personified as women with appropriate attributes, surrounding the recumbent Sixtus.

Not to be outdone, in his 1568 edition Vasari incorporated Condivi's view, suggesting that some of the figures of *Prisoners* represented the liberal arts while others were subjugated provinces. Condivi had claimed that each of the *Prisoners* as the liberal arts would have had its symbol, 'so by this each one would be easily recognized for what it was'.[14] 'Easily recognized' now seems remote from what the *Prisoners* have become, cut loose from Julius's tomb. It is, however, easier to accept Condivi's assessment of the two complete prisoners, that 'those who have seen them judge that nothing has ever been created more praiseworthy'.[15]

The *Dying Prisoner* (p. 196), carved in about 1513–15, is Michelangelo's most openly homoerotic statue. This nude, with tight bands around his body that would have bound him to the tomb, flings back his head in surrender, slipping into unconsciousness – or losing himself in ecstasy. His companion is the *Rebellious Prisoner*, who is struggling against his bonds, his face pleading for help (p. 196). Today they stand in empty space, their contrasting responses to their bondage

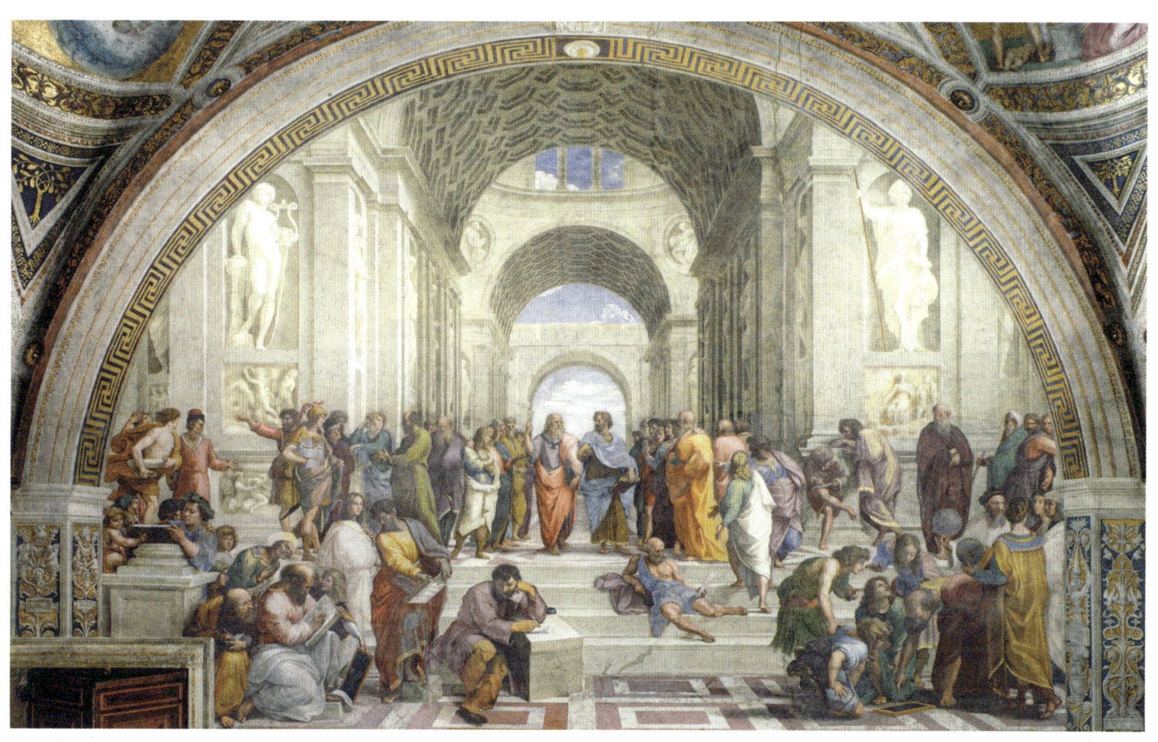

Raphael,
School of Athens,
c. 1510–12.

inviting thoughts on mortality. To struggle is to be alive: restless, unhappy, but hopeful. To give in to your fate is death. Yet their meaning is ambiguous: to struggle and rage is to be endlessly frustrated; surrender is sweet ecstasy.

Another set of captives, created in the 1520s, are such unfinished fragments that they were used as decorations in a Medici garden grotto for centuries. Their elegiac power was seen afresh in the age of Rodin. These four crushed giants seem enslaved not just by Julius but by matter itself. Their immense, hulking chests and bowed, bearded heads push against masses of raw stone. The pathos and beauty of the male body that so moved Michelangelo is punished here, shattered into fleeting memories of flesh – a muscular torso, an arm reaching over a head. It is as if the little swarming nudes from his youthful *Battle of the Centaurs* have reached gigantic proportions. Michelangelo's mental image of the tomb of Pope Julius II has in no way shrunk. Instead, it has become a formless outcrop, like the quarry at Carrara, a staggering mountain out of which human bodies push in an endless drama of longing and defeat.

Michelangelo, *Rebellious Prisoner*, 1513–15.

Michelangelo, *Dying Prisoner*, 1513–15.

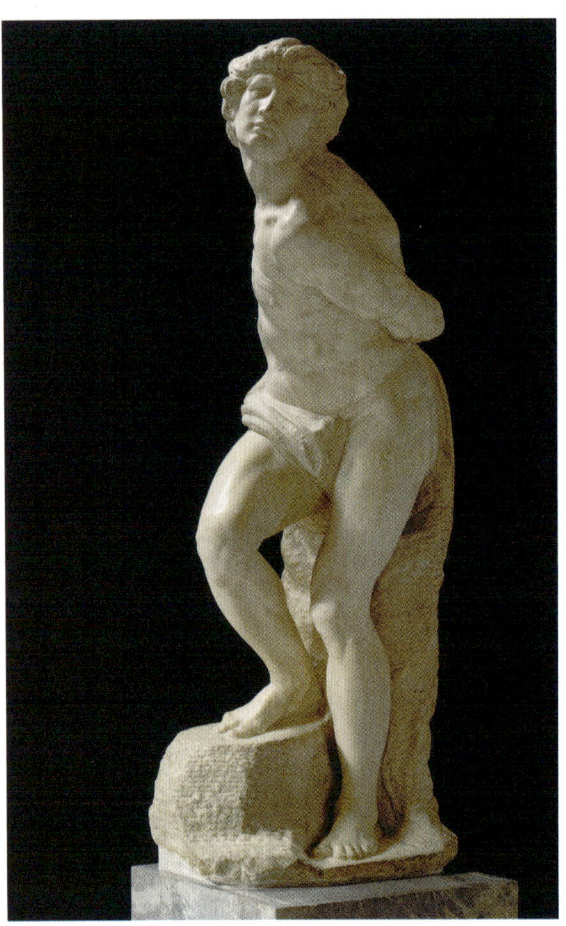

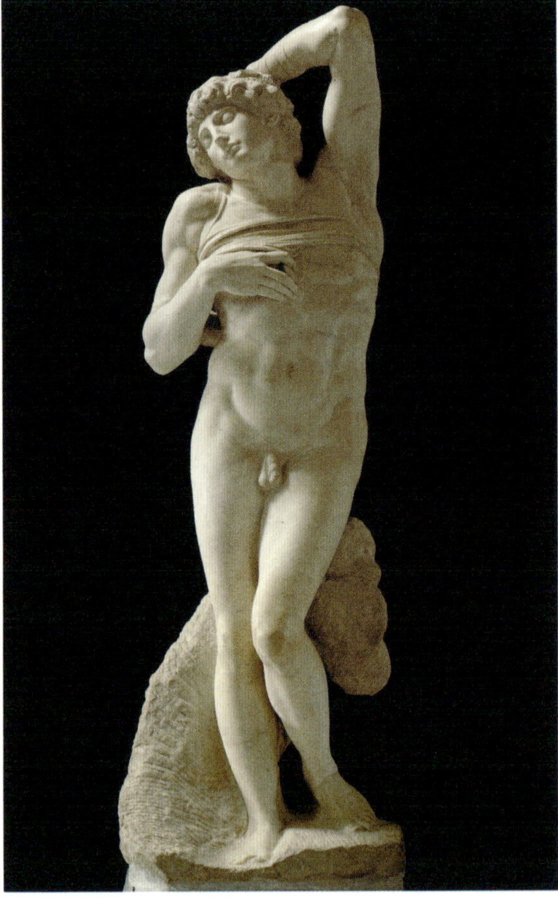

Michelangelo, *Awakening Prisoner*, c. 1520s.

Michelangelo, *Young Prisoner*, c. 1520s.

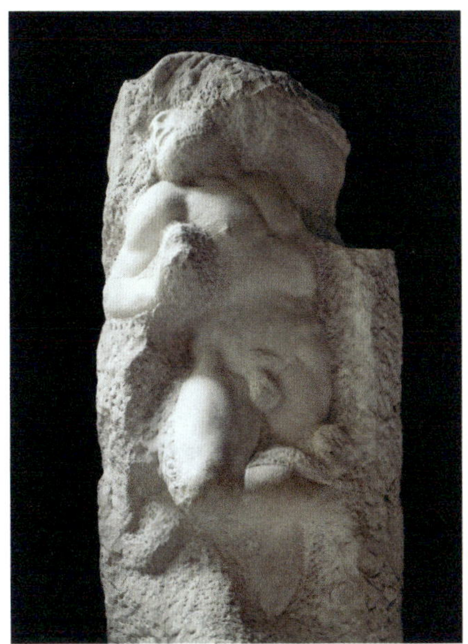

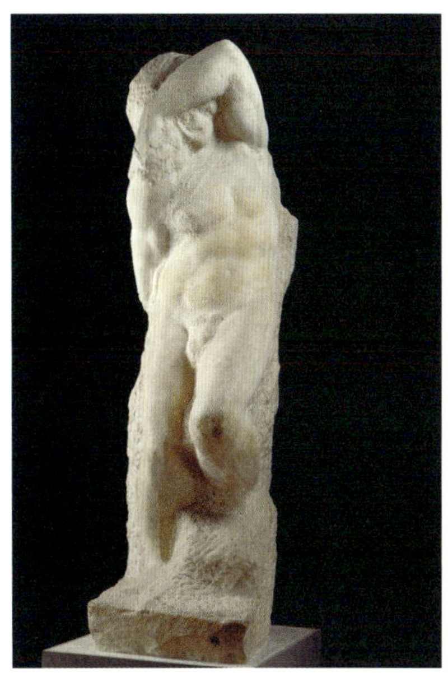

Michelangelo's definitive image for Julius is enthroned on the otherwise undistinguished tomb that was finally built in the hilltop church of San Pietro in Vincoli (overleaf). Moses turns to his left, staring challengingly at anyone who approaches him through the church. You feel that this must be how Julius burned you with his eyes when he was angry. He has horns, medieval attributes of Moses that add to his prickly aura. Yet he fingers a beard that flows like river. This facial hair, tenderizing a tough demeanour, has the same softening effect as a portrait of Julius that Raphael painted from life in 1511, when the downcast and frail-looking pope had grown a beard to mourn the loss of Bologna. Raphael makes Julius seem introspective rather than wrathful. Michelangelo's *Moses* is a more uneasy homage. You could claim Julius II was, like Moses, a leader of his people – if you wanted to be kind. The statue was so irresistible that Vasari says the Jewish community in Rome adopted it as their own and often came to see it.

The tomb of Julius II may seem the great failure of Michelangelo's career – Condivi calls it a 'tragedy' – and it got him into bitter financial wrangles with the dead pope's family. The artist wrote in a letter that he had been 'bound' to it, like one of his prisoners.[16] Yet when he gave away the *Dying* and *Rebellious Prisoners* to his friend Roberto Strozzi in the 1540s, who took them to France, he seemed deliberately to be ensuring that this tomb would never be a single, imposing image of papal power but instead experienced as fragments. Surely the tragedy would be if he had completed it as planned and produced a pompous folly. Anyone lucky enough to see the scattered sculptures he did create perceives a pathos totally free from bombast. The *Prisoners* are undying images

Michelangelo, *Moses*, c. 1513–15.

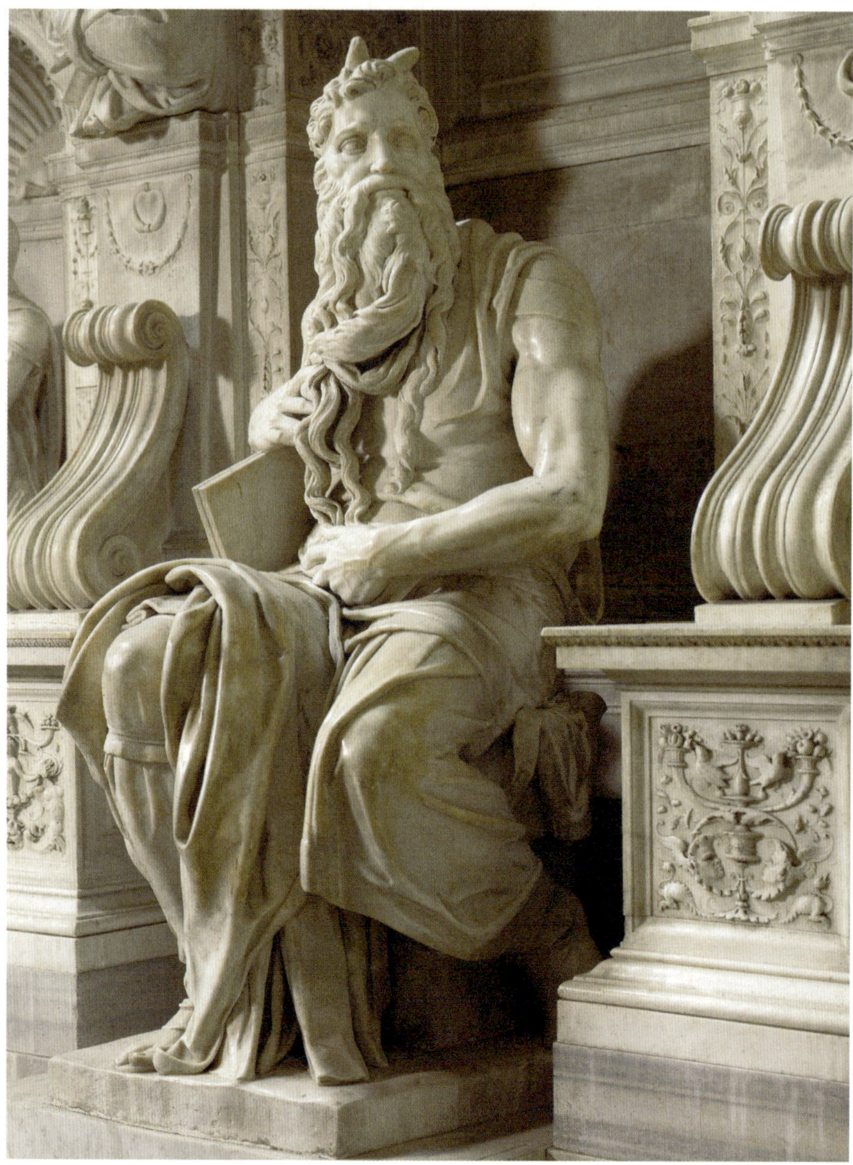

of the flux and pain of existence. Burckhardt was disappointed that the Italian Renaissance had produced no great tragedy; but at the time he was writing the Florentine *Prisoners* were still in the grotto of the Boboli Gardens behind the Pitti Palace. Since they entered the gallery of the Accademia in 1909 and were added to the other relics of the tomb, we can see that this is the Italian tragic masterpiece of the age, the brooding poetry of an age of war, the art of the inferno.

Julius had raised Rome from the ruins and set in motion a great age of building, sculpting and fresco painting that matched the ancients. The city now staked a claim to be the capital of Europe, even the world. It came with unexpected consequences. The new St Peter's would take many decades, several popes and numerous designers, including Michelangelo, to finish. The costs would spiral. And the church reaped the money from Christians. In 1515 a special sale of indulgences – papal guarantees of time off from purgatory – was instigated to raise money for the new basilica. It was targeted north of the Alps with the help of the Augsburg banker Jacob Fugger.

But one theologian at the University of Wittenberg was getting sick of the petty, mercantile answers the church offered to the question of how sinners can be saved. His view of human life resembled that of Bosch's *Haywain*: sin is universal, everyone is headed to hell. Pathetic nostrums like indulgences won't help: only the gratuitous mercy of God can save any of us brands from the fire. So in 1517 the theologian – named Martin Luther – wrote a letter protesting against the sale of indulgences and included a set of proposals for an academic debate on the subject, making the first gesture of a Reformation that would convulse Northern Europe. Julius II had transformed Rome, and helped to shatter the Christian world.

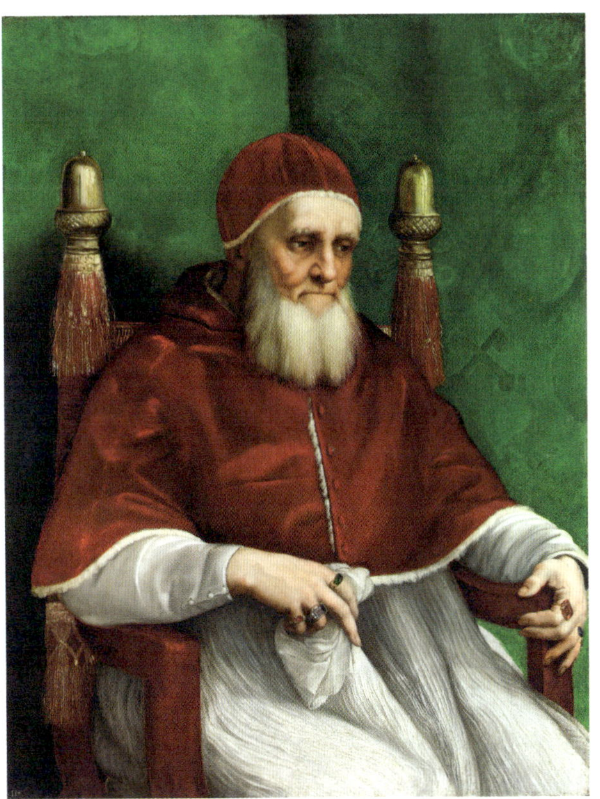

Raphael, *Portrait of Pope Julius II*, 1511.

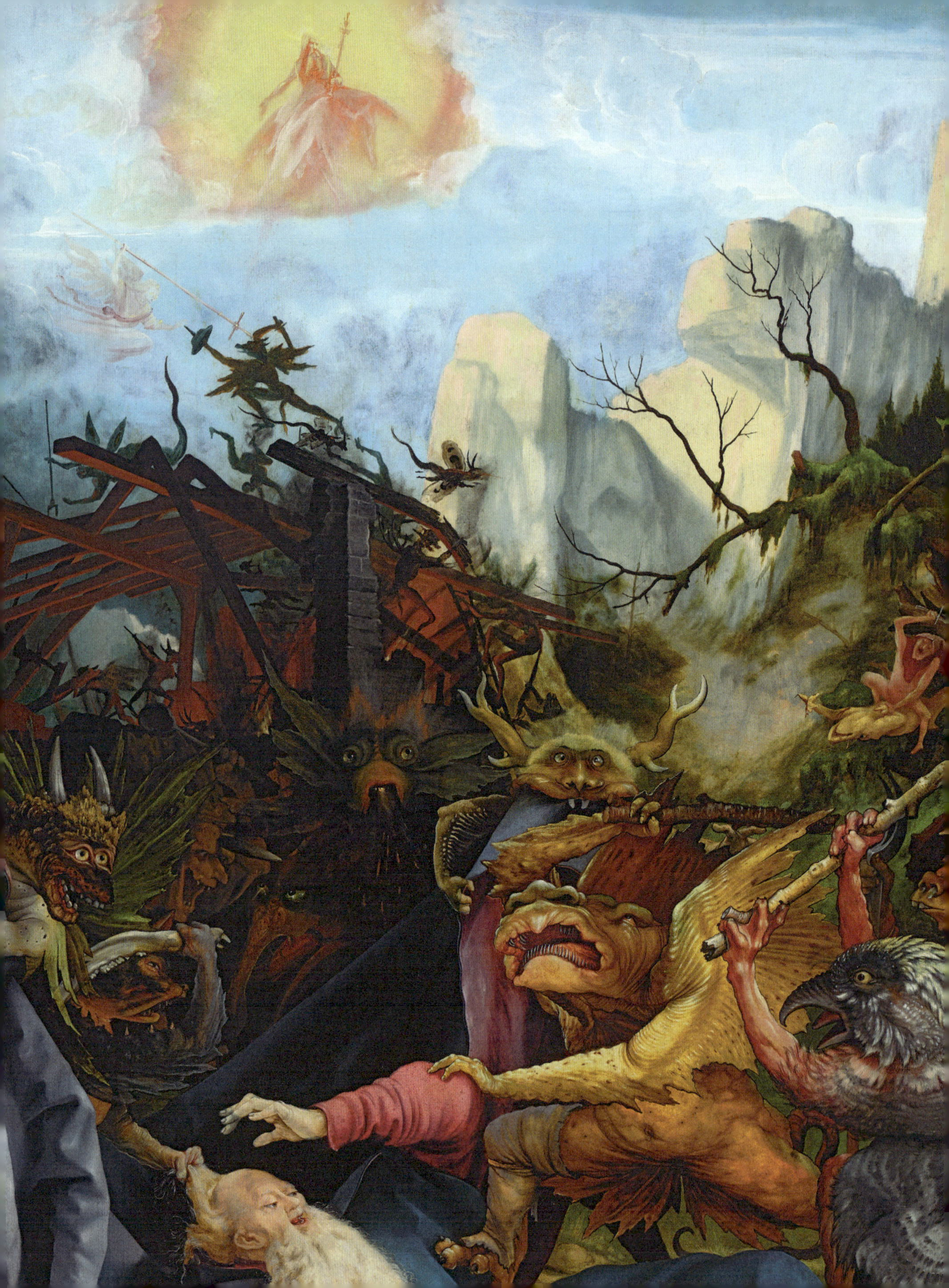

9 Melancholia

The man is dead, that's obvious. His eyes are horribly half open, but the pupils loll unseeingly. His mouth is agape, teeth visible. His beard, weirdly, grows up, towards the top of the long, narrow box in which he lies. His hair straggles. Most agonizing of all, his face has turned the grey-green colour of decay. This corpse rots from the extremities. The right hand, which we can see, is a livid hue, and the toes are black. The torso has a more lifelike tint, albeit terribly pale, the lance wound in its side a red gash against the white ribcage. Hans Holbein must have spent hours observing a recently deceased man, about 30 years of age, to see how the first marks of decay appear, how the skin lies drily on shrinking muscles, how the fingers close and claw.

Holbein painted the *Dead Christ in the Tomb* (overleaf), from 1521 to 1522, in a city where the Reformation was already a topic of discussion. Basel, on the river Rhine north-west of the Alps, would become officially Protestant (to use the modern term for this new kind of Christian) by the decade's end. It was a city of printers and thinkers, where Desiderius Erasmus, the greatest humanist scholar north of the Alps, moved to be near his publisher, Frobenius. Only in a free intellectual atmosphere could this picture of the repulsive corpse of Christ have been painted. It has nothing to soften the blow. There's no hint of heavenly light in those empty eyes. The tomb looks inescapable. The Russian

Matthias Grünewald, *Temptation of St Anthony* (detail), c. 1512–16.

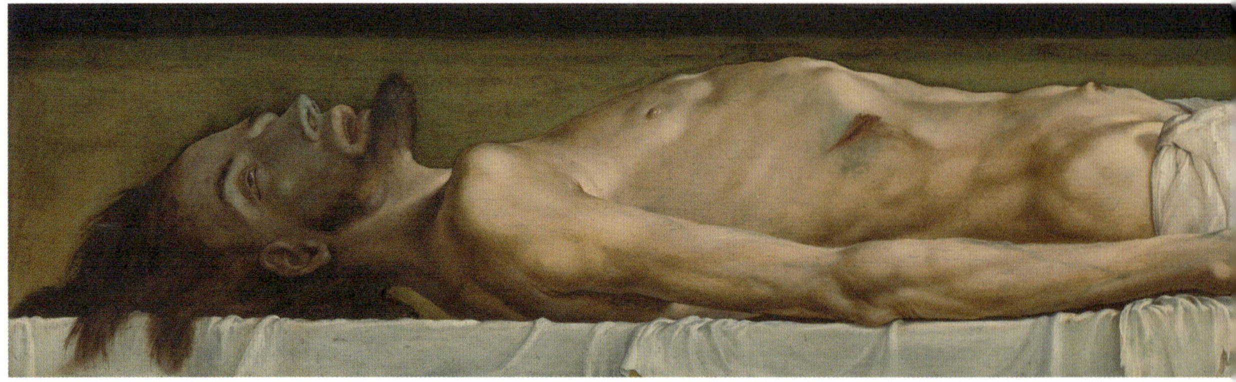

Hans Holbein, *Dead Christ in the Tomb*, 1521–22.

novelist Fyodor Dostoevsky was so perturbed when he saw this painting that he has Prince Myshkin, hero of *The Idiot*, see a copy and declare: 'Why, a man's faith might be ruined by looking at that picture!'[1]

The cold precision with which Holbein contemplates death and sees Christ as a specimen of morbid anatomy is avant-garde, even for an age when artists were studying the human body more closely than ever before. Leonardo kept his dissections separate from his religious art; even so, he had trouble with the church. In 1513 the Tuscan, who was now spending far more time on science than on painting, headed for Rome with his household, 'Giovanni, Francesco Melzi, Salaì, Lorenzo and il Fanfoia', to live in the Belvedere Palace as a guest of the Medici.[2] The head of the family, Lorenzo the Magnificent's son Giovanni, had just been chosen as Pope Julius II's successor, taking the name Leo X. It was an extraordinary posthumous triumph for the Magnifico, who started his son's church career to get the Medici the kind of religious power long taken for granted by Italian noble dynasties. Having reimposed their rule in Florence the previous year, the Medici were more commanding than ever.

Leonardo seemed to have had a comfortable new role, with plenty of space in Bramante's majestic palace for his experiments on parabolic mirrors that he promised could be used as burning weapons on the battlefield. However, suspicions were sparked by his anatomical research at the nearby Hospital of the Holy Spirit. Could such dissections be Christian? When he fell out with a German lens-grinder, the technician spread malign gossip about what Leonardo was up to. This man, complained Leonardo in a draft of a letter he may never have sent, 'has hindered me in anatomy blaming it before the Pope and likewise at the hospital'.[3]

One of the questions Leonardo asked – and that contravened all piety – was, what makes the human body mortal? Why does this beautiful machine fail?

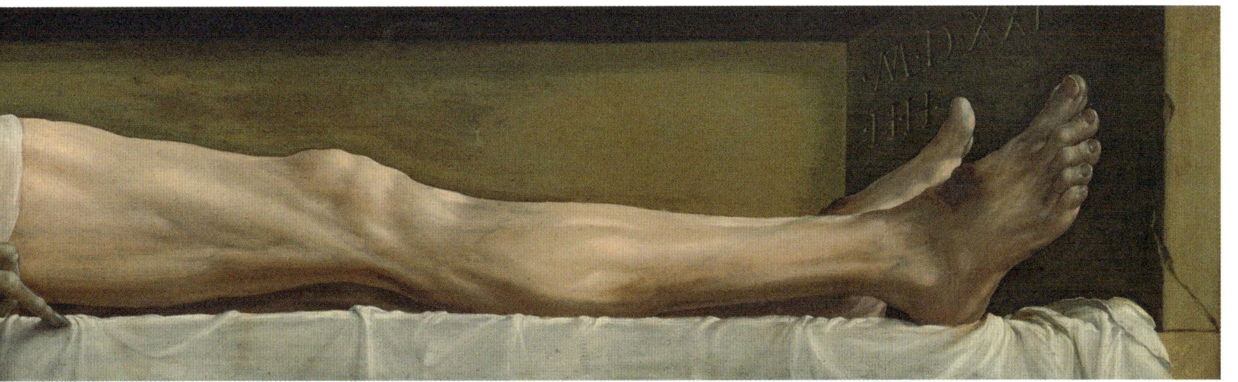

An especially graceful sheet of his dissection drawings depicts an arm flayed to expose interfolding muscles and webs of veins. Among these studies is the serene face of an old man who has just died. It could be the same man whose end he witnessed at Santa Maria Nuova hospital in Florence. In his notes he describes how

> this old man, a few hours before his death told me that he had lived a hundred years, and that he did not feel any bodily ailment other than weakness, and thus while sitting upon a bed ... without any movement or sign of anything amiss, he passed from this life.[4]

Here is a glimpse of Leonardo the doctor, sitting by the old man's hospital bed, talking to him gently, watching him with compassion. Then he dissected him:

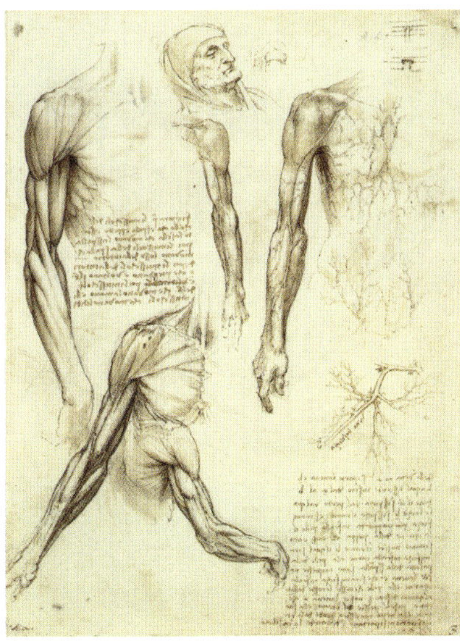

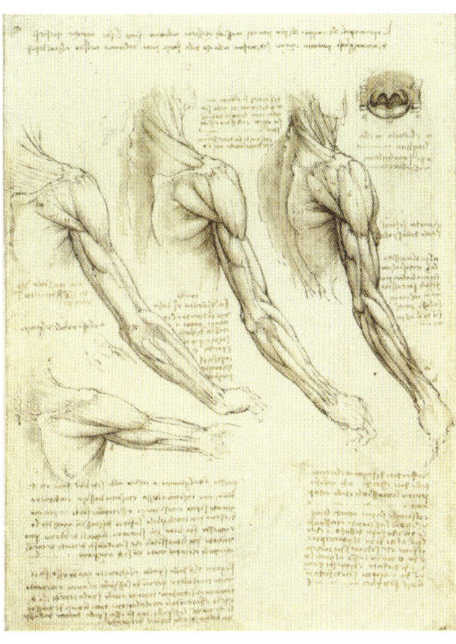

Leonardo da Vinci, *The muscles of the arm, and the veins of the arm and trunk*, c. 1510–11.

Leonardo da Vinci, *The muscles of the shoulder, arm and neck*, c. 1510–11.

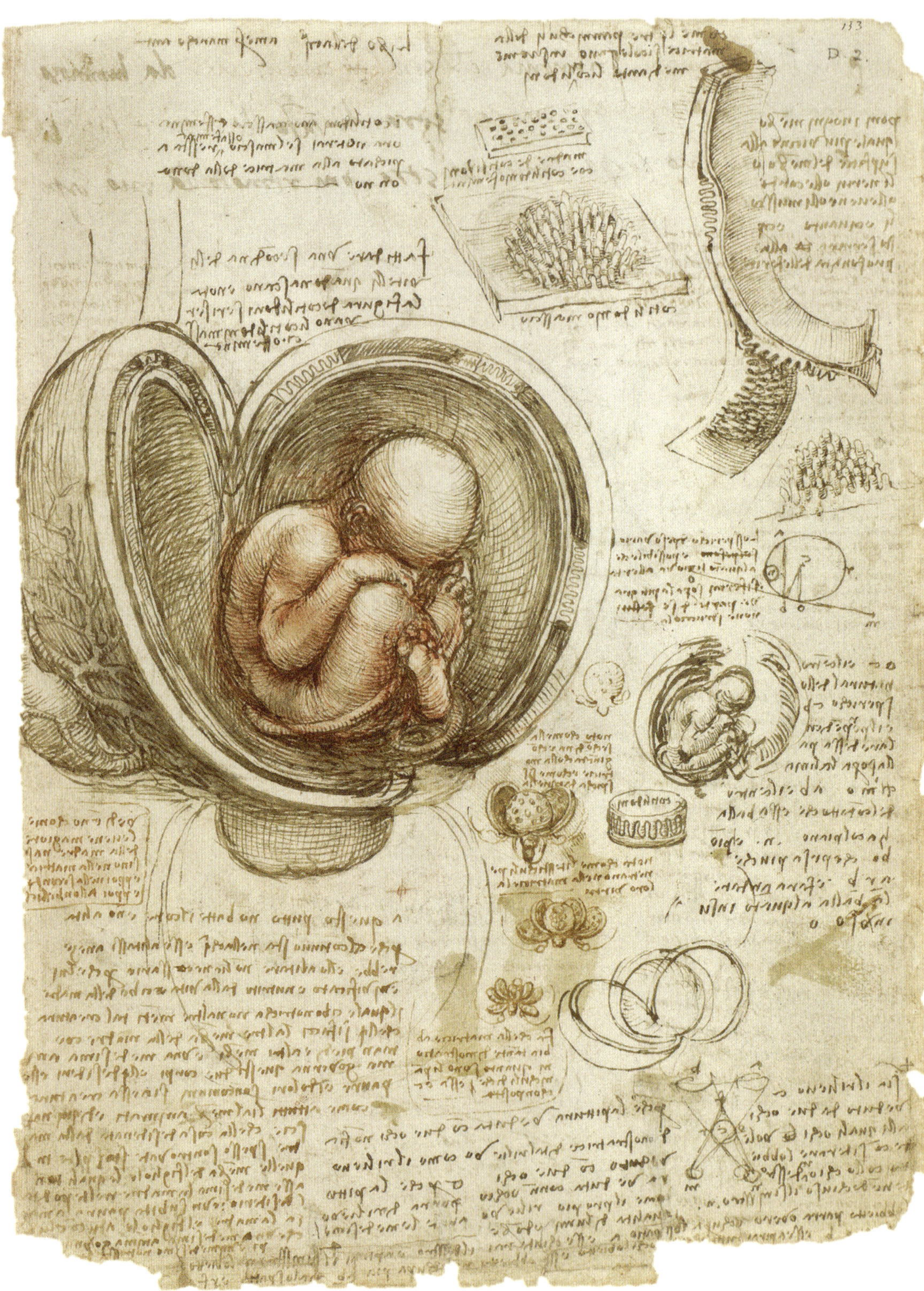

Leonardo da Vinci, *The foetus in the womb*, c. 1511.

> And I made an autopsy in order to ascertain the cause of so peaceful a death, and I found that it proceeded from weakness through failure of blood and of the artery that feeds the heart and the other lower members, which I found to be very parched and shrunk and withered; and the result of this autopsy I wrote down very carefully and with great ease, for the body was devoid of either fat or moisture, and these form the chief hindrance to the knowledge of its parts.[5]

It wasn't the only dissection he carried out:

> And the other autopsy was on a child of two years, and here I found everything the contrary of what it was in the old man.[6]

Death is the scientific problem at the centre of Leonardo's anatomy. All the bodies he dissected were obviously dead – as was the human foetus he drew. Death was everywhere, but it could be understood, believed Leonardo. The narrowing of arteries, the drying of the body with age, was not a divine curse but a mechanical process. The skin thickens and pressurizes the arteries: 'and from this it comes to pass that the old dread the cold more than the young, and that those who are very old have their skin the colour of wood or dried chestnut'.[7]

Leonardo was nervous that such matter-of-fact science was being painted as irreligious by vicious rumour. Leo X was a relaxed, even sybaritic pope, but that confidence went with a simple, happy promotion of the faith. Unnerving investigations rocked the broad-bottomed boat. In fact, anything melancholy or challenging was out of favour. Michelangelo was too saturnine for this pontiff, who remembered him as the brooding genius favoured by his father, Lorenzo de' Medici. Leo called Michelangelo 'terribile': awesome but scary. The artist who thrived most during his pontificate was Raphael, the most poised and reassuring of High Renaissance geniuses. Raphael's portrait of Leo X painted in 1518, a year after Luther's opening salvo, shows him studying an illuminated manuscript with a magnifying glass. It's significant. The angry evangelicals in Germany used print to spread their message; Leo lives in a comfortable world of expensive, hand-copied books.

Scrutiny of his science in the papal precincts may be one of the reasons Leonardo ended up an artist of the north. He plainly did not feel loved in Leo X's Rome. In 1516 he crossed the Alps to take up the offer of Francis I, the new king of France, to be his royal painter, 'peintre du Roy', with his own chateau near the royal palace of Amboise in the Loire Valley. He took with him his notes and the handful of paintings he was still refining.

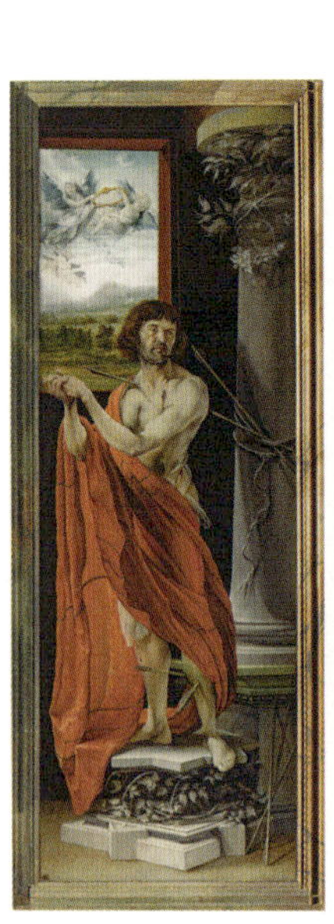
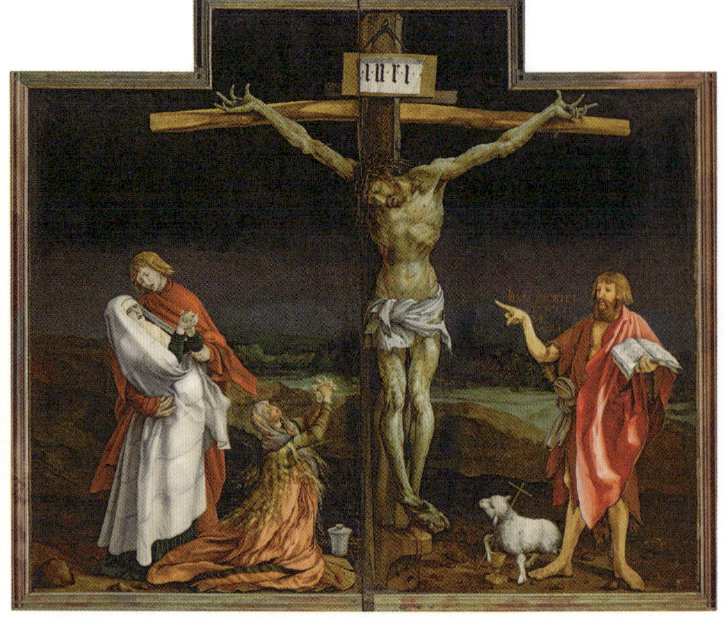

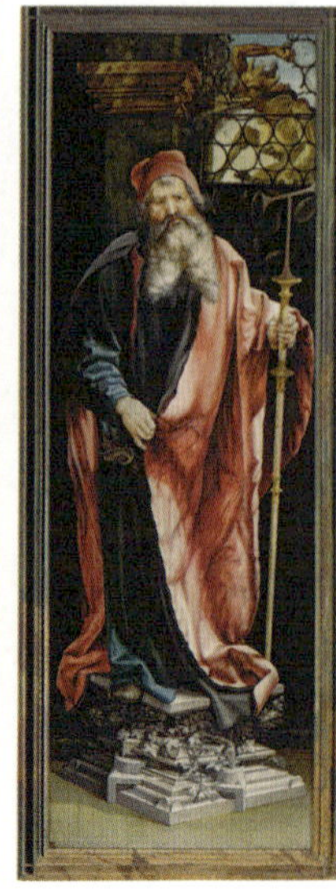
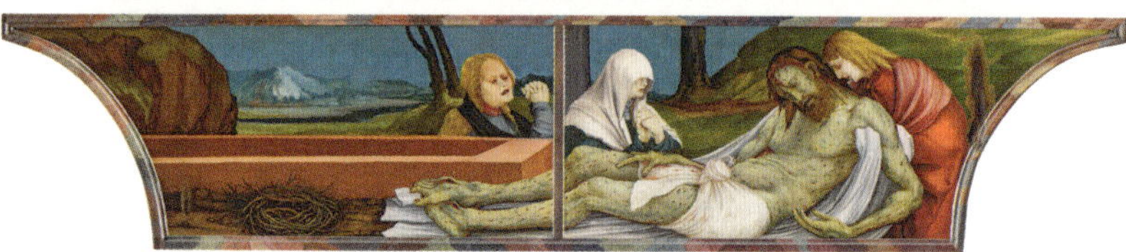

Matthias Grünewald, Isenheim Altarpiece, c. 1512–16.

* * *

The *Dead Christ in the Tomb* is as explicit as any of Leonardo's dissection drawings in its eye for biological facts. Holbein did not look at this body to find out more about the living, however. His painting is a merciless observation of what happens to a corpse. This was not a new theme in German art; the disturbing novelty is that Holbein strips it of any visible promise of the Resurrection and the life to come.

Just before the start of the Reformation, near Colmar, a day's ride north of Basel – or you could go by boat on the Rhine – a crucifixion was painted that still horribly enthrals. Matthias Grünewald's Christ appears to have started rotting even before his final breath. His body on the cross, as he finally slumps his head, is a gangrenous mass of sores. Black spots erupt all over his brown, grey, green and yellow skin. His fingers tighten and bend as if the tendons were shrinking. His feet have succumbed to septic necrosis. No wonder his mourners don't seem in any hurry to touch him. They pray and sob from a safe distance. They do take him down, of course, and in the panel below lament over his putrescent corpse beside the waiting tomb. It is a second chance to study the tumescent shadows that burst from his lifeless skin.

This horrible corruption of Christ's flesh is a clinical rendering of a real medical condition. Grünewald painted his polyptych for a monastery that specialized in helping people suffering from 'St Anthony's fire'. Grünewald, like Leonardo, has gone into a hospital and spent time with the sick and dying. His masterpiece, the Isenheim Altarpiece, is art as therapy and a tour de force of the kind of magical thinking Luther wanted to abolish. The complex wooden structure unfolded like a gripping piece of cinema, panel after panel, to take the patients who saw it on a spiritual journey from despair to salvation. They might not recover, in an age that had no real medicine. But they could hope for deliverance in the life to come.

Those afflicted with St Anthony's fire became blotched and discoloured as gangrene developed in their hands and feet. The monks gave them fortified wine impregnated with physical relics of St Anthony and applied a herbal salve. Who knows, perhaps this helped psychologically. In reality, this common medieval illness was caused by rye infected with ergot, a fungus.

Christ's suffering in Grünewald's painting is a faithful image of the agonies of ergotism. On another panel, visible only when the altarpiece is fully open, patients could perceive the same tell-tale signs of fungus-induced necrosis on a figure in the foreground of the *Temptation of St Anthony* (overleaf). Above this sufferer, a scene of the desert saint's torment explodes in hideous forms and hallucinatory colours. The white-bearded holy man is plucked and mocked by demons. A bird-man clubs at him. A toothy face with antlers peeps over an orange creature with dragon wings, shark head and thick, humanoid legs. A tonsured, werewolfish character attacks a gnome-like man who is straddling a toad. These horrors materialize not in a faraway desert but in a German landscape, with winter branches and distant fir trees rising towards Alpine peaks. It's a nightmare taking place in a sweaty delirium.

Yet Grünewald brings hope. The horrors in the Isenheim Altarpiece are matched and – for the believer – outdone by luminous visions of redemption. The *Annunciation* and *Nativity* blaze with red and gold and pay homage to Mary, the most merciful of heaven's intercessors. Mary looks at the Infant Christ with infinite maternal love, and the patient is invited to bask in that love. Between these two scenes a choir of angels performs under a gilded Gothic canopy, like the musicians at the Red Cloister who played for the mentally ill Hugo van der Goes. Most dazzling of all, Christ rises from his tomb, his body shining, his hair golden as he floats in a bronze disc of heavenly light. Every trace of the sores and gangrene that covered his dead body has vanished. Purity emanates from him and promises rapturous renewal to ailing and dying humanity.

Matthias Grünewald, *Temptation of St Anthony*, inner wing of the Isenheim Altarpiece, c. 1512–16.

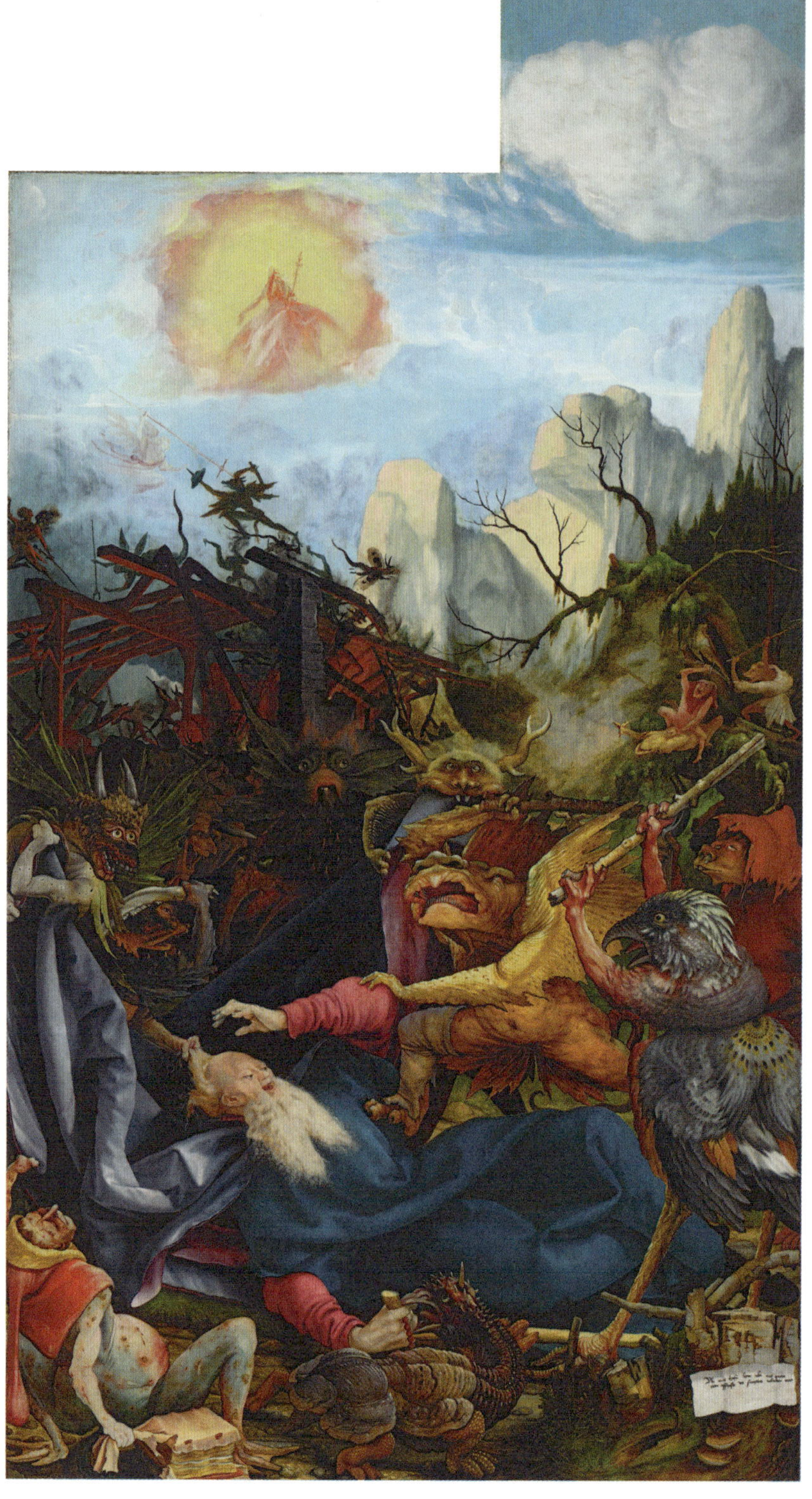

This is how art soothed the suffering and brought light to the downcast as late as 1516, in a place not so far from Basel. By 1521 Holbein dared picture a dead Christ with no promise he'll ever get out of that box. It is as if the logic of medieval art has suddenly collapsed, shorn of its choirs of angels and gentle Madonna, reduced to an image of a dead man shut in a tomb, with no context, in a disenchanted world. What can have caused this fall?

* * *

In 1519 a stonemason from Regensburg in Bavaria called Jacob Kern had a serious accident and wasn't given much hope of survival. His wife prayed to a local relic, the 'Beautiful Virgin', which was believed to be a portrait of Mary painted from life by St Luke. Her prayers were answered: the man made a miraculous recovery. Word of the painting's efficacy spread like a virus, and crowds came from far and wide to seek the aid of the 'Schöne Maria'. Pope Leo recognized its status, and the artist Albrecht Altdorfer created souvenir prints you could buy at the shrine.

Martin Luther was appalled, although not for the reasons we are today. Kern sustained his injury as part of a mob tearing down Regensburg's synagogue after the city had expelled its Jewish community. That didn't worry Luther. He was simply furious that, at a time when his condemnation of empty superstition was creating a stir, yet another idiotic instance of Mariolatry proved it was still big business. Such shrines should all be destroyed, he insisted, putting the

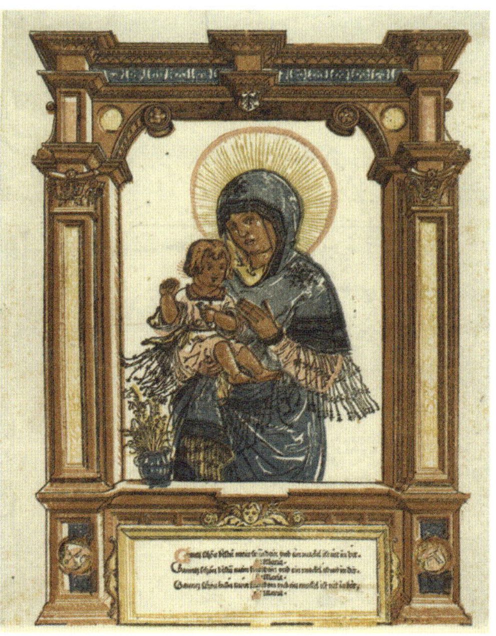

Albrecht Altdorfer, *Beautiful Virgin of Regensburg*, c. 1519–20.

spark to what became firestorms of iconoclasm: in the decades to come, radical Protestants smashed stained glass, attacked statues with hammers and tore down places of pilgrimage to free Christianity from its false accretions of claptrap.

It was an extreme rebellion within the religion shared by most Europeans. Luther's arguments were rooted in a close reading of the Bible made possible by the new humanist scholarship, yet he risked being seen as another in a long line of offbeat cultists, like the Cathars in south-west France or the Lollards in England, persecuted as heretics by the medieval church. To Rome, Protestants would be just that, 'heretics', for a long time to come. And there was some rationale for this. They were turning the faith of their parents, and parents' parents, upside down. Venerating Mary was now wrong; art in church was idolatrous; the pope was a fraud. There was no need for monks, nuns, a celibate priesthood. As for purgatory, relics and the rest – God help us. For nothing else can.

We are all born into mortal sin. God's bountiful grace alone can redeem such lost souls. Even a brand-new work of religious art such as the Isenheim Altarpiece was worthless in this belief system. Yet Luther did not hate art. When he married Katherine von Bora in 1525 – an ex-monk marrying an ex-nun – the Wittenberg artist Lucas Cranach was his best man.

Cranach's 1529 painting *The Law and the Gospel* tries to explain Luther's teaching in images: the true Christian who puts his faith in the love of Christ is saved, while one who relies on human lawgivers such as Moses is doomed to hell. It's not his most alluring work. More piquant were the hard-hitting, anti-papist prints his workshop churned out. *The Papal Ass in Rome*, published in 1523, gives the pope a donkey's head and an androgynous, scaly body; female

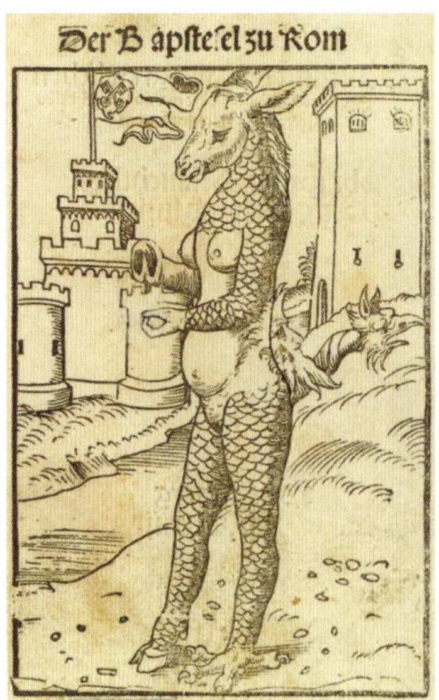

Workshop of Lucas Cranach the Elder, *The Papal Ass in Rome*, 1523.

Lucas Cranach the Elder, *Venus in a Landscape*, 1529.

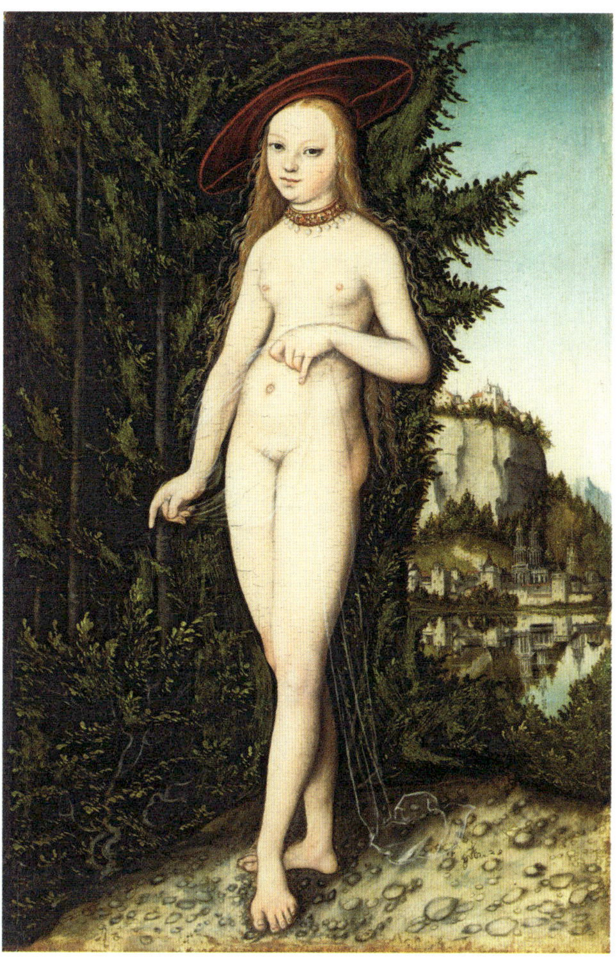

breasts poke out from a sleek reptilian form which also has a bearded face emerging from its arse.

This gender-bending satire is not so far from the products of Cranach's day job as an erotic artist for aristocratic clients. Where the young Dürer had anguished over the classical nude, Cranach exults in its sinfulness: he has a penchant for it. His female nudes are slender and small-breasted, any hint of maternal fecundity effaced. They look like modern models. Yet his women need not be naked to be sexualized. Cranach's Salome is bedecked in finery as she shows the severed head of John the Baptist on a platter: her gold and velvet and silks underline her cool, commanding beauty. The Baptist's head has its gory neck towards us, an image of castration and submission at the hands of the bejewelled seductress.

Cranach's eroticism is perfectly in tune with Luther, for whom the Fall defines us, with lust its inevitable human fruit. Cranach depicts a fallen world where every woman is a wicked Eve. In his 1526 painting *Cupid Complaining to Venus*, the little god of love has tried to steal honey from a bees' nest and got stung. Yet the picture itself is also a honeytrap: Venus reaches up to an apple tree that reminds you of the first sin in Eden. In 1529 Cranach painted *Venus in a Landscape* (p. 211). With a dimpled chin and disingenuous gaze, the goddess looks like a real woman wearing a rakishly angled, bloody-coloured hat, a pearl collar, and nothing else except for some transparent silk she dangles in front of her. There's a castle in the distance, but no fortification can stop fornication. We are in a wicked place. Cranach's *Venus* is barely a goddess at all: she is simply bare.

* * *

The *Dead Christ in the Tomb* comes from the heart of a moment when the relics and saints that had reassured people for centuries were being denigrated, when Christians were satirizing the leader of the church as a scaly ass-headed monster, when an artist like Holbein faced an uncertain future if religious images were to be condemned as idolatrous. The Reformation was an attempt to purify faith, but it was so rationalist that it risked negating what many meant by belief. Holbein dares to show a Christ who is dead in a world without ritual or reassurance. He depicts an extreme implication of the revolution in belief: no belief at all.

That must have been a melancholy thought. But melancholy, suggests Albrecht Dürer in an engraving he published in 1514, is the natural state of the true artist. Dürer's print shows a winged female spirit, or genius, sitting paralysed and disconsolate – her face in shadow, her cheek resting on her hand in a traditional medieval pose denoting the melancholy humour – listlessly holding a pair of dividers. A carpenter's plane, saw and nails lie discarded at her feet, while other tools and instruments are chaotically scattered about; two perfect geometrical sculptures, a sphere and a polyhedron, show what she is capable of on a good day. A balance, an hourglass, a bell and a number square – in fact a magic square, in which the numbers in all the rows, columns and quadrants add up to 34, and symmetrical numbers about the centre add up to 17 – suggest both science and mortality. The year 1514 can be seen in the grid of numbers as if flashed up by a doomsday clock. A putto looks as downcast as the genius. Over a grey sea of horizontal ink lines, lit by a sun that pierces the sky with its rays and creates a rainbow, flies a bat-like creature with a banner that reads 'MELENCOLIA I'.

This image of what looks like a stalled architectural and sculptural project was created soon after the death of Pope Julius II. It might have seemed that his desire to rebuild Rome had died with him. Michelangelo's *Dying* and *Rebellious Prisoners* date from this period, as the tomb of Julius turned into exactly the kind of stop-and-start, stupendously ambitious yet tragically unfinished artistic work Dürer depicts here. It was at this time too, according to Vasari, that

Albrecht Dürer, *Melencolia I* (first state), 1514.

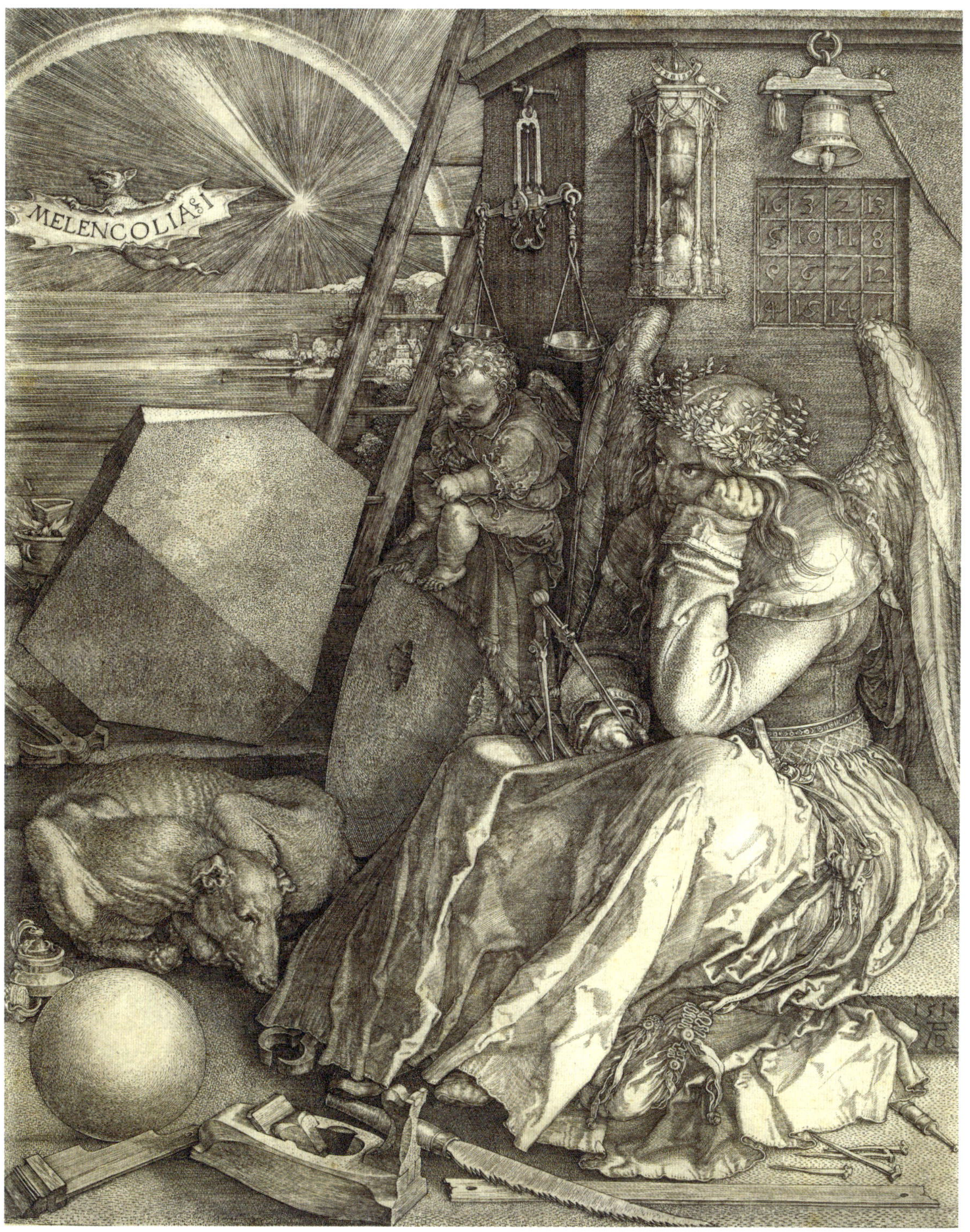
MELENCOLIA § I
16 3 2 13
5 10 11 8
9 6 7 12
4 15 14 1

Leonardo was being dismissed by Pope Leo X as someone who never finished his projects: 'Alas! this man will never do anything, for he begins by thinking of the end of the work, before the beginning.'[8]

Dürer had been to Italy and was smitten by its artists. He pays homage to Leonardo in his prints of knot designs based on the procrastinating polymath's works. So it is no exaggeration to say that Dürer is diagnosing the malady of the Italian geniuses of his age, based on information from Rome. Dürer is a genius himself, of course. He suggests it is necessary to be melancholy, to let your mind wander over dreary seas of nothingness. Only then will you see the light of inspiration blast the sky apart.

* * *

Holbein too drifts on that melancholy ocean. His painting of the decaying corpse of Christ risks a distressing thought: what if there were no Resurrection? Yet all is not quite as it seems. In fact, the very meaning of this painting is that things are not always what they seem. They may be the opposite.

The *Dead Christ in the Tomb* is not a Protestant painting, nor an atheist one. It is philosophical. Holbein knew the towering northern intellectual Desiderius Erasmus in Basel and read his wittiest work, a satire called *Praise of Folly*. Erasmus had seen Julius II's Italy and was not impressed. He called for a Catholic renewal, and his new Greek edition and Latin translation of the Gospels provided the material for one. The renewal turned out to be the root-and-branch Reformation, however. Erasmus didn't want to change the Christian faith as absolutely as Luther, but in *Praise of Folly*, published in 1511, he adopts the voice of the mock-goddess Folly to point out such abuses as a pope going to war. Folly, in other words, isn't such a fool as she looks.

Folly gets philosophical and reaches for an image in the *Symposium* to justify her paradoxical satire, pointing out that truth itself is elusive. In Plato's dialogue, Alcibiades compared Socrates to ceramic figurines of Silenus, the old, drunk and corpulent companion of the god Dionysus. These 'Sileni' possessed a secret, for they were hollow inside, and when you took them apart you saw that they contained little figures of gods. For Alcibiades, Socrates is a 'Silenus' because, despite appearances, he contains treasure within. Erasmus interprets this image as an expression of the fundamental ambiguity of 'all human affairs' – even life and death:

> It is a given that all human affairs are like the Sileni of Alcibiades which have sides that are completely dissimilar from each other. So what at first sight, as they say, is death, if you look within it, is life: and the opposite, what is life is death.[9]

Hans Holbein and his brother, Ambrosius, who was the illustrator of More's *Utopia*, left doodles in the margins of the copy of *Praise of Folly* they studied, so Hans definitely read it. The *Dead Christ in the Tomb* could be a Silenus. What is death at first sight is life if you look within. In another masterpiece more than a decade later and in a different country, Holbein would explore the other side of the paradox, that what looks like life may really be death.

The Renaissance was expanding. Its networks of merchants, humanists, printers and artists were latticing Europe and looking beyond it. In July 1520 Dürer and his wife, Agnes, set out on a year-long trip to the Netherlands that took in a microcosm of this ebullient international society. The real purpose of the trip was to make sure that he continued getting his pension from the Holy Roman Emperor. Maximilian was dead, and his grandson was due to be crowned Charles V at Aachen. It would be a weighty moment in European history. As a result of Maximilian's dynastic plans, Charles ruled not only German lands but Spain and the former Duchy of Burgundy. He governed Spain's colonies, including the newest, Mexico.

The Dürers sailed up the Rhine to the Netherlands and stayed in Antwerp. There they met friends from the Fugger banking family, as well as Peter Giles, who appears in Thomas More's *Utopia*, and the artist Quentin Metsys (or Quinten Massys), creator of the painting of an old woman with a distorted jaw and face

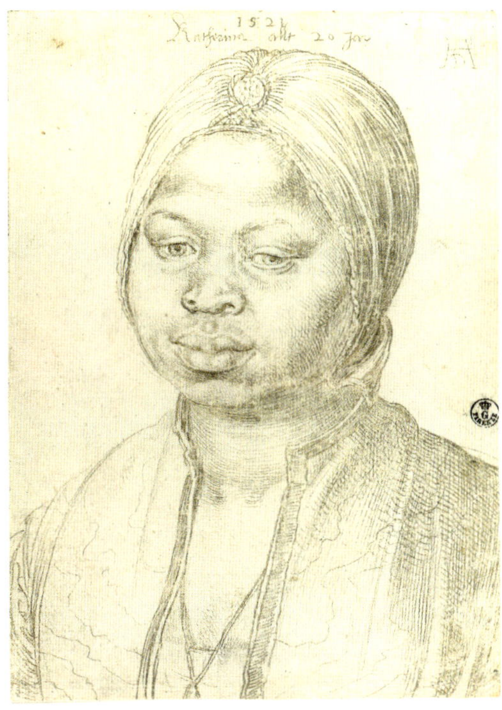

Albrecht Dürer,
Portrait of Katharina,
1521.

known as the *Ugly Duchess* that is intimately related to a drawing by Leonardo. They also encountered some friendly Portuguese merchants. Dürer visited Ghent to see the van Eyck altarpiece, dined out constantly and drew portraits of the people he met, including a 20-year-old African woman whose name he records as Katharina (p. 215). She was a servant of one of the Portuguese merchants with whom he dined. Katharina looks down sadly as he carefully portrays her: a study in melancholy.

While in Antwerp, Dürer got the shocking news from Germany that Luther had been captured and might be dead. He wrote emotionally in his journal: 'Whether he lives yet or whether they have put him to death, I know not. If he has suffered, it is for the sake of Christian truth.'[10] Dürer's vehement reaction to what turned out to be a false alarm shows how much he was drawn to Luther's new ideas. But then he had an appetite for novelties. In the Netherlands he drew a walrus, his eye feasting on its distinctive anatomy. When he saw Aztec treasures on display in Brussels, sent to Charles V by the conquistador Hernán Cortés, he was so awestruck that he declared:

> All the days of my life I have seen nothing that reaches my heart so much as these, for among them I have seen wonderfully artistic things and have admired the subtle ingenuity of men in foreign lands; indeed, I don't know how to express what I there found.[11]

It's the most enthusiastic response on record by a Renaissance artist to art made outside Europe. Dürer looks at the golden sun discs and turquoise daggers of Moctezuma and admires their craftsmanship with open mind and heart.

Back home, Dürer discussed Luther's ideas with intellectual friends. His portrait of the beady-eyed, thin-faced Philip Melanchthon, who taught Greek at Wittenberg, was executed when this collaborator of Luther was staying with Dürer's friend Pirckheimer. Yet Luther was not just a hero to the educated elite. In 1524 his impact was felt in a way that terrified Luther himself. German peasants rose up in the biggest popular rebellion in Europe before the French Revolution. They quoted Luther freely. The Reformation was shaking the social order.

Dürer commemorates this uprising and its bloody defeat in a work of bitter irony. For Luther had turned on the peasants and called for their suppression – a crackdown the ruling orders were happy to enact. Dürer proposes a monument to the peasants in which a milk jug, wheatsheaf, hoes, forks and other agricultural implements are balanced one on top of the other to create a column. At its summit sits a peasant resting his head on his hand, a rustic figure of Melancholy. He has a sword in his back.

It is a Silenian satire. Is Dürer mocking the peasants or mourning them? His monument can be seen both ways: as a cruel taunt, or as a furious denunciation of the educated Lutherans who stabbed their poor brethren in the back.

* * *

Dürer never sailed across the North Sea to England. The closest he came was a boat trip off the Dutch coast that nearly ended in disaster when the wind caught the sails and pulled the vessel back out to sea when they were disembarking; in the panic it was Dürer who held his nerve, commanded the ship and saved the day. Had he crossed those treacherous waters, he would have found the Tudor dynasty imposing its proud image on England. Henry Tudor took the crown from Richard III at the Battle of Bosworth Field in 1485 after decades of aristocratic feuding and what Thomas More described in a biography of Richard as the rule of a tyrant antichrist. England was now producing its own Renaissance scholarship and writing. More and the educational reformer John Colet were leading lights of humanism in the English capital. And More was on the up in court politics, bringing his serious wit into the privy council of Henry VIII.

Erasmus dedicated *Praise of Folly* to More; its first title, *Moriae encomium*, is a pun on his name. In the preface he compares More to the ancient Greek Democritus, the so-called 'Laughing Philosopher', for 'Though indeed through the exceptional character of your intelligence you are accustomed to diverge in your views far and wide from the crowd, by the incredible sweetness and grace of your manners you are able to, and rejoice in your ability to get on with all men at all times.'[12]

Erasmus thought More might get on with Hans Holbein, the artist he knew in Basel. In 1526 Holbein headed for England with a letter of recommendation to More from Erasmus. More duly commissioned a group portrait of himself and his family, for which Holbein drew intimate, precise studies of the royal adviser's household and kin at his riverside home in Chelsea. The painting is lost, but Holbein's compositional drawing suggests it contained a memento mori amid the vivacious family: a state-of-the-art wall clock, ticking life's time away.

It was ticking away for More. By October 1529 he was Lord Chancellor, but Henry VIII wanted to divorce his wife, Catherine of Aragon, to marry Anne Boleyn. The pope would not allow it – naive politics at a time when Protestant ideas were raging in Northern Europe. As Henry looked for ways out of his marriage, he became interested in the new Lutheran beliefs that were shared by Anne Boleyn. More opposed the divorce, putting him on a collision course with a monarch prepared to transmute religion for the sake of what he believed was true love.

* * *

In Holbein's life-sized drawing of Henry, the king looks like an elephantine parody of a Renaissance man. He wears fine cloth and jewelry, like one of Cranach's women. His body is as broad as a wall. The dagger at his side is phallic enough, but to ram the point home he wears a bulbous codpiece. Here's a man whose virility needs a Reformation to satiate it. Yet this is not a parody. Surviving suits of tournament armour prove that Henry really was as big as Holbein makes him. And the codpiece too is matched by a steel example from the king's armoury. But the face is impenetrable, a piggy-eyed blank. We cannot read the ruler's thoughts, and it's best not to try.

This is the surviving half of a cartoon – a full-size final design – for a mural of Henry and his family commissioned in 1537 that Holbein painted in London's Whitehall Palace. Everyone else in this imposing work was dead. The wraithlike

Hans Holbein the Younger, *Henry VIII*, c. 1536–37.

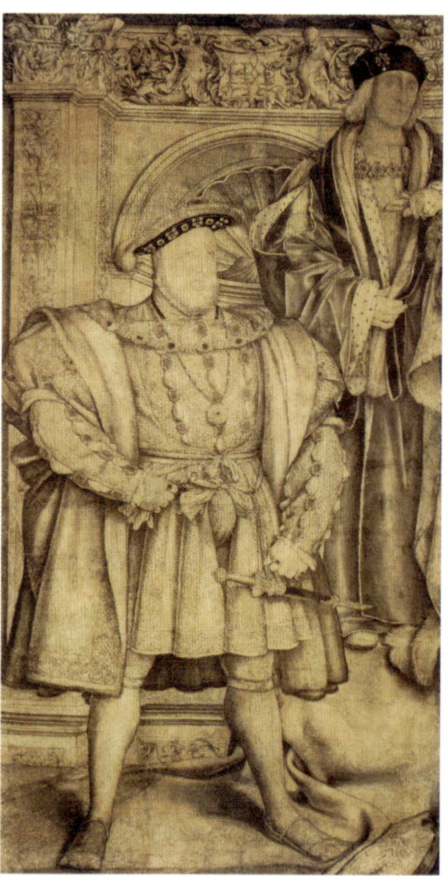

figure behind the colossal king is his father, Henry VII. The mural, destroyed when Whitehall Palace burned down in 1698, also included Henry VII's queen, Elizabeth of York, and Henry VIII's wife, who died in childbirth soon after – or even before – the painting was completed.

The doomed woman is Jane Seymour. Henry had Anne Boleyn executed for treason in 1536 after accusing her of multiple adulteries and incest, and immediately married Jane, who died bearing him a son to succeed as head of the new English church. More had gone to the executioner's block at Tower Hill in 1535. John Fisher, the bishop of Rochester – another friend of Erasmus portrayed by Holbein – died the same year for his opposition to the state-ordered upheaval of beliefs. Holbein's English portraits are sensitive yet ominous images of the soon to be dead: scaffold snapshots. They make you think of the heads, including More's, that were placed on spikes above the Stone Gateway of London Bridge.

* * *

Even sculptures got their heads chopped off. The 14th-century Lady Chapel in Ely, in the English fen country, is a ravishing yet disquieting place. Under the new pro-Reformation bishop of Ely, Thomas Goodrich, a singularly systematic destruction of the chapel's 'idols' was carried out. Every figure in its many delicate Gothic niches was destroyed or decapitated. The decorative arches and festoons of foliage were carefully left intact (these were not idolatrous, so they were acceptable), but the saints were mutilated with precise malice.

By the Act of Suppression in 1536, monasteries across England were demolished, their artistic embellishments ransacked if they were thought valuable or smashed if they weren't. We think of the Renaissance as a time of creativity, yet it was also an age when art was deliberately destroyed. In England, Renaissance art took hold at court just as attacks on religious images were about to be launched across the country. This violent break with the past made the modernity of the Renaissance distinctive and uneasy in England. Holbein was the perfect artist to portray this new age of apprehension.

* * *

In a world where the rules of Christian conformity could be changed overnight, Holbein painted masks. His portraits are hypnotically lifelike images of what people show on their faces but betray nothing of the soul. Everyone is an enigma to him. He does not ask their faith, their beliefs. He observes what they look like, exactly: a German merchant in his office in the Steelyard, the walled community of the Hanseatic League in London; a potential bride for Henry VIII; the mercurial king himself. They are all studied with a clarity that

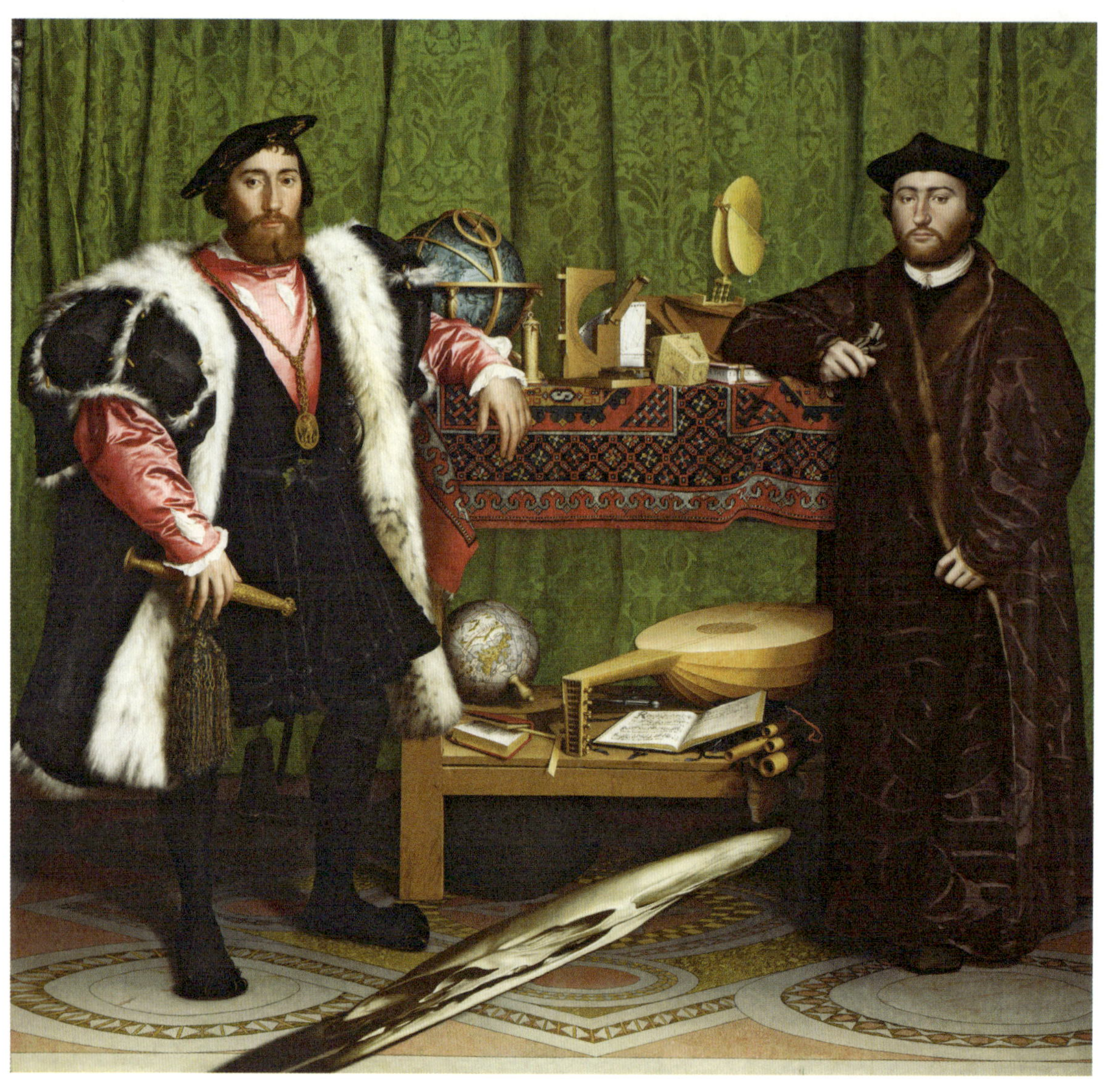

Hans Holbein
the Younger,
The Ambassadors, 1533.

makes them present to us even after five centuries. Yet they are allowed to keep their thoughts secret behind opaque expressions. This does not rob Holbein's portraits of seriousness: on the contrary, it is a rejection of caricature, a refusal to make faces easily readable.

The unfathomable nature of existence haunts his melancholy English masterpiece. In London in 1533, two visiting Frenchmen posed for Holbein. On the left side of a dresser stands Jean de Dinteville, a diplomat on a mission for the French king. His friend Georges de Selve, bishop of Lavaur, poses on the other side of it. Between them is a gathering of musical instruments, mathematical and scientific tools, and earthy and celestial globes that directly allude to Dürer's *Melencolia I*.

Holbein's clients may not have known this. They probably wanted to look like educated men of the world. For anyone who has seen Dürer's image of creative paralysis, however, this assemblage of Renaissance objects has a futile air. The two globes recall the sphere in *Melencolia I*, and a polyhedral wooden sundial reflects its stone equivalent in the print. Holbein extends Dürer's imagery to compose a snapshot of the Renaissance world in 1533. There's a Turkish carpet slung over the upper shelf; the spherical earth shows America. Every object is planned out in glorious perspective, as is the tiled floor. And yet this full perspectival reality is oddly cut off by a thick, green curtain across the back of the picture, from the edge of which peeps a crucifix, with its silver effigy of the dying or dead Christ.

The perspective is undermined even more drastically by a black-and-white smear that bleeds across the space of the painting, a visitation from another dimension imposing itself between the two well-dressed, bland-faced men. It exists outside the realistically constructed space, in its own otherplace, or, as More would say, 'no-place'. But it is equally real. Walk around, get close, look from the correct angle at the right, and you see it for what it is – a skull.

The skull is black and white, like an engraving. It possesses the bare-bones truth of a woodcut. Holbein created a series of just such lethal woodcuts, a *Dance of Death* in which a skeleton taps ladies and their lovers, rulers and peasants on the shoulder to call them from life. The inky black and white of the skull in *The Ambassadors* is an antidote to all the colours of life the painting shows. Yet the painting is not a medieval plague image, a crude memento mori: it is much more alienated. With its constellation of finely made objects representing the latest advances in science, the arts and exploration, the painting suggests that the more we learn, the less we know. It acknowledges that a meticulous perspective picture is just one view of truth. It is a paradox – or, as Folly would say, a Silenus. The young friends stand there proud, fashionable and in their prime, but – as Erasmus wrote – if you look within, what is life is death.

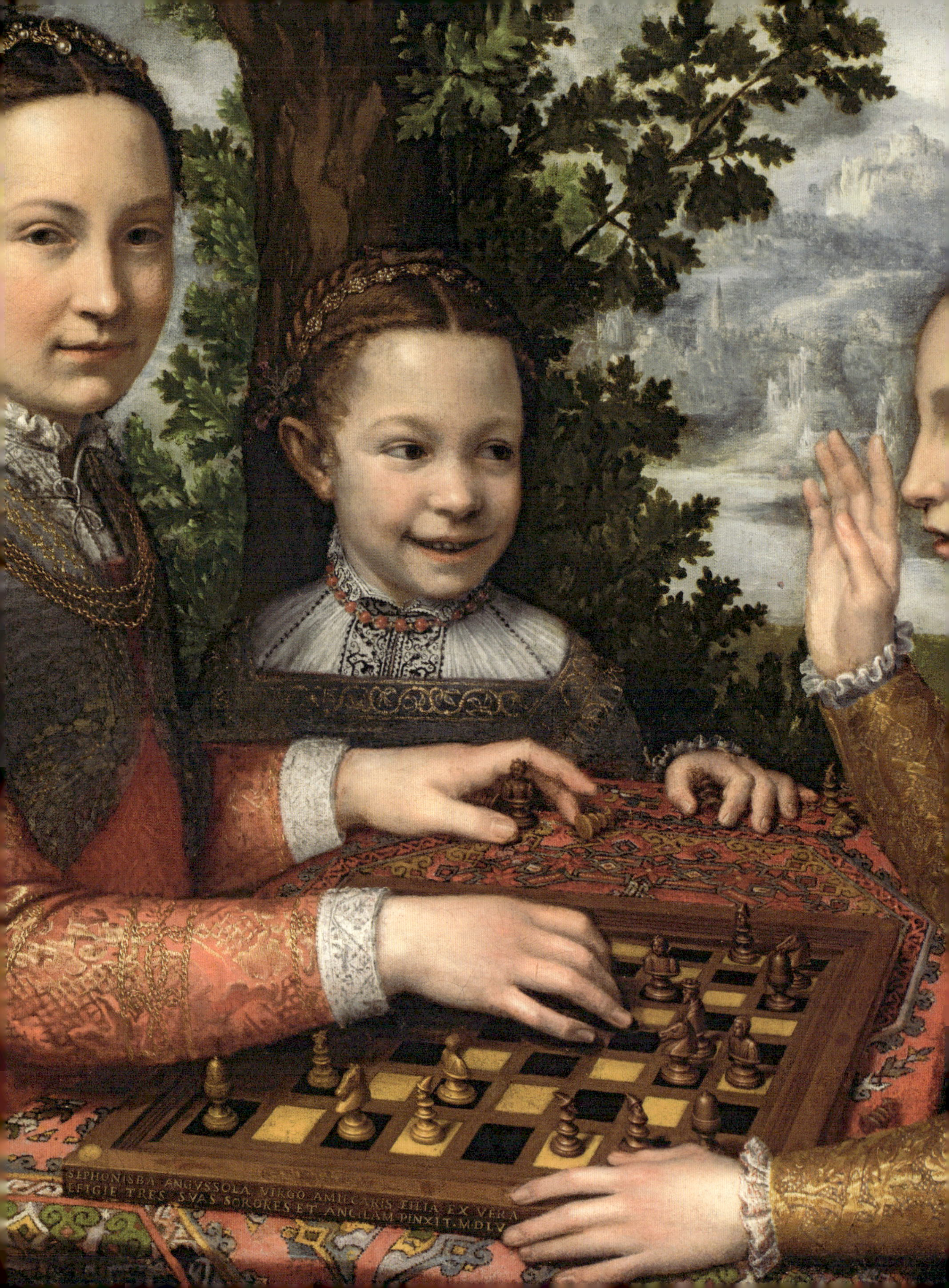
SEPHONISBA ANGVSSOLA VIRGO AMILCARIS FILIA EX VERA
EFIGIE TRES SVAS SORORES ET ANCILAM PINXIT MDLV

10 The Pulse of Life

In a garden in Cremona in 1555 two young women are playing chess while their little sister laughs between them, her whole face creasing up. An elderly servant attends, her lined face a contrast with their youthful vibrancy. Lucia Anguissola, the eldest, composed and mature, is making a move. Her sister Minerva stares intensely, holding up a hand in surrender or surprise. Perhaps it is because Lucia is winning, for with her left hand she lightly touches pieces she has captured as she turns to us with a half-smile. The girls are wearing expensive, courtly garb. Do they always dress this well to play in the garden? Yet there is nothing excessively formal about the image. Their physical closeness and social ease tell us that this is a painting of a happy family.

It is the artist's own family. Sofonisba Anguissola was 23 years old when she painted this portrait of her sisters. In this jewel of domestic realism, she takes us into the lives of a group of 16th-century girls, albeit a distinctive one: for few women before them had had the artistic training their parents arranged for their daughters. The Cremona couple Amilcare Anguissola and Bianca Ponzona, both from noble families, decided that all their daughters should learn to paint. Her younger sisters showed considerable ability, but Sofonisba's gifts would lead to an international career.

Sofonisba Anguissola, *Game of Chess* (detail), 1555.

* * *

Sofonisba Anguissola, *Game of Chess*, 1555.

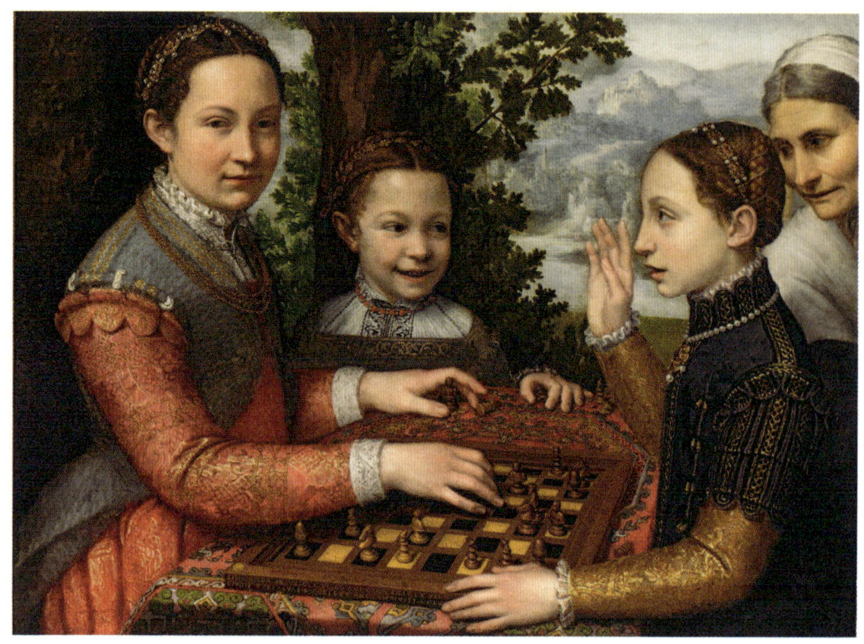

This idea would have been impossible a century earlier. There was no such thing as an 'artist' in the medieval world. There were only craftsmen, who belonged to guilds. They started out as apprentices, living with a master craftsman, to whom they were bound for a number of years and who stood *in loco parentis* over the trainee boys in the household. The craft of painting was regulated by Guilds of St Luke, named after the evangelist who was said to have portrayed the Virgin Mary from life. Women did not belong to guilds. This literally patriarchal, father-and-son model excluded women from the male world of skilled work.

The emergence of women artists in 16th-century Europe was not unprecedented: the ancient Roman natural historian Pliny the Elder, for instance, names celebrated professional female painters from the Greco-Roman world whose works he has seen. They are, however, the first group of women artists in history about whom we have anything like detailed knowledge.[1] In the first edition of Vasari's *Lives*, Sofonisba Anguissola appears as an addendum to a chapter on the sculptor Properzia de' Rossi from Bologna. Vasari also mentions two Florentine women painters: Lucrezia Quistelli, who painted a *Mystical Marriage of St Catherine*, and Plautilla Nelli, a prioress, both of whom were living at the same time as him. Of the numerous religious works by Plautilla that Vasari reports in Florence's churches and private residences, only a few have survived, including an epically scaled, recently restored *Last Supper* painted for a convent refectory. In it, John leans on Christ's shoulder asleep, or rapt with love.

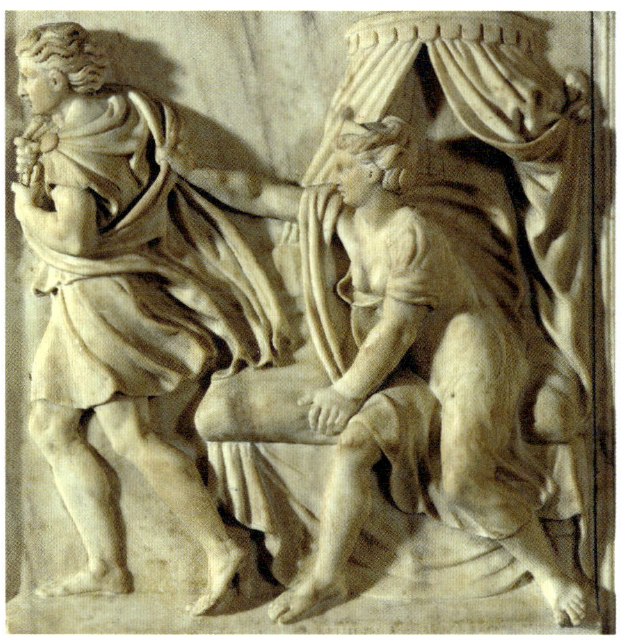

Properzia de' Rossi, *Joseph and Potiphar's Wife*, c. 1526.

Properzia de' Rossi's works include a forceful relief of *Joseph and Potiphar's Wife* for Bologna's cathedral – a story of a woman sexually pursuing a man. As a female sculptor, Properzia was a rarity not just in the 16th century but for centuries to come. It would be interesting to know how she was trained. Unfortunately, Vasari provides little information on her artistic background except to say that she started off carving peach stones, and instead burdens his account with waffle. We learn that Properzia was excellent in household matters and a good musician. She carved *Joseph and Potiphar's Wife* in a fit of unrequited passion for a man who didn't care for her. This is all a poor match with Properzia's appearances in Bologna's court records for 1520 and 1525, in which she is charged with wrecking a neighbour's garden, and throwing paint at and scratching the eyes of a male artist.[2] She sounds as if she could have given the big egos of male High Renaissance artists a run for their money. She would probably have needed a tough hide to become a sculptor, because she was not from a stone-carving dynasty: training within the family was the most likely route by which a girl could become an artist.

* * *

There was still no general term 'artist', only words for specific activities: painting, sculpture, architecture. It was Michelangelo who redefined what an artist was by practising them all; his feats were connected by a single expressive idea, a unique vision. Michelangelo's precociously modern concept of art may have primed him to recognize female talent, for he advised and encouraged Sofonisba

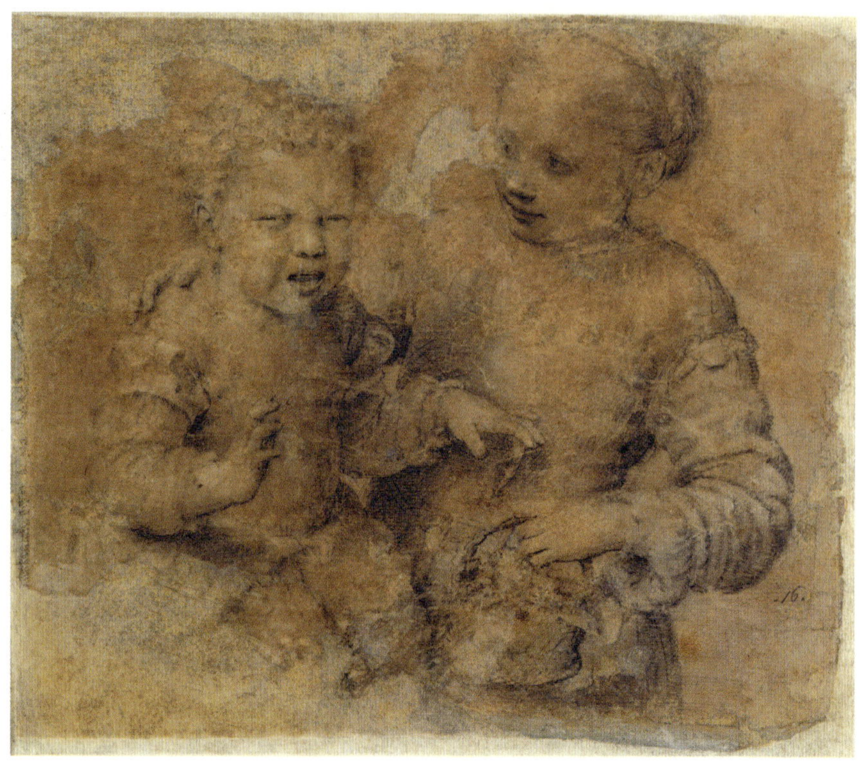

Sofonisba Anguissola, *Child Bitten by a Crayfish*, c. 1554.

Anguissola. She may have visited him, or just sent him her drawing of a girl laughing, like her young sister in the *Game of Chess*. His close friend Tommaso de' Cavalieri recalled in a letter that Michelangelo wrote to her saying he would prefer to see a weeping boy, a much more difficult thing, and Sofonisba obliged by making her younger brother cry and drawing him from life.[3] The drawing still survives, a funny yet compassionate study of a small boy in tears. A crayfish has bitten his finger, and his face crumples in a mask of distress. Four decades later it would be given a darker twist by Caravaggio when he painted a sensual youth twisting his features in pain because a lizard has its jaws clamped on his finger.

* * *

It may have been the recommendation of his friend and hero Michelangelo that made Vasari set out for Cremona to discover more about Sofonisba for his second edition of the *Lives*. He visited the family home, but she was long gone. Cremona was under the sway of the Habsburg Empire, and Sofonisba's fame had reached the capital in far-off Madrid and the court of Philip II, who summoned her to be painter and art tutor to his queen. Her parents seem to have boasted to Vasari of how much money Sofonisba made in Spain and shown him her youthful masterpiece: 'portraits of her three sisters playing chess, and with them an old woman of the household, all done with such care and such spirit, that they have all the appearance of life'.[4] The figures in another family portrait 'appear to be breathing' and are 'absolutely alive'. Other examples of her painting 'lack nothing save speech'. This is Vasari's habitual way of praising a portrait; here, however, he adds a provocative and gender-specific postscript: 'If women know so well how to produce living men, what marvel is it that those who wish are also so well able to create them in painting?'

Portraiture would turn out to be a professionally useful choice for women artists since it was so marketable: a good portraitist could get work whoever she was. In England and France there was a particular vogue for miniature portraits, portable tokens of love and esteem. In his second edition, Vasari includes a list of women miniaturists in a chapter on 'Divers Flemings'. Two of these, Susanna Horenbout and Levina Teerlinc, worked at the English court. Women were also at the forefront of self-portraiture – a fact that shows how closely the rise of the female artist was bound up with the growing cult of the artist. Portraying yourself was a self-conscious declaration of artistic identity, and women were pioneers in this. In 1548 the 20-year-old Flemish artist Catharina van Hemessen portrayed herself facing the viewer, sitting at an easel with her paints, an outline of a face on her canvas. The Latin inscription, 'I Caterina van Hemmesen have painted myself', suggests a spin on Vasari's sentiment: an artist can create herself through art. In about 1556 Sofonisba Anguissola also depicted herself at the easel, putting the finishing touches to a Madonna and Child: a significant subject in an Italy that still adored Mary.

* * *

Vasari's speculation about women's reproduction and creativity is a quintessentially Italian Renaissance thought. At its core was the double-edged sword of female reproductive power. This reverence for the maternal continued unchallenged in 16th-century Italy even as it was attacked in many places north of the Alps. Wherever the Reformation took hold, the medieval cult of Mary, mother of Christ, with its images of a breastfeeding and nurturing woman, was literally dismantled. In England, the shrine of Our Lady of Walsingham – one of Europe's most popular Marian pilgrimage sites, which contained a relic of Mary's milk – was destroyed in 1538; the serial wife-killer Henry VIII was behind its downfall. Protestant art replaced Mary with Cranach's wicked devil-women.

In Italy, where the Old Church still ruled, artists were painting Madonnas more realistically than ever in the early 1500s, the climax of a development that had started in the 13th century when Tuscan artists began softening her relationship with Jesus. In early Renaissance Florence the Carmelite painter Fra

Filippo Lippi created especially tender, and earthly, Madonnas: Mary is both beautiful woman and exhausted mother. It's possible that they are portraits of Lucrezia Buti, a novice nun who eloped with Fra Filippo and had children with him. Raphael's *Madonna with the Goldfinch*, painted in about 1505–6, takes such tenderness into a sublime High Renaissance stratosphere, as Mary watches over Christ and the young John the Baptist playing with a pet bird. Raphael's delicate drawings of nursing mothers prove that he rooted this and his other paintings of Mary in relaxed observation of women he seems close to.

That same intimate sense of reality colours the erotic art that was one of the outstanding achievements of Venice from the start of the 1500s. What connected the Virgin Mary with female nudes were the conventions of courtly love – still very much alive in the 16th century. The most enigmatic masterpiece of the age reaffirms courtly love's power to turn a mortal, and apparently unimportant, woman into a new kind of divinity. It makes a tantalizing appearance in the travel journal of the inquisitive canon Antonio de Beatis, who raved about seeing the *Garden of Earthly Delights* in Brussels.

After departing Brussels, Cardinal d'Aragona, Antonio and their company journeyed into France, taking in fairy-tale chateaux in a slow summer drift that found them by autumn among the royal palaces of the Loire Valley. Here they visited Francis I's castle in Amboise. As de Beatis writes in his journal for 10 October 1517, they also went to a mansion in the suburbs 'to see Messer Leonardo da Vinci of Florence, an old man of more than seventy, the most outstanding painter of our day'. The cardinal was shown three paintings: 'one of a certain Florentine woman portrayed from life at the request of the late Magnificent Giuliano de' Medici', a young John the Baptist, and a Madonna and Child seated on the lap of St Anne, 'all ... quite perfect'.[5]

* * *

Leonardo was in his sixties, not his seventies, but perhaps seemed older because he was frail. He was also suffering from a paralysis in his right hand, which, according to Antonio, meant that nothing more could be expected from Leonardo's brush – although in reality the genius was left-handed. The visitors marvelled at his anatomical drawings.

Leonardo spent his last years in his fine house in Cloux, which he justifiably called a 'palace', as painter to Francis I, king of France. He was still able to design courtly entertainments: at a royal wedding uniting the Medici family with the French crown, the guests processed from Amboise to Cloux to dance under a vault he created in his courtyard, with luminous stars and planets conjuring an illusion of the night sky. For another royal festivity he devised a robot lion.

He lived with his noble-born pupil Francesco Melzi, to whom he would leave his notebooks. A late drawing shows the same youth who posed as Leonardo's *John the Baptist*, who may well be his less respectable companion Salaì, with finger pointing upwards, long hair in ringlets – and an erection. So Leonardo enjoyed himself to the end, and died at Cloux on 2 May 1519.

Melzi wrote a letter to Leonardo's brothers, assuming they already knew of the death of their brother and his own 'so excellent a father', and saying it would be impossible for him to express the scale of his grief as long as he lived, 'deservedly so since he daily carried for me a visceral and most passionate love'.[6]

Decades later Vasari acknowledged how devotedly Leonardo's notes and drawings were treasured by Melzi, 'a gentleman of Milan, who in the time of Leonardo was a very beautiful boy, and much beloved by him, and now is a no less beautiful and gentle old man'.[7] As for the three paintings Leonardo showed his guests, they ended up in the French royal collection and entered the Louvre after the 1789 Revolution. The one that draws the crowds is the 'Florentine Lady', or, as she is better known, the *Mona Lisa*.

* * *

That name is accurate. This is a painting of Monna Lisa Gherardini del Giocondo, the wife of a Florentine merchant called Francesco del Giocondo; *Monna* was a respectful Florentine term of address, short for *Madonna*, 'My Lady'. So even the name we know this painting by is an echo of courtly love.

Leonardo started his portrait of Monna Lisa in Florence in 1503, as confirmed by a note from Agostino Vespucci, who worked for Machiavelli in the government palace. Vespucci compares Leonardo with the ancient Greek painter Apelles and says he's working on an as yet unfinished head of Lisa del Giocondo.

When Leonardo showed the painting much later to Cardinal Luigi d'Aragona and his scribe Antonio, he appears to have told them it was a portrait of 'a certain Florentine woman' commissioned by Giuliano de' Medici, the duke of Nemours – not the brother of Lorenzo, but the Magnifico's third son, named after his murdered uncle. Such a fabrication makes sense in the dreamy setting of the French court. Medieval chivalry was alive and well in France: the greatest native work of art from this period is a tapestry cycle portraying splendidly dressed youths in a hunt for an allegorical unicorn. So Leonardo invented a Medici commission, and told his visitors that this was an enigmatic Florentine woman, implicitly the mistress or idol of Giuliano.

Looked at through the lens of courtly love, the *Mona Lisa* teases us. Without getting up from her chair, this quietly powerful *donna* summons attention and incites speculation. The half-smile suggests secrets she is not going to tell. You can't help waiting for words to fall from those lips, which, like her bone structure, are precise applications of Leonardo's anatomical research.

To Vasari, the Mona Lisa seemed actually to be alive. Not only did her eyes have moisture in them and her nose look as rosy as living flesh, but 'in the pit of the throat, if one gazed upon it intently, could be seen the beating of the pulse'.[8]

Maybe it was awkward for Leonardo to explain why his most bewitching portrait was not of a noble or royal personage but a middle-class merchant's wife. He would certainly have had trouble accounting for the choice to Isabella d'Este, marchioness of Mantua. When the cardinal and de Beatis returned to Italy, they stopped off at Mantua as her guests; for twenty days there was dancing and festivities, 'one long round of pleasures'.[9] Isabella took an interest in Antonio's travel writing and urged him to make a copy for her. She would certainly have been intrigued by his account of Leonardo. For Isabella d'Este had wanted to be the *Mona Lisa*.

Married at age 15 to Francesco Gonzaga, the ruler of Mantua, Isabella carved out an autonomous role as a supporter of some of Italy's greatest artists. One ambition was to get Leonardo to do a painting of her. He stayed in Mantua as her guest after the fall of Milan and drew her portrait. In his subtly shaded study he gives her classical authority by turning her head in profile, like a Roman emperor on a coin. Yet this also makes her distant. Did she scare him? The artist soon moved on, returning to his native Tuscany. Although she sent people to chase up her painting, he was elusive. Leonardo was so busy studying geometry he had no time to paint, her correspondent reported in 1501; his day-to-day life was chaotic and erratic.[10] In the end she made do with a younger painter, Titian, who would excel in the job Leonardo had ducked, portraying her three times, including in a painting done in her last years that shows her as a young woman – a trick later adopted by Elizabeth I.

In his letter the go-between addresses Isabella d'Este as a 'Most Illustrious, Excellent and Singular Lady'. Yet she wasn't singular enough for Leonardo. His drawing of her is respectful rather than intimate.

It was not true that Leonardo was done with painting. By 1503 he was working on the *Mona Lisa*.

The *Mona Lisa* may not be a noble, but she is a queen of courtly love. She communicates inner tranquillity and concealed knowledge. The depth of her eyes, the dark nimbus of her hair, the elision between Lisa and the landscape all create a sense of psychological complexity. The landscape flows in and out of this woman, its blues and greens interacting with the shadows on her face and grotto-like hollows made by her hair. The misty mountains, water, road and bridge are both unreal and specific, insinuating a symbolism no more explicable

Leonardo da Vinci,
Mona Lisa, c. 1503–7.

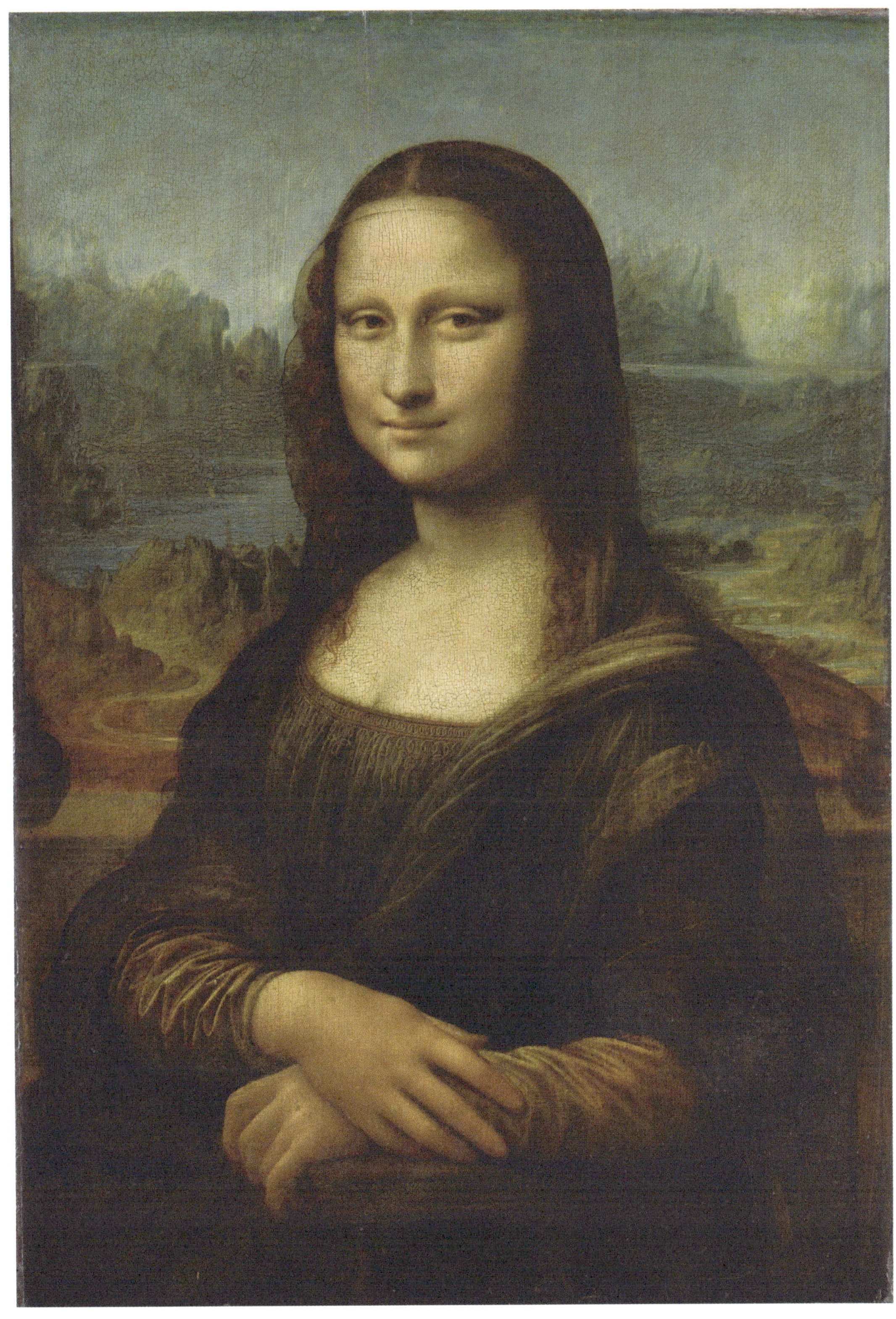

Raphael, *Portrait of Maddalena Doni*, c. 1505–7.

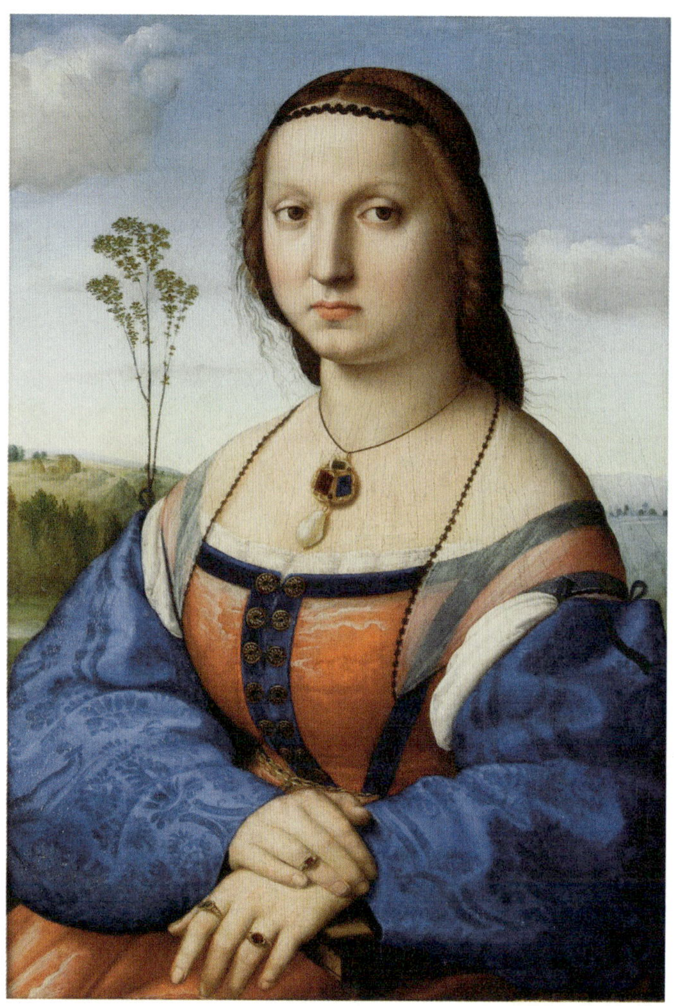

than her fleeting yet eternal smile. She has an authority that has made all the world her enslaved courtly lover for five centuries now.

As early as 1505 the *Mona Lisa*'s pose, twisting towards us in her seat, one hand over the other, was being imitated by Raphael. He saw the unfinished portrait in Leonardo's workshop next to Santa Maria Novella in Florence, and quickly offered clients a string of *Mona Lisa* lookalikes. His portrait of Maddalena Doni shows her with hands folded and body turned; another portrait known as *La Muta*, the 'Silent One', combines the Leonardesque template with an un-Leonardesque religiosity: the sitter wears a prominent cross.

* * *

It was one thing to portray wives such as Gherardini and Maddalena Doni with quiet dignity. In Venice in the first decade of the 1500s, a new generation of painters had begun to portray a group of women in sexual encounters and personal reveries.

This was a second revolution in Renaissance painting, just as consequential as the invention of perspective. Michelangelo was giving sculpture lifelike freedom and expressiveness at the start of the 16th century; two young artists in Venice did the same for oil painting by making perspective and classical proportion secondary to the poetry of colour. This turned the grass a more complex living green, the sky a more intense blue in their art, yet it started as an attempt to express their feelings about women.

The Serene Republic's most glamorous young artist at the start of the new century was Giorgione da Castelfranco. Born in a small town in Venice's territory on the Italian mainland, the *terraferma*, Giorgione was known for his skill with the lute. It was said he used his musical talents, along with his good looks and courtly ways, to seduce ladies. One woman whose confidence he certainly seems to have won is known to history only as 'Laura' because of the laurel bush he painted behind her. This detail could imply that she is the Laura to whom Petrarch dedicated his life of lyric poetry; Petrarch himself commissioned a portrait of Laura by Simone Martini, so maybe this is a re-creation of that lost work. But given the painting's audacious sense of reality, perhaps Laura was the sitter's name and Giorgione plays on it, like Leonardo depicting a juniper bush behind Ginevra de' Benci.

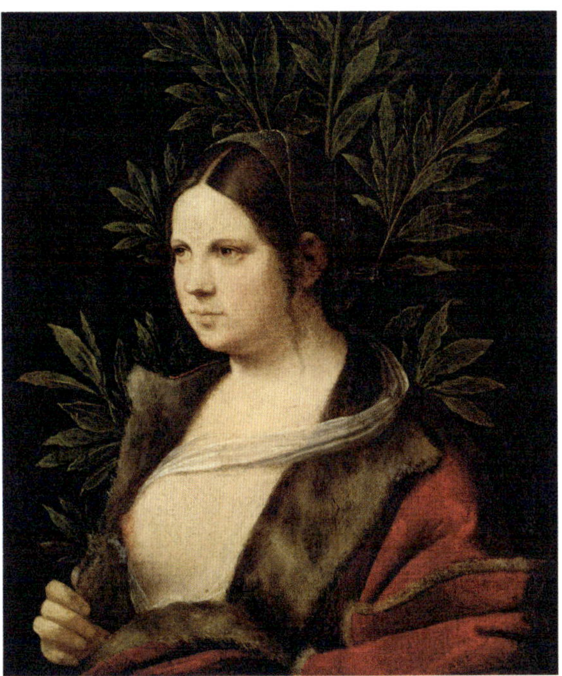

Giorgione, *Portrait of a Young Woman ('Laura')*, 1506.

Laura replaces the mythological goddesses of the early Renaissance with a woman of living flesh and blood. And she shows that flesh. Giorgione portrays the decision as hers, for her brown eyes look intently towards someone we cannot see as she opens her fur-lined gown to expose a breast that's so softly painted it seems like mist. This is a new use of oil paints, not to model sharp classical forms, but to evoke the body breathing, the flesh vibrating. The portrait was painted on canvas, a material ready to hand in Venice where sails for ships were always needed. Oil paint on canvas can create a greater variety of textures than oil on wood. Venetian painters in the early 1500s seized on this development to brush dappled leaves, blossoming clouds, fine brocades – and this breast.

Giorgione's younger friend Titian took this new genre of sexual portraiture to luxurious heights. Titian came from Cadore in the foothills of the Dolomites, where he was born in about 1490, moving to Venice to train as a painter at the start of the new century. His *Head of a Venetian Girl*, painted in about 1509 – and long attributed to Giorgione – is challenging and erotic: the model holds her shawl as if about to remove it, revealing more of the creamy chest that's showing through the lace of her chemise. Her head is confidently cocked, her hair loosened, her gaze provocative. Similarly frank portraits followed. In *Flora*, painted in about 1516–18, a woman in a loose, white undergarment proffers a

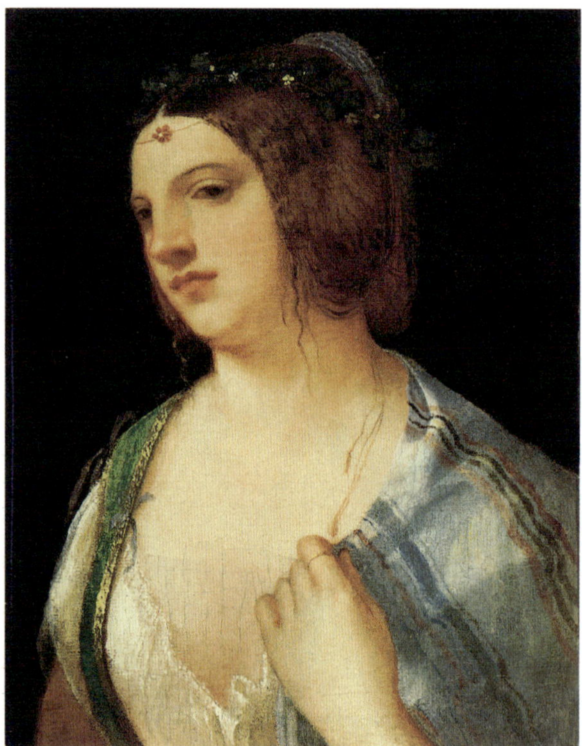

Titian,
Head of a Venetian Girl,
c. 1509.

Titian,
Flora, c. 1516–18.

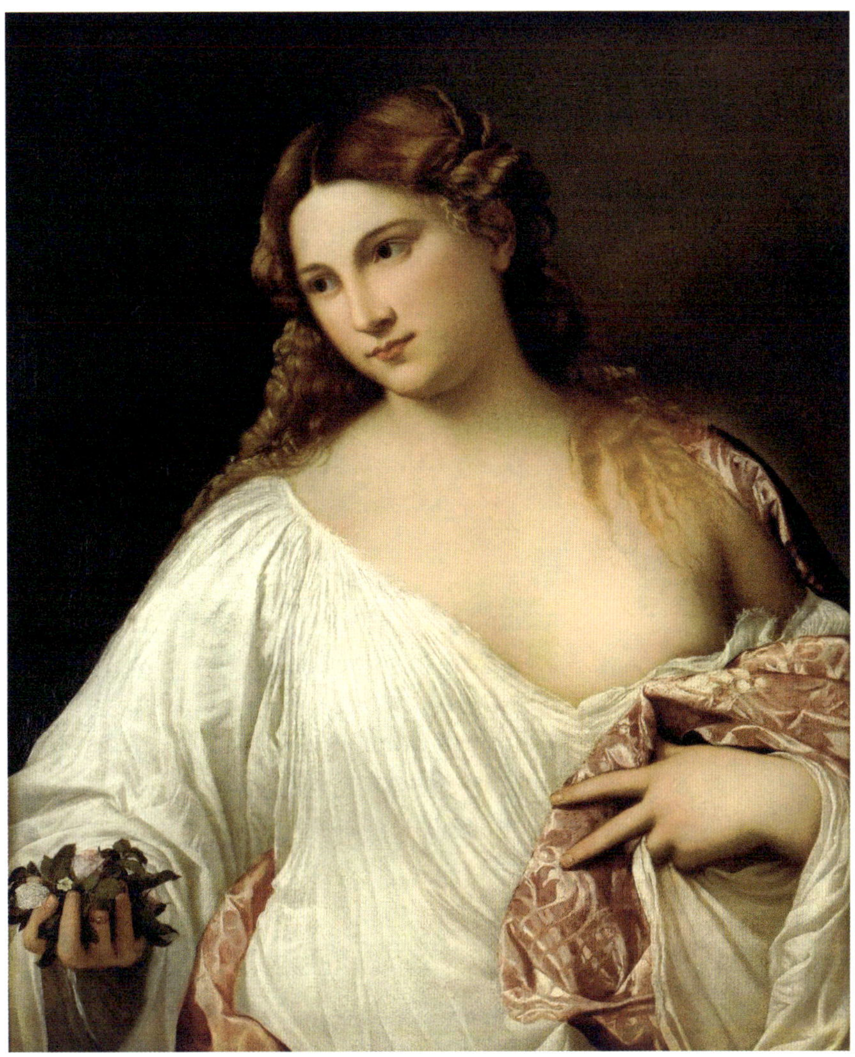

handful of flowers as she exposes a breast and looks tenderly at someone we cannot see. In its refinement of the bedroom portrait, this is Titian's answer to Giorgione's *Laura*. Flora is painted with an ardour verging on religiosity, and yet she helps pin down who these women are: courtesans. Flora was the goddess of spring and vegetation, but there were earthier connotations. In ancient Rome, the festival of Flora, the Floralia, featured performances by the city's sex workers. It was their day. This is why in Venetian art Flora is the symbol of the *cortigiana*.

* * *

Renaissance Italy was a world in which marriage followed by reproduction was expected to be universal, except for Christian celibates including monks, nuns and, in theory, the pope. This created a huge undertow of illicit sexual behaviour. The Serene Republic of Venice detected a commercial (and anti-sodomitical) opportunity, and took the step of commodifying and taxing sex with women. The women who sold sex fell broadly into two groups, though there was no legal distinction. There were those who were in effect streetwalkers. Then there were the elite 'honest courtesans' who charged high prices and whose patrons included men at the top of Venetian society. A list, with their tariffs, was published in 1565. The names include Veronica Franco, who would publish her poetry and correspondence, and campaign for the protection of poorer women.

It was a precarious existence. In 1531 the patrician poet Lorenzo Venier published two invectives against the courtesans Elena Ballerina and Angela del Moro, nicknamed 'La Zaffetta'. In the first, he imagines the supposedly undiscriminating Elena ending up as a syphilitic streetwalker, and in the second Angela, who refuses the attentions of a noble lover, is gang-raped. Venier's misogynistic fantasy points to the real risks of their profession.

The honest courtesans who negotiated the sexual market were often cultured and sophisticated: they published literary works, and wielded political influence. They were not just selling sex but were engaged in a commercialization of courtly love. In the wealthy Republic of Venice, where regular contact with the Ottoman Empire had introduced the idea of the harem, it became a big-spending upper-class male entertainment – and courtesans' portraits formed part of the burlesque. The English travel writer Thomas Coryat, who visited Venice in the early 1600s, was dazzled by these women. You visit them in their 'palaces', he says, where your senses are stimulated by sumptuous tapestries and gilt leather, perfumes and wine: 'You seeme to enter into the Paradise of Venus.'[11] He also reports that the courtesan is likely to have a portrait of herself hanging up: 'Besides you may see the picture of the noble Cortezan most exquisitely drawen.'[12]

One of Veronica Franco's correspondents was the painter Tintoretto; in a letter she praises his portrait of her and reassures him that she is not like the Narcissus of Greek mythology so won't fall in love with her own image.[13] It is very likely that some of the vivid paintings of women by Titian and his contemporaries are portraits of courtesans commissioned by the women themselves. Palma Vecchio, a less gifted artist who brings the genre helpfully down to earth, painted a blonde woman as Flora in about 1520, with a bunch of flowers and a bared breast. It looks as much advert as portrait.

This Flora can be recognized, posing nude, in another painting, *Venus and Cupid in a Landscape*. She looks bored as she lies holding Cupid's arrow towards herself, with a rustic vista thrown in. It suggests that the same women who posed for courtesan portraits could also be engaged as nude models. Who else would the sumptuous nudes of Venetian oil painting be?

There was an attempt to control the dress of Venetian courtesans through sumptuary restrictions, whose purpose was to distinguish them from respectable noblewomen. In reality the codes were flouted. Such confusion of categories may lie behind the misidentification of a portrait of a courtesan as one of the most famous noblewomen of Renaissance Italy. Bartolomeo Veneto's painting of a young woman with long, golden ringlets, looking at us as she exposes a breast beside an expensive necklace and holds up a posy of flowers like a scientific specimen, was for a long time fancifully identified as Lucrezia Borgia, sister of Cesare and daughter of Pope Alexander VI. In reality the portrait has all the traits of the courtesan-as-Flora genre. And it is one of the most dynamic examples. The slender woman moves sensationally through space as she engages your eye and holds out the flowers.

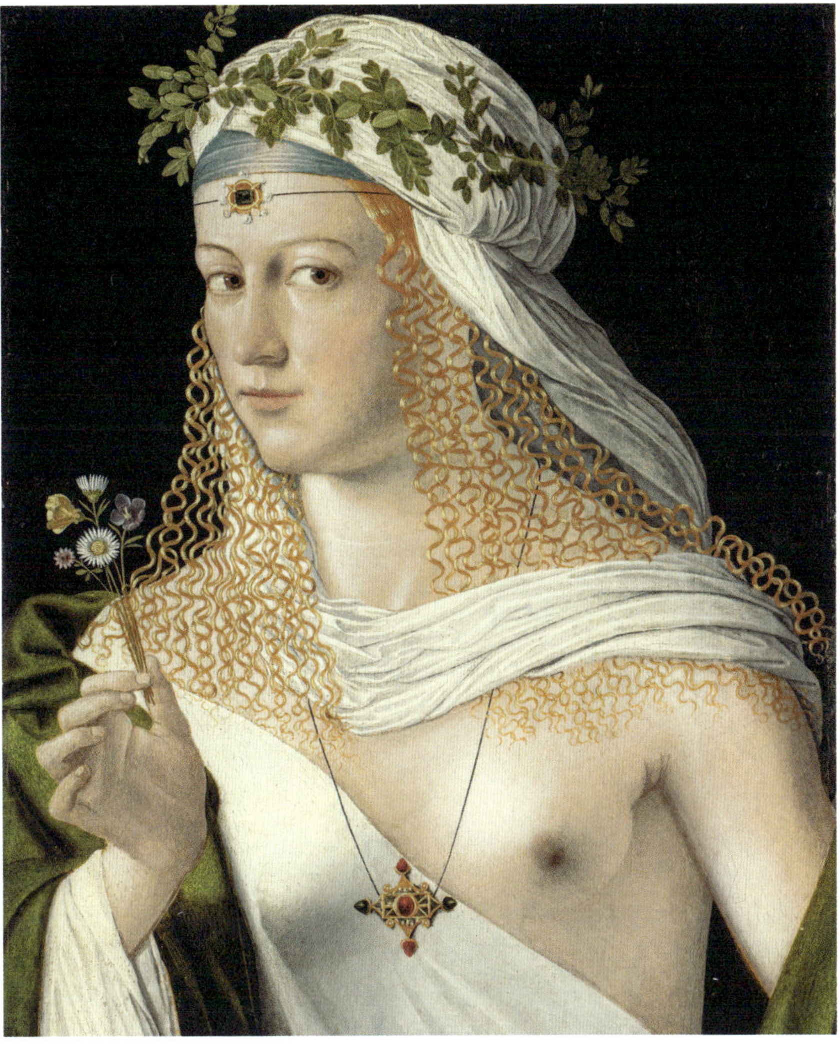

Bartolomeo Veneto, *Portrait of a Young Woman as Flora*, c. 1520.

This is not Lucrezia, but its overt sexuality matches her myth. Lucrezia's infamy goes back to the 16th century, when the historian Francesco Guicciardini recorded widespread gossip that not only her two brothers but also her father 'competed' for her love. More plausible portraits of Lucrezia that survive are quite dull. No wonder people prefer to see her in Veneto's arresting picture of a courtesan. In reality, the controversial pope's daughter married Alfonso d'Este, ruler of Ferrara, and died at 39 after giving birth to her tenth child, a short-lived girl named after her sister-in-law Isabella d'Este.

* * *

What courtesans offered was a fascinating performance for their clients. Their portraits are part of it. Giorgione died of plague in 1510, but Titian honed his art of women over a long lifetime. His courtesan models are great actors and creative collaborators. The same women who perform the role of ideal lovers also play their many parts as saints, nymphs and classical heroines. This helps Titian create an art of pitch-perfect emotional nuance. The courtesans' acting abilities emerge in Titian's religious paintings such as the *Noli me tangere*, with its impassioned Magdalene looking intensely at the resurrected Christ in the dawn light, and his *Penitent Magdalene*, who manages to be both passionately pious and flamboyantly sexual in an outrageous triumph of performance art.

In Catholic Italy there was a continuum between painting nude women and painting holy women, for sacred and profane art alike paid homage to beauty. At the same time that Titian was lavishing his oils on golden flesh, he also painted the Virgin ascending into the brilliant vault of heaven in his 1516–18 masterpiece the *Assumption*, set mystically against the luminous windows of Venice's Frari church.

This female heroic imagery of Catholicism was no longer available to Protestant Europe. That didn't stop women, even south of the Alps, exploring the new ideas of Luther and Calvin. After all, the Reformation emphasized personal study of the Bible, valued the literacy and individual journeys of female as well as male converts, and stressed inner freedom. The reality of women's lives was clearly not entirely encompassed by cosy idylls of courtly love.

* * *

Agnolo Bronzino's portraits of women hint at this edgier truth. Born in Florence in 1503, Bronzino was the favourite portraitist of the Medici court after Cosimo I de' Medici became Grand Duke of Tuscany in 1537 and secured his family's absolute hereditary rule until the 18th century. Yet Bronzino's paintings don't flatter so much as estrange.

Titian,
***Penitent Magdalene*,**
1531–35.

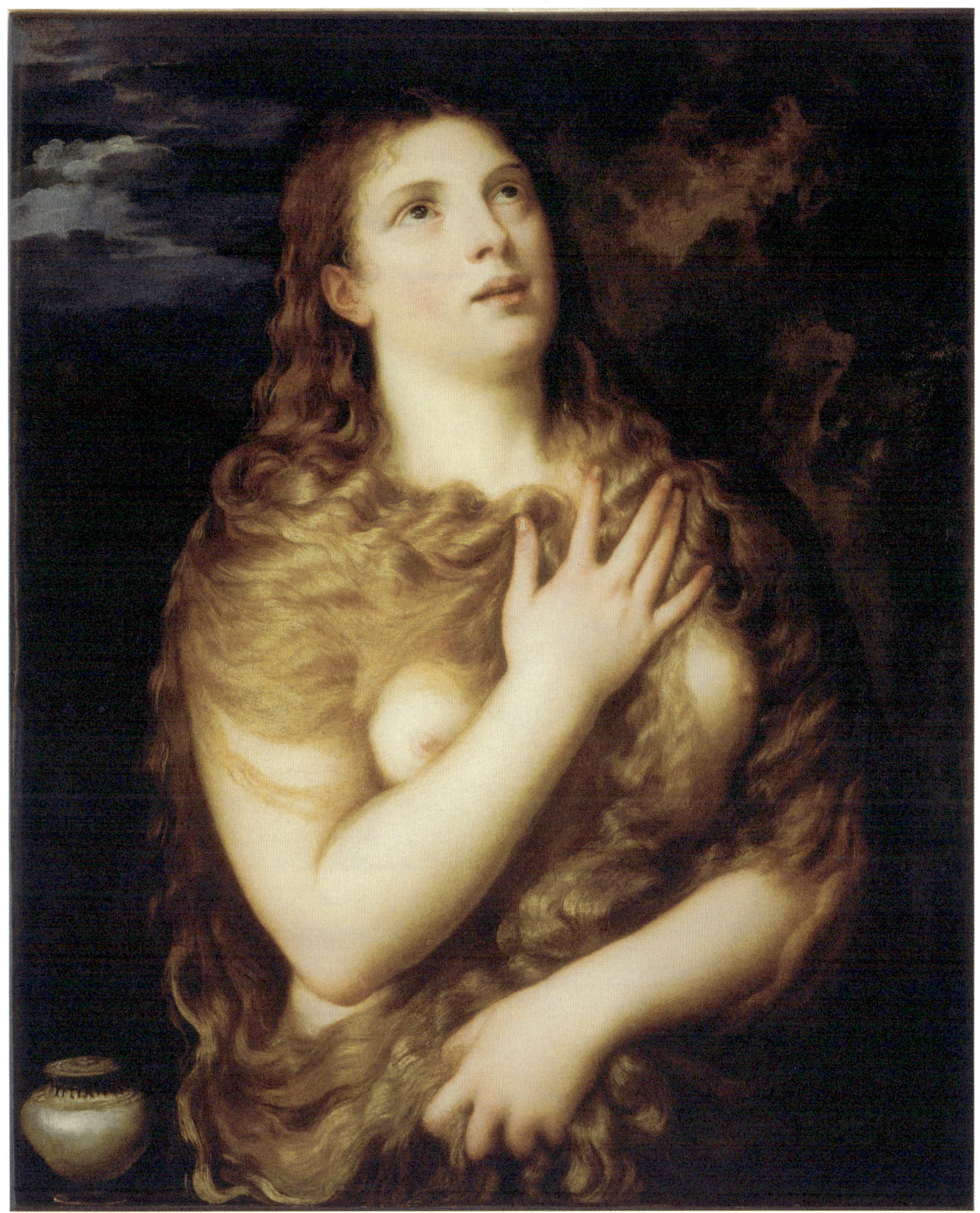

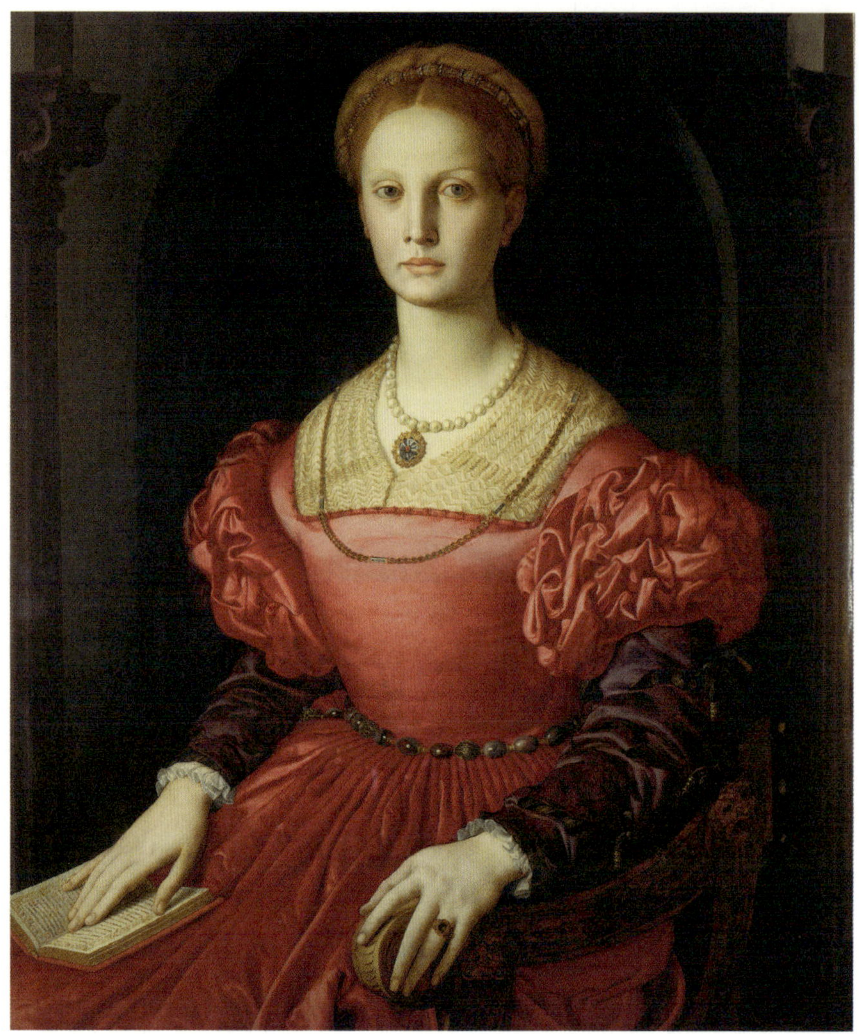

Agnolo Bronzino, *Portrait of Lucrezia Panciatichi*, c. 1540.

Lucrezia Panciatichi, portrayed by Bronzino in about 1541, sits tensely, a hand clutching the arm of her chair, in a flaming red dress. Yet Bronzino points us from her outer appearance to what may lie behind it. She has an open book, her long fingers resting on its words. Her face is menaced by shadow, her eyes bleary as if she has been crying. The length of her nose and height of her cheeks are distortions, but not for some empty stylistic reason, artifice for its own sake. Panciatichi's tall, thin, almost sallow face suggests hunger and illness under its beauty. Inwardly she's being eaten away – even as she sits in bejewelled, crimson splendour. 'Love lasts forever,' it says in French on her locket. But this love causes agony, an emaciation of the soul. It could mean the love of God, for Panciatichi converted to Protestantism. It's an exceptional portrait, simultaneously depicting the outer, social image Lucrezia shows to the world and letting us see past it as we register her nervous fingers and heavy eyes.

Laura Battiferri too puts her trust in words. One of the female humanists mentioned by Vasari in a catalogue of eminent women throughout history, this friend of Bronzino's belonged to his milieu of Florentine artists: her husband, Bartolomeo Ammanati, created sensual fountains for the Medici. She was a poet, as was Bronzino himself: they conducted a Platonic romance through verse. She holds a book of Petrarch open, with those refined hands, in a commanding way. Her head is shown in aquiline, distinguished profile: just as Leonardo drew Isabella d'Este like an emperor on a coin, so Bronzino makes us look at Battiferri with respect for her authority and intellect. He portrays her as Petrarch's heir, a visionary artist whose mysterious profile is tense with creative fury.

Agnolo Bronzino, *Portrait of Laura Battiferri*, 1555–60.

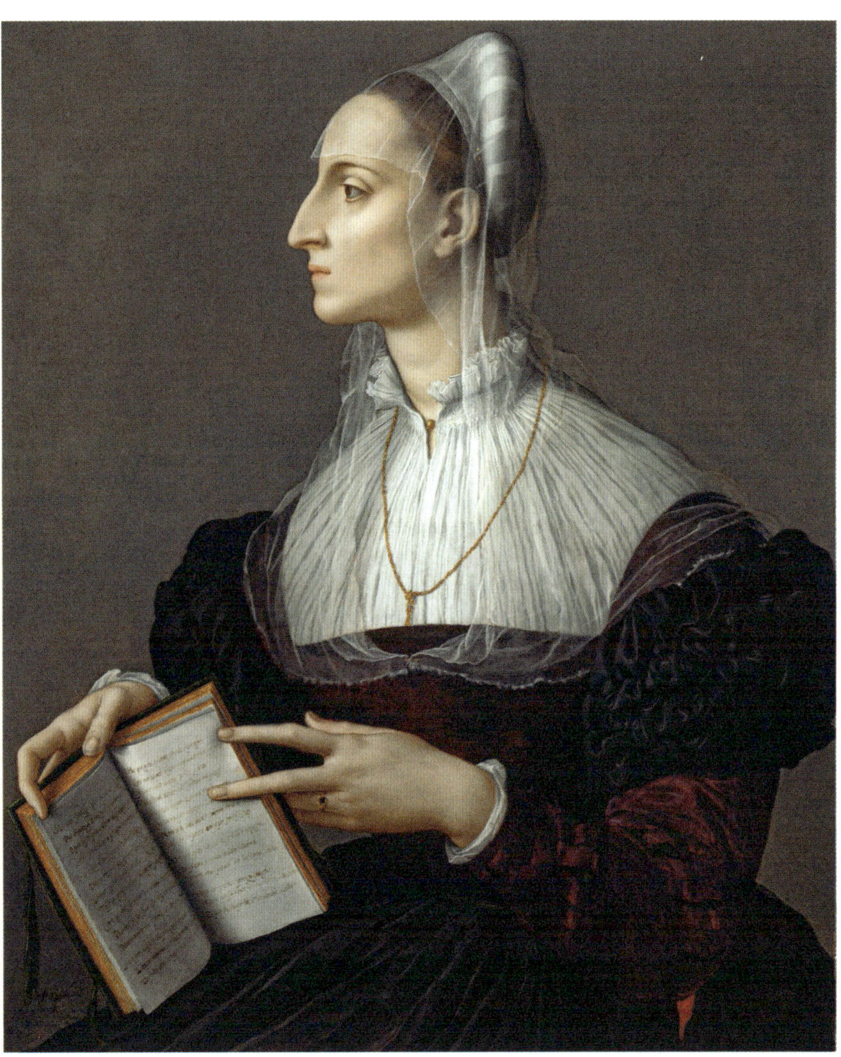

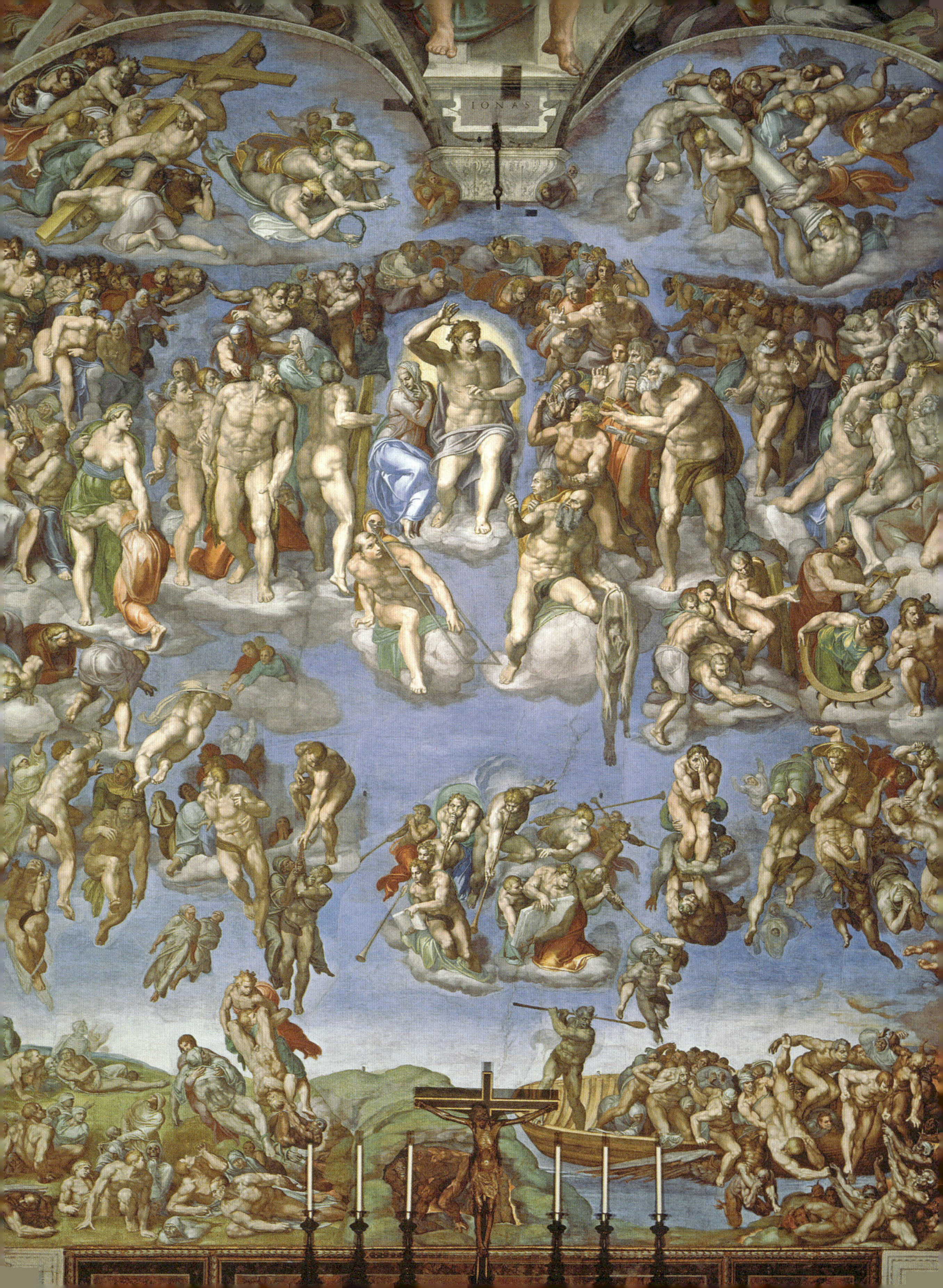
IONAS

11 Judgments

Nudity ran riot at the climax of the Italian Renaissance. The depiction of naked people that had started with van Eyck's nudes and been energized through encounters with 'noble savages' now reached unprecedented, perhaps unmatched, heights. This Italian empire of the senses conquered the courts and imaginations of the north, crossing denominational lines and making nudity a common culture of Europe. Yet it also collided with the revival of Christianity that was sweeping the continent. As the Catholic church sought to renew itself in the face of the Lutheran challenge, the nude – that 'new-found-land', as the English poet John Donne called the naked body of his mistress[1] – became a battlefield between Renaissance exuberance and religious scruple, free expression and moral control. Michelangelo headed right into the heart of this conflict as he began his greatest painting and his enemies sharpened their knives. In fact, the road to the *Last Judgment* started on an actual battlefield.

* * *

In 1527 an army of northern mercenaries, many of them Lutherans, attacked Rome and rampaged through the pope's city. The Wars of Italy that started with the French invasion in 1494 had brought disasters, but this was true tragedy. As many as 10,000 people were killed. Looting and rape went unchecked. It was a

Michelangelo, *Last Judgment* (detail), 1536–41.

humiliation not just for Italy but also for the Holy Roman Emperor Charles V, in whose name the atrocities were carried out. Charles neither ordered the Sack of Rome nor incited its barbarities. He saw himself as a mediator of Europe's conflicts, a wise overlord who was firmly Catholic but wanted reconciliation with Protestants. But it was hard to control Habsburg dominions that stretched from Bohemia to Mexico. The attack was a spontaneous move by his commander, the duke of Bourbon, that left Charles shamefaced. The pope was holed up in the Castel Sant'Angelo, the great drum of a fortress by the Tiber converted from the mausoleum of the Emperor Hadrian.

Luckily for the pontiff, Benvenuto Cellini was there. This pugnacious Florentine goldsmith and sculptor, later to write an autobiography, was inspired by Michelangelo not only to sculpt but to live in a staggeringly egotistical way. His life as he recorded it was compulsively transgressive. He committed crimes, including murder, and got away with them because of his status as an artist. He had frightening form in street fighting. Now Cellini discovered a perfect, and legal, use for his dexterity, keen eye and casual readiness to kill. As the imperial army rushed Rome's poorly defended city walls, he took his harquebus and, together with two companions, fired at the attackers. They killed the duke of Bourbon, or so he claimed.

Even with its leader dead, the invasion was unstoppable. Retreating to Castel Sant'Angelo, Cellini was put in charge of an artillery post. One reason he was so effective, he says, was that he didn't share the qualms of comrades who held back from firing lest they hurt their own families out there in the chaos. Cellini spotted a Spanish officer of the Habsburg army and aimed a falconet, a slender artillery piece. He took his shot and saw the distant Spaniard sliced clean in two at the waist: Cellini had hit the soldier's sword, slung across his front, and it cut right through him. Pope Clement VII happened to be watching and was impressed.

In 1523 Clement became the second pope from the Medici family, two years after the death of his cousin Leo X. Now, on the battlements of Castel Sant'Angelo, he asked Cellini how he had halved the imperial officer so neatly:

> The pope, who had not expected such a thing, was very pleased and amazed, because it seemed to him impossible that a gun could hit accurately from so far away and because the man was cut in two pieces and it did not seem that this was possible; he ordered for me to be called so that I could be asked about it.[2]

Cellini obliged, but wanted something from the pope too:

> Kneeling, I begged him to absolve me of this murder and others I had committed in the Castello in service of the church. At this, the pope raised his hands and made a clear sign of the cross above my body, saying to me that he blessed me and pardoned me of all the murders I had committed and all those I would commit in the service of the apostolic church.[3]

So Cellini went on firing his guns and slaughtering Habsburg soldiers until Clement paid a ransom, preserving the papacy but leaving the city a wasteland of unburied bodies and ransacked buildings.

Michelangelo, meanwhile, was in Florence. The Medici family's control of the papacy had given the heirs of Lorenzo the Magnificent a new source of power, but it was Janus-faced. The humiliation of Clement VII in Rome offered Florentine republicans an opportunity. They drove out the Medici, again, and restored a popular republic.

Michelangelo had never hidden his politics. The *David* was, among other things, a symbol of republican vigilance. Yet the reason he was living in Florence in the 1520s was to work on an ambitious Medici commission.

Even before becoming pope, when he was still Cardinal Giulio de' Medici, Clement had tasked Michelangelo with the creation of a suite of architectural and sculptural marvels at the Medici family's parish church, San Lorenzo. In the New Sacristy he started in the early 1520s, as Vasari observes, Michelangelo rejected the submission to classical rules and harmony of his hated rival Bramante. He used classical columns and pilasters, pediments and niches, but in an allusive way, as if he were creating an ominous stage set. Heavy, blank marble niches framed by fluted pilasters hang over the doors and replicate their height, like ghost portals existing in another dimension. Above are dark-grey window frames in the local stone, *pietra serena*, sounding another bleak bass note. This is a poet's design. Architecture, previously an art of rules and harmony, was being twisted into expressive forms to produce uneasy feelings and sinister impressions.

* * *

In the statues Michelangelo carved to go on the Medici tombs in the New Sacristy, he applied the same wilfulness to the human figure. Giuliano de' Medici, the duke of Nemours, sits atop his tomb in grotesque armour emblazoned with a satyr on his chest. When you go to one side to meet his eye, you see that his neck is impossibly, horribly long, like a serpent emerging from the armour. Below him, nudes representing *Night* and *Day* rest on the sarcophagus (overleaf). On the opposite wall Lorenzo de' Medici, duke of Urbino, is enthroned with his hand pensively on his chin and his elbow on a money box with the face of a mouse or bat, while below him nude figures of *Dawn* and *Dusk* disport themselves (p. 247).

Giuliano and Lorenzo were minor members of the Medici family, less memorable than their 15th-century namesakes, yet they got the biggest and best tombs. The price they pay is to be subsumed into Michelangelo's personal meditation on mortality. Giuliano and Lorenzo are ghosts in an opera, overshadowed by the nudes embodying light and darkness, the rising and falling of the sun, in a mythology forged by Michelangelo from classical, and perhaps even Egyptian, lore.

One nude stands out. *Night* is accompanied by sinister symbols: a mask with empty eye holes and an owl. If the room as a whole expresses death and pensiveness, she is its conclusion. She is melancholy in stone: the room's ideal inhabitant.

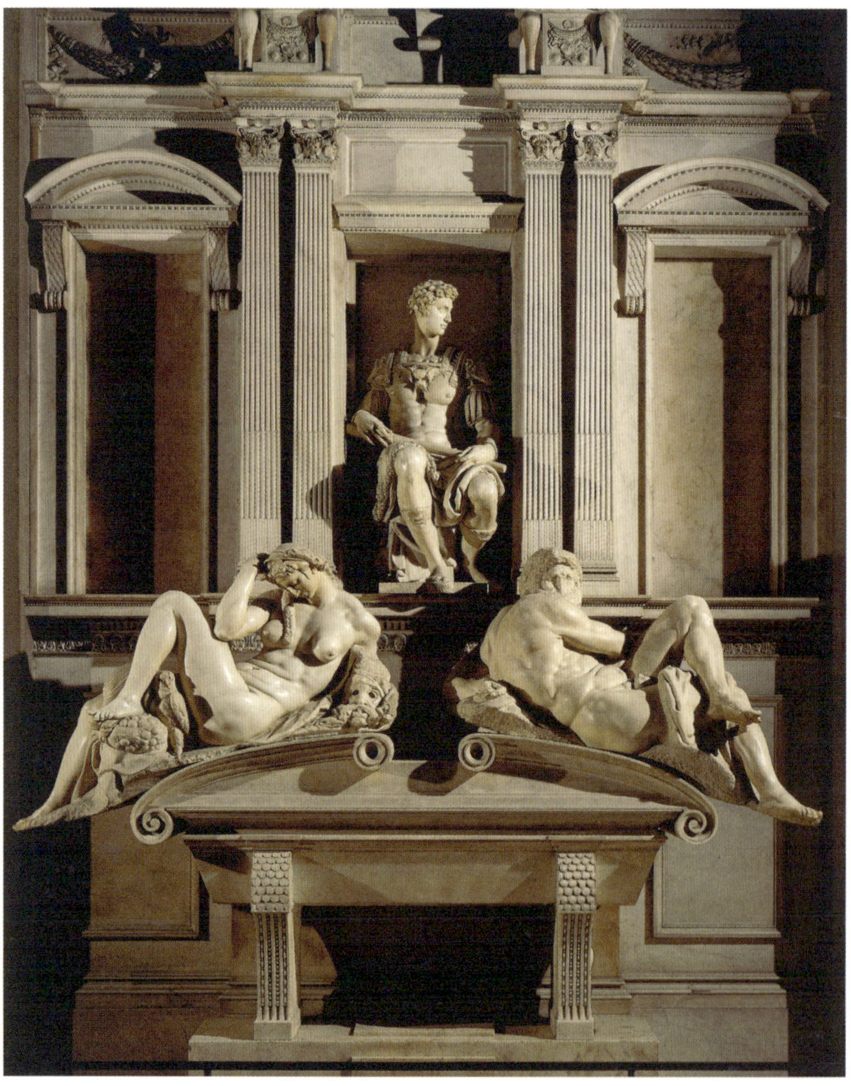

Michelangelo, *Tomb of Giuliano de' Medici*, 1526–33.

Night's little death renews us, suggests Michelangelo in verses he wrote about this figure. Its blackness is benign and, 'With peace ends all our work at day's end.'[4] In a later poem he speaks bitterly from the mouth of his statue to express other reasons to embrace unconsciousness. Another poet had urged Michelangelo's sleeping nude to awake. She refuses: 'For as long as damage and shame last.'[5] He wrote this after Florence's defiance of the Medici had been crushed.

Michelangelo was braver than the braggadocious Cellini, who wisely sided with his patron, the Medici pope. Michelangelo stayed in the new republic, downed tools at San Lorenzo and started designing bastions that translate his psychically disturbing architecture into forbidding gatehouses. He was put in

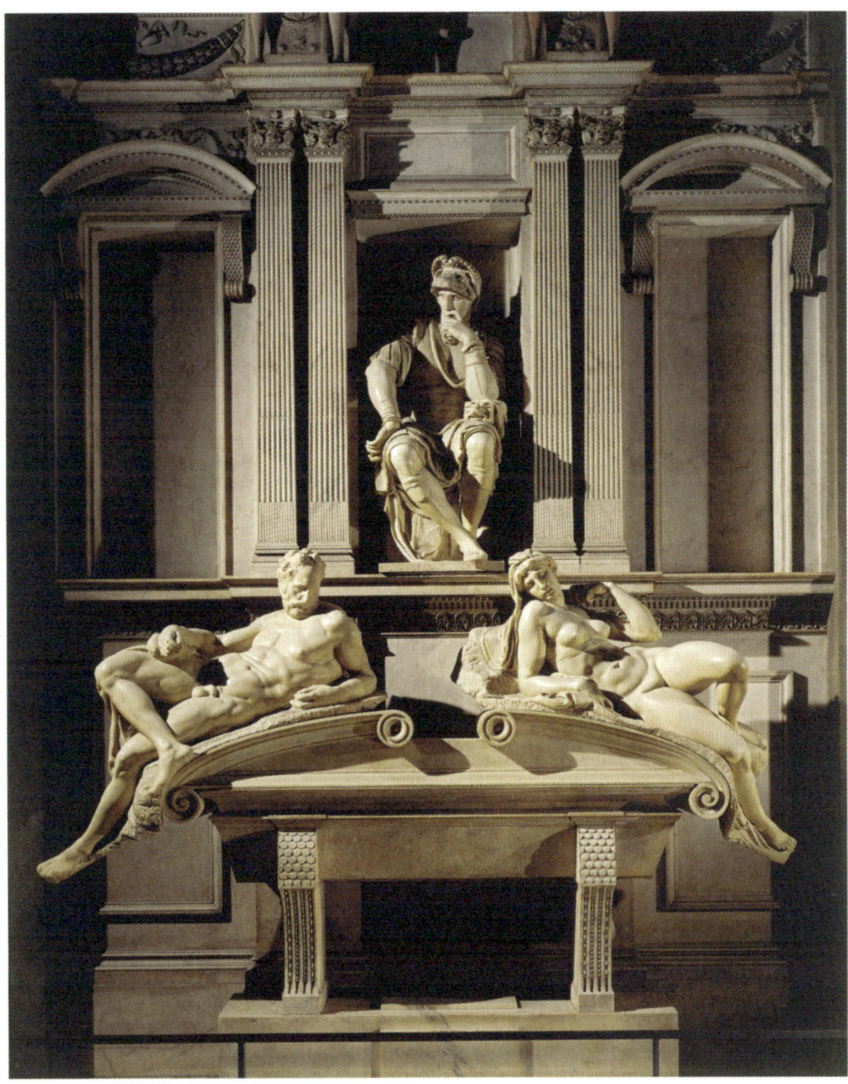

Michelangelo, *Tomb of Lorenzo de' Medici*, 1524–31.

charge of building fortifications – but in the event there was no time to construct these complex defences.

The pope and Charles V not only made peace, but the emperor, embarrassed by the assault in his name on Rome, sent an army in 1529 to make Florence bow to the Medici. Michelangelo had a panic attack and fled, but returned to stand with his fellow citizens. Instead of fancy architecture, he designed brutally practical earthworks that were raised by crowds working through the night. He turned the hill of San Miniato south of the city into a fortress aiming its guns at the imperial onslaught. Guicciardini says that the falconet fired from San Miniato's church tower was crucial in pinning down the assailants, forcing them to besiege the city.

The fortifications held. The imperial troops camped on hillsides outside the walls eating roast hogs (as later depicted in a fresco in the Palazzo Vecchio), while hunger and disease spread inside the defences. Meanwhile, Michelangelo worked on a painting with an outlandish, sexual theme.

* * *

While planning his defences Michelangelo had visited Alfonso d'Este, ruler of Ferrara, a noted military expert whose weaponry reputedly included the Giulia, the cannon cast from the statue of Julius II. While giving Michelangelo a tour of the city walls, Alfonso also showed off his 'Rooms of Alabaster', for which he had commissioned lavish bacchanalian paintings.

Renaissance artists knew about the cult of the wine god Bacchus from Livy and Ovid, and from bacchanalian-themed carved reliefs on ancient sarcophagi. They ranged from depictions of vines and putti to processions involving Bacchus riding a panther or pulled on a chariot by panthers, accompanied by satyrs, maenads and Silenus. Donatello included a bacchanal with putti on the base of *Judith and Holofernes* – biblical morality apparently mocked by pagan play. Andrea Mantegna created two intense prints with bacchanal themes, *Bacchus with a Wine Vat* and *Bacchus and Silenus*. Alfonso set out to commission the best artists in early 16th-century Italy to paint pagan-themed, orgiastic partying.

The project was begun cautiously by the veteran Venetian painter Giovanni Bellini with the *Feast of the Gods* in 1514, a stately depiction of the classical pantheon. It was supposed to be joined by works from Italy's leading artists, but the scheme ended up being monopolized by Titian: he would even be asked to overpaint Bellini's canvas in his own style. Titian's *Worship of Venus* is a gold-lit explosion of sheer joy, as a crowd of little cupids frolics in front of a statue of the love goddess. He followed it with the *Bacchanal of the Andrians* – the most elegantly decadent picnic in art. The wine we see in a glass jug held aloft against

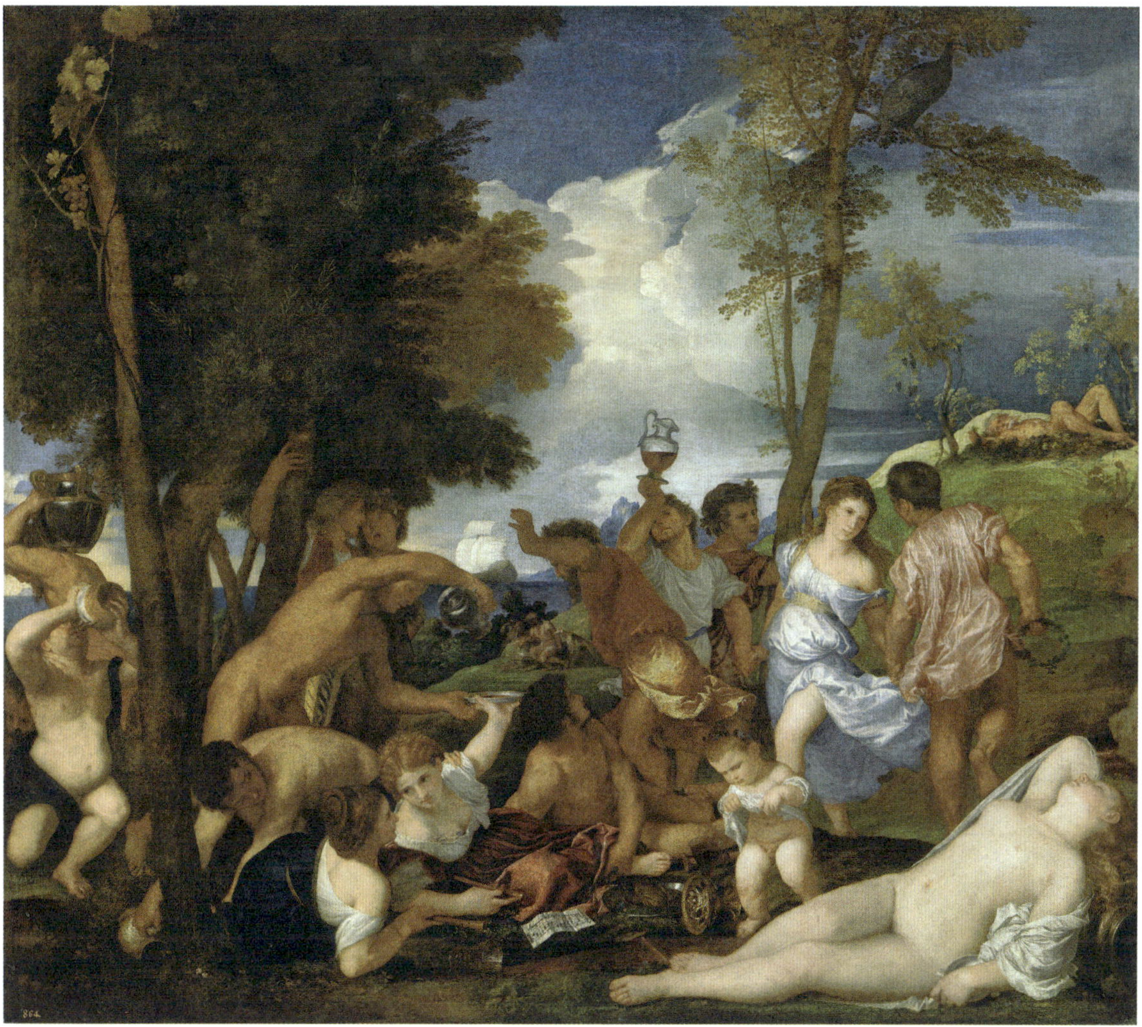

Titian, *Bacchanal of the Andrians*, 1523–26.

silvered clouds is fuelling a wild rave under the trees. Among the celebrants, two women with their tops loosened lie on the ground deep in conversation. One holds up her cup to be refilled; another shows a leg and her blue dress falls off the shoulder as she dances with a man in pink. In the foreground a nude throws back her head, her face full of satisfaction.

The last painting in the series, done in 1520–23, is the most mysterious. *Bacchus and Ariadne* depicts the fate of a princess, the daughter of King Minos of Crete. Having helped the Greek hero Theseus kill the Minotaur and escape her father's island, she was abandoned by him on the isle of Naxos. Titian shows the moment when Ariadne is found by Bacchus. The constellation above Ariadne's head is a promise of immortality up there in the blue. Yet the azure, heavenly side of the painting is rammed against a frenzied procession. Bacchus, riding on a chariot pulled by leopards, comes with his crazy retinue of maenads and satyrs. A goat-legged boy at the front of the dangerous parade pulls, like a toy on a rope, a donkey's severed head. Behind him a maenad clashes cymbals while snakes writhe on the sun-browned flesh of a naked satyr. Another satyr behind him holds up the leg of the donkey they have torn apart. Meanwhile the fat, naked Silenus slumps at the rear.

* * *

Alfonso d'Este pressed Michelangelo to paint a mythological canvas to hang with his masterpieces by Titian. Michelangelo would work on it during the Siege of Florence. As he painted, Michelangelo knew that the imperial army might burst through any moment and unleash savagery – a bloody bacchanal. Michelangelo dealt with the atmosphere of dread by transforming the seductive paintings he had seen in Ferrara into something more perturbing. His subject was *Leda and the Swan*.

The story of Leda concerns one of the shape-shifting love affairs of Jupiter, chief of the gods. Jupiter came to Leda as a swan, had sex with her and impregnated her. This exotic theme fascinated Leonardo, whose drawings for a lost painting have the bird's long, phallic neck twist in a serpentine curve towards

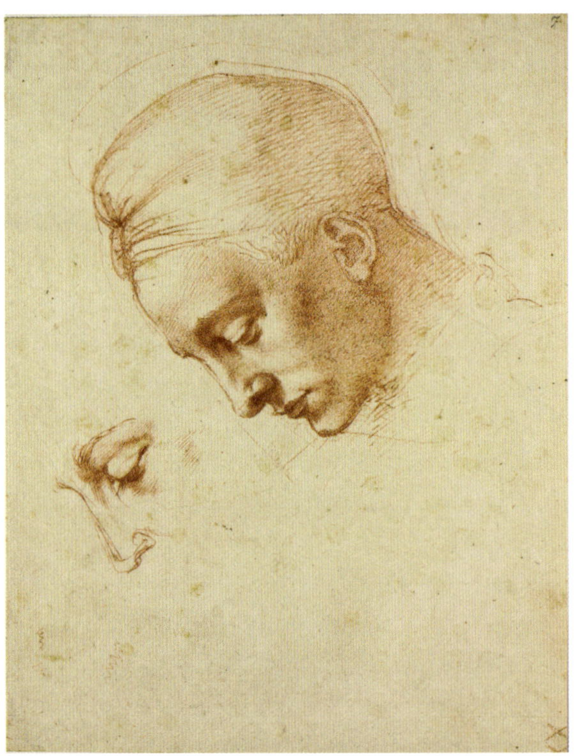

Michelangelo, *Studies for the Head of Leda*, c. 1530.

the nude Leda. In one sketch the swan caresses her ear with its beak; she smiles. Michelangelo made a drawing for the face of his own Leda, looking downwards, as if lost in a dream, like his statue of *Night* (see p. 246). This is not a woman's face. It is a portrait of his assistant Antonio Mini.

Putting Mini's face on a female nude holding the same pose as his *Night*, he inserted a swan between her legs, its long, tubular neck reaching over 'her' body to thrust its beak against Mini's lips. It seems a deliberately obscene act of despair at a moment when he had reason to think he was going to die, his corpse left to rot among the broken bodies of his fellow citizens. When starvation and sickness forced the fall of the city in 1530, leaving thousands dead, Michelangelo was on a list of republicans to be killed. He hid in a cubby-hole in a friend's house until the personal intervention of Pope Clement saved his life. He was ordered back to work on the Medici tombs.

A gentleman came from the Ferrara court to collect the *Leda*. He was not impressed. Michelangelo asked him his profession. He sneered that he was a merchant, which Michelangelo took to be a mockery of the commercial people of Florence, says Condivi. He refused to hand the painting over and instead gave it to Mini, who took it to France, where it later vanished, with the result that it is known to us only from painted and engraved copies.

* * *

With the fall of the republic, Michelangelo had no desire to remain in Florence. In Rome in autumn 1532 he fell in love with a young nobleman called Tommaso de' Cavalieri. Michelangelo was in his late fifties, and Tommaso in his late teens or perhaps 20 years old. The artist never consummated his passion for Tommaso, but they became friends, and the younger man accepted this love. Michelangelo insisted that it was like Ficino's 'Platonic love'. In a poem he attests that, simply by looking in Tommaso's face, his soul has risen many times to God:

> And if the wicked mob, cruel and stupid,
> point out in others what they feel themselves,
> no less gratifying is my intense wish,
> and my love, my faith and my honest desire.[6]

Michelangelo weaves together longing and Neo-Platonist thought in one of the great love poems of the Renaissance. In an age when you could be burned for 'sodomy', he proclaims his adoration for a man. Those who see something dirty in this are themselves base.

Michelangelo also gave drawings with mythological themes to Tommaso. They are more carnal than his verse, because art is always more provocative than words. One of them depicted Jupiter in the form of an eagle carrying off the beautiful mortal Ganymede. Michelangelo makes Ganymede a young man rather than a boy, as Ovid calls him. Preserved in what is either the original or an early copy, *Ganymede* portrays a love between men, or at least between a man and an eagle. The naked beauty of the young man is theatrical, his legs held apart by the giant bird's talons to stress the visibility of his genitals. He swoons in the eagle's clutches: it's the *Dying Prisoner* all over again. Yet the bird is solicitous, its neck embracing Ganymede, its wings protective. Jupiter's talons hold his lover like fetters; at the same time there is tenderness. And the eagle is flying high, towards heaven. Michelangelo leaves most of the sheet of paper blank to give us a dramatic sense of upward flight in the empty air.

* * *

The bodies rising and falling in Michelangelo's drawings for Tommaso are austerely delineated forms of compacted muscle surrounded by empty space. These ascents and descents reflect Michelangelo's knowledge of Plato. The love of an older man for a younger one can give the soul wings, according to Plato's *Phaedrus*. This vertiginous imagery of bodies in the sky also has a source far back in Michelangelo's past: Martin Schongauer's *Temptation of St Anthony*, the print he copied in his early teens – a small, intense sheet in which the ground falls away as the desert saint is borne upwards by demons.

That intertwining of the classical nude with old-time Gothic was about to produce a much more stupendous spectacle. In 1534 Clement VII commissioned Michelangelo to return to the scene of his greatest triumph and paint the *Last Judgment* on the wall above the altar of the Sistine Chapel. A few days later Clement died, but his successor, the Farnese family's Pope Paul III, stuck with the plan. It took Michelangelo until 1536 to start painting, and five years more to finish. He was in his early sixties now.

The echoes of northern art in the *Last Judgment* are explicit. Before the Reformation, every church in England had its Doom. In 15th-century Flanders, the naked souls of the dead rising from their tombs were robustly painted by Rogier van der Weyden, Dirk Bouts and Hans Memling. As Protestants challenged traditional beliefs about salvation, the decision to paint this venerable Christian subject in the pope's chapel reasserted the Catholic doctrine of grace. Pray and perform good works and you will be saved: otherwise hell awaits.

Naked souls were traditional, but Michelangelo gives his saints and sinners an enhanced athletic beauty that mixes the Bible with a bacchanal. Ripe sensuality is released like a fine wine, and a lifetime's passion for the male body runs free in the chapel. He shows more than rippling flesh in the tall painted

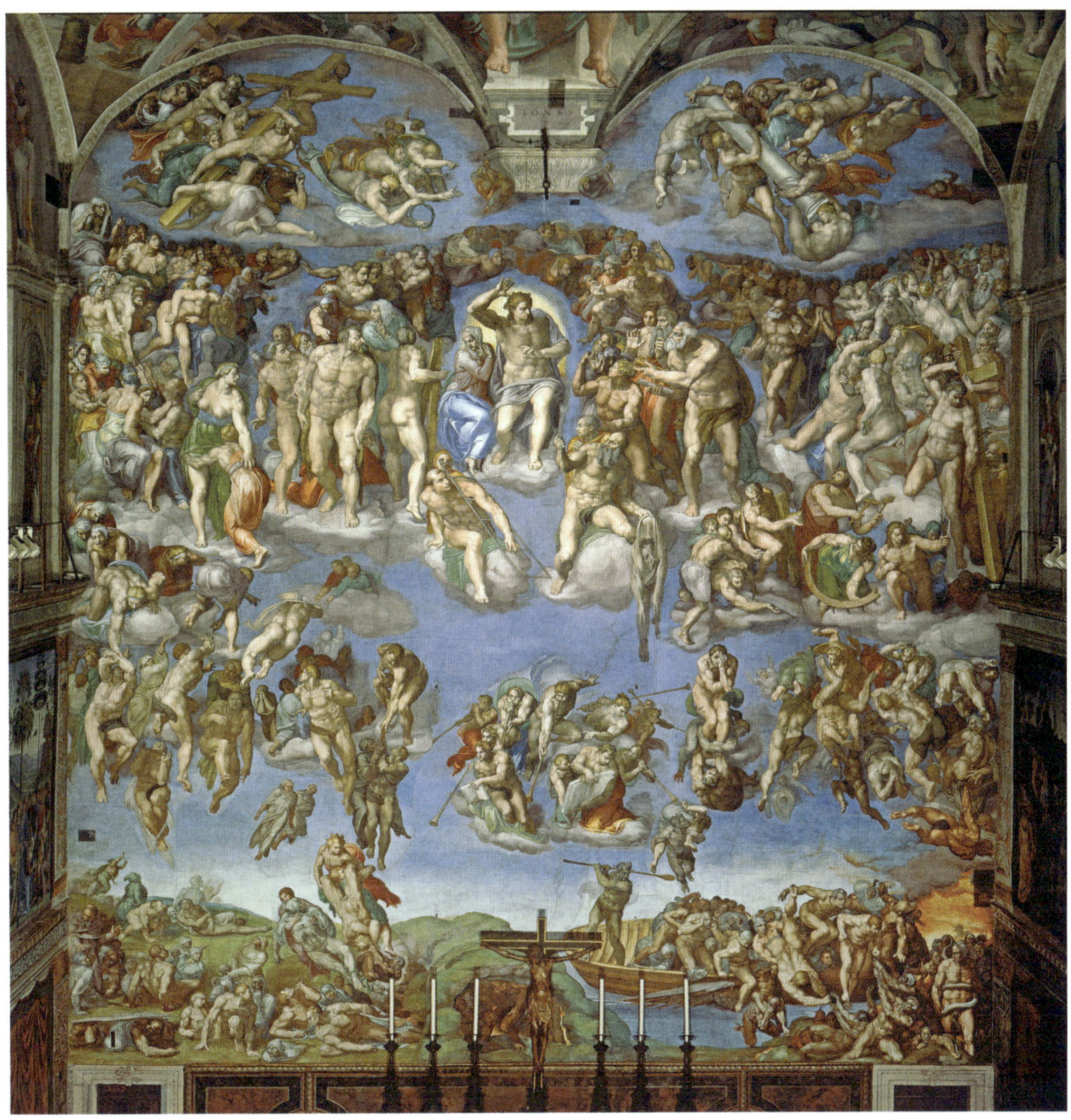

Michelangelo, *Last Judgment*, 1536–41.

sky. Two youths hug each other with powerful arms; another pair make explicit lip contact. These male embraces take place among the saints, in the heights. Michelangelo here explores his dream of the winged soul on a colossal scale, his fresco a cosmic drama of rising and falling flesh. In a deep, warm blueness, resurrected humans either lightly float upwards or are dragged down by demons. Michelangelo doesn't have to show the horrors of hell – although he does – to get his message across. To see a soul being pulled back down, forbidden to rise in that blue ether, produces a thud of despair. Emotion is conveyed through the suggestion of weight. Each body's fate expresses a different state of the soul. We hope to rise. So often we fall.

The painting is full of subversions that could be seen as 'heresy'. Two African men, perhaps Muslim, are pulled upwards.[7] Michelangelo ignores traditional Christian iconography to show angels without their gaudy wings. Christ appears like the god Apollo, a beardless, muscular nude in a glowing ovoid sun. The artist seems to have simply expected his audience to accept his personal philosophy of body and soul, however idiosyncratic.

* * *

Michelangelo had always identified with his figures: now he makes his sexuality his signature. The drawings for Tommaso de' Cavalieri were not secret: Tommaso showed them to powerful people, including the pope. Michelangelo's love poems also circulated widely. This gave plenty of ammunition to the 'wicked mob, cruel and stupid'.

Attacks began inside the Vatican before the fresco was even finished. When Paul III came to see how it was going, tells Vasari, he was accompanied by his master of ceremonies, Biagio da Cesena. This 'person of great propriety' denounced Michelangelo's three-quarters-finished work, right there in the Sistine Chapel, in front of the artist and the pope. He said that

> it was a very disgraceful thing to have made in so honourable a place all those nude figures showing their nakedness so shamelessly, and that it was a work not for the chapel of a pope, but for a *bagnio* or tavern.[8]

There was no escaping the implication. Bath houses were associated with illicit sex, including homosexual encounters. A crackdown on sodomy in Florence after the death of Lorenzo de' Medici singled out these venues, and taverns too. Biagio was accusing Michelangelo of bringing sexual lowlife into the Vatican.

No contemporary erotic frescoes from such meeting places survive. However, an extant decorated Renaissance room certainly implies that bathing was seen as sensual. It's in the Vatican. The *stufetta*, 'little warm room', commissioned by Cardinal Bibbiena, not only had the rare ancient Roman luxury of heating: it was decorated by Raphael and his team in imitation of ancient Roman wall paintings, found at the end of the 15th century in the buried palace of Nero and known as 'grotesques' because they seemed to come from a *grotto*, or cave. Stories of Venus, including her birth and love affair with Adonis, are depicted against a rich red background. The attempted rapes of Minerva by Vulcan and the nymph Syrinx by Pan also feature, along with playful vignettes of a river god's hair being washed and frolicking putti. The message seems to be that getting naked in a heated bathroom was a potentially arousing experience for a cardinal, and perhaps also for the pope. It was this atmosphere Michelangelo was accused of introducing into the Sistine Chapel.

Michelangelo was not pleased with Biagio's reaction. Nor was he cowed. When Biagio exited the chapel, the artist painted his face into the fresco as Minos, the judge of hell. His features are preserved among the infernal flames as he stands, naked and muscular, with a giant snake wrapped round his body. In Dante's *Divine Comedy*, the number of times Minos coils his serpentine tail announces the circle of Hell to which a sinner must go. Michelangelo added a twist, in which the snake clamps its mouth on Minos's penis. So just as his Leda symbolically fellated the swan, so Biagio is fellated by the serpent. He, not Michelangelo, is the base spirit who secretly desires what he condemns.

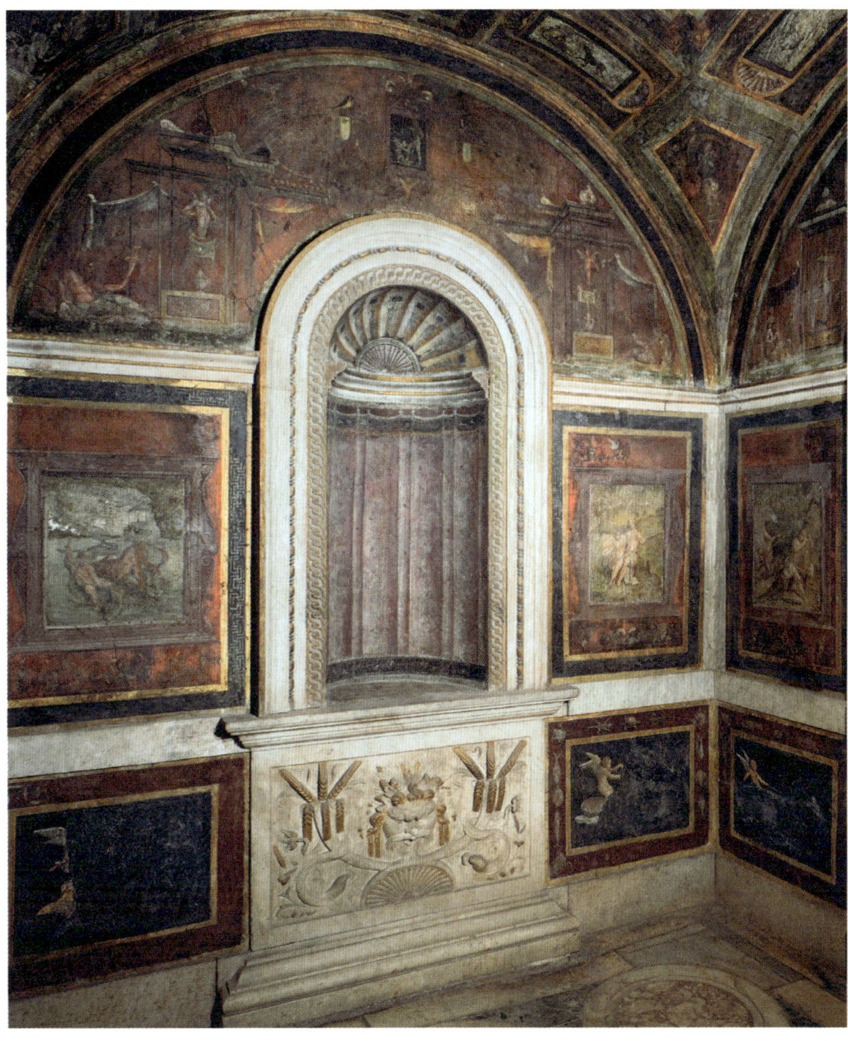

Raphael and studio, the *stufetta* of Cardinal Bibbiena, 1516.

It was just the beginning of the spite. Now that Michelangelo had made his love for a young man public, the naked male bodies in the *Last Judgment* were targets for censors and hypocrites. The most vicious attack was mounted by Pietro Aretino, the celebrity writer who corresponded with monarchs and emperors from his home in Venice. Aretino had made his name with pornographic poems to illustrate *I Modi* (The Ways) – an album of sex-guide images drawn by Raphael's assistant Giulio Romano and engraved by Marcantonio Raimondi. He also wrote a dialogue in which Nanna, a prostitute, explains to her daughter why sex work offered a better life than marriage or the convent. So his onslaught on Michelangelo was a masterpiece in hypocrisy.

Their correspondence started in flattery. 'The world has many kings, but only one Michelangelo,' Aretino wrote to the living legend in 1537. He corresponded regularly with the likes of Francis I of France and Henry VIII of England, distributing praise, blame and demands for gifts, but Michelangelo is greater than all of them, he says, before offering advice on the *Last Judgment*. He unfolds his own design as if pitching a film script: 'I see Nature there standing apart, full of terror, barren with her decrepit age. I see Time, parched and trembling, who is near to his end and seated on a dry tree-trunk.'[9] And so on. It all added up to an absurd, dry allegory. Michelangelo replied to Aretino's misguided letter that, sadly, he had already painted a lot of the fresco. Aretino kept bothering him, and in 1538 begged to be sent a piece of the cartoon. He did not get it. But a few years later he did get his revenge.

In the four years since its completion the fresco had proved a target for bigots. Just after it was unveiled in 1541, the Theatines, a religious order set up to renew Catholicism, denounced Michelangelo's vast display of nudity in the Sistine Chapel. Aretino waited until 1545, when it was clear a chill wind was blowing, to send his poisonous critique to Michelangelo, and in a revised form to others.

As a baptized Christian, Aretino 'blushes' at the licence taken in the *Last Judgment*.[10] He asks how it is possible that you, the 'divine' Michelangelo, 'who do not deign to consort with mortal men', have done this, above the highest altar in the most sacred temple on earth? Aretino prides himself that he dealt with the immodest themes of his Nanna dialogue in a modest fashion, whereas Michelangelo has presented saints and angels without even earthly decency and 'deprived of every celestial ornament', going further even than the ancients: 'For when they created statues of Diana, they clothed them, and when they sculpted Venuses, they made them cover with a hand the parts that should not be seen'. He accuses Michelangelo of valuing art above faith and believing it a royal spectacle to portray martyrs and virgins in an improper manner, with such an ecstatic display of genital organs, before which even those in brothels would shut their eyes in order not to gaze at them. Your art would suit some voluptuous *bagnio*, not the supreme chapel.

Aretino follows up his accusations with more clumsy artistic advice. But all might not be lost if Michelangelo changed

> the shameful parts of the damned to flames, and those of the blessed to rays of the sun; or imitate Florentine modesty, which hides the shame of your colossus under some golden leaves.[11]

* * *

There was a new atmosphere, a thickening mood, and Aretino could smell it. In December that year, the first session of the Council of Trent began, opening a grand inquiry into the tenets of Catholicism as the church faced up to the heretics' critique of lax old ways. The Theatines, who were so disturbed by the *Last Judgment*'s nudes, were shock troops of what would later become known as the Counter-Reformation. Aretino aped its language to damage Michelangelo.

* * *

In the same year that Aretino denounced Michelangelo and the Council of Trent took shape, the writer's Venetian friend Titian brought an incandescent nude to Rome. It was a painting of the mythological tale of Danaë. The church might be having scruples about nudity, but there were sybaritic clerics in its upper echelons who hadn't got the message: this sensual masterpiece was commissioned by Cardinal Alessandro Farnese, grandson of Pope Paul III. When Titian was working on it, the papal legate reassured Farnese that it made Titian's frank nude the *Venus of Urbino* look like a 'Theatine nun'.[12]

Titian paints an impossible metamorphosis: the king of the gods, Jupiter, comes to the princess Danaë, imprisoned in a bronze chamber, as a shower of gold (overleaf). Titian makes the gold a fine mist, floating above her bed, out of which globules of coins materialize. Danaë lies back to receive the homage, pensive, her face in shadow, as we look at her glowing, ample body, the gold-touched fluidity of her skin, the way Titian can make human flesh look substantial and unfixed at the same time. Danaë's contemplation of the gold mist is as awestruck as our own: for this glowing mystery is in fact a god.

It is also a metamorphosis of Michelangelo. Titian has given *Danaë* the pose shared by *Night* and *Leda*, thigh raised as she lies back awaiting her divine cash shower. This is an act of competition, or compliment, an aesthetic game played

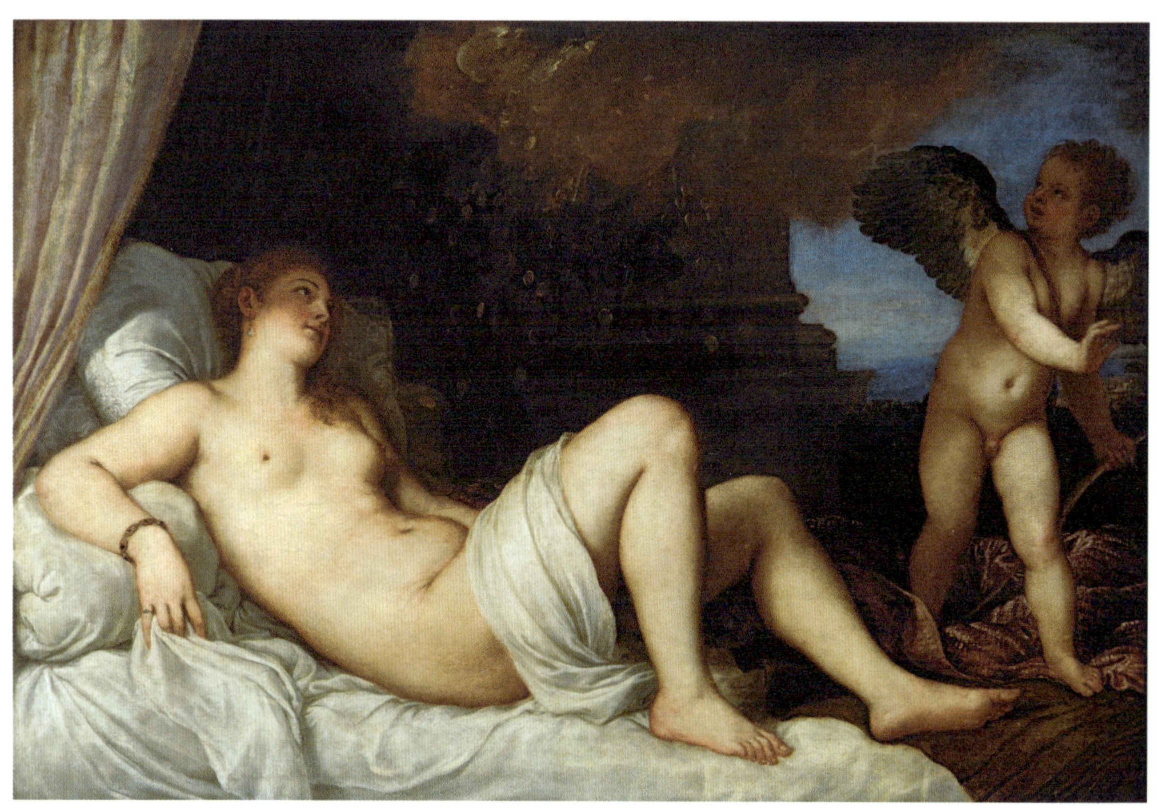

Titian,
Danaë,
1544–45.

between two artistic titans who agree on one thing: the greatness of the human body as an artistic theme.

Is it also a dig at Michelangelo, like Aretino's? There is nothing modest about Titian's *Danaë*. It's been suggested that her face is that of Cardinal Farnese's mistress, and in the context of the upper-crust culture of commercial sex the cascade of coins can be seen as a cynical joke. Yet it is an inexplicable encounter. In Titian's Venice the most mesmerizing art of the divine was and is the ceiling of St Mark's, with its shimmering golden mosaics – a sighing visual music of the heavens. The shower of gold that approaches Danaë has this same sublimity. The borrowing from Michelangelo may imply that, while he reduced religious art to decorations for a brothel, Titian can turn a courtesan getting paid into a divine encounter.

Vasari describes how he went with Michelangelo to visit Titian, who was staying in Rome at the Belvedere, and saw *Danaë*. They praised it, he says pointedly, 'as one does in the painter's presence'. On the way home Michelangelo said it was good, but 'it was a pity that in Venice men did not learn to draw well from the beginning ... if this man had been in any way assisted by art and design, as he is by nature, and above all in counterfeiting the life, no one could do more or work better'.[13]

Michelangelo's suggestion that Venetian artists don't learn to draw like Florentines has been used to suggest a far too easy contrast between Venetian *colore* and Tuscan *disegno*. In reality he and Titian were thinking in similar ways as they competed to paint the most lavish nudes. Michelangelo is not just a draughtsman but a scintillating colourist, as restorations of his paintings – especially the *Last Judgment* – have revealed. And Titian, as in his transformation of *Night* into *Danaë*, was riveted by Michelangelo's delineations of the body in space.

The spatial splendour of the *Last Judgment*, that rising and falling of flesh in the sky, has echoes in the mythological paintings that grew out of Titian's success with the *Danaë*: the tremendous canvases for Philip II of Spain that he called his *poesie*, poems. In a continent fretting and fighting over the nature of God's grace, the world of classical myth offered an escape, a pagan Arcadia where you could take a break from theological arguments. And you had to have Italians to create these hedonist playgrounds. The cult of Italy united the continent's courts just as Luther and his enemies were dividing them. Baldassare Castiglione's *Book of the Courtier*, published in 1528, was a continent-wide bestseller. In it, he gives a handy checklist of artists the good courtier should know: Leonardo, Mantegna, Raphael, Michelangelo, Giorgione – all Italian.

* * *

Francis I had a head start, having attracted Leonardo to France. He also gave the painter Rosso Fiorentino, who headed over the Alps after fleeing the Sack of Rome, a highly paid post to decorate a hunting lodge at Fontainebleau, to the south of Paris, that he had begun transforming into a palace. Fontainebleau is the birthplace of classicism in France, a love letter to the Italian Renaissance. Yet it wasn't graceful harmony or perspective that took hold here, but elongated bodies, over-the-top grotesques, fantastic gaudiness for gaudiness's sake. In the long *galerie*, Rosso Fiorentino's paintings include a giant elephant and are set among bulbous white stuccoes overflowing with nudes and love gods, fruits and scrolls, busts and sphinxes.

After a typical series of misadventures, a more unruly Italian ended up employed by Francis. Benvenuto Cellini justified the king's confidence by completing a delicate masterpiece: a gold salt cellar featuring two nudes, male and female, personifying the sea and earth. They face each other next to the bowl, their legs nearly touching as they lean back on seats of bubbling green and gold, as if relaxing at the sea shore.

Cellini also created a large bronze of a female nude with a masculine face, elongated form and muscular stomach embracing a stag, to go above the gate at Fontainebleau. It was instead appropriated by Francis's mistress, Diane de Poitiers, for her new château in the Loire. The identification of Diane de Poitiers with the ancient goddess, whose power is not to be trifled with, took off.

The political and military struggles of early 16th-century Europe were shaped by the rival ambitions of Francis and the Holy Roman Emperor Charles V, who was slower off the mark when it came to decorating his palaces with erotic Italian art. The ruler of Mantua gave Charles a group of mythological paintings by Correggio that portray the loves of Jupiter in what might have been flattery of the godlike power of the Habsburg global emperor. As the greatest of the gods, who had his way with whomever he liked, Jupiter was a suitable stand-in for the supposedly omnipotent ruler. In one work, *Jupiter and Io*, a woman is embraced by a cloud. Ovid says that Jupiter propositioned Io, but she ran away, so he swathed the countryside in a deep mist and raped her under its cover. Correggio represents not a rape but a fantastical seduction, making the mist itself Io's lover: a human face forms to kiss her, and a vaporous arm embraces her. Correggio makes tenderness the defining feature of the transformed Jupiter: he literally has a soft touch.

Sensational stuff, but Charles V preferred portraits of himself. And he liked them to be by Titian. The Venetian master pictured him standing, seated and, most impressively, on horseback, in a masterpiece that's almost apocalyptic in

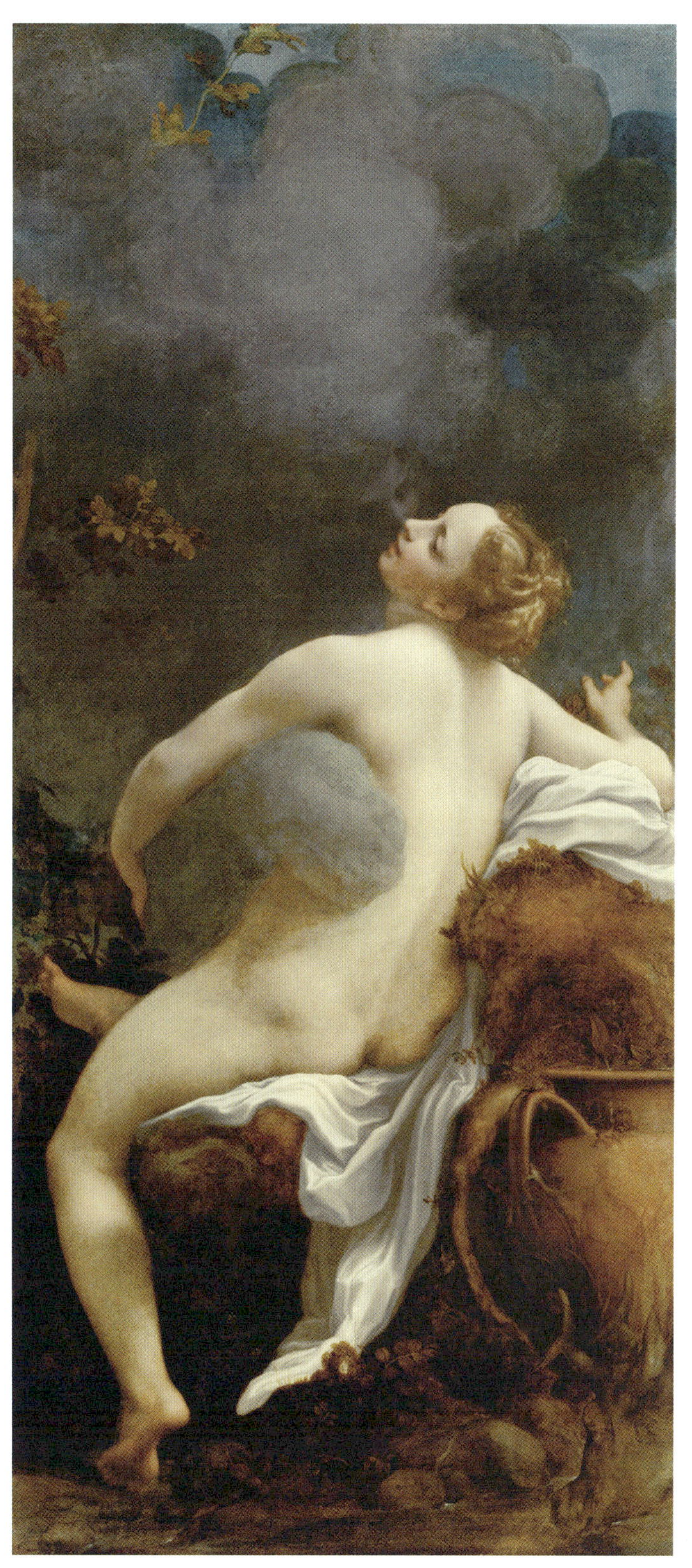

Correggio,
Jupiter and Io, c. 1530.

its depiction of a ruler, armoured for war, in a landscape that seems to contain the entire world – much of which Charles in theory commanded.

Titian's equestrian portrait of Charles was painted to celebrate his 1547 victory over a German Protestant alliance called the Schmalkaldic League. For a moment the Holy Roman Emperor seemed to have subdued the 'heretics' and restored Catholicism as Europe's true faith. It quickly became clear, however, that Luther and the even more radical theologian John Calvin, who held that salvation and damnation are completely predetermined in the mind of God, had captured too many souls at all social levels for the old order to be reimposed. Charles decided to retire. He split the Habsburg inheritance: his brother, Ferdinand, took over Central Europe as Holy Roman Emperor, while his son Philip became king of Spain and its growing dominions, including the Netherlands, Mexico, Peru and the Philippine Islands, which were named after him.

Philip also inherited Titian. He had a more adventurous eye for art than his father. And despite being a zealot for Catholicism, he had a taste for erotica. By 1554, while he was still prince, he and Titian had agreed on an ambitious series of canvases making visible Ovid's *Metamorphoses*. The artist would do them at his leisure in Venice and send them across the continent to Philip.

The first subject Titian tackled was a remake of the sensational *Danaë*, but this version, from the early 1550s, is less spiritual drama than ironic comedy. Danaë has an old servant who holds up a cloth to catch the coins; the cloud of gold is painted with less abstract mysticism. Titian must have reckoned that the young Prince Philip just wanted some titillating fun. And he was right: their long-distance working relationship flourished.

When Philip received the second painting he was in England, where he married Mary I in July 1554. It was a political marriage brokered by his father as another stratagem in the religious wars. England's Reformation looked like it was over. When Henry VIII died in 1547 he was succeeded by his 9-year-old son Edward, an enthusiastic Protestant surrounded by keen reformers. Following Edward's early death, and in spite of a desperate attempt at a Protestant coup during which the doomed Lady Jane Grey was installed as puppet ruler, Catherine of Aragon's Catholic daughter Mary took the throne.

By marrying Mary, Philip underlined the shift back to the Roman church, potentially added England to the Habsburg Empire and maintained the Habsburg tradition of cousin-marriage. So here he was, in London. In November 1554 the heresy laws were revived, and the following year burnings of recalcitrant Protestants began. Philip had agreed to marry Mary, said an adviser, 'for no fleshly consideration'.[14] She soon sequestered herself with what turned out to be a false pregnancy, possibly the result of ovarian cancer.

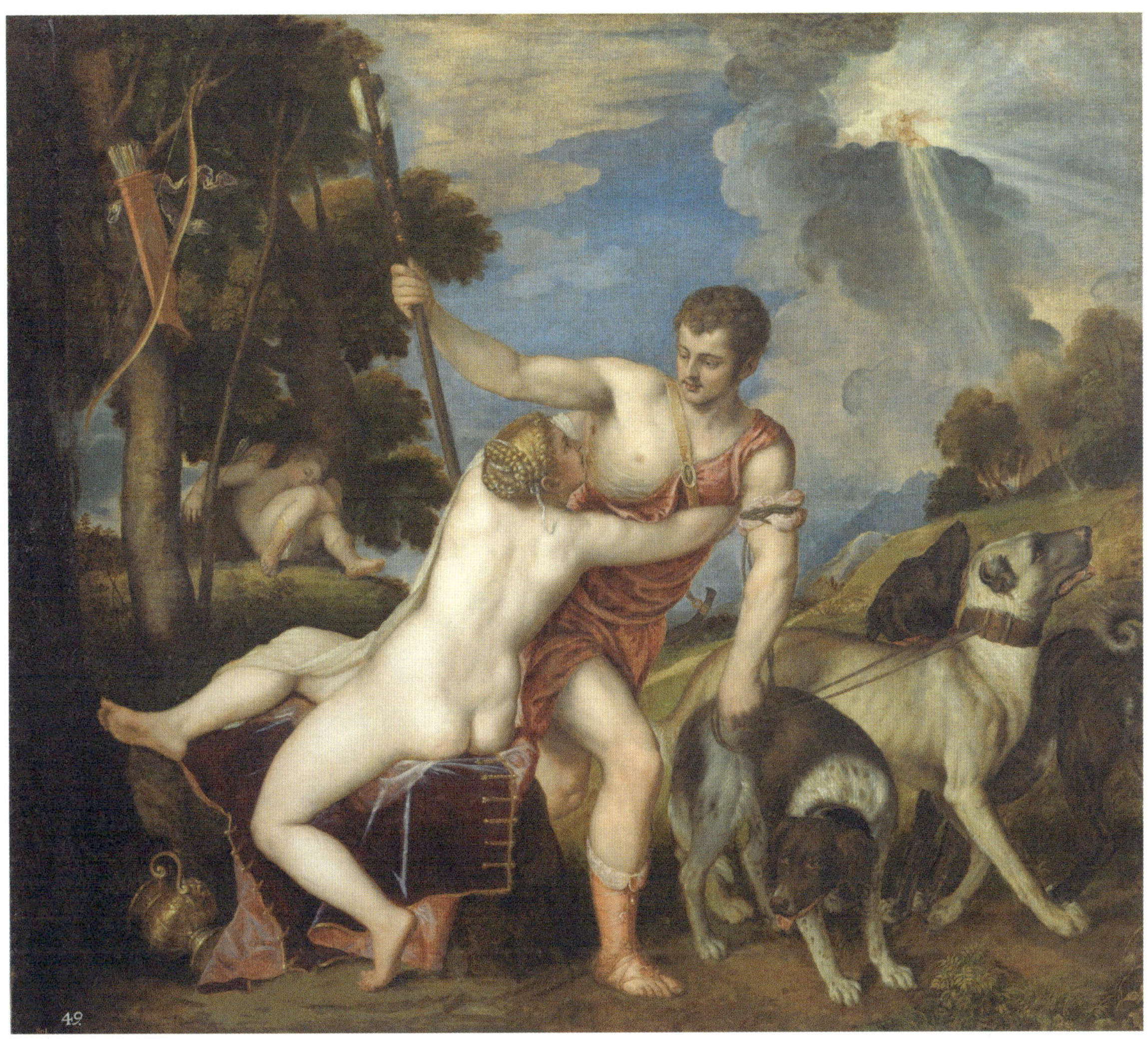

Titian,
Venus and Adonis,
1554.

Titian's second painting for Philip, *Venus and Adonis*, was not a simple piece of erotic escapism. Venus has her back to the onlooker as she puts her arms around Adonis and begs him not to go hunting: with divine foresight she knows that he will get killed. He pulls away; she pleads. She's nude and sitting on her corset, yet the mood is tragic. We feel Venus's pain. It didn't help Philip to see things from the unhappy Mary's point of view. He left England in 1555, taking his canvas with him.

The memory of this painting lingered in the British Isles. Shakespeare's *Venus and Adonis* reads like an amplification of it, giving a voice to Venus's pleas. The poet imagines himself into the role of Venus, begging and cajoling. There's a curious ambiguity to Titian's Venus too. Looking at her from behind, she is not entirely female: her back and rump are almost muscular.

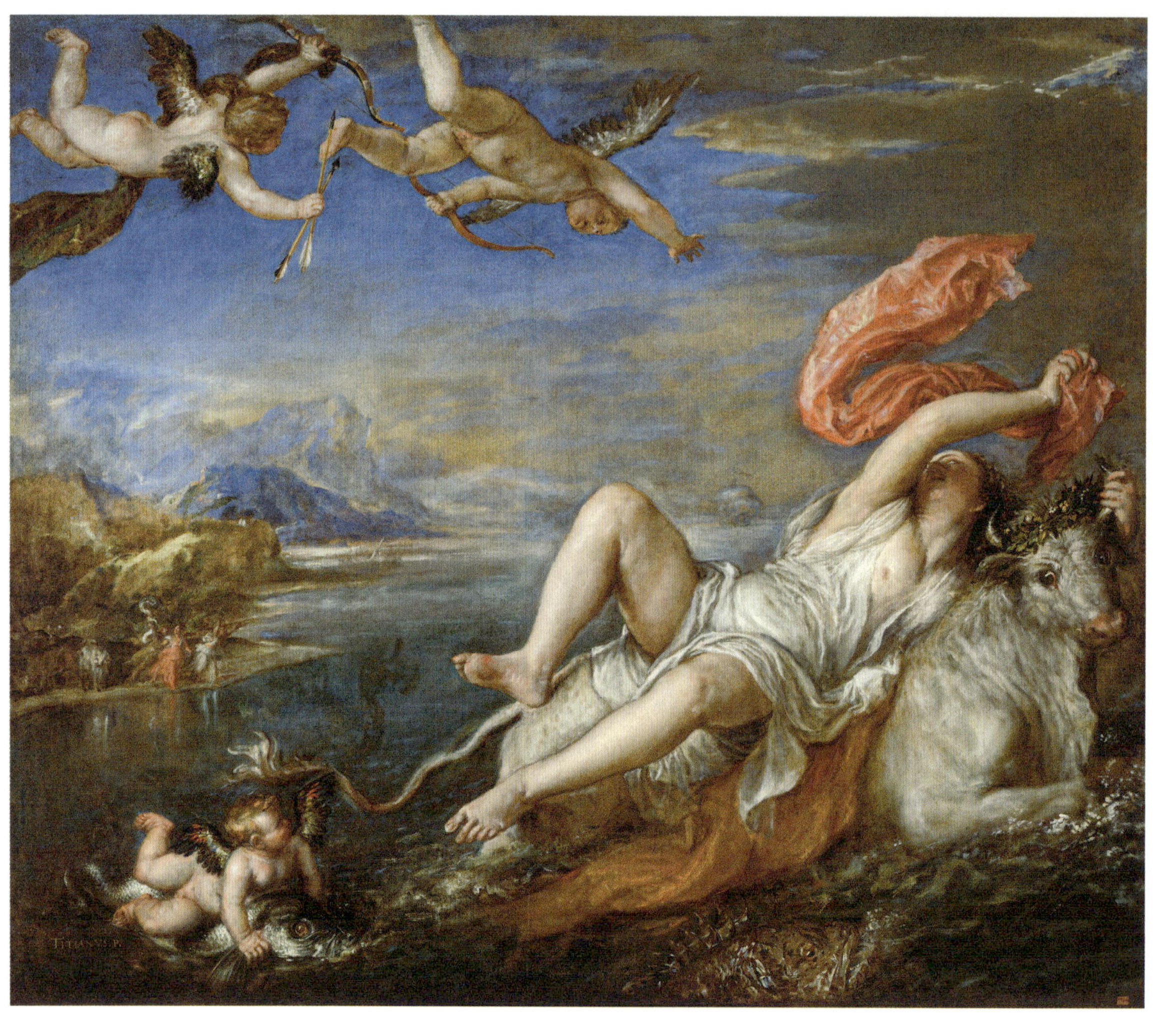

Titian,
Rape of Europa,
1559–62.

She looks like a homage to one of Michelangelo's favourite subjects, the male back.

* * *

Over the years Philip took delivery of more and better works, their poetry created by bodies in poignant groupings, in epic landscapes. *Diana and Actaeon* is a haunting mix of solidity and fleeting light. As the woodland goddess and her nymphs flinch in horror at being observed by the young hunter Actaeon, a fountain putters in their forest hideaway. It is the most magically painted fountain in art: a luminous trickle of silver, so wet you can feel its coldness, so fresh it seems to move.

The presence of Michelangelo's wall of painted bodies is hard to miss in Titian's later *poesie*. *Perseus and Andromeda* is in poor condition but that doesn't stop you seeing how Perseus flies and wheels in the air like a Michelangelo nude. In the *Rape of Europa*, the last of the cycle, the foaming green sea and deep-blue sky hung with fiery clouds merge into one great instability. Nothing supports Europa except the monster that is carrying her away from the shores of Asia Minor to become the emblem of the Western continent. This huge beast is a bull with a glaring eye and massive horns that she holds onto as her limbs splay precariously, trapped on this terrifying voyage. Or is she trapped? Titian urges us to contemplate the possibility that she's chosen to ride the bull, chosen this adventure. The story struck Renaissance eyes as erotic and ambiguous: Poliziano wrote of the bull turning to kiss Europa's feet, while on a relief by Giovanni Francesco Rustici it tongues her nipple.

Titian gives the myth a sublime twist. The intense colours of the sky, rhyming with Europa's fluttering bit of pink silk, transfigure the physical into the ethereal. The bull's gaze feels more than animal. This is not just a beast: it is a god. It may even be God. Titian hints at the new era of heightened religious intensity in this unlikely subject. Europa's fate anticipates the paintings of suffering saints that would become the archetypal art of the Counter-Reformation. Europa is a martyr.

By the time he received this painting, in 1562, the fervently Catholic Philip had the same problems as his father in controlling people far across the continent. The Spanish Netherlands was increasingly frustrated by his distant rule and religious impositions. Protestant preachers were whipping up passions that focused on removing the hated chief counsellor Cardinal de Granvelle, who seemed determined to entomb the Netherlands in Spain's distinctive Catholicism. Philip was forced to agree. Then in 1566 a full-scale revolt started, including iconoclastic attacks on religious images, known as the 'Beeldenstorm' ('Image Storm').

The Netherlandish region, with its stupendous artistic heritage, had plenty of idolatrous images to tear down. The van Eyck brothers' Ghent Altarpiece was saved by being taken apart, raised on ropes and hidden in the bell tower of St Bavo's. Soon the Spanish would be breaking human bodies in turn. An artist with a sharp eye for suffering would be there to watch as the horses' nostrils steamed and Spanish plate armour clanked in the frosty, snowbound landscape.

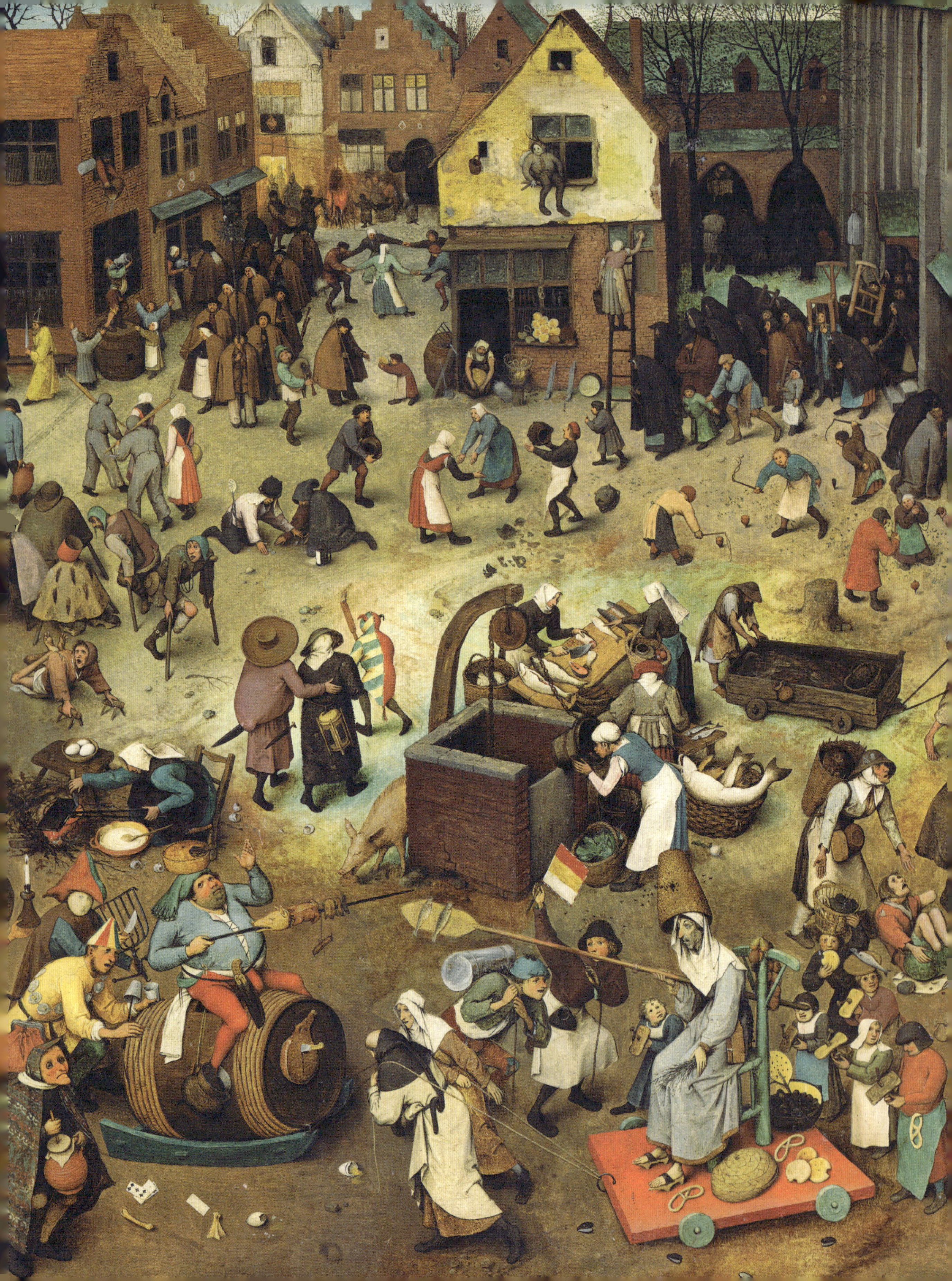

12 Carnival and Lent

Pieter Bruegel's *Battle between Carnival and Lent* transports us to a lost world of European popular customs and rites. Painted in 1559, it is a document of festivals that were far older. It offers a way to interpret one of Bruegel's inspirations – Hieronymus Bosch – and a window on the folk culture of people who had no contact with the high art of the Renaissance.

The *Battle between Carnival and Lent* is, you could say, a painting of time, or two times. The calendrical seasons of feast and fast clash at the heart of a town square and fight for dominance of the pictorial space. The forty days of Lent commemorate the period Christ spent living in the wilderness. Carnival has no such biblical justification; this 'farewell to flesh' could stretch from the feast of Epiphany to its culmination on the eve of Ash Wednesday with 'Mardi gras', or 'Fat Tuesday'. On the right-hand side of Bruegel's painting is order, where Lent dominates. On the left, the scene is given over to riot and abandon. Some of the roisterers wear masks.

These masks are varied. Some are ghostly white face coverings, moulded to show mouth, nose and eyes, yet without visible holes to see or breathe through. Behind the fat embodiment of Carnival, a stumpy figure has a crude face-covering of bark, cork or rags, with two bulging eyes. Close by is a cloaked figure in a finely crafted mask of a clenched-up, russet face with a long chin.

Pieter Bruegel, *Battle between Carnival and Lent* (detail), 1559.

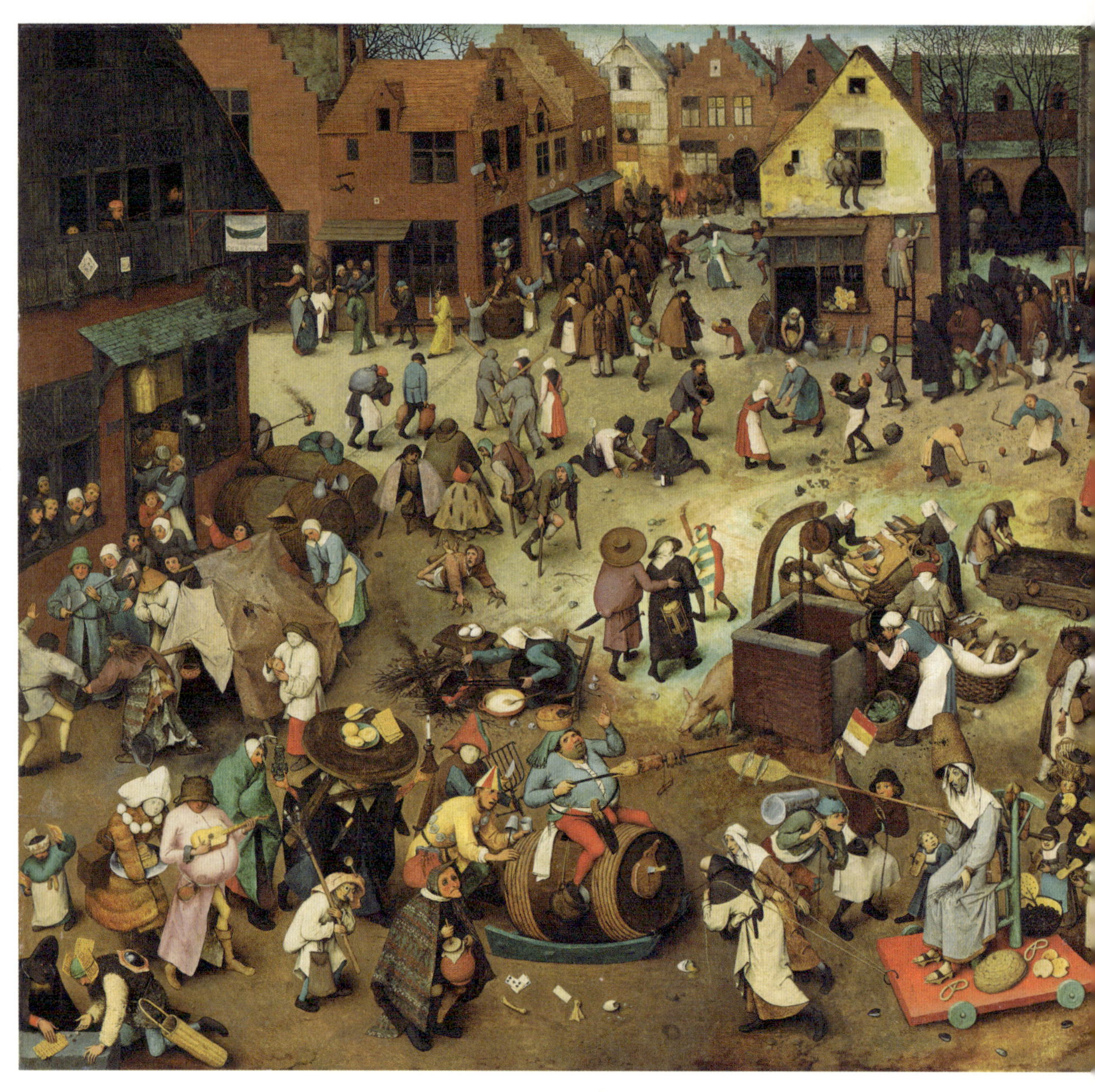

Pieter Bruegel,
Battle between Carnival and Lent, 1559.

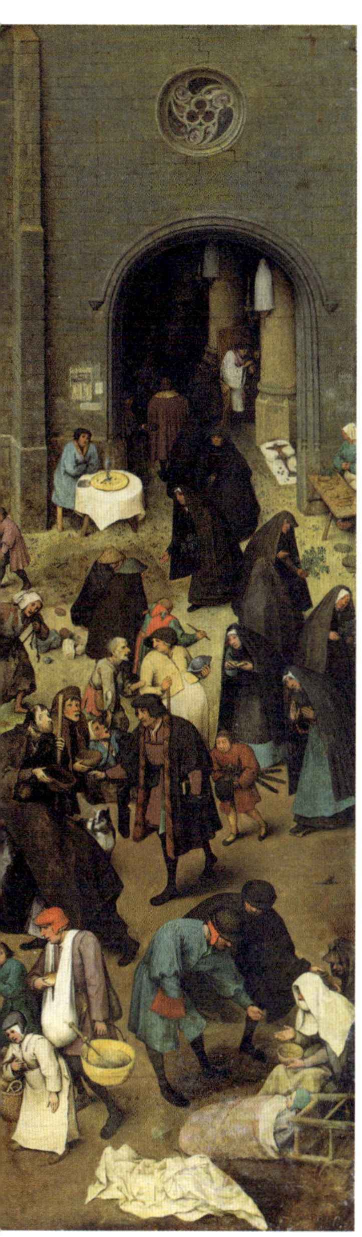

A dice player wears a black domed hood that covers his features. A particoloured jester wears a crown.

Europeans were sailing the oceans and encountering new peoples in the 16th century, but Europe was not some rationalist, advanced civilization that stood above the rest of the world. Bruegel shows us rituals that are hard to decipher, behaviour from an alien way of life. The people in white masks could be in medieval Japan or 19th-century Africa: all over the world, masking has been part of ceremonies in which people literally blank out their conventional selves to enact what is usually forbidden.

In the struggle between carnival and Lent, it is not certain whose side Bruegel is on. He might be saying carnival is foolery, Lent spiritual truth. Yet he scarcely makes the life of prayer look appealing. In their respectable corner, the good folk of Lent give to charity, but the way they drop coins to the poor is ostentatious. Disabled beggars helplessly solicit aid in front of the church. Across the square, at the heart of the carnival, a group of cripples dances and cavorts. There's no charity at carnival because there are no hierarchies of status or wealth. In the Lenten corner it is not just patronizing charity that grates: the monk pulling Lent's trolley exchanges a look with his female colleague. There's hypocrisy as well as injustice in the Lenten world.

Is carnival even a Christian festival, or does it exist beyond the Christian order altogether? Bruegel implies the latter by depicting its ruling palace as the inn as opposed to the church. People gather here, outside and in, to watch a crazy costumed procession and to dance and laugh. They don't seem to be sinning enormously. Only at the edges of the feast do we glimpse untamed excess: a man vomiting out of the window, a couple having sex. The festival is quite well organized. There is street theatre and music. People dressed as mythological archetypes can be seen in the crowd – Wild Man, King, Jester.

Bruegel shows these personae clashing with those of the church as a fraternity of penitents in brown cloaks marches into the square, bringing relief to the forces of Lent. Of course carnival can't win. Lent may look like a pathetic wraith, yet she has time on her side – and the church. It looms up like a stone fortress, the most permanent building on the square. Where carnival is a fleeting phenomenon embodied by dancers, guzzlers and drinkers, the power of Lent lies in the solidity of this Gothic place of worship, in front of which Lenten folk give alms and do penitence, and into whose shadows they go to do reverence.

* * *

The modern view of Bruegel is that he was not a peasant. The claim made by his early 17th-century biographer Karel van Mander that he was born into the peasantry in the village of 'Brueghel' has been dismissed as a fable. That may be unfair. Although Bruegel became a highly skilled, successful urban artist after training in Antwerp and Brussels with the painter Pieter Coecke van Aelst, a lack of documentation surrounding his birth means it is possible he was indeed of peasant stock. In any case he was born some time in the second quarter of the 16th century, when the Netherlandish north had become part of the Habsburg Empire. This context created an international appetite for Flemish 'peasant' art. The *Garden of Earthly Delights* was acquired in the 1560s by the duke of Alba, the tough Spanish general sent by Philip II to subdue the region, and in 1591 it would enter the collection of Philip himself. Bruegel too got snapped up by the Habsburgs soon after his death. In 1595 a batch of his paintings entered the extensive, eccentric collections of Rudolf II, the Habsburg Holy Roman Emperor, at his court in Prague. These fiercely original painters appealed to Renaissance courts as well as to wealthy townspeople in Antwerp. Yet popular imagery is integral to Bruegel's art. He shows us peasant lives and minds from the inside: what it was to dream of meat while trudging through the snow with an empty stomach.

Bruegel is an artist of food. Contrasting diets mark out the territories of carnival and Lent. The plump, drunken man acting out the part of Carnival has a game pie on his head and is mounted on a booze barrel, to which a chop is pinned by a knife. A roasted pig is skewered on his lance, its body partly eaten away; this flesh-clock ticks away the time of freedom. The foods of carnival are fatty, buttery, warm. There are waffles galore, not only to eat but to wear – a man inserts them in his headband. Eggs are worn as jewelry by a masked woman who has on a straw suit and carries more waffles. An old woman holds what looks like a waffle iron to a fire in the open square, to cook a new batch from her bowl of batter. Meanwhile, not far from the fat flesh-king, a respectably covered woman sells fish. They look cold and wintry, as if they were born from ice. The fish are laid out, gutted, chopped up, yet there are few buyers because Lent is only just beginning. Soon everyone will be eating those silvery creatures.

Lent looks thin, grey, worn out, her weakly held lance a long wooden spade with two measly fish on it. Pretzels and thin bread are scattered on the trolley platform: dry, salty Lenten fare. Lent's followers carry hard, flat loaves for shields.

* * *

The symbolic power of food in Bruegel rests on the fact that, in his world, access to it could never be assumed. There was always the fear of famine in the countryside, and in lean years the price of bread escalated, hitting the urban poor. Bruegel's prints of the *Fat Kitchen* and the *Thin Kitchen* imply that the opposition of abundance and want was a brute psychological framework for his contemporaries, all the time. In the *Fat Kitchen*, comically rotund people, from plump children to a big-stomached patriarch with a sausage in his belt, all crowd into their kitchen to enjoy roast porkers, chicken, hams, sausages. A starveling man is driven away from the door while a fat cat sleeps by the fire, a fat mother breastfeeds her fat baby, and the well-covered people wash down their meat with beer and wine. They don't bother with vegetables. In the *Thin Kitchen* a turnip lies on the table, while a woman who is too emaciated to feed her baby gives it milk or water from a horn. Like the fatties, these skinnies crave protein rather than carrots and onions, but their only source of it is a bowl of mussels. Modern Belgium's national dish of *moules et frites* would have baffled Bruegel and his peers: mussels are poverty food, just as fish are Lenten fare.

Bruegel's 1567 painting the *Land of Cockaigne* visualizes the folk fantasy of a land of milk and honey, where everyone will be satiated, without effort. The good life is again defined by fat. A pig provides its own knife to carve it; a fowl offers its head on a platter; an egg cracked open scuttles about on chicken legs. A table laden with cooked meats tilts itself towards three adventurers – a knight, a peasant and a scholar – who have found this magic land. Another knight rests in a hut whose roof is covered in bowls of porridge or soup, while a man is tunnelling with his bare hands into a mountain of butter. Even the sea is made of milk. This is wish-fulfilment on a cornucopian scale. To interpret the *Land of Cockaigne*, as some do, as a grim condemnation of the sin of gluttony is to ignore its comic exuberance. It's no more condemnatory of earthly pleasures than is François Rabelais. The French Renaissance writer's literary works *Gargantua* and *Pantagruel* are rampant celebrations of gorging and, especially, boozing.

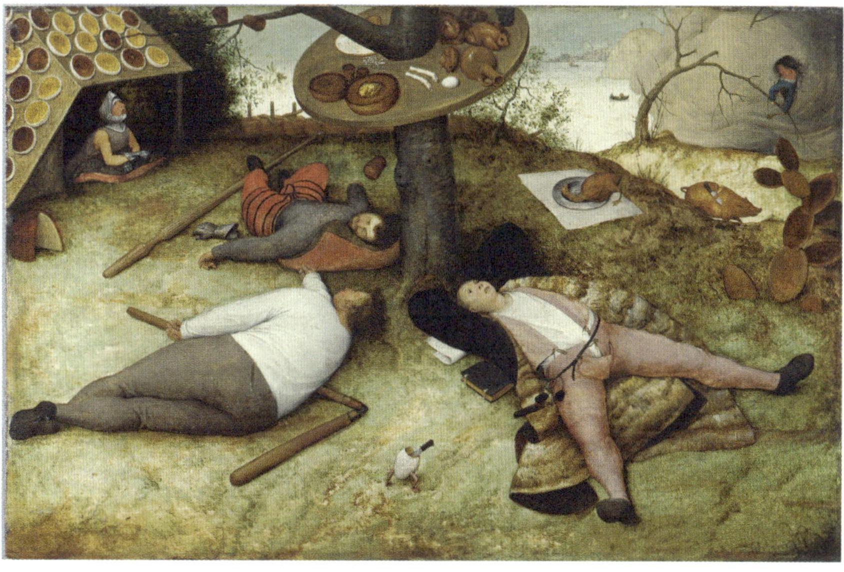

Pieter Bruegel, *Land of Cockaigne*, 1567.

Gargantua is born calling for a drink. As a baby he consumes the milk of 17,913 cattle a day, a veritable Cockaigne's worth.

* * *

Van Mander tells a story about Bruegel that is more subtle than reducing him to a folk artist. Bruegel, he says, often dressed up as a peasant and went to country weddings, claiming to be related to the bride or groom and bringing gifts: 'It gave Bruegel pleasure to study the ways of peasants in eating, drinking, dancing, leaping, larking.'[1] This tale makes Bruegel seem like an anthropologist on fieldwork. One of his most realistic rural scenes is the *Peasant Wedding*, a depiction of the kind of party van Mander says he crashed. It's a detailed view of village society: while two well-off rural families, just joined by marriage, are celebrating with their neighbours in a barn where the bride looks supremely contented and musicians pipe rustic music, a crowd of lesser villagers watch from the door. Yet the people at the trestle table are only comparatively well-off. They are not eating meat with their beer but bowls of porridge. A boy licking the last drop off his finger looks glad to get it. In the *Peasant Wedding*, the entertainment is just as basic: drink, bagpipe music and dancing. What more do you want?

The appeal of Bruegel for us today is precisely that he brings us down to earth, puts us in touch with humble pleasures. We want to join in with his squat figures as they skate on icy ponds. We would love to be invited to his jamborees. This recollection of forgotten basics is the consequence of some bold artistic decisions. For there was nothing obvious about painting peasants in the 16th century. In fact, they were the least likely social group you would make art about. Bruegel's leap in the snow is a moment of true discovery.

When European intellectuals began studying folklore in a systematic way in the Romantic age, they were often motivated by a quest for national identity. The Grimm brothers collected German tales at a moment when the nature of Germanness was being mythologized. Much earlier, and with a passion for region and place that had nothing to do with nationalist ideology, Bruegel discovered the people. He did this at a time when the Low Countries – both modern Belgium and the modern Netherlands – were chafing at the tether of Spanish rule. The cities of Flanders had a long history of defending their rights, even when they were ruled by the locally based Burgundian court. Now the remote Catholic rule of Spain sparked protests and dissent. Bruegel digs deep into his local world to find the roots of Netherlandish freedom in peasant merry-making. Yet the route he took to discover 'home' was surprising. For this peasant painter had seen Italy.

* * *

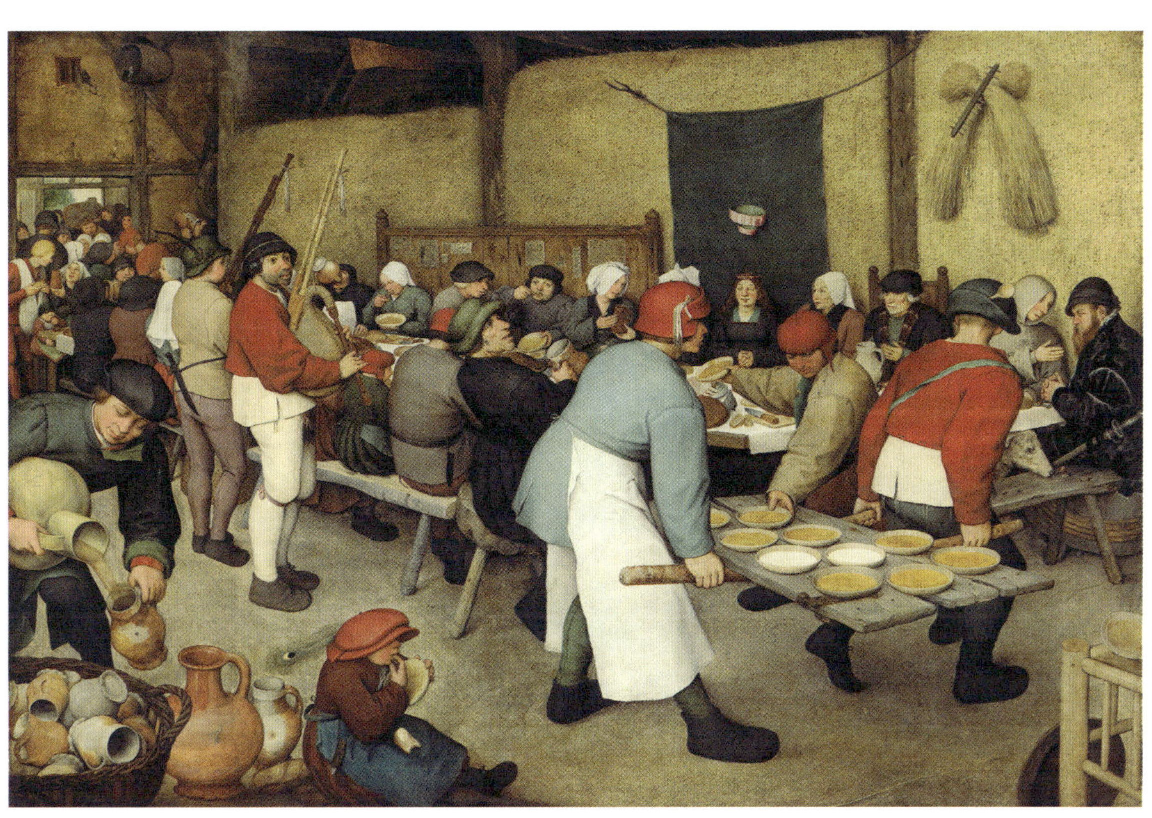

Pieter Bruegel,
Peasant Wedding, 1568.

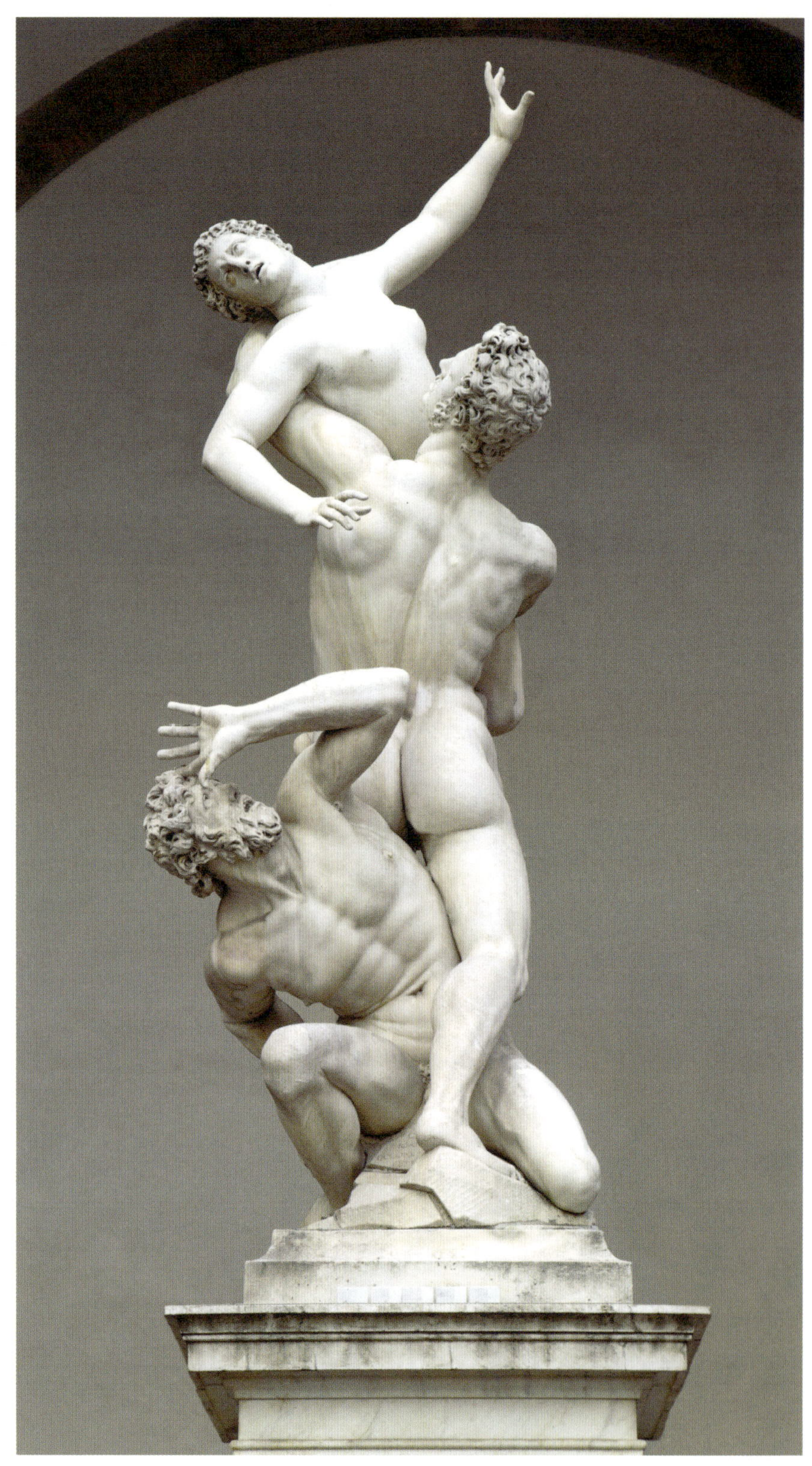

Giambologna,
Rape of a Sabine, 1582.

The cult of Italian classicism that seized 16th-century Europe had a complicated effect in Flanders. Artists felt obliged to import pagan mythology and classical proportion that often looked ill at ease combined with homely Netherlandish portraits and Gothic architecture. It could produce ungainly nudes, awkward bacchanals. Nonetheless, artists from the north now saw a journey to Italy as crucial to their education. Some stayed. Jean de Boulogne from Douai settled in Florence and became Giambologna, the most brilliant classical sculptor after Michelangelo: his genius in this quintessentially 'Italian' form shows that there was nothing innate about the styles of different regions.

Then again, Giambologna's mastery of classical grace is in creative tension with an appetite for fantasy that distantly connects him with Bosch. His masterpiece, the *Rape of a Sabine*, is a tottering tower of human bodies that he conceived without a story in mind: it was named by another artist after its creation. He also brought a Bosch-like imagination to garden sculpture for the Medici, creating dreamlike fountains and a colossal personification of the Apennines as a snow-bearded giant.

* * *

In 1552 Bruegel set out on his journey to Italy. We know that he traversed mountain passes high above plummeting valleys and saw ice-covered peaks and even volcanoes, for they all appear in his art. His 1565 painting *Hunters in the Snow* (overleaf) encloses a waterlogged Netherlandish plain between two dramatic uplands. Our vantage point is a snowy hillside where the hunters and their dogs trudge home past a fire blazing in front of the Stag Inn, while white-cloaked houses look as though they have gathered together for warmth. On the frozen water in the valley people play, skating and sledging on the blue ice. Beyond, the horizon is closed off by sheer rock faces rising to Alpine pinnacles. We are simultaneously in a Flemish winter and in a more forbidding territory of stone and ice.

Bruegel may have had an unprecedented interest in the people and customs of his own region, yet he invents landscapes composed of everywhere he had seen. His paintings are encyclopaedic and cartographic. The vision of earth Bosch painted on the closed wings of the *Garden of Earthly Delights* may have inspired this urge to capture the world in a painting – or at least Europe. Bruegel's debt to his fantastical predecessor has been recognized since the Renaissance. The Habsburgs collected both artists, and van Mander noted that Bruegel

> made a study of Hieronymus Bosch and he too created many spookeries and drolleries, for which reason he was called 'Pieter the Droll'.[2]

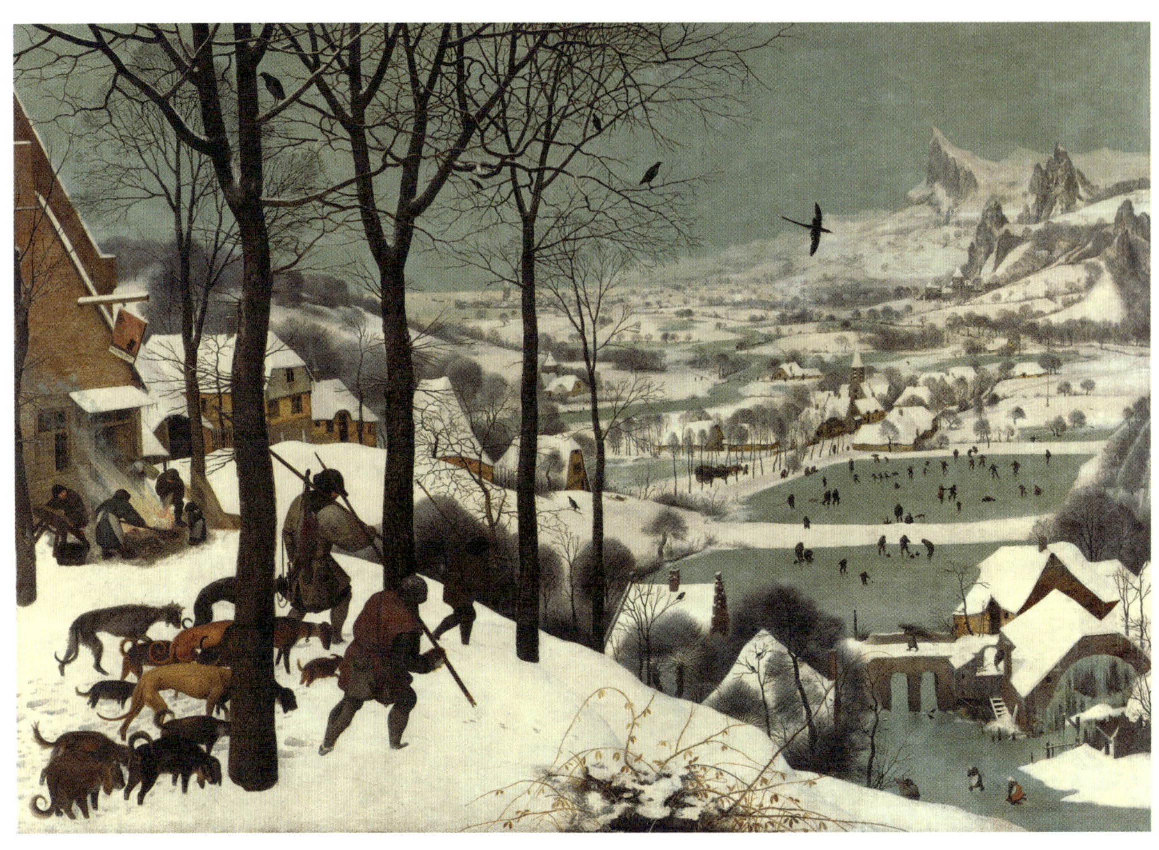

Pieter Bruegel,
Hunters in the Snow,
1565.

Bruegel's genius lay in translating the carnival humour and night terrors of Bosch to a more realistic landscape. His two-year journey to Italy and back enabled him to do so, and it's clear from sketches that survive how subtly he observed new places. Other northerners depicted tourist sights. The Haarlem artist Maarten van Heemskerck, who stayed in Rome in the 1530s, portrayed himself, after returning to the Netherlands, in front of the weed-covered Colosseum in a souvenir selfie. In Rome he drew Michelangelo's *Bacchus* standing in the garden of the banker Jacopo Galli; he also sketched the building site of St Peter's.

These are precious records of Renaissance Rome, yet Bruegel took a more sidelong view. His only extant drawing of the pope's capital is a quiet depiction of the Ripa Grande port on the river Tiber. There are no famous landmarks in this workaday scene: you sense the stillness of a hot, subdued, southern afternoon. Bruegel finds time, as he sits on the river bank, to portray a dog watching from the shore as a rowing boat pulls out to ferry someone over the river, a donkey waiting while its owner trawls the shallows, people hanging around lackadaisically on the far shore. It is a drawing of the edge of city life, not its glamorous centre.

Bruegel went further south, and further from the obvious. He got as far as the city of Reggio Calabria and the Strait of Messina that divides mainland Italy from Sicily. He drew Reggio, making it appear as sleepy as his view of Rome's river port – except that parts of it are on fire. A print Bruegel designed explains the mystery: it has been attacked as European and Ottoman ships battle it out in the Strait. The text accompanying this print indicates that Bruegel was not

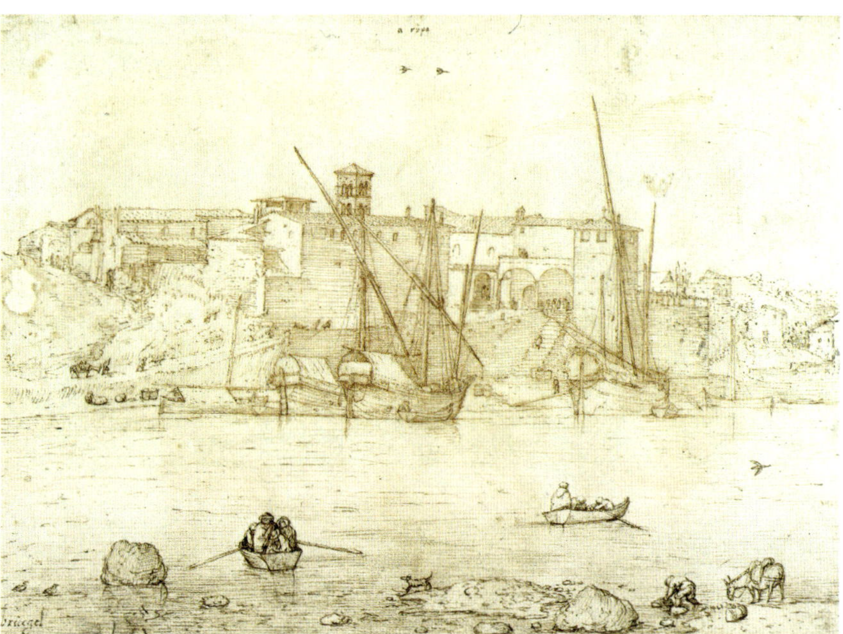

Pieter Bruegel, *View of the Ripa Grande, Rome*, 1552–53.

deaf to the siren calls of classical culture as he journeyed in a landscape saturated with it. The Strait of Messina, the inscription points out, is home to the 'terrible monster' Scylla, the scourge of sailors. There's no sign of sea monsters in the picture. But another Mediterranean scene by Bruegel – or, if not by Bruegel, then faithfully copied from a lost work by him – is perhaps the most moving of all Renaissance depictions of classical mythology.

* * *

The story of Daedalus and Icarus was familiar to Bruegel and his contemporaries from Ovid's *Metamorphoses*. The tale of the imprisoned craftsman who devises an escape plan involving flight on constructed wings, but whose foolish son ignores his advice to take the middle way, offered thrilling material for a painter. Yet there is nothing obvious about Bruegel's approach. His painting of the story is known to us through two versions. One is a typically poor, late 16th-century copy. The other is a superb painting long regarded as Bruegel's original, until a combination of technical examinations and connoisseurship convinced the museum where it hangs that it owns a copy. That's baffling, for whoever painted it is as gifted as Bruegel. Who can this non-Bruegel have been?

A pair of legs is being swallowed by warm, green water, vanishing for ever without stirring anything in the wider scene. Icarus has fallen into an inlet shaded by rocks, above which we find ourselves. There are others here with us – except that they see nothing. A ploughman concentrates on his heavy work, head down, following his familiar furrow. Even if he were to raise his head from drudgery, he is facing away from the drowning boy. So are a shepherd and his dog, who also ignore their flock scattered precariously on the rocky slope leading down to the sea. On the ship, sailors are too busy in the rigging to notice.

Bruegel has pointedly changed Ovid's imagery. Witnesses to the flight of Daedalus and Icarus are specified in the *Metamorphoses*. As Arthur Golding's English translation from the 1560s has it:

> The fishermen
> Then standing angling by the sea and shepherds leaning then
> On sheephooks, and the ploughmen on the handles of their plough,
> Beholding them, amazèd were: and thought that they that through
> The air could fly were gods.[3]

Bruegel depicts just such bystanders – ploughman, shepherd, sailors – but they see nothing. They fail to bear witness. They don't see either the miracle of flight or the tragedy of the falling boy: it's as if they inhabit a different world. A tale from Ovid has come to life, but they are stuck in routines of 'real life'. The

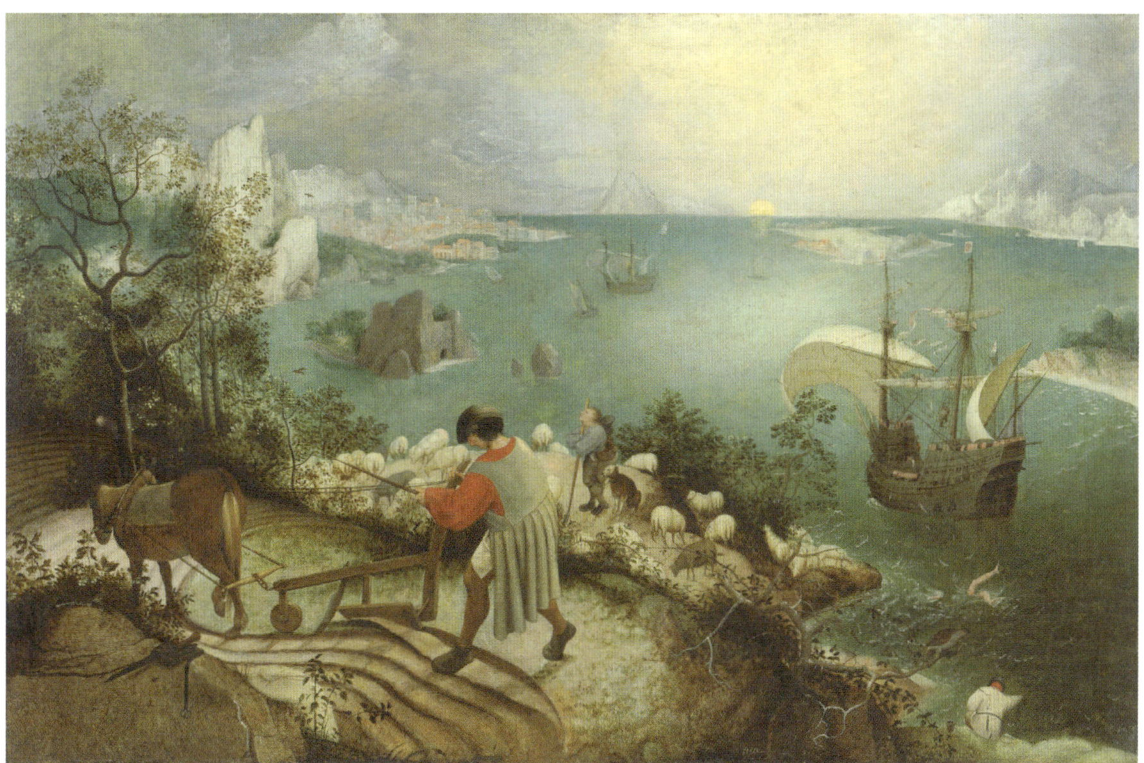

Pieter Bruegel or follower, *Landscape with the Fall of Icarus*, c. 1555–60.

ploughman wears wooden clogs like a northern peasant. Bruegel's Mediterranean vista is too sunny for him to notice as he toils in heavy clothes, as if it were a cold Flanders day in a flat land where things like this just don't happen. Myth rubs up against rustic, working lives, a dullard ploughman, an irresponsible shepherd.

The spread of Italian art and its cult of classical antiquity did not put some conformist stamp on European culture. Instead it released the most nuanced phase of the Renaissance through interaction with local customs, folklore and climate. Bruegel sees mythology as a Netherlandish peasant might; a tale from Ovid becomes a bleak proverb.

This crab-like, ironic perspective on the action, panning away from the individual tragedy to take in the epic sweep of a wider reality, resembles the off-centre views Bruegel drew of Italy: a quiet afternoon in an unpicturesque part of Rome; smoke rising from Reggio Calabria. *Landscape with the Fall of Icarus* stands back from a supposedly central drama to reveal the complex human moment in which it just happens to happen.

Bruegel's sustained interest in this myth is reflected by a print he did of a sailing ship in which the sun's spear-like rays destroy Icarus's wings while his father flies wisely in the middle air. It was one of a series of prints of ships in which mythological characters crop up. In fact, there is another sailing ship that

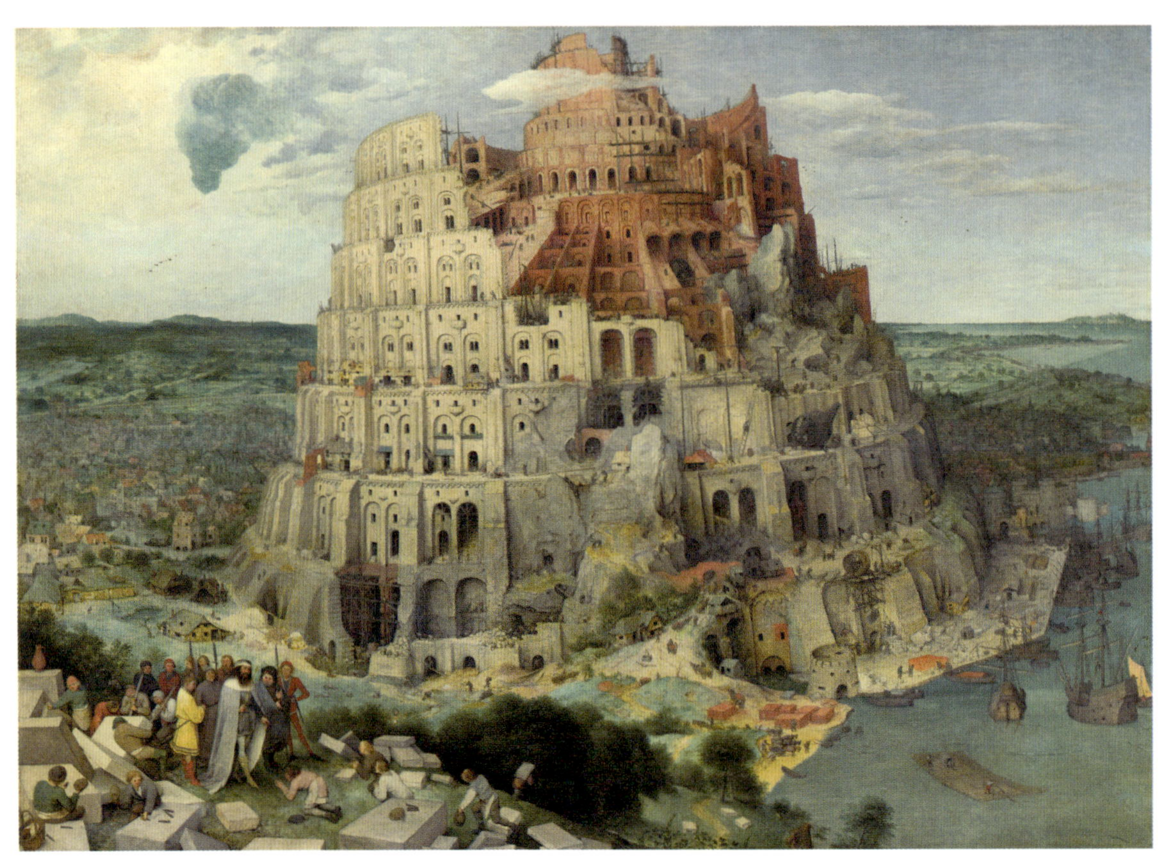

Pieter Bruegel,
Tower of Babel, 1563.

proves that the conception of *Landscape with the Fall of Icarus* is pure Bruegel. Or, rather, the sailor in its rigging who is clambering up the lattice of ropes on the ship's starboard side. This tiny figure in Bruegel's painting the *Tower of Babel* is in an identical position, and wearing the same clothes, as the man climbing the rigging in the vista of the fallen boy.

* * *

The *Tower of Babel* also shares *Icarus*'s radical shift of viewpoint. Bruegel painted more than once the biblical story of the tower: built to touch heaven, it so angered God that he punished humanity by turning the single tongue spoken by the first people into a chaos of mutually incomprehensible languages. The spellbinding details and strange perspective of the version owned by Rudolf II make it one of Bruegel's most mind-bending creations.

The impossible citadel rises from its immense base, reducing the houses around it to toys and the people swarming its galleries to ants. This 1563 panel is not immense – yet Bruegel uses surreal contrasts of scale to make the tower a vertigo-inducing prodigy, a Gargantua among buildings. He takes your imagination on a ride into its excesses by letting you explore details: at the lowest level an apparatus operated by a treadmill raises a block of stone from the harbour, while workers struggle to shift the blocks already brought up so that they can be raised by another, bigger crane to the next tier. Another machine is lifting materials still higher. The tower is partly supported by a grey mountain, making the building site seem like a quarry. Meanwhile, on the town side of the structure, people are already living inside arched alcoves as scaffolding supports the lower stories. The fatal tower is crumbling at its base even as its summit soars among the clouds.

Bruegel uses the skill of a miniaturist to define each aspect with a clarity that makes the tower Brobdingnagian. It's possible he learned how to paint on a small scale from Mayken Verhulst, the wife of his master, Pieter Coecke van Aelst. She was a painter in watercolour and tempera, a miniaturist and a print publisher. Aside from her publications, her works don't survive, but her legacy may live on in Bruegel's eye for the small scale. In 1563 he married the Aelsts' daughter Mayken Coecke, so the relationship was close. In fact, Bruegel supported himself in Rome by working as a miniaturist with the renowned manuscript illuminator Giulio Clovio. Like Bruegel, this artist was an outsider in Italy, a Croatian whose birth name was Juraj Julije Klovi. Clovio, as he Italianized it, created luxury masterpieces, including the Farnese Hours, for a Roman elite still wedded to expensive handmade books well into the age of print. Bruegel's work too has been detected in them.

Bruegel deploys microscopic detail to create a bewildering vastness. As his tower rises, it turns into a distorted version of a building whose name defines the colossal: the Colosseum. So Bruegel had seen Rome's sights after all. This monumental ancient amphitheatre, begun in about 70 to 72 CE in the reign of Vespasian, had been quarried for stone and left to rot, yet still stood as a daunting memorial to the ancient Romans. But Bruegel insists, always, on looking from an unexpected angle. Exposed ribs of red brick are seen in the unfinished top part of the edifice, radiating to support an inner tower. They unmistakably resemble the ruinous seating and undercroft of the great arena in Rome. Arched, cavernous openings and galleries are also visible, as if the guts of the behemoth have been exposed by an anatomist.

Bruegel's *Tower of Babel*, like the Rome he knew, is both wreckage and habitation. People live in the unfinished yet collapsing structure, just as life in Renaissance Rome burrowed into ancient stone husks. In the early 16th century the architect Baldassarre Peruzzi built a palace for the wealthy Orsini family inside and on top of the ancient Theatre of Marcellus. The popes' Castel Sant'Angelo was perched on the sepulchral corridors of Hadrian's mausoleum. Bruegel's *Tower of Babel* is Renaissance Rome, a dilapidated, unfinished human warren.

Like Bruegel's titanic mound of entropy, it was hard to tell if the building site of St Peter's was unfinished or already in ruins. Maarten van Heemskerck's drawings show incomplete vaults open to the sky, as if the greatest building project of the Renaissance were a folly of Babel-like proportions. The potential insanity of this venture, begun decades ago and still far from completion, surely looms large in Bruegel's satire.

But there was hope. When Antonio da Sangallo the Younger, the third architect of St Peter's after Bramante and Raphael, died in 1546, Pope Paul III put Michelangelo in charge. While accusations of obscenity swirled around his *Last Judgment*, Michelangelo took over building the most prestigious basilica on earth. And saved it. The first thing he did was not architectural but managerial: he shut down a network of corruption that had clogged the project in the four decades since it began. Michelangelo brought a moral fervour to his task: he even argued against having too many hideaway corners in the great church where crime and vice might fester. His design for St Peter's was bigger, clearer, and lit from above by a dome on a scale that would represent heaven itself.

Michelangelo had already reshaped the top of the Capitoline Hill, the sacred centre of ancient Rome, into an open civic space flanked by cultural and political buildings: an optimistic image of public life that is truly utopian in its beauty. But Michelangelo's old age was Lenten. He fixed his eyes on God, as a man whose span had passed the life expectancy of the era should. Michelangelo dedicated himself to the holy task of saving St Peter's.

As he took charge of Rome's supreme modern building, Michelangelo's philosophical interests put him at the forefront of religious reform. With his friends Vittoria Colonna and the exiled English cardinal Reginald Pole he discussed Catholic renewal. His art increasingly put the suffering of Christ at its centre. His two last sculptures are unfinished, revolutionary rethinkings of the *Pietà*. In the Florentine *Pietà*, which he was working on when Bruegel was in Rome, the group supporting the collapsed corpse of Christ is dominated not by Mary but by a hooded old man. This is Nicodemus, the Pharisee who, according to the Gospel of St John, assisted with the deposition and embalming of the corpse. He stands upright, lending Christ his verticality, literally giving his strength to the lifeless body so that it can almost stand on its feeble legs. He has the bearded, ravaged face of the artist himself.

* * *

Michelangelo died in 1564, leaving Rome transformed. St Peter's was now a real building, not a vainglorious fantasy. Over gigantic vaults and pilasters it had a mighty circular drum rising into the sky, ready for the dome to be raised. There was still plenty to be done, and the dome itself would be modified from his semi-spherical design into something more egg-like. Nonetheless, thanks to him, papal Rome now had a wonder to match the achievements of the Caesars. Michelangelo's fascination with the colossal culminated in a building on God's scale.

Michelangelo's corpse was spirited back to his native city, concealed in a hay bale. The new Florentine Academy, instituted by Cosimo I, Grand Duke of Tuscany, organized extravagant obsequies that celebrated Michelangelo as art's greatest hero. He takes the palm from both the living and the dead, as Vasari says. If the logic of the Renaissance was that of 'rebirth', a renewal of a vanished antiquity, Michelangelo seemed to his contemporaries its climactic genius. He not only equalled but exceeded the ancients: while classical painting remained a mystery, known chiefly through the shadowy frescoes of Nero's Golden House, it was easy to see that Michelangelo's sculpture had more life, more force than ancient statues on display in Rome like the Apollo Belvedere or Farnese Hercules. What now?

Italian art started to stall. It had already entered a Mannerist phase, in which artists emulated Michelangelo's stylistic audacity by distorting forms and taking liberties with colour and space. This licensed the daring art of Pontormo, Bronzino, Giambologna, Cellini, Rosso, Parmigianino and more, but in the long run it could also justify slack, pretentious art. The falling-off is personified by

Michelangelo,
Rondanini *Pietà*,
c. 1550–64.

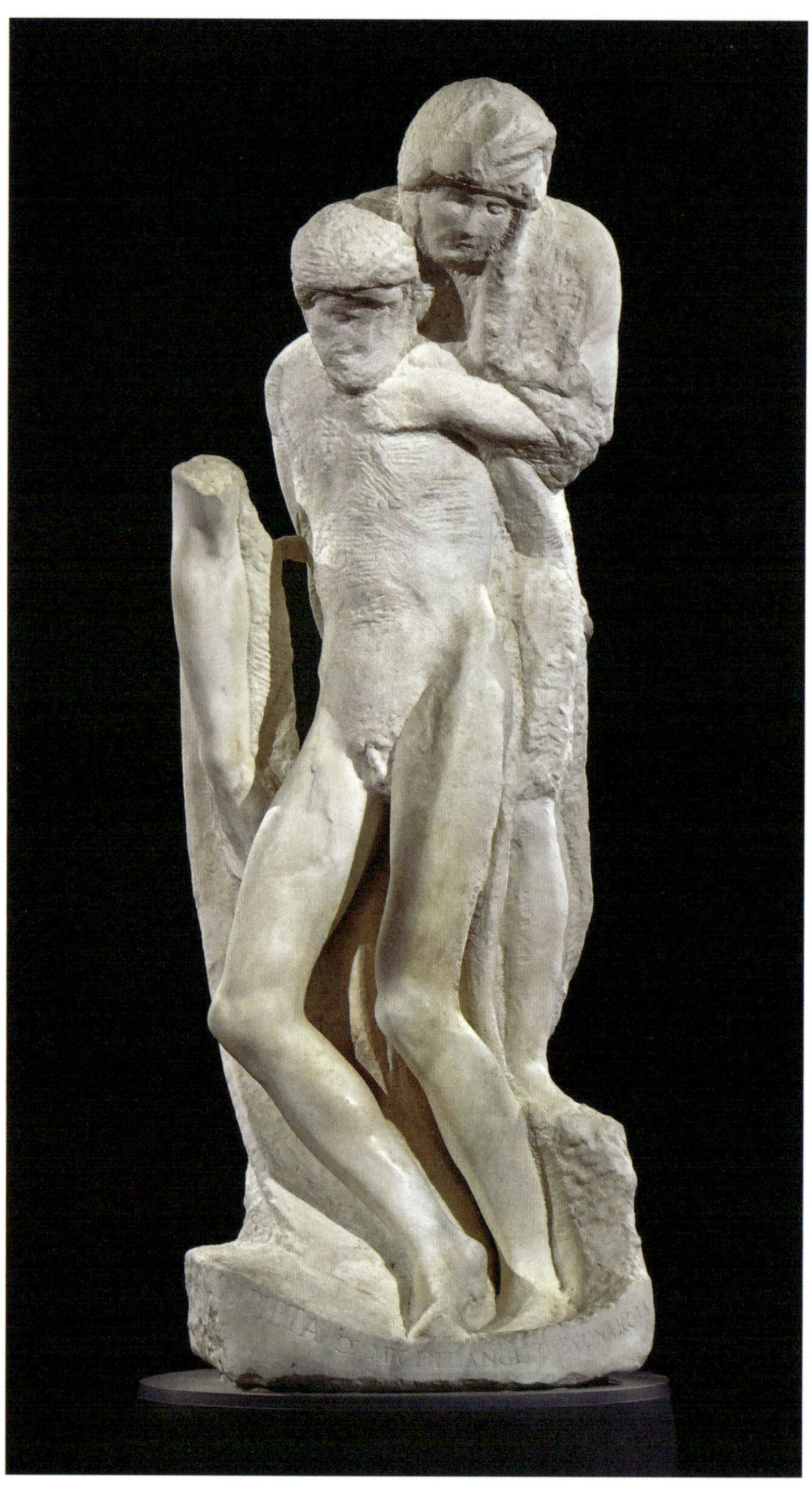

Vasari himself. While giving the Renaissance a written history, self-consciously constructing a lineage of genius from Cimabue to Michelangelo, he painted frescoes that fill space confidently – but lack purpose. It didn't help that he served the Medici dukedom as a propagandist. His scenes of Tuscan history in the Palazzo Vecchio are emotionally hollow. Only the grotesques that he and his team created in its corridors and staircases bubble with fun.

* * *

The year of Michelangelo's death saw Italy's triumph of Lent. The final session of the Council of Trent took place in 1563, and its edicts became official in early 1564. Its rigorous regime of literary censorship ended the intellectual freedom of the Italian Renaissance. From now on all books published in the Catholic world would need a papal licence. There was also an index of forbidden books, in which Rabelais appeared at the top of the 'Heretics of the First Class'; he would be joined by many other scientific and political authors before the index was abolished in 1966. The Council of Trent gave Catholic practice a chastening rigour while reasserting core medieval beliefs: selling indulgences was banned, but venerating relics, praying to the saints and belief in purgatory were affirmed. Art in churches received special scrutiny: it must communicate faith and doctrine, not celebrate the artist. The 'Tridentine' reforms called for an end to pagan frolics in religious art, commanding that

> all lasciviousness be avoided; in such wise that figures shall not be painted or adorned with a beauty exciting to lust; nor the celebration of the saints, and the visitation of relics be by any perverted into revellings and drunkenness.[4]

A year later the most notorious work of art in the Catholic world received its correction. Daniele da Volterra was hired to paint draperies over the most provocative details in Michelangelo's *Last Judgment*. No one had dared it while the great artist was alive. Now crudely daubed loincloths covered penises and male buttocks. St Catherine and St Blaise were also subjected to a highly destructive reworking to remove any suggestion of heterosexual intimacy. Nor has the Vatican ever got around to removing all these pious underpants.

* * *

Bruegel's *Massacre of the Innocents* (p. 287) was also censored early in its history. It was not impiety that caused the fuss but brutal reality, as a column of soldiers is shown riding into a village and causing mayhem. The painting's owner, Rudolf II, was apparently troubled by the conjunction of a contemporary setting with the depiction of soldiers killing babies. For these are plainly Habsburg soldiers in Spanish military dress who have been sent, not by Herod, but by Rudolf's uncle, Philip II.

Spain didn't wait for the Council of Trent's say-so to start its own Counter-Reformation. The long Reconquista that had driven out the Muslims made religious war a habit. One result was persecution of the Jewish population. Another was the brutality of conquistadors in the New World and Asia. That same crusading spirit came to Flanders when Fernando Álvarez de Toledo y Pimentel, 3rd duke of Alba, arrived to restore order there in 1567.

Bruegel shows how unchristian a Christian army could be. A column of mounted men heads straight down the main street of a village in the middle of winter. Amid the snow the soldiers terrorize helpless peasants. One man is kicking in a door while another comes with a battering ram. They climb in a window looking for suspects, run rampage with swords, brusquely ignore pleading villagers while women weep or sit on the ground in despair.

It is disturbing enough even after being bowdlerized. At Rudolf's command the slaughtered innocents have been replaced with packs of goods, but we can still feel terror in the midwinter air. Van Mander knew this picture before the emendations. He shudders at traumatic details, singling out 'a whole family pleading for a peasant child which a murderous soldier has caught, the mothers collapsing with grief'.[5]

Bruegel does not show peasants as comedy boors. He paints their precarious existence in a world where soldiers might ride into your village any time, plague strike, or a harsh winter kill next year's crop in the ground. He sides with the poor folk. That's clear in his illustration of a proverb of how the powerful prey on the powerless. In his print *Big Fish Eat Little Fish*, published in 1557, an old fisherman in a boat says to his son, look – the big fishes eat the small! The old codger is pointing at a giant fish on the shore, its belly sliced open to expose hosts of smaller fish in its gut that have even smaller fish in their mouths. It's a North Sea scene, with fishermen hanging up their gutted and salted catch from a tree to dry, a lone angler, a northern town visible across the bay. Yet these familiar details are juxtaposed with a phantasmagoria straight out of Bosch. A fish walks on human legs. Another flies on moth-wings, like one of St Anthony's demons.

In these same years Bruegel was experimenting with landscape art. In the *Penitent Magdalene*, one of a print series of *Large Landscapes*, Mary is shoved into a corner by the grand view behind her. Mighty peaks rise above a valley in the kind of vista he might have seen as he crossed the Alps. For Bruegel, landscape is more than a setting for stories: his people become figures in an imposing space rather than the space existing to heighten their reality. The road to

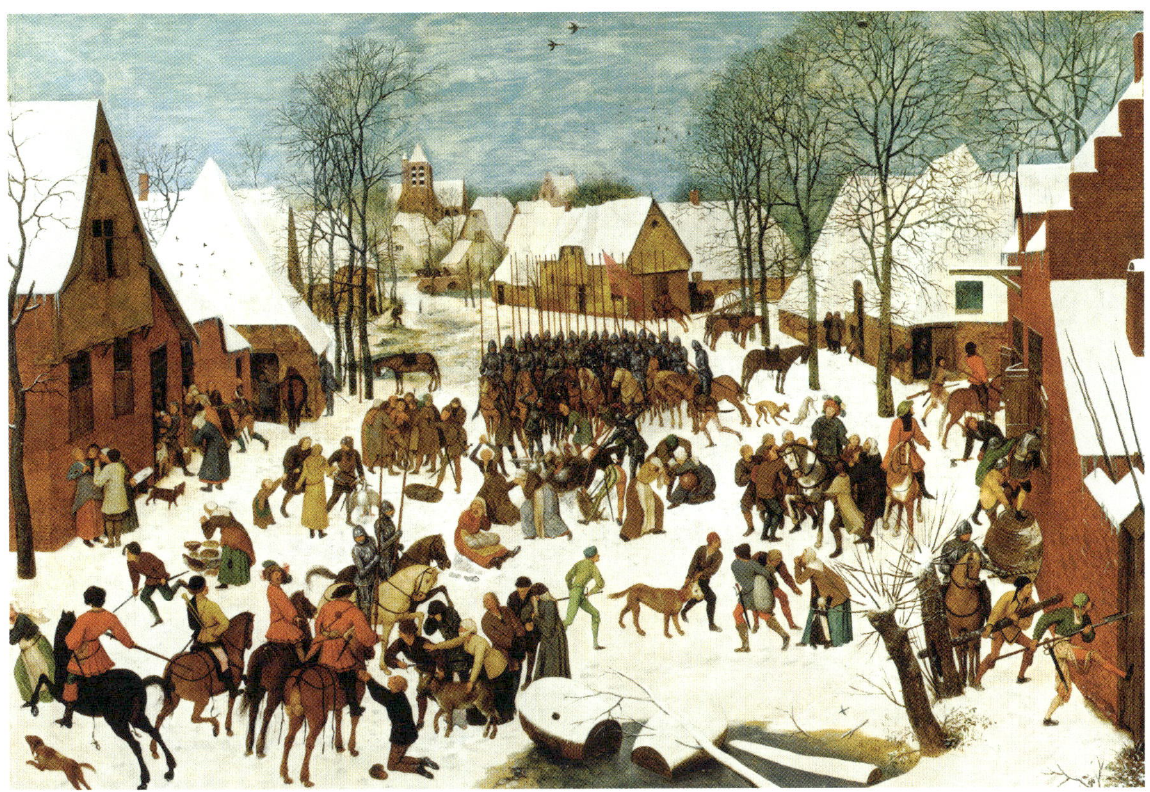

Pieter Bruegel, *Massacre of the Innocents*, c. 1565–67.

landscape art had been a winding one. Leonardo was drawing the Arno Valley for its own sake in 1473, and his misty mountains were never just 'background' to his paintings. The German painter Albrecht Altdorfer created landscapes with no stories or even people in the early 1500s. But Bruegel thinks more ambitiously about landscape. It is the arena that can encompass his interest in the miniature and the epic, the local and the universal.

Bruegel mixed with intellectuals and wealthy collectors in Antwerp and Brussels. The most brilliant of them, Abraham Ortelius, was a revolutionary geographer and cartographer. After Bruegel's death, Ortelius wrote a eulogy for 'our friend', saying he 'was the most perfect painter of his century'; no one would deny this 'except a man who is envious, jealous, or ignorant'.[6] Ortelius was no mean artist himself, and a scientific thinker. He produced a map of the world in 1564 in which the continents start to look as we know them and the southern polar continent of 'Terra Australis' is projected. He went on to publish the first world atlas, which included fifty-three maps. Ortelius corresponded with mapmakers across Europe, learning the principles of geography from his Dutch friend Gerardus Mercator, inventor of the 'Mercator projection', a revolution in mathematical mapping.

* * *

Bruegel's friendship with Ortelius is illuminating, for they are both world-mappers. In the series of *Seasons* he painted in 1565 for the merchant Nicolaes Jongelinck, he synthesizes Europe's variety. *Hunters in the Snow* is not the only painting in the cycle that sums up a whole continent's uplands, valleys, villages and coasts. The *Gloomy Day* also has it all: across a storm-tossed river mouth, where boats battle the waves, loom harsh mountains sheltering a castle. Closer, a cosy village nuzzles a hillside where peasants are collecting firewood. You can sample the heterogeneity of life in this painted atlas of a continent that can be wild or cosy, sublime or small.

Bruegel is a Renaissance artist in a more comprehensive way than anyone before him. Like a natural philosopher, he tries to give a totalizing account of the world, from Mount Vesuvius in a scene of the Bay of Naples to country people lunching on porridge in his painting *Harvesters*, another of the *Seasons*. No other 16th-century artist shows us as many sailing ships. These little wooden realms fascinate him. They are images of the Renaissance at its most expansive, a conveyance by which to reach a world beyond Europe.

Yet the Renaissance hits the rocks in his art. The peasant in him looks up at the Tower of Babel with a cynical grin: it's bound to come tumbling down. For the truth about European life was that it hadn't changed. A happy wedding, a vicious attack by overlords were the timeworn bedrock of life for most of Europe's inhabitants. Nor was it better for townspeople, who endured even higher mortality rates than their country cousins. The Renaissance hoped to create a more civilized and beautiful world by reviving the classics of Greece and Rome, but behind those texts lay a material life that it still couldn't match. When the young William Shakespeare, who was born in 1564, was studying Ovid in a half-timbered schoolroom by a street reeking of animal and human ordure in an English market town, what was he to make of an image the classical poet uses in his tale of Pyramus and Thisbe to describe blood spurting from a wound:

> It was just as when a leak in a damaged lead pipe splits open
> And with a squeal through the narrow crack sprays out
> Long jets of water.[7]

Shakespeare grew up in a glover's house with a vat of urine out back for leather tanning, and no plumbing. Ovid describes an ancient Rome whose language and literature the Renaissance revived yet whose running water remained an extreme rarity.

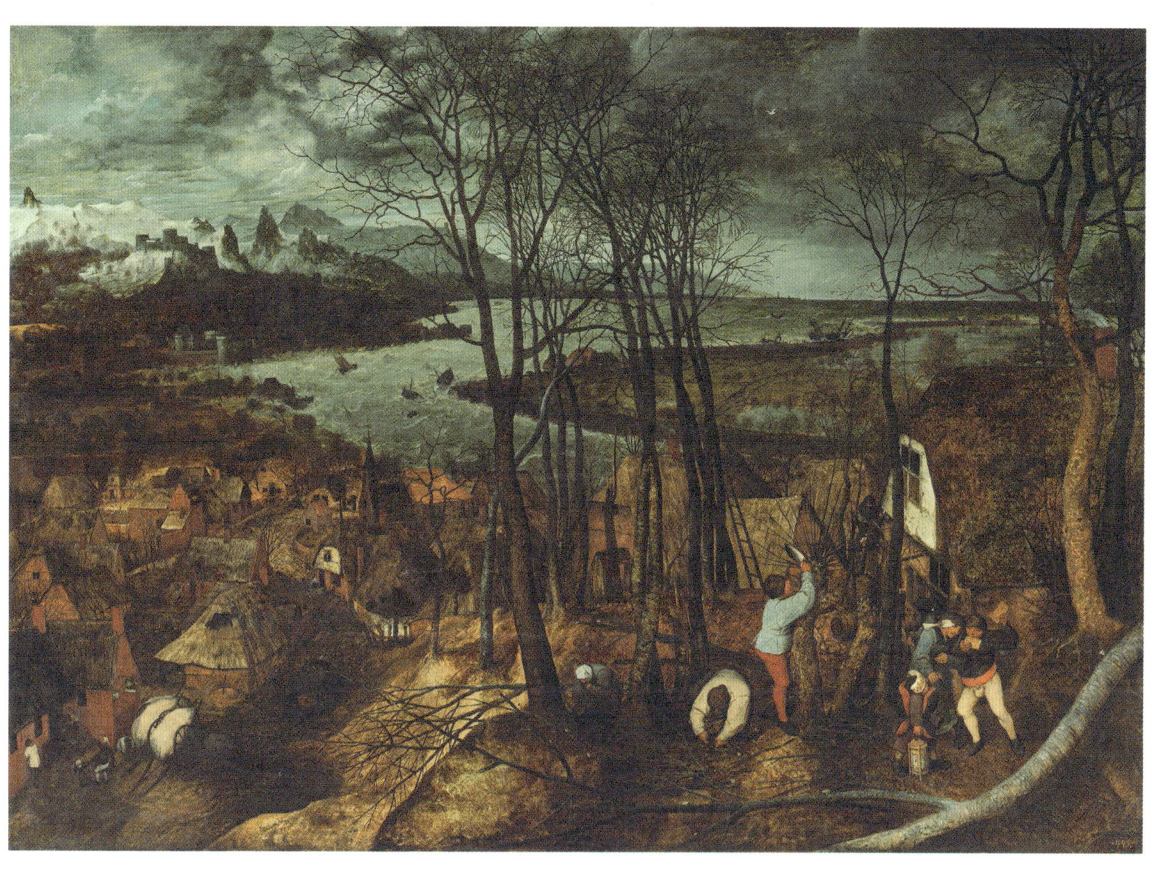

Pieter Bruegel,
Gloomy Day, 1565.

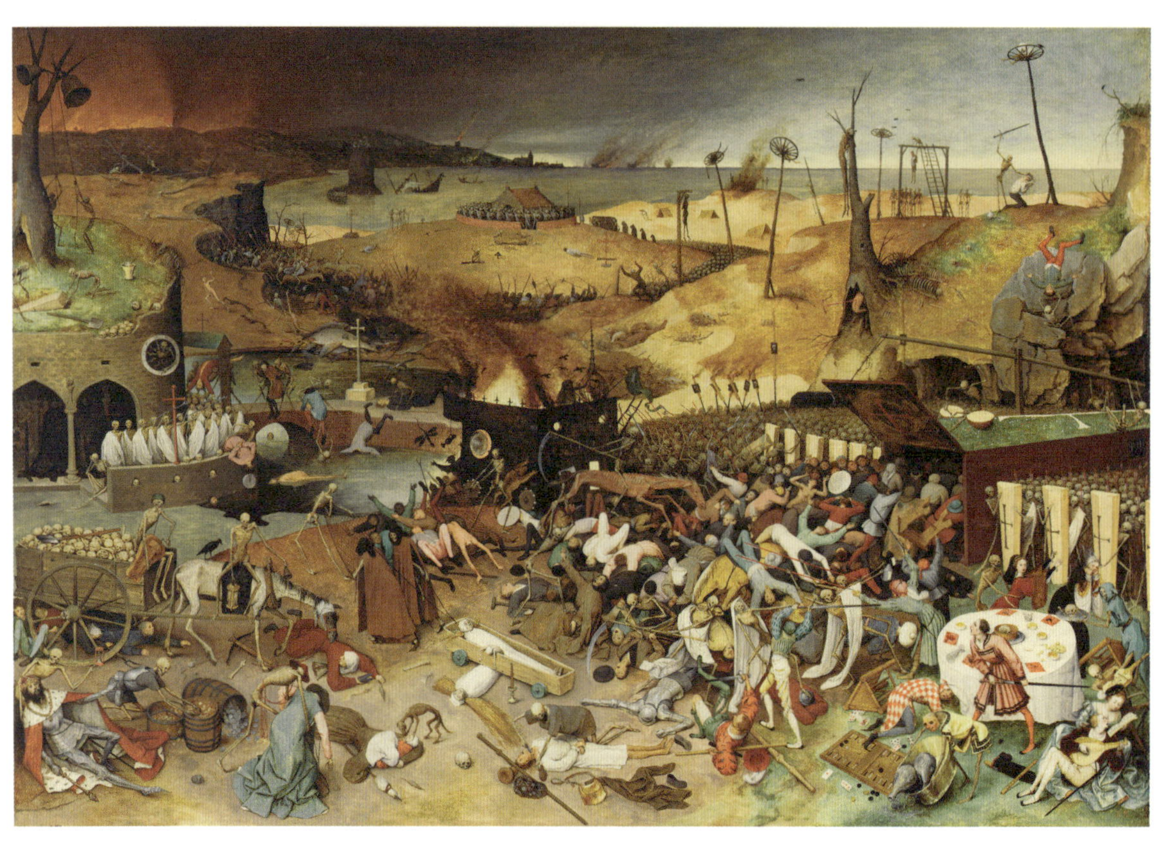

Pieter Bruegel,
Triumph of Death,
1562–63.

Technology had not seriously changed since the 14th century. Bruegel shows us people trudging behind horse-drawn wagons, crossing rivers in little boats, braving oceans in matchstick vessels. Leonardo had the genius to see further. His notebooks outline a utopia of machines. Forget myths: if we can master mechanics, his inventions urge, we can unlock humanity's hidden possibilities. We might even fly.

Bruegel reports on a world where none of that has happened. It is still the Middle Ages. That is the message of his sardonic masterpiece the *Triumph of Death*. It out-Bosches Bosch. Skeletons rampage, like the Spanish, across a ravaged landscape where people try any expedient to escape, yet are doomed alike – old or young, rich or poor. Bodies lie atop gibbets that have wheel-like platforms, lovers are interrupted by bony intruders, people are herded into a giant coffin. The skeleton army enact a cosmic carnival of death, driving a cart full of skulls, holding an hourglass to a dying king, clubbing and scything haphazardly. One skeleton wears a carnival mask.

Matthias Grünewald and Hans Holbein had looked death in the face, but Bruegel piles the corpses higher. It is nauseating, funny, terrifying. But is it new? The 'Dance of Death' had first appeared in art in the wake of the 14th-century Black Death. The art of death did not need to change because death had not changed. Plague was still a regular visitor; no one was free from life-threatening disease; sudden fevers took children. To reach adulthood was itself an achievement, to attain what today's Europeans regard as old age unusual. Bruegel's painting catches the failure of the Renaissance.

Bruegel himself died of unknown causes in 1569, leaving his wife and two young sons. As his coffin was taken to Notre-Dame de la Chapelle in Brussels, perhaps a child skating on the frozen river failed to look up, a man driving a mule ignored the procession, and a woman carried on cooking waffles.

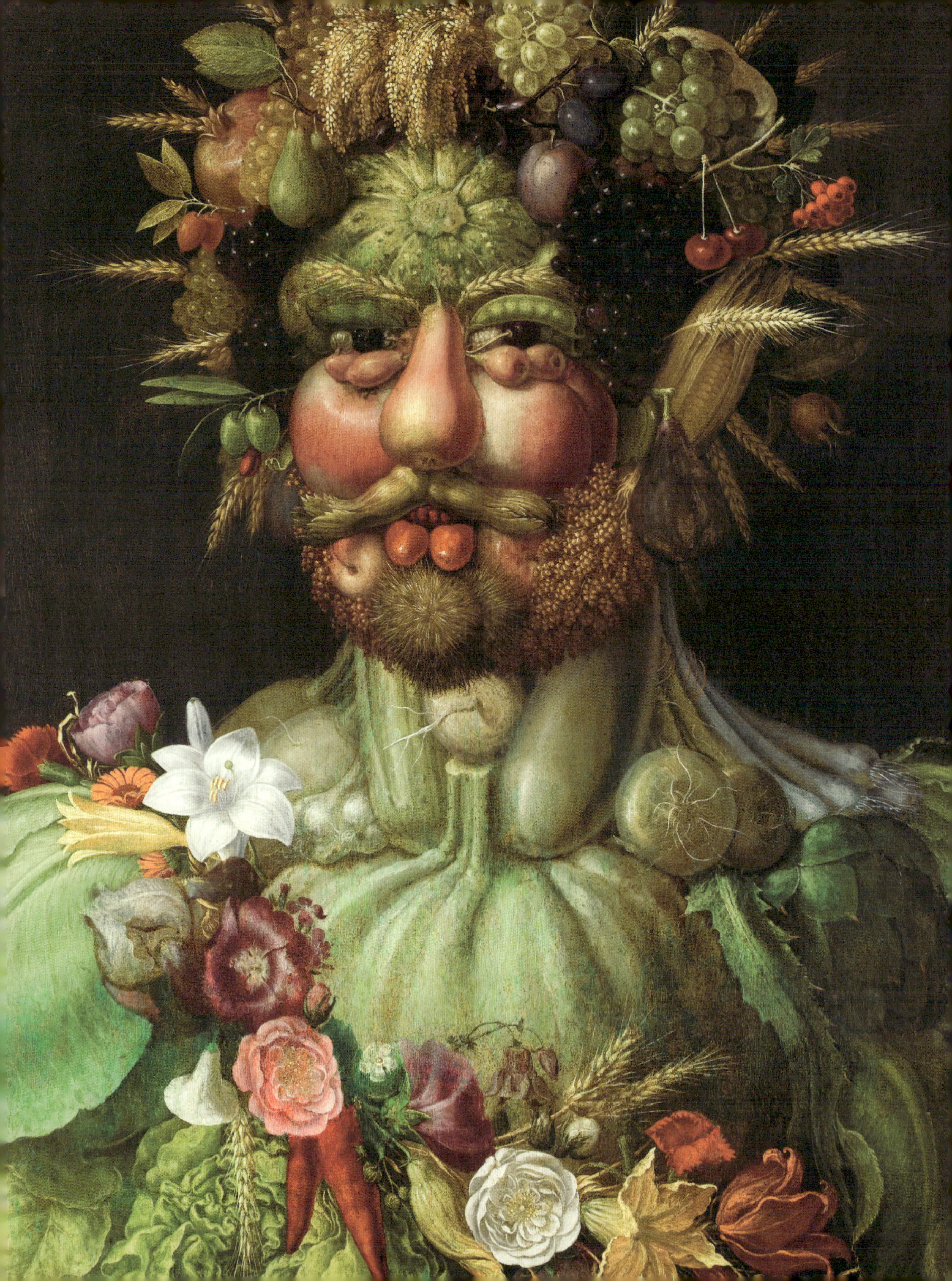

13 Curiosities

In 1561 a Bristol innkeeper called Hew Draper carved symbols of his beliefs into the wall of his prison in the Tower of London (overleaf). Draper had been arrested for sorcery. He claimed that, although he did have a passing interest in the occult, he had given it up and thrown his magic books away. Yet the works of art he left in the Salt Tower, where he was confined, suggest that he was unrepentant. While other prisoners scratched Christian marks, he laboriously carved an astrological sphere and celestial globe. He was no country bumpkin summoning imps, and perhaps was determined to tell posterity as much; his esoteric engravings show that he was a learned magician, skilled in sophisticated arts of divination. The Renaissance was a golden age of what might be called 'noble magic'. It was a world this prisoner wanted to join.

Perhaps Hew Draper aspired to be a magus like John Dee, the university-educated mathematician and occult philosopher who served Queen Elizabeth I as an astrologer, alchemist and dreamer of magical empire. Dee provided horoscopes for the new queen upon her accession in 1558, but what she most valued was his advice on alchemy, which she practised in her workshops at Hampton Court Palace. The royal greed for gold took on a global scope as Britain started to challenge Spain in the Americas, with Dee advising on navigation – in which he was expert – and on the quest for King Arthur's mythical New World colony.

Giuseppe Arcimboldo, *Vertumnus*, 1591.

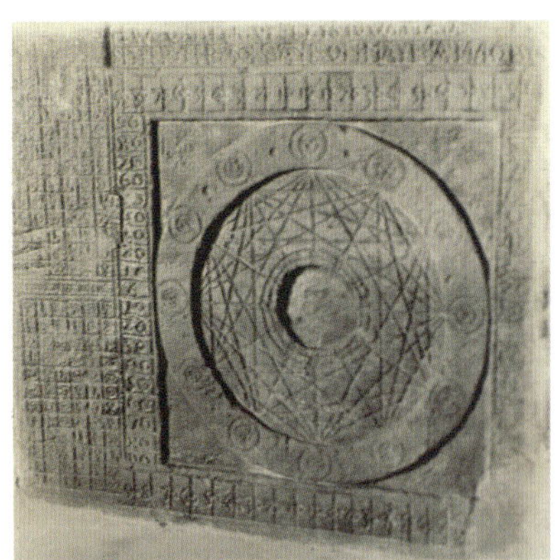

Hew Draper's astrological carvings in the Salt Tower, Tower of London.

Yet as Dee's court career slipped – there were flashier alchemists who promised greater riches – the dangerous side of his magic was exposed. He was fascinated by the evocation of spirits. His surviving equipment associated with this enterprise includes a mirror made of polished black obsidian to capture spirits and converse with them in a special language. It is an Aztec artefact that reached England from 16th-century Mexico: another example, like the masked rituals of carnival, of the similarity between Renaissance Europe and the world on which its sailors and conquerors were making landfall. This mirror was made for supernatural purposes by an Aztec artist and put to similar use by Dee.

Magic was the perfect expression of the ambition of Renaissance Europe. To dream of marvellous new powers and human capabilities in a pre-industrial world, you needed to defy nature. Leonardo dreamt of doing this with technology. He despised necromancers as frauds, yet his argument is telling: if they really could control spirits, they would rule the world, and we would see proof of their power everywhere. He shares the aspiration – he just does not believe magic is the way.

It was in the Florence of Leonardo's youth that magic became respectable. By mixing medieval Islamic spell books with Hermetic texts, Marsilio Ficino created the image of the learned and benign magus. A century later it was a role

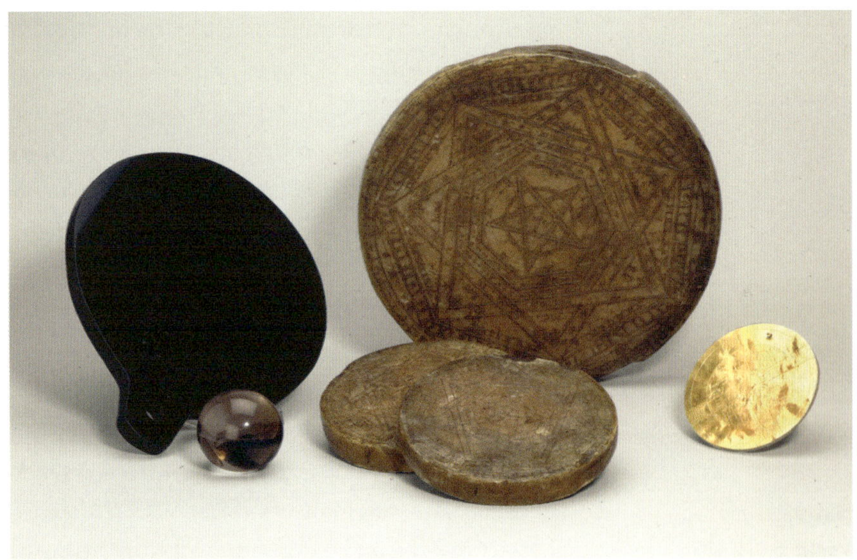

John Dee's magical mirror, possibly 14th–16th century.

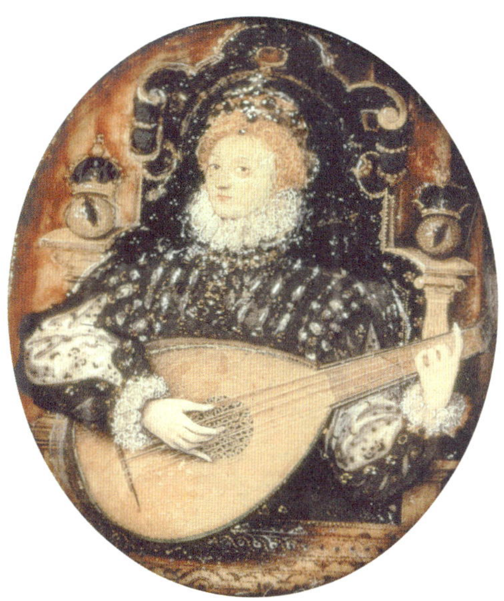

Nicholas Hilliard, *Elizabeth I Playing the Lute*, c. 1580.

coveted by Draper and Dee. Perhaps the true Elizabethan magus was the queen herself. Encouraging the royal image of the 'Faerie Queene', Elizabeth conjured English folk beliefs into glamorous enchantment. Nicholas Hilliard's miniature portrait of her playing the lute could almost be a talisman: the music her fingers create is a symbol of harmony – as she would explain to courtiers – but may also suggest an invisible order throughout the cosmos, a music of the spheres with which the Fairy Queen charms her subjects.

* * *

Renaissance high magic was a paganizing, pluralistic experiment that neatly sidestepped Christian fears. But those fears were deepening as the stress of the Reformation and Counter-Reformation kept people awake at night, worrying about witches. The Renaissance magician claimed to be benign, but witches were believed to worship Satan at night in the woods. They were typecast as ignorant rural women with no magical arts except those they got from their master and lover, the Devil.

German artists had helped shape this fantasy. In 1510 Hans Baldung Grien created a tenebrous woodcut of witches (overleaf). They have gathered at midnight in a desolate clearing in a German forest. The tree trunk beside them is decaying, cursed; there are human and animal bones on the ground; a cat and a goat are nearby. Two women sit on the ground by a brazier inscribed with mystic letters spewing out the filthy potion that will enable them to fly, while between them a third, older woman rears up on her knees, holding aloft a platter of sacrificial meats. There's a fourth figure lurking behind. All are naked.

Hans Baldung Grien, *Witches*, 1510.

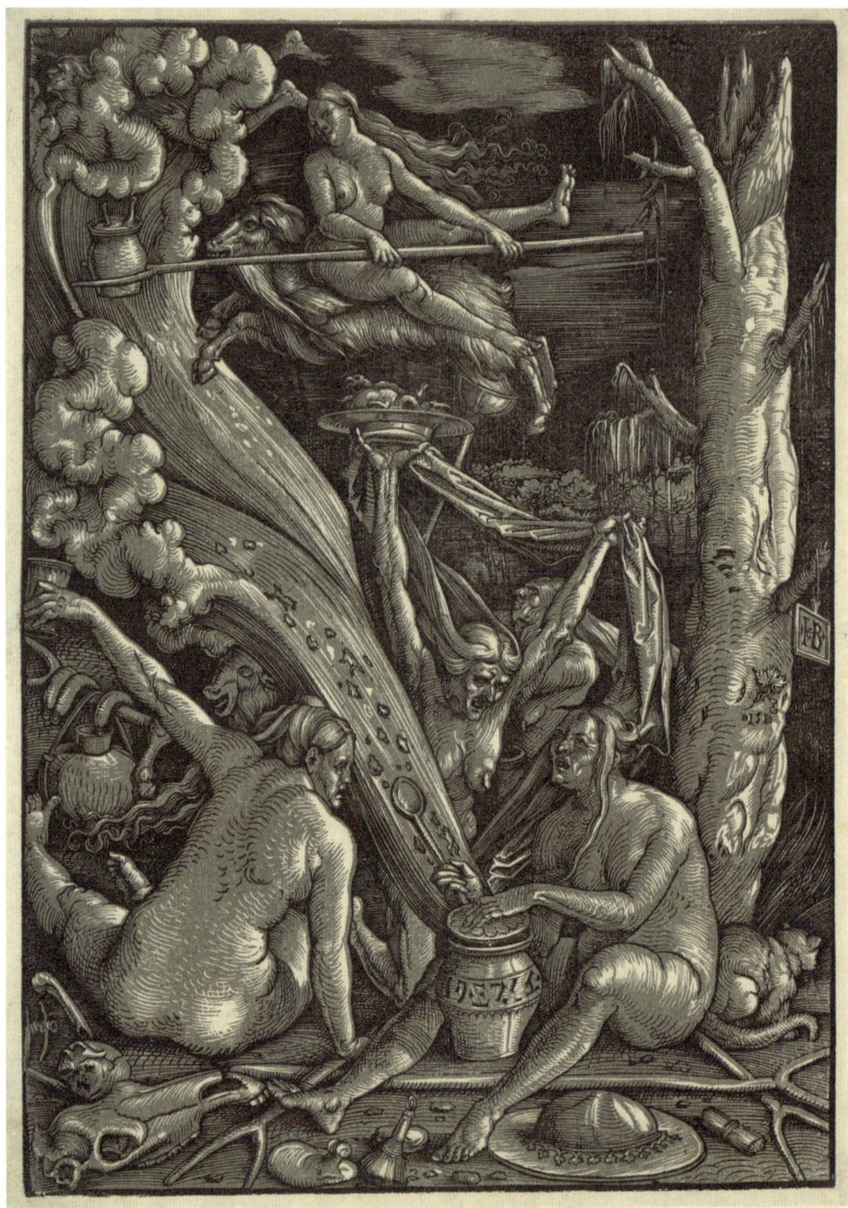

A fifth nude woman rides another goat backwards through the sky, spreading her body, extending her legs. Baldung uses thick ink to plunge us into night, weaving the cauldron's vomitus to cut streaks of grey into the blackness, dappling the scene with shimmers of moonlight. Baldung was the pupil of Albrecht Dürer, whose print of four witches dancing in a ring gave the eroticism of the Italian classical nude a frisson of hell. Baldung shares his master's ambivalence: these women may be Satanic crones, but their naked, rippling flesh has the power to ensnare.

To believe in witches you had to first believe in the demons they consorted with. Almost everyone did. In the art of Bosch, we glimpse how demons were visualized, as flying creatures with hybrid bodies. His hallucinations resemble anonymous woodcuts depicting witches and their familiars, or 'imps', that appeared in accounts of witch trials. A pamphlet of the 'confession' of the English witch Elizabeth Stile in 1579 is illustrated with a clawed and winged demon balancing on the hand of a coven member; in another vigorous woodcut the hook-nosed Stile spoon-feeds blood to toadlike and feline familiars. Even for the more socially elevated, the demons of Renaissance art were 'real'. The claws, wings and grimacing faces of devils in paintings and prints by Bouts, Grünewald and Michelangelo were not just artistic play but reflected and shaped beliefs. In fact, all the satyrs and centaurs, nymphs and zephyrs in Renaissance art, painted with such irresistible conviction, might be sophisticated versions of the demons, familiars and spirits that woke people in the night and cursed their crops. In the later Renaissance the attempt to control the world through magic engrossed the same intellectuals who were pioneering science; it served the same longing for knowledge.

In 1600 Giordano Bruno was burned alive in the Campo de' Fiori in Rome. Bruno supported the heliocentric theory of the Polish thinker Nicolaus Copernicus, which stated that the earth was one of a group of planets orbiting the sun. Copernicus had published *The Revolutions of the Celestial Spheres* just before his death, in 1543, yet the church did not immediately realize the threat it posed to the Book of Genesis. It was Bruno who made the danger overt by going spectacularly further than Copernicus to claim that our solar system is only one of many in a potentially infinite cosmos, in which alien species may live on distant planets. Bruno would refuse to retract his views before the Inquisition. It is still debated whether he was a martyr for cosmology, heresy or magic, which also interested him.

* * *

The midnight world of the witches was not really so far from the activities of the skilled magus. Benvenuto Cellini openly confesses to dabbling in black magic. His interest began when he befriended an educated Sicilian priest who raised the subject of *negromanzia*, or necromancy – trafficking with infernal spirits:

> And on this subject I said: 'I have had the greatest desire for my whole life to see or experience something of this art.' To this declaration the priest replied: 'A strong and stable mind are needed for a man who embarks on such a deed.'[1]

That was a red rag to an egomaniac. Benvenuto and the Sicilian chose the most atmospheric place in Rome for their rites: the Colosseum. The priest drew magic circles and pentacles on the ground, lit fires and wafted perfumes in the air. After an hour's incantations 'several legions of devils appeared, in such a fashion that the Colosseum was totally full'. Cellini makes the summoning of fiends sound like opera or performance art. With the intoxicating mix of incantations, scents and flames in the night-time setting of the ruinous amphitheatre, anyone might have seen demons.

That sensual, disturbing theatricality of magic was put to sensational use in 1590s London when Christopher Marlowe's *Tragical History of the Life and Death of Doctor Faustus* was staged. Marlowe's play could be justified to the censors as a Christian work in which Faustus is dragged off to hell at the end. Yet even today a staging can be unsettling. In a world that overwhelmingly believed in magic, it must have been hair-raising – especially since Dr Johann Faust was a real historical figure. Marlowe's Faustus performs necromancy on stage: he draws the magic circle, recites the dreadful words, and the demon Mephistopheles appears. The first published edition of the play in 1616 was illustrated with an arresting woodcut of Faustus standing in his circle and holding his book of spells as Mephistopheles rises through the floor – a scandalous, scary scene.

For 1590s audiences the jolt of seeing magic on stage may have brought to mind John Dee, whose experiments had by now acquired a dubious reputation. In the 1580s the former royal adviser travelled to Europe's courts, where he demonstrated his 'scrying mirrors'. He met the Polish king and was introduced to the Holy Roman Emperor, Rudolf II, in Prague. Rudolf's interest was piqued by every kind of novelty. In his heavily fortified castle on a steep hill above the Bohemian city, where he had moved the imperial court in 1583, Rudolf assembled a human collection of artists and scientists in addition to his menagerie. One find was Tycho Brahe, a formidable Dane who wore a prosthetic nose because his real one had been sliced off in a duel. Brahe was part of a growing community of 'natural philosophers' whose work was escaping the realms of isolated speculation to become a systematic enterprise of theory and evidence.

This process would be termed the 'Scientific Revolution'. Copernicus was a brilliant theorist, but the first modern scientist is generally held to be the Brussels-born anatomist Andreas Vesalius, who published his masterwork *On the Fabric of the Human Body* in 1543. Its frontispiece is a visual manifesto for the scientific method: Vesalius stands among a crowd of enthralled witnesses gesturing at a corpse he has dissected. This was a radical break with the way medicine was taught at medieval universities, where a lecturer read from the ancient Greek while an assistant tackled a specimen. Vesalius is urging scientists

Frontispiece of Andreas Vesalius, *On the Fabric of the Human Body* (1543).

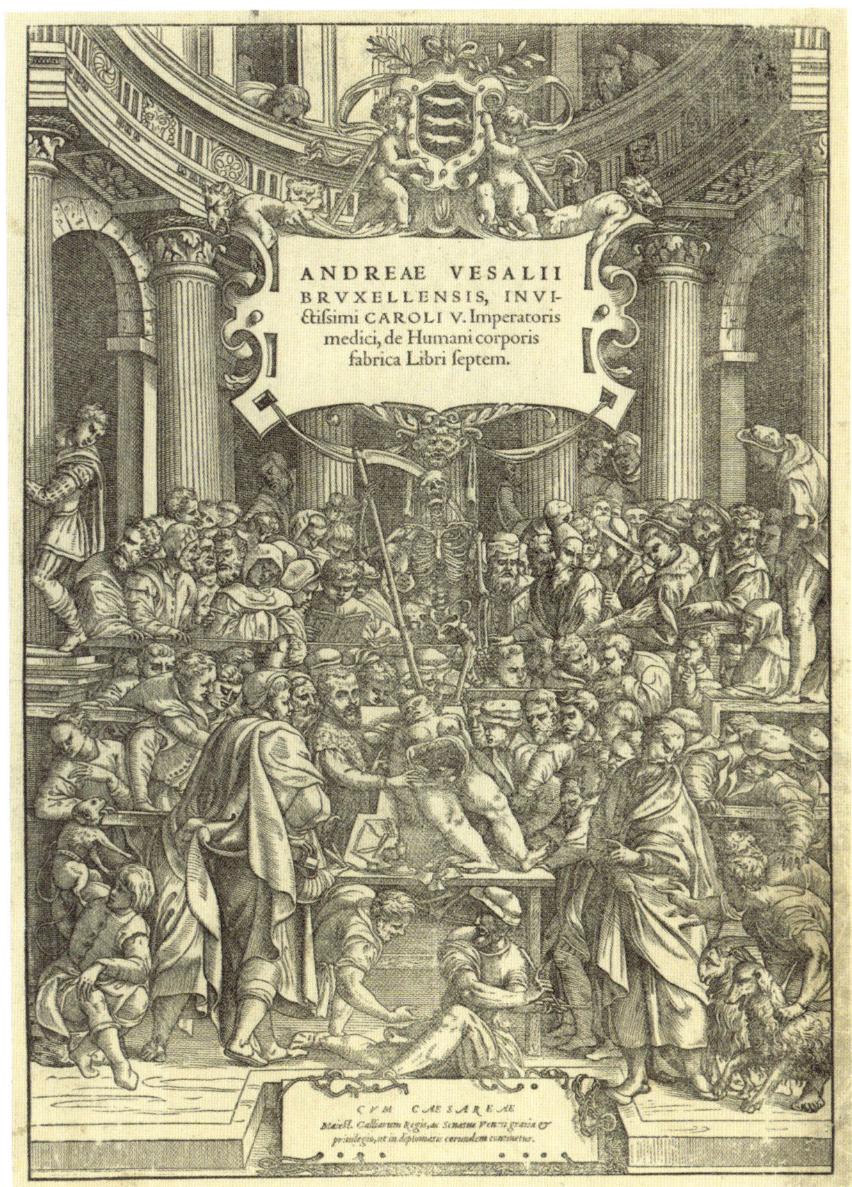

to study nature for themselves rather than accept the words of Galen as gospel. Inside the book are forceful, intricate illustrations, probably by Titian's pupil Jan Stefan van Kalkar: bodies are flayed to expose muscles, flayed more to reveal bones. They are macabre as well as factual, turning the book into a learned memento mori.

* * *

Tycho Brahe, who arrived at Rudolf's court in 1599, was a living example of how the new science connected Europe, using printing and the 'universal' languages

Giuseppe Arcimboldo, *Fire*, 1566.

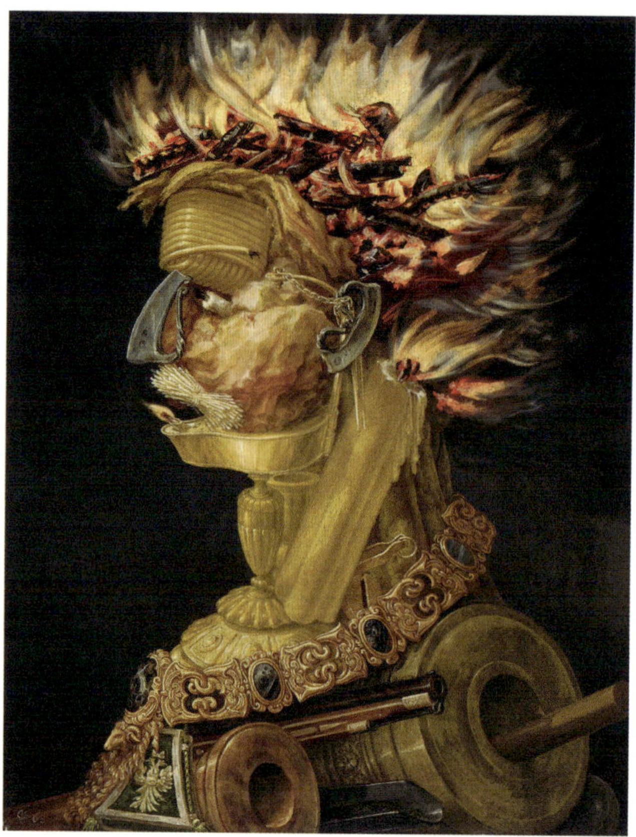

of Latin and mathematics to create a continent-wide network of discovery. Born into a noble Danish family and educated at German universities, he had created a research centre on an island between Copenhagen and Sweden. There he compiled a star catalogue of unprecedented accuracy. This was all the more impressive since the telescope was not yet in use, and he relied on medieval measuring devices and the naked eye.

The Holy Roman Emperor, however, was more interested in astrological advice. Brahe obliged, to secure Rudolf's patronage. He was joined by a second great scientist drawn by Rudolf's generosity, the humbly born German mathematician Johannes Kepler. When he succeeded Brahe, inheriting his tables of star positions, Kepler made crucial progress towards vindicating Copernicus by proposing that planets orbit the sun in ellipses, not circles. Yet he too had to keep the emperor happy with horoscopes.

Artists too came to Prague from all over Europe to serve Rudolf, including the Flemish painter Bartholomaeus Spranger, who produced kinky mythological canvases, probably in consultation with the emperor. Yet Rudolf inherited the court's greatest artist from his father, Maximilian II. The Milanese painter

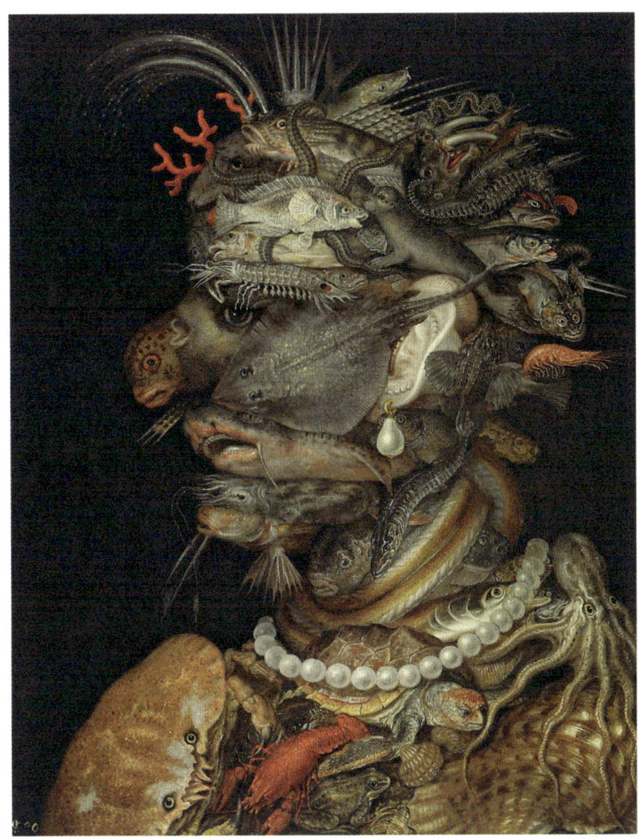

Giuseppe Arcimboldo, *Water*, 1566.

Giuseppe Arcimboldo created hybrids of portraits and still-lifes, fantastic faces of related objects that are ingeniously juxtaposed to create human features while remaining eerily inhuman. They have too much conviction and reality – or surreality – to be simply comic, but seem to come from the magical realm of folklore. They are sprites, fiends, preternatural beings. Arcimboldo's figure of *Fire*, with its metal nose, could almost be a portrait of Brahe, but that's a coincidence, for it belongs to a group called the *Elements* he painted in the 1560s. The series assumes the medieval model of the terrestrial sphere, in which the elements of earth, water, air and fire are compounded to constitute everything in nature. The personification of *Fire* is made of things that are flammable or produced by flames: a gunpowder box, a fuse, cannon and a firearm, phosphorus, candles, gold cast in a furnace, and a blazing bonfire of hair. It lingers in the mind as more than a courtly entertainment. The being that Arcimboldo has assembled has conscious agency. In a world haunted by demons and spirits, here is an elemental deity come to life.

Fire is also an image of war's frenzy. Gunpowder and artillery were making armed conflict more fiery all the time. In the later 16th century, decisive sea battles saw ships in flames, sailors and soldiers leaping into the sea. In 1571 Christian and Ottoman fleets clashed at the Battle of Lepanto – a European victory that quelled fears, for a while, of Turkish conquest; and in 1588 English fireships ravaged Philip II's storm-tossed Armada.

Arcimboldo merges magic and science. His paintings are supernatural, yet also empirical: he seems to have conducted experiments on the science of colour. For Rudolf, his paintings were *Wunder*, wonders, to be displayed in his 'cabinet of curiosities' in the north wing of Prague Castle. A wonder might be natural or cultural, as long as it was rare, bizarre or precious enough to stimulate the senses and thoughts of a collector. Rudolf II's Kunstkammer was the largest of a number of such assemblages in later Renaissance Europe. These forerunners of the modern museum gathered together natural marvels, such as sea shells, ostrich eggs, narwhal horns, mermaids, amber, minerals, fossils, alongside human marvels: clocks, mechanisms and art from the Old World and New.

* * *

Rudolf's combination of esotericism and cutting-edge technology suggests not so much a retreat from the world as a fantasy of commanding it. He loved automata and astronomical instruments, and owned a 'mechanical celestial clock' that landed its maker in hot water when Rudolf discovered he had made a superior model for his brother, the archduke Ernst. Alongside these man-made items were natural objects full of invisible power: red coral, which was good for the gut, blood and sexual potency and a defence against witchcraft; and bezoars, formed in the guts of large ruminants, which were prized as antidotes to poison and as a cure for melancholia and epilepsy. Such treasures were often displayed in ornate golden receptacles.

Rudolf's collection was not a haphazard hoard.[2] It celebrated the interconnectedness of all things and all branches of knowledge represented in a microcosm of the world. That would make Arcimboldo's paintings a microcosm of a microcosm, for they too are collections. For example coral, with its magical properties, is one of the marine marvels that constitute his portrait of *Water* (p. 301). It appears among a 'museum' of fish whose alien eyes and silver scales come from another element. The painter outdoes the collector, for while fish could be preserved in a cabinet only as shrivelled specimens, they keep their freshness in Arcimboldo's painted museum.

Arcimboldo turns precise observations into the art of dreams. His 1591 portrait of Rudolf II as Vertumnus – the Roman god of the seasons and growth – casts the emperor as a spectacular constellation of fruit and veg (p. 292). Rudolf must have had a sense of humour to appreciate being pictured with a pear for a nose, apple cheeks, peapod eyebrows, berry eyes, cherry lips. Yet there is flattery too. He is transfigured into a supremely fertile, generative deity, his face blooming with abundance and health. The ears of yellow wheat that grow like hairs from his face attribute to him the power to ensure good harvests. His headdress of green, black and gold grapes makes him lord of the vintage. Artists had previously tried to associate the Habsburgs with Jupiter but this work trumps them as an image of the emperor as a folk deity who can guarantee a bounteous diet for his subjects. Rudolf's mask of fruit and flowers, crops and vegetables, is the face of a green man, a corn dolly, a totem.

Arcimboldo shared his ability to breathe life into vegetation with a fellow Milanese artist, Fede Galizia, whose work he introduced to Rudolf's court. She was a painter of still-lifes, a genre that flourished in Lombardy maybe because of its openness to influences from the north, maybe because precise depictions of food and drink in Leonardo's *Last Supper* could be studied there. Her work that survives was done after Arcimboldo's death in 1593, but it's not hard to see what engaged him about her style if you look at *Crystal Fruit Stand with Peaches, Quinces and Jasmine Flowers.* There's a ghostly sense of expectancy in this highly naturalistic configuration of knobbly fruit.

* * *

Cabinets of curiosities were preoccupied with anomalies, including human ones. The Kunst- und Wunderkammer of Rudolf's cousin Ferdinand II in Ambras Castle, Innsbruck, features portraits of people whose bodies defied nature: they include a man who survived with a lance head stuck through his skull, and another with shrunken, twisted limbs. Ferdinand also maintained a 'live' collection of human curiosities in his Habsburg castle, including visiting members of the Gonsalvus, or Gonzalez, family, who had hair entirely covering their bodies and faces. Portraits of Pedro Gonzalez and his three daughters, which Ferdinand and Rudolf commissioned, were exhibited as perplexing examples of those who straddled the border between the human and bestial, bringing myths of wild men, werewolves and satyrs into real life.

The best is a graceful study by Lavinia Fontana of the young Antonietta Gonzalez (overleaf). She stands holding up a written document relating her origins, showing that she is a human, capable of literacy, and not a monkey in a dress. Fontana depicts her face as almost birdlike, finding unique beauty in her bright eyes surrounded by fur. Lavinia Fontana, who was born in Bologna in 1552, is often credited with being the first truly successful professional woman artist of the Renaissance, since she ran her own workshop and was not dependent on a court position. Although she painted large-scale biblical and mythological scenes,

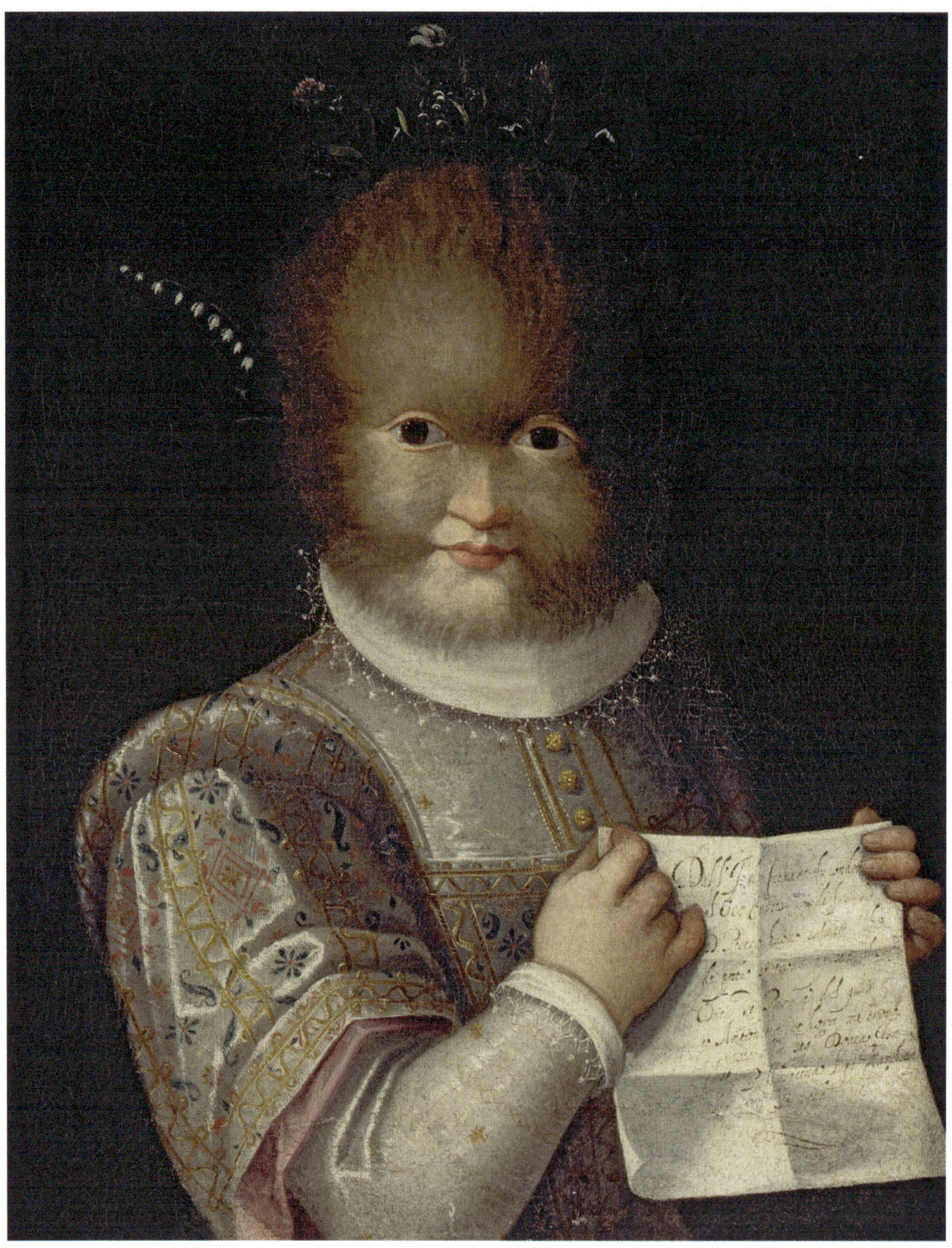

Lavinia Fontana, *Portrait of Antonietta Gonzalez*, c. 1583.

she was known chiefly as a portraitist of the noble and wealthy. Here, Fontana turns her eyes upon the ultimate outsider. She does not look at Gonzalez as an anomaly, however, but engages sympathetically with her. Stressing Antonietta's intelligence and charm, her image compels the onlooker to consider the mystery of nature that has such people in it.

The French philosopher Michel de Montaigne, too, ponders the case of a hairy child in his essay published in 1580, 'Of the Force of Imagination'. Among examples of the fancies of the mind having consequences in the physical world, he recalls that

> There was presented to Charles the Emperor and King of Bohemia, a girl from about Pisa, all over rough and covered with hair, whom her mother said to be so conceived by reason of a picture of St. John the Baptist, that hung within the curtains of her bed.[3]

So potent is the imagination that, simply by staring at the image of the wildman saint, a woman might give her baby a coat of fur.

Montaigne is the great philosopher of this age of curiosities. He is immersed in classical texts but has his eyes and ears open to the local life surrounding the town of Montaigne in south-western France, of which he was lord and where he retired to write. His essays value wonder and investigation rather than fixed conclusions. The very form of the *essai* that he pioneered suggests trying things out, rolling ideas and facts about playfully, meditatively. As a young lawyer he witnessed the trial of 'Martin Guerre', who was accused of stealing another man's identity and life – and typically thought the verdict overconfident: he wasn't at all sure who was the real Martin. Montaigne transforms the interweaving of magic and science, folklore and classical learning into an ethical principle: it is good to see all sides of an argument, bad to lapse into dogmatic certainty. All customs are relative: our own deepest moral assumptions may be repulsive to peoples brought up in different beliefs.

* * *

The mutability and flux Montaigne recognizes in himself infects the whole of nature in Titian's last paintings. The Venetian master was a natural wonder himself, living and painting well beyond the average lifespan, outlasting even Michelangelo. His late style is unrivalled: a dappled, suggestive poetry of paint in which there is no longer any need to define form, just to conjure it into life with splashes of colour. He painted the *Flaying of Marsyas* around 1579, when he was in his eighties. It creates a world where nothing is fixed or solid (p. 307). The trees and clouds are swirling maelstroms. Michelangelo's ungenerous remark that Venetians don't learn to draw becomes a credo, for Titian has completely escaped the early Renaissance commitment to delineating solid bodies in space. This painting is a veil of blood and smoke. Marsyas is a thin strip of flesh, a slash of brown and yellow. He accepts his fate, as Apollo and a helper carefully remove his skin, their knives resembling brushes, their attentive manner like the concentration of painters. The onlookers watch this spectacle carefully, like students in an anatomy theatre. Is Titian thinking of Vesalius and his students as portrayed by his pupil Kalkar?

As his last works lay bare, Titian is not just entertained by tales in Ovid's *Metamorphoses*: he is gripped by the idea of metamorphosis itself. Apollo uses the body of Marsyas to give a lesson in the nature of transmutation. As he cuts, red blood flows, and a little dog laps it up. Death bleeds into life.

Titian's Venice remained an intellectual and libertine haven while other places in Italy and beyond were being muffled by Christian renewal. When the Inquisition tried to crush the freedom of Venetian art, it was practically laughed out of the city. In 1573 Titian's younger friend Paolo Veronese was hauled before this tribunal of religious enforcement to account for a sprawling scene of the *Last Supper* he had painted for the Venetian monastery of SS Giovanni e Paolo. It was set in a classical arcade worthy of his contemporary the architect Palladio, where Christ and his well-dressed disciples enjoy a sophisticated supper served by a team of black and white waiters. It was not the presence of Africans that upset the Inquisition, but other 'scurrilous' additions: 'What is the meaning of the armed man, clothed like a German, holding a halberd?' The interrogators were also troubled by a man with a nosebleed, a dog, and a jester with a parrot: 'Do you think it is fitting that the Last Supper of Our Lord include jesters, drunks, Germans, dwarves and other outrageousness?'[4]

The Council of Trent had called for religious art to focus tightly on communicating the faith. Instead of this Lenten purity, Veronese imagines the *Last Supper* as a convivial party, with participants more likely to be seen at a street festival than in church (pp. 308–9). He answered his questioners breezily. The Inquisition's powers were strictly limited in Venice: it was the last great self-governing city in Italy, had its own Mediterranean empire, and was not about to let the papacy control it. Veronese did not just tease his would-be tormentors. He eloquently defended artistic freedom, saying: 'Painters take the same licence as poets and madmen.'[5]

It's another allusion to the 'fury' of the poet, the idea that 15th-century humanists had found in Plato. Veronese's contempt was obvious. About all he did was to change the painting's title to *Feast in the House of Levi*. In another of his giant religious party scenes, the *Wedding at Cana*, women join the carnival

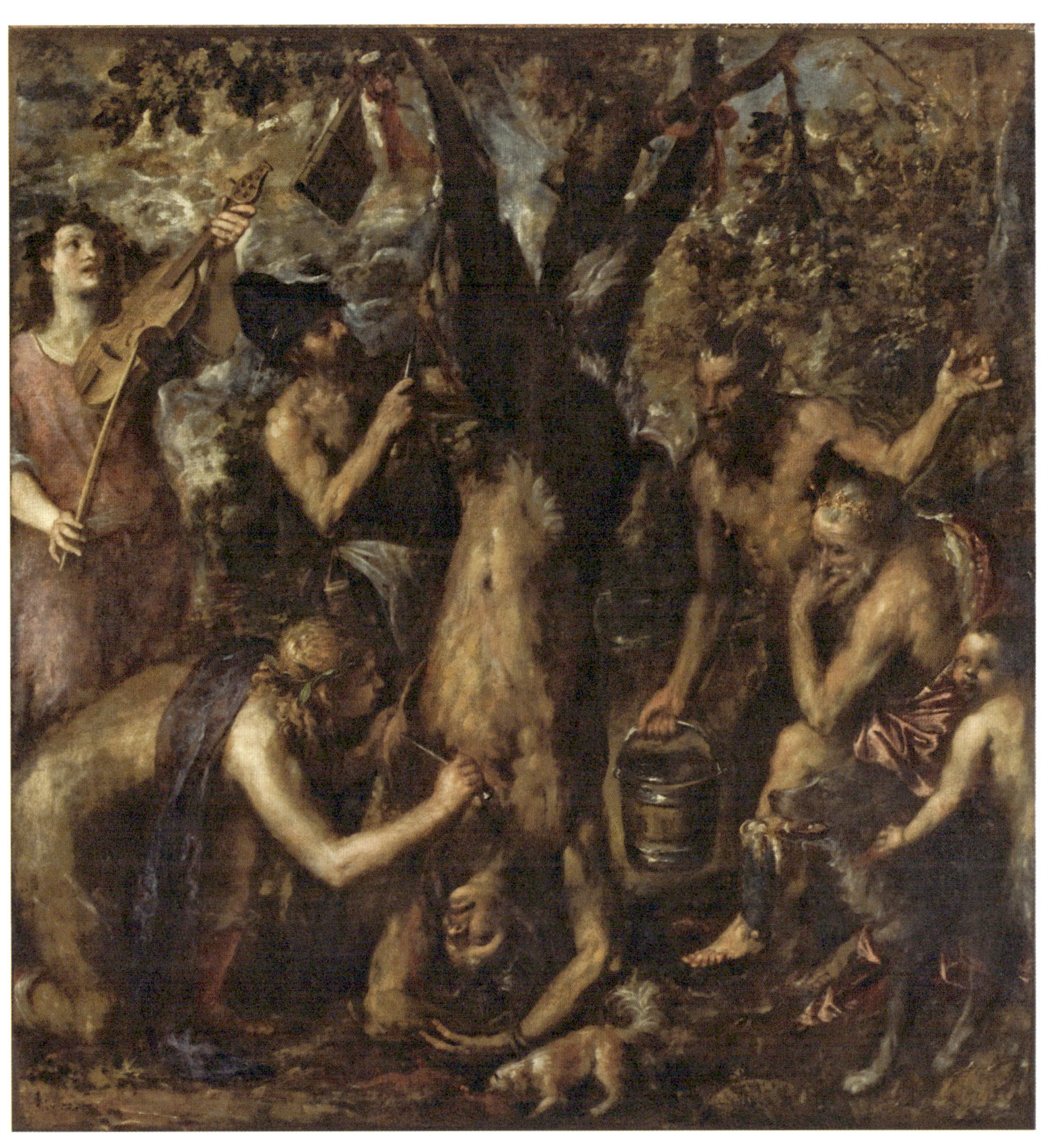

Titian,
Flaying of Marsyas,
c. 1579.

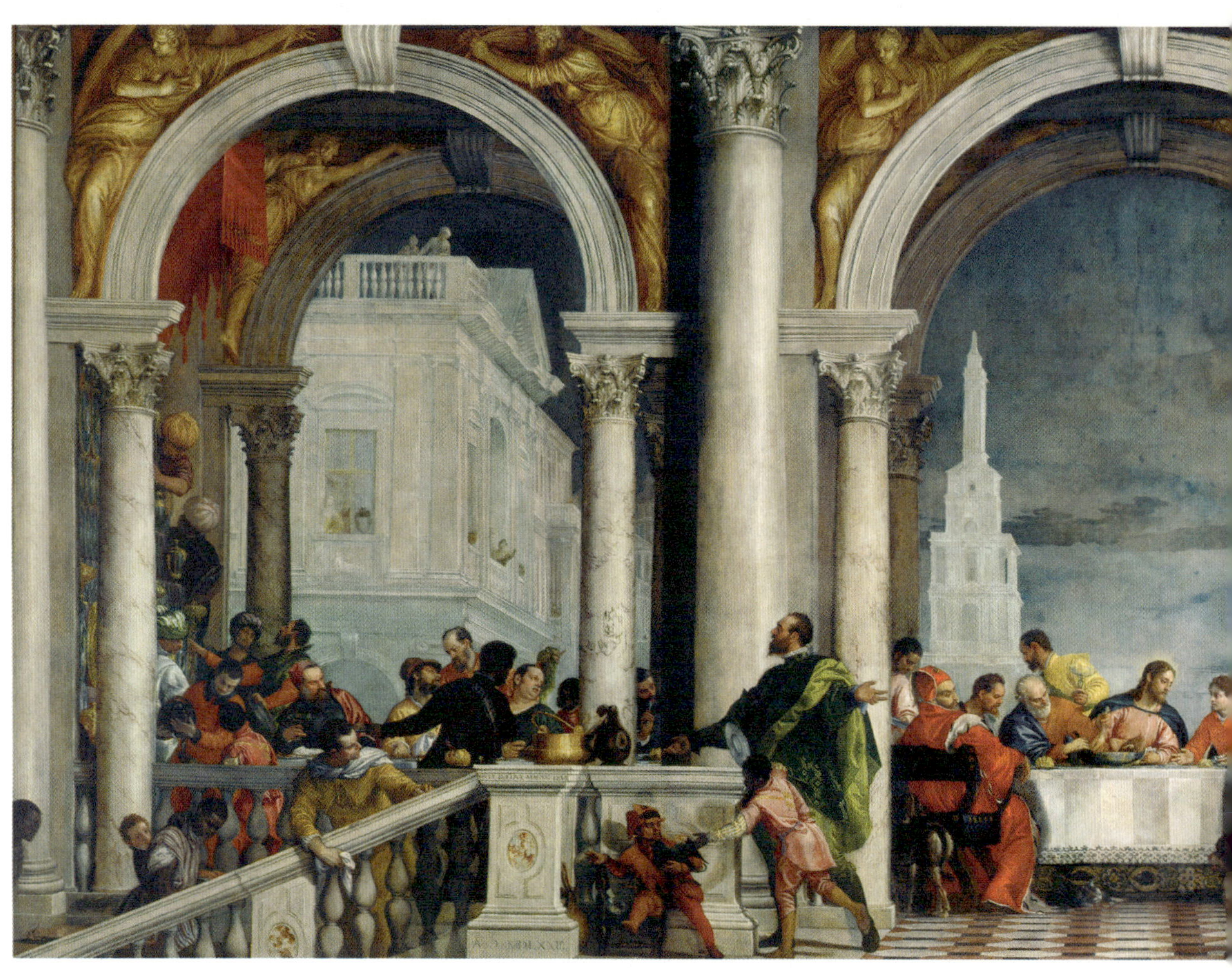

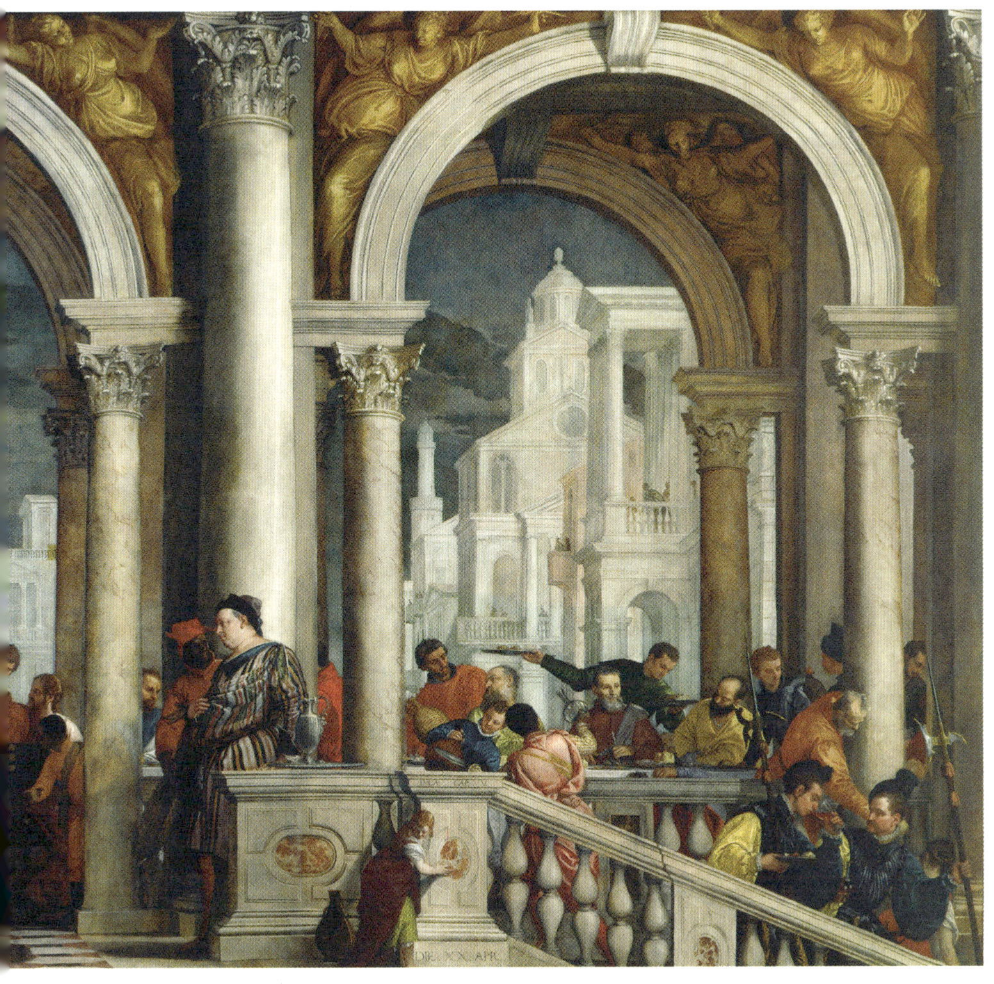

Paolo Veronese, *Feast in the House of Levi*, 1573.

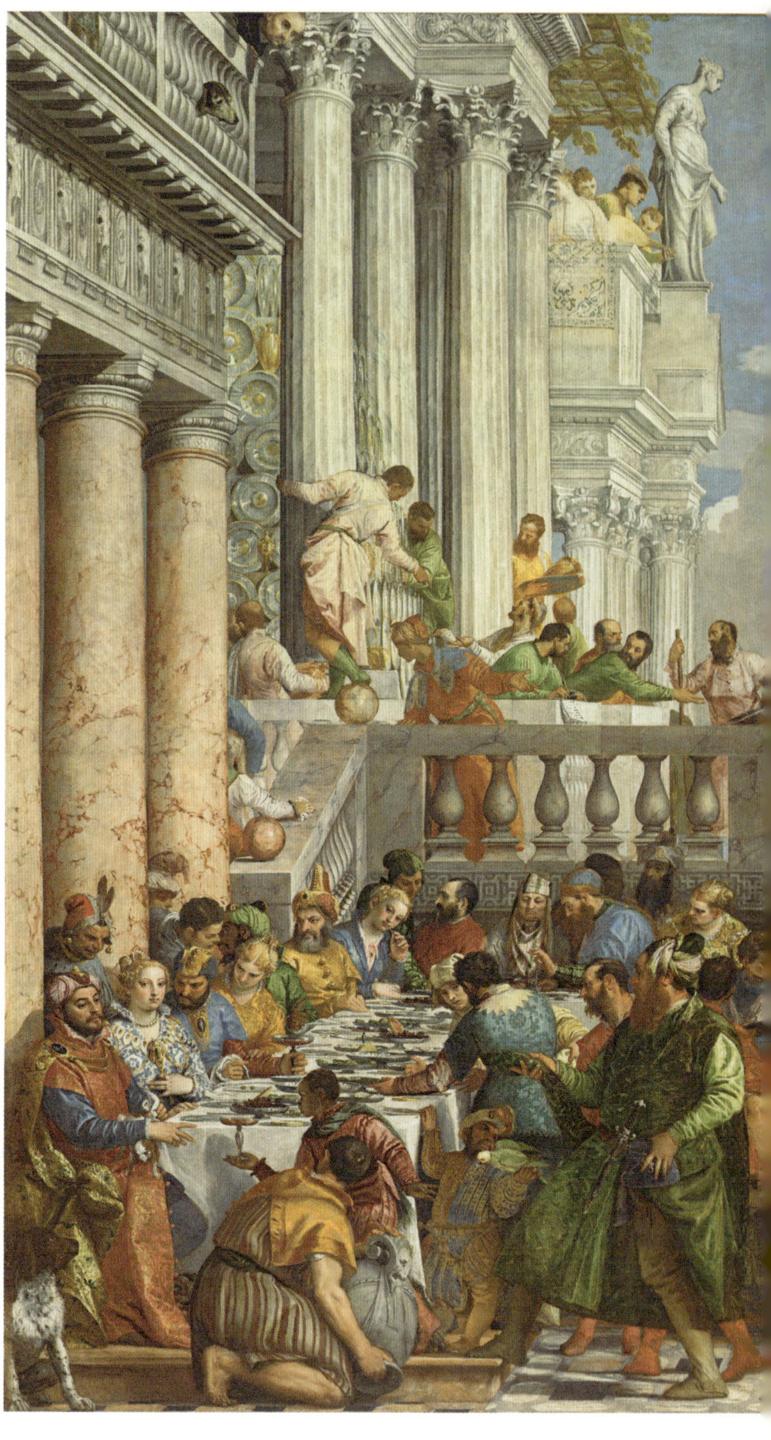

Paolo Veronese,
Wedding at Cana,
1562–63.

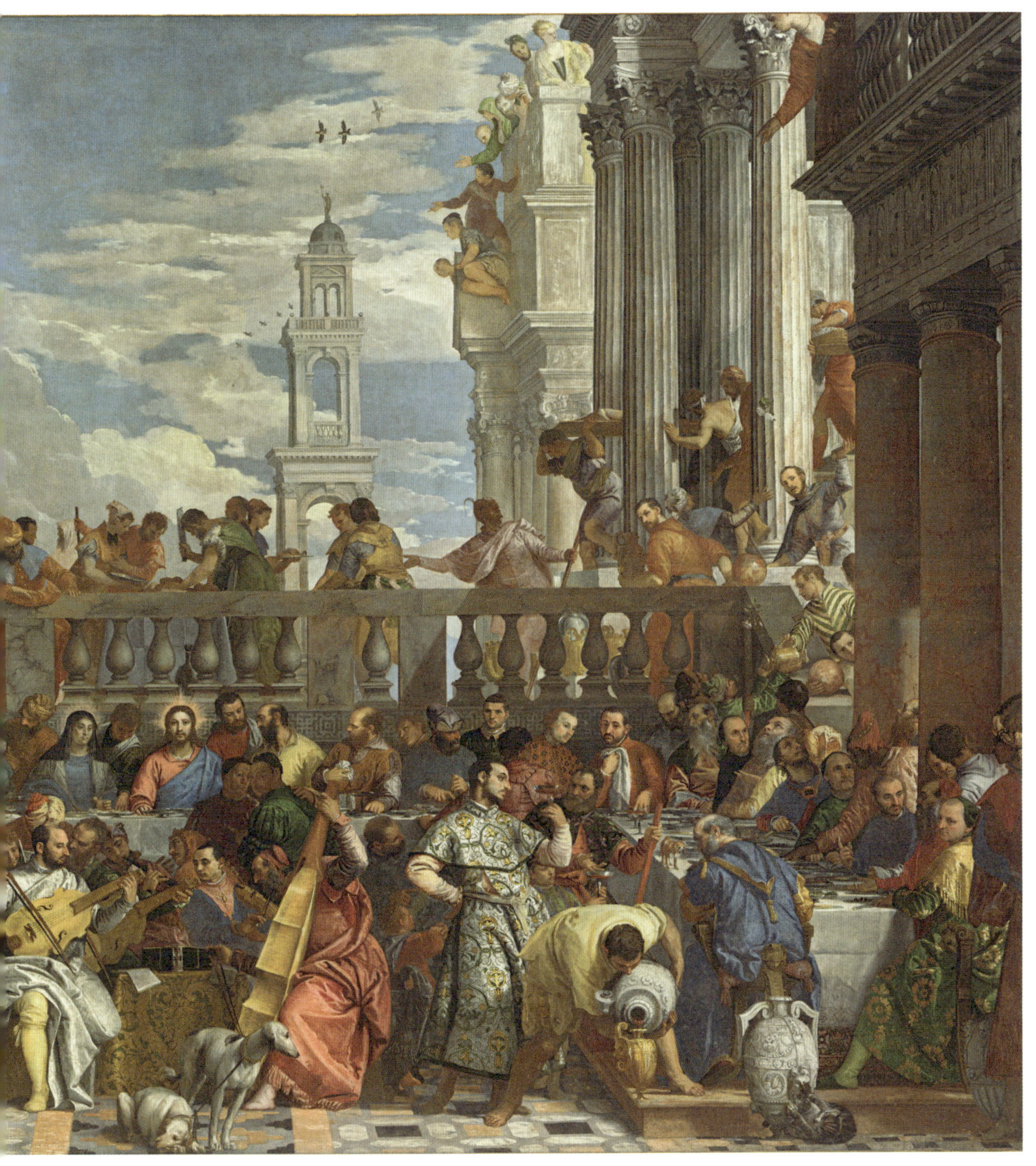

(pp. 310–11). Superbly dressed men and their girlfriends enjoy fine wines and antipasti; a waiter proffers a broad-rimmed glass held skilfully on the palm of his hand; a man who has already had too much stares intently at a woman to his right, to the displeasure of his girlfriend. They are entertained by musicians who include portraits of Veronese himself and Titian.

Another of the musicians is Jacopo Robusti – Tintoretto – who would work on into the 1590s. Destroying the conventions of perspective with sweeping vistas that hurtle away into space, he creates an unreal visual world almost as expressive as the last works of Titian. His painting *Susanna and the Elders* uses this freedom to celebrate and question the Renaissance nude. A young woman sits bathing in a garden, contemplating herself in a mirror, but two old men are creeping round a leafy trellis to spy on her. Tintoretto, like Titian in his *Diana and Actaeon*, dramatizes the voyeurism his painting solicits. Yet he also creates one of the most beautiful and intimate of all female nudes. The fact that we don't want to be like those old fools makes Susanna the hero of this painting. She is an observer too: while the elders

Jacopo Tintoretto, *Susanna and the Elders*, c. 1555–56.

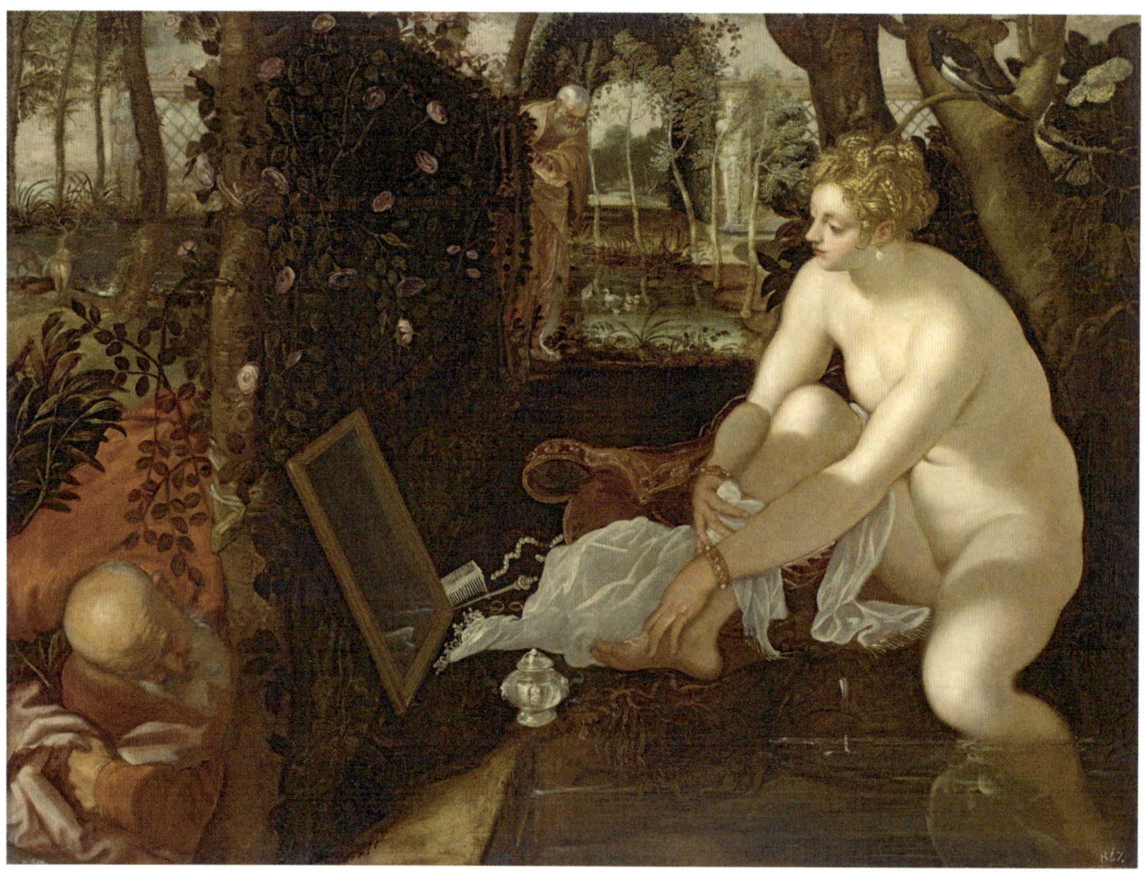

furtively sneak a peek, she beholds herself in a mirror, the true possessor, Tintoretto suggests, of her own beauty.

* * *

Tintoretto was religious, but not because anyone forced him to be. His decoration of a meeting place for a lay brotherhood dedicated to the plague saint St Roch – the Scuola Grande di San Rocco – with fervent, spectacular biblical scenes was a personal obsession. Meanwhile the Venetian Republic's intellectuals were openly flouting the pieties preached elsewhere in Italy. In 1607 the pope excommunicated the entire republic for refusing to submit to his authority. In response a defender of Venetian liberty, Paolo Sarpi, would publish a *History of the Council of Trent* under an alias in London in 1619. He used it to scathingly claim that this Catholic 'reform' was a cynical product of papal politics.

Sarpi's radical friends in Venice included Galileo Galilei, a Pisan who lectured at Padua. The climate of intellectual freedom that prevailed in Venice and its territories was ideal for his pursuit of experimental science. Galileo was the first scientist to consistently practise the experimental method. He was also a fierce sceptic: he saw the ancient ideas of Aristotle that still dominated natural philosophy as so much moribund rubbish. Only testable theory and evidence could create science worth its salt.

While recovering from an assassination attempt in 1607, probably arranged by the Vatican, Sarpi told Galileo some news that might interest him: a Dutchman had invented an optical instrument that made far-off objects appear close. He was right: the telescope was of great interest to Galileo. Once the scientist had made his own device, more powerful than any previously constructed, Sarpi helped get him an audience to demonstrate it to Venice's Great Council.

In the *Origin of the Milky Way*, Tintoretto painted our galaxy being born from milk spurted from the breast of Juno. As a jet of milk shoots upwards from her left nipple, it turns into a speckle of stars. Tintoretto's stretched and raked pictorial space creates a drama of the universe. Galileo was a doubter, Tintoretto a mystic, yet they both thought on a cosmic scale.

Galileo became the first person to see other worlds in detail. He pointed his telescope at the heavens and saw landscapes with astonishing sharpness. The surface of the moon was not a smooth disc, as it was said to be, but a rugged, cratered terrain. He observed moons orbiting Jupiter, suggesting that our moon orbits us. Galileo was a skilled artist, drawing what he saw, publishing the results in an illustrated book, the *Starry Messenger*. Traditional thought held the so-called 'sublunary sphere' where we live (literally 'below the moon') to be mortal and mutable, and this is our curse; the heavens are eternal and fixed, therefore perfect. Galileo saw no such fixity in heaven through his telescope. He saw moons orbiting other planets, and the scarred face of our moon. He theorized that there was no such thing as absolute space or motion, only relative space and relative motion. This was the discovery with which the Renaissance culminated. Everything moves. Everyone changes. Planets orbit suns, and moons orbit planets. The world is flux. Life is change.

* * *

Venice was a liberating place to work, but Galileo wanted success in his native Tuscany. So he dedicated his book about the new universe seen through the telescope to Cosimo II de' Medici, the new grand duke, and named the moons of Jupiter the 'Medicean Stars'. It got him the position he coveted at the court of Florence. There, if he ever happened to wander into the ducal armoury, he might have contemplated an arresting sight.

At the centre of this martial collection – in a city that no longer enjoyed any military significance – were two mannequins on wooden horses wearing suits of Persian armour, presented to the Medici by Shah Abbas I. One of the dummies wore a shield on its arm, round and convex, painted with what looked like a still-living severed head with a wriggling nest of black snakes for hair, suspended in its green circle like the moon in a telescope eyepiece. This too was a gift, from the Medici diplomatic representative in Rome, Cardinal Francesco Maria del Monte. It was a work by his protégé, a gifted young painter called Michelangelo Merisi, from Caravaggio in Lombardy.

Caravaggio had turned up in Rome in the early 1590s with no connections and no plan but was soon selling paintings at a humble art shop near del Monte's palace. They were thrilling, enticing, incorporating superb natural details of fruit and flowers even fresher than those of his fellow Lombards Arcimboldo and Galizia. Caravaggio combined the still-life with the old Venetian genre of the courtesan portrait, except that Caravaggio's models were young men and – to judge from his use of floral symbolism – homosexual prostitutes. One wears a pink flower in his hair, as overt a sexual use of Flora's iconography as you could get.

Yet something has gone badly wrong. This youth wears a loose sheet falling off his shoulder, and is depicted in a room with dingy walls. Light from a window glints on luscious cherries on the table, but as the boy reaches for the fruit with his filthy fingers a sneaky lizard has given him a nasty bite. He scrunches his face in pain, his whole body rearing as the shock sears through him.

Is this a sombre Christian warning against sin? It would seem not, for Caravaggio's dangerous erotic masterpiece transforms an earlier, more playful work, Sofonisba Anguissola's *Child Bitten by a Crayfish*. She wasn't making a heavy-handed point about hell, and neither is he – except in order to give his scene extra depravity.

Cardinal del Monte, who was homosexual according to contemporary gossip, was impressed by this artist with street dirt under his nails. Caravaggio moved into his palace and strutted around, armed, claiming the cardinal's protection and patronage. This ruffian was the real thing, a painter of genius, del Monte could see. What better way to prove it than by taking on the greatest Renaissance polymath of all and presenting the results to the Medici?

* * *

Caravaggio painted the *Medusa* on canvas stretched over a wooden buckler in an act of rivalry with the memory of Leonardo da Vinci. His patron – and probably the painter too, who owned books for all his thuggery – would have been familiar with the story told by Vasari that we have already encountered, of the Tuscan artist in his youth creating a monster by combining snakes, insects, bats

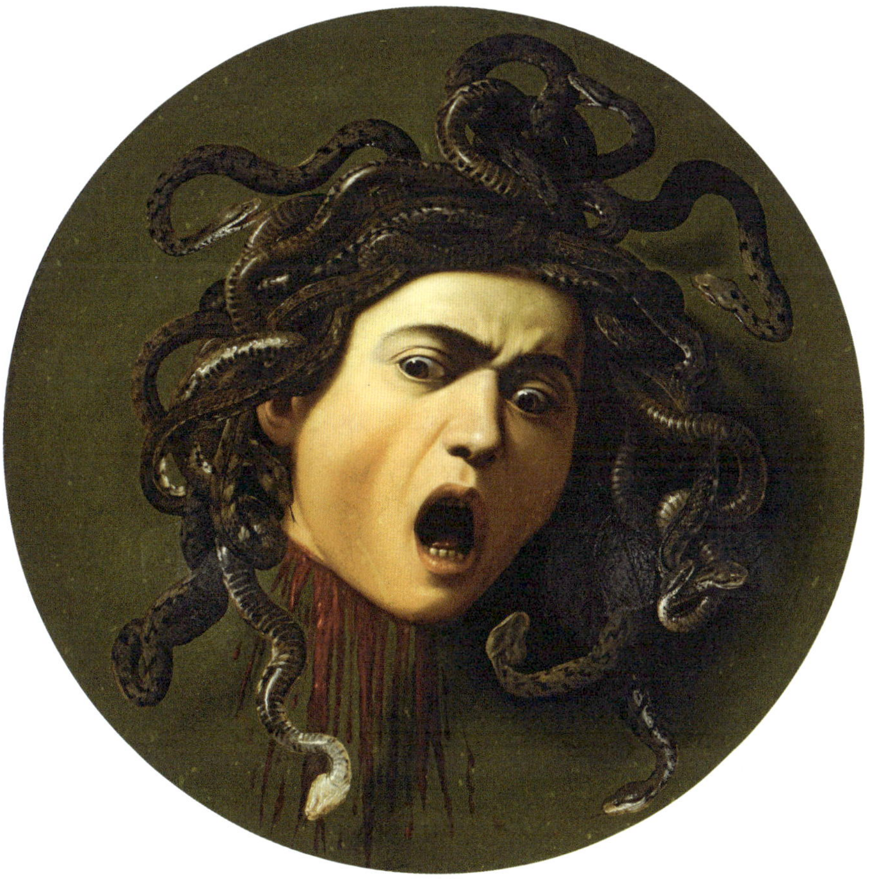

Caravaggio, *Medusa*, c. 1597.

and other animals to paint on a circular shield. Leonardo strove to produce an effect comparable to the basilisk stare of the Gorgon of classical mythology. His creature was not literally a Medusa: it was an idiosyncratic folk version produced with the same desire to horrify as Caravaggio's classicizing shocker. Vasari claims that Leonardo also painted an actual Medusa, owned by the Medici. If the work ever existed it is lost, though a fake version was created in the 17th century. It was considered a treasure of the Uffizi in the 19th century, when Caravaggio's shield was treated as a trifle.

Caravaggio's *Medusa* is sensational because it is painted from life. We have no doubt that he had real snakes slithering around his studio. As for the face, it is his: an impossible self-portrait, decapitated, with eyes turned away in horror and despair. How did Caravaggio look in a mirror to portray himself if his eyes don't look back? It is a paradox. In his *Self-Portrait in a Convex Mirror*, the Mannerist Parmigianino has his eyes attentively on his own reflection, as he reproduces what the mirror shows. But Caravaggio sees his eyes drop downwards in frozen rage. He looks at himself like a stranger. It is a portrait of the artist as a monster, the work of an artist who shared the egotism and pride of Cellini and Michelangelo but with a heightened capacity for self-knowledge, even self-hatred.

Caravaggio's *Medusa* refers artfully both to Leonardo's youthful gargoyle and his painting of the Gorgon, and to the portrait they help Vasari create of Leonardo's genius as a power to scandalize and confound, like Coleridge's vision of the poet's fury: 'Beware! Beware! / His flashing eyes! His floating hair!'[6] The Renaissance had translated the ancient Greek idea of poetic mania from literature to visual art. Leonardo's unsettling creation of a living Medusa is Vasari's symbol of his manic mystery. Caravaggio claims it, but with a new sense of the genius as not only mysterious, but fated and cursed. He is the Gorgon with hair of floating snakes.

Caravaggio's edge got him noticed and brought him work, but in Counter-Reformation Italy the drive to galvanize, terrify and absorb worshippers demanded religious public art that dwelt on martyrdom and suffering. He painted them with the same stunning authority as his early sensual art. The exalting of faith so dominated the new artistic agenda that Caravaggio's secular paintings seemed like eccentricities, which was how the Medici treated his *Medusa*.

In 1606 Caravaggio's uneasy paradoxes collapsed in on themselves when his nightlife as a violent troublemaker ended his glittering years as Rome's most coveted Christian painter. He killed a man and fled. He sought absolution by joining the crusading order of St John on the heavily fortified island of Malta. There he painted another oddity that was sent to Florence and that again shows

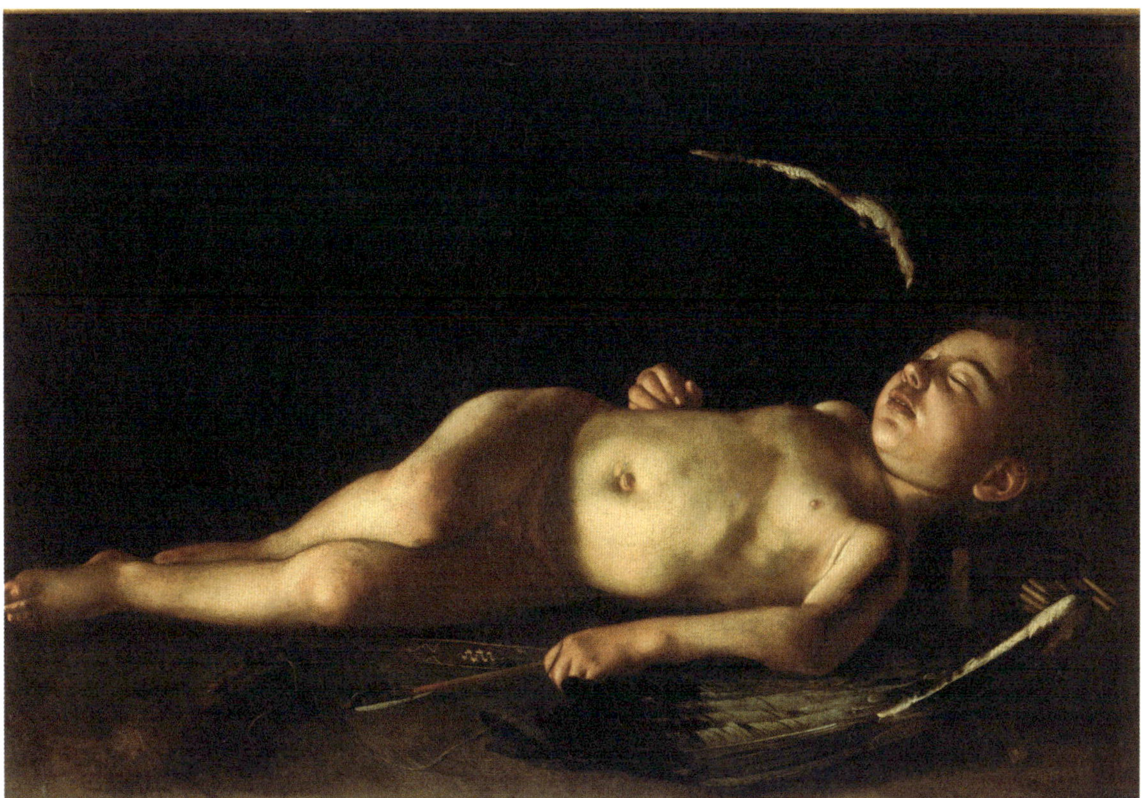

Caravaggio,
Sleeping Cupid, 1608.

his sense of rivalry with the art of the past: he restaged the famous fake that got Michelangelo noticed in 1490s Rome, a *Sleeping Cupid*.

Caravaggio's Cupid is not a classically inspired, beautiful god. This Cupid is sick. His body is mature and stunted, his face prematurely adult, his pose ungainly and twisted, his slumber deathly as his black wings lie useless in the shadows that surround him. The bronze light on his flesh is like the last glow of the Mediterranean sun coming through Caravaggio's window in the Maltese citadel. It is a farewell to delight, a funeral monument for an age of discovery and desire.

One of Michelangelo Buonarroti's grand-nephews, a knight of Malta, wrote to his brother in Florence to say that the *Cupid* had been sent there where experts may see it for themselves.[7] The letter about this ailing and exhausted love god was sent on 20 July 1609. It's as good a date as any for the end of the Renaissance.

Notes

All translations are the author's unless otherwise stated.

Introduction

1 In L. Beltrami, *Documenti e memorie riguardanti la vita e le opere di Leonardo da Vinci in ordine cronologico* (Milan: Fr. Treves, 1919), nos 88 and 89, p. 51.
2 J. M. Roberts and Odd Arne Westad, *The Penguin History of the World* (London: Penguin, 6th edn 2013), p. 528.

Chapter 1 The Arnolfini Nude

1 Michael Baxandall, 'Bartholomaeus Facius on Painting: A Fifteenth-Century Manuscript of the *De Viris Illustribus*', *Journal of the Courtauld and Warburg Institutes*, vol. 27 (1964), p. 103.
2 Ibid., p. 105.
3 Ibid.
4 Dante Alighieri, *La commedia, secondo l'antica vulgata*, ed. Giorgio Petrocchi, vol. 2: *Inferno* (Milan: Mondadori, 1966–67), Canto 1.
5 Ibid., Canto 3.
6 Baxandall, p. 102.
7 *Della Pittura* (Italian edition, 1436), in Leon Battista Alberti, *Opere volgari*, ed. C. Grayson (Bari: Laterza, 1973).

Chapter 2 The Naked Citizen

1 See Beata Możejko, *Peter von Danzig: The Story of a Great Caravel, 1462–1475* (Leiden: Brill, 2019).
2 Dante Alighieri, *La commedia, secondo l'antica vulgata*, ed. Giorgio Petrocchi, vol. 3: *Purgatorio* (Milan: Mondadori, 1966–67), Canto 11.
3 Ibid., vol. 2: *Inferno*, Canto 15.
4 See Karen Rose Mathews, 'Recycling for Eternity: The Reuse of Ancient Sarcophagi by the Pisan Merchant Elite in the 12th to 14th century,' in Anne Leader (ed.), *Memorializing the Middle Classes in Medieval and Renaissance Europe* (Kalamazoo, Mich.: Medieval Institute Publications, 2018), pp. 25–48.

Chapter 3 The Triumph of Love

1 Dante Alighieri, *La commedia, secondo l'antica vulgata*, ed. Giorgio Petrocchi, vol. 2: *Inferno* (Milan: Mondadori, 1966–67), Canto 5.
2 Geoffrey Chaucer, *The Canterbury Tales*, General Prologue, lines 1–4.
3 Lucretius, *De rerum natura* 1.31–34.
4 Angelo Poliziano, *The Stanze of Angelo Poliziano*, parallel text, trans. David Quint (Pennsylvania: Pennsylvania State University Press, 1993), 2.4, p. 68 (author's translation).
5 Ibid., 1.43, p. 22.
6 Ibid., 1.52, p. 26.
7 Giorgio Vasari, *Lives of the Painters, Sculptors and Architects*, trans. Gaston du C. de Vere (London: Macmillan/Medici Society, 1912–15), vol. 3, p. 248.
8 Poliziano 1.72, p. 36.
9 Ibid., 1.99, p. 50.
10 Ibid., 1.100, p. 50.

Chapter 4 Nature's Child

1 Codex Urbinas fol. 33[v], Vatican Apostolic Library, Urb. lat. 1270.
2 Ibid., fol. 34[r].
3 Cristoforo Landino, *Poems*, trans. Mary P. Chatfield (Cambridge, Mass.: Tatti Renaissance Library, Harvard University Press, 2008), *Carmina Varia* 5, lines 5–6 and 8–12, p. 282 (author's translation).
4 Marsilio Ficino, *Commentaries on Plato*, vol. 1: *Phaedrus* and *Ion*, ed. Michael J. B. Allen (Cambridge, Mass.: Harvard University Press, 2008), *Phaedrus* 2.1.2, p. 40.
5 Giorgio Vasari, *Lives of the Painters, Sculptors and Architects*, trans. Gaston du C. de Vere (London: Macmillan/Medici Society, 1912–15), vol. 3, p. 271.
6 Codex Forster III, fol. 66[r], National Art Library, Victoria & Albert Museum, London, in Jean Paul Richter, *The Notebooks of Leonardo da Vinci* (London: 1888), vol. 1, no. 498, p. 250.
7 Vasari, vol. 4, p. 93.
8 Codex Atlanticus, fol. 186[v], in Jean Paul Richter, vol. 2, no. 1363, p. 414.
9 Codex Atlanticus fol 18[v], in *Leonardo da Vinci Notebooks*, selected by Irma Richter, ed. and trans. Thereza Wells, (Oxford and New York: Oxford University Press, 2008), p. 271.
10 25 April 1483, Archivio di Stato di Milano; reproduced in *Leonardo on Painting*, ed. and trans. Martin Kemp and Margaret Walker (New Haven and London: Yale University Press, 1989), pp. 268–70.
11 One theory was that the earlier painting was sold to Ludovico Sforza. For the confusing implications of the documentary evidence, see Cecil Gould, 'The Newly Discovered Documents concerning Leonardo's Virgin of the Rocks and their Bearing on the Problem of the Two Versions', *Artibus et Historiae*, vol. 2, no. 3 (1981), pp. 73–76.
12 Jacobus de Voragine, *The Golden Legend*, trans. William Caxton (London, 1483), vol. 2.
13 'A Folio containing Papers chiefly related to Ecclesiastical Affairs', British Library, Harley MS 6848, (Baines) fols. 185[r]–86[r], (Kyd) 154[r].

Chapter 5 Worldly Knowledge

1 Codex Leicester, fol. 10[r], in Domenico Laurenza and Martin Kemp (eds), *Leonardo da Vinci's Codex Leicester: A New Edition* (Oxford and New York: Oxford University Press, 2019), vol. 3, p. 86 (author's translation).

2 Ibid.
3 Ibid.
4 Ibid., fol. 31^r, p. 268.
5 MS A (Paris), fol. 3^r, in Jean Paul Richter, *The Notebooks of Leonardo da Vinci* (London: 1888), vol. 1, no. 50, pp. 29–30. (Richter translates 'la pittura' as 'drawing'.)
6 Forster II, fol. 18^r, in ibid., no. 14, p. 16.
7 MS D (Paris), fol. 8^r, in ibid., no. 71, p. 45.
8 Codex Atlanticus, fol. 1082^r, in ibid., vol. 2, no. 1340, p. 397.
9 MS I (Paris), fol. 128 [80]^v, in *The Notebooks of Leonardo da Vinci*, ed. and trans. Edward MacCurdy (London: Jonathan Cape, 1938), vol. 2, XXVI, p. 834.
10 Codex Urbinas, fol. 15^v.
11 Codex Atlanticus, fol. 417^r, in Richter and Wells, p. 6.
12 Fogli B (On Anatomy, Royal Library, Windsor), fol. 919047^v, in MacCurdy, vol. 1, III, p. 148.
13 Giorgio Vasari, *Le Vite de' piú eccellenti architetti, pittori, et scultori* (1550), ed. Luciano Bellosi and Aldo Rossi (Turin: Einaudi, 1986), p. 550.
14 Codex Atlanticus 120^r, in MacCurdy, vol. 2, XLIX, p. 1163.
15 Niccolò Machiavelli, *Il Principe*, ed. Giorgio Inglese (Turin: Einaudi, 1995), 14.8, trans. W. K. Marriott (London and Toronto: J. M. Dent, 1908), p. 116.
16 Ibid., 'Dedication' 5, in Marriott, p. 2.
17 Ibid., 7.28 (author's translation).
18 Ibid., 11.12, in Marriott, p. 93.

Chapter 6 Haywain to Hell

1 Thomas More, *Utopia*, Book 1, trans. Ralph Robinson (London: Abraham Vele, 1551), p. 29.
2 In W. Stechow (ed.), *Northern Renaissance Art, 1400–1600: Sources and Documents* (Englewood Cliffs, N.J.: Prentice Hall, 1966), p. 16.

Chapter 7 The Garden of Earthly Delights

1 Psalms 33: 9.
2 Entry for 30 July 1517, in *The Travel Journal of Antonio de Beatis*, trans J. R. Hale and J. M. A. Lindon (London: Hakluyt Society, 1979), p. 94.
3 Bosch Research and Conservation Project, *Hieronymus Bosch, Painter and Draughtsman: Catalogue Raisonné* (New Haven, Conn., and London: Yale University Press, 2016), p. 582.
4 Christopher Columbus, *Epistola Christofori Colom. ... de insulis Indie supra Gangem* (Rome, 1493), trans. The Gilder Lehrman Collection, GLC01427, p. 2.
5 Ibid., pp. 1–2.
6 Amerigo Vespucci, *Lettera di Amerigo Vespucci* (Princeton, N.J.: Princeton University Press, 1916), p. 5; translation by C. R. Markham in *The Letters of Amerigo Vespucci* (New York: Burt Franklin, 1894), 'First Voyage', p. 3.
7 Ibid., p. 9, in Markham, p. 7.
8 Giorgio Vasari, *Lives of the Painters, Sculptors and Architects*, trans. Gaston du C. de Vere (London: MacMillan/Medici Society, 1912–15), vol. 4, p. 127.
9 Johan Huizinga, *The Autumn of the Middle Ages* (1919), trans. R. J. Payton and U. Mammitzsch (Chicago: Chicago University Press, 1996), p. 2.
10 Lucretius 5.1105–6.
11 Vasari, trans. de Vere, vol. 4, pp. 128–29.
12 Letter, *c.* 13 October 1506, trans. R. Tombo, *Memoirs of Journeys to Venice and the Low Countries* (Auckland: The Floating Press, 1913). I have also used here Jeffrey Ashcroft, *Albrecht Dürer: Documentary Biography*, 2 vols (New Haven, Conn., 2017), who corrects earlier English translations that have preferred to see Dürer, less grossly, warning Willibald against having sex with Agnes *because* she would be endangered by Pirckheimer.

Chapter 8 Render unto Caesar

1 Giorgio Vasari, *Lives of the Painters, Sculptors and Architects*, trans. Gaston du C. de Vere (London: Macmillan/Medici Society, 1912–15), vol. 4, p. 84.
2 Ibid., vol. 8, p. 42.
3 Ascanio Condivi, *Vita di Michelagnolo Buonarroti*, ed. G. Nencioni (Florence: Studio per Edizioni Scelte, 1998), p. 10.
4 Niccolò Machiavelli, *Il Principe*, ed. Giorgio Inglese (Turin: Einaudi, 1995), 7.45–46, trans. W. K. Marriott (London and Toronto: J. M. Dent, 1908), p. 63.
5 Condivi, p. 13.
6 Plutarch, *Plutarch's Lives*, trans. Bernadotte Perrin (Cambridge, Mass.: Harvard University Press, 1916), vol. 3, 1.31.4., pp. 91–92.
7 Condivi, p. 62.
8 *Symposium* 216d, trans. Benjamin Jowett (Oxford: Clarendon Press, 1871).
9 Ibid., 219d.
10 Amerigo Vespucci, *Lettera di Amerigo Vespucci* (Princeton, N.J.: Princeton University Press, 1916), p. 5; translation by C. R. Markham in *The Letters of Amerigo Vespucci* (New York: Burt Franklin, 1894), 'First Voyage', p. 3.
11 Jacob Burckhardt, *The Civilization of the Renaissance in Italy*, trans. S. G. C. Middlemore (London: C. K. Paul, 1878), p. 149.
12 *Il Principe*, trans. W. K. Marriott, p. 110.
13 Michelangelo, *Le lettere di Michelangelo Buonarroti pubblicate coi ricordi ed i contratti artistici*, ed. G. Milanesi (Florence: Le Monnier, 1875), no. 343, p. 378.
14 Condivi, p. 24.
15 Ibid.
16 Cited in Maria Ruvoldt, 'Michelangelo's *Slaves* and the Gift of Liberty', *Renaissance Quarterly*, vol. 65, no. 4 (2012), p. 1029.

Chapter 9 Melancholia

1 Fyodor Dostoevsky, *The Idiot* (1869), trans. Eva Martin (London: J. M. Dent, 1914), Chapter 4.

2 MS E (Paris), fol. 1r, in *The Notebooks of Leonardo da Vinci*, ed. and trans. Edward MacCurdy (London: Jonathan Cape, 1938), vol. 2, XLVIII, p. 1161.

3 Codex Atlanticus, fol. 500r, in Jean Paul Richter, *The Notebooks of Leonardo da Vinci* (London: 1888), vol. 2, 1353, p. 410.

4 Royal Collection, Windsor, fol. 919027v, in MacCurdy, vol. 1, III, p. 116.

5 Ibid.

6 Ibid.

7 Ibid., pp. 116–17.

8 Giorgio Vasari, *Lives of the Painters, Sculptors and Architects*, trans. Gaston du C. de Vere (London: Macmillan/Medici Society, 1912–15), vol. 4, p. 104.

9 Desiderius Erasmus, *Moriae encomium, id est Stultitiae laus*, in *Opera omnia*, vol. IV.3, ed. Clarence H. Miller (Amsterdam and Oxford: North Holland Publishing Company, 1979), p. 104, lines 577–81. Erasmus would apply the image specifically to the church in *Sileni Alcibiadis* (1515).

10 Letter, Antwerp, 17 May 1521, trans. R. Tombo, *Memoirs of Journeys to Venice and the Low Countries* (Auckland: The Floating Press, 1913).

11 Letter, Brussels, August–September 1520, in ibid.

12 Erasmus, *Moriae encomium*, pp. 67–68, lines 15–19.

Chapter 10 The Pulse of Life

1 For an overview into current research on neglected women artists of the Italian Renaissance, see Sheila Barker (ed.), *Women Artists in Early Modern Italy* (Turnhout: Brepols, 2016).

2 See Fredrika H. Jacobs, 'The construction of a life: Madonna Properzia De' Rossi "Schultice" Bolognese', *Word & Image*, vol. 9, no. 2 (1993), pp. 122–32.

3 Letter to Duke Cosimo, 20 January 1562, cited in Michael W. Cole, *Sofonisba's Lesson: A Renaissance Artist and Her Work* (Princeton, N.J.: Princeton University Press, 2020), pp. 266–67.

4 Giorgio Vasari, *Lives of the Painters, Sculptors and Architects*, trans. Gaston du C. de Vere (London: Macmillan/Medici Society, 1912–15), vol. 8, pp. 45–46.

5 Entry for 10 October 1517, in *The Travel Journal of Antonio de Beatis*, trans. J. R. Hale and J. M. A. Lindon (London: Hakluyt Society, 1979), p. 132.

6 Letter, 2 May 1519, in L. Beltrami, *Documenti e memorie riguardanti la vita e le opere di Leonardo da Vinci in ordine cronologico* (Milan: Fr. Treves, 1919), no. 245, p. 155.

7 Vasari, trans. de Vere, vol. 4, p. 99.

8 Ibid., p. 101.

9 Entry for 6 January 1518, in *The Travel Journal of Antonio de Beatis*, p. 187.

10 Letter, 3 April 1501, Archivio di Stato, Mantua, Archivio Gonzaga. See *Leonardo on Painting*, ed. and trans. Martin Kemp and Margaret Walker (New Haven and London: Yale University Press, 1989), p. 34.

11 Thomas Coryat, *Coryat's Crudities* (London: W. S., 1611), vol. 1, p. 265.

12 Ibid.

13 Veronica Franco, *Lettere familiari a diversi* (Venice, 1580), pp. 38–40. Discussed in Norman E. Land, 'Veronica Franco, Tintoretto, and Narcissus', *Notes in the History of Art*, vol. 22, no. 2 (2003), pp. 25–28.

Chapter 11 Judgments

1 John Donne, 'To His Mistress Going to Bed' (1633, pub. 1654), line 27.

2 *Vita di Benvenuto Cellini*, 1.37, in *Tutta l'opera del Cellini*, ed. E. Camesasca (Milan: Rizzoli, 1955).

3 Ibid.

4 Sonnet 102, in *The Poetry of Michelangelo: An Annotated Translation*, ed. James M. Saslow (New Haven, Conn. and London: Yale University Press, 1991), p. 232 (author's translation).

5 Sonnet 247, in ibid.

6 Sonnet 83, in ibid.

7 See John Turner, 'Michelangelo's Blacks in "The Last Judgment"', *Notes in the History of Art*, vol. 33, no. 1 (2013), pp. 8–15.

8 Giorgio Vasari, *Lives of the Painters, Sculptors and Architects*, trans. Gaston du C. de Vere (London: Macmillan/Medici Society, 1912–15), vol. 9, p. 57. Vasari uses the word 'stufe', which de Vere renders as 'bagnio'.

9 15 September 1537, in Pietro Aretino, *Lettere*, ed. F. Nicolini (Bari: Laterza, 1913), no. 192.

10 In J. W. Gaye, *Carteggio inedito d'artisti dei secoli XIV, XV, XVI*, 3 vols (Florence: G. Molini, 1839–40), vol. 2, pp. 332–35.

11 Ibid.

12 Letter, 20 September 1544, cited in R. Zapperi, 'Alessandro Farnese, Giovanni della Casa and Titian's *Danae* in Naples', *Journal of the Warburg and Courtauld Institutes*, vol. 54 (1991), pp. 159–71.

13 Vasari, trans. de Vere, vol. 9, p. 171.

14 Ruy Gómez, letter dated 12 August 1554, cited in Linda Porter, *Mary Tudor: The First Queen* (Boston, Mass.: Little, Brown, 2007), p. 320.

Chapter 12 Carnival and Lent

1 Karel van Mander, *Het Schilder-Boeck* (Haarlem, 1604; repr. Utrecht: Davaco, 1969), fol. 233r.

2 Ibid.

3 Ovid, *Metamorphoses*, trans. Arthur Golding (London: William Seres, 1567), 8.292–96.
4 Council of Trent, Session 25, 2nd decree, trans. J. Waterworth (London: Dolman, 1848), pp. 235–36.
5 Van Mander, fol. 234r.
6 In W. Stechow (ed.), *Northern Renaissance Art, 1400–1600: Sources and Documents* (Englewood Cliffs, N.J.: Prentice Hall, 1966), p. 37.
7 Ovid, *Metamorphoses* 4.122–24.

Chapter 13 Curiosities

1 *Vita di Benvenuto Cellini*, 1.64, in *Tutta l'opera del Cellini*, ed. E. Camesasca (Milan: Rizzoli, 1955).
2 See Thomas DaCosta Kaufmann, 'Remarks on the Collections of Rudolf II: The *Kunstkammer* as a Form of *Representatio*', *Art Journal*, vol. 38, no. 1 (1978), pp. 22–28.
3 *Les Essais*, trans. C. Cotton as *The Essays of Montaigne* (1877), Chapter 20.
4 Holy Tribunal, 18 July 1573, cited in Gino Fogolari, 'Il processo dell'inquisizione a Paolo Veronese', *Archivio Veneto*, vol. 5, no. 17 (1935), pp. 352–85.
5 Ibid.
6 *Kubla Khan* (1816), lines 49–50.
7 Cited in Catherine Puglisi, *Caravaggio* (London: Phaidon, 1998), Appendix IX, p. 421.

Further Reading

David Abulafia, *The Discovery of Mankind: Atlantic Encounters in the Age of Columbus* (New Haven, Conn., and London: Yale University Press, 2008)

Albrecht Dürer, ed. Christoph Metzger, exh. cat. (Munich, London and New York: Prestel, 2019)

Dante Alighieri, *The Divine Comedy of Dante Alighieri*, ed. Robert M. Durling, 3 vols (Oxford: Oxford University Press, 1997–2003)

Pietro Aretino, *Selected Letters*, trans. George Bull (Harmondsworth: Penguin, 1976)

Jeffrey Ashcroft, *Albrecht Dürer: Documentary Biography*, 2 vols (New Haven, Conn.: Yale University Press, 2017)

Sheila Barker (ed.), *Women Artists in Early Modern Italy* (Turnhout: Brepols, 2016).

Michael Baxandall, *Painting and Experience in Fifteenth-Century Italy* (Oxford: Clarendon Press, 1972)

Bosch Research and Conservation Project, *Hieronymus Bosch, Painter and Draughtsman: Catalogue Raisonné* (New Haven, Conn., and London: Yale University Press, 2016)

William J. Bouwsma, *The Waning of the Renaissance, 1550–1640* (New Haven, Conn.: Yale University Press, 2000)

Stefan Bower and Simon Ditchfield (eds), *A Renaissance Reclaimed: Jacob Burckhardt's 'Civilisation of the Renaissance in Italy' Reconsidered* (Oxford: Oxford University Press, 2022)

Alison Brown, *Return of Lucretius to Renaissance Florence* (Cambridge, Mass.: Harvard University Press, 2010)

Michelangelo Buonarroti, *The Letters of Michelangelo*, trans. E. H. Ramsden, 2 vols (Stanford, Calif.: Stanford University Press, 1963)

—— *The Poetry of Michelangelo: An Annotated Translation*, trans. James M. Saslow (New Haven, Conn., and London: Yale University Press, 1991)

—— and Ascanio Condivi, *Michelangelo: Life, Letters and Poetry*, trans. George Bull and Peter Porter (Oxford and New York: Oxford University Press, 1987)

Jacob Burckhardt, *The Civilization of the Renaissance in Italy*, intro. Peter Burke, trans. S. G. C. Middlemore (London: Penguin, 2004)

Peter Burke, *Popular Culture in Early Modern Europe* (London: Temple Smith, 1978)

Benvenuto Cellini, *My Life*, trans. Julia Conaway Bondanella and Peter Bondanella (Oxford and New York: Oxford University Press, 2002)

Fernando Cervantes, *Conquistadores: A New History* (New York: Viking, 2021)

Martin Clayton and Ron Philo, *Leonardo da Vinci: Anatomist* (London: Royal Collection Trust, 2012)

Norman Cohn, *The Pursuit of the Millennium* (Oxford: Oxford University Press, rev. edn. 1970)

Michael W. Cole, *Sofonisba's Lesson: A Renaissance Artist and Her Work* (Princeton, N.J.: Princeton University Press, 2020)

Virginia Cox, *Women's Writing in Italy 1400–1650* (Baltimore: Johns Hopkins University Press, 2008)

Anthony D'Elia, *Pagan Virtue in a Christian World: Sigismondo Malatesta and the Italian Renaissance* (Cambridge, Mass.: Harvard University Press, 2016)

Charles Dempsey, *The Portrayal of Love: Botticelli's Primavera and Humanist Culture at the Time of Lorenzo* (Princeton, N.J.: Princeton University Press, 1992)

Eamon Duffy, *The Stripping of the Altars*, 2nd edn. (London and New Haven, Conn.: Yale University Press, 2005)

J. H. Elliott, *Empires of the Atlantic World: Britain and Spain in America, 1492–1830* (New Haven, Conn.: Yale University Press, 2007)

Sylvia Ferino-Pagden (ed.), *Arcimboldo 1526–1593* (Milan: Skira, 2008)

Galileo Galilei, *Sidereus Nuncius*, trans. A. van Helden (Chicago: University of Chicago Press, 1989)

Martin Gayford, *Michelangelo: His Epic Life* (London: Penguin, 2013)

Carlo Ginzburg, *The Enigma of Piero*, foreword by Peter Burke, trans. Martin Ryle and Rate Soper (London: Verso, 1985)

Richard A. Goldthwaite, *Wealth and the Demand for Art in Italy, 1300–1600* (Baltimore: Johns Hopkins University Press, 1993)

Stephen Greenblatt, *The Swerve: How the World Became Modern* (New York: W. W. Norton, 2011)

Francesco Guicciardini, *The History of Italy*, ed. and trans. Sidney Alexander (Princeton, N.J.: Princeton University Press, 1984)

Sabine Haag (ed.), *Bruegel: The Master* (London and New York: Thames & Hudson, 2018)

J. R. Hale, *Florence and the Medici* (London and New York: Thames & Hudson, 1977)

James Hankins (ed.), *The I Tatti Renaissance Library* (Cambridge, Mass.: Harvard University Press, 2001–)

Craig Harbison, 'Sexuality and Social Standing in Jan van Eyck's Double Arnolfini Portrait', *Renaissance Quarterly*, vol. 43, no. 2 (1990), pp. 249–91.

Johan Huizinga, *The Autumn of the Middle Ages* (1919), trans. R. J. Payton and U. Mammitzsch (Chicago: Chicago University Press, 1996)

In the Age of Giorgione, ed. Simone Facchinetti and Arturo Galansino, exh. cat. (London: Royal Academy, 2016)

Frederika H. Jacobs, 'Woman's Capacity to Create: The Unusual Case of Sofonisba Anguissola', *Renaissance Quarterly*, vol. 47, no. 1 (1994), pp. 74–101

Paul Joannides, *Titian to 1518* (New Haven, Conn., and London: Yale University Press, 2001)
Martin Kemp, *Leonardo da Vinci: The Marvellous Works of Nature and Man* (London: J. M. Dent, 1981)
—— *The Science of Art: Optical Themes in Western Art from Brunelleschi to Seurat* (New Haven, Conn., and London: Yale University Press, 1990)
Robert E. Lerner, *The Heresy of the Free Spirit in the Later Middle Ages* (Berkeley: University of California Press, 1972)
Leonardo da Vinci, *The Notebooks of Leonardo da Vinci*, ed. and trans. Edward MacCurdy, 2 vols (London: Jonathan Cape, 1938)
Leonardo on Painting, ed. and trans. Martin Kemp and Margaret Walker (New Haven, Conn.: Yale University Press, 2001)
Roberto Longhi, *Piero della Francesca* (1927), trans. David Tabbat, introduction by Keith Christiansen (New York: Sheep Meadow Press, 2002)
Diarmaid MacCulloch, *Reformation* (London: Allen Lane, 2003)
Niccolò Machiavelli, *The Essential Writings of Machiavelli*, trans. Peter Constantine (New York: Random House, 2007)
Christopher Marlowe, *The Tragical History of Doctor Faustus*, in *The Complete Plays*, ed. Frank Romany and Robert Lindsey (London: Penguin, 2003)
Michel de Montaigne, *The Complete Essays*, ed. and trans. M. A. Screech (London: Penguin, 1991)
Thomas More, *Utopia*, trans. Dominic Baker-Smith (London: Penguin, 2012)
John M. Najemy, *A History of Florence, 1200–1575* (Malden, Mass.: Blackwell, 2006)
Ovid, *Metamorphoses*, trans. Arthur Golding (London: William Seres, 1567)
Steven Ozment, *The Serpent and the Lamb: Cranach, Luther and the Making of the Reformation* (New Haven, Conn., and London: Yale University Press, 2011)
Erwin Panofsky, *Perspective as Symbolic Form* (1927), trans. Christopher S. Wood (Princeton, N.J.: Princeton University Press, 1997)
—— *Studies in Iconology: Humanistic Themes in the Art of the Renaissance* (New York: Oxford University Press, 1939)
Geoffrey Parker, *Imprudent King: A New Life of Philip II* (New Haven, Conn.: Yale University Press, 2014)
Glyn Parry, *The Arch-Conjuror of England: John Dee* (New Haven, Conn.: Yale University Press, 2012)
Angelo Poliziano, *The Stanze of Angelo Poliziano*, parallel text, trans. David Quint (University Park, Penn.: Pennsylvania State University Press, 1993)
Catherine Puglisi, *Caravaggio* (London: Phaidon, 1998)
François Rabelais, *Gargantua and Pantagruel*, trans. M. A. Screech (London: Penguin, 2006)
Carol M. Richardson, Kim W. Woods and Michael W. Franklin (eds), *Renaissance Art Reconsidered: An Anthology of Primary Sources* (Oxford: Blackwell, 2007)
Michael Rocke, *Forbidden Friendships: Homosexuality and Male Culture in Renaissance Florence* (Oxford: Oxford University Press, 1996)
William Shakespeare, *Venus and Adonis*, in *The Complete Sonnets and Poems*, ed. Colin Burrow (Oxford: Oxford University Press, 2008)
Niketas Siniossoglou, *Radical Platonism in Byzantium: Illumination and Utopia in Gemistus Plethon* (Cambridge: Cambridge University Press, 2011)
Wolfgang Stechow (ed.), *Northern Renaissance Art 1400–1600: Sources and Documents* (Englewood Cliffs, N.J.: Prentice Hall, 1966)
Griet Steyaert et al. (eds), *The Ghent Altarpiece: Research and Conservation of the Interior: The Lower Register* (Turnhout: Brepols, 2021)
Titian: Love, Desire, Death, ed. Matthias Wivel et al., exh. cat. (New Haven, Conn., and London: Yale University Press, 2020)
Richard C. Trexler, *Public Life in Renaissance Florence* (Ithaca, N.Y.: Cornell University Press, 1980)
Giorgio Vasari, *Lives of the Painters, Sculptors and Architects*, trans. Gaston du C. de Vere, 10 vols (London: Macmillan/ Medici Society, 1912–15)
Edgar Wind, *Pagan Mysteries in the Renaissance* (London: Faber, 1958)
David Wootton, *The Invention of Science* (New York: Harper Collins, 2015)
Francis A. Yates, *Giordano Bruno and the Hermetic Tradition* (Chicago: University of Chicago Press, 1964)

Acknowledgments

The idea for this book was concocted over a hearty lunch with Roger Thorp at a French restaurant round the corner from Thames & Hudson. I recommend the snails. And I am profoundly grateful to Roger for commissioning such a book on a theme that has fascinated me all my life, then sticking with it through the years of the pandemic and finally overseeing the beautifully produced volume in your hands. I am indebted to everyone on the superb T&H team, especially Mohara Gill, Sam Wythe, Adam Brown, Susanna Ingram and Nikos Kotsopoulos for their immaculate and precise work on images, layout, production and editing.

Years before that lunch, I wrote an article in the *Guardian* about Jacob Burckhardt and his classic *The Civilization of the Renaissance in Italy*. Professor Simon Ditchley of York University and Dr Stefan Bower of King's College London were kind enough to say that it 'planted the seed' for their 2018 British Academy conference 'Burckhardt at 200' and invited me to speak at its opening event at the Warburg Institute. It was a crash course in the latest academic thinking on the Renaissance, especially my conversation with Dr Martin Ruehl of Cambridge University about Burckhardt. I've separately been lucky enough to discuss Leonardo with Martin Kemp. A few years ago my historical hero Simon Schama suggested I read van Mander on northern art, and I am still plundering this source.

When we were students, Sarah Currie and I ate bad pizza in Florence and visited the Uffizi. Since then the food has got better, but we're still exploring art and history together along with our daughter, Primavera. It's an endless delight.

List of Illustrations

Illustrations are listed by page number. Dimensions are given height before width

2 Francesco del Cossa, *April, Triumph of Venus*, *c.* 1467–70 (detail of **70–71**).

6 Leonardo da Vinci, *Lady with an Ermine*, *c.* 1489. Oil and tempera on panel, 54.8 × 40.3 cm (21⅝ × 15⅞ in.). National Museum, Kraków.

8 Leonardo da Vinci, *Virgin and Child with a Cat*, *c.* 1478–81. Pen and brown ink, brown wash, on paper, 13 × 9.4 cm (5⅛ × 3¾ in.). British Museum, London.

10 Hieronymus Bosch, *Garden of Earthly Delights* (detail), 1490–1500. Oil on oak panel, overall dimensions 185.8 × 249 cm (73¼ × 98⅛ in.). Museo del Prado, Madrid. Photo Museo Nacional del Prado/Scala, Florence.

12 Andrea Palladio and Vincenzo Scamozzi, Teatro Olimpico, Vicenza, 1580–85. Photo Edwin Smith/ RIBA Collections.

14 Jan van Eyck, *Arnolfini Portrait*, 1434. Oil on oak panel, 82.2 × 60 cm (32⅜ × 23⅝ in.). National Gallery, London.

17 Willem van Haecht, *The Gallery of Cornelis van der Geest*, 1628. Oil on canvas, 99 × 129.5 cm (39 × 51 in.). Rubenshuis, Antwerp. Photo Bart Huysmans and Michel Wuyts.

18 After Jan van Eyck, *Woman at Her Toilet*, early 16th century. Oil on oak panel, 27.2 × 16.3 cm (10¾ × 6½ in.). Fogg Art Museum, Harvard Art Museums, Cambridge, Mass. Francis H. Burr, Louise Haskell Daly, Alpheus Hyatt Purchasing and William M. Prichard Funds/Photo President and Fellows of Harvard College.

20 Jan van Eyck, *Portrait of Margaret van Eyck*, 1439. Oil on panel, 32.6 × 25.8 cm (12⅞ × 10¼ in.). Groeningemuseum, Bruges.

21 Hubert van Eyck and Jan van Eyck, *Eve* and *Adam*, from the Ghent Altarpiece, 1432. Oil on panel, overall dimensions 340 × 520 cm (133⅞ × 204¾ in.). St Bavo's Cathedral, Ghent.

23 Jan van Eyck, *Virgin and Child with Canon van der Paele*, 1434. Oil on panel, 124.5 cm × 160 cm (49⅛ × 63 in.). Groeningemuseum, Bruges. Photo Lukas – Art in Flanders VZW/Bridgeman Images.

26 Unknown artist, *Love Magic*, *c.* 1470–80. Oil on panel, 24 × 18 cm (9½ × 7⅛ in.). Museum der Bildenden Künste, Leipzig. Photo akg-images.

28 Piero della Francesca, *Baptism of Christ*, after 1437. Tempera on poplar, 167 × 116 cm (65¾ × 65⅜ in.). National Gallery, London.

33 Antonello da Messina, *Virgin Annunciate*, *c.* 1476. Oil on panel, 45 × 34.5 cm (17¾ × 13⅝ in.). Palazzo Abatellis, Palermo. Photo Scala, Florence.

34 Giovanni Bellini, *Madonna and Child Enthroned*, *c.* 1487. Oil on panel, 471 × 292 cm (185½ × 115 in.). Gallerie dell'Accademia, Venice. Photo G.A.VE Archivio fotografico, foto Intraprese fotografiche, 2021/ Courtesy of the Ministero della Cultura.

35 Titian, *Woman with a Mirror*, 1525–50. Oil on canvas, 99 × 76 cm (39 × 30 in.). Musée du Louvre, Paris. Photo RMN-Grand Palais (Musée du Louvre)/ Franck Raux.

36, 38 Hans Memling, *Last Judgment*, 1467–71. Oil on panel, 223.5 × 306 cm (88 × 159⅞ in.). National Museum, Gdańsk.

40 Giotto, *Kiss of Judas*, 1304–6. Fresco, 200 × 185 cm (78¾ × 72¼ in.). Scrovegni Chapel, Padua.

41 Cimabue, *Flagellation of Christ*, *c.* 1280. Tempera on panel, 24.8 × 20 cm (9⅞ × 7⅞ in.). Frick Collection, New York. Photo akg-images.

43 Rogier van der Weyden, *Pietà*, *c.* 1441. Oil on panel, 32.5 × 47.2 cm (12⅞ × 18⅝ in.). Musées Royaux des Beaux-Arts de Belgique, Brussels.

44–45 Rogier van der Weyden, *Last Judgment*, 1443–51. Oil on panel, 215 × 560 cm (84¾ × 220½ in.). Musée de l'Hôtel-Dieu, Beaune. Photo Bridgeman Images.

48 Masaccio, *Expulsion from Paradise*, *c.* 1427. Fresco, 214 × 90 cm (84⅜ × 35½ in.). Brancacci Chapel, Santa Maria del Carmine, Florence.

51 Fra Angelico, *Mocking of Christ*, 1440–42. Fresco, 181 × 151 cm (71⅜ × 59½ in.). Museo Nazionale di San Marco, Florence. Photo Scala, Florence/Courtesy of the Ministero Beni e Att. Culturali e del Turismo.

55 Donatello, *David*, *c.* 1440. Bronze, height 158 cm (62¼ in.). Museo Nazionale del Bargello, Florence. Photo © Arte & Immagini srl/Vincenzo Fontana/Corbis via Getty Images.

56 Donatello, *Judith and Holofernes*, 1455–60. Bronze, height 236 cm (93 in.). Piazza della Signoria, Florence. Photo Edizione Brogi/Rijksmuseum, Amsterdam.

59 Antonio Pollaiuolo, *Battle of the Nudes*, *c.* 1470–90. Engraving, 38.4 × 58.9 cm (15⅛ × 23¼ in.). Metropolitan Museum of Art, New York. Purchase, Joseph Pulitzer Bequest, 1917.

60, 69 Master of Charles of Durazzo, *Triumph of Venus*, *c.* 1400. Oil on panel, diameter 51 cm (20⅛ in.). Musée du Louvre, Paris. Photo RMN-Grand Palais (Musée du Louvre)/Tony Querrec.

62–63 Andrea del Verrocchio, *Death of Francesca Pitti Tornabuoni*, *c.* 1477–80. Marble, 45 × 170.5 cm (17¾ × 67¼ in.). Museo Nazionale del Bargello, Florence. Photo akg-images/Rabatti & Domingie.

64 Domenico Ghirlandaio, *Birth of the Virgin*, 1486–90. Fresco, length 450 cm (177¼ in.). Tornabuoni Chapel,

Santa Maria Novella, Florence. Photo Scala, Florence/ Fondo Edifici di Culto – Min. dell'Interno.

65 Domenico Ghirlandaio, *Birth of John the Baptist*, 1486–90. Fresco, length 450 cm (177¼ in.). Tornabuoni Chapel, Santa Maria Novella, Florence. Photo Scala, Florence/Fondo Edifici di Culto – Min. dell'Interno.

66 Apollonio di Giovanni, *Triumph of Love*, *c.* 1460–70. Tempera on poplar panel, 72 × 72 cm (28⅜ × 28⅜ in.). Victoria and Albert Museum, London.

68 Enamelled casket, Limoges, *c.* 1180. Copper, enamel, gold, 21.7 × 11.6 × 16.5 cm (8⅝ × 4⅝ × 6½ in.). British Museum, London. Photo © The Trustees of the British Museum.

70–71 Francesco del Cossa, *April, Triumph of Venus*, *c.* 1467–70. Fresco, overall dimensions, 320 × 500 cm (126 × 196⅞ in.). Salone dei Mesi, Palazzo Schifanoia, Ferrara. By permission of the Musei di Arte Antica di Ferrara.

73 Andrea Mantegna, ceiling fresco, *c.* 1474. Camera degli Sposi, Palazzo Ducale, Mantua. Photo DeAgostini/ Getty Images.

74 Sandro Botticelli, *Venus and Mars*, *c.* 1485. Tempera and oil on poplar, 69.2 × 173.4 cm (27¼ × 68⅜ in.). National Gallery, London.

78 Sandro Botticelli, *Pallas and the Centaur*, *c.* 1480–85. Tempera on canvas, 207 × 148 cm (81½ × 58⅜ in.). Uffizi, Florence. Photo Gabinetto Fotografico delle Gallerie degli Uffizi.

80–81 Sandro Botticelli, *Primavera*, *c.* 1480. Tempera grassa on panel, 207 × 319 cm (81½ × 125⅝ in.). Uffizi, Florence. Photo Gabinetto Fotografico delle Gallerie degli Uffizi.

83 Sandro Botticelli, *Birth of Venus*, *c.* 1485. Tempera on canvas, 172.5 × 278.5 cm (68 × 109¾ in.). Uffizi, Florence.

84, 94 Leonardo da Vinci, *Annunciation*, *c.* 1472. Oil on panel, 90 × 222 cm (35½ × 109¾ in.). Uffizi, Florence. Photo Scala, Florence.

86 Leonardo da Vinci, *Drawing of an Arno Valley Landscape*, 1473. Ink on paper, 19.7 × 28.6 cm (7⅞ × 11⅜ in.). Gabinetto dei Disegni e delle Stampe, Uffizi, Florence.

87 (left) Andrea del Verrocchio, *Putto with a Dolphin*, *c.* 1470. Bronze, height (without base) 70 cm (27⅝ in.). Palazzo Vecchio, Florence. Photo White Images/Scala, Florence.

87 (right) Leonardo da Vinci, *Study of the Christ Child with a Cat*, *c.* 1478–81. Pen and brown ink on paper, 21.2 × 14.8 cm (8⅜ × 5⅞ in.). British Museum, London.

89 Leonardo da Vinci, *Ginevra de' Benci*, *c.* 1474–78. Oil on panel, 38.1 × 37 cm (15 × 14⅝ in.). National Gallery of Art, Washington, DC. Ailsa Mellon Bruce Fund.

91 Petrus Christus, *Portrait of a Young Woman*, *c.* 1470. Oil on oak panel, 29 × 22.5 cm (11½ × 8⅞ in.). Gemäldegalerie, Berlin.

92 Andrea del Verrocchio and Leonardo da Vinci, *Baptism of Christ*, 1470–75. Tempera and oil on panel, 177 × 151 cm (69¾ × 59½ in.). Uffizi, Florence. Photo Scala, Florence.

97 Leonardo da Vinci, *Study of the Hanged Bernardo Baroncelli*, 1479. Pen and ink on paper, 19.2 × 7.3 cm (7⅝ × 2⅞ in.). Musée Bonnat-Helleu, Bayonne.

98 Leonardo da Vinci, *Adoration of the Magi*, *c.* 1482. Drawing in charcoal, watercolour ink, tempera and oil on panel, 244 × 240 cm (96⅛ × 94½ in.). Uffizi, Florence.

100 Leonardo da Vinci, *Virgin of the Rocks*, 1483–94. Oil on canvas, 199.5 × 122 cm (78⅝ × 48⅛ in.). Musée du Louvre, Paris.

103 Leonardo da Vinci, *Last Supper*, 1495–98. Tempera mural with pitch and mastic, 460 × 880 cm (181⅛ × 346½ in.). Santa Maria delle Grazie, Milan.

104, 106 Leonardo da Vinci, *Virgin of the Rocks*, *c.* 1491–1508. Oil on poplar, 189.5 × 120 cm (74⅝ × 47¼ in.). National Gallery, London. Photo National Gallery, London/Scala, Florence.

108 Leonardo da Vinci, *A Ravine*, *c.* 1482–85. Pen and ink, 22 × 15.8 cm (8¾ × 6¼ in.). Royal Collection Trust, London.

109 Leonardo da Vinci, *Virgin and Child with St Anne*, 1503–19. Oil on panel, 168 × 130 cm (66¼ × 51¼ in.). Musée du Louvre, Paris. Photo RMN-Grand Palais (Musée du Louvre)/René-Gabriel Ojeda.

110 Leonardo da Vinci, *Perspectival Study for the 'Adoration of the Magi'*, *c.* 1481. Pen and ink, traces of silverpoint and white on paper, 16.4 × 29 cm (6½ × 11½ in.). Gabinetto dei Disegni e delle Stampe, Uffizi, Florence. Photo Leemage/Corbis via Getty Images.

112 Leonardo da Vinci, *The skull sectioned*, 1489. Pen and ink, traces of black chalk, 18.8 × 13.4 cm (7½ × 5⅜ in.). Royal Collection Trust, London.

113 Leonardo da Vinci, *The layers of the scalp and the cerebral ventricles*, *c.* 1490–92. Red chalk, pen and ink, 20.3 × 15.3 cm (8 × 6⅛ in.). Royal Collection Trust, London.

114 Leonardo da Vinci, *The cranial nerves*, *c.* 1506. Pen and ink over traces of black chalk, with scratching out, 19 × 13.6 cm (7½ × 5⅜ in.). Royal Collection Trust, London. Photo Royal Collection Trust/His Majesty King Charles III, 2023/Bridgeman Images.

116 Leonardo da Vinci, *A scene in an arsenal*, *c.* 1485–90. Pen and ink, 25 × 18.3 cm (9⅞ × 7¼ in.). Royal Collection Trust, London

117 Leonardo da Vinci, *Mortars firing into a fortress*, *c.* 1503–4. Black chalk, pen and ink, wash, 32.9 × 48 cm (13 × 19 in.). Royal Collection Trust, London.

120 Leonardo da Vinci, *Study for a flying machine with a hand- and foot-driven mechanism*, *c.* 1487–90. Paris MS B, fol. 79. Pen and ink on paper, 23 × 16 cm (9⅛ × 6⅜ in.). Institut de France, Paris.

124 Leonardo da Vinci, *A map of Imola*, 1502. Black chalk, stylus lines, pen and ink, coloured washes, 44 × 60.2 cm (17⅜ × 23¾ in.). Royal Collection Trust, London.

126, 144–45 Hieronymus Bosch, *The Haywain*, 1512–15. Oil on panel, 147.1 × 224.3 cm (58 × 88⅜ in.). Museo del Prado, Madrid. Photo Museo Nacional del Prado, Madrid/Scala, Florence.

129 Hieronymus Bosch, *Adoration of the Magi*, *c.* 1494. Oil on oak panel, 147.4 × 168.6 cm (58⅛ × 66½ in.). Museo del Prado, Madrid.

130 Unknown Sapi-Portuguese artist, lidded saltcellar, 15th–16th century. Ivory, height 29.8 cm (11¾ in.). Metropolitan Museum of Art, New York. Gift of Paul and Ruth W. Tishman, 1991.

133 Martin Schongauer, *Temptation of St Anthony*, 1470–75. Engraving, 31.5 × 23.2 cm (12½ × 9¼ in.). National Gallery of Art, Washington, DC. Rosenwald Collection.

136 Sandro Botticelli, *Mystic Nativity*, 1500. Oil on canvas, 108.6 × 74.9 cm (42⅞ × 29½ in.). National Gallery, London.

138 Albrecht Dürer, *St Michael Fighting the Dragon*, from the *Apocalypse* series, 1498. Woodcut, 39.2 × 28.3 cm (15½ × 11¼ in.). Metropolitan Museum of Art, New York. The George Khuner Collection, Gift of Mrs George Khuner, 1975.

140–41 Hieronymus Bosch, *Temptation of St Anthony*, 1505–6. Oil on panel, 131.5 × 225 cm (51⅞ × 88⅝ in.). Museu Nacional de Arte Antiga, Lisbon. Direção-Geral do Património Cultural/Arquivo e Documentação Fotográfica. Photo Luísa Oliveira.

142 Hieronymus Bosch, *The Wood has Ears, the Field has Eyes*, *c.* 1500. Pen on paper, 20.2 × 12.7 cm (8 × 5 in.). Kupferstichkabinett, Berlin. Photo Fine Art Images/A. Burkatovski/Superstock.

143 Hieronymus Bosch, *The Wayfarer*, *c.* 1500. Oil on panel, diameter 71 cm (28 in.). Museum Boijmans V an Beuningen, Rotterdam.

147 Dirk Bouts, *Fall of the Damned*, *c.* 1468. Oil on panel, 115 × 69.5 cm (45⅜ × 27⅜ in.). Palais des Beaux-Arts, Lille. Photo RMN-Grand Palais (PBA, Lille)/Stéphane Maréchalle.

148 Hugo van der Goes, *Fall of Man*, *c.* 1470–75. Oil on panel, 33.8 × 22.9 cm (13⅜ × 9⅛ in.). Kunsthistorisches Museum, Vienna.

150, 153, 154–55, 157, 158 Hieronymus Bosch, *Garden of Earthly Delights*, 1490–1500. Oil on oak panel, overall dimensions 185.8 × 249 cm (73¼ × 98⅛ in.). Museo del Prado, Madrid. Photo Museo Nacional del Prado/Scala, Florence.

152 Hieronymus Bosch, *Ship of Fools*, *c.* 1475–1500. Oil on panel, 58 × 33 cm (22⅞ × 13 in.). Musée du Louvre, Paris.

162 Piero di Cosimo, *Return from the Hunt*, *c.* 1494–1500. Tempera and oil on panel, 70.5 × 168.9 cm (27⅞ × 66¼ in.). Metropolitan Museum of Art, New York. Gift of Robert Gordon, 1875.

163 Piero di Cosimo, *Forest Fire*, *c.* 1505. Oil on panel, 71.2 × 202 cm (28⅛ × 79⅝ in.). Ashmolean Museum, Oxford. Photo Ashmolean Museum/Bridgeman Images.

167 Albrecht Dürer, *Hercules at the Crossroad*, *c.* 1498. Engraving, second state of two, 32.3 × 22.5 cm (12¾ × 8⅞ in.). Metropolitan Museum of Art, New York. Fletcher Fund, 1919.

168 Albrecht Dürer, *Death of Orpheus*, 1494. Engraving, 28.9 × 22.5 cm (11½ × 8⅞ in.). Hamburger Kunsthalle. Photo Bridgeman Images.

169 Albrecht Dürer, *Men's Bath*, *c.* 1496–97. Woodcut, 38.3 × 27.8 cm (15⅛ × 11 in.). Cleveland Museum of Art. Fiftieth anniversary gift of The Print Club of Cleveland 1969.271.

171 Albrecht Dürer, *Portrait of Oswolt Krel*, 1499. Oil on panel, central panel 49.6 × 39 cm (19⅝ × 15⅜ in.), left panel 49.3 × 15.9 (19½ × 6⅜), right panel 49.7 × 15.7 cm (19⅝ × 6¼ in.). Bayerische Staatsgemäldesammlungen – Alte Pinakothek, Munich.

172 Dürer, *The Sea Monster*, *c.* 1498. Engraving, 24.8 × 18.9 cm (9⅞ × 7½ in.). Metropolitan Museum of Art, New York. Fletcher Fund, 1919.

173 Albrecht Dürer, *Self-portrait*, 1500. Oil on panel, 67.1 × 48.9 cm (26½ × 19⅜ in.). Bayerische Staatsgemäldesammlungen – Alte Pinakothek, Munich.

174, 192–93 Michelangelo, *Ceiling of the Sistine Chapel*, 1508–12. Fresco. Sistine Chapel, Vatican, Rome.

177 Michelangelo, *Torment of St Anthony*, 1487. Tempera on panel, 47 × 34.9 cm (18⁵⁄₇ × 13¾ in.). Kimbell Art Museum, Fort Worth.

181 Michelangelo, *Battle of the Centaurs*, 1490–92. Marble, 80.5 × 88 cm (31¾ × 34⅝ in.). Casa Buonarroti, Florence. Photo Scala, Florence.

183 Michelangelo, *Bacchus*, 1496. Marble, height 203 cm (80 in.). Museo Nazionale del Bargello, Florence. Photo Arte & Immagini srl/Vincenzo Fontana/Corbis via Getty Images.

185 Michelangelo, *Pietà*, 1498–99. Marble, height 174 cm (68⅝ in.). St Peter's, Vatican, Rome. Photo Leemage/Corbis via Getty Images.

187 Michelangelo, *David*, 1501–4. Marble, height 517 cm (203⅝ in.). Galleria dell'Accademia,Florence. Photo Michael Nitzschke/imageBROKER/Shutterstock.

195 Raphael, *School of Athens*, c. 1510–12. Fresco, 550 × 770 cm (216⅝ × 303¼ in.). Stanza della Segnatura, Vatican, Rome.

196 (left) Michelangelo, *Rebellious Prisoner*, 1513–15. Marble, height 227.7 cm (89½ in.). Musée du Louvre, Paris. Photo © RMN-Grand Palais (Musée du Louvre)/René-Gabriel Ojeda.

196 (right) Michelangelo, *Dying Prisoner*, 1513–15. Marble, height 227.7 cm (89½ in.). Musée du Louvre, Paris. Photo © RMN-Grand Palais (Musée du Louvre)/René-Gabriel Ojeda.

197 (left) Michelangelo, *Awakening Prisoner*, c. 1520s. Marble, height 267 cm (105⅛ in.). Galleria dell'Accademia, Florence. Photo Leemage/Corbis via Getty Images.

197 (right) Michelangelo, *Young Prisoner*, c. 1520s. Marble, height 256 cm (100⅞ in.). Galleria dell'Accademia, Florence. Photo Bridgeman Images.

198 Michelangelo, *Moses*, c. 1513–15. Marble, height 235 cm (92⅝ in.). San Pietro in Vincoli, Rome. Photo Leemage/Corbis via Getty Images.

199 Raphael, *Portrait of Pope Julius II*, 1511. Oil on poplar panel, 108.7 × 81 cm (42⅞ × 32 in.). National Gallery, London.

200, 208 Matthias Grünewald, *Temptation of St Anthony*, inner wing of the Isenheim Altarpiece, c. 1512–16. Tempera and oil on panel, 265 × 141 cm (104⅜ × 55⅝ in.). Musée Unterlinden, Colmar. Photo RMN-Grand Palais (Musée d'Unterlinden)/Stéphane Maréchalle/Mathieu Rabeau.

202–3 Hans Holbein, *Dead Christ in the Tomb*, 1521–22. Oil on limewood panel, 32.4 × 202.1 cm (12⅞ × 79⅝ in.). Kunstmuseum Basel. Amerbach-Kabinett 1662.

203 (left) Leonardo da Vinci, *The muscles of the arm, and the veins of the arm and trunk*, c. 1510–11. Black chalk, pen and ink, wash, 28.9 × 19.9 cm (11½ × 7⅞ in.). Royal Collection Trust, London.

203 (right) Leonardo da Vinci, *The muscles of the shoulder, arm and neck*, c. 1510–11. Black chalk, pen and ink, wash, 28.9 × 19.9 cm (11½ × 7⅞ in.). Royal Collection Trust, London.

204 Leonardo da Vinci, *The foetus in the womb*, c. 1511. Red chalk and traces of black chalk, pen and ink, wash, 30.4 × 22 cm (12 × 8¾ in.). Royal Collection Trust, London.

206 Matthias Grünewald, Isenheim Altarpiece, c. 1512–16. Tempera and oil on panel, 269 × 307 cm (106 × 120⅞ in.). Musée Unterlinden, Colmar. Photo RMN-Grand Palais (Musée d'Unterlinden)/Stéphane Maréchalle/Mathieu Rabeau.

209 Albrecht Altdorfer, *Beautiful Virgin of Regensburg*, c. 1519–20. Colour woodcut, 12.2 × 9.4 cm (4 × 3¾ in.). Metropolitan Museum of Art, New York. Harris Brisbane Dick Fund, 1925.

210 Workshop of Lucas Cranach the Elder, *The Papal Ass in Rome*, 1523. Engraving, 20.9 × 14.6 cm (8¼ × 3¾ in.). New York Public Library, Rare Book Division.

211 Lucas Cranach the Elder, *Venus in a Landscape*, 1529. Oil on beechwood panel, 38 × 52 cm (15 × 20½ in.). Musée du Louvre, Paris. Photo RMN-Grand Palais (Musée du Louvre)/Tony Querrec.

213 Albrecht Dürer, *Melencolia I* (first state), 1514. Engraving, 23.9 × 18.7 cm (9½ × 7⅜ in.). National Gallery of Victoria, Melbourne. Felton Bequest, 1956.

215 Albrecht Dürer, *Portrait of Katharina*, 1521. Silverpoint on paper, 20 × 14 cm (7⅞ × 5⅝ in.). Gabinetto dei Disegni e delle Stampe, Uffizi, Florence.

218 Hans Holbein the Younger, *Henry VIII*, c. 1536–37. Ink and watercolour, 257.8 × 137.2 cm (101½ × 54⅛ in.). National Portrait Gallery, London. Accepted in lieu of tax by H.M. Government and allocated to the Gallery, 1957.

220 Hans Holbein the Younger, *The Ambassadors*, 1533. Oil on oak, 207 × 209.5 cm (81½ × 82½ in.). National Gallery, London.

222, 224 Sofonisba Anguissola, *Game of Chess*, 1555. Oil on canvas, 72 × 97 cm (28⅜ × 38¼ in.). National Museum in Poznań, Poland. Raczyński Foundation at the National Museum in Poznań.

225 Properzia de' Rossi, *Joseph and Potiphar's Wife*, c. 1526. Marble, 53.5 × 54 cm (21⅛ × 21⅜ in.). Basilica di San Petronio, Bologna.

226 Sofonisba Anguissola, *Child Bitten by a Crayfish*, c. 1554. Black chalk and charcoal on brown paper, 33.3 × 38.5 cm (13⅛ × 15¼ in.). Museo Nazionale di Capodimonte, Naples. Photo Scala, Florence.

231 Leonardo da Vinci, *Mona Lisa*, c. 1503–7. Oil on panel, 77 × 53 cm (30⅜ × 20⅞ in.). Musée du Louvre, Paris.

232 Raphael, *Portrait of Maddalena Doni*, c. 1505–7. Oil on panel, 63.5 × 45 cm (25 × 17¾ in.). Uffizi, Florence.

233 Giorgione, *Portrait of a Young Woman ('Laura')*, 1506. Oil on canvas mounted on panel, 43.6 × 36.5 cm (17¼ × 14⅜ in.). Kunsthistorisches Museum, Vienna.

234 Titian, *Head of a Venetian Girl*, c. 1509. Oil on panel, transferred to canvas, 31.8 × 23.8 cm (12⅝ × 9⅜ in.). Norton Simon Foundation, Pasadena.

235 Titian, *Flora*, *c.* 1516–18. Oil on canvas, 79.7 × 63.5 cm (31½ × 25 in.). Uffizi, Florence.

237 Bartolomeo Veneto, *Portrait of a Young Woman as Flora*, *c.* 1520. Mixed media on poplar panel, 43.7 × 34.7 cm (17¼ × 13¾ in.). Städel Museum, Frankfurt am Main.

239 Titian, *Penitent Magdalene*, 1531–35. Oil on canvas, 85.8 × 69.5 cm (33⅞ × 27⅜ in.). Uffizi, Florence.

240 Agnolo Bronzino, *Portrait of Lucrezia Panciatichi*, *c.* 1540. Oil on panel, 102 × 85 cm (40¼ × 33½ in.). Uffizi, Florence. Photo Scala, Florence.

241 Agnolo Bronzino, *Portrait of Laura Battiferri*, 1555–60. Oil on canvas, 83 × 60 cm (32¾ × 23⅝ in.). Museo di Palazzo Vecchio, Florence.

242, 253 Michelangelo, *Last Judgment*, 1536–41. Fresco, 13.7 × 12 m (44 × 39 ft). Sistine Chapel, Vatican, Rome.

246 Michelangelo, *Tomb of Giuliano de' Medici*, 1526–33. Marble, 630 × 420 cm (248⅛ × 165⅜ in.). Sagrestia Nuova, San Lorenzo, Florence. Photo DeAgostini/G. Dagli Orti/Getty Images.

247 Michelangelo, *Tomb of Lorenzo de' Medici*, 1524–31. Marble, 630 × 420 cm (248⅛ × 165⅜ in.). Sagrestia Nuova, San Lorenzo, Florence. Photo DeAgostini/G. Dagli Orti/Getty Images.

249 Titian, *Bacchanal of the Andrians*, 1523–26. Oil on canvas, 175 × 193 cm (69 × 76 in.). Museo del Prado, Madrid.

250 Michelangelo, *Studies for the Head of Leda*, *c.* 1530. Red pencil, 35.4 × 26.9 cm (14 × 10⅝ in.). Casa Buonarroti, Florence.

255 Raphael and studio, the *stufetta* of Cardinal Bibbiena, 1516. Vatican Palace, Rome. Photo Scala, Florence.

258 Titian, *Danaë*, 1544–45. Oil on canvas, 120 × 172 cm (47¼ × 67¾ in.). Museo e Real Bosco di Capodimonte, Naples. Courtesy of the Ministero della Cultura – Museo e Real Bosco di Capodimonte.

261 Correggio, *Jupiter and Io*, *c.* 1530. Oil on canvas, 162 × 73.5 cm (63⅞ × 29 in.). Kunsthistorisches Museum, Vienna.

263 Titian, *Venus and Adonis*, 1554. Oil on canvas, 186 × 207 cm (73¼ × 81½ in.). Museo del Prado, Madrid.

264 Titian, *Rape of Europa*, 1559–62. Oil on canvas, 178 × 205 cm (70⅛ × 80¾ in.). Isabella Stewart Gardner Museum, Boston.

266, 268 Pieter Bruegel, *Battle between Carnival and Lent*, 1559. Oil on oak panel, 118 × 163.7 cm (46½ × 64½ in.). Kunsthistorisches Museum, Vienna. Photo KHM-Museumsverband.

271 Pieter Bruegel, *Land of Cockaigne*, 1567. Oil on panel, 51.5 × 78.3 cm (20⅜ × 30⅞ in.). Bayerische Staatsgemäldesammlungen – Alte Pinakothek, Munich. Photo Scala, Florence/bpk, Bildagentur für Kunst, Kultur und Geschichte, Berlin.

273 Pieter Bruegel, *Peasant Wedding*, 1568. Oil on oak panel, 113 × 164 cm (44½ × 64⅝ in.). Kunsthistorisches Museum, Vienna.

274 Giambologna, *Rape of a Sabine*, 1582. Marble, height 410 cm (161½ in.). Loggia dei Lanzi, Florence. Photo Peter Barritt/Superstock.

276 Pieter Bruegel, *Hunters in the Snow*, 1565. Oil on oak, 116.5 × 162 cm (45⅞ × 63⅞ in.). Kunsthistorisches Museum, Vienna.

277 Pieter Bruegel, *View of the Ripa Grande, Rome*, 1552–53. Pen and brown ink, 20.7 × 28.3 cm (8¼ × 11¼ in.). Chatsworth House, Devonshire Collections, Derbyshire.

279 Pieter Bruegel or follower, *Landscape with the Fall of Icarus*, *c.* 1550–60. Oil on canvas, 73.5 × 112 cm (29 × 44⅛ in.). Musées Royaux des Beaux-Arts de Belgique, Brussels.

280 Pieter Bruegel, *Tower of Babel*, 1563. Oil on panel, 135 × 176 cm (53¼ × 69⅜ in.). Kunsthistorisches Museum, Vienna. Photo KHM-Museumsverband.

284 Michelangelo, Rondanini *Pietà*, *c.* 1550–64. Marble, height 190 cm (74⅞ in.). Castello Sforzesco, Milan.

287 Pieter Bruegel, *Massacre of the Innocents*, *c.* 1565–67. Oil on panel, 109.2 × 158.1 cm (43 × 62¼ in.). Royal Collection Trust, London. Photo Royal Collection Trust/His Majesty King Charles III, 2023/Bridgeman Images.

289 Pieter Bruegel, *Gloomy Day*, 1565. Oil on oak panel, 118 × 163 cm (46½ × 64¼ in.). Kunsthistorisches Museum, Vienna.

290 Pieter Bruegel, *Triumph of Death*, 1562–63. Oil on panel, 117 × 162 cm (46⅛ × 63⅞ in.). Museo del Prado, Madrid.

292 Giuseppe Arcimboldo, *Vertumnus*, 1591. Oil on panel, 70 × 58 cm (27⅝ × 22⅞ in.). Skokloster Castle, Sweden.

294 (above) Hew Draper's astrological carvings in the Salt Tower. Photograph by Sir Benjamin Stone, 1898. Royal Collection Trust, London. Photo Royal Collection Trust/His Majesty King Charles III, 2023.

294 (below) John Dee's magical mirror, possibly 14th–16th century. Obsidian, diameter 21 cm (8⅜ in.). British Museum, London. Photo © The Trustees of the British Museum.

295 Nicholas Hilliard, *Elizabeth I Playing the Lute*, *c.* 1580. Watercolour on paper, 4.8 × 3.9 cm (2 × 1⅝ in.). Berkeley Castle, Gloucestershire. Photo Bridgeman Images.

296 Hans Baldung Grien, *Witches*, 1510. Chiaroscuro woodcut in two blocks, second state of two, 38.9 × 27 cm (15⅜ × 10¾ in.). Metropolitan Museum of Art, New York. Gift of Felix M. Warburg and his family, 1941.

299 Andreas Vesalius, *On the Fabric of the Human Body* (1543), frontispiece of 2nd edn (1555). Rijksmuseum, Amsterdam.

300 Giuseppe Arcimboldo, *Fire*, 1566. Oil on limewood, 66.5 × 51 cm (26¼ × 20⅛ in.). Kunsthistorisches Museum, Vienna.

301 Giuseppe Arcimboldo, *Water*, 1566. Oil on alder wood, 66.5 × 50.5 cm (26¼ × 20 in.). Kunsthistorisches Museum, Vienna.

304 Lavinia Fontana, *Portrait of Antonietta Gonzalez*, *c.* 1583. Oil on canvas, 57 × 46 cm (22½ × 18⅛ in.). Musée des Beaux-Arts, Château Royal de Blois. Photo RMN-Grand Palais/Michèle Bellot.

307 Titian, *Flaying of Marsyas*, *c.* 1579. Oil on canvas, 220 × 204 cm (86⅝ × 80⅜ in.). Olomouc Museum of Art.

308–9 Paolo Veronese, *Feast in the House of Levi*, 1573. Oil on canvas, 560 × 1309 cm (220½ × 515⅜ in.). Gallerie dell'Accademia, Venice. Photo Cameraphoto/Scala, Florence.

310–11 Paolo Veronese, *Wedding at Cana*, 1562–63. Oil on canvas, 677 × 994 cm (266⅝ × 391⅜ in.). Musée du Louvre, Paris. Photo RMN-Grand Palais (Musée du Louvre)/Michel Urtado.

312 Jacopo Tintoretto, *Susanna and the Elders*, *c.* 1555–56. Oil on canvas, 146 × 193.6 cm (57½ × 76¼ in.). Kunsthistorisches Museum, Vienna.

315 Caravaggio, *Medusa*, *c.* 1597. Oil on canvas mounted on wood, diameter 58 cm (22⅞ in.). Uffizi, Florence.

317 Caravaggio, *Sleeping Cupid*, 1608. Oil on canvas, 75 × 105 cm (29⅝ × 41⅜ in.). Palazzo Pitti, Florence. Photo akg-images/Mondadori Portfolio/Mauro Magliani.

Index

Page references in *italic* refer to illustrations

Abbas I, Shah 314
Adorno family 23, 46–47
Aelst, van, family 281
Africa 11, 122, 128
African art objects 129–30
'Aisling Meic Conglinne', poem 165
Alba, duke of *see* Álvarez de Toledo, Fernando, 3rd Duke of Alba
Alberti, Leon Battista 9, 53, 58
  On Painting 29, 30–31, 111
Albizzi family 49
alchemy 293–94; *see also* magic
Alcibiades 181–82, 214
Alexander VI, Pope (Rodrigo de Borja) 123–25, 137, 177, 178
Alfonso V of Aragon 17
Altdorfer, Albrecht, *Beautiful Virgin of Regensburg* 209, *209*
Álvarez de Toledo, Fernando, 3rd Duke of Alba 270, 286
Ammanati, Bartolomeo 241
anatomical study 94, 96, 113, 119, 202–6, 228, 298–99
Angelico, Fra 184
  Mocking of Christ 50, *51*
Anguissola, Sofonisba 224–27
  Child Bitten by a Crayfish 226, *226*, 315
  Game of Chess 223–24, *224*
Anguissola family 223, 226–27
Antonello da Messina 32
  St Jerome in his Study 32
  Virgin Annunciate 32, *33*
Antonio da Sangallo, the Younger 282
Antwerp 16, 128–32, 215–16
  Brotherhood of Our Lady 131–32
Apelles 229
Aquinas, Thomas, *Summa Theologiae* 12
Aragona, Cardinal Luigi d' 153, 228, 229
Arcimboldo, Giuseppe 301–2
  Fire 300, 301–2
  Vertumnus 292, 302–3
  Water 301, 302
Aretino, Pietro 256–57
Aristotle 52, *53*, *65*, 68, 74, 135
Arnolfini, Giovanni di Nicolao di *14*, 15–16, 19–20, 22, 25, 26, 29, 31
Arnolfini family 46–47
art for art's sake 92–93
artists, status of 224, 225, 227, 244
astrology 118, 293, *293*, 300
astronomy 52, 300–302; *see also* telescopes
Augsburg 199
Aztec art objects 216, 294, *294*

bacchanalian painting 248–52
Baines, Richard 103
Baldung Grien, Hans, *Witches* 295–96, *296*
Ballerina, Elena 236
Bandello, Matteo, *Novellas* 153
Bardi, Simone dei 46
Bardi bank 46
Baroncelli, Bernardo 96–97, *97*
Bartolomeo Veneto, *Portrait of a Young Woman as Flora* *237*, 237–38
Basel 134, 201
Battiferri, Laura 241, *241*
Beatis, Antonio de 153–56, 228, 230
Beaune 42
Belgium 271
Bellini, Giovanni 8
  Feast of the Gods 248
  Madonna and Child Enthroned 32–33, *34*
Bembo, Bernardo 88, 90
Benci, Ginevra de' 88–89, *89*, 93
Benci, Giovanni 122
Bernardino of Siena 54
Biagio da Cesena 254, 255
Bibbiena, Cardinal 254
birth trays (*desci da parto*) 64–70, *66*, *69*
Black Death/plague 41–42, 291
Boccaccio, Giovanni 30
  Decameron 66
Boleyn, Anne 217–19
Bologna 191, 197, 225
Borgia, Cesare 123, 125, 137, 177, 178
Borgia, Lucrezia 237–38
Borgia, Rodrigo de *see* Alexander VI, Pope
Borgia family 123–25, 137, 177, 179
Bosch, Hieronymus 128–32, 139–46, 161, 162, 172, 297
  Adoration of the Magi 128–31, *129*
  Garden of Earthly Delights *10*, 151–60, *154–55*, *157*, *158*, 162, 164–66, 170, 228, 270; with panels closed 151, *153*, 275
  The Haywain *144–45*, 146–49, 151, 157, 165
  Last Judgment 134, 143, 146, 151, 157–59
  Ship of Fools 151, *152*, 157
  Temptation of St Anthony 139–42, *140–41*, 165
  The Wayfarer *143*, 143–46
  The Wood has Ears, the Field has Eyes 142, *142*
Botticelli, Sandro 76, 85, 90, 94, 97, 98, 135–37
  Adoration of the Magi 76–77
  Birth of Venus 16–17, 39, 82–83, *83*
  Mystic Nativity 135–36, *136*
  Pallas and the Centaur 78, *78*
  Primavera 9, 79–82, *80–81*
  Venus and Mars 72–75, *74*, 77
Bouts, Dirk, *Fall of the Damned* 146, *147*
Bracciolini, Poggio 49
Brahe, Tycho 298, 299–300
Bramante, Donato 190, 191
Brethren of the Free Spirit 22, 27
Bristol 293
Bronzino, Agnolo 238–40
  Portrait of Laura Battiferri 241, *241*
  Portrait of Lucrezia Panciatichi *240*, 240–41
Bruegel, Pieter the Elder 165, 269–70, 275–78, 286–88, 291
  Battle between Carnival and Lent 165, 267–71, *268–69*
  Big Fish Eat Little Fish 286
  Fat Kitchen and *Thin Kitchen* 270–71
  Gloomy Day 288, *289*
  Hunters in the Snow 275, *276*, 288
  Land of Cockaigne *271*, 271–72
  Landscape with the Fall of Icarus 278–79, *279*
  Massacre of the Innocents 285–86, *287*
  Peasant Wedding 272, *273*
  Penitent Magdalene 286
  Tower of Babel *280*, 281–82
  Triumph of Death *290*, 291
  View of the Ripa Grande, Rome 277, *277*
Bruges 10, 16, 17, 22–23, 29, 31, 37, 39, 45–47, 58, 61, 90, 128
Brunelleschi, Filippo 29, 30, 52, 58, 111
Bruni, Leonardo 49, 53
Bruno, Giordano 297
Brussels 42, 45, 153, 216, 228
  Rood Klooster 149
Burckhardt, Jacob 9, 188, 198
Buti, Lucrezia 228
Byzantine Empire 50–52, 178

cabinets of curiosities 302–3
Caesar, Julius 178
Calvin, John 262
camera obscura 113–15
Campin, Robert 90
Caravaggio 226, 314–17
Medusa 315, 315–16
Sleeping Cupid 317, *317*
carnival 164–66, 172
Carrara marble 189–90
cartography 122–25, 287–88
Castiglione, Baldassare, *Book of the Courtier* 259
Catholicism 238, 256–57, 262, 283
Fourth Lateran Council 40
papal indulgences 199, 285
see also Council of Trent; Counter Reformation
Cattaneo, Simonetta 77–79
Cavalieri, Tommaso de' 226, 251–52, 254
Cellini, Benvenuto 244–45, 247, 260, 297–98
censorship 256, 285–86
Cereta, Laura 66
Charlemagne 49
Charles the Bold, duke of Burgundy 47
Charles V, Emperor 215, 216, 244, 248, 260–62
Charles VIII of France 135
Chaucer, Geoffrey 72
The Canterbury Tales 15
China 122
Christendom 178, 199
Reconquista 121, 286
Christianity 22–23, 39, 53, 63, 101–2, 146, 178, 210; *see also* Catholicism; crusades; Mandaeanism; Protestantism
Christus, Petrus, *Portrait of a Young Woman* 90, *91*
Cicero 49
Cimabue, *Flagellation of Christ* 40–41, *41*
classicism 63, 72, 184, 260, 275, 278, 279, 305; *see also* Greece, ancient; mythology, classical; nudes, classical; Rome, ancient; sculpture, classical
Clement VII, Pope (Giulio di Giuliano de' Medici) 244–45, 251, 252
Cloux 228–29
Clovio, Giulio 281
Colet, John 217
Colmar 206
Colonna, Vittoria 283
Columbus, Christopher 11, 121–22, 134, 156–57, 159–60, 162
Condivi, Ascanio, *Life of Michelangelo* 175, 176, 181–82, 194, 197
Constantine, Emperor 189
Copernicus, Nicolaus 297
Correggio, *Jupiter and Io* 260, *261*
Cortés, Hernán 216
Coryat, Thomas 236
Cossa, Francesco del, *Triumph of Venus 70–71*, 71
Council of Florence 52
Council of Trent 257, 285, 286, 306, 313
Counter Reformation 243, 257, 265, 316
courtesans 168, 235–38, 259, 314
courtly love 67–71, 74–76, 88, 228, 229–32
Cranach, Lucas the Elder 227
Cupid Complaining to Venus 211–12
The Law and the Gospel 210
The Papal Ass in Rome (workshop of) *210*, 210–11
Venus in a Landscape 211, 211–12
Cremona 223, 226
crusades 25, 178

Daniele da Volterra 285
Dante Alighieri 30, 41, 46, 54
Divine Comedy 24–25, 46, 67–68, 135, 255
The New Life 46, 68
death 42, 68, 202–5, 291
Dee, John, magical mirror 293–94, *294*, 298
demons 297–98
Diane de Poitiers 260
dissection *see* anatomical study
Donatello 54, 58
Cantoria 63
David 54–58, *55*, 59
Judith and Holofernes 54–57, *56*
St George 54
Donati, Lucrezia 75–76
Doni, Maddalena 232, *232*
Donne, John 243
Dostoevsky, Fyodor, *The Idiot* 202
Draper, Hew, astrological carvings 293, *294*
Duccio 10
Dürer, Albrecht 130, 137–38, 166–73, 179, 214–17, 296
Apocalypse series *138*, 138–39, 168
Death of Orpheus 168, 168–69
Dream of the Doctor 170
Hercules at the Crossroad 166, *167*
Melencolia I 212, *213*, 216–17, 221
Men's Bath 169, 170
Portrait of Katharina 215, 216
Portrait of Oswolt Krel 171, *171*
The Sea Monster 171–72, *172*
Self-Portrait 173, *173*
Dyck, Anthony van 16

Edward III of England 46
Elizabeth I of England 230, 293, 295, *295*
Elmina Castle 11, 122
Ely 219
engineering 115–16, 121
Erasmus, Desiderius 12–13, 201, 219
Praise of Folly 214–15, 217, 221
eroticism 16, 27, 54, 211–12, 228, 234, 254–55, 260–65
Escorial 157
Este, Alfonso d' 191, 238, 248, 250
Este, Isabella d' 8, 230
Eyck, Jan van 10, 17–19, 22, 24, 25, 29–32, 35, 89–90
Annunciation 27, 32
Arnolfini Portrait 14, 15–16, 19–20, 22, 25, 26, 29, 31
Ghent Altarpiece (and Hubert van Eyck) 20–22, *21*, 26–27, 216, 265
Portrait of Margaret van Eyck 19, *20*
St Jerome in his Study 90
Virgin and Child with Canon van der Paele 23, 23–24
Woman at Her Toilet (lost) 16–20, *18*, 26–29, 31, 35
Eyck, Margaret van 19, *20*

Facio, Bartolomeo 17–19, 27, 29, 35
Farnese, Alessandro *see* Paul III, Pope
Farnese, Cardinal Alessandro 257
Ferdinand II, Emperor 160, 262, 303
Ferrara 52, 70, 72, 179, 191, 248–51
Hall of the Months, Palazzo Schifanoia *70–71*, 70–72, 74
Ficino, Marsilio 52–54, 88, 182, 294
Fisher, John 219
Flemish art 32, 42, 61, 68, 89–90, 92, 179, 186, 252, 270, 272, 275, 286
flight 101, 123, 176
Florence 9, 10, 29–30, 39, 46–54, 57–58, 61–62, 75–76, 88, 134–35, 161,

164–65, 186, 189–90, 202, 227–28, 245, 248
Accademia Gallery 198, 283
Baptistery 30, 181
Cathedral 29, 30, *63*, *96*
Guild of St Luke 86
Medici palace 54, 182, 188, 196, 198
Office of the Night 95
San Lorenzo 245–48
San Marco 50, 96, 134, 135, 137
San Miniato 248
Santa Maria Novella 58, 63
Santa Maria Nuova hospital 61, 202, 203
Siege of 250, 251
Uffizi Gallery 10, 39
folk traditions 77, 142, 268–72, 295
folklore 74, 102, 165, 171–72, 272, 279, 301, 305; *see also* paganism
Fontainebleau 260
Fontana, Lavinia, *Portrait of Antonietta Gonzalez* 303–5, *305*
food 270–71
Francis I of France 205, 228, 260
Franco, Veronica 236
Freud, Sigmund 97
Frey, Agnes (Dürer) 166–67, 169, 170, 215
Fugger, Jacob 199
Fugger family 215

Galileo Galilei 313–14
Galizia, Fede 303
Gallerani, Cecilia *6*, 7–9, 12
Galli, Jacopo 184, 277
Gdańsk (Danzig) 37–39
Geest, Cornelis van der 16, *17*, 19
Genoa 19, 23, 41–42, 46
geography 24, 125, 287; *see also* cartography
geology 108–10
fossils 105–8
Ghent Altarpiece 20–22, *21*, 26–27, 216, 265
Gherardini del Giocondo, Monna Lisa 229–32, *231*
Ghiberti, Lorenzo 181
Ghirlandaio, Domenico 63, 175, 180
Birth of John the Baptist 63–64, *65*
Birth of the Virgin 63–64, *64*
Giambologna, *Rape of a Sabine* *274*, 275
Giles, Peter 127, 215
Giorgione 233, 238
Portrait of a Young Woman ('Laura') *233*, 233–34
Giotto 10
Kiss of Judas *40*, 40–41
Giovanni, Apollonio di, *Triumph of Love* 65–66, *66*
Giuliano da Sangallo 190
Giulio Romano 176, 256
Goes, Hugo van der
Fall of Man *148*, 149
Portinari Altarpiece 61
Golden Age, classical mythology 162
Gonzaga, Francesco 230
Gonzaga family 72
Gonzalez, Antonietta 303–5, *305*
Gonzalez family 303
Goodrich, Thomas 219
Gothic style 54, 58, 61, 72, 131, 252, 269
Gramme, Agneese de 128, *129*
Granada 121
Granvelle, Cardinal de 265
Grass, Günter, *The Tin Drum* 39
Greece, ancient 9, 13, 16–17, 29, 30, 31, 47–58, 96, 180, 186, 194; *see also* classicism
Grimm bothers 272
Grimston, Edward 90
Grünewald, Matthias, Isenheim Altarpiece *206*, 206–7
Temptation of St Anthony, inner wing 207, *208*
Guicciardini, Francesco 238, 248
guilds 86, 224
Gutenberg, Johannes 132

Haarlem 277
Habsburgs 179, 226, 244–45, 262, 270, 275, 285–86, 303
Haecht, Willem van, *The Gallery of Cornelis van der Geest* 16, *17*, 19
Hanseatic League 37, 61
Heemskerck, Maarten van 277, 282
Hemmesen, Catharina van 227
Henry VIII of England 217–19, 227, 262
's-Hertogenbosch 128, 131
Hesiod, *Works and Days* 162
Hilliard, Nicholas, *Elizabeth I Playing the Lute* 295, *295*
Holbein, Ambrosius 215
Holbein, Hans 215, 217–21
The Ambassadors *220*, 221
Dance of Death 221
Dead Christ in the Tomb 201–2, *202–3*, 206, 209, 212, 214
Henry VIII *218*, 218–19
Holy Roman Empire 49, 179, 215; *see also* Habsburgs
homoeroticism 194–96
homosexuality 53–54, 57–58, 88, 101–3, 169–70, 182, 251–56, 314–15; *see also* sodomy
Horenbout, Susanna 227
Huizinga, Johan 161
humanism 52–53, 58, 66, 134–35, 182, 184, 210, 217, 241

Ibn al-Haytham, Hasan (Alhazen) 30
iconoclasm 210, 219, 265
Iron Age, classical mythology 162
Isabella I of Castile 160
Islam 13, 31, 52, 121–22, 134–35, 178, 254
ivory 129–30

Jacobus de Voragine, *Golden Legend* 102
Jewish communities 197, 209, 286
jousting 68, 75, 76, 88
Judaism 13, 134–35
Julius II, Pope (Giuliano della Rovere) 178, 179, 188–91, 194–99, *199*, 212

Kalkar, Jan Stefan van 299
Kepler, Johannes 300
Kern, Jacob 209
Krel, Oswolt 171, *171*
Kyd, Thomas 103

Landino, Cristoforo 88
landscape painting 85–86, 89, 105, 142–43, 156, 275–77, 286–87
Latin 49, 52, 66, 88
Latini, Brunetto 54
Leo X, Pope (Giovanni di Lorenzo de' Medici) 202, 205, 214, 244
Leonardo da Vinci 10, 12, 47, 85–125, 142, 161, 178, 202–5, 214, 228–32, 294, 315–16
Adoration of the Magi (and study for) *98*, 99, *110*, 110–11
anatomical drawings *112*, 113, *113*, *114*, *203*, 203–5, *205*
Annunciation *94*, 94–95, *96*
Baptism of Christ (and Andrea del Verrocchio) 91–93, *92*, 95
Drawing of an Arno Valley Landscape 86, *86*
Ginevra de' Benci 88–89, *89*, 93
Lady with an Ermine *6*, 7–9, 12
Last Supper 102–3, *103*

Leda and the Swan (lost) 250–51
Madonna Litta 7
Madonna of the Carnation 7
A map of Imola *124*, 125
Mona Lisa 229–32, *231*
Mortars firing into a fortress *117*, 117–18
notebooks 107–19, 229, 291
A Ravine *108*
A scene in an arsenal 116, *116*
Study for a flying machine with a hand- and foot-driven mechanism *120*, 121
Study of the Christ Child with a Cat 87, *87*
Study of the Hanged Bernardo Baroncelli 96–97, *97*
Virgin and Child with a Cat 7, *8*
Virgin and Child with St Anne 108–10, *109*
Virgin of the Rocks (1483–94) 99–101, *100*
Virgin of the Rocks (*c.* 1491–1508) 101, 105–7, *106*, 108, 115
Vitruvian Man 171
libraries 49–50
Limoges, enamelled casket 68, *68*
Lippi, Fra Filippo 10, 227–28
literature 30, 49, 50, 52, 53, 162, 165
Lomazzo, Giovanni Paolo 97
Lombardy 303
London, Tower of 293, *294*
Louis XII of France 178
Love Spell, The (unknown artist) 25–27, *26*, 35
Lucca 47
Lucretius, *On the Nature of Things* 49, 50, 74, 82, 163–64
Luther, Martin 199, 209–11, 216
Lutheranism *see* Protestantism

Machiavelli, Niccolò 12–13, 189, 229
Florentine Histories 76
The Prince 123, 125, 177–78
Madrid 226
magic 13, 25, 52–53, 293–98, 302, 305; *see also* alchemy
Malatesta, Sigismondo 53
Malta 316–17
Mandaeanism 101
Mander, Karel van 269–70, 272, 275, 286
mania 184, 194
Mannerism 283–85
Mantegna, Andrea 176
Chamber of the Newlyweds (Camera degli Sposi) 72, *73*
Death of Orpheus 168
Mantovana, Diana (Mantuana) 175–76
Mantovano, Giovanni Battista 175–76
Mantua 175–76, 230, 260
manuscript illumination 22, 205, 281
Marian imagery 227–28
Marlowe, Christopher 103
Doctor Faustus 298
Martini, Simone 10, 233
Mary I of England 262–63
Masaccio 47–48
Expulsion from Paradise 48, *48*
masks 246, 269
Master of Charles of Durazzo, *Triumph of Venus* 69, *69*
Maximilian I, Emperor 179, 215
Maximilian II, Emperor 300
Medici, Cosimo de' 46, 47, 49, 50, 52, 54, 57, 58, 67, 76, 238
Medici, Cosimo II de' 314
Medici, Giovanni di Lorenzo de' *see* Leo X, Pope
Medici, Giuliano de' 76–77, 88, 96, 228
Medici, Giuliano de', duke of Nemours 229, 245–46, *246*
Medici, Giulio di Giuliano de' *see* Clement VII, Pope
Medici, Lorenzo de' (the Magnificent) 62, 67, 75–76, 88, 93, 96, 97, 98, 116, 134, 135, 179–80, 182, 184
Medici, Lorenzo de', duke of Urbino 245–46, *247*
Medici, Piero de' 67, 75, 76, 135, 182
Medici bank 37, 39, 46–47, 96, 99
Medici family 46, 49, 50, 57, 59, 75–76, 90, 135, 180, 182, 202, 228, 238, 244–47, 285
Medici palace, Florence 54, 182, 188, 196, 198
medieval period *see* Middle Ages
Meervenne, Aleid van der (Bosch) 132
Melzi, Francesco 229
Memling, Hans 45
Last Judgment 37–39, *38–39*, 44–45, 47, 58, 59, 61
Mercator, Gerardus 287
Metsys, Quentin (Quinten Massys), *Ugly Duchess* 215–16
Michelangelo Buonarroti 47, 175–76, 179–97, 205, 225–26, 243–59, 265, 282–85
Bacchus *183*, 183–84, 186, 277
Battle of the Centaurs 180–81, *181*
David 186–89, *187*
Entombment 184
Ganymede 252
Last Judgment 243, 252–57, *253*, 259, 285
Moses 197, *198*
Pietà (*c.* 1550–64) 283, *284*
Pietà, Rondanini (1498–99) 184–86, *185*
Prisoners 194–98, *196*, *197*, 212
Sistine Chapel Ceiling 176–78, 191–94, *192–93*
Studies for the Head of Leda *250*, 250–51
Tomb of Giuliano de' Medici 245–47, *246*
Tomb of Lorenzo de' Medici 245–47, *247*
Torment of St Anthony 176, *177*
Michelet, Jules 9
Michelozzo 49–50, 58
Middle Ages 9, 10, 22, 24–25, 31, 42, 46–47, 49, 68, 75, 106, 129, 161, 165, 207, 209, 224, 229, 291
church and theology 12–13, 22, 25, 30, 40
see also courtly love; jousting
Milan 98–99, 116, 178, 230
San Francesco Grande 99, 101
Santa Maria delle Grazie 102
military *see* warfare
Mini, Antonio 251
miniature art 227, 281–82
Mino da Fiesole 49
mirrors 19–20, 25–26, 29–31, 35
magical 293–94, *294*, 298
Montaigne, Michel de 13, 305
Monte, Cardinal Francesco Maria del 314, 315
More, Thomas 12–13, 217, 219
Utopia 127–28, 160, 215
mythology, classical 69–74, 77–82, 161–62, 168–71, 180, 183–84, 278–81

nakedness *see* nudity/nakedness
Naples 17

national identity 272
naturalism 17, 22–24, 25
navigation *see* seafaring
Nelli, Plautilla 224
Last Supper 224
Neroni, Dietisalvi 49
'New World' 122–23, 127, 156–57, 159–60, 162, 163, 188, 293
Niccoli, Niccolò de' 49
Northern European art 10–19, 30, 31–32, 89–90, 252
Vesperbild or *Pietà* 41, 184–86
nudes 16–22, 24, 27–29, 31, 35, 39, 44–45, 54, 57–59, 74–75, 168–71, 246–47
body of Christ 40–41, 50
censorship of 285
classical 17, 54, 57–59, 161, 166, 170–72, 186–88, 252
female 16–17, 82, 166, 170, 211–12, 228, 236–38, 251, 260, 296, 312–13
male 33, 47–48, 57, 59, 65, 181–84, 194–96, 252–56, 264
nudity/nakedness 16, 19–22, 25–27, 39, 42–48, 54, 57–70, 139, 143, 146, 153, 157–61, 188, 243, 256, 257
Nuremberg 137, 169–71
Nuremberg Chronicle 134, 137, 156, 159

occult *see* magic
oil painting 20, 22, 32–33, 89–92, 99, 111, 234
optics 23, 25, 29, 30, 111, 313; *see also* mirrors; telescopes
Ortelius, Abraham 287–88
Ottoman Empire 50, 178, 236, 277
Ovid 49, 288
Fasti 82
Metamorphoses 162, 169, 262, 278–79, 306

Padua 40
Paele, Canon Joris van der *23*, 23–24
paganism 13, 52, 53, 58, 83, 135, 164, 166, 269, 285, 295; *see also* folklore
Palladio, Andrea 11–12, *12*, 306
Palma Vecchio, Jacopo 236
Panciatichi, Lucrezia *240*, 240–41
Panofsky, Erwin 31
Paris, Louvre 229
Parmigianino, *Self-Portrait in a Convex Mirror* 316
Pater, Walter 9, 97
Paul III, Pope (Alessandro Farnese) 252, 254, 282
Pazzi family 96–97
peasantry *see* folk traditions
Persians 52, 314
perspective 8–12, 16, 30–31, 72, 111–15, 181, 221
Peruzzi, Baldassarre 282
Petrarch (Francesco Petrarca) 30, 66–68, 233, 241
Pheidias 180
Philip II of Spain 125, 157, 226, 259, 262–65, 270, 286
Philip the Good, duke of Burgundy 22, 116
Pico della Mirandola, Giovanni 134–35, 188, 194
Piero della Francesca 29
Baptism of Christ 27–29, *28*, 31, 33, 52
Piero di Cosimo 161–64, 172
Battle of Lapiths and Centaurs 164
carnival float 164–65
Forest Fire 163, 164
Return from the Hunt 162, 162–63
Pirckheimer, Willibald 170
Pitti, Francesca 62–63
Pius III, Pope (Francesco Todeschini Piccolomini) 177
plague/Black Death 41–42, 291
Plato 30, 52–54, 59, 88, 184, 252, 306
Phaedrus 53–54, 88, 184, 252
Republic 127–28
Symposium 53, 88, 182, 214
Platonism 52–54, 88, 184, 241, 251
Plethon, George Gemistus 52, 53
Pliny the Elder 224
Pole, Reginald 283
Poliziano, Angelo 77, 180, 194, 265
Verses for the Joust of Giuliano de' Medici 77–79, 82–83
Pollaiuolo, Antonio 75
Battle of the Nudes 59, *59*
Martyrdom of St Sebastian (and Piero Pollaiuolo) 58–59
Tomb of Sixtus IV 194
Polykleitos 57, 171
Pontormo, Jacopo 46
Portinari, Beatrice 46
Portinari, Tommaso 39, 45–47, 58, 59, 61, 149
Portinari family and bank 46
portraiture 49, 89–90, 227, 236–37
Prague 298, 300
Praxiteles 16–17
printmaking 132–34, 137–38, 168, 175–76, 179, 205
prostitution 42, 82, 95, 256, 259, 314; *see also* courtesans
Protestantism 201, 210, 217, 227, 238, 240, 243–44, 252, 262, 265; *see also* Reformation
Pucci family 59
purgatory 25, 46, 146, 199, 285

Quintilian 49
Quistelli, Lucrezia 224

Rabelais, François 12–13, 271–72, 285
Raimondi, Marcantonio 256
Raphael 191
Madonna with the Goldfinch 228
Portrait of Maddalena Doni 232, *232*
Portrait of Pope Julius II 197, *199*
Portrait of Pope Leo X 205
School of Athens 194, *195*
stufetta of Cardinal Bibbiena (and studio) 254–55, *255*
Reformation 199, 201, 206, 209–16, 227, 238, 252, 262
Act of Suppression 219
Regensburg 209
Reggio Calabria 277–79
Regiomontanus, Johannes 118
Renaissance, concept of 9–13
republicanism 47–49
Riario, Cardinal Raffaele 179, 183
Rimini, Tempio Malatestiano 53
Roberts, J. M. 9–10
Rolin, Nicolas 42
Romanticism 272
Rome 25, 58, 135, 177, 179, 182–83, 189, 191, 198–99, 202, 212, 277, 283, 314
Castel Sant'Angelo 244, 282
Colosseum 277, 282, 298
Sack of 243–45, 248, 260
St Peter's 189–91, 199, 277, 282–83
see also Sistine Chapel
Rome, ancient 9, 13, 16–17, 29–31, 47–58, 63, 96, 171, 179–80, 224, 235; *see also* classicism
Rossi, Properzia de' 224
Joseph and Potiphar's Wife 225, *225*
Rosso Fiorentino 260
Rovere, Francesco della *see* Sixtus IV, Pope
Rovere, Giuliano della *see* Julius II, Pope

Rubens, Pieter Paul 16
Rudolf II, Emperor 270, 281, 285, 286, 298, 300–303

St Anthony's fire (illness) 207
Saltarelli, Jacopo d'Andrea 95
Sapi-Portuguese lidded saltcellar 130, *130*
Sarpi, Paolo 313
Sarto, Andrea del 67
Savonarola, Girolamo 134, 135, 137
Scamozzi, Vincenzo 11, *12*
Schedel, Hartmann 134, 137
Scheyfve, Peeter 128, *129*
Schongauer, Martin 138
  Temptation of St Anthony 132–34, *133*, 176, 252
Scientific Revolution 298–302, 305, 313
sculpture, classical 54, 57–58, 82, 96, 179–80, 183, 275
seafaring 24, 121–23, 134, 162, 172, 288, 293
self-portraiture 227
sex 67, 74, 76, 93, 166–70, 211, 250, 254, 259, 269; *see also* courtesans; prostitution; sodomy
sexuality 41, 62, 71, 182, 238, 254; *see also* homosexuality
Seymour, Jane 219
Sforza, Ludovico 7, 8, 98, 116, 178
Shakespeare, William 13, 288
  Venus and Adonis 263
Sigüenza, José de 157
Sistine Chapel, Vatican, Rome
  Ceiling 176–78, 191–94, *192–93*
  Last Judgment 243, 252–57, *253*, 259, 285
Sixtus IV, Pope (Francesco della Rovere) 178, 194
Socrates 53, 182, 184, 214
Soderini, Piero 188, 189, 190–91
sodomy 54, 57, 101, 169, 176, 251, 254
  accusations of 95–97, 282
Spranger, Bartholomaeus 300
Stile, Elizabeth 297
still-lifes 303
Strozzi, Alessandra 75
Strozzi, Roberto 197

Tanagli, Catarina 47
Tani, Angelo 47
Teerlinc, Levina 227
telescopes 313–14
Tintoretto, Jacopo (Robusti) 236, 312–13
  Origin of the Milky Way 313
  Susanna and the Elders *312*, 312–13
Titian 35, 230, 234, 236, 238, 260–62, 305–6
  Bacchanal of the Andrians 248–49, *249*
  Bacchus and Ariadne 249–50
  Danaë 257–59, *258*, 262
  Diana and Actaeon 264–65, 312
  Flaying of Marsyas 305–6, *307*
  Flora 234–35, *235*
  Head of a Venetian Girl 234, *234*
  Penitent Magdalene 238, *239*
  Perseus and Andromeda 265
  Rape of Europa *264*, 265
  Venus and Adonis *263*, 263–64
  Woman with a Mirror 35, *35*
  Worship of Venus 248
Tornabuoni, Giovanni 62–63, 67
Tornabuoni, Leonardo 95
Trento 134
Tudor dynasty 217
Uccello, Paolo, *Battle of San Romano* 10
Urbino 27
utopianism 13, 127–28

Vasari, Giorgio
  frescoes 285
  Lives of the Artists 31–32
    Jan van Eyck 31–32
    Leonardo da Vinci 91, 93–94, 97, 98, 119, 121, 229, 230, 316
    Michelangelo 175–76, 180, 194, 197, 212–14, 245, 254, 259, 283
    Piero di Cosimo 161, 164
    Sandro Botticelli 79
    women artists 224, 225, 226–27, 241
Venice 31–35, 49, 167–68, 170, 178, 228, 232–38, 256, 257, 259, 262, 306, 313–14
  St Mark's 259
  Scuola Grande di San Rocco 313
  SS Giovanni e Paolo 306
Venier, Lorenzo 236
Verhulst, Mayken 281
Vermeer, Johannes 16
Veronese, Paolo
  Feast in the House of Levi 306, *308–9*
  Wedding at Cana 306–12, *310–11*
Verrocchio, Andrea del 86, 87, 91–93
  Baptism of Christ (and Leonardo da Vinci) 91–93, *92*, 95
  Death of Francesca Pitti Tornabuoni 62–63, *62–63*
  Putto with a Dolphin 87, *87*
Vesalius, Andreas, *On the Fabric of the Human Body* 298–99, *299*
Vespucci, Agostino 123, 229
Vespucci, Amerigo 122–23, 127, 159, 160, 162, 188
Vespucci family 75
Vicenza, Teatro Olimpico 11–12, *12*
Vision of MacConglinne, The ('Aisling Meic Conglinne') 165
Vitruvius 49, 57, 171

Waldseemüller, Martin 122
Walsingham shrine 227
warfare 115–18, 125, 178–79, 301–2
Webster, John, *The Duchess of Malfi* 153
Westad, Odd Arne 9–10
Weyden, Rogier van der 19, 42, 90
  Deposition 184
  Last Judgment 42–45, *44–45*
  Pietà 42, *43*
White, John 163
witches 295–97
Wolgemut, Michael 137
women 62–70, 228, 233–38, 241
  artists 224–27
  see also courtesans; nudes: female; witches